Lecture Notes in Computer Science 13620

More information about this series at https://link.springer.com/bookseries/558

Chunhua Su · Dimitris Gritzalis ·
Vincenzo Piuri (Eds.)

Information Security Practice and Experience

17th International Conference, ISPEC 2022
Taipei, Taiwan, November 23–25, 2022
Proceedings

Springer

Editors
Chunhua Su
University of Aizu
Fukushima, Japan

Vincenzo Piuri
Università degli Studi di Milano
Milan, Italy

Dimitris Gritzalis
Athens University of Economics and Business
Athens, Greece

ISSN 0302-9743 ISSN 1611-3349 (electronic)
Lecture Notes in Computer Science
ISBN 978-3-031-21279-6 ISBN 978-3-031-21280-2 (eBook)
https://doi.org/10.1007/978-3-031-21280-2

This Springer imprint is published by the registered company Springer Nature Switzerland AG
The registered company address is: Gewerbestrasse 11, 6330 Cham, Switzerland

Preface

This volume contains the papers presented at ISPEC 2022: The 17th International Conference on Information Security Practice and Experience held during November 23–25, 2022, in Taipei. ISPEC 2022 was organized by National Donghwa University (NDHU), National Taiwan University of Science and Technology (NTUST), and National Sun Yat-sen University (NSYSU), Taiwan. The main goal of the ISPEC 2022 conference was to promote research on new information security technologies, including their applications and their integration with IT systems in various vertical sectors. Previous ISPEC conferences have taken place in Singapore (2005), Hangzhou, China (2006), Hong Kong, China (2007), Sydney, Australia (2008), Xi'an, China (2009), Seoul, South Korea (2010), Guangzhou, China (2011), Hangzhou, China (2012), Lanzhou, China (2013), Fuzhou, China (2014), Beijing, China (2015), Zhangjiajie, China (2016), Melbourne, Australia (2017), Tokyo, Japan (2018), Kuala Lumpur, Malaysia (2019), and Nanjing, China (2021). For all editions, the conference proceedings were published by Springer in the Lecture Notes in Computer Science series. Note that ISPEC 2020 was postponed to 2021 due to the COVID-19 pandemic.

This year, the ISPEC 2022 conference received 87 submissions. Each submission was carefully reviewed by an average of 2.3 Program Committee members in terms of novelty, practical application, and technical quality to reach a common conclusion. Eventually, the Program Committee decided to accept 33 papers and two invited papers, giving an acceptance rate of 37.9%. The accepted papers cover multiple topics of cyber security and applied cryptography. We are grateful to the Program Committee, which was composed of more than 50 well-known security experts from 16 countries; we heartily thank them as well as all external reviewers for their time and valued contributions to the tough and time-consuming reviewing process. In addition to the paper presentations, the program also featured four invited talks and we are grateful to each speaker for accepting our invitation to participate in the conference.

ISPEC 2022 was organized through the joint efforts of numerous people around the world, and we would like to thank the Organization Committee for their continual dedication and support. In addition, we would like to express our gratitude to the authors and attendees for their support, and we thank all of our generous sponsors.

November 2022

Chunhua Su
Dimitris Gritzalis
Vincenzo Piuri

Organization

Honorary Chair

Robert H. Deng — Singapore Management University, Singapore

General Chairs

Kuo-Hui Yeh — National Dong Hwa University, Taiwan
Han-Chieh Chao — National Dong Hwa University, Taiwan
Nai-Wei Lo — National Taiwan University of Science and Technology, Taiwan

Program Chairs

Chunhua Su — University of Aizu, Japan
Dimitris Gritzalis — Athens University of Economics and Business, Greece
Vincenzo Piuri — Università degli Studi di Milano, Italy

Special-Issues Chairs

Weizhi Meng — Technical University of Denmark, Denmark
Zhiyuan Tan — Edinburgh Napier University, UK
Chi-Yuan Chen — National Ilan University, Taiwan
Saru Kumari — Chaudhary Charan Singh University, India

Execution Chairs

Hsin-Hung Cho — National Ilan University, Taiwan
Wei-Che Chien — National Dong Hwa University, Taiwan
Fan-Hsun Tseng — National Cheng Kung University, Taiwan
Yu-Chun Lin — National Dong Hwa University, Taiwan

Publication Chairs

Jia-Ning Luo — National Defense University, Taiwan
Nakamura Akihito — University of Aizu, Japan

Sepcial Session Chair

Chia-Mu Yu	National Yang Ming Chiao Tung University, Taiwan

Publicity Chairs

Yingjiu Li	University of Oregon, USA
Chan Yeob Yeun	Khalifa University, UAE
Ito Ryoma	National Institute of Information and Communications Technology, Japan
Bagus Santoso	The University of Electro-Communications, Japan
Ilsun You	Soonchunhyang University, South Korea
Valentina E. Balas	Aurel Vlaicu University of Arad, Romania
Mian Ahmad Jan	Abdul Wali Khan University Mardan, Pakistan
Chin-Tser Huang	University of South Carolina, USA

Local Arrangement Chair

Jheng-Jia Huang	National Taiwan University of Science and Technology, Taiwan

Web Chair

Wei-Yang (Wayne) Chiu	Technical University of Denmark, Denmark

Conference Secretaries

Siang-Yin Chen	National Dong Hwa University, Taiwan
Tzu-I Shih	National Dong Hwa University, Taiwan

Program Committee

Joonsang Baek	University of Wollongong, Australia
Aniello Castiglione	University of Naples Parthenope, Italy
Xiaofeng Chen	Xidian University, China
Chen-Mou Cheng	Kanazawa University, Japan
Nathan Clarke	University of Plymouth, UK
Mauro Conti	University of Padua, Italy
Francesco Flammini	Malardalen University, Sweden
Sara Foresti	Milan University, Italy
Steven Furnell	University of Nottingham, UK
Bela Genge	Petru Maior University, Romania

Dieter Gollmann	Hamburg University of Technology, Germany
Stefanos Gritzalis	University of Piraeus, Greece
Shoichi Hirose	University of Fukui, Japan
Xinyi Huang	Fujian Normal University, China
Dong-Seong Kim	Kumoh National Institute of Technology, South Korea
Kwangjo Kim	Korea Advanced Institute of Science and Technology, South Korea
Panayiotis Kotzanikolaou	University of Piraeus, Greece
Lukasz Krzywiecki	Wroclaw University of Science and Technology, Poland
Noboru Kunihiro	University of Tsukuba, Japan
Costas Lambrinoudakis	University of Piraeus, Greece
Albert Levi	Sabanci University, Turkey
Shujun Li	University of Kent, UK
Giovanni Livraga	University of Milan, Italy
Javier Lopez	University of Malaga, Spain
Rongxing Lu	University of New Brunswick, Canada
Jia-Ning Luo	Chung Cheng Institute of Technology, Taiwan
Ioannis Mavridis	University of Macedonia, Greece
Weizhi Meng	Technical University of Denmark, Denmark
Haralambos Mouratidis	University of Essex, UK
Maria Papadaki	University of Derby, UK
Günther Pernul	University of Regensburg, Germany
Nikolaos Pitropakis	Edinburgh Napier University, UK
Rodrigo Roman-Castro	University of Malaga, Spain
Pierangela Samarati	University of Milan, Italy
Jun Shao	Zhejiang Gongshang University, China
Yannis Stamatiou	University of Patras, Greece
George Stergiopoulos	University of the Aegean, Greece
Chunhua Su	University of Aizu, Japan
Willy Susilo	University of Wollongong, Australia
Emmanouil Vasilomanolakis	Aalborg University, Denmark
Cong Wang	City University of Hong Kong, China
Ding Wang	Peking University, China
Edgar Weippl	University of Vienna, Austria
Qianhong Wu	Beihang University, China
Shouhuai Xu	University of Colorado Colorado Springs, USA
Toshihiro Yamauchi	Okayama University, Japan
Wun-She Yap	Universiti Tunku Abdul Rahman, Malaysia
Kuo-Hui Yeh	National Dong Hwa University, Taiwan
Xun Yi	RMIT University, Australia

Additional Reviewers

Almani, Dimah
Brighente, Alessandro
Cao, Yanmei
Carpent, Xavier
Chrysoulas, Christos
Friedl, Sabrina
Groll, Sebastian
Halder, Subir
Hong, Zhao
Kalogeropoulos, Panagiotis
Kelarev, Andrei
Kim, Suri
Lian, Zhuotao
Lin, Chao
Luo, Junwei
Mahmood, Khalid
Mayer, Rudi
Ning, Jianting
Qiu, Chen
Rios, Ruben
Roman, Rodrigo
Schlette, Daniel
Stifter, Nicholas
Tian, Guohua
Wang, Ziyue
Yang, Xu
Yang, Xuechao
Zhou, Xiaotong

Contents

Authentication and Biometric Security

Cryptography

Blockchain

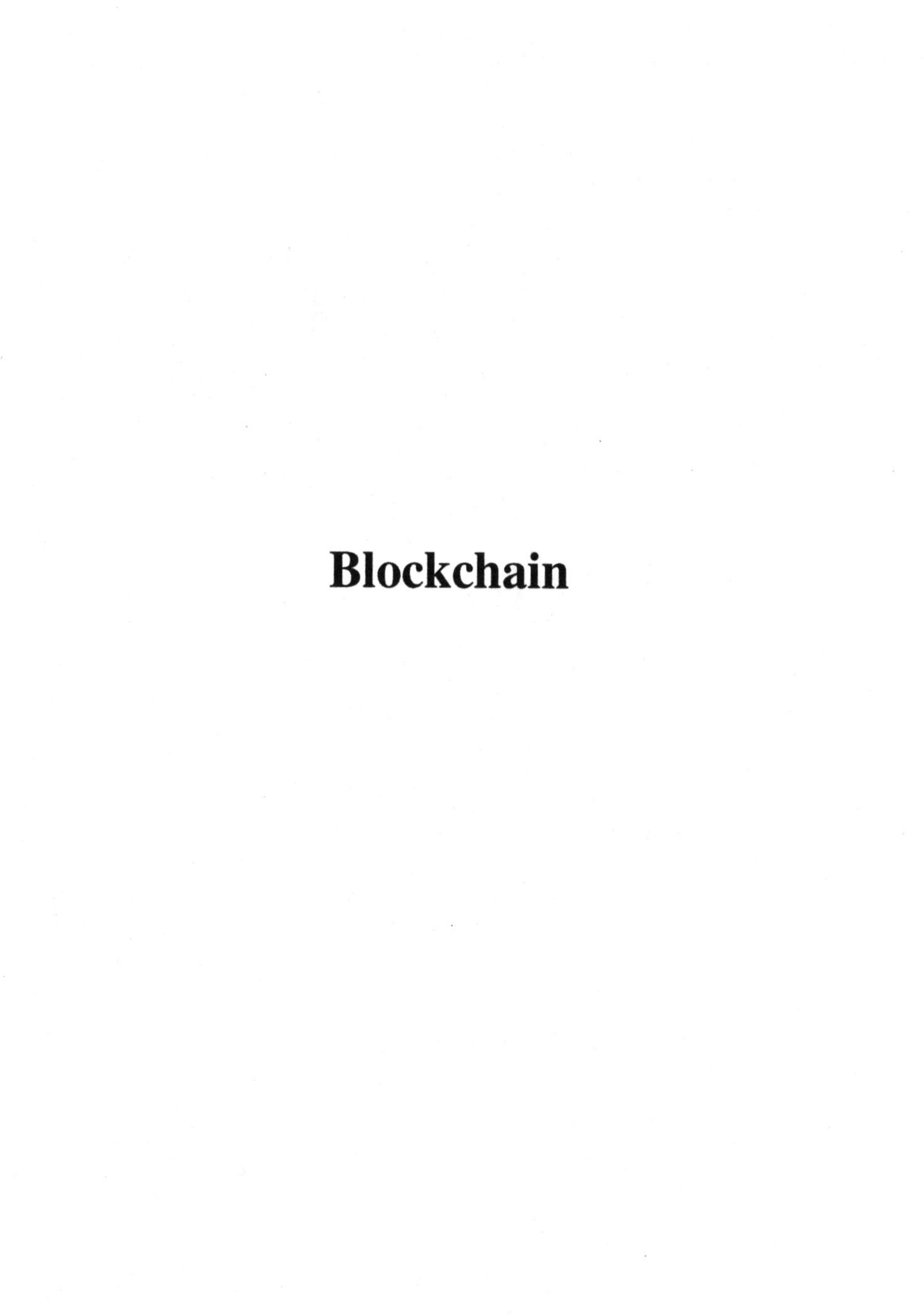

Towards Blockchain-Enabled Intrusion Detection for Vehicular Navigation Map System

Bodi Bodi, Wei-Yang Chiu, and Weizhi Meng(✉)

SPTAGE Lab, Department of Applied Mathematics and Computer Science, Technical University of Denmark, Lyngby, Denmark
weme@dtu.dk

Abstract. In recent years, with the fast development of autonomous driving technology, the Internet of Vehicles (IoV) has received much more attention regarding the security aspect. The traditional security defense strategies are not enough to cope with the risks faced by the IoV. The mature V2X communication protocols such as C-V2X and DSRC are not widely deployed because they have not reached consensus among telecom operators, vehicle manufacturers, and even governments. In the literature, some researchers proposed to combine blockchain technology, especially consortium blockchain, with IoV. However, we find that the consortium blockchain solution may also face some challenges that once an attacker gains control of permissioned nodes, they can upload fake or false data (e.g., forged geographic information and road information) to affect the system performance and security. Motivated by this issue, this paper focuses on vehicular navigation map and develops a blockchain-enabled intrusion detection scheme for vehicular navigation map systems. It can detect malicious nodes that exist in the blockchain in order to ensure the integrity of navigation map data when uploading.

Keywords: Blockchain technology · Intrusion detection · Internet of Vehicles · Navigation map · Data security · IoV

1 Introduction

In recent years, with the rapid development of wireless communication, artificial intelligence, Internet of Things (IoT) and other technologies, the world has gradually entered the era of so-called *Industry 4.0*. Almost all industries are trying to use new technologies to carry out technological revolution. In the field of transportation, many countries are preparing for the construction of an intelligent transportation system (ITS) [3,22].

According to the design requirements of the intelligent vehicles, on the basis of using more sensors to make the vehicle more intelligent, the concept of vehicle to everything (V2X) is added as a supplement of sensors, enabling a vehicle to have a more accurate perception of the surrounding environment [8,15]. The V2X technology includes the Vehicle to Vehicle (V2V), Vehicle to Infrastructure

C. Su et al. (Eds.): ISPEC 2022, LNCS 13620, pp. 3–20, 2022.
https://doi.org/10.1007/978-3-031-21280-2_1

(V2I), Vehicle to Pedestrian (V2P) and Vehicle to Network (V2N) communications. However, more parties in such system may pose a higher security risk. For example, the interface used by V2X in the communication may bring risks to the whole system [1]. The V2X interface could allow an attacker to launch a remote attack and hack the vehicle, i.e., gaining control of the vehicle or the data stored in the vehicle. Meanwhile, mature V2X communication protocols such as C-V2X and DSRC have not been widely deployed, because they did not reach consensus among telecom operators, vehicle manufacturers, and even governments [2]. This is the same for the Internet of Vehicles (IoV) [9], empowered by the adoption of Internet of Things (IoT).

As the information in a V2X network is often decentralized stored and shared between vehicles and infrastructures, some researchers proposed to combine the bloackchain technology with vehicular network to ensure the confidentiality and privacy of the shared data. For example, Yuan and Wang [25] discussed the ITS risk and supported the integration with the blockchain technology, in order to ensure the decentralization of the system as well as the integrity and confidentiality of the shared data. However, the blockchain-based solution may still face the risks and attacks due to the adoption of blockchain. As the ITS serves the public infrastructure, it has to be highly secure and subject to some degree of third-party oversight. In this case, there is a need to control whether unknown users can join this network who might be malicious. The consortium blockchain or the private blockchain could be an option [7]. In particular, the private blockchain and the consortium blockchain can set up an enrollment mechanism for the users: the private blockchain only allows one organization to handle the access control, while the consortium blockchain allows more organizations to take the responsibility. Hence, the consortium blockchain should be an expected solution for ITS and IoV to achieve multi-party governance and fulfill the decentralization.

Motivation. Due to the feature of multi-party governance of a consortium blockchain, it can mitigate the impact of some attacks such as the 51% attack. However, with more nodes joining into the consortium blockchain, the risk of internal data leakage will also increase [4,11]. For example, all information in the consortium blockchain can be leaked by one malicious node. In the context of ITS and IoV, navigation map system will provide critical services to help drivers find a destination with a suitable route. However, attackers may take control of some nodes to download and share the wrong map to others via the V2X network. The wrong information (e.g., map update) may lead to traffic congestion, off the right path, and even traffic accidents.

Contribution. The literature has figured out the importance of High-definition (HD) map to the auto-driving cars [23]. Hence, it is believed that maintaining the map integrity and consistence will become an important security standard in the future design of ITS and IoV. Motivated by this observation, we aim to develop a blockchain-enabled intrusion detection approach to protect the vehicular navigation map system. Our contributions can be summarized as below:

- We focus on the detection of malicious nodes in the blockchain-based ITS network, which can share false or wrong navigation maps with other nodes.

Our key idea is to develop a blockchain-enabled intrusion detection approach to detect any false map information shared among vehicles.
- We use the Fabric platform to construct the consortium blockchain-based vehicular network and implement the logic of intrusion detection via smart contract. In the evaluation, we analyze our system performance in terms of detection accuracy and system scalability.

In Sect. 2, we briefly introduce the background of navigation map system and present related work. Section 3 illustrates the design of our proposed system. Section 4 evaluates the system performance in the aspect of scalability and discusses the limitations. We conclude the work in Sect. 5.

2 Background and Related Work

2.1 High Definition Map

Vehicle-automation system (VAS) is an important part of ITS, while how to locate itself is one of the challenges for auto-driving. A typical solution to mitigate this issue is the cooperative work among GPS, sensors and a high-definition map (HD map) [26]. HD map as a central component of the auto-driving vehicle, it can provide so called "lane-level definition" service to the auto-driving car, which is used to help the intelligent vehicle to gain accurate surrounding information when the sensors cannot feel the environment perfectly in some situations.

Currently, there are two main technical routes for collecting HD map data. One is represented by Google's mapping car, and the other is represented by Tesla's FleetLearning Network. It is equivalent to crowd-sourcing mapping tasks by utilizing mass-produced cars to mobilize all the sensors in the fleet to collect and upload data via the cloud to a central database, where eventually each car will be a contributor and a recipient of map data. For this purpose, Zhong *et al.* [27] proposed the combination of blockchain technology with the HD-map update management system. They also introduced a prototype system based on Hyperledger Fabric to allow vehicles uploading the collected data onto blockchain, which can ensure the data integrity and traceability of map update.

However, HD-map is still facing some other threats. Sinai *et al.* [20] presented a Sybil attack against the vehicular navigation system. They trained 15 bots to simulate the vehicles on road, which sent fraud speed data to the server. When driving on a road with 2–8 km/h speed, they found that a traffic jam could be caused on the navigation application. Traditionally, the system will recommend the road that is not having jam to the users; however, if the attacker could tamper and falsify map data, then it may lead to a huge security incident. Besides, the attacker could track other users who are using the same application via the malicious vehicles or fake bots. Another attack – Message Falsification Attack [16] can upload forged vehicle locations and events to update the HD map. It is similar to writing dirty data to the database.

2.2 Related Work

The security of ITS and IoV has been widely explored in the literature [21]. With the development of decentralized ledger technology, blockchain has been applied in many different domains, such as data management [10,13], intrusion detection [6,14] and smart city [3,5,12].

In the area of blockchain-based vehicles. Chiu and Meng [3] focused on the Electronic Toll Collection (ETC) system and introduced a blockchain-based ETC system called EdgeTC. Yin *et al.* [24] developed a blockchain-based data storage system to support incremental data updating for intelligent vehicle systems, which can decrease the overhead and enhance data reliability. Vishwakarma and Das [17] introduced an incentive mechanism, called SmartCoin, for vehicles based on a consortium blockchain. Their scheme aimed to mitigate the impact of fraud messages in traffic congestion and road accidents.

For the navigation map system in ITS, Poggenhans *et al.* [19] introduced an HD map framework for the automotive vehicles. They argued that the complex environment in downtown should provide more detailed information on the HD map and then serve the automated vehicles. In fact, the HD map can bring a significant improvement to the automated vehicles. It can not only bring the information services but also mitigate the attacks to the sensors. For instance, if one of the sensors is hacked by sending fraud data to other vehicles (e.g., speed or location), the HD map can provide the correct location data to detect whether the data from the sensor is correct. However, to the best of our knowledge, the robustness of navigation map system was not extensively studied. This motivates our work to explore and enhance the security of map system.

3 Our Proposed System

3.1 System Design

Figure 1 show the system overview of our blockchain-enabled intrusion detection scheme, including five main entities:

- **Consortium Blockchain**: In our system, consortium blockchain is used to ensure the integrity and confidentiality of the data, and also help implement the intrusion detection scheme via smart contract. In addition, the consortium blockchain can provide multi-party maintenance of the system.
- **Certificate Authority (CA)**: This is used for the enrollment mechanism of the system. That is, only authorized nodes can connect to the blockchain network. It prevents a large number of malicious nodes from randomly connecting to the network.
- **Intelligent Vehicle**: These vehicles can join the blockchain network as edge nodes with certain computing power. It can calculate the hash value of a map or track and upload the data to the blockchain system. Hence we can use the generated data to detect malicious nodes within the system.

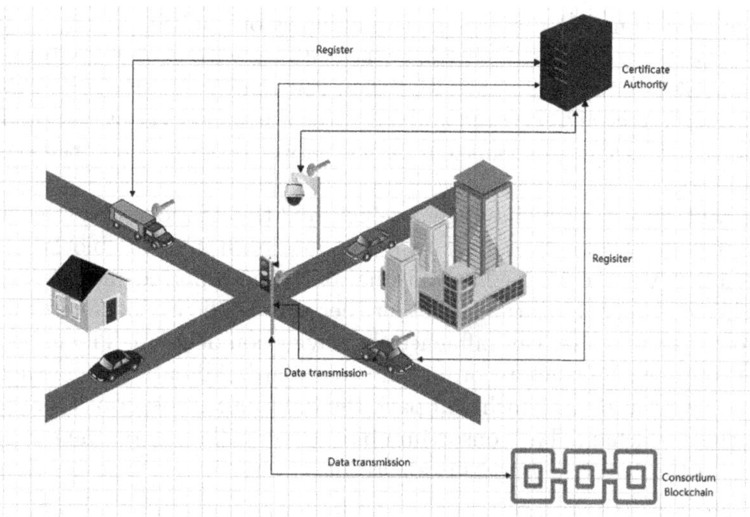

Fig. 1. System overview

- **Road Side Unit (RSU)**: This is a device that communicates with On Board Unit (OBU), which can help identify and communicate with vehicles, receiving and forwarding data and other functions. In our system, the RSU mainly provides the communication interface for the vehicles to publish and confirm transactions in the blockchain.
- **Track Recording Unit (TRU)**: This unit is a kind of OBU, which can record the vehicle's track path based on GPS. The track path will be an output as a JSON file for usage and storage. In our system, we use the track path as a parameter for our intrusion detection scheme, which validates the places where the vehicle passed.

Below are the main steps on how the system works.

- **Registration.** Each intelligent vehicle and RSU should be registered in the CA with their unique ID (V_{id},R_{id}), in order to get the permission to join the consortium blockchain. Once the registration is completed, both of the registered vehicle and the RSU can obtain a certificate and a key pair. Meanwhile, the CA will enroll the registered vehicle and RSU in the system and upload them onto the consortium blockchain.
- **Authentication.** This is the process how an intelligent vehicle establishes a connection with the RSU to join the consortium blockchain. This step proves that a vehicle has indeed passed a particular area at a certain time aiming to prevent malicious nodes from accessing driving tracks and uploading malicious information. It is worth noting that RSU is not trusted by default. When a vehicle enters an area, the RSU initiates the authentication process with the incoming intelligent vehicle. The RSU sends its R_{id} and the signed R_{id} to the intelligent vehicle that is signed by its private key. The vehicle will

validate the signed R_{id} by using the public key of the RSU. After the vehicle has authenticated the RSU, it can encrypt its V_{id} with the vehicle private key by the public key of the RSU, and then can send it to the RSU. The RSU decrypts the received message and validates the signed V_{id} by the public key of the vehicle. Hence, the authentication between the RSU and the vehicle is completed.
- **Transaction.** Once the intelligent vehicle and the RSU complete the authentication step, it can generate data report and push it to the blockchain as a transaction via the RSU. The information to be reported includes: current speed, geographical location, whether there are traffic accidents on the road, and other factors that can influence the navigation decision. The information is collected by the track recording unit on board. All data will be encrypted and sent to the RSU, which will pack the data into transactions and push it onto the blockchain. The consortium blockchain will agree on the transaction based on the selected consensus algorithm.

In this work, we aim to build a consortium blockchain-based vehicular network within a limited region, where vehicles can join dynamically and upload real-time map data (e.g., road conditions, congestion information) and all the data can be stored onto the blockchain. However, it can only ensure that the data will not be tampered during transmission. This is because if the trusted node is compromised, we cannot guarantee that the data uploaded by these compromised nodes is reliable. Therefore, we develop a blockchain-enabled intrusion detection scheme to verify the correctness of data sources and the legitimacy of node operations.

3.2 Threat Model

Before introducing our intrusion detection scheme, we first define the capability of an attacker against the navigation map system as follows. Firstly, the attacker can gain the control of some nodes in the consortium blockchain, i.e., caused by clicking on phishing sites or failing to update the vehicle system. We assume that most of the nodes should update the system regularly, but only a small number of nodes may be vulnerable. Hence, once the attacker obtains the full control of some nodes, they can be used to download the fake map, and share the tampered map data, e.g., road information, to the consortium blockchain. For example, when some malicious nodes exist in the blockchain within a region, they can upload false information about car accidents in that region to the consortium blockchain. If other nodes that are not in the zone receive a false message, they may change the navigation plan. This is similar to a *fake data injection attack* to the navigation map system.

3.3 Blockchain-Enabled Intrusion Detection

HD-map is one of the most important factors to ensure the safety of IoV and V2X, such as autonomous vehicles. If someone malicious can share forged map data, the driving safety of normal vehicles will be seriously affected. Our main idea for building an intrusion detection scheme will be based on the consistency of maps. In particular, we will define normal and malicious nodes within the system according to the legitimacy of uploaded data, so as to identify malicious nodes. The intrusion detection scheme will be implemented via smart contracts deployed on the blockchain.

- **Detection rule.** In our system, we assume that the vehicles will use the same brand's HD-map, and stipulate the legal behaviors and malicious behaviors based on the consistency of the HD-map in each intelligent vehicle, as shown in Table 1.

Table 1. Node behaviors

	Legal node	Malicious node
Map version	Latest official version	Unknown/old version
Road conditionreport	Correct	False
Traffic report	Correct	False
POI report	Correct	False
Traffic signs report	Correct	False
Vote	Vote yes for the correct result	Vote no for the correct result

  In our scenario, the malicious node acts similarly to one bot node, where external attackers can gain the control of some nodes by means of single point attack, but users themselves do not know that they have been attacked. Hence, the attacker can share and upload forged data with other nodes in the network to affect the driving safety of normal users.
  To ensure the consistency of HD-map in our system, every legal node must maintain the latest official version map locally. The malicious node might use a forged map or an old version of HD map to influence the consistency of the map. The real-time data includes the traffic report, road condition report, point of interest (POI) report, and traffic signs report. The legal node must share the correct report, which can be verified by other legal nodes. It means that each kind of map data must be reported and published as a transaction on the blockchain. Therefore, how to identify the reported data becomes the key to distinguish the normal node and the malicious node. In our case, we decide to design a smart contract to realize a double-vote function that can verify the integrity of uploaded data.
- **Detection logic.** Table 2 shows the parameter description, and the detection flow chart is shown in Fig. 2. There is a trigger to start the intrusion detection process, and the main steps are introduced as below.
  1. **Initiation**: One node initiates the voting process by hashing the locally stored map and publishing both *Hash* and *Sender* to call the smart contract of `vote`. It means that when a node publishes a transaction on

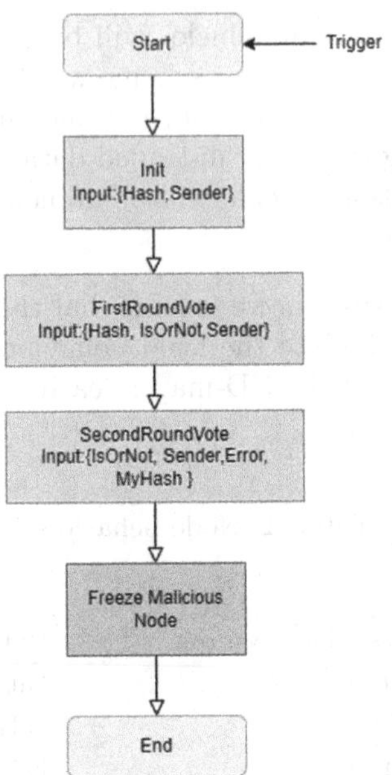

Fig. 2. Smart contract design

Table 2. Parameter description

Parameter	Description
Hash	Node's local map version's hashReal-time map data
Sender	Node's unique identifier
IsOrNot	Vote yes or not
Error	Error report of the specific map data
MyHash	Node's track record hash

the blockchain, other nodes know who initiates a voting process and the transaction detail. The primary goal of this real-name voting is to avoid someone uploading malicious data but the system cannot trace the source of malicious node.

2. **FirstRoundVote**: Once a node starts the voting process, the other nodes should join it. In particular, the nodes have to input their own *Hash* and vote for *yes* or *no* by comparing the local map's hashes with the published *Hash*. If there is a match, then it should vote *yes*, vice versa. Meanwhile, each node has to input their unique identifier in the transaction for real-name voting. Once the system finishes the first round vote, it can perform the consistency check of the local map data among nodes in the network. Therefore, the nodes can be divided into three groups:

(a) **Vote Yes**: These nodes have the same hash value as the *Hash* in the first step. It means that these nodes are using the same map or uploading the same data as the vote originator.
(b) **Vote No**: These nodes have a different hash value against the *Hash*. It means that these nodes are using a different map or disagree with the uploaded data from the vote originator.
(c) **Nonvoters**: These nodes do not join the voting process due to unknown reasons. They might either have Internet connection issues or not join the process on purpose.

According to the detection rule, the malicious nodes will upload false real-time map data or use a non-latest official map. We only need to check the correctness of the initiated *Hash*, then the system can identify which group's nodes are malicious.

3. **SecondRoundVote**: The second round vote is the process that other nodes should verify the correctness of the initiated *Hash*. For the consistency of map version and real-time map data, these nodes should verify the information by themselves and vote their opinion. Therefore, the nodes can also be divided into three groups:
(a) **Vote Yes**: These nodes agree with the initiated *Hash*. That is, they have verified the initiated *Hash* and there is no error reported. They also attach the track record as the verification proof. They should input their unique identifier in the transaction for real-name voting.
(b) **Vote No**: These nodes disagree with the initiated *Hash*. It means that the result failed to pass the node verification and an error was reported. They also attach the track record as the verification proof.
(c) **Nonvoters**: These nodes do not join the vote process due to unknown reasons. They might either have Internet connection issues or not join the process on purpose.

For instance, if the initiated *Hash* is the map version, then other nodes should verify the current map version. If it is unusable such as missing roads, impassable roads, destination incorrectly located and so on, then the node votes *no* to the initiated *Hash* and attaches the node's track record as a proof. The track record is regarded as the proof of verification, it claims that the node does pass a path on map to verify the uploaded data. It is the same solution when the initiated *Hash* is the real-time map data. For the two rounds of voting, each round can divide the nodes into three groups, we thus summarize the relationships into two cases as shown in Fig. 3.

Our voting detection mechanism is based on the principle of majority rule. Once the initiated *Hash* is authenticated, it can identify which groups of nodes are good or malicious from the first and second round vote. However, there are some nonvoters during the voting process. There are two major scenarios: one is for network reasons, and the other is deliberately done by malicious nodes. Due to the complexity, the handling of nonvoters will be addressed in our future work.

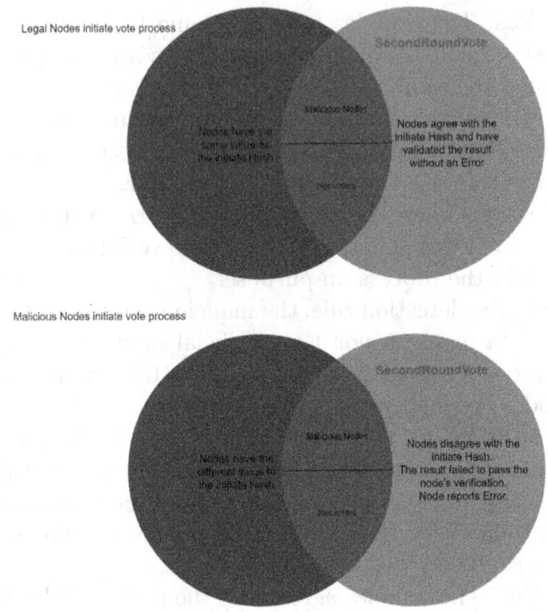

Fig. 3. Venn of nodes

4. **Freezing**: In our system, the countermeasure designed against malicious nodes is freezing. After the second round vote, the system will freeze the malicious nodes, making them unable to participate in blockchain transactions. Hence, malicious nodes cannot impact the consistency and integrity of the system.

- **Detection Scenario.** As shown in Fig. 2, there is a trigger to start the detection process. According to different triggers, we can divide the detection into two conditions: one is the consistency detection of map version, and the other is the consistency detection of data uploaded by nodes. Table 3 shows the description of triggers.

Table 3. Trigger description

Trigger	Map version	Map data
Time	When the map company releases the new version	A node reports information about road conditions (traffic jam, accident, POI, etc.)
Area	Limited area	Limited area
Initiate Hash	Map version's hash	Reported information's hash

1. **Map version**: For the first scenario, when the map company releases the latest map update, the system should select a random node to start the detection process within a limited area (e.g., a few blocks). It means that only these nodes within the area can join the detection process. This can

Fig. 4. The initiation vote process

avoid those nodes outside the area disrupting the voting results, who are unable to provide proof of presence.

2. **Map data**: For this scenario, when a node wants to report the information about the issues on road, it triggers the detection process within a limited area (e.g., cross road, main road). Normally it happens when a node meets a traffic jam, accident, and a new Proof of Insurance report. Therefore, the initiated *Hash* will be the real-time map data.

4 Evaluation

This section introduces the environmental setup, system implementation and evaluation results.

4.1 Environmental Setup

We created a network with three nodes to implement the voting process, with two legitimate nodes (*Node* 0, *Node* 1) and one malicious node (*Node* 2). Table 4 presents the environmental configuration including hardware and software.

Table 4. System environment

Environment			
Hardware		Software	
CPU	AMD Ryzen 9 3900XT12-Core Processor 3.80 GHz	Virtual machine	Ubuntu 18.04
Storage	Force MP600 SSD	Blockchainplatform	Hyperledger Fabric 1.4.4
Memory	32GB DDR4 2660	Smart contract	Chaincode
Network	Vmware virtual network	Container	Docker, Docker-compose,curl

4.2 System Implementation

- **Init.** Based on the system design, when an event triggers the intrusion detection scheme, there is a node will initiate the voting process. It only needs to upload the data hash (e.g., map version, or real-time map data) with its address. Hence, each node in the blockchain network can know who initiates the voting process and the vote. The initiation process is shown in Fig. 4.

Fig. 5. First round vote

Fig. 6. Second round vote

- **FirstRoundVote.** Once a node initiates a voting process, the other nodes should join the process. The voting of each node will invoke a smart contract, and the voting process will be regarded as a transaction to be recorded on the chain. Figure 5 shows the process of a node participating in the first vote. It indicates that *Node* 1 agreed with this map but *Node* 2 disagreed with the initiated data. To avoid malicious node re-voting in the first round vote, we also implemented a function to ensure that each node can vote only once. Then the system records the address, ballot and the status of all nodes participating in the first round vote. The parameters and descriptions are summarized in Table 5.

Table 5. Parameters of firstVote

Function: firstVote		
Parameter	Value	Description
Addr	64 bits Hash	Hash of voting node's address
IsOrNot	0,1	0 = node votes no to the init Hash 1 = node votes yes to the init Hash
AddrStatus	0,1	0 = node is frozen 1 = node is active

- **SecondRoundVote.** When a node completes the first round of voting, it has to examine the information being voted. The system assumes that malicious nodes are a small part of all nodes in the system. Hence, we only need to consult a large number of nodes regarding the correctness of the voted information, and determine whether the initialized information is correct. Figure 6 shows the process of nodes participating in the second round vote.

When the node completes validation of the voted information, the node can invoke the *secVote* function of the smart contract and input parameters as shown in Table 6. The node has to attach its address as the first round vote for real-name voting. It should vote *yes* or *no* for the voted information. Then it should upload the error report and its hash of track record as a proof. We also set up a protection mechanism to prevent the malicious nodes from voting multiple times.

Table 6. Parameters of secVote

Function: secVote		
Parameter	Value	Description
Addr	64 bits Hash	Hash of voting node's address
IsOrNot	0,1	0 = node votes no to the init Hash 1 = node votes yes to the init Hash
Error	0,1	0 = There is no error in voted information 1 = There is an error in voted information
MyHash	64 bits Hash	Hash of node's track record

- **Freezing.** According to Fig. 3, there is no matter whether the malicious node or legal node initiates the voting process. Based on the consistency of voted data, the system considers the nodes that oppose the mainstream opinion as malicious nodes in the two voting rounds. The system will freeze the malicious nodes after two rounds of voting.

4.3 Scalability Evaluation

This is an important metric when we evaluate the performance of blockchain-based systems. The scalability issue is mainly caused by the number of nodes, and the number of contract invokes (number of transactions) executed concurrently within the system. We chosen *Solo* as the consensus algorithm in Hyperledger Fabric and stressed our system by using the *Tape* [18] to simulate the multi-node transaction process.

Assumption. As our detection scenario is based on data exchange between vehicles and the blockchain network, our detection does not require a high response speed similar to traditional host-based intrusion detection. It means that we allow the detection finished in several minutes. In addition, our detection will be conducted in phases of two-round voting, so that we can find the relationship between the maximum transaction volume to be processed by all nodes within the current blockchain network in a given period of time. The derivation is shown as below:

- **One node**: During the detection process, one legal node can initiate three transactions at most within the limited time: namely, *init*, *FirstRoundVote*, *SecRoundVote*.

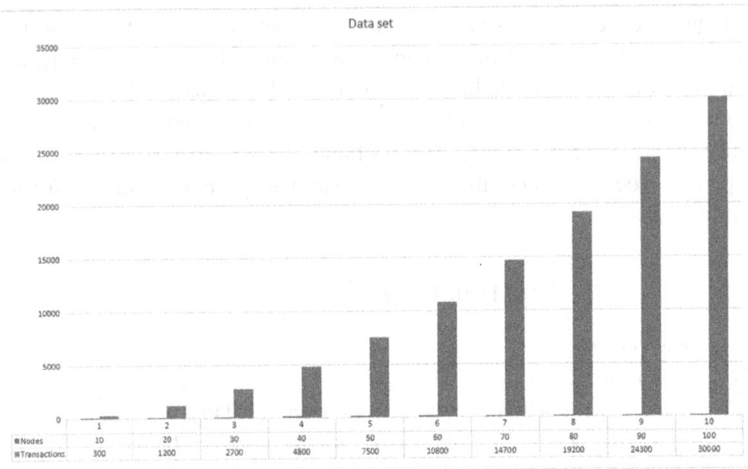

Fig. 7. Dataset information

- n **nodes**: We assume that in the current blockchain network, there are n legal nodes that can join the voting process. Hence, if one node initiates a voting process, then the transactions in the system can be computed as follows:

$$Transactions = 2 \times n \tag{1}$$

- **The worst case**: The worst scenario in the detection process is that all nodes in the system are initiating a voting process concurrently. Then each node should initiate three transactions in the limited time. The transaction volume in this case will reach the system peak as below:

$$Transactions = 3 \times n \times n = O(n^2) \tag{2}$$

Dataset. Based on the relationship that we found between the numbers of nodes and transaction volume above, we designed ten different sets of data to simulate the maximum transaction volume faced by the system. For each dataset, the number of nodes and the maximum transaction are different. We used *Tape* to simulate the process of multi-node transaction packaging and loaded in the blockchain network, and thus explored the generation time of each block and the duration to complete the transaction. The dataset is shown in Fig. 7.

It shows that with the number of nodes in the network increasing, the transaction volume will increase exponentially, which could bring a great challenge to the system.

Result and Analysis. As illustrated in Fig. 8, we used *Tape* to simulate the configured nodes and invoke specific smart contract functions. It can complete the process of transaction packaging and uploading blocks onto the chain, which is similar in a real-world environment. We thus can get the duration of completing all transactions and the transaction per second (TPS).

Fig. 8. Experimental case

Once we finished these 10 groups of experiments, we got the trend of duration and TPS with the number of nodes and transactions increasing. The experimental results are shown in Fig. 9 and Fig. 10. We can have the following observations:

1. As the number of nodes increases, there was a slight decreasing trend on TPS, but the value decrease would not affect the performance of the system.
2. As there is no significant change in TPS, it can be considered that the speed of transaction processed by the system does not change. Therefore, with the increase of nodes, the amount of transactions will go up.
3. With more nodes, the time of transaction processed by the system can increase significantly, and the time duration may increase exponentially with the increase of transaction volume.

Limitation and Discussion. Our system is still under development, and some improvements have to be made in future work.

- We did not solve the challenge on how to handle nonvoters. If we freeze nonvoters, it is very likely that we may freeze legal nodes that cannot vote due to network reasons accidentally. This will reduce the number of legal nodes in the system and undermine the premise of a blockchain system. Hence, we plan to design a new punish mechanism to replace freezing. The basic idea is that we design a credit management system, and each node will have a credit attribute. If a node votes and the majority of the nodes agree with the result, then its credit will increase, and vice versa. If the node does not vote, the credit of the nonvoter will gradually decrease. The credit of the nodes will be taken into account in the voting process, and we can carry out a weighted calculation.

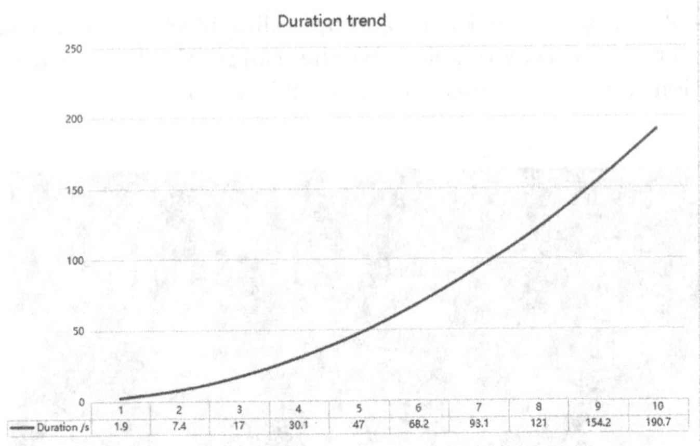

Fig. 9. Duration trend

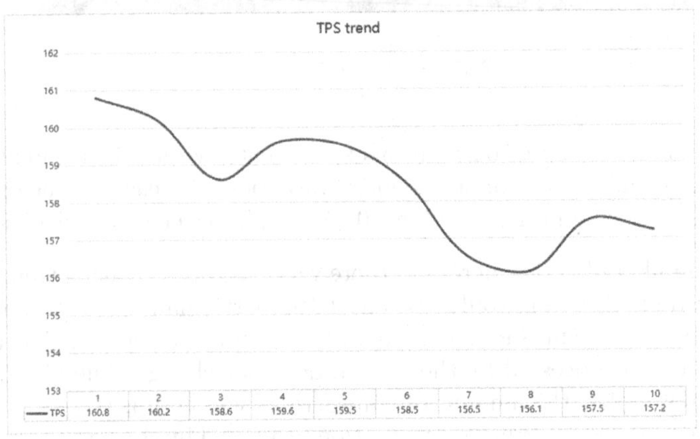

Fig. 10. TPS trend

- The current work adopts Solo provided by Fabric, which is a lab-level consensus algorithm with lower performance than the algorithm applied in the actual production (e.g., PBFT, Raft). Hence, we plan to investigate the scalability using commercial consensus algorithms. We also plan to implement a practical network environment to explore the impact of network speed on system scalability.

5 Concluding Remarks

Currently, with the rapid development of intelligent vehicle and autonomous driving, the security of navigation map has become more important. In this work, we developed a blockchain-enabled intrusion detection scheme for vehicular navigation map system, in order to ensure the security of shared map data in the vehicular networks against data tampering and false data uploading. Our intrusion detection scheme adopted the specification-based detection by defining both legal and malicious operations. We also designed a smart contract to realize a two-round voting process. To investigate the system scalability, we conducted a stress test and found that our proposed system could provide good scalability, i.e., with the increasing nodes, there was only a slight decrease on TPS, so that it would not affect the performance of the system.

Acknowledgments. This work was partially funded by the EU H2020 DataVaults project with GA Number 871755.

References

1. Alnasser, A., Sun, H., Jiang, J.: Cyber security challenges and solutions for V2X communications: a survey. Comput. Networks **151**, 52–67 (2019)
2. Agudo, I., Montenegro, M., Lopez, J.: A blockchain approach for decentralized V2X (D-V2X). IEEE Trans. Veh. Technol. **70**(5), 4001–4010 (2021)
3. Chiu, W.Y., Meng, W.: EdgeTC - a PBFT blockchain-based ETC scheme for smart cities. Peer-to-Peer Network. Appl. **14**, 2874–2886 (2021)
4. Chiu, W.Y., Meng, W.: Mind the scraps: attacking blockchain based on selfdestruct. In: Proceedings of The 26th Australasian Conference on Information Security and Privacy (ACISP), pp. 451–469 (2021)
5. Chiu, W.Y., Meng, W., Li, W.: LibBlock - towards decentralized library system based on blockchain and IPFS. In: Proceedings of The 18th International Conference on Privacy, Security, and Trust (PST), pp. 1–9 (2021)
6. Meng, W., Li, W., Zhou, J.: Enhancing the security of blockchain-based software defined networking through trust-based traffic fusion and filtration. Inf. Fus. **70**, 60–71 (2021)
7. Diego, G.: Private blockchain vs consortium blockchain (2021). https://101blockchains.com/private-blockchain-vs-consortium-blockchain/
8. Ganesan, K., Mallick, P.B., Lohr, J., Karampatsis, D., Kunz, A.: 5G V2X architecture and radio aspects. In: Proceedings of CSCN, pp. 1–6 (2019)
9. Hbaieb, A., Ayed, S., Chaari, L.: A survey of trust management in the Internet of Vehicles. Comput. Networks **203**, article 108558 (2022)
10. Chiu, W.Y., Meng, W., Jensen, C.D.: My data, my control: a secure data sharing and access scheme over blockchain. J. Inf. Secur. Appl. **63**, 103020 (2021)
11. Hofmann, A., Gwinner, F., Winkelmann, A., Janiesch, C.: Security implications of consortium blockchains: the case of ethereum networks. JIPITEC **12**(4), 1–13 (2021)
12. Chiu, W.Y., Meng, W.: Towards decentralized bicycle insurance system based on blockchain. In: The 36th ACM/SIGAPP Symposium on Applied Computing (ACM SAC), pp. 249–256 (2021)
13. Chiu, W.Y., Meng, W., Jensen, C.D.: NoPKI - a point-to-point trusted third party service based on blockchain consensus algorithm. In: The 3rd International Conference on Frontiers in Cyber Security (FCS), pp. 197–214 (2020)
14. Meng, W., Li, W., Zhu, L.: Enhancing medical smartphone networks via blockchain-based trust management against insider attacks. IEEE Trans. Eng. Manage. **67**(4), 1377–1386 (2020)

15. Husain, S.S., Kunz, A., Prasad, A., Pateromichelakis, E., Samdanis, K.: Ultra-high reliable 5G V2X communications. IEEE Commun. Stand. Mag. **3**(2), 46–52 (2019)
16. Karnouskos, S., Kerschbaum, F.: Privacy and integrity considerations in hyperconnected autonomous vehicles. Proc. IEEE **106**(1), 160–170 (2018)
17. Vishwakarma, L., Das, D.: SmartCoin: a novel incentive mechanism for vehicles in intelligent transportation system based on consortium blockchain. Veh. Commun. **33**, article 100429 (2022)
18. Liu, D.: Hyperledger-TWGC/tape: a simple traffic generator for Hyperledger Fabric (2020). https://github.com/Hyperledger-TWGC/tape
19. Poggenhans, F., et al.: Lanelet2: a high-definition map framework for the future of automated driving. In: Proceedings of ITSC, pp. 1672–1679 (2018)
20. Sinai, M.B., Partush, N., Yadid, S., Yahav, E.: Exploiting Social Navigation. CoRR abs/1410.0151 (2014)
21. Sun, X., Yu, F.R., Zhang, P.: A survey on cyber-security of connected and autonomous vehicles (CAVs). IEEE Trans. Intell. Transp. Syst. **23**(7), 6240–6259 (2022)
22. Veres, M., Moussa, M.: Deep learning for intelligent transportation systems: a survey of emerging trends. IEEE Trans. Intell. Transp. Syst. **21**(8), 3152–3168 (2020)
23. Vardhan, H.: HD Maps: new age maps Powering Autonomous vehicles (2019). https://www.geospatialworld.net/article/hd-maps-autonomous-vehicles/
24. Yin, Y., Li, Y., Ye, B., Liang, T., Li, Y.: A blockchain-based incremental update supported data storage system for intelligent vehicles. IEEE Trans. Veh. Technol. **70**(5), 4880–4893 (2021)
25. Yuan, Y., Wang, F.Y.: Towards blockchain-based intelligent transportation systems. In: Proceedings of ITSC, pp. 2663–2668 (2016)
26. Zang, A., Li, Z., Doria, D., Trajcevski, G.: Accurate vehicle self-localization in high definition map dataset. In: Proceedings of AutonomousGIS@SIGSPATIAL, pp. 2:1–2:8 (2017)
27. Zhong, L., Onishi, R., Wang, L., Ruan, L., Tan, S.J.: A scalable blockchain-based high-definition map update management system. In: Proceedings of ISC2, pp. 1–4 (2021)

Blockchain-Based Self-Sovereign Identity System with Attribute-Based Issuance

Yi-Hsiu Lee[1], Zi-Yuan Liu[1,2], Raylin Tso[1(✉)], and Yi-Fan Tseng[1]

[1] National Chengchi University, Taipei 11605, Taiwan
109753123@nccu.edu.tw, {zyliu,raylin,yftseng}@cs.nccu.edu.tw
[2] Kanazawa University, Kanazawa 920-1192, Japan

Abstract. With the rapid development of blockchain applications, digital identity management systems have started being deployed on decentralized networks. However, the inherent transparency of blockchain technology poses a challenge to privacy-conscious applications. To address this challenge, we adopt a DDH-based oblivious transfer and trust execution environment (TEE) to hide users' private attributes. Furthermore, we propose a concrete system that includes transferring users' attributes from a legacy server for verifying and issuing on the blockchain. In verifying protocol, we apply TEE in confidential smart contracts that execute the verification logic privately. Users can control their data and freely compose their identities using verified attributes. We also leverage smart contracts to record the status of attributes to achieve batch revocation of identities. Security analysis and comparison demonstrate that our system achieves privacy protection and is more user-centric in revocation than existing blockchain-based identity systems.

Keywords: Batch revocation · Blockchain · Decentralized identity · Self-sovereign

1 Introduction

1.1 Background and Related Work

At present, a considerable amount of data is transmitted over and stored on cloud applications such as online games, social media platforms, and membership systems. For flexible management, users usually need to register their accounts on the cloud servers. The cloud servers will store the properties uploaded by the users and record users' online activities for further analysis. As mentioned by Laurent and Bouzefrane [14][1], this information (*i.e.,* accounts, properties, and activities) represents the *digital identities* of the users.

In the original model of *digital identities*, each service is usually isolated, so there will be multiple sets of identifiers (ID) and credentials associated with each

[1] A digital identity refers to the information needed to activate an account, as well as any traces an individual leaves as a result of their activities.

C. Su et al. (Eds.): ISPEC 2022, LNCS 13620, pp. 21–38, 2022.
https://doi.org/10.1007/978-3-031-21280-2_2

service. This kind of model has the disadvantage that users need to memorize a large amount of login information. To overcome this challenge, the concept of *digital identity management system (DIMS)* is gradually attracting attention [6,14]. A DIMS enables digital identities to connect with individuals and makes them easier to maintain and manage. In general, there are many entities in DIMS, such as registry or identity providers (IdPs), which manage digital identities and execute the authenticate functions, and service providers (SPs). Once users register their digital identities with an IdP, they will receive a token or credential as proof, and then they can authenticate themselves at multiple SPs using the same digital identities to avail of various services.

With increased development of decentralized networks such as bitcoin [18] in recent years, people have gradually started to research DIMS on the blockchain network [8,12]. Owing to the features of the blockchain [9], such as that no one can tamper with the user's data once it is recorded on the blockchain or that anyone can become a node and host the distributed ledger with the consensus algorithm on the blockchain, we have opportunities to build new DIMSs with special properties that differ from traditional ones. We can build a trusted and decentralized DIMS in an untrusted internet environment, allowing users to have complete control of their identity attributes without depending on a single authority. This kind of DIMS also avoids the single point of failure problem in traditional centralized DIMS. With these advantages, new approaches of DIMS called *decentralized identity systems* [5,17,21] emerging. In some decentralized identity systems, users are allowed to possess an account under the *decentralized identifiers (DIDs)* [5,21]. With DID, users have full control over their own identities and attributes, achieving a user-centric model. The DID is regarded as a unique key of a person that integrates many attributes to compose an identity. By controlling the private key of DID, the user interacts with the service provider and freely discloses his attributes of identity in exchange for services. Users also allow some operations upon their identities, such as deleting and de-authorizing the attributes. We also note that the above conditions comply with the General Data Protection Regulation (GDPR) [24] proposed by European Union. If a system comply with such conditions, it is called a self-sovereign identity system [10].

Although some decentralized identity systems have been proposed, they encounter challenges in building systems through decentralized platforms. For example, decentralized identity systems require privacy protection, but the transparency feature of the blockchain has the opposite requirements. To solve the issue of protecting the user's privacy in decentralized identity systems on the blockchain, Yang *et al.* proposed a zero-knowledge-based decentralized identity system (BZDIMS) [27]. In this system, they implement zk-SNARK in an existing claim identity system to keep users' privacy, secretly transferring and authenticating the ownership of private attributes. Although they try to address privacy problems using zero-knowledge proof, the execution suffers from efficiency issues. Another decentralized identity system proposed by Deepak *et al.*, called CanDID [16], ports identities and credentials securely by the oracles (either DECO [29] or

Town Crier [28]) from the existing server to blockchain. Using the oracles, they preserve the user's privacy by means of the special protocol or trust execution environment, which may substantially improve the execution efficiency.

In addition, the systems that use a centralized authority to achieve revoking and issuing identities function usually cause overly centralized power issues. This issue will leave users unable to fully control their identities, making the systems unsuitable for self-sovereign identity systems. In BZDIMS, users cannot arbitrarily revoke or control their own identities' permissions by themselves; instead, they need the IdP who issues the identity attribute to execute revocation. In contrast, the revocation situation of the CanDID system needs the committee that issues the DIDs to create a public revocation list for the revoking process. Once the user's DID is recorded in the list, all credentials of the user will be revoked. This invalidates all credentials instead of revoking some specific problematic credentials. Furthermore, when the committee has the ability to issue and revoke credentials concurrently, it may have the aforementioned centralized power issue. To keep the privacy of the revocation list, CanDID performs privacy-preserving fuzzy matching through secure multiparty computation, which needs to develop special solutions for special cases to avoid impacting efficiency [7,11].

1.2 Motivation and Contribution

Decentralized identity systems suffer from privacy-related concerns, and a trade-off relationship between efficiency and privacy. Furthermore, we need to identify entity with potentially too much power on the decentralized network, which would make the whole system centralized so that the user would not be able to fully control his identity. We also consider the possibility of self-sovereign identity systems. With regard to revocation, there are few efficient methods that can accurately revoke specific attributes without affecting other valid attributes.

Aiming to address the aforementioned concerns, our main contributions in this study are as follows. We present a decentralized attribute-based self-sovereign identity system supporting issuance and batch revocation over the blockchain. In our system, we separate the power of issuing and revoking attributes into two entities instead of one centralized authority. This avoids concentration of the power within a specific entity, such as an IdP, avoiding this entity having too much power to adjudicate users and thus avoids having a single point of failure. Furthermore, we store the current status of every attribute transferred from the legacy server to the blockchain for the revocation mechanism. We use a smart contract as the method for recording because of its property of transparency, and it is also a native method on the blockchain. Considering the privacy protection of user's attributes in our system, we present a method for transferring attributes from the legacy server by oblivious transfer (OT), hiding users' data usage footprint. We also adapt the confidential smart contract with a trust execution environment that transforms the operation of smart contracts from transparent to private and improves processing efficiency. Finally, a comparison in terms of security analysis of our system and others is provided.

2 Blockchain-Based Self-sovereign Identity System with Attribute-Based Issuance

2.1 Problem Statement

We consider the current problems in decentralized identity systems on the blockchain.

- If we want to transfer a user's data from a legacy server to the blockchain, we need to consider the data privacy problem during the transmission. Specifically, when transmitting or retrieving users' identity data from/to in insecure channels, their data may be stolen or monitored and their personal information might be exposed.
- The legacy servers can obtain the data usage footprint of a user, which may result in privacy exposure of personal data usage footprint. As this data can be regarded as important commercial assets, the legacy servers will prevent unrelated entities from using this legacy server-authenticated data.
- When a user submits his attributes from the legacy server to the smart contract for verification, all execution steps and states inside the smart contract will be known to the public. Therefore, how to prevent this information from being leaked to other users is an important concern.
- Some blockchain-based identity issuance systems only transfer user's credentials (*e.g.,* a student credential composed of many attributes), instead of a unit of identity attributes, from the legacy server to the blockchain. This raises an issue with regard to revoking identity credentials—it is difficult to revoke a specific credential for a user who has a bunch of related and hierarchically structured credentials.

2.2 System Description

Our proposed system aims to resolve the above issues. It comprises four entities, namely the legacy server, user with attributes (user), verifier of attributes (verifier), and service provider, as shown in Fig. 1.

- Legacy server: The legacy server is an entity that ensures compliance with GDPR. Users can arbitrarily add and delete their personal data in accordance with the content of regulations. The legacy server is responsible for allowing users to retrieve their attribute data. In addition, the legacy server needs to instantly update the smart contract that manages the status of attributes. We note that in practice we can employ multiple legacy servers in the system in order to avoid single point of failure on the legacy server. However, for the convenience of discussion, we assume that there is only a legacy server in the system.

- User: The user is the owner of the attributes stored on the legacy server and has control over those attributes. He can choose which attributes he wants to transfer from the legacy server to the verifier. After receiving the verified identity attributes from the verifier, the user can compose his attributes into an identity for requesting a specific service provided by the service provider. For example, as people need to be over 18 years old to buy alcohol, buyers can add their verified age attribute into the identity and prove it to the wine merchant.
- Verifier: The verifier is responsible for drafting the requirements that the smart contract should verify, including verifying that the signature is signed using a designated legacy server's private key, timestamp, and attributes are eligible, and then deploying the smart contract to the blockchain. In addition, when the verifier receives unverified attributes from the user, he transfers them to the smart contract for verification. Then, the verifier binds the attributes that are already verified by the smart contract to the user and finally signs on the result and issues.
- Service provider: Upon receiving a service request from a user along with an identity, the service provider verifies the information in the identity, such as signatures on attributes and status of attributes, and decides whether the user should be served.

We consider an model of identity issuance and revocation system on the blockchain that is different from the traditional identity system in which one centralized authority has the power of revoking and issuing identity attributes. In our model, there are four types of parties: legacy server, user, verifier, and service provider. For instance, a user stores his age data on a legacy server, and the legacy server first verifies the authenticity of the data by interacting with the user off-chain. After data authentication, we can trust that the data is correct if the legacy server validates the identity attribute properly. We assume that the legacy server in this model is honest and GDPR-compliant. Hence, the user can delete or update his identity attributes directly through the legacy server. If the user wants to transfer and issue his legacy attributes from the legacy server to the blockchain, he first needs to send a query requesting attributes. Then, the legacy server sends the attribute with his signature to the user via OT, which leaves the legacy server unable to identify which message is transferred by the user, providing privacy for the attribute and the user. Meanwhile, the legacy server records a hash value of the message in a smart contract for checking the real-time status of attributes. When receiving the message from the legacy server, the user extracts the real information from the OT and signs their signature on the message for the next step of verification.

Before receiving the message from the user, the verifier first writes the verification logic inside a confidential smart contract for checking whether the transferred identity data satisfies the necessary conditions, and the verifier also needs to set a legacy server's public key for the signature verifying process which can prove that the data is indeed come from the legacy server. Afterward, the user encrypts the data by the public key of the confidential smart contract to protect his privacy. In addition, the user sends the data with his signature to the verifier. Then, the verifier signs on the data and sends it to the confidential smart contract for verification. When the confidential smart contract receives the user's data from the verifier, it starts executing the computation process without leaking any information and then outputs an encryption result to the verifier. For example, if the confidential smart contract is about verifying whether the user is an adult, this condition can simply be represented as a statement "your age > 18 years old." The confidential smart contract first checks if the data of the user's birth really comes from the legacy server by verifying the signature of the legacy server. Then, the confidential smart contract checks if the input age passes the inequality, encrypts the result which is a bit of true or false of the verification by the verifier's public key, and then sends the ciphertext to the verifier. Next, the verifier needs to bind the verified data to the user, prevent the data from being substituted, and then send the binding result and verified data with the verifier's signature as verified proof of issuance back to the user.

When the user receives a verified proof of issuance of his attribute, he composes an identity of his attributes according to the requirements of the service provider and proves them to the service provider to obtain services. On the side of the service provider, he needs to check each attribute value within the user identity, *e.g.,* if the issuer of the verified proof is an accredited verifier, and then compare the status and timestamp of each attribute to the smart contract that records the real-time status of attributes. Furthermore, the attributes recorded in the smart contract are managed by the legacy server. After passing all verification, the service provider can provide services to the user.

For attribute revocation, we consider two types of revocation situations in our system. One situation is executed by an authority as the government, while the other is performed by the users. If some specific identity attributes of the user are revoked owing to external reasons, such as the driver's license (the attribute of the ability to drive) being revoked by the authorities in charge, the executive authority will instruct the legacy server to perform revocation. Then, the legacy server updates its database and updates the status of attributes on the smart contract simultaneously. Additionally, the user can also decide whether to revoke or update his attributes on the blockchain by deleting or editing them on the legacy server. Once the attributes are revoked or updated, all changed attributes renew their status and timestamp on the smart contract. All identities that contain the revoked attribute will also become invalid, achieving batch revocation. Thus, all changed attributes need to be re-validated through the verification process again in order for the changed attributes to get activated.

3 Preliminaries

3.1 DDH-Based Oblivious Transfer

Oblivious transfer (OT) is a two-party protocol between sender and receiver introduced by Rabin [20], achieving the following functionalities. In the beginning, the receiver chooses a bit b as a private input, and the sender does not need to provide any private input. At the end of the protocol, the receiver gets either a bit b or an undefined value, but the sender cannot discover which value the receiver has learned with a probability of 50%. In this way, the receiver can obtain information from the sender but the sender does not know which information has been chosen. In this study, we adopt Naor and Pickas's 1-out-of-2 OT protocol ($\binom{1}{2}$-OT) [19]. Let $\mathbb{G}$ be a group with order p and g be a generator of $\mathbb{G}$. The messages m_0, m_1 owned by the sender are also the elements in $\mathbb{G}$. The protocol runs as follows:

- The receiver first randomly picks a private bit $b \in \{0, 1\}$ and $x, y, z_{1-b} \in \mathbb{Z}_p$. Then, he computes $z_b = xy$.
- The receiver sets $(A, B, C_0, C_1) \leftarrow (g_x, g_y, g^{z_0}, g^{z_1})$ and sends it to the sender.
- After the sender receives the tuple (A, B, C_0, C_1), he first checks whether $C_0 \neq C_1$. He then randomly picks $r, s \in \mathbb{Z}_p$ and computes $U = A^r g^s$, $\pi_i = C_i^r B^s$ for $i \in \{0, 1\}$. In addition, he computes $V_i = \pi_i m_i$ for $i \in \{0, 1\}$. He then returns (U, V_0, V_1) to the receiver.
- Finally, the receiver computes $\pi_b = U^y$, where b is the value he chose at first step. He can then obtain the message m_b by computing $m_b = V_b / \pi_b$.

3.2 Confidential Smart Contract

Smart contract [25,26] is proposed to enrich functions of the blockchain, and it also follows the properties of the blockchain platform, such as transparency. Anyone can write code for the logic of smart contracts and deploy it on the blockchain, interacting with other nodes on the platform, resulting in a variety of applications on the decentralized network, which are called Dapps. The entire process of executing inside the smart contract is also obvious to people. However, the transparency for those privacy-demanding applications and users becomes a shortcoming. Users do not want their private information to be disclosed to the world but hope to have limited disclosure only when there is a need for use. Consequently, many cryptographic tools, such as zero-knowledge proofs [2,4, 13], homomorphic encryption [22], and multi-party computation [30], have been applied to the smart contracts of Dapps in recent years in order to achieve the purpose of protecting privacy. However, these mathematics-based methods have encountered bottlenecks in the efficiency of execution.

Therefore, a trust execution environment (TEE) [15] solution has been proposed for the confidential smart contracts, which moves complex computations into secure hardware and has good performance, also providing applications privacy. TEE uses the CPU hardware to prevent adversaries from tampering with personal sensitive data. The TEE has the ability to provide a secure environment for executing the computation in the contract code. The code is running in an isolated location on the processors, guaranteeing the integrity of its execution and the confidentiality of the state. For example, Intel SGX usually ensures that the TEE has an isolation place in the chip called *secure enclave* for running contract code in privacy, without leaking any information, and cannot be compromised even by the TEE operator. It also has *remote attestation*, which can prove that code is running on a remote machine. Furthermore, the *sealing* enables the enclave to encrypt its secret data to prevent the information from leaking when being transferred in an untrusted environment. Current systems having privacy issues have adopted TEE in their system. For instance, Szalachowski [23] proposed password-authenticated decentralized identities systems that used confidential smart contracts. Brandenburger *et al.* [3] proposed a solution of trusted computing on the Hyperledger Fabric [1] using confidential smart contracts.

Each created confidential smart contract generated a special key pair and published them. This key pair can protect the contract and identify it. The confidential smart contract must ensure that before a transaction is sent to the confidential contract, it can be encrypted as a ciphertext by the TEE's public key, which can transfer the user's private message in a public environment. We assume that our system exposes the public key of a confidential smart contract, allowing users to encrypt the private data by the contract public key and then send encrypted transactions to the contract for verification, and then computes the entire process confidentially to maintain the user's privacy.

4 Proposed System

In this section, we first propose a concrete system shown in Fig. 1 and illustrate each step in detail.

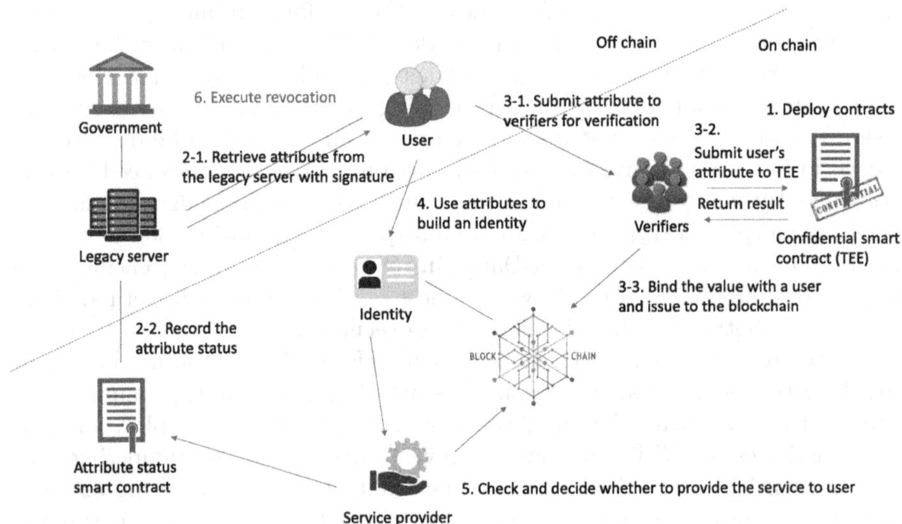

Fig. 1. Overview of the proposed system

Phase 1 - Deploy Contracts. In our system, the attribute status smart contract shows the user's attributes status instantly, which are maintained by the legacy server, and while the other attribute-verifying contract is deployed and written by the verifier.

Table 1. Meaning of attribute status data in smart contract

Types	Descriptions
$hash(attr_i)$	Hash value of user's attribute
$status$	Real-time attribute status
$time_{sign}$	Timestamp of transferring this attribute from the legacy server

Table 2. Meaning of user's attribute list data

Types	Descriptions
$name$	The name of this attribute
$\sigma_{verifier}$	The verifier (issuer) of this attribute, *e.g.*, represent as verifier's signature
$resultValue$	The resultValue illustrates that the result of an attribute whether to pass the attribute-verifying smart contract
$hash(attr_i)$	The hash value of user's attribute
$statusAddr$	A smart contract address which directs to the smart contract containing the real-time status of this attribute
$time_{issue}$	The timestamp of issuing this attribute from verifier

- Attribute status smart contract: This smart contract has a function that creates a map to record the attribute transferred from the legacy server to the user. After the legacy server has transferred the attribute, it needs to call the smart contract function as Algorithm 1 to add a new attribute. Furthermore, the legacy server needs to instantly update and maintain the status of attributes on this smart contract if the attribute is invalid because of expiration, being revoked by the government, or being revoked by the user himself, as synchronized with the records in the legacy server's database. For example, if the government rescinds a specific attribute of a person such as the ability to drive a car owing to the user committing a crime, the legacy server not only needs to update the status in their own database but in this smart contract as well. The data of attributes recorded in the smart contract is summarized in Table 1, containing a hash value $hash(attr_i)$ of attribute value $attr_i$, a current status $status$, and a timestamp of status $time_{sign}$, which represents the transferring time from the legacy server.

  Another useful function is that when the service provider or attribute-verifying smart contract wants to query the information of a specific attribute,

Algorithm 1. statusRecordFunction()

Input: $hash(attr_i), time_{sign}, status$

Output: $LogCreateInfo()$

$require(msg.sender == serverAddress)$
//create a mapping from hash to attribute information
attrInfos$[hash(attr_i)].hashValue = hash(attr_i)$
attrInfos$[hash(attr_i)].timestamp_{sign} = time_{sign}$
attrInfos$[hash(attr_i)].attrStatus = status$
Emit the event $LogCreateInfo(hash(attr_i), time_{sign}, status)$

Algorithm 2. statusQueryFunction()

Input: $hash(attr_i)$

Output: $LogInfo()$

//mapping from attribute hash to get attribute information
$qTime_{sign} =$ attrInfos$[hash(attr_i)].timestamp_{sign}$
$qStatus =$ attrInfos$[hash(attr_i)].attrStatus$
Emit the event $LogInfo(hash(attr_i), qTime_{sign}, qStatus)$

they use $hash(attr_i)$ as a key for mapping in this smart contract function to get the information, as presented in Algorithm 2.

- Attribute-verifying smart contract: This contract is in charge of validating the attributes transferred from the legacy server, which the user wants to issue on the blockchain. This smart contract, which is made by TEE, is considered as a secure environment for running contract logic in isolated hardware. For example, Intel Software Guard Extension (Intel SGX) allows a user to create a secure place, called an enclave, for computing. As TEE has its own key pairs, the user establishes a secure channel where the messages are all encrypted with the TEE remote hosts. Then, SGX runs trusted contract logic in enclaves and uses hardware to prevent adversaries from knowing or tampering with private data. In this manner, TEE guarantees execution integrity and state confidentiality of blockchain, and no one, not even the TEE host, knows the computing process inside this contract.

Phase 2 - Retrieve Attribute from the Legacy Server. In this phase, we transfer an attribute from a legacy server that is GDPR-compliant to the user by OT. The attribute record on the legacy server has been verified for authenticity before the transfer starts. We assume that the transfer attribute is m_b. At first, the user picks a bit b from $\{0, 1\}$, picks random x, y from $\mathbb{Z}_p$, and then computes $Z_b = xy$, and picks a random Z_{1-b} from $\mathbb{Z}_p$. Then, $(g^x, g^y, g^{z_0}, g^{z_1})$ is set as (A, B, C_0, C_1) and (A, B, C_0, C_1) is sent to the legacy server. At the legacy server side, it first checks if $C_0 \neq C_1$. Then, he randomly picks r, s from $\mathbb{Z}_p$, and computes

$$U = A^r g^s; \quad \pi_i = C_s^r B^s \text{ for } i \in \{0,1\}.$$

Next, for $i = 0, 1$, the legacy server generates a signature σ_{server_i} by signing algorithm $Sign(sk_s, m_i)$, where

$$m_i = (attr_i \| hash(attr_i) \| statusAddr \| time_{sign}).$$

Finally, for $i = 0, 1$, the legacy server computes $V_i = \pi_i \sigma_{server_i}$, and sends (U, V_0, V_1) back to the user. After receiving these parameters, the user gets the true σ_{server_b}, which he actually wants to transfer from the legacy server secretly, by computing $\pi_b = U^y$ and $\sigma_{server_b} = V_b/\pi_b$. The user finally gets σ_{server_b}, and by the signature-verifying algorithm he received $m_b = (attr_b \| hash(attr_b) \| statusAddr \| time_{sign})$, where m_b is the attribute the user wants to transfer, where $b = 1$. The $attr_b$ is the attribute value for verifying. The $hash(attr_b)$ is used as a key value for mapping in the attribute status smart contract whose address is $statusAddr$. Later, the user uses the public key of TEE pk_c to encrypt the data m_1 as ciphertext c_1, then uses his secret key sk_u to sign a signature on the ciphertext and send it to the verifier for the next verifying phase.

Through OT, the user transfers his value from the legacy server and keeps the privacy of the attribute. Meanwhile, the transferred data along with the legacy server's signature is considered as proof that this attribute indeed came from the legacy server, which is GDPR-compliant and has already verified the attribute. We use OT to construct a secure channel to prevent external adversaries and prevent the legacy server from knowing the information of the transferred data. Using the public key pk_c of TEE, the user encrypts his attribute data which may contain his private information, preventing the data from exposure.

When the transfer is completed, the legacy server calls the function in Algorithm 1 to create a mapping for the attribute status. Both the messages transferred in OT need to be registered because the legacy server does not know which attribute transferred but it is the one the user indeed needs.

Phase 3 - Verify and Issue Attributes to the Blockchain. After the verifier receives the ciphertext c_1 with the user's signature σ_{user} from the user, he then signs his signature on the ciphertext using his private key sk_v. Next, the verifier sends the c_1 and signatures to the attribute-verifying smart contract for verification. When the attribute-verifying smart contract receives the input data from the verifier, it first verifies signatures $\sigma_{verifier}$ and σ_{user}; if they are verified, then the ciphertext c_1 is decrypted using the private key of TEE sk_c to get m_1 with the signature of the legacy server. If the signature of the legacy server passes the verification, it means that this attribute indeed transfers from the legacy server. Next, the attribute-verifying smart contract verifies whether the attribute value $attr_1$ meets the statement in this contract, which represents the verified conditions of this contract ($e.g., verify\ the\ age\ value > 18$). If the data form of birthday value $attr_i$ is $yyyy/mm/dd$, the logic of this contract can be written as $today's\ yyyy/mm/dd - birthday's\ yyyy/mm/dd = r$. If $r > 18$

passes the verification, it means the person's age attribute is older than 18 years old. Then, this contract verifies the timestamp of m_1, *i.e.*, whether $time_{sign}$ is earlier than $time_{now}$. This means that the attribute is actually generated earlier. If all verification criteria are met, the TEE encrypts the result using the verifier's public key pk_v to protect the user's private information. Finally, the verifier uses his private key to decrypt the result and binds the result with the user's public key pk_u by signing on the statement:

$$resultValue\|hash(attr_b)\|statusAddr\|time_{issue}\|pk_u.$$

Then, the verifier encrypts the entire data of the verification procedure as c_{attr} using the user's public key pk_u and sends them back to the user. The entire protocol of submitting and verifying the user's attribute is described in https://gist.github.com/identity-system-protocol/0fa46c8385dbb0a1035a29313ccb78d1.

Phase 4 - Use Attributes to Build an Identity. After receiving a verified result of the attribute with the verifier's signature, which represents that the result was bound with the user, the user gets the attributes as a list, presented in Table 2. According to the user's verified-attributes list, the user can freely compose his identity by several attributes, according to the requirements of the service provider he submits. In this way, the smallest unit that constitutes identity is turned into an attribute, and when a specific attribute of the user is revoked, the identity containing the revoked attribute will also be revoked. In contrast, if the identity does not contain the revoked attributes, it will not be affected. The advantage of this method is that when a specific attribute is revoked, the identities containing this attribute can be revoked in batches, but the use of other identities is not affected, which makes the management of users more convenient.

Phase 5 - Use Identity to Avail of the Service. When receiving the user's identity, the service provider needs to check whether every attribute in the identity meets the conditions he proposed. First, the service provider checks if the attribute is $verifiedAttr$ with the verifier's signature. Then, the service provider checks the attribute status and compares the timestamp of the attribute issuance with the timestamp recorded in the attribute status smart contract. If the timestamp in this contract is generated earlier than the timestamp of issuance, this attribute is valid; otherwise, the timestamp of issuance is earlier than the timestamp in this contract, indicating that an attribute update has occurred in the attribute status smart contract, so the user needs to re-do all the steps from retrieving the attribute to verifying the attribute. If all verification criteria are met, the service provider provides the service to the user.

Phase 6 - Update and Revoke Attribute. In our system, we consider two situations for revocation: revocation by a government authority, such as the driving license being revoked because of a serious traffic violation, and the user's self-revocation, to meet the regulations of GDPR. In the situation of revocation by the government, the government informs the legacy server that the identity attributes of a particular user have been revoked. As the legacy server is a legal server, it obeys the government's instructions. When the legacy server receives the instruction for revoking an attribute, it first changes the attribute status stored in the database inside the legacy server. Meanwhile, it sends a transaction to change the attribute status in the attribute status smart contract. When the service provider checks each attribute in the user's identity before providing the service, it will re-compare the current status of the attribute recorded in the attribute status smart contract. If the status shown as "revoke" is checked, it regards the user's identity as invalid and the service provider will not provide services.

Next, we consider the situation of updating the attributes, *e.g.,* there are some attributes that may have validity periods like student identity status. If the expiration date of the attribute is approaching, the legacy server updates the attribute status and renews the timestamp proactively. Until the user re-does the phase of retrieving the attribute from the legacy server to attribute verification again, the timestamp $time_{sign}$ in the attribute status smart contract is later than the timestamp $time_{issue}$ in the user's attribute list. This means the identity which contains the updated attribute cannot pass the checking procedure of the service provider until the user re-verifies his attributes. As the identity submitted to the service provider is composed of attributes, which the service provider wants to check, the attributes are units in our system. Furthermore, a user also has many identities concurrently. For example, an identity as a student ID contains attributes such as age, validity period, and department. The identity as a driver's license includes attributes such as whether they passed the driver's license test, age, and validity period. However, in some special cases, for example, the legacy server has doubts about the user's age and needs this age attribute to be re-verified, that particular attribute is temporarily revoked. This causes the status recorded in the attribute status smart contract to change and causes the age attribute in the identities submitted to the service provider to be invalidated, thereby causing all identities containing this attribute to be invalidated. Under our system, batch revoking identity is achieved by simply revoking attributes.

5 Security Analysis

In this section, we first analyze our system in terms of the security constraints presented in Table 3. Before our analysis, we first consider the following preconditions:

1. The legacy server is a GDPR-compliant entity, which verifies the user's attributes by interacting with the user.
2. The verifier is a trusted party, and the running codes of the attribute-verifying smart contract deployed by the verifier are honest, not malicious, and vulnerable.

3. The service provider does not disclose the identity submitted by the user, and can only obtain the minimized data of the user.
4. The security of a confidential smart contract is guaranteed by the hardware of TEE. No parties can retrieve the information from the hardware.

Table 3. Security constraints

Security constraint	Condition	Purpose
Unlinkability of attributes	A user's identity cannot be known by cross-comparing the attributes recorded on the attribute status smart contract and the attributes on the user's identity	Prevent the user's identity information from being leaked
Privacy of the user	A user's private data cannot be known when operating in the system	Prevent the user's privacy data from being leaked by others entities
Data minimization of the user	A user only needs to submit the minimized data to the service provider	Prevent the user from exposing unnecessary information to others
Attribute authorization	The authenticity of the source of the user data can be verified	Prevent the user data from forging by third parties
Verified attribute substituting attack	A user's verified attribute cannot be used by others entities	Prevent the user's verified attribute be substituted by an adversary
Single point of failure	A single point of verify or legacy server failure does not affect the entire system	Prevent an adversary from attacking a single server and paralyzing the entire system

Unlinkability of Attributes. The information stored in the attribute status smart contract is in the form of hash values, instead of the plaintext (*i.e.*, attributes) stored via the hash value. Therefore, if an adversary tries to retrieve the attributes of identity, he has to find the inverse of a hash value. In other words, no adversary can obtain the information of the attributes if the underlying hash function is secure.

Privacy of the User. We consider four scenarios as follows:

- Retrieve attributes from the legacy server: Our system adopts OT protocol to prevent the legacy server and third parties from obtaining what attributes data the user wants to retrieve. In other words, if there exists an adversary that can obtain attribute information, then there exists another adversary that can successfully break the security of the underlying OT protocol.
- Submit attributes to the verifier: When a user submits a transferred attribute σ_{server_b}, which is obtained from legacy server via OT protocol, to verifiers on the blockchain, our system will compute a ciphertext $c \leftarrow Enc(pk_c, \sigma_{server_b})$ by using the public key of TEE. Therefore, no adversary can obtain any information from this insecure channel.
- Verify the confidential smart contract: We set TEE as the attribute-verifying smart contract running environment. The key pair of TEE can be used to securely transmit data. In addition, TEE is a hardware-based computing environment that exists in an isolated place (enclave) in the chip; therefore,

no one, not even the chip holder, can obtain information about the computing process.

– Return the attribute from confidential smart contract: After passing the verification of the attribute that is verified by attribute-verifying smart contract, the $resultValue$ will be encrypted by verifier's public key pk_v as

$$\hat{c} \leftarrow Enc(pk_v, resultValue||hash(attr_b)||statusAddr||time_{issue}),$$

and be returned to the verifier. As our system only renders the $resultValue$ value (True/False) as the answer to the verification, instead of presenting the entire attribute data to the service provider, there exists no information leakage.

Data Minimization of the User. When the attribute passes the verification process in the attribute-verifying smart contract, it returns the verification result called $verifiedAttr$ instead of the entire attribute values transferred from the legacy server. After the user receives the $verifiedAttr$, he can compose his own identity using several $verifiedAttr$ according to the requirements of the service provider. This means the user only needs to reveal the necessary attributes to the service provider.

Attribute Authorization. To ensure that the source of the attributes is correct and has been authorized by legacy server, the legacy server is required to generate the corresponding signature by $Sign(sk_s, m_i) \rightarrow \sigma_{server_i}$ for $i = 0, 1$. In addition, the verification of the signature is performed in the attribute-verifying smart contract, which is deployed by the verifier. After the signature passing the verification of the attribute-verifying smart contract, a verifier issues a $verifiedAttr$ with his signature. When a user's $verifiedAttr$ contains the verifier's signature, its attribute has been authorized by the legacy server and verified by the attribute-verifying smart contract. Therefore, if the underlying signature scheme is secure and the attribute-verifying smart contract works correctly, our system provides attribute authorization.

Verified Attribute Substituting Attack. As the verified attribute that a verifier receives from the attribute-verifying smart contract is an $unbindAttr$, it may be stolen and used by an adversary if it does not bind to the owner of the attribute. To prevent this, in our system, the verifier binds the $unbindAttr$ to a user by adding the pk_u to the statement. The verifier then generates a signature on the statement and produces a $verifiedAttr$.

Single Point of Failure. In the analysis below, we consider two entities with concerns about the single point of failure—verifier and legacy servers. As any TEE-capable user can act as a verifier, a single point of failure is avoided even if the verifier is disconnected. In contrast, our system comprises multiple legacy servers to transfer the attributes with signatures as the proof of the source. It thus also avoids single-point failure even if some of the legacy servers are disconnected.

6 Comparisons

We now compare our proposed system with the existing systems [16,27] in terms of revocation entity, revocation unit, and building blocks. As summarized in Table 4, we introduce a novel revocation mechanism that decentralizes the power of revocation to the legacy server and user. In contrast, the revocation entity in BZDIMS and CanDID is only a single entity. Furthermore, compared with CanDID, the revocation unit of our system is the attribute that is the same as BZDIMS, instead of the user's pre-credential in CanDID. Consequently, users can manage their identities more flexibly. In terms of building blocks, our system adopts smart contracts and TEE as the building blocks. Therefore, compared to other systems, our system can not only protect privacy but maintain efficiency when executing confidential smart contracts.

Table 4. Comparisons of blockchain-based identity systems

Properties	Ours	BZDIMS	CanDID
Revocation entity	Server & User	IDP	Government
Revocation unit	Attribute	Attribute	User
Building blocks	SC & TEE	SC & ZKP	Oracle

7 Conclusion

In this paper, we present a self-sovereign identity system supporting attribute-based issuance by using the OT scheme and TEE in the confidential smart contract. Compared with other systems, our system comprises two attributes issuing entities: verifiers and attributes revoking entities to decentralize the power of issuance and revocation. In addition, the smallest unit to constitute the identity of a user is the attribute. When a specific attribute of the user is revoked, the identities related to that attribute are also revoked. Furthermore, users can freely delete and update their attributes on the legacy server that is synchronously updated to the blockchain. Therefore, the proposed system meets the requirements of GDPR.

However, our system adopts OT to achieve the indistinguishability of transfer attributes. This method requires the attribute domain to be large. If the domain is small (such as for the gender attribute), then the adversary can obtain the attribute information by simply using a brute force attack over OT. Preventing this is an open problem that we will investigate in a future study.

Acknowledgments. The authors thank the anonymous reviewers of ISPEC 2022 for their insightful suggestions on this work. This research is partially supported by the National Science and Technology Council, Taiwan (ROC), under grant numbers NSTC 109-2221-E-004-011-MY3, NSTC 110-2221-E-004-003-, NSTC 110-2622-8-004-001-, and NSTC 111-2218-E-004-001-MBK.

References

1. Androulaki, E., et al.: Hyperledger fabric: a distributed operating system for permissioned blockchains. In: EUROSYS 2018, pp. 1–15 (2018)
2. Baghery, K.: On the efficiency of privacy-preserving smart contract systems. In: Buchmann, J., Nitaj, A., Rachidi, T. (eds.) AFRICACRYPT 2019. LNCS, vol. 11627, pp. 118–136. Springer, Cham (2019). https://doi.org/10.1007/978-3-030-23696-0_7
3. Brandenburger, M., Cachin, C., Kapitza, R., Sorniotti, A.: Blockchain and trusted computing: problems, pitfalls, and a solution for hyperledger fabric. CoRR abs/1805.08541 (2018). http://arxiv.org/abs/1805.08541
4. Bünz, B., Bootle, J., Boneh, D., Poelstra, A., Wuille, P., Maxwell, G.: Bulletproofs: short proofs for confidential transactions and more. In: S&P 2018, pp. 315–334. IEEE (2018)
5. Decentralized identity foundation.https://identity.foundation/, Accessed 20 June 2022
6. Digital identity management. https://www.raulwalter.com/government/digital-identity-management/. Accessed 20 July 2022
7. Du, W., Atallah, M.J.: Secure multi-party computation problems and their applications: a review and open problems. In: NSPW 2001, pp. 13–22. ACM (2001)
8. Dunphy, P., Petitcolas, F.A.: A first look at identity management schemes on the blockchain. IEEE S&P **16**(4), 20–29 (2018)
9. Efanov, D., Roschin, P.: The all-pervasiveness of the blockchain technology. Procedia Comput. Sci. **123**, 116–121 (2018)
10. Ferdous, M.S., Chowdhury, F., Alassafi, M.O.: In search of self-sovereign identity leveraging blockchain technology. IEEE Access **7**, 103059–103079 (2019)
11. Goldreich, O.: Secure multi-party computation. Manuscript. Preliminary version **78**(110) (1998)
12. Jacobovitz, O.: Blockchain for identity management. Technical report, The Lynne and William Frankel Center for Computer Science Department of Computer Science, Ben-Gurion University, Beersheba, Israel (2016). https://www.cs.bgu.ac.il/frankel/TechnicalReports/2016/16-02.pdf
13. Kosba, A., Miller, A., Shi, E., Wen, Z., Papamanthou, C.: Hawk: the blockchain model of cryptography and privacy-preserving smart contracts. In: S&P 2016, pp. 839–858. IEEE (2016)
14. Laurent, M., Bouzefrane, S.: Digital Identity Management. Elsevier (2015)
15. Li, R., Wang, Q., Wang, Q., Galindo, D., Ryan, M.: SoK: TEE-assisted confidential smart contract. Proc. Priv. Enhancing Technol. **2022**(3), 711–731 (2022)
16. Maram, D., et al.: CanDID: Can-Do decentralized identity with legacy compatibility, sybil-resistance, and accountability. In: S&P 2021, pp. 1348–1366. IEEE (2021)
17. Naik, N., Jenkins, P.: uPort open-source identity management system: an assessment of self-sovereign identity and user-centric data platform built on blockchain. In: ISSE 2020, pp. 1–7. IEEE (2020)
18. Nakamoto, S.: Bitcoin: a peer-to-peer electronic cash system (2008). http://www.bitcoin.org/bitcoin.pdf
19. Naor, M., Pinkas, B.: Oblivious transfer with adaptive queries. In: Wiener, M. (ed.) CRYPTO 1999. LNCS, vol. 1666, pp. 573–590. Springer, Heidelberg (1999). https://doi.org/10.1007/3-540-48405-1_36

20. Rabin, M.O.: How to exchange secrets with oblivious transfer. IACR Cryptol. ePrint Arch. **187** (2005). https://eprint.iacr.org/2005/187
21. Reed, D., et al.: Decentralized identifiers (DIDs) v1.0. Technical report, W3C (2020). https://www.w3.org/TR/did-core/
22. Solomon, R., Almashaqbeh, G.: smartFHE: privacy-preserving smart contracts from fully homomorphic encryption. IACR Cryptol. ePrint Arch. **133** (2021). https://eprint.iacr.org/2021/133
23. Szalachowski, P.: Password-authenticated decentralized identities. IEEE Trans. Inf. Forensics Secur. **16**, 4801–4810 (2021)
24. Voigt, P., Von dem Bussche, A.: The EU General Data Protection Regulation (GDPR). Springer, Cham (2017)
25. Wang, S., Yuan, Y., Wang, X., Li, J., Qin, R., Wang, F.Y.: An overview of smart contract: architecture, applications, and future trends. In: IV 2018, pp. 108–113. IEEE (2018)
26. Wood, G., et al.: Ethereum: a secure decentralised generalised transaction ledger. Yellow paper, Ethereum project (2014). https://files.gitter.im/ethereum/yellowpaper/VIyt/Paper.pdf
27. Yang, X., Li, W.: A zero-knowledge-proof-based digital identity management scheme in blockchain. Comput. Secur. **99**, 102050 (2020)
28. Zhang, F., Cecchetti, E., Croman, K., Juels, A., Shi, E.: Town crier: an authenticated data feed for smart contracts. In: CCS 2016, pp. 270–282 (2016)
29. Zhang, F., Maram, D., Malvai, H., Goldfeder, S., Juels, A.: DECO: liberating web data using decentralized oracles for TLS. In: CCS 2020, pp. 1919–1938 (2020)
30. Zyskind, G., Nathan, O., Pentland, A.: Enigma: decentralized computation platform with guaranteed privacy. CoRR abs/1506.03471 (2015). http://arxiv.org/abs/1506.03471

Blockchain-Based Confidential Payment System with Controllable Regulation

Yu-Chen Liao[1], Raylin Tso[1(✉)], Zi-Yuan Liu[1,2], and Yi-Fan Tseng[1]

[1] National Chengchi University, Taipei 11605, Taiwan
109753124@nccu.edu.tw, {raylin,zyliu,yftseng}@cs.nccu.edu.tw
[2] Kanazawa University, Kanazawa 920-1192, Japan

Abstract. Blockchain-based payment systems (e.g., Bitcoin) have been wildly adopted for many scenarios since the transaction details are publicly accessible. Blockchain-based anonymous payment systems (e.g., Monero and Zerocash) have also been proposed to protect on-chain privacy, such as the sender's or receiver's balance, and the transaction amount. However, overly privacy preserving systems are sometimes abused for malicious behavior in lieu of suitable regulation. Thus, balancing between requirements for regulation and privacy has become an important issue for such systems. This paper proposes a blockchain-based confidential payment system with controllable regulation. To protect user privacy and provide controllable regulations, we realized the proposed system using threshold homomorphic encryption to encrypt user transaction values and balance. The encryption was performed with thresholded regulators' keys and hence limits regulator abilities to decrypt a transaction. In addition, we can update the user's balance using the homomorphic property, without decrypting the transaction value or user's balance, preserving on-chain privacy, while satisfying all security requirements. A prototype implementation is provided for performance analysis.

Keywords: Accountability · Blockchain · Confidential transaction · Threshold homomorphic encryption

1 Introduction

Blockchain has been applied to many applications for its immutability, verifiability, and decentralization. Financial service, such as cryptocurrency, is a very popular blockchain utilization. However, although cryptocurrency has several advantages over traditional finance tools, including improved accessibility and instant remittances, privacy remains a concern due to the underlying nature of blockchain. In a blockchain system, in order to verify the correctness of a transaction, nodes need to access details within a blockchain system, e.g., sender, receiver, and transaction amount. However, it may not be appropriate to reveal sensitive information to everyone for some scenarios. Hence most cryptocurrencies employ pseudonym mechanisms to offer some level of anonymity, e.g., Bitcoin [17] and Ethereum [3]

C. Su et al. (Eds.): ISPEC 2022, LNCS 13620, pp. 39–56, 2022.
https://doi.org/10.1007/978-3-031-21280-2_3

However, studies have shown that using methods like transaction graph analysis [8] and address clustering [22], adversaries can de-anonymize users and subsequently trace their transactions. Some cryptocurrencies, e.g., bitcoin, allow users to create distinct and anonymous accounts as payers for a transaction. However, an adversary can use graph analysis, turning every account and transaction flow into a graph, and hence treat different payer accounts in one transaction as one entity. The adversary can then de-anonymize different anonymous accounts by following the whole transaction graph on the blockchain. Thus, simply creating multiple anonymous accounts is insufficient. To solve the above issue, various decentralized anonymous payment (DAP) schemes have been proposed to further improve privacy, including Monero [23] and Zerocash [2]. Such DAP schemes use cryptographic techniques, including zero-knowledge proof and ring signatures, and offer strong privacy that hides sender, receiver, and amount in a transaction.

Although DAP schemes can greatly enhance user privacy, they can also be abused in the absence of regulation. Since no authority controls user identities, and transaction details are hidden in DAP schemes, it is difficult to devise suitable regulatory measures. Consequently, cryptocurrency can be used to conduct illegal acts such as money laundering and terrorist funding [24].

One relatively simple approach to tackle this problem is to introduce an additional regulator to the DAP scheme that can decrypt and check every transaction before appending it to the blockchain. However, although this can eliminate regulatory concerns discussed above, it also gives regulators access to all transaction details, and regulator(s) can secretly exclude certain transactions from the system to gain unfair advantages for others, since every transaction must pass through a regulator before being appended to the blockchain. An alternate approach is to eliminate a central regulator by adding zero-knowledge proofs for every transaction. Zero-knowledge proofs ensure each transaction follows certain regulatory policies, such as limiting transaction frequency or other anti-money laundering measures. Thus, zero-knowledge proofs can achieve regulatory requirements without introducing any central authorities, such as regulator(s).

However, zero-knowledge proof is also insufficient for practical regulatory needs. Rules need to be provided beforehand and encoded in the system, so that any transaction that passes the rule check cannot be subsequently monitored or analyzed. As little as 0.1% to 0.3% of money laundering is currently detected with present anti-money laundering policies [20]. Being able to subsequently analyze transactions to identify money laundering is critical to tackle the problem [16], and relying solely on regulatory policies is insufficient.

1.1 Contribution

In this paper, we try to find the balance between privacy and regulation. Although the regulator does not check every transaction's content before appending it to the blockchain, it must be able to perform regulatory tasks if necessary. To achieve this goal, we first encrypt the transaction amount and user balance with the regulator's key to maintain privacy. This ensures that no one except the regulator will be able to observe the transaction amount. Then we partition validator and regulator roles, where validators only check the correctness of a transaction and are responsible for updating the blockchain, as with nodes in some blockchain systems. Zero-knowledge proofs validate transaction correctness without leaking transaction details. In addition, the user's balance is correctly updated by homomorphic encryption. Thus, the validator does not have to decrypt every transaction before validating it and updating the blockchain.

In contrast, regulators are special entities that do not participate in any transactions and are only responsible for regulatory tasks. To prevent the regulator from decrypting any transaction at will, we set a threshold number t at the system setup. Transaction amount can only be revealed only if at least t regulators participate in a decryption. We employ threshold encryption to split the private key between regulators, and they must go through a "voting" process to decrypt a transaction. Thus, threshold encryption allows regulator powers to be controlled within the system. Furthermore, we provides a proof-of-concept implementation of the proposed system. Note that we only hide the transaction amount but leave the sender and the receiver in plaintext. This is due to the need for accountability. If we hide the transaction as well as the sender and the receiver, the regulators will have no choice but to decrypt every transaction in order to supervise the system. This would break the threshold design and also damage user privacy.

1.2 Related Works

Cryptonote [21] and Zerocoin [13] are two seminal confidential blockchain payment schemes. Cryptonote utilizes traceable ring signatures to hide transaction sender and recipient details, creating the Monero protocol which uses similar techniques. Zerocoin uses zero-knowledge proof and an accumulator scheme to break the linkage between different transactions. Ben-Sasson et al. [2] proposed Zerocash based on Zerocoin, which formulates decentralized anonymous payment (DAP) schemes and provides strong anonymity through SNARKs [19] and commitment schemes. In contrast, Ethereum uses the AZTEC protocol [25] combining uses zero-knowledge proof and commitment schemes to provide verifiable confidential transactions.

Previous studies have proposed many approaches to allow regulation in DAP schemes. Garman et al. [12] included user and coin tracing in Zerocash using zk-SNARKs. Lin et al. proposed a decentralized condition anonymous payment system DCAP [15] that hides transaction sender and recipient. However, DCAP manager(s) needs the sender and recipient real addresses to validate each transaction and append the transaction on the blockchain, hence the manager can reject any transaction. Cecchetti et al. [5] proposed Solidus, employing publicly verifiable oblivious RAM, only allowing users' banks to obtain their identity;

whereas others can only learn the bank identities. This approach is suitable for modern financial systems. Chen et al. [7] proposed PGC using zero-knowledge proof to ensure transactions follow certain policies. Xue et al. [26] also proposed a payment system using zero-knowledge proof to ensure compliance with certain transactional policies. However, although zero-knowledge proof can maintain decentralization while providing regulatory means, it may not be sufficient for all regulatory requirements described above.

1.3 Organization

The remainder of this paper is organized as follows. Section 2 presents cryptographic primitives that used to construct the proposed system and describe the security. Section 3 provides a high-level view of the proposed system and then defines the system and security models. Section 4 subsequently presents an in-depth view for the proposed system. Section 5 presents an efficiency analysis for the proposed system and proof-of-concept implementation. Finally, Sect. 6 summarizes the paper and discusses future research directions.

2 Preliminaries

2.1 Threshold Cryptosystem Without A Trusted Party

Informally, in threshold cryptosystems [18], a secret key is split among n members, and a ciphertext can only be decrypted if more than t members ($1 \leq t \leq n$) cooperate. In particular, if the selecting and distributing of a secret key can be achieved without assistance from a trusted party, then the threshold cryptosystem is further called a threshold cryptosystem without a trusted party.

Formally, a threshold cryptosystem without a trusted party comprises six algorithms $(Setup, GenPK, GenSharedSK, Encrypt, Decrypt, CombineShare)$, as follows.

- $Setup(\lambda) \rightarrow pp$. On inputting of a security parameter λ, it outputs public parameters pp. Here, the threshold value t is implicitly contained in pp.
- $GenPK(pp) \rightarrow \{pk_1, pk_2, \cdots, pk_n\}$. On inputting of the public parameters pp, each member of the group generates his or her share of the public key pk_i where $i \in \{1, 2, \cdots, n\}$ and then broadcasts it to other users. After receiving all other's shares, each member can calculate and output the same public key pk.
- $GenSharedSK(pp, pk_i, pk) \rightarrow sk_i$. On inputting of the public parameters pp, a share of public key pk_i, and the public key pk, each member of the group outputs his or her share of the secret key sk_i.
- $Encrypt(pk, m) \rightarrow c$. On inputting of the public key pk and the message m, it outputs the ciphertext c of the message.
- $DecryptShare(sk_i, c) \rightarrow sh_i$. On inputting of a share of the secret key sk_i and the ciphertext c, it outputs a share of the message sh_i of member i.
- $CombineShare(sh_1, sh_2, \cdots, sh_j) \rightarrow m$. On inputting of j shares of the message m for some $j \geq t$, it outputs the message m of the ciphertext c.

2.2 Additive Homomorphic Encryption

Additive homomorphic encryption is a cryptosystem that permits the user to perform additive computation in the form of a ciphertext. Formally, additive homomorphic encryption comprises five algorithms $(Setup, KeyGen, Encrypt, Decrypt, Add)$, as follows.

- $Setup(\lambda) \rightarrow pp$. On inputting of the security parameters λ, it outputs public parameters pp.
- $KeyGen(pp) \rightarrow (pk, sk)$. On inputting of the public parameters pp, it outputs a pair of public/private keys (pk, sk).
- $Encrypt(pk, m) \rightarrow c$. On inputting of a public key pk and a message m, it outputs a ciphertext c of the message m.
- $Decrypt(sk, c) \rightarrow m$. On inputting of a secret key sk and a ciphertext c, output the origin message m of ciphertext c.
- $Add(c_1, c_2) \rightarrow c_{1+2}$. On inputting of two ciphertext c_1, c_2 related to the same public key pk, it outputs a ciphertext c_{1+2} such that $Decrypt(sk, c_{1+2}) = Decrypt(sk, c_1) + Decrypt(sk, c_2)$.

2.3 Zero-Knowledge Proofs

For a language $L := \{x \mid \exists w \text{ s.t. } R(x, w) = 1\}$, where w is a witness of x, zero-knowledge proofs allow a prover who possesses w to prove $x \in L$ without leaking any additional knowledge about w. In particular, zero-knowledge proof scheme must satisfy the following properties:

1. *Completeness*: If a statement $x \in L$, then the prover must succeed in convincing the verifier.
2. *Soundness*: If a statement $x \notin L$, then the prover must fail to convince the verifier.
3. *Zero-knowledge*: Besides the correctness of a statement, the process must not reveal any additional information.

Σ-protocols [6,14] can be regarded as interactive zero-knowledge proofs with three phases: *Commitment*, *Challenge*, and *Response*, interacting between a prover P and a verifier V. Let G be a multiplicative cyclic group with generator g, then the following Σ-protocol proves the possession of $x \in \mathbb{Z}_p$ such that $y = g^x$.

1. *Commitment*: P randomly chooses $r \in \mathbb{Z}_p$ and calculate $T = g^r$. Afterward, P sends T to V.
2. *Challenge*: V chooses a random $c \in \mathbb{Z}_p$ and send c to P as a challenge.
3. *Response*: P calculates a response $s = r - cx \mod p$ and sends the response to V.
4. V verifies the response by validating whether $y^c g^s$ is equal to T, if so, outputs 1. Otherwise, V outputs 0.

The Fiat-Shamir transform [10], i.e., using the hash of commitment produced by P as a challenge without interacting with V, makes the above process a non-interactive protocol.

3 Confidential Blockchain Payment System with Regulation

3.1 System Description

To reach our goal of protecting user privacy while being regulated, we introduce a novel confidential blockchain payment system with regulation. As shown in Fig. 1, we focus on distributing the power of regulators and separating the roles of regulators and validators. Entity details are as follows.

- *Users*: Users have their own ledger public keys and secret keys, and can send and receive transactions via their secret keys and public keys. respectively. The balance for each user is encrypted by using the regulators' public key.
- *Validators*: Validators are entities for validating each transaction, but they only validate the correctness of a transaction rather than legitimacy. They may also initiate a transaction. We intentionally separate the role of regulators and validators to ensure the proposed system can still function like a normal blockchain payment system even without regulators. Validators can be regarded as miners of blockchains, similar to Bitcoin or Ethereum.
- *Regulators*: Regulators are special nodes on the system who are capable of checking the legitimacy of certain transactions. They cannot send or receive a transaction. Regulators share a single common public key, with the corresponding secret key thresholdized and split between each regulator. Note that in the concrete construction of the system, the public key is required to be additive homomorphic in order to correctly update the balance of both parties of a transaction.
- *Identity Authority*: Identity authority is in charge of linking users' public keys to their real identities. The identity authority is independent of the system and can be differently implemented depending on the system setup.

Workflow for the proposed system can be simplified as follows. The number of regulators n is defined depending on the security parameter, along with a threshold $t \leq n$ (i.e., the minimum number of regulators required to cooperate to decrypt one transaction. Large t makes it more difficult for the regulators to decrypt a transaction, hence prevents regulators from arbitrarily decrypting transactions. The proposed system employs ElGamal encryption with threshold private keys [9], since this simplifies constructing a suitable additive homomorphic ElGamal encryption.

Regulators are special entity on the blockchain, and first generate the shared regulator public key, then calculate their own private key based on t and the public key. Users employ regulator's public key to encrypt their balance and transaction amount. The system creates a public key pair for the identity authority to link an account to its real identity. Each user must register with the identity authority using their personal information to acquire their public key and certificate on the blockchain. The certificate is included in every transaction and checked by the validator using the identity authority public key.

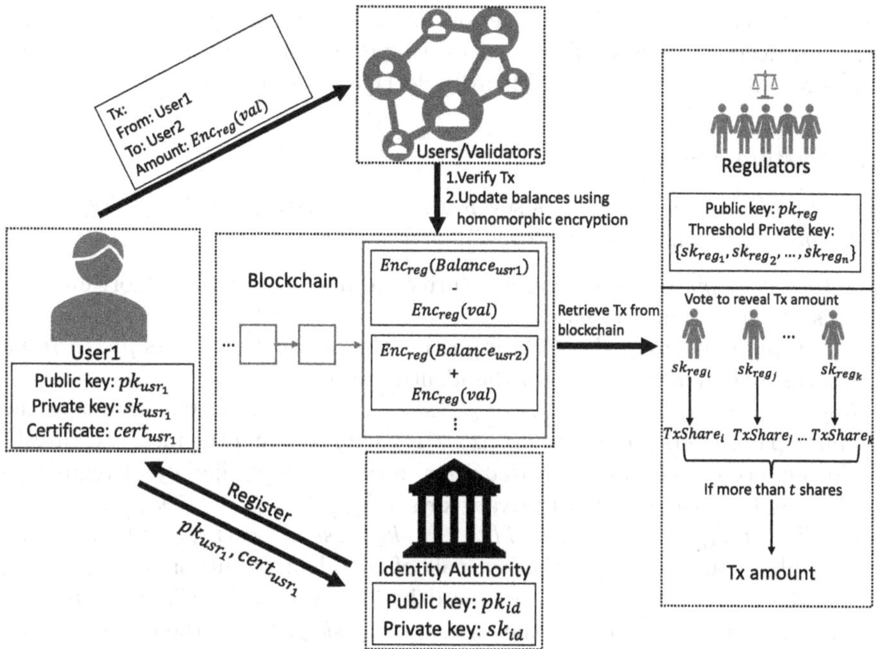

Fig. 1. The description of the proposed systems

To initiate a transaction, the user first encrypts the transaction amount using the regulator's public key, and must include the random one-time key used for encryption in the transaction to ensure the receiver can see the amount. This random one-time key is encrypted with the recipient's public key. Users must also encrypt the random key with their own public key to recover their balance since it is also encrypted by the regulator's key. There can be several ciphertexts within a transaction, hence the transaction must also include zero-knowledge proofs for the validators to check ciphertext correctness. The user then signs the generated transaction with their private key and broadcasts it on the network.

Upon receiving a transaction, the validators validate the transaction by checking its zero-knowledge proofs, signature, and certificate before appending it to the blockchain. Since we encrypt both the transaction amount and the balance, we rely on the encryption scheme's additive homomorphic property to correctly update the balance.

When a regulator wants to decrypt a transaction, he or she sends the transaction to other regulators since it needs to be decrypted. If a regulator agrees, he or she generates a decryption share for the transaction using his or her own secret key and sends the decryption share to other regulators. Regulators can then decrypt the transaction after gathering more than t decryption shares. Thus, collecting decryptions is analogous to a voting process between regulators, which helps prevent regulators from arbitrarily decrypting every transaction.

3.2 System Model

The proposed system comprises seven algorithms (*Setup*, *IdSetup*, *RegSetup*, *UsrRegister*, *Send*, *Validate*, *Reveal*), as described below.

- $Setup(\lambda) \rightarrow pp$. On inputting a security parameter λ, *Setup* algorithm outputs public parameters pp.
- $IdSetup(pp) \rightarrow (pk_{id}, sk_{id})$. On inputting the public parameters pp, *IdSetup* returns a key pair pk_{id}, sk_{id} of the identity authority.
- $RegSetup(pp, n, t) \rightarrow (pk_{reg}, \{sk_{reg_1}, sk_{reg_2}, \cdots, sk_{reg_n}\})$. On inputting the public parameters pp, the group size of regulators n, and the intended threshold number of the system t, *RegSetup* returns the public key of regulators pk_{reg} and the thresholdized private keys $\{sk_{reg_1}, sk_{reg_2}, \cdots, sk_{reg_n}\}$.
- $UsrRegister(pp, pk_{id}, sk_{id}, usrID_i) \rightarrow (pk_{usr_i}, sk_{usr_i}, cert_{usr_i})$. On inputting the public parameters pp, the key pair of the identity authority (pk_{id}, sk_{id}), and the user identity $usrID$ required by the system, *UsrRegister* returns a public/private key pair of the user, (pk_{usr_i}, sk_{usr_i}), and the corresponding certificate $cert_i$ generated by the identity authority.
- $Send(pp, pk_{usr_i}, sk_{usr_i}, pk_{usr_j}, val, cert_{usr_i}) \rightarrow (tx, \sigma_{tx})$. On inputting the public parameters pp, the public/private key pair (pk_{usr_i}, sk_{usr_i}) of the sender, the receiver's public key pk_{usr_j}, a transaction amount val, and the certificate $cert_{usr_i}$ of the sender, *Send* outputs a transaction tx and a corresponding signature σ_{tx} generated by the sender.
- $Validate(tx) \rightarrow 1/0$. On inputting a transaction, *Validate* outputs 1 if tx is valid; otherwise, it outputs 0.
- $Reveal(pp, tx, \{sk_{reg_i}, sk_{reg_j}, \cdots, sk_{reg_k}\}) \rightarrow val/\perp$. On inputting the public parameters pp, a transaction tx, and a set of regulators' keys, *Reveal* returns the original amount val of the transaction or $\perp$ indicates failure.

3.3 Security Model

The proposed regulated confidential payment system should provide *Authenticity*, *Confidentiality*, and *Balance* as with other payment systems, detailed below.

1. *Authenticity* requires that the sender of a transaction must own the account (knows the private key of the sender's account), nobody else is capable of making a transaction from this account.
2. *Confidentiality* requires that besides the sender, receiver, and regulators, no one can obtain any information about the hidden amount of a confidential transaction.

3. *Balance* requires that the balance of sender and receiver should be correctly updated with the transaction amount.

In addition, we further consider the *ConsistentAmount* property in the proposed system. More concretely, since the transaction amount will be encrypted by regulators' public key, we need this property to ensure the transaction amount should be consistent when viewed by a sender, receiver, or regulators.

We formally define the properties by the following games interacted between a challenger $\mathcal{C}$, an adversary $\mathcal{A}$. The adversary $\mathcal{A}$ can send $\mathcal{C}$ with following queries include *UsrRegister*, *Send*, and *Reveal*. After getting the queries, $\mathcal{C}$ checks the formality and forwards the queries to an oracle $\mathcal{O}^{CBP}$ of the payment system. Here, $\mathcal{O}^{CBP}$ is initialized by $\mathcal{C}$, and $\mathcal{O}^{CBP}$ maintains a ledger followed by the system and updates it correspondingly with the queries from $\mathcal{A}$. Note that $\mathcal{A}$ cannot acquire the private inputs of a transaction. $\mathcal{A}$ can only query *Reveal* to reveal the amount of a transaction sent by or send to a user created by $\mathcal{A}$ with *UsrRegister* and reveal the balance of a user created by $\mathcal{A}$. The *Reveal* query reveals the amount or balance encrypted with the regulators' key, which is the amount or balance stored on the ledger.

Game - Authenticity:

- *Initialization*: $\mathcal{C}$ initializes an oracle $\mathcal{O}^{CBP}$ which maintains a ledger L and follows the system with different queries. $\mathcal{O}^{CBP}$ provides $\mathcal{A}$ with the view of L and also maintains a user list U that is created by $\mathcal{A}$ with *UsrRegister* queries.
- *Queries*: $\mathcal{A}$ adaptively sends queries to $\mathcal{C}$ who then forwards the queries to $\mathcal{O}^{CBP}$ if they pass the formality test. $\mathcal{O}^{CBP}$ then updates the ledger corresponding to different queries and returns the result to $\mathcal{C}$. Finally, $\mathcal{C}$ forwards the result to the $\mathcal{A}$.
- *Output*: $\mathcal{A}$ outputs a transaction tx' where the sender of tx' is denoted by S'. We say $\mathcal{A}$ wins the game if $Validate(tx') = 1$ and $S' \notin U$.

The advantage of $\mathcal{A}$ in winning the above game is defined as

$$Adv^{Aut}_{CBPS,\mathcal{A}}(\lambda) := \Pr[Validate(tx') = 1 \wedge S' \notin U].$$

Definition 1. *(Authenticity)* A confidential blockchain payment system satisfies authenticity if, for any PPT $\mathcal{A}$, $Adv^{Aut}_{CBPS,\mathcal{A}}(\lambda)$ is negligible.

Game - Confidentiality:

- *Initialization*: $\mathcal{C}$ randomly selects $b \in \{0, 1\}$. Then, he/she also initializes an oracle $\mathcal{O}^{CBP}$ as the previous game.
- *Queries*: $\mathcal{A}$ can submit queries to $\mathcal{C}$ freely, but each time $\mathcal{A}$ submit *Send* query to $\mathcal{C}$, $\mathcal{A}$ also provides the value v inside the transaction to $\mathcal{C}$. Upon receiving a *Send* query from $\mathcal{A}$, $\mathcal{C}$ creates a transaction tx' where the sender and receiver are not in U. The value in tx' is set to v if $b = 0$ or a random number r if $b = 1$. Afterward, $\mathcal{C}$ returns tx' to $\mathcal{A}$.

- *Output*: $\mathcal{A}$ outputs a bit $b' \in \{0,1\}$. We say $\mathcal{A}$ wins the game if $b' = b$.

The advantage of $\mathcal{A}$ in winning the above game is defined as

$$Adv_{CBPS,\mathcal{A}}^{Con}(\lambda) := \left|\Pr[b' = b] - \frac{1}{2}\right|.$$

Definition 2. *(Confidentiality)* A confidential blockchain payment system satisfies confidentiality if, for any PPT $\mathcal{A}$, $Adv_{CBPS,\mathcal{A}}^{Con}(\lambda)$ is negligible.

Game - Balance:

- *Initialization, Queries*: These two phases are the same as phases in the Authenticity game.
- *Output*: $\mathcal{A}$ outputs a transaction tx'. Let val be the transaction amount in tx', S be the sender, and R be the receiver. In addition, let S's and R's balance difference before and after the transaction be S_{dif} and R_{dif}, respectively. We say $\mathcal{A}$ wins the game if $Validate(tx') = 1$ and the equation $-S_{dif} = R_{dif} = val$ does not hold.

The advantage of $\mathcal{A}$ in winning the above game is defined as

$$Adv_{CBPS,\mathcal{A}}^{Bal}(\lambda) := \Pr[Validate(tx') = 1 \wedge -S_{dif} = R_{dif} = val \text{ does not hold}].$$

Definition 3. *(Balance)* A confidential blockchain payment system satisfies balance if, for any PPT $\mathcal{A}$, $Adv_{CBPS,\mathcal{A}}^{Bal}(\lambda)$ is negligible.

Game - ConsistentAmount:

- *Initialization, Queries*: These two phases are the same as phases in the Authenticity game.
- *Output*: $\mathcal{A}$ outputs a transaction tx'. Let $v_{am,S}$, $v_{amo,R}$, and $v_{amo,reg}$ be the view of amount for sender, receiver, and regulators. We say $\mathcal{A}$ wins the game if $Validate(tx') = 1$ and $v_{am,S} = v_{amo,R} = v_{amo,reg}$ does not hold.

The advantage of $\mathcal{A}$ in winning the above game is defined as

$$Adv_{CBPS,\mathcal{A}}^{ConAmo}(\lambda) := \Pr[Validate(tx') = 1 \wedge v_{am,S} = v_{amo,R} = v_{amo,reg} \text{ does not hold}].$$

Definition 4. *(ConsistentAmount)* A confidential blockchain payment system satisfies consistentAmount if, for any PPT $\mathcal{A}$, $Adv_{CBPS,\mathcal{A}}^{ConAmo}(\lambda)$ is negligible.

4 The Proposed System

In this section, we describe the details of the proposed system.

Setup. With the input of a security parameter λ, this algorithm chooses a generator g of a group G with prime order q. Then, it sets the public parameter as $pp = (q, g, G)$.

IdSetup. The identity authority randomly chooses private key $sk_{id} \xleftarrow{\$} \mathbb{Z}_q$ and sets public key as $pk_{id} = g^{sk_{id}}$.

RegSetup. The regulators invoke this algorithm to get their shared public key and their own thresholdized private keys. Let n be the number of regulators, and $t \leq n$ be the threshold size. The regulators are described as $R = \{R_1, R_2, \cdots, R_n\}$. Let $C(m, r)$ denote a commitment on $m \in \{0,1\}^*$ with a random r. The regulators generate a shared public key pk_{reg} as follows:

1. For each $R_i \in R$, R_i randomly chooses $x_i \xleftarrow{\$} \mathbb{Z}_q$ and computes $h_i = g^{x_i}$. Afterward, R_i chooses another random $r_i \in \mathbb{Z}_q$ and generates a commitment $C_i = C(h_i, r_i)$. Finally R_i broadcasts C_i to all members belong to R.
2. After all members in R have broadcast their commitments, each R_i opens its commitment C_i.
3. The shared public key pk_{reg} is set as $pk_{reg} = \prod_{i=1}^{n} h_i = g^{\sum_{i=1}^{n} x_i}$.

Although all regulators have obtained the public key pk_{reg}, they cannot compute the corresponding private key $sk_{reg} = \sum_{i=1}^{n} x_i$ unless they collude with each other. Therefore, each R_i in R has to run the following procedure to obtain his/her private key:

1. R_i randomly generates a $t-1$ degree polynomial $f_i(z) = f_{i,0} + f_{i,1}z + \cdots + f_{i,t-1}z^{t-1}$ with $f_{i,0} = x_i$ (i.e., $f_i(0) = x_i$).
2. R_i calculates $F_{i,j} = g^{f_{i,j}}$ for $j = 0, \cdots, t-1$ and broadcast $(F_{i,1}, \cdots, F_{i,t-1})$ to other regulators. Here we note that $F_{i,0} = g^{f_{i,0}} = g^{x_i} = h_i$ is already known by other members.)
3. R_i sends $s_{i,j} = f_i(j)$ to R_j for $j = 1, \cdots, n$ via a secure channel.
4. R_i verifies $s_{j,i}$ sent from R_j by checking $g^{s_{j,i}} \stackrel{?}{=} \prod_{\ell=0}^{k-1} F_{j,\ell}^{i^\ell}$. If failed, R_i publish $s_{j,i}$ and terminates.
5. Finally, R_i computes his or her thresholdized private key $sk_{reg_i} = \sum_{j=1}^{n} s_{j,i}$. Then, if more than t members cooperate, they can decrypt a ciphertext encrypted with pk_{reg}.

UsrRegister. Each user in the system must register to the identity authority before enacting a transaction for accountability purposes. Identity requirements for a user can differ depending on system implementation. Although the identity authority could be omitted, so that users could create new accounts at will, that would make tracing a user on the chain significantly more difficult.

The initial balance for every user is set to zero and encrypted by regulator public key. We employ additive homomorphic ElGamal as the encryption scheme to enable the balance to be correctly updated while encrypted. The proposed system uses the certified key generation protocol [1], i.e., each user's public key must be certified by the identity authority. The protocol runs between user *usr* and identity authority *id* as follows:

1. *usr* randomly chooses k in $[0, q-1]$, computes $z = g^k$ and sends to *id*, including his identity information required by the system.

2. After receiving the identity information and z from usr. id first verifies the identity information. If this fails, it aborts the protocol; otherwise id picks random k' in $[0, q-1]$ and computes $cert_{usr} = z \cdot g^{k'}$, $\bar{x} = k' + cert_{usr} \cdot sk_{id}$. Afterward, id sends $(cert_{usr}, \bar{x})$ to usr.
3. After receiving $(cert_{usr}, \bar{x})$ from id, usr sets his or her private key as $sk_{usr} = \bar{x} + k$ and public key as $pk_{usr} = g^{sk_{usr}}$. Here, anyone can easily verify the correctness of the public key by using $cert_{usr}$ as follows:

$$\begin{aligned} pk_{usr} &= g^{sk_{usr}} = g^{k+k'+cert_{usr} \cdot sk_{id}} \\ &= g^{k+k'} \cdot g^{cert_{usr} \cdot sk_{id}} \\ &= cert_{usr} \cdot pk_{id}{}^{cert_{usr}}. \end{aligned}$$

   We also note that usr's public key pk_{usr} and certificate $cert_{usr}$ should be included in every transaction such that anyone can verify them.
4. The balance of usr is set to zero and encrypted with the regulators' public key pk_{reg}. The random number used in the ElGamal encryption scheme is also set to zero and will be updated when the user receives or sends a new transaction. Here, the random number is used to generate a zero-knowledge proof for a transaction, as described in the next algorithm. Finally, the initial balance after encryption is as follows:

$$bal_{usr} = (g^0, g^0 \cdot pk_{reg}{}^0).$$

Send. This algorithm enables a user to send a transaction without revealing the amount, although the sender and receiver remain visible for regulation purposes. To achieve this requirement, we use ElGamal encryption to encrypt the transaction amount and the balance of every user. Since ElGamal encryption is additive homomorphic, we are able to correctly maintain the balance of each account even if the transaction is hidden. The sender must also generate zero-knowledge proofs to prove transaction correctness, and ensure the sender follows the protocol when generating a transaction.

Let sender usr_i's encrypted balance be $enc\text{-}bal_{usr_i} = (g^{r_i}, g^{bal_{usr_i}} \cdot pk_{reg}{}^{r_i})$ and a receiver usr_j's encrypted balance be $enc\text{-}bal_{usr_j} = (g^{r_j}, g^{bal_{usr_j}} \cdot pk_{reg}{}^{r_j})$, where r_i and r_j are the random numbers of usr_i and usr_j, respectively; bal_{usr_i} and bal_{usr_j} are the balances of usr_i and usr_j, respectively. The process to send a transaction is as follows:

1. The sender usr_i first encrypts the amount val with the regulator's public key pk_{reg}. usr_i randomly chooses $r, r_1, r_2 \xleftarrow{\$} [0, q-1]$ and calculates

$$e_{reg} = (g^r, g^{val} \cdot pk_{reg}{}^r);\ rd_{usr_i} = (g^{r_1}, r \cdot pk_{usr_i}{}^{r_1});\ rd_{usr_j} = (g^{r_2}, r \cdot pk_{usr_j}{}^{r_2}).$$

   In order for the receiver to see the amount, usr_i encrypts the random number r used in e_{reg} with receiver's public key as rd_{usr_j}. Since the balance of every user is also encrypted by the regulators' public key, usr_i also encrypts r used in e_{reg} with his own public key as rd_{usr_i} so that he can recover his own balance by scanning through the blockchain history. By including r, users can also keep track of their current random number used to encrypt their balance in order to generate correct zero-knowledge proofs.

2. usr_i needs to prove the encrypted balance after the transaction $enc\text{-}bal'_{usr_i}$ is greater than or equal to 0. Therefore, usr_i generate proof π_{bal} for the statement $(enc\text{-}bal'_{usr_i}, g, pk_{reg}) \in L_{bal}$, where the language L_{bal} is defined is as:

$$\begin{aligned}L_{bal} := \{&(enc\text{-}bal'_{usr}, g, pk_{reg}) \mid \\ &\exists (r', val') \text{ s.t. } enc\text{-}bal'_{usr} = (g^{r'}, g^{val'} \cdot pk_{reg}{}^{r'}) \wedge val' \geq 0\}.\end{aligned}$$

$enc\text{-}bal'_{usr_i}$ will be calculated by the validators on the blockchain using the additive homomorphic ElGamal encryption, where

$$\begin{aligned}enc\text{-}bal'_{usr_i} &= Add(enc\text{-}bal_{usr_i}, (e_{reg})^{-1}) \\ &= (g^{r_i}, g^{bal_{usr_i}} \cdot pk_{reg}{}^{r_i}) \times (g^{-r}, g^{-val} \cdot pk_{reg}{}^{-r}) \\ &= (g^{r_i - r}, g^{bal_{usr_i} - val} \cdot pk_{reg}{}^{r_i - r}).\end{aligned}$$

3. usr_i needs to prove the random number used in e_{reg} is the same as the one encrypted in rd_{usr_j}, and the keys used in e_{reg} and rd_{usr_j} are pk_{reg} and pk_{usr_j}. usr_i generate a proof π_{eq} for the statement $(g, pk_{usr_j}, pk_{reg}, rd_{usr_j}, e_{reg}) \in L_{eq}$, where the language L_eq is defined as follows:

$$\begin{aligned}L_{eq} = \{&(g, pk_{usr}, pk_{reg}, rd_{usr}, e_{reg}) \mid \\ &\exists (r, val, r_2) \text{ s.t. } rd_{usr} = (g^{r_2}, r \cdot pk_{usr}{}^{r_2}) \wedge e_{reg} = (g^r, g^{val} \cdot pk_{reg}{}^r)\}.\end{aligned}$$

4. usr_i needs to prove the amount encrypted in e_{reg} is greater than 0 and smaller than some value m where m is much smaller than the group size used in the modular arithmetic. usr_i generate a proof π_{range} for the statement $(g, pk_{reg}, m, e_{reg}) \in L_{range}$ which is defined as follows:

$$\begin{aligned}L_{range} = \{&(g, pk_{reg}, m, e_{reg}) \mid \\ &\exists r, val \text{ s.t. } e_{reg} = (g^r, g^{val} \cdot pk_{reg}{}^r) \wedge 0 \leq val \leq m\}.\end{aligned}$$

5. usr_i generates a signature σ signed the transaction tx where

$$tx = (pk_{usr_i}, pk_{usr_j}, e_{reg}, rd_{usr_i}, rd_{usr_j}, \pi_{bal}, \pi_{eq}, \pi_{range}, cert_{usr_i})$$

and broadcast the signature σ and tx to the blockchain.

Validate. After the validators receive a transaction, they use the algorithm to validate the transaction. Although the transaction amount is encrypted, we can ensure the correctness of the transaction by verifing the zero-knowledge proofs. We can also update the balances of both sender and receiver by using the additive homomorphic ElGamal encryption. The processes for a validator V to validate a transaction tx are as follows:

1. V first validates the signature σ of the transaction. If failed, abort the algorithm.
2. V validates the certificate of the sender using the identity authority's public key. If failed, abort the algorithm.
3. V calculates the balance of sender and receiver, $enc\text{-}bal'_{usr_i}$ and $enc\text{-}bal'_{usr_j}$ as follows.

$$\begin{aligned}
enc\text{-}bal'_{usr_i} &= Add(enc\text{-}bal_{usr_i}, (e_{reg})^{-1}) \\
&= (g^{r_i}, g^{bal_{usr_i}} \cdot {pk_{reg}}^{r_i}) \times (g^{-r}, g^{-val} \cdot {pk_{reg}}^{-r}) \\
&= (g^{r_i - r}, g^{bal_{usr_i} - val} \cdot {pk_{reg}}^{r_i - r}); \\
enc\text{-}bal'_{usr_j} &= Add(enc\text{-}bal_{usr_j}, e_{reg}) \\
&= (g^{r_j}, g^{bal_{usr_j}} \cdot {pk_{reg}}^{r_j}) \times (g^{r}, g^{val} \cdot {pk_{reg}}^{r}) \\
&= (g^{r_j + r}, g^{bal_{usr_j} + val} \cdot {pk_{reg}}^{r_j + r}).
\end{aligned}$$

4. V validates the zero-knowledge proofs in the transaction. This process ensures the correctness of the transaction. If failed, abort the algorithm.
5. V updates the balance of sender and receiver on the blockchain.

The process of updating the blockchain is based on the underlying blockchain and can be changed depending on different setups. Note that the validators do not have the power to decrypt the transaction amount and the balance of the user. Thus they only check the correctness of a transaction but not the legitimacy.

Reveal. The regulators use this algorithm to decrypt the amount of a transaction or the balance of a certain user. Any of the regulators can initiate the process of decrypting a transaction. The regulator who initiates it acts as the master of the process and sends a decrypting request to other regulators. Once other regulators receive the request, they may decide whether to decrypt the transaction/balance or not. For a regulator reg_{mas} who initiates the algorithm, the process is as follows:

1. reg_{mas} sends a request $request_{dec}$ for decryption and a transaction id tx_{id} to all regulators.
2. For a regulator reg_i who received the request, he or she retrieves the encrypted amount of the transaction $e_{reg_{tx}} = (g^{r_{tx}}, g^{val_{tx}} \cdot {pk_{reg}}^{r_{tx}})$ from the blockchain with tx_{id}.

3. If reg_i decides to participate in decrypting the transaction, he or she calculates a share of the transaction $txShare_i = g^{r_{tx} \cdot sk_{reg_i}}$, where sk_{reg_i} is the private key share of reg_i. Then, he or she broadcasts $(txShare_i, i)$ to other regulators via a secure channel. Otherwise, reg_i broadcasts $\perp$ via a secure channel.
4. After a regulator receives more than t shares from other regulators, he or she randomly selects t shares from these shares to form a group S. Without loss of generality, let k be one of the share indexes randomly chosen from S. The regulator calculates

$$a_n = txShare_k^{\prod_{j \neq k, j \in S} \frac{j}{j-k}} = g^{r_{tx} \cdot sk_{reg_k} \cdot \prod_{j \neq k, j \in S} \frac{j}{j-k}}.$$

5. The regulator calculates $\prod_{n=1}^{t} a_n = g^{pk_{reg}{}^{r_{tx}}}$ and can thus retrieve $g^{val_{tx}}$ by using the second part of $e_{reg_{tx}}$. That is, $g^{val_{tx}} = (g^{val_{tx}} \cdot pk_{reg}{}^{r_{tx}}) \cdot (g^{pk_{reg}{}^{r_{tx}}})^{-1}$. Finally the regulator calculates the discrete logarithm of $g^{val_{tx}}$ to get the amount val_{tx}.

The regulators can decrypt the balance of a user by a similar process. Instead of a transaction id, reg_{mas} sends the public key of a user to other regulators.

Security. The following we provide four security theorems to show that the proposed system satisfies *Authenticity*, *Confidentiality*, *Balance*, and *ConsistentAmount*. Here we note that due to the page limit, the corresponding security proofs will be provided in the full version of this work.

Theorem 1. *The proposed system satisfies Authenticity if the underlying signature scheme is existentially unforgeable under the chosen message attacks.*

Theorem 2. *The proposed system satisfies Confidentiality if the underlying threshold cryptosystem and the public-key encryption scheme are indistinguishable under the chosen plaintext.*

Theorem 3. *The proposed system satisfies Balance if the underlying encryption scheme is additive-homomorphic and the zero-knowledge proof scheme is sound.*

Theorem 4. *The proposed system satisfies ConsistentAmount if the underlying zero-knowledge proof scheme is sound.*

5 Performance Evaluation

We implemented a proof-of-concept system using Rust language for efficiency analysis. The experiment was conducted on a MacBook Pro 2017 laptop (macOS Monterey version 12.3) with Intel(R) i5-7360U CPU clocked at 2.5GHz and 8GB of system memory.

In our implementation, we leveraged BulletProof [4] as the zero-knowledge range proof protocol and sigma protocol with Fiat-Shamir [6,14] transform as the zero-knowledge proof protocol. In addition, we selected secp256k1 elliptic curve, which has 256-bit security and is broadly used in cryptocurrencies such as Bitcoin and Ethereum. Each point on the curve can be stored as 88 bytes, and the scalar for the finite field can be stored as 56 bytes.

Table 1. The computation cost of confidential transaction

	Size (bytes)	Generation time (ms)	Verify time (ms)
Confidential tx	1992	126	52

Here we set the max value of the transaction as $2^\ell - 1$ where $\ell = 64$. The computation cost of generating and verifying a transaction, as shown in Table 1, is efficient to compute. The transaction size is also feasible for the use of blockchain. Note that when using elliptic curve setup, we need to encode the random number used in e_{reg} to a point on the curve when encrypting in rd_{usr_i} and rd_{usr_j}. The encoding method may be different when using different curves and could impact transaction time and size.

Table 2. The computation cost of decrypting threshold ElGamal

	Calculate share time (ms)	Combine share time (s)
Threshold ElGamal	0.2	224.8

In addition, we use threshold ElGamal encryption with 5 members and the threshold is set to 3. We encrypt a value of 10,000,000 and use a simple brute force method in decryption. As shown in Table 2, the regulators can easily decrypt the transaction even if they need to compute the discrete logarithm problem when combining decryption shares. The decryption time is feasible for our use case since the regulators do not have to run the decryption algorithm with every transaction. In addition, the decryption time can be further reduced if run in parallel.

6 Conclusion and Future Works

This paper proposed a confidential payment system with controllable regulation based on blockchain. The regulation procedure included a voting process to limit regulator power, and we attempted to balance between privacy and regulation.

Below we describe possible improvements for future work. As noted in Section 5, when we adopt an elliptic curve in the proposed system, the random number used in e_{reg} needs to be encoded to a point over the curve. Although lots of encoding algorithms have been introduced in [11], how to obtain an efficient encoding algorithm that fits our system is an open problem.

Another aspect that needs to consider is how to improve efficiency. Since the proposed system requires users to verify zero-knowledge proofs over the blockchain, it may cause additional computational costs. A possible solution is to adopt a curve that is more suitable for this usage, and how to find this curve is also an interesting problem.

Acknowledgments. The authors thank the anonymous reviewers of ISPEC 2022 for their insightful suggestions on this work. This research is partially supported by the National Science and Technology Council, Taiwan (ROC), under grant numbers NSTC 109-2221-E-004-011-MY3, NSTC 110-2221-E-004-003-, NSTC 110-2622-8-004-001-, and NSTC 111-2218-E-004-001-MBK.

References

1. Ateniese, G., Faonio, A., Magri, B., de Medeiros, B.: Certified Bitcoins. In: Boureanu, I., Owesarski, P., Vaudenay, S. (eds.) ACNS 2014. LNCS, vol. 8479, pp. 80–96. Springer, Cham (2014). https://doi.org/10.1007/978-3-319-07536-5_6
2. Ben Sasson, E., et al.: Zerocash: decentralized anonymous payments from Bitcoin. In: IEEE S&P 2014, pp. 459–474. IEEE (2014)
3. Buterin, V.: Ethereum: a next-generation smart contract and decentralized application platform (2014). https://nft2x.com/wp-content/uploads/2021/03/EthereumWP.pdf
4. Bünz, B., Bootle, J., Boneh, D., Poelstra, A., Wuille, P., Maxwell, G.: Bulletproofs: short proofs for confidential transactions and more. In: IEEE S&P 2018, pp. 315–334. IEEE (2018)
5. Cecchetti, E., Zhang, F., Ji, Y., Kosba, A., Juels, A., Shi, E.: Solidus: confidential distributed ledger transactions via PVORM. In: CCS 2017, pp. 701–717. ACM (2017)
6. Chaidos, P., Groth, J.: Making Sigma-protocols non-interactive without random oracles. In: Katz, J. (ed.) PKC 2015. LNCS, vol. 9020, pp. 650–670. Springer, Heidelberg (2015). https://doi.org/10.1007/978-3-662-46447-2_29
7. Chen, Y., Ma, X., Tang, C., Au, M.H.: PGC: decentralized confidential payment system with auditability. In: Chen, L., Li, N., Liang, K., Schneider, S. (eds.) ESORICS 2020. LNCS, vol. 12308, pp. 591–610. Springer, Cham (2020). https://doi.org/10.1007/978-3-030-58951-6_29
8. Conti, M., Sandeep Kumar, E., Lal, C., Ruj, S.: A survey on security and privacy issues of Bitcoin. In: IEEE Communications Surveys and Tutorials, vol. 20, pp. 3416–3452. IEEE (2018)
9. Desmedt, Y., Frankel, Y.: Threshold cryptosystems. In: Brassard, G. (ed.) CRYPTO 1989. LNCS, vol. 435, pp. 307–315. Springer, New York (1990). https://doi.org/10.1007/0-387-34805-0_28
10. Fiat, A., Shamir, A.: How to prove yourself: practical solutions to identification and signature problems. In: Odlyzko, A.M. (ed.) CRYPTO 1986. LNCS, vol. 263, pp. 186–194. Springer, Heidelberg (1987). https://doi.org/10.1007/3-540-47721-7_12

11. Fouque, P.A., Joux, A., Tibouchi, M.: Injective encodings to elliptic curves. In: Boyd, C., Simpson, L. (eds.) ACISP 2013. LNCS, vol. 7959, pp. 203–218. Springer, Heidelberg (2013). https://doi.org/10.1007/978-3-642-39059-3_14
12. Garman, C., Green, M., Miers, I.: Accountable privacy for decentralized anonymous payments. In: Grossklags, J., Preneel, B. (eds.) FC 2016. LNCS, vol. 9603, pp. 81–98. Springer, Heidelberg (2017). https://doi.org/10.1007/978-3-662-54970-4_5
13. I. Miers, C.G., M. Green, A.D.R.: Zerocoin: anonymous distributed E-cash from Bitcoin. In: IEEE S&P 2013, pp. 397–411. IEEE (2013)
14. Krawczyk, H.: SIGMA: the SIGn-and-MAc' approach to authenticated diffie-hellman and its use in the IKE protocols. In: Boneh, D. (ed.) CRYPTO 2003. LNCS, vol. 2729, pp. 400–425. Springer, Heidelberg (2003). https://doi.org/10.1007/978-3-540-45146-4_24
15. Lin, C., He, D., Huang, X., Khan, M.K., Choo, K.K.R.: DCAP: a secure and efficient decentralized conditional anonymous payment system based on blockchain. IEEE Trans. Inf. Forensics Secur. **15**, 2440–2452 (2020)
16. McCarthy, K.J., van Santen, P., Fiedler, I.: Modeling the money launderer: microtheoretical arguments on anti-money laundering policy. In: International Review of Law and Economics, vol. 43, pp. 148–155. Elsevier (2015)
17. Nakamoto, S.: Bitcoin: a peer-to-peer electronic cash system (2008). https://bitcoin.org/bitcoin.pdf
18. Pedersen, T.P.: A threshold cryptosystem without a trusted party. In: Davies, D.W. (ed.) EUROCRYPT 1991. LNCS, vol. 547, pp. 522–526. Springer, Heidelberg (1991). https://doi.org/10.1007/3-540-46416-6_47
19. Petkus, M.: Why and how zk-SNARK works (2019). http://arxiv.org/abs/1906.07221
20. Pietschmann, T., Walker, J.: Estimating illicit financial flows resulting from drug trafficking and other transnational organized crimes (2011). https://www.unodc.org/documents/data-and-analysis/Studies/Illicit_financial_flows_2011_web.pdf
21. Saberhagen, N.V.: Cryptonote v 2.0 (2013). https://bytecoin.org/old/whitepaper.pdf
22. Shen, X.S., et al.: Data management for future wireless networks: architecture, privacy preservation, and regulation. In: IEEE Networking, vol. 35, pp. 8–15. IEEE (2021)
23. Sun, S.F., Au, M.H., Liu, J.K., Yuen, T.H.: RingCT 2.0: a compact accumulator-based (Linkable Ring Signature) protocol for blockchain cryptocurrency monero. In: Foley, S.N., Gollmann, D., Snekkenes, E. (eds.) ESORICS 2017. LNCS, vol. 10493, pp. 456–474. Springer, Cham (2017). https://doi.org/10.1007/978-3-319-66399-9_25
24. van Wegberg, R., Oerlemans, J.J., van Deventer, O.: Bitcoin money laundering: Mixed results? an explorative study on money laundering of cybercrime proceeds using Bitcoin. In: Journal Financial Crime, pp. 419–435. Emerald Publishing Limited (2018)
25. Williamson, Z.J.: The AZTEC protocol (2018). https://raw.githubusercontent.com/AztecProtocol/AZTEC/master/AZTEC.pdf
26. Xue, L., Liu, D., Ni, J., Lin, X., Shen, X.S.: Enabling regulatory compliance and enforcement in decentralized anonymous payment. In: IEEE Transactions on Dependable and Secure Computing. IEEE (2022)

Designing Enhanced Robust 6G Connection Strategy with Blockchain

August Lykke Thomsen, Bastian Preisel, Victor Rodrigues Andersen, Wei-Yang Chiu, and Weizhi Meng(✉)

SPTAGE Lab, Department of Applied Mathematics and Computer Science, Technical University of Denmark, Lyngby, Denmark
{weich,weme}@dtu.dk

Abstract. With the rapid evolution of wireless communication technologies, the new generation of 6G is already under development, due to the next step-change in performance from Gigabit to Terabit capacities as well as reaching sub-millisecond response time. For example, 6G connectivity is expected to support speeds of one Terabyte per second. This level of capacity and latency will be in support of increasing demand in the areas of wireless cognition, detection and imaging. The 6G connection strategy is made to cope with the major traffic growth, especially in a crowded area, e.g., under holiday celebration. However, without a proper connection strategy, an attacker can cause the traffic jam to one or more nodes in a 6G network. In this work, we consider the benefits of blockchain, and showcase a practical implementation of blockchain-enabled connection strategy for 6G, where telecom companies can use in order to provide the best connection experience and robustness for each device through connection strategies deployed on the chain. We also implement an Android application on mobile devices to demonstrate the viability of our approach.

Keywords: Blockchain technology · 6G · Connection strategy · Decentralized database · Smart contract · Blockchain application

1 Introduction

The advancement of information technology creates method of communications more than verbal and physical, it creates multiple method of data transmission through several types of media. However, in the recent years of development, it has shown the trend of utilizing various medium to reach the final goal of the proposed communication system. For example, Long Term Evolution (LTE) [13] provides options for network operators to offload the data flow through local 802.11 access points, and later, LTE-M was released, as a suitable access media for Internet of Things (IoT), under the hood of LTE specification. Its successor, the New-Radio (NR) further branched the method of access detailly, such as Ultra Reliable Low Latency Communications (URLLC) for critical applications that require real-time response and Enhanced Mobile Broadband (eMBB) for applications that need huge amounts of bandwidth.

C. Su et al. (Eds.): ISPEC 2022, LNCS 13620, pp. 57–74, 2022.
https://doi.org/10.1007/978-3-031-21280-2_4

It has no doubt that the later successor of 6G will have a similar system architecture [6]. It has become important to exploit the knowledge of different connection media types to provide the best user experience. For example, it is unreasonable for a 6G user to access a public macro-cell tower, which can be quite packed, when the distributed fento-cells are deployed in/or near the residency that can provide a faster response and better bandwidth-per-user ratio [1].

However, the current implementation of wireless devices is equipped with an elegant but not a future-proof method of choosing the current access point, whichever shows the strongest signal toward the device, it will be the current access point of the device. Although such implementation can be reasonable when single media types were involved, it can be quite questionable when dealing with various medium and applications – The cell that shows the best reception does not always prove to have the best connection quality. Furthermore, based on different applications, several of its connections can be offloaded differently [7]. For example, a pre-recorded video can be transmitted through connections that have broader bandwidth but with slightly higher latency. Video and phone calls require real-time response, while bandwidth only has to be satisfiable to complete the task. Lastly, as the ubiquitous data access can be considered as the basic component of our daily life, the ability for dynamic and instant response toward the change of environment should be considered and included. For example, as congestions can be easily occurred during rush hours in packed areas, if operators can have the capability to provide reference guidelines for devices not to use the macro-cell tower by-default, such issue can be partially resolved.

Motivation. As the network operators have the full knowledge of their own networks, they are suitable for providing guidelines. However, the data distribution of these guidelines has become an issue since there are countless customers on the network. Having a centralized system may become costly for operators to maintain. Furthermore, as the deployment of connection strategy can heavily affect the user experience and system revenue, a system with high-availability and auditability is preferred. Blockchain proves itself as a better alternative compared with traditional database, since it satisfies the above requirements [4].

Contribution. Blockchain technology has been studied in various domains such as trust management [15,16], smart cities [3,17], intrusion detection [14], vehicular network [8,9], etc. It is a kind of distributed database that can be shared among nodes within a network, providing enhanced trust, security, transparency, and traceability of the data. Motivated by its benefits and the issues of connection strategy in 6G, in this work, we design and showcase a practical implementation of blockchain-enabled connection strategy scheme in 6G. Our contributions can be summarized as below:

- Typically, 6G allows devices to connect with a much wider variety of access medias, ranging from older cell towers to dedicated satellites and smaller cells. We design a blockchain-enabled 6G connection strategy for a more robust 6G environment, including smart contract design, client application design, web platform design, and Android App design.

- We then introduce how to implement the proposed strategy, based on an open-source blockchain development platform – DevLeChain, including user interface, workflow of the client class, and diagram of the client application. In the evaluation, we initially discuss the performance of our system, and demonstrate its viability.

The rest of the work can be summarized as follows. In Sect. 2, we briefly present the background of 6G and related work on blockchain-based 6G vision. Section 3 introduces the design of our blockchain-enabled 6G connection strategy. Section 4 details how to implement the system and strategy, and Sect. 5 discusses the system performance under several tests and use cases. Finally, we conclude the work in Sect. 6.

2 Background and Related Work

2.1 6G Technology

6G is the sixth generation of wireless technology. A 6G network follows up on 4G and 5G, building on the revamped infrastructure and advanced capacity currently being established on millimeter-wave 5G networks. Using higher-frequency radio bands, it will give networks much faster speeds and lower latency, in order to support sophisticated mobile devices and systems [6]. It is anticipated that 6G networks will be able to use higher frequencies than 5G networks, which will enable higher data rates to be reached. This involves expanding into Tera-Hertz (THz) communications, due to its extremely short wave length, it becomes possible to meet the need for large-capacity short-distance communication, as well as high-precision positioning and sensing.

Many 5G's private wireless communication implementations involving LTE, 5G and edge computing for enterprise and industrial customers, have helped lay the groundwork for 6G [12]. Next-generation 6G wireless networks will further improve this and bring it to the next level. 6G technology is expected and envisioned to provide fully immersible interaction and support precise spatial interaction to meet the requirements for multiple senses, feeling, and mind communications. Communication for sensing and inclusive intelligence will realize the digitalization and intelligence of physical objects. Native intelligence, communication for sensing, digital twins, and native security are some of the key capabilities that 6G is planned to support.

Some of the other driving forces of 6G development are changes in social structure, since digital technologies are required to increase inclusiveness across unbalanced income levels and demographic imbalance calls for digital technology to improve human capital. High-quality economic growth is another critical aspect of its development, as sustainable economic growth is fueled by the impetus brought by new technologies, and the globalization of services requires lower cost in all-round information communications. Lastly, environmental sustainability also contributes to this scenario, given that lower carbon emissions and carbon neutrality call for improved energy efficiency and green development.

2.2 6G with Blockchain

Introducing blockchain technology to the 6G environment brings many beneficial features and characteristics to the system. Hewa *et al.* [18] introduced an intelligent resource management method with the exponential expansion of the tenants future, the resource management operations such as spectrum sharing, orchestration and decentralized computation may require to be compatible with massive infrastructure volumes. They also mentioned the proposal of an intelligent network architecture, which utilized blockchain technology by handling the relationship between operators and users via smart contracts.

Wang *et al.* [20] introduced a Blockchain Radio Access Network for 6G (B-RAN). They described it as an open and unified framework for diverse applications to achieve resource pooling and sharing across sectors, which is an attractive solution for future 6G networks. B-RAN unites inherently untrustworthy network entities without any middleman, and it manages network access, authentication, authorization and accounting via trustful interactions. With B-RAN, a multi-sided platform (MSP) is established to connect different parties and facilitate resource and data sharing in a cooperative, flexible and secure way. B-RAN can not only dynamically share computing, caching and communicating capabilities, but also deliver and spread intelligence across subnetworks.

The 6G network is expected to be 3D integrated, such that we have 6G elements present in all three dimensions. This will help provide guaranteed Quality-of-Service (QoS). The 6G infrastructure will be made of dense deployment of communication devices, by operators or specialized asset service providers. By implementing the blockchain into the network, we can help reduce latency. Users will connect to a relay, and the relay will check the users' information and the network from the blockchain and provide the desired connectivity. It can be achieved by checking a smart contract, which contains the desired SLAs (Service-Level Agreement) made by the specialized service providers [11].

Other opportunities that come from implementing the blockchain with the 6G network can be summarized as below [21].

- Simplifying roaming terms and agreements between different providers.
- Helping the implementation of network slicing, by keeping track of how each resource is being used and how providers perform against the SLAs.
- Managing money transfers across borders.
- Managing users and authentication.

More related work on the combination of blockchain and 6G can refer to several recent studies [5,10,19,22]. To the best of our knowledge, there is no prior work discussing how to use blockchain technology to optimize and secure connection strategies in 6G era. This motivates our work on implementing a prototype of blockchain-enabled 6G connection strategy.

3 Our Proposed System

The main goal of our work is to deploy and maintain connection strategies for telecommunication companies in a 6G environment, and validate the feasibility and viability of this approach. Figure 1 describes the overview of system design. The system can interact with a private Ethereum-based blockchain, by integrating **Ethers** with the **Web3j** Ethereum APIs and libraries. The design also involves a web application that retrieves and sends information through a smart contract running on a private blockchain and an end-user application retrieving this information and acting accordingly.

Based on this design, telecom companies can have an easily accessible platform to deploy, manage and visualize the deployed strategies. The end-user application may vary from device to device as there might be different versions on which the device is running, such as smartphone, computer or cell server. While it allows the rest of the system to remain untouched and consistent throughout the entire network. This also provides reliable, secure and consistent data across the setup given that it is built up on blockchain technology.

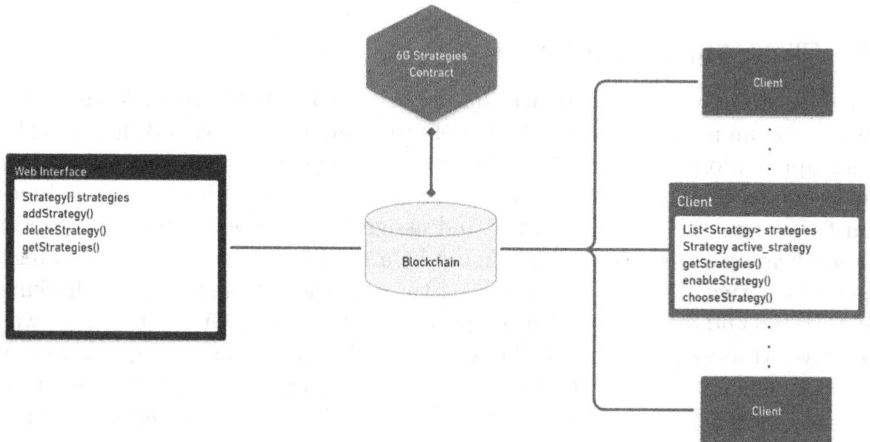

Fig. 1. Overview of the system design

3.1 Smart-Contract Design

When designing a smart contract, we need to consider what kind of strategy should be involved in terms of fields and relevant information. First, we need a field to store what type of **connection** should be used, such as Wi-Fi, Satellite or Cellular. This field would have the main responsibility for what action has to be performed when it is active. Then we need to decide a strategy to hold the **dates** regarding when the strategy is active. We also need to choose a strategy with a **priority** value to decide which of the strategies with overlapping time frames should be the active one.

In addition, we also need a strategy to hold a **location** where it should be active. This means that the device would have to be in the given area defined by the location in order for the strategy to become active. A **location** is composed of **latitude** and **longitude** coordinates for the center of a circle, along with a **radius**, in order to define a circular area for each strategy. This could be relevant if a user is in an area where people are usually outside in large crowds, where a lot of traffic to the nearest cell tower could overload it. To round it out, a strategy should also have a **name** and a **description**. Every strategy also has a unique **ID**.

In order to pass the information to the client devices, when a new strategy has been added, we decided to use events provided by Solidity. These events will broadcast to all devices connected to the blockchain and the contract. In our case, an event is emitted whenever a change has been made to the array, i.e., being the addition of a new strategy, removal of one, or a change in priority. This signals that a re-evaluation of the array is needed at each device in order to figure out which strategy has to be active among the new constellation.

3.2 Client Application Design

When designing the client application, we select Java as the programming language as it can integrate with Ethereum blockchain with the **Web3j** library. The client application should retrieve the currently deployed strategies and decide which one of them should be active. For this purpose, it should have a function to retrieve the strategies array and assign it to a global data structure in the application. After that, there should be a method to choose which strategy should be active. This involves iterating through the list of strategies, checking its start and end date along with the priority and location. Given that there was no active strategy prior to such check, the one that meets the former conditions should be the chosen one. Should there be two or more that apply for the given date and location, the one with the highest priority will be chosen in the end. Also, should two strategies have the same priority, the first one encountered will be chosen.

Once the strategy is chosen, it has to be enabled. Thus, the application needs a function that performs the necessary changes on the device in order to suit the chosen strategy. This may vary from device to device, while in our case, it will include the code needed to enable or disable a Wi-Fi or Bluetooth interface on a Linux distribution either on a laptop or a Raspberry Pi. Then a listener is needed to the event that is emitted every time a change is made to the strategy list. Should the event be triggered, it fetches the list again and runs the same process described before. Other than the event listener, the application checks periodically whether the current active strategy is expired or not valid for the current location; in that case, it should choose a new one if there is a fit with the new location and time.

3.3 Web Platform Design

The motivation for having a web platform is to be able to manage the deployed strategies, especially the deployment and the deletion. The platform also serves the purpose of providing an overview of which strategies are currently deployed, in what location, and their additional information, such as start- and end-time. This will be useful for the people responsible for this on the company side.

One of the essential design choices is to include a map, which can display the current strategies and their locations. This allows users to have an easy overview of the strategies. However, only having a map to display the strategies can easily become unmanageable, as strategies can overlap each other. Therefore we decided to also have a grid displaying the strategies in addition to a map. Displaying the map and the grid beside each other will then allow users to easily create an overview of all the strategies on the blockchain.

3.4 Android App

Having a smartphone version also allows us to work with a different environment and make use of different parameters when deciding which strategy should be active. Also, providing the client's computer with current location is a challenge; thus, having a smartphone version allows us to include this easily in the code that is already made for the computer application.

The design consists of two pages. The first one is where the user sets up the information to connect to the blockchain such as IP, port and so on, as well as the information for the account to be used, such as the key file and password. Once this is properly inserted and a connection has been established, the second screen is shown, which displays the current state of the system, i.e., the current active strategy, or that no strategy is active at the current time.

4 System Implementation

4.1 Blockchain

To communicate with the blockchain, we need to connect to an Ethereum node. In this work, we used the JSON-RPC protocol to interact, which allows us to execute code on another machine. JavaScript Object Notation (JSON) is a lightweight data-interchange format, which can represent numbers, strings, ordered sequences of values, and collections of name/value pairs. Combining JSON and RPC (Remote Procedure Call), it can communicate with the blockchain, where the blockchain acts as a server deployed on a network, and the clients use the JSON-RPC protocol to make changes on the blockchain.

The blockchain platform was developed based on DevLeChain [2], which can provide various functions, i.e., creating a new local chain with multiple accounts. We could also start peering multiple nodes with each other, by having two nodes with the same genesis file and network ID, but having different ports. We could add them as peers using the JavaScript command – `admin.addPeer(enode)` in the Geth console. The enode is viewable by using `admin.nodeInfo`. We could also peer two nodes from two different computers over the same network, by changing the IP in the **enode**.

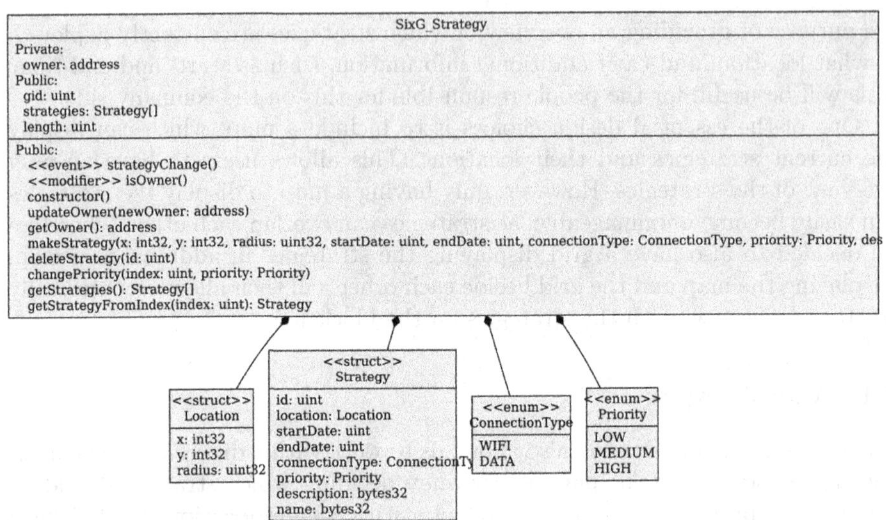

Fig. 2. UML diagram of smart contract

4.2 Smart Contract

Programming in Solidity using Remix IDE was the most optimal choice since it is a combo of an object-oriented programming language designed to implement smart contacts. RemixIDE also allows smart contracts to be easily tested as functions, which can be called directly from the user interface, and it also allows testing by deploying the contract on JavaScript VMs available within the IDE, instead of setting up own chain and deploying it.

Figure 2 depicts a diagram of the smart contract. A `Strategy` was implemented including a *struct* containing the fields, with the `Location` *struct* that includes **latitude** and **longitude** coordinates as 32 byte integers, and a **radius** that is the same size but unsigned. The **id** is also an unsigned integer, alongside the **startDate** and **endDate** for the strategy in question. The dates are stored as UNIX timestamps. The `ConnectionType` and `Priority` were implemented as `enums` in order to have predefined constants that can be chosen from, in this case being `(DATA, WIFI)` and `(LOW, MEDIUM, HIGH)` respectively.

Then the **name** and the **description** fields were both implemented as `bytes32`, meaning that they were byte arrays instead of regular Strings. This has to be done because **Web3j** is used for the client application, which cannot handle and generate proper data structures and methods for Solidity `Strings`, due to the dynamic size.

As global fields for the contract, there is an **id** integer in order to keep track of unique ids given to each strategy, the address of **owner** to commit changes to the strategies and add or remove them. The global **id** counter is initialized to 0 and only incremented by 1 every time when a strategy is added, indicating that new strategies will have a unique ID never used, not even by strategies that have been deleted. This also means that a maximum of strategies that can be made during the lifetime of the contract, since the ID is a `uint256`. This means there is a max amount of $2^{256} - 1$ strategies that can be created.

When it comes to the functions the smart contract is also composed of, we first have the methods related to the owner of the smart contract: `isOwner()` to check whether the *callee* is the owner of the contract, `updateOwner()` to update the owner of the contract and `getOwner()` to return the address of the owner. In order to add or remove strategies from the list, we implemented `makeStrategy()` and `deleteStrategy()`. The first one takes all the necessary parameters formerly described that a strategy has and creates the struct, pushes it into the array, increments the global ID counter and emits the event broadcasting a change in the strategy list. The `deleteStrategy()` method deletes a strategy from the list by given its ID.

Should a situation arise where the company has to change the **priority** of a strategy in order to activate it because some conditions changed or because another should take its place, we decided to implement a `changePriority()` function that takes the index of the strategy whose priority should be changed, and sets the priority to the new value.

The smart contract should also naturally allow users and clients to connect to it, aiming to retrieve the information stored. For that purpose, the functions `getStrategies()` and `getStrategyFromIndex()` have been implemented. The first one simply returns the list of strategies in its current state, while the second one returns a strategy object given an index from the list.

4.3 Web Platform

To communicate with the blockchain, we used the `ethers.js` library, which handles interaction with the blockchain and its ecosystem. We also used this library to set up the JSON-RPC connection to the blockchain.

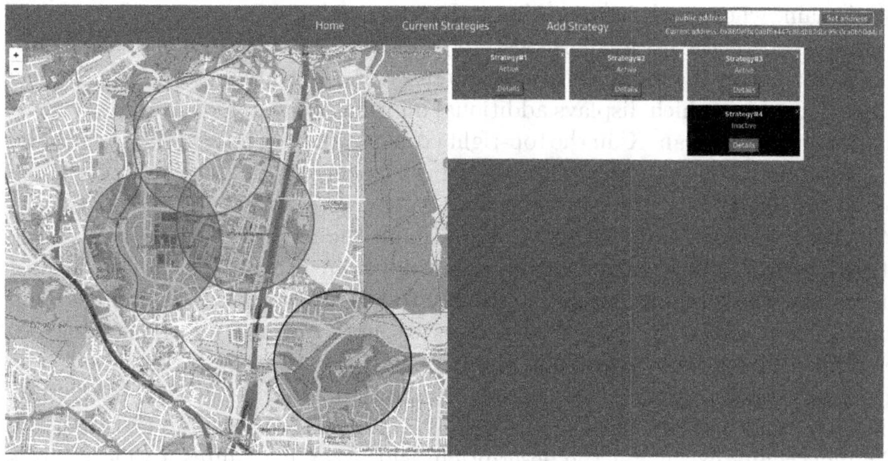

Fig. 3. User interface for viewing the current strategies on the blockchain

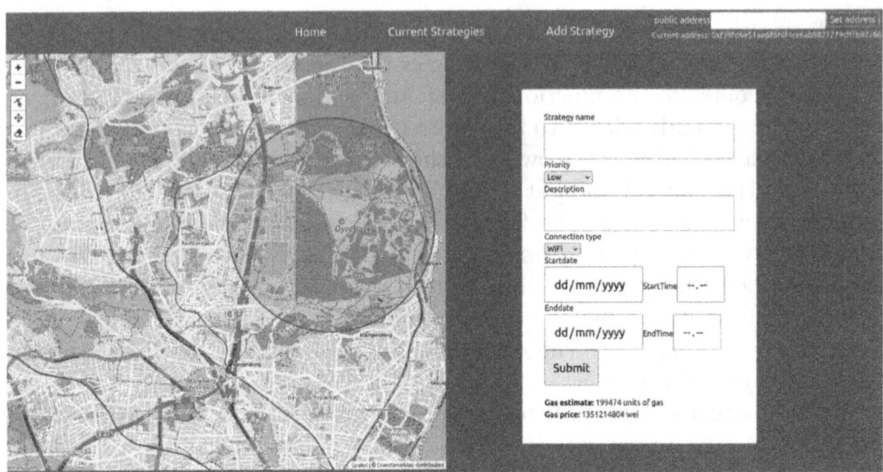

Fig. 4. User interface for adding a new strategy to the blockchain

The component that shows the current strategies is shown in Fig. 3. As mentioned in Sect. 3.3, it contains a map and a grid, where the map shows the location of the strategies, and the grid contains other details about the strategies. The grid uses the `react-grid-layout` package, in order to dynamically change the grid.

The strategies displayed on the map are color-coded based on their priority, where green is low, yellow is medium, and red is high. The edge color is also color-coded, based on whether the strategy is active, inactive, or expired, with the colors orange, black, and purple respectively. If a strategy is selected, it will display information about the clicked strategy.

The grid changes, depending on what strategies are currently on the blockchain, where each item on the grid corresponds to a strategy. The color of each strategy on the list is color-coded the same way as the edge color of the strategies. This makes it more intuitive for the user. Each strategy then has a button labeled 'details', which displays additional information in a popup modal, such as its description, and an 'X' in the top-right corner to remove it from the blockchain.

To update the map and grid displaying the current strategies, an event listener was made to listen for when new blocks were added on the blockchain. When a new block is added to the blockchain, the map and grid will fetch the strategies from the contract again, this time from the newest block. Figure 4 shows how the user can upload a strategy to the blockchain. It contains a map and a form, where the map allows users to mark an area for the strategy to be added, and a form containing the details of the strategy to be added. The fields are: name, priority, description, connection type, start-date, start-time, end-date, and end-time. All of the fields are necessary to deploy a strategy to the blockchain, except for the description field. Also, it requires a valid address as the sender and a marked area to deploy a strategy to the blockchain. If one or more of the required information is missing, a popup will inform the user.

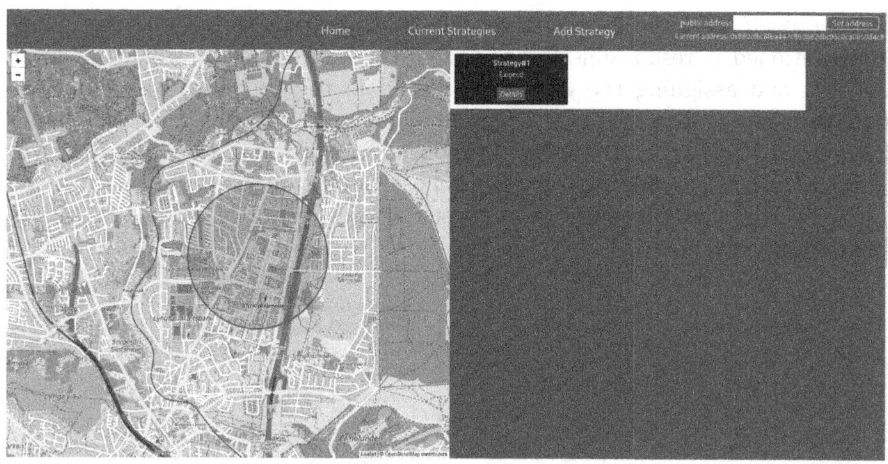

Fig. 5. Expired strategy with invalid address

The navigation-bar contains links to the other parts of the page, an input field that takes the address of the user and also displays the last address entered. This address is used for transactions on the blockchain, i.e., adding or removing a strategy. This address is saved in the computer's local storage, so it will be saved when the page is closed or refreshed.

We can also remove the expired strategies, as shown in Fig. 5, which can be done automatically by removing the expired strategies when the website is rendered, if the user has entered a valid address as the one calling the `deleteStrategy()` method from the smart contract. If not, the expired strategies will be displayed as expired, until the user enters a valid address.

4.4 Client Application

As mentioned in Sect. 3.2, the client application was implemented in Java and with a wide use of the `Web3j` blockchain library. Web3j is a Java and Android library for working with Smart Contracts and integrating with clients (nodes) on the Ethereum network. It allowed us to work with the Ethereum blockchain, without the additional overhead of having to write our own integration code for the platform.

As shown in Fig. 6, the application is divided in classes where the **Client** class is the main class, responsible for all the logic of how the strategies are handled and all the others are support classes storing information and providing functions ranging from interactions with the contract to credentials storage.

To achieve the defined goals for the `Client` class, three particular functions such as `setStrategies()`, `chooseActiveStrategy()` and `enableStrategy()` were implemented. Other than these, the class also contains the `main()` method. The file also keeps track of the stored information by having a `Strategy` object **active_strategy**, which holds the currently active strategy, an object for the contract itself, and the list of strategies at its current state. The first function mentioned is responsible for retrieving the strategy array from the smart contract, and assigning the global list stored in the program, by calling the `getStrategies()` function in the generated contract class by Web3j. The function `enableStrategy()` is the one responsible for running the code that will interact with the operating system or host device, in order to execute the necessary commands to match the chosen strategy; mainly by looking at its `ConnectionType` value.

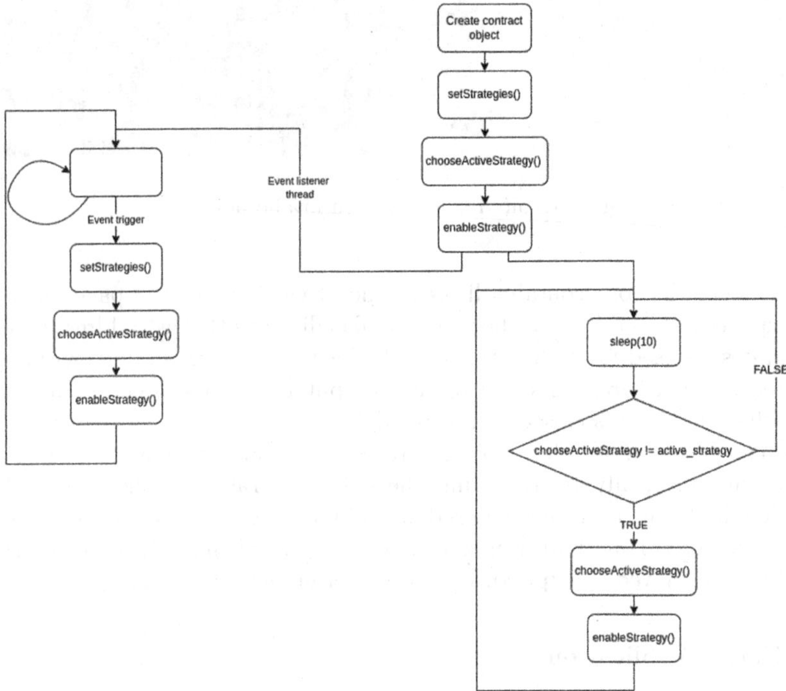

Fig. 6. Workflow of the client class

The workflow of the program starts with creating the contract object, and then a list of strategies is retrieved and a check is run to decide which should be the active one. Once it is completed, should there be an active strategy, it is then enabled and the device settings are tweaked in order to suit it. Then the event listener thread is created, which will keep listening for an event trigger when a change has been made to the list. As soon as that happens, the process of retrieving, choosing, and enabling strategies is run once again, and finally the thread waits again for another trigger. After the creation of the thread, an infinite loop is initiated so that a check can be made every 10 s to explore whether the current strategy is expired or time has come for a new strategy to be the active one. This is done by running the `chooseActiveStrategy()` method to figure

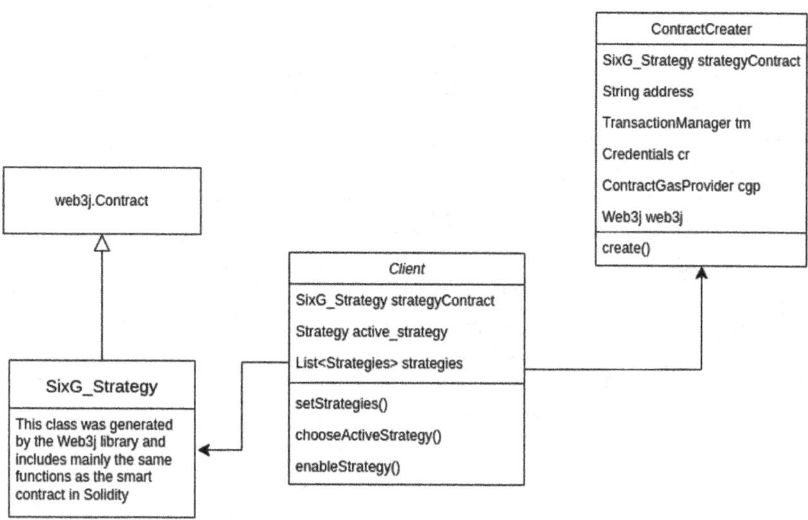

Fig. 7. Diagram of the client application

out which strategy should be active. If the returned object is different than the current one, a change should be made, and the new one is set to be active and enabled through `enableStrategy()`. Once it has been done, the program loops and sleeps for 10 s again before running another check.

Another class was the `ContractCreater`, whose job is to establish the connection between the client application, the smart contract, and the contract object itself, which will be used and interacted in the `Client` class.

Its code is primarily built by Web3j objects and functions, in order to set up the connection with the blockchain network, a series of steps need to be followed so that the contract can be loaded. The **address** of the contract on the chain has to be stored and a `HttpService` has to be created based on the IP address and port number that the chain has as endpoint. Thereafter a new account is created by generating a new key pair of public and private key, followed by a wallet as well. In our implementation, a new account is made every time when the program is running again, but in a real network, it would only be created if there is no account already created on the running device. The credentials are then used to create a `RawTransactionManager` followed by the creation of a `DefaultGasProvider` object as well.

The `SixG_Strategy` class is also a major component of the application, which contains all the functions that correspond to the ones in the smart contract. However it is automatically generated by the Web3j package when being given the `.abi` file for the compiled contract alongside its binary code in a `.bin` file. Thereafter the package generates all functions, event listeners and classes, so that everything in the smart contract is accessible in Java in a class of its own. The diagram of the client application is depicted in Fig. 7.

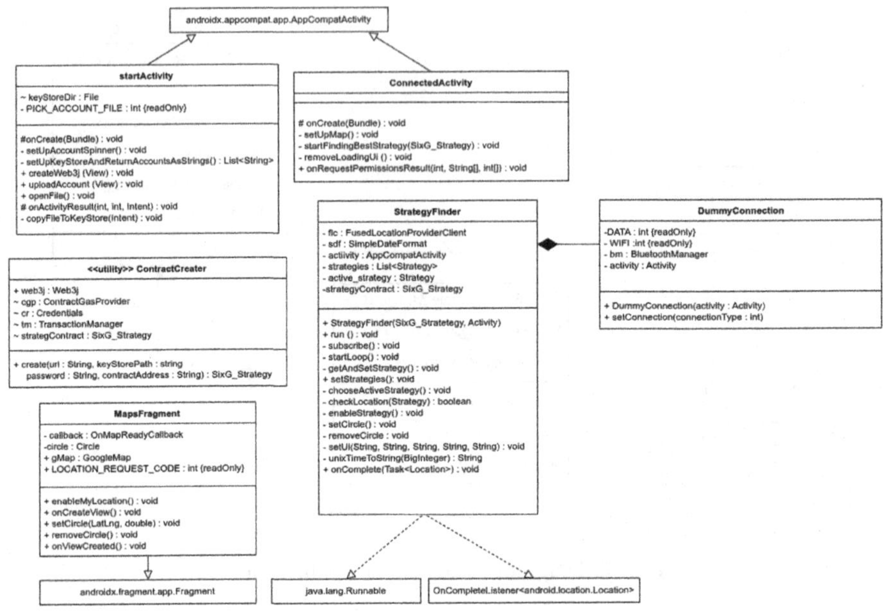

Fig. 8. Class diagram of the App

4.5 Android App

Figure 8 illustrates the class diagram of the App design. We have two Android activities: the start activity to input connection data, and the main `ConnectedActivity`, which runs after connecting to the node. The `ContractCreater` class holds a method that takes the necessary arguments, and creates a `Web3j` object by using an HTTP service to the given URL. This returns a `SixG_Strategy` that is a subclass of the Web3j's `Contract` class, and is generated by Web3j's command line interface.

The `StrategyFinder` class implements the `runnable` interface, so that it can run in the background without stopping the UI thread. It is responsible for retrieving the strategies on the contract, and finding the most suitable one. It holds a list of *Strategies*, which is a java representation of the *struct* in the contract, automatically created by Web3j. It runs a loop that checks the strategies in the list every 10 s and updates the list every time when the contract calls `StrategyChangedEvent`.

The map fragment is a subclass of an Android fragment, which is attached to the `ConnectedActivity`. It holds a **GoogleMap** field, and with the methods of `setCircle()` and `removeCircle()`, we can show the area where the active strategy is valid. We used the class `DummyConnection` to symbolize the change of connection method. The class contains `setConnection(int connectionType)`, where the argument is corresponding to the `connectType` enum in the smart contract. This method can be changed in the future, in order to support changing the connection type of our mobile data.

5 Evaluation and Discussion

As a case study, we implemented unit tests and run different testing frameworks for each component of the system, since each was implemented in its own programming language and environment. For example in the case of testing the smart contract, RemixIDE has a built-in unit testing tool, which can generate a generic test file that can be expanded and customized to implement the tests for our contract.

We then programmed unit tests for the methods implemented in the smart contract, mainly `makeStrategy()`, `deleteStrategy()` and `changePriority()`. For the case of the first function, we tested whether the strategy was actually added to the list and with the correct given ID. For the second function we tested with a check whether the length of the new list is less than the previous one, meaning not only that the strategy was deleted but the size of the array was also dynamically changed. For the `changePriority()` test, we issued a check whether the new priority is the same as the one that the method was called on the list. The performance and correctness of the smart contract was also tested in the overall tests we did on the system.

When it came to testing the client application, we decided to bundle the tests with the Android app, since the logic is exactly the same, apart from location checks on the Android version. The most important aspect to be tested was the process of choosing which strategy has to be chosen from the list. Thus, we made a unit test for the app, by checking the logic for the `chooseActiveStratgy()` method. This is because it contains a large boolean logic check. The tests we performed can be summarized as below.

- No strategies are uploaded (an empty list is received).
- A strategy that should get applied or added.
- Going from one strategy to one with higher priority.
- A strategy that is expired gets added.
- Applying a strategy that later expires, and then choosing a strategy with lower priority.
- A strategy that far away gets added.

In order to test the overall performance of the system, manual tests had to be performed as there was no unified unit testing framework that we could work with, which suited every platform and application of the system we implemented. For this reason, we came up with different scenarios in which the program should behave as expected. We added the following use cases.

- No strategy is on the list and a strategy is added that should instantly become active.
- No strategy is active and we reached `startDate` for a strategy on the list. Meaning it should be activated.
- The active strategy expires and no other is valid for the time being.
- A strategy is currently active but another has been added valid for the same time as the current one, but with higher priority.

- A strategy with high priority expires but another with lower priority is still valid.
- A strategy that is currently active is deleted but another is still valid.
- A strategy that is currently active is deleted but there is no other on the list.

Observations and Results. In all these cases, the system behaved as expected and in the correct way according to our goals. For example, Fig. 9 shows that our app can correctly display the strategy status. When it comes to the performance and efficiency, the system depends mainly on the amount of time it takes to mine each transaction, as the event trigger is instant as soon as the transaction has been mined, initiating the selection process in the client application.

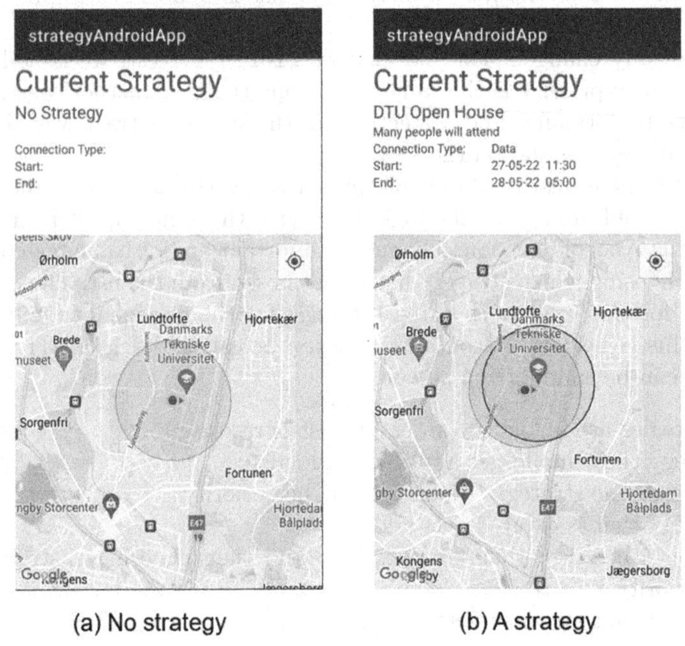

Fig. 9. The test for exploring the strategy. (a) No strategy is used, and (b) A strategy is being used.

Discussion. After setting up the blockchain, the platform run smoothly as a whole, and the response time was reasonable from the moment a change is committed from the web platform to the client application reacted, by considering the mining process the transaction has to go through. From the client application's perspective, the worst case scenario is only dependent on the time it takes for a transaction to finish being mined, given how as soon as that happened, the event listener is triggered, starting the entire strategy selection process as previously mentioned, meaning that it has nothing to do with the `while` loop checking for strategy validity. The latter, on the other hand, has a worst case scenario when a strategy expires or another should become active, just as the loop enters the 10 s sleep-period and then has to unnecessarily wait that time before it performs the changes needed. This means that the device can lose 10 s of optimal connection but given how strategies probably have a period of at least a few hours rather than days or months, then 10 s is not significant for the end user.

6 Concluding Remarks

The connection strategy is important to ensure the 6G performance, such as real-time response according to the change of environment. However, traditionally centralized schemes are expensive with low-availability, low-adaptivity, and low-auditability. In this work, we explored the use of blockchain for a more robust connection strategy and provided a practical implementation of blockchain-enabled connection strategy in 6G era. The main goal of our work was to assess the viability of using blockchain to control the connectivity of a network through connection strategies applied to diverse devices on the grid in 6G. In our test, the results demonstrated the viability of our proposed system.

Further, our proposed system can also be used in a way that the clients can provide information about the quality of the connection currently in a certain location to the smart contract and the telecommunications company in a way that a strategy can be made activated according to the information gathered. It means that a large amount of data on the connectivity can be gathered from several clients, which can generate something like a map of the connection quality for different places, in order to help everyone involved for achieving a better and more robust connection.

Acknowledgments. This work was partially funded by the EU H2020 DataVaults project with GA Number 871755. All the source code for the project is available at https://github.com/Bassusour/Blockchain-Connection-Strategy.

References

1. Arai, S., Kinoshita, M., Yamazato, T.: Optical wireless communication: a candidate 6G technology? IEICE Trans. Fundam. Electron. Commun. Comput. Sci. **104-A**(1), 227–234 (2021)
2. Chiu, W.Y., Meng, W.: DevLeChain - an open blockchain development platform for decentralized applications. In: Proceedings of the 5th IEEE International Conference on Blockchain (IEEE Blockchain), IEEE (2022)
3. Chiu, W.Y., Meng, W.: EdgeTC - a PBFT blockchain-based ETC scheme for smart cities. Peer-to-Peer Network. Appl. **14**, 2874–2886 (2021)
4. Chiu, W.Y., Meng, W., Jensen, C.D.: My data, my control: a secure data sharing and access scheme over blockchain. J. Inf. Secur. Appl. **63**, article 103020 (2021)
5. Faisal, T., Dohler, M., Mangiante, S., Lopez, D.R.: BEAT: blockchain-enabled accountable and transparent network sharing in 6G. IEEE Commun. Mag. **60**(4), 52–56 (2022)

6. Holslin, P.: What Is 6G Internet and What Will It Look Like?. https://www.highspeedinternet.com/resources/6g-internet. Accessed 27 June 2022 https://www.highspeedinternet.com/resources/6g-internet
7. Je, D.H., Jung, J., Choi, S.: Toward 6G security: technology trends, threats, and solutions. IEEE Commun. Stand. Mag. **5**(3), 64–71 (2021)
8. Jensen, W.L., Jessing, S., Chiu, W.Y., Meng, W.: AirChain - towards blockchain-based aircraft maintenance record system. In: Proceedings of The 2022 IEEE International Conference on Blockchain and Cryptocurrency (IEEE ICBC), pp. 1–3 (2022)
9. Jensen, W.L., Jessing, S., Chiu, W.Y., Meng, W.: A practical blockchain-based maintenance record system for better aircraft security. In: Proceedings of The 4th International Conference on Science of Cyber Security (SciSec) (2022)
10. Kumari, A., Gupta, R., Tanwar, S.: Amalgamation of blockchain and IoT for smart cities underlying 6G communication: a comprehensive review. Comput. Commun. **172**, 102–118 (2021)
11. Khan, A.H., et al.: Blockchain and 6G: the future of secure and ubiquitous communication. IEEE Wirel. Commun. **29**(1), 194–201 (2022)
12. Kranz, G., Christensen, G.: What is 6G? Overview of 6G networks & technology. https://www.techtarget.com/searchnetworking/definition/6G. Accessed 27 June 2022 https://www.techtarget.com/searchnetworking/definition/6G
13. Li, T., Zhang, M., Cao, H., Li, Y., Tarkoma, S., Hui, P.: "What Apps Did You Use?": understanding the long-term evolution of mobile app usage. WWW **2020**, 66–76 (2020)
14. Li, W., Wang, Y., Li, J.: Enhancing blockchain-based filtration mechanism via IPFS for collaborative intrusion detection in IoT networks. J. Syst. Architect. **127** (2022)
15. Meng, W., Li, W., Zhu, L.: Enhancing medical smartphone networks via blockchain-based trust management against insider attacks. IEEE Trans. Eng. Manage. **67**(4), 1377–1386 (2020)
16. Meng, W., Li, W., Zhou, J.: Enhancing the security of blockchain-based software defined networking through trust-based traffic fusion and filtration. Inf. Fus. **70**, 60–71 (2021)
17. Meng, W., Li, W., Tug, S., Tan, J.: towards blockchain-enabled single character frequency-based exclusive signature matching in IoT-assisted smart cities. J.. Parallel Distrib. Comput. **144**, 268–277 (2020)
18. Hewa, T.M., Gur, G., Kalla, A., Ylianttila, M., Bracken, A., Liyanage, M.: The role of blockchain in 6G: challenges, opportunities and research directions. In: Proceedings of 6G SUMMIT, pp. 1–5 (2020)
19. Velliangiri, S., Manoharan, R., Ramachandran, S., Rajasekar, V.: Blockchain based privacy preserving framework for emerging 6G wireless communications. IEEE Trans. Ind. Inf. **18**(7), 4868–4874 (2022)
20. Wang, J., Ling, X., Le, Y., Huang, Y. You, X.: Blockchain-enabled wireless communications: a new paradigm towards 6G, Natl. Sci. Rev. **8**(9) (2021)
21. Xu, H., Klaine, P.V., Onireti, O., Cao, B., Imran, M., Zhang, L.: Blockchain-enabled resource management and sharing for 6G communications. Digit. Commun. Networks **6**(3), 261–269 (2020)
22. Xie, J., Zhang, K., Lu, Y., Zhang, Y.: Resource-efficient DAG blockchain with sharding for 6G networks. IEEE Netw. **36**(1), 189–196 (2022)

Blockchain-Based Multi-keyword Search on Encrypted COVID-19 Contact Tracing Data

Zheng Yao Ng(✉) and Iftekhar Salam

School of Computing and Data Science, Xiamen University Malaysia, Sepang 43900, Malaysia
{swe1904870,iftekhar.salam}@xmu.edu.my

Abstract. Contact tracing data contain highly sensitive information in which any form of leakage will significantly threaten the security and privacy of the individual. Encryption schemes can be used to ensure confidentiality; however, the usability of the retrieval system will be reduced considerably as the encrypted data does not support searchability. Hence, searchable encryption could be applied to contact tracing data. This paper introduces our implementation of a blockchain-based multi-keyword searchable encryption for COVID-19 contact tracing data. We used Advanced Encryption Standard as the symmetric primitive for encrypting datasets and Attribute-based Encryption as the asymmetric primitive for encrypting the search index. We incorporated Blockchain-based storage into our scheme to assure the integrity of the datasets and search index. It provides immutable storage and ensures data integrity and non-repudiation, as any form of access will be logged automatically. The results show that the scheme works efficiently without compromising any security goals. Compared to the existing searchable contact tracing schemes, it provides more features and maintains efficiency even if a large search index was used within the system.

Keywords: COVID-19 contact tracing data · Attribute-based searchable encryption · Blockchain · Smart contract

1 Introduction

It has been widely reported that the COVID-19 pandemic altered the economics and lifestyle around the world due to its ease of transmission through close physical contact. As a countermeasure against the transmission of the virus, the government of different countries enforced Movement Control Order (MCO) alongside systematic control methods by utilizing mobile applications such as TraceTogether [4], PriLok [7], Pronto-C2 [5], DP3T [15], BeepTrace [16], and MySejahtera [3]. These applications collect personal details such as names, identity card numbers, real-time location, and recently visited places. This information is utilized to generate contact tracing data and to track clusters infected by the COVID-19 virus. Therefore, the security of the information possesses high priority since leakage of confidential information will cause unwanted negative

C. Su et al. (Eds.): ISPEC 2022, LNCS 13620, pp. 75–92, 2022.
https://doi.org/10.1007/978-3-031-21280-2_5

consequences. For example, a study conducted by Jung et al. [10] shows that even if the names of the personnel have not been collected, from the visited location and their frequency, 70% of the data successfully reveals the owner's exact location of residence, workplace, as well as their hobbies and routine behavior and thus causing the security and privacy of the owner to be violated. Other than the application's security issues, the security of cloud storage should be concerned as well. The convenience of ease to access properties of cloud storage made majority cloud users maintained "trusted-but-curious" attitudes towards the security of cloud storage. Cases such as Socialarks data leak [1] and Microsoft's cloud storage leak [2] show that even without malicious party deliberately breaching the databases, there are possibilities where the database is accidentally leaked to the public by the organization. Hence, applying effective practices to sensitive information is essential before outsourcing them.

Cryptographic schemes can be used to assure the confidentiality of sensitive contact tracing data. However, the usability of the retrieval system will be significantly reduced as the encrypted data does not support searchability. Searchable encryption with Blockchain could be a viable solution to address the security of the data without affecting functionality. In this work, we implement a blockchain-based multi-keyword searchable encryption scheme for COVID-19 contact tracing data that assures confidentiality, integrity, and non-repudiation.

1.1 Related Work

Contact tracing data has only gained attention recently due to the COVID-19 pandemic. Hence, only a few schemes address the topic of searchable contact tracing. Many contact tracing schemes tend to involve blockchain due to their security properties [5,9,16]. These schemes mainly focus on privacy-preserving proximity tracing but may not involve search functionality. On the other hand, a few existing schemes propose privacy-preserving processing of contact tracing data with searchable encryption. Tahir et al. [13] proposed a blockchain-based searchable encryption scheme for contact tracing data. In this scheme, all data are encrypted and decrypted by a single entity, the enterprise that developed the system. This entity perform all processes before any other operations are executed. This may lead to an unwanted situation where the third party misuses the data. Moreover, in this scheme, authorized personnel are decided by the enterprise. The enterprise administrator decides on authentication for viewing contact tracing data. If any malicious party are registered into the system with the aid of an insider, the data confidentiality will be breached as no access policy is applied to the system. Also, this scheme only supports single-keyword search.

Nabil et al. [12] proposed a surveillance system that supports searchable encryption over encrypted COVID-19 data. The system calculates the similarity score between visitors' and patients' embedding vectors without retrieving data from the server. An offline key distribution center distributes the keys in this scheme. Each party involved uses different keys, and since the key distribution center is an offline entity, it frequently updates the keys to prevent any security issues. This work guarantees that the server will not learn any useful data for its calculation process. However, the integrity of the results or data used for the calculation was not emphasized. Moreover, as all the data were swarmed into a single cloud service platform, the cloud server might be overloaded with resources, decreasing the efficiency and accuracy of data retrieval.

In general, multi-keyword searchable encryption is more practical than single-keyword as the COVID-19 cluster analysis typically involves large datasets. Hence using a single-keyword scheme will result in lower efficiency. We must also avoid centralized storage to address the data misuse [14].

1.2 Our Contribution

We adopted and implemented Guo et al.'s Attribute-Based Searchable Encryption (ABSE) [8] that supports multi-keyword searching for the COVID-19 contact tracing data. We tweaked their scheme by incorporating an attribute authority center to address the unstandardized key generation of multiple data owners. In our implemented scheme, the contact tracing data is encrypted via Advanced Encryption Standard (AES), and the searchable index is encrypted using ABSE. This way, the confidentiality of the outsourced data and search index is assured. On top of that, blockchain and smart contracts are used to store and access encrypted search indexes and retrieve files. InterPlanetary File System (IPFS) has also been used to outsource encrypted data. With the aid of blockchain technology, the access of files and search index are logged, thus achieving non-repudiation. The immutability of blockchain ensures the integrity of the stored content. Our implemented system proves efficient and practical as the search efficiency is approximately linear to the size of the search index and the deployment costs of the smart contract are low.

2 Framework of the Developed System

Implementing an attribute-based encryption (ABE) scheme allows users with different authorities to access information according to their roles. Combining ABE with searchable encryption is a convenient system where users can retrieve information based on their roles. This could easily fulfill the access policy of the dataset storage within an organization, which helps eliminate several security risks when the dataset is outsourced to a cloud storage server. The proposed framework assumes that the data should only be accessible by the government and other government-authorized organizations such as research companies and hospitals. The contact tracing datasets content consists of name, identity card number, gender, check-in date, time, and visited location. Four keywords are used to identify the datasets: the organization that provides the data, the location area coverage for the contact tracing data, and the month and year of the collected data. Since the contact tracing datasets are confidential and not allowed to be shared publicly, the dataset used in this paper is randomly generated dummy data following the type of values that the MySejahtera app uses.

2.1 High-Level Overview of the Proposed System

The system mainly consists of four parties, Data Owner (DO), Data Requester (DR), Attribute Authority Center (AAC), and Cloud Service Platform (CSP). Figure 1 shows a high-level overview of the proposed system. A brief discussion of these entities are discussed below:

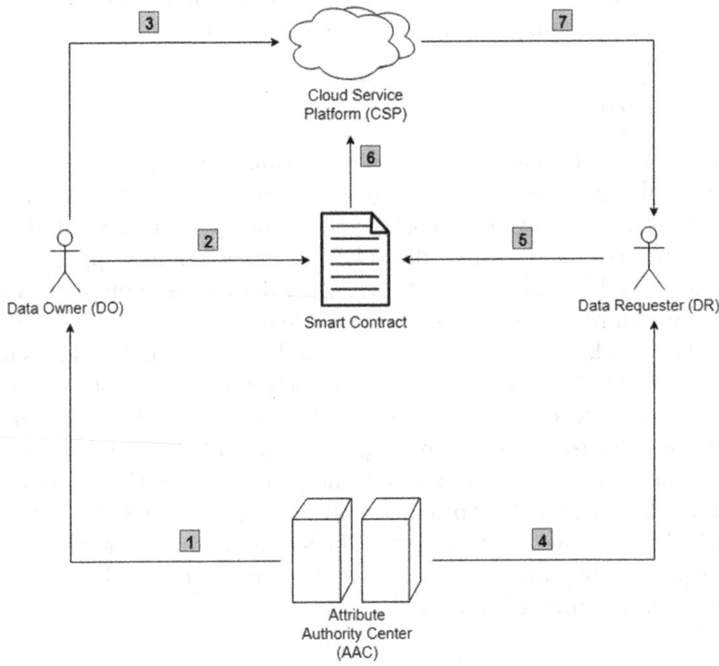

Fig. 1. High-level overview of the proposed system.

1. Data Owner (DO): DO is the entity sharing the contact tracing data with the system. Mainly, the data owner could consist of the local hospital or the center that collects contact tracing data for that particular area. They will hold the original content of the contact tracing data and are responsible for encrypting it and uploading the file to the CSP. They are also responsible for uploading the encrypted search index and the access policy to the smart contract so that DR can access the content.
2. Data Requester (DR): DR is the entity requesting encrypted data from the system. An example of DR includes a government department or a research center authorized by the government. Each of them has its corresponding attributes, and they will only be able to decrypt the data if their attributes match the access policy set by DO.
3. Attribute Authority Center (AAC): AAC is the entity responsible for the generation and distribution of the public and private keys for all system users.

Depending on the system, AAC could be a trusted third-party or an internal department of the organization.

4. Cloud Service Platform (CSP): CSP is the entity that will be responsible for the storing of encrypted data. The results returned from the smart contract can be used to retrieve the desired files.

Aside from the interaction between these parties, the smart contract will be used by both DO and DR to interact with the encrypted data. DO will upload the index to the smart contract to be stored securely within the blockchain network, whereas DR will interact with the smart contract to retrieve the encrypted data that matches the desired keywords.

2.2 Workflow of the System

The workflow of the system is demonstrated as a sequence diagram in Fig. 2. The steps involved in the sequence diagram include:

1. AAC generates the system parameters and a master private key. Then, the system parameters are distributed to DO through a secure communication channel.
2. DO generates an encrypted keyword search index with an access policy and encrypts the contact tracing data with AES-GCM. The encrypted contact tracing data will be outsourced to CSP for storing purposes.
3. DO stores the encrypted search index into a smart contract and deploys it onto the blockchain network for fair payment and searching purposes.
4. AAC generates a private key based on the attributes of DR and distributes it to that particular DR through a secure communication channel.
5. DR generates a search token, deploys a smart contract for search-related functions and sends it to the blockchain to make a transaction. The search operation will proceed only if a sufficient fee is given.
6. After executing the search operation, a list of files that fulfill the desired keywords will be retrieved from the CSP.
7. The result is sent to DR; upon receiving the encrypted data file, DR decrypts the encrypted files.

3 Construction of the Proposed Scheme

This section provides the details of the implemented system[1]. For our implementation, the datasets are encrypted via Advanced Encryption Standard (AES), whereas the search index is encrypted via Attribute-Based Searchable Encryption scheme referred from Guo et al. [8].

AES is a type of symmetric block cipher encryption with higher efficiency in encryption and decryption than asymmetric encryption. Hence, it is used for the

[1] The source code for the implementation can be accessed via GitHub repository: https://github.com/Wise-Neko/SWE1904870-FYP.

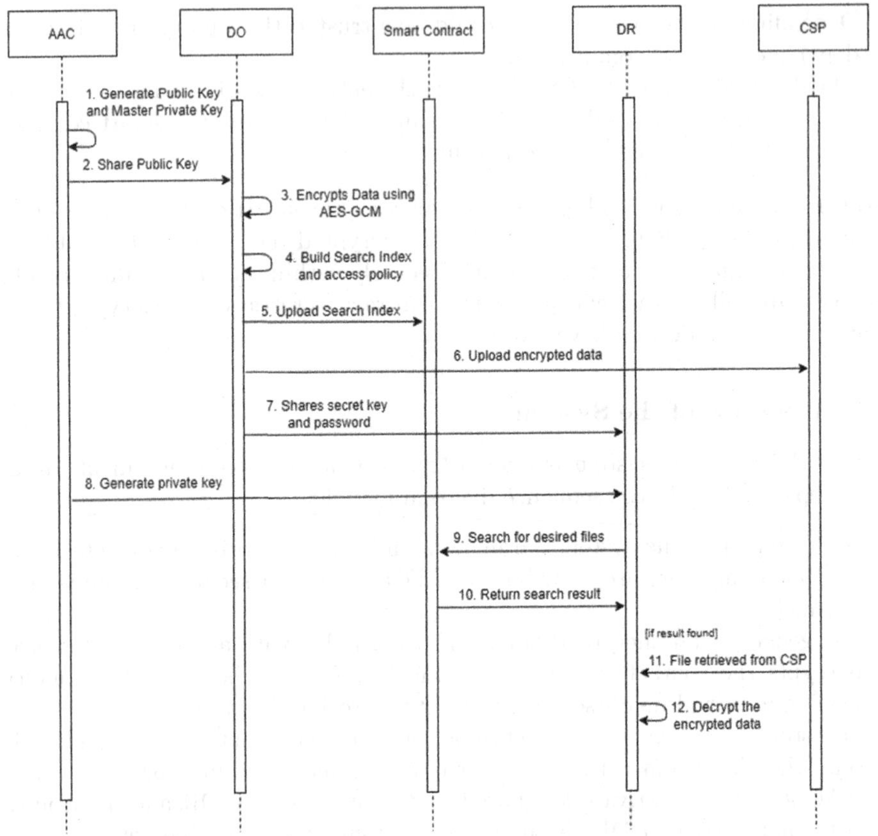

Fig. 2. Sequence diagram of the proposed system.

encryption of datasets. AES-Galois/Counter Mode (AES-GCM) is chosen particularly for this system [11]. It utilizes an authentication tag during the decryption process to determine whether the user is permitted to perform decryption. This proposed system will store the authentication tag within the encrypted data. During the decryption operation, if the generated tag does not match the authentication tag stored within the encrypted dataset, the decryption results will not be displayed to the user.

On the other hand, the search index is encrypted by Guo's asymmetric encryption scheme [8] to provide a higher degree of security. The encrypted search index is stored within a smart contract, whereas the encrypted datasets are stored within a distributed storage system network called InterPlanetary File System (IPFS). IPFS is a distributed file system network for storing and sharing data. It has a unique identifier for each file stored within the system. Since it is a peer-to-peer storage network, the content that is stored within could be accessed by peers located anywhere. In this work, IPFS has been used to replace the CSP because CSP is a centralized authority which increases the risk of the data stored within getting abused by authorities. Since IPFS stores its content across several nodes, it also assures the availability and accuracy of content stored within, even if malicious actions were acted upon the content. It also provides a more reliable uptime for storing and retrieving data. The IPFS that is used in this implementation is the IPFS desktop. Compared to other IPFS that require a terminal command line for operation, the IPFS desktop provides an interface. Hence, it is easier for the users to manage the node content, link to any service or platform used, and keep track of the peers connected to the nodes.

3.1 System Setup

First, the AAC will initialize the system by getting all possible user's attribute, $U = \{attr_1, attr_2, \cdots, attr_n\}$, where n is the size of the attribute sets. For each attribute within the system, there are two values v_i and $\neg v_i$. The value of $attr_i = v_i$ when the the data requester possess the attribute $attr_i$. If the data requester does not possess the attribute $attr_i$, the value of $attr_i = \neg v_i$. These values are important as they are used to determine whether or not the data requester's attribute set contain the attribute. The AAC will then start the generation of the public key and master private key. A bilinear group $e : G * G \rightarrow G_T$, where p is the prime order of G and G_T, and $H : \{0,1\}^* \rightarrow Z_p$ as the one-way hash functions is computed. Then, the following variables are randomly selected.

$$a, b, c \leftarrow Z_p \tag{1}$$

$$\{r_1, r_2, \ldots, r_{2n}\} \leftarrow Z_p \tag{2}$$

$$\{x_1, x_2, \ldots, x_{2n}\} \leftarrow G \tag{3}$$

Then, let $u_i = g^{r_i}$ and $y_i = e(x_i, g)$, where $1 \leq i \leq 2n$. After setting all the variables, the public key, pk and master private key, msk are generated.

$$pk = (g, g^a, g^b, g^c, (u_i, y_i)|1 \leq i \leq 2n) \tag{4}$$

$$msk = (a, b, c, (r_i, x_i)|1 \leq i \leq 2n \tag{5}$$

Afterwards, the encryption can be done by the data owner. First, $t_1, t_2 \in Z_p$ are chosen randomly and the access policy structure $S = \wedge_{v_i \in u} v_i'$ is defined, where $v_i' = v_i$ or $\neg v_i$. Next, we compute $u_{gate} = g^{t_2} \prod_{i=1}^{n} u_i'$. Each keyword w is then encrypted with $W' = g^{ct_1}$, and $W = g^{a(t_1+t_2)} g^{bH(w)t_1}$. The associated file will be encrypted using the AES algorithm. Here, u_{gate} is the access policy, whereas W' and W are used for verification purposes. Algorithm 1 shows the key generation process during the system setup. For prime number mapping purposes, JPBC library [6] has been imported for the generation of keys for attribute-based encryption. In Algorithm 1, the public key was generated using a preset properties file provided by JPBC for bilinear prime mapping.

3.2 File Encryption

The data owner will first generate a secret key to be distributed to the data requester beforehand. The secret key will be used in AES-GCM for the encryp-

Algorithm 1: Key Generation Algorithm

Input: All possible user attributes
Output: Public Key and Master Private Key

Initialize JPBC for bilinear mapping using it.unisa.dia.gas.jpbc library
Set new Element for each parameter
for *each attribute* **do**
  Get the grouping for each attribute in master private key
  Get the grouping for each attribute in public key
Perform multiplicative operations for each element

Algorithm 2: File Encryption via AES-GCM

Input: Contact tracing data in plaintext form and password
Output: Encrypted contact tracing data file

Initialize AES-GCM for encryption using javax.crypto library
Convert the plaintext file into a byte
Generates a random salt and IV
Encrypts the byte file with salt, IV, and password
if *file encryption succeeds* **then**
  Writes the encrypted byte file into the same directory

tion and decryption of the file. The data owner can set a password during the encryption; hence, the data requester also needs to know the password to decrypt the file. Algorithm 2 shows the process of file encryption via AES-GCM. First, AES-GCM is initialized using javax.crypto library. After the initialization, it will read the plaintext file into byte form for encryption usage. A random salt and IV alongside the password will be generated to be used for the encryption by the data owner. If the encryption succeeds, the encrypted file bytes will be written into a file and stored within the directory of the file. Next, the data owner generates a search index and encrypts it using AES-GCM but with another key that will be preinstalled within the system. The key is different from the key used for file encryption, and with the aid of using a password during encryption, the adversary will not be able to encrypt/decrypt the file easily even if the keys were to be learnt. After successfully encrypting the COVID-19 contact tracing data, the encrypted data can then be uploaded to IPFS.

3.3 Index Generation

The encrypted search index for the particular file will then be uploaded onto the smart contract. The smart contract possesses an array class mapped to a SearchIndex structure. The uploaded search index will be added to the array class for searching purposes. The structure consists of seven variables: id, ipfsHash, organization, location, month, year, and token. Algorithm 3 shows the process of index encryption and upload, and Table 1 shows the summary of the SearchIndex

Algorithm 3: Index Generation and Uploads

Input: Keyword Index in plaintext form and token for access policy
Output: Encrypted search index uploaded to smart contract

1 Convert the keyword index into encrypted keyword index
2 Pass the access policy into ABSE
3 Generates a file token based on the access policy
4 Upload the encrypted index along with token to smart contract
5 Smart contract stores the encrypted index and token in a new position within the SearchIndex structure array
6 A unique ID corresponding to the particular file position is generated

Table 1. Summary of search index structure

Search index structure	Explanation
id	The unique ID number for each file
ipfsHash	The hash values for the file within IPFS
organization	The organization that owns the data
location	The location area of the collected data
month	The month of the data collection
year	Year of the data collection
token	Token generated from access policy

structure. Smart contract stores the SearchIndex structure and maps it with an incremental count representing its location within the structure.

First, a comparison between access policy and attribute sets is performed to generate a file token. Algorithm 4 shows the generation of the file token. Firstly, set $v = g^{ac}$ and for each attribute that the data requester possesses, set $y_i^* = y_i$; else set $y_i^* = y_{i+n}$. Similarly, set $\sigma_i^* = x_i v^{r_i}$ if the data requester possesses the attributes; else set $\sigma_i^* = x_{i+n} v^{r_{i+n}}$. Afterwards, set $\sigma_{user} = \prod_{i=1}^{n} \sigma_i^*$ and the data requester private key, sk is generated.

$$sk = (y_{user} = \prod_{i=1}^{n} y_i^*, < v, \sigma_{user} >) \tag{6}$$

After the private key is generated, the user can generate a search token for their desired keyword. The user selects $s \leftarrow Z_p$ and generates the search token for the file associated with the desired keywords and access policy.

$$token1 = (g^a g^{bH(w)})^s \tag{7}$$

$$token2 = g^{cs} \tag{8}$$

$$searchtoken = (y_{user}^s, < v^s, \sigma_{user}^s >, token1, token2) \tag{9}$$

Algorithm 4: File Token Generation

```
Input: Access policy of the file and attribute included in system
Output: File token for authentication purpose
Initialize JPBC using it.unisa.dia.gas.jpbc library
for each attribute in the system do
    if the attribute is within the access policy then
        Multiply the token and the public parameters with the attribute
    else
        Multiply the token and the public parameters without the attribute
    Perform multiplicative operations for each element
```

3.4 Searching and Access Control

Algorithm 5 shows the process of the searching algorithm that is used within the system. Data requester will first enter their attribute set and desired keywords to generate a search token. Then, a transaction will be invoked to retrieve five string arrays from the smart contract to the client for searching functions. First, a comparison between searched keywords and four string arrays, organization[], location[], month[] and years[], is performed. If the searched keyword for the corresponding array is not null and is contained within the array, the position of the keyword will be stored in an array, position[]. Once every array has been compared, the last array retrieved from the smart contract, token[], will be used to verify whether or not the data requester has met the requirements to access the encrypted data. If the token were to verify first before searching for the file

Algorithm 5: Searching and Access Control Algorithm

```
Input: Desired keywords in plaintext and attribute set of data requester
Output: Hash value for encrypted file associated with desired keywords
Generate search token based on the attribute sets of data requester
Retrieve five string arrays from smart contract, organization[], location[],
  month[], year[] and token[]
for each array do
    if desired keywords NOT null then
        Check for searched keyword locations
        Store the result within results[]
    Remove duplicate values within results[]
for each element in results[] do
    Compare search token with token[results]
    if search token != token[results] then
        Remove the element from results[]
    Retrieve ipfsHash from smart contract using results[]
    Download the encrypted data using the ipfsHash
```

that fulfills the desired keywords, the system needs to run through all of the tokens retrieved from the smart contract, where the size is essentially the size of the whole search index. This will significantly affect the efficiency of the system. If the search token of the data requester matches the token retrieved, then the encrypted data is permitted to be viewed by the data requester. For this, E is computed for the search token purpose. The variables used for the calculations are encrypted keywords and the user token.

$$E = \frac{e(u_{gate}, v^s)e(\sigma^s_{user}, g)}{(y^s_{user})} \tag{10}$$

If the data requester's attributes match the access policy, then the data requester is permitted to download the encrypted data and perform decryption. The access policy is determined based on the below computation:

$$e(W', token1)E = e(W, token2) \tag{11}$$

This process will be repeated for each file that satisfies the desired keywords. After that, the ipfsHash will be retrieved from the smart contract. The file can then be downloaded using the hash value taken from the smart contract. Refer to the appendix to find examples of the dataset and search operations.

3.5 File Decryption

Once the index of the file is retrieved from the search results, a transaction can be made to retrieve the IPFS hash value for the file. The value can then be used to download the encrypted data from IPFS and decrypt it using AES-GCM. The data requester needs to input the password and secret key. If both inputs match the values used during encryption, then only the decryption functions will be performed successfully. Algorithm 6 shows the decryption process of the encrypted file downloaded from IPFS.

Algorithm 6: File Decryption

Input: Input: Password and secret key
Output: Printed decrypted file in plaintext form

Initialize AES-GCM for decryption using javax.crypto library
Buffers the IV, Salt and Ciphertext
Reads and initialize the secret key
Upload the encrypted index and token to smart contract
if *password invalid* **then**
  Decryption process failed
else
  Decrypts the encrypted file using the secret key
Print the decryption output into a file

4 Security Analysis and Performance Evaluation

We discuss the performance and security level of the proposed scheme. First, we discuss the proposed system's properties that help to satisfy the security goals. Next, we evaluate the performance of the implemented system in terms of encryption efficiency, search efficiency, and cost factor. Lastly, we present a feature comparison between the implemented system and other similar systems.

4.1 Security Analysis

In the implemented scheme, the security of the contact tracing data is being prioritized over the searching efficiency and computational overhead. Hence, several security goals are inspected.

Confidentiality of Contact Tracing Data. Throughout the storing, IPFS cannot learn any meaningful data from the outsourced datasets. Suppose the adversary successfully gained access to the encrypted file. In that case, they will not be able to read the datasets directly or perform common attacks such as known ciphertext attacks on the encrypted datasets to recover the original file.

Proof. We used AES-GCM for the encryption of datasets, along with a password chosen by the data owner. The encryption process has been performed with a symmetric key generated by the data owner and a password. After the encryption has been done, the encrypted file will then only be uploaded to the IPFS storage network. Hence, the knowledge of both values, the key and the password, must be known for the file decryption operation to produce the original file. An adversary without the knowledge of these values will not be able to decrypt the file and learn any meaningful data. Aside from that, the AES-GCM encryption mode operates in a more complex method than the other AES block cipher modes. Multiple XOR functions have been applied to one single plaintext block before converting it into a ciphertext block, and with the involvement of IV, the pattern of the ciphertext block will be randomized completely. The properties of the authentication tag will enable detecting any modification of the data. Hence, the confidentiality and integrity of the outsourced contact tracing data are assured.

Non-repudiation and Immutability of Data Storage. Storing a search index on the local server or outsourcing data to the CSP may risk the confidentiality and integrity of data as the CSP may view or modify the content. We used a smart contract for the search index and stored the outsourced data in the IPFS. This allows any accidental or deliberate modification attempts to be identified and prevented. Any access to the data will also be logged so that the data requester will not be able to deny their transactions.

Proof. In this scheme, the search index is uploaded to the Ethereum blockchain, which possesses immutability properties and distributed ledgers. Therefore, anything stored within the blockchain network must check its validity with the network participants before any transactions can be made. Any tampers made to the data within the network can be easily identified. Aside from the search index, the outsourced data stored within IPFS possess the same properties. Any amendments to the content of the stored data in the IPFS will significantly affect the hash values within the blockchain network. When the value for one participant has been changed, the other nodes will not be affected. Hence, any form of amendment will be recognized immediately.

4.2 Performance Evaluation

In our implemented system, dummy data is generated to assess the performance, as contact tracing datasets are not publicly available due to their sensitive nature. Multiple aspects are considered, including encryption and decryption efficiency, index searching efficiency, and cost efficiency.

Encryption Efficiency. The encryption efficiency is assessed by the speed of completion of the encryption operations over the different sizes of datasets. The test file sizes are 10 MB, 50 MB, 100 MB and 200 MB. System.currentTimeMillis() function is used to record the time that is used for encryption. By running the function before and after the encryption operation, the time to complete the operation is found by calculating the interval. Figure 3a illustrates a slight curve in the time taken for encryption operation to be completed when the data size increases from 10 MB to 200 MB. This indicates a potentially exponential growth in the time required for the encryption operation when the file size increases. This is mainly due to the trade-off to achieving stricter security goals. The same pattern is observed for the decryption time, as illustrated in Fig. 3b.

Index Searching Efficiency. The index search efficiency is assessed by the time required for the system to search through the search index to get the desired file. This process includes comparing each keyword array and computing token to see whether the data requester is permitted to retrieve the encrypted file from IPFS. The search index is filled with various keywords and up to 80 file's search index.

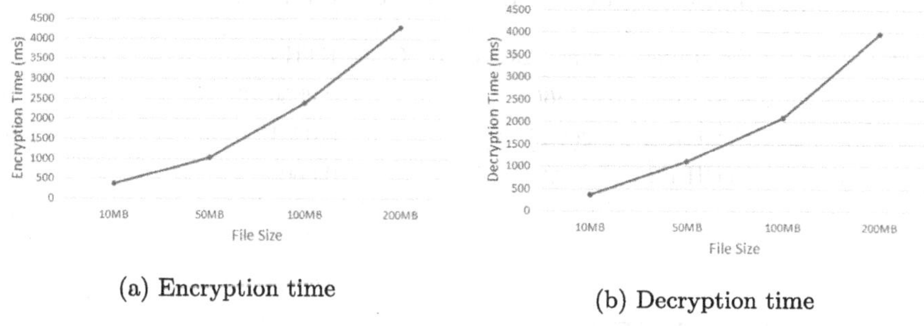

(a) Encryption time

(b) Decryption time

Fig. 3. Time taken for encryption and decryption algorithms.

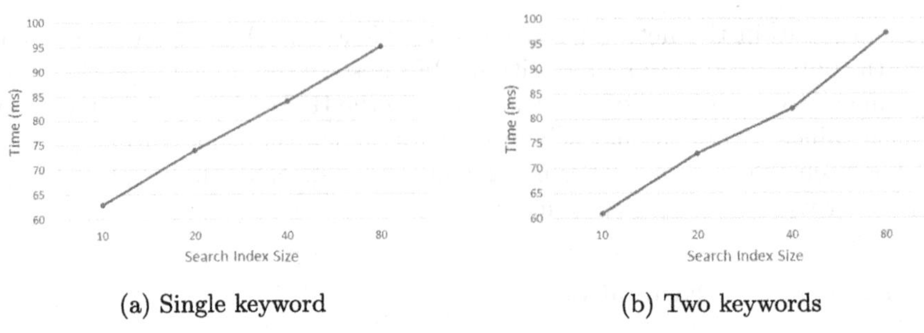

(a) Single keyword (b) Two keywords

Fig. 4. Time taken for the searching operation.

Figure 4a shows the graph of time taken to search through the search index for a single desired keyword. It can be seen that the time taken for the searching operation to be completed is directly proportional to the search index size. Figure 4b shows the graph of time taken to search through the search index for two desired keywords. It is observed that there is no considerable difference between the time taken for searching for one desired keyword or searching for multiple keywords. Hence, this scheme supports the searching without an exponential increase in search time.

Ethereum Gas Price. To successfully deploy the smart contract for storing and accessing the search index, it requires 1131872 gases. As of 2nd July 2022, one gas costs five gwei, meaning the smart contract costs 5659360 gwei (equivalent to 0.00565936 ETH). This deployment cost is considered low as the smart contract does not require large storage or complex operations that may increase its deployment costs. Aside from the deployment costs, the search index upload and retrieval and IPFS hash retrieval require gas. Table 2 shows the estimated costs for each function within the smart contract in ETH. The amount of ETH needed is low for each transaction as adding the index only requires approximately 6 USD per transaction and 0.14 USD per search.

Table 2. Estimated ETH costs for each function

Functions	Transaction costs (Gas)	ETH
Add Index	1131860	0.0056593
Get Index	26227	0.000131135
Get IPFS	41830	0.00020915

4.3 Comparison with Existing Schemes

A set of features has been compared between related work and the proposed scheme. The result of the comparison is shown in Table 3. It can be seen that

Table 3. Comparison of our scheme with other related works

Features	Schemes		
	[13]	[12]	Our implementation
Search Index Encryption	SSE	SSE	ABSE
Multi-Keyword	✗	✓	✓
Dynamic Update	✗	✗	✓
Storage Integrity	Search Index Only	Search Index Only	✓
Non-Repudiation	✓	✓	✓
Encrypted Search Index	✓	✓	✓
Encrypted Search Query	✗	✓	✓

aside from our implementation that utilizes attribute-based encryption, the rest of the schemes use symmetric searchable encryption where a search token is generated whenever a search request has been received. There are no advanced access policies as anyone that has the search token is permitted to search for the encrypted contact tracing data. Aside from that, the scheme proposed by Tahir et al. [13] only supports single-keyword searching. This means that the searching efficiency for the particular scheme will be lower when there is a large number of datasets within the storage. For both related works, the search index must be reconstructed each time a new file is added. However, our system supports a dynamic update of the search index by adding a new column and row to the search index each time new data has been added. Hence, any modification does not require the index to be rebuilt. Aside from that, our scheme assures the integrity of both search index and encrypted data. This is because the search index is stored within a smart contract, and the encrypted data is stored within IPFS. Both smart contract and IPFS could easily identify any modifications that are being made to the content. Since the search index is stored within a smart contract, all schemes support non-repudiation as the access of the search index and encrypted file will be automatically logged by the transactions. Aside from that, all schemes encrypted their search index before storing it within the smart contract. In this way, the adversary is not able to learn the keywords for each individual file that is requested. However, Tahir et al. did not encrypt the search query when the data requester searched for the encrypted file using the keywords; hence, the adversary can easily learn the keywords of the retrieved file. Once the file's keyword has been retrieved, any file with the same keywords will reveal the encrypted search index.

5 Conclusion

We implemented a searchable encryption system with blockchain technology to enable secure and efficient storage of COVID-19 contact tracing data. Our implementation used AES for encrypting the contact tracing data and attribute-based searchable encryption to achieve a systematic access policy within an organization. A slight exponential curve is observed in the encryption and decryption performance; however, as the typical datasets are around 200 MB, it is expected not to exceed 6ms per encryption/decryption operation. The time required for searching function through the search index proves to be efficient as the time needed to complete the searching and access verification is approximately linear to the size of the search index regardless of the number of keywords being searched. The implemented scheme also performs well even with large sizes of the search index. While achieving high efficiency, the security goals of confidentiality, integrity and non-repudiation are maintained. Overall, compared to the existing schemes related to COVID-19 contact tracing data, our implemented system provides more features on searchability over encrypted contact tracing data while maintaining security goals. We conclude that attribute-based searchable encryption with blockchain is practical for storing and searching over encrypted contact tracing data and allowing a group of users to access and perform decryption that fulfilled the access policy.

Acknowledgements. This work was funded by Xiamen University Malaysia Research Fund (XMUMRF) under Grants XMUMRF/2019-C3/IECE/0005 and XMUMRF/2022-C9/IECE/0032.

Appendix A Example of Search Function

Table 4 shows a sample of the generated data, whereas Table 5 shows the example of keywords for the data. For each dataset, four keywords are registered for the corresponding data owner. The sample from Table 4 shows the datasets within a plaintext form, associated with the keywords in Table 5. If the data requester intends to search for this data file, they need to search for keywords that the data owner sets. For example, in this case, to retrieve the datasets from Table 4, the data requester can search either one of the four keywords: "OrganizationABC", "Salak Tinggi", "February", and "2022" to get this file. The results will be more specific as more keywords are searched by the data requester. For example, if only "February" is searched, all datasets associated with "February" will be produced. They could be datasets with keywords ("February", "2021"), or ("OrganizationABC", "February"), and so on. Hence, if the data requester wishes for a specific set of datasets as the results, more keywords must be entered.

Table 4. Sample datasets of generated contact tracing data

Name	IC Number	Gender	Date	Time	Visited location
Daron Robe	000-33-4851	Female	05-02-22	7:28 AM	Kip Mall
Lucas Smith	254-75-5861	Male	06-02-22	6:24 AM	Aeon Mall
Matt Thompson	471-32-3650	Male	04-02-22	1:30 PM	Aron Mall
Kieth Ulyatt	872-61-2400	Male	08-02-22	5:29 AM	KFC

Table 5. Sample keywords for the data

Organization	Location	Month	Year
OrganizationABC	Salak Tinggi	February	2022

Table 6. Example of a sample organization array retrieved from smart contract

organization[0]	organization[1]	organization[2]	organization[3]
OrgA	OrgB	OrgC	OrgA

Table 7. Example of a sample location array retrieved from smart contract

location[0]	location[1]	location[2]	location[3]
Klang	Nilai	Klang	Sepang

Table 6 shows an example of the organization array retrieved from the smart contract. In this example, the file hash value associated with the keyword"OrgA" is stored in indexes 0 and 3 in the structure. If the searched keyword is "OrgA", the tokens in the corresponding positions, i.e., 0 and 3, can be used to calculate whether the data requester fits the access policy. If the data requester is permitted access, they could request the ipfsHash value from the smart contract and access the encrypted file. If the data requester searches for two keywords, the same operation will be applied to two arrays, and their results will be compared. Table 7 shows an example of a location array retrieved from the smart contract. If the data requester's desired keywords for organization value is "OrgA" and location value is "Klang", the only fitted index is 0. Hence, in this case, only a token from index 0 needs to be computed to verify the access policy of the data requestor. The same logic applies to scenarios where more keywords were added within the system.

References

1. Chinese start-up leaked 400gb of scraped data exposing 200+ million facebook, instagram and linkedin users. https://www.safetydetectives.com/blog/socialarks-leak-report/. Accessed 11 Oct 2022
2. Microsoft leaves 250m customer service records open to the web. https://threatpost.com/microsoft-250m-customer-service-records-open/152086/. Accessed 11 Oct 2022
3. Mysejahtera. https://mysejahtera.malaysia.gov.my/. Accessed 30 Jan 2022
4. Tracetogether app. https://support.tracetogether.gov.sg/hc/en-sg. Accessed 30 Jan 2022
5. Avitabile, G., Botta, V., Iovino, V., Visconti, I.: Towards defeating mass surveillance and sars-cov-2: the pronto-c2 fully decentralized automatic contact tracing system. Cryptology ePrint Archive, Report 2020/493 (2020). https://ia.cr/2020/493 https://ia.cr/2020/493

6. De Caro, A., Iovino, V.: jpbc: Java pairing based cryptography. In: 2011 IEEE Symposium on Computers and Communications (ISCC), pp. 850–855. IEEE (2011). https://doi.org/10.1109/ISCC.2011.5983948
7. Esteves-Verissimo, P., Decouchant, J., Völp, M., Esfahani, A., Graczyk, R.: Prilok: citizen-protecting distributed epidemic tracing. arXiv preprint arXiv:2005.04519 (2020)
8. Guo, W., Dong, X., Cao, Z., Shen, J.: Efficient attribute-based searchable encryption on cloud storage. In: Journal of Physics: Conference Series, vol. 1087, p. 052001. IOP Publishing (2018). https://doi.org/10.1088/1742-6596/1087/5/052001
9. Hee, Z., Salam, I.: Blockchain based contact tracing: a solution using bluetooth and sound waves for proximity detection. Cryptology ePrint Archive, Report 2022/209 (2022). https://eprint.iacr.org/2022/209
10. Jung, G., Lee, H., Kim, A., Lee, U.: Too much information: assessing privacy risks of contact trace data disclosure on people with covid-19 in south korea. Front. Public Health **8**, 305 (2020). https://doi.org/10.3389/fpubh.2020.00305
11. McGrew, D., Viega, J.: The galois/counter mode of operation (GCM). Submission NIST Modes Oper. Process **20**, 0278–0370 (2004)
12. Nabil, M., Sherif, A., Mahmoud, M., Alsmary, W., Alsabaan, M.: Privacy-preserving non-participatory surveillance system for covid-19-like pandemics. IEEE Access **9**, 79911–79926 (2021). https://doi.org/10.1109/ACCESS.2021.3082910
13. Tahir, S., Tahir, H., Sajjad, A., Rajarajan, M., Khan, F.: Privacy-preserving covid-19 contact tracing using blockchain. J. Commun. Networks **23**(5), 360–373 (2021). https://doi.org/10.23919/JCN.2021.000031
14. Tan, T.L., Salam, I., Singh, M.: Blockchain-based healthcare management system with two-side verifiability. PLOS ONE **17**(4), 1–25 (2022). https://doi.org/10.1371/journal.pone.0266916
15. Troncoso, C., et al.: Decentralized privacy-preserving proximity tracing (2020). https://doi.org/10.48550/arXiv.2005.12273
16. Xu, H., Zhang, L., Onireti, O., Fang, Y., Buchanan, W.J., Imran, M.A.: Beeptrace: Blockchain-enabled privacy-preserving contact tracing for covid-19 pandemic and beyond. IEEE Internet Things J. **8**(5), 3915–3929 (2020). https://doi.org/10.1109/JIOT.2020.3025953

UCC: Universal and Committee-based Cross-chain Framework

Yi Zhang, Zhonghui Ge, Yu Long(✉), and Dawu Gu(✉)

Shanghai Jiao Tong University, Shanghai, China
{zy0105,zhonghui.ge,longyu,dwgu}@sjtu.edu.cn

Abstract. One most potential solution to enhance the interoperability of various kinds of blockchains is to utilize the cross-chain mechanism. This mechanism, however, still faces some challenges. One is to find a universal cross-chain solution, independent of the underlying heterogeneous blockchains. The other is the lack of formal security definitions. To address these challenges, we propose UCC, a universal cross-chain framework using the cross-chain committees. We provide the formal security definition of the cross-chain framework and prove that UCC is secure when each well-defined module meets its security requirement. To demonstrate the feasibility of UCC, we implement it with efficient components and make the experimental evaluation. The result shows that UCC achieves a secure cross-chain with a low cost in comparison to the underlying chains.

Keywords: Blockchain · Cross-chain · Atomicity · Termination

1 Introduction

The past dozen years have witnessed the rapid development of blockchains, and various kinds of chains have been created. With more and more assets and data being recorded on different blockchains, the interoperability between them becomes a crucial problem. The key to the problem is cross-chain technology.

At the beginning of the study, researchers mainly focus on the cross-chain technology of two specified chains. In 2016, Buterin divided the non-universal cross-chain methods into 3 types [14], namely the notary-based method, the relay-based method, and the hash-locking method. Firstly, in a notary-based cross-chain mechanism, a trusted entity (or set of entities) is responsible for handling cross-chain transactions. To guarantee security, the assumption that the majority of notaries are honest needs to be satisfied. The well-known Corda [15] belongs to this type. Secondly, the relay-based cross-chain mechanism enables cross-chain transactions by facilitating another blockchain (i.e., the relay chain). ETH Relay [16] utilizes this solution. Besides, hash timelock is proposed to

This work is supported by the National Natural Science Foundation of China (No. 61872142), the Key (Keygrant) Project of Chinese Ministry of Education (No. 2020KJ010201), the Key Research and Development Plan of Shandong Province (No. 2021CXGC010105).

C. Su et al. (Eds.): ISPEC 2022, LNCS 13620, pp. 93–111, 2022.
https://doi.org/10.1007/978-3-031-21280-2_6

achieve the atomic swaps within one chain. Hash-locking extends it to the cross-chain scene by deploying hash contracts on different chains. Different as they are, all these non-universal cross-chain methods suffer from the hardness to be promoted to heterogeneous blockchains.

Recently, some researchers have shifted their focus to universal cross-chain solutions, which focus on the transfer of assets between each pair of chains as long as they meet certain requirements. Among the existing universal cross-chain solutions, Polkadot [1] is the most well-known one. It has two layers, the parachains, and the relay chain. To perform cross-chain transactions, a blockchain should connect to one of Polkadot's parachains in a pluggable manner. Thus, blockchains connecting to different parachains will be able to perform cross-chain transactions with the help of the relay chain. Although being applied in many cross-chain scenes, Polkadot is short of security proof, which limits its further applications.

In [4], Herlihy *et al.,* defines the cross-chain protocols' properties including safety and liveness and proposes a new cross-chain protocol named the cross-chain deals and adversarial commerce (CDAC), by utilizing the *smart contract* for the first time. The other cross-chain protocol utilizing the smart contract is the Hash time-lock contracts (or HTLC contracts [5]), which uses a hash-time lock contract to realize the cross-chain atomic swaps. Both CDAC and HTLC depend on the Turing-complete smart contract, which causes potential incompatibilities with chains such the Bitcoin. They also require that the transaction graph is strongly connected, disabling uni-directional transactions. Thus, a cross-chain user must have an account on both chains to form the directed transaction graph. In 2020, Shadab *et al.*, improve CDAC [13]. They introduce the concept of leaders and followers and support non-strongly-connect transaction graphs.

In 2022, Thyagarajan *et al.,* propose the universal atomic swaps (UAS) protocol [3], which improves the HTLC contract by concealing the dependence on smart contracts. Specifically, the protocol uses several cryptographic tools, such as verifiable timed signatures (VTS) [11] and 2-party computation (2PC) [10] protocols, to realize the function of HTLC contracts. Besides, UAS provides an efficient instantiation based on adaptor signatures [12] and time-lock puzzles. However, a user still has to create two accounts on both chains in UAS. Thus uni-direction cross-chain transactions are not permitted. Furthermore, to guarantee the security of UAS, an (unreasonable) assumption that one party can estimate others' computing power needs to be satisfied.

In practice, to achieve interoperability between heterogeneous blockchains, including the transfer of value and data, a unidirectional cross-chain protocol has a wider range of applications. Thus, utilizing the common ground of heterogeneous blockchains which are built upon different consensus, and proposing a universal cross-chain framework are significant. To the best of our knowledge, a smart contract independent universal cross-chain protocol with formal security proof and the support of unidirectional transactions is still an open problem.

1.1 Our Contribution

This work proposes a universal cross-chain framework named UCC, which provides the cross-chain framework for any two underlying blockchains without the help of a smart contract. Table 1 compares our protocol with previous solutions. Our contributions are as follows.

- *Practical universal cross-chain solution.* By utilizing the cross-chain committees rather than smart contracts, we eliminate the dependence on smart contracts, and therefore our protocol can be applied to non-Turning-complete chains. Unlike previous works focusing on the atomic swap of assets, our protocol supports unidirectional transactions and only requires a cross-chain user to have one account on its chain, which expands its scope of application. Besides, we propose a pipeline structure to batch the transactions.
- *Formal security definition and proof.* We formalize the security goals of UCC and provide the formal security proof by reduction.
- *Efficient instantiation and valid evaluation.* We instantiate UCC with the verifiable random function (VRF) [9] based committee member selection, Rapidchain's intra-committee consensus and cross-committee gossip modules. The evaluation results show that UCC's cross-chain cost is cheap compared with the intra-chain consensus.

Table 1. Comparison with previous solutions

Scheme	Security proof	Contract independent	No power knowledge	Unidirectional tx support	Need only one account (1 to 1)
Polkadot [1]	✗	✓	✓	✓	✓
HTLC [5]	✓	✗	✓	✓	✗
CDAC [4]	✓	✗	✓	✗	✗
UAS [3]	✓	✓	✗	✓	✗
Ours	✓	✓	✓	✓	✓

2 Preliminary

In this section, we introduce the definitions of permissioned and permissionless consensus protocols, and committee construction protocols. Parts of the definitions are borrowed from Dumbo [6] and Hybrid Consensus [7].

2.1 Permissionless Consensus

Permissionless blockchains use permissionless consensus, where anyone can join the chain without the permission of some centralized party. Among all the permissionless consensus, the PoW consensus is the most popular one. In 2015, Garay and Kiayias [8] introduced three important security requirements for permissionless consensus, namely *common prefix*, *self-consistency*, and *liveless*, to formally guarantee the security of the protocol. We use $\mathscr{L}$ to denote the set of confirmed transactions in the permissionless consensus protocol.

2.2 Permissioned Consensus

In permissioned blockchains, users who get the permission of some centralized party can run permissioned consensus to achieve agreements. A system of n users can output the correct answer, as long as the number of Byzantine users

f satisfies $3f + 1 < n$. The security properties of permissioned consensus are *consistency* and *liveness*.

Though this kind of protocol is designed for achieving agreements within a permissoned environment, it can be utilized in the permissionless setting by running a committee construction protocol. The main idea is to publicly select and rotate members in a committee, and the committee can run the permissioned consensus. This is the so-called hybrid scheme. In this case, a "good" committee construction protocol is required, as described in the next section.

2.3 Committee Construction

In the blockchain, the committee construction is a protocol used to form a committee. Assume the committee size is n, to run the permissioned consensus, no more than f Byzantine nodes are allowed in each committee. Assume the committee members' candidate set has size N, and F of them are Byzantine nodes. The committee construction protocol needs to satisfy the *termination*, *agreement*, *validity*, and *unpredictability*.

Intuitively, these properties guarantee the successful and fair construction of a valid committee which can be committed by each honest chain user. See Appendix A, Definition 2 for more details.

3 Security Model and Definition

3.1 Security Model

Network Model. There are three kinds of message propagation in our model, that is, propagation within the blockchain, propagation within the committee, and propagation among different committees. We suppose all the underlying chains are realized in a synchronous peer-to-peer network[1], where a message sent by an honest node will be received by all honest blockchain nodes within a known fixed time δ, while the order of the messages can be arbitrary. We also assume that all messages are transferred with authenticated communication channels.

Blockchain Model. We assume that the two blockchains involved in cross-chain transactions satisfy security definitions mentioned in Sects. 2.1 and 2.2, i.e., for permissionless blockchains, they satisfy common prefix, self-consistency, and liveness. For permissioned blockchains, they satisfy consistency and liveness.

Threat Model. Without loss of generality, we assume that each node has the same mining power. We assume that the number of the Byzantine nodes (which can deviate from the protocol in arbitrary ways) will not exceed a known ratio. For instance, it has been proved that to ensure responsiveness and security against self-mining attacks, this ratio is no larger than 1/3 [7].

---

[1] It is worth noting that the cross-chain committee running upon each chain could work in the partially synchronous model, as long as it satisfies the security properties of the BFT consensus.

3.2 Security Definition of the Cross-Chain Framework

To generically describe the cross-chain scene, we suppose that there are two blockchains, chain A and chain B, and the sender Alice has an account on chain A and the receiver Bob has an account on chain B. The cross-chain interaction is defined as follows: *Alice's value or data on chain A is transferred to chain B, resulting the change of Bob's account state on chain B.* To make a more concrete explanation, consider the case of asset transfer, which is the most common use case of the cross-chain interaction. Specifically, Alice's assets decrease by a coins on chain A, while Bob's assets increase by b coins on chain B, where a coins on A have the same value as that of b coins on B. We use this to illustrate the cross-chain procedure in the following.

To solve this problem even with the presence of Byzantine nodes (under a bounded ratio) in chain A and chain B, two security properties need to be satisfied, including atomicity and termination. For convenience, we denote the incident that Alice's asset decreases by a coins as I_A, and Bob's asset increases by b coins as I_B.

Definition 1. In a cross-chain framework, each cross-chain transaction satisfies the following properties,

- **Atomicity** The probability that only one of I_A and I_B happens is negligible.
- **Termination** If a cross-chain transaction is invoked at time t_A, and the finishing or refunding happen at time t_B, then there exists a certain time interval T_L, such that the probability of $t_B - t_A > T_L$ is negligible.

Intuitively, these two properties guarantee that neither of the two honest users, who form a cross-chain pair (i.e., (Alice, Bob)), would lose money, and a cross-chain transaction can always terminate within a given time-bound. Note that we ignore the liveness in [4], because it is trivial to achieve this goal in our UCC by including multiple committees on both chains.

4 Construction Overview

In this section, we provide the overview of our scheme, which is consisted of 4 modules: chain message passing module, committee consensus module, inter-chain message passing module, and committee member selection module.

Without loss of generality, we assume that Alice and Bob are two users that take part in chain A and chain B respectively, and Alice wants to launch cross-chain payment toward Bob. To achieve this procedure, chain A and chain B maintain their own (rotation) cross-chain committees, denoted as $\mathsf{cccom}_\mathrm{A}$ and $\mathsf{cccom}_\mathrm{B}$, respectively. Each committee controls an account on its belonging chain.

Roughly speaking, when Alice tries to transfer some assets to Bob, she first sends a coins along with Bob's address to $\mathsf{cccom}_\mathrm{A}$ on chain A. Then the members of $\mathsf{cccom}_\mathrm{A}$ receive Alice's transaction through **the chain message passing (CMP) module**. After some predefined time, the members of $\mathsf{cccom}_\mathrm{A}$ commit to the outwards cross-chain transactions through **the committee consensus**

(CC) module, and then start to inform cccom_B of this transaction through **the inter-chain message passing (IMP) module**.

Meanwhile, the members of cccom_B receive the corresponding inwards cross-chain requirement from cccom_A through the inter-chain message passing module. After some time, the members of cccom_B commit to the validity of the inwards transaction and send the assets from the committee's account to Bob's address if the check passes. Else cccom_B reject this requirement. In both cases, cccom_B return the cross-chain processing result back to cccom_A through the inter-chain message passing module. Figure 1 provides an overview of our scheme.

Simple as it seems, the above construction suffers from two main problems.

- First, a long-term cross-chain committee is undesired since it always suffers from bribery attacks, which ruins the *atomicity* of the cross-chain protocol.
- Secondly, to achieve *termination*, the whole procedure must be precisely designed, to guarantee that the honest user's coins will not be locked for a long time in this protocol.

To solve the above problems, we introduce **the committee member selection (CMS) module** to achieve the smooth rotation of the committee members. By smooth we mean that each committee works in a pipeline mode to avoid the potential conflict and the long-term domination.

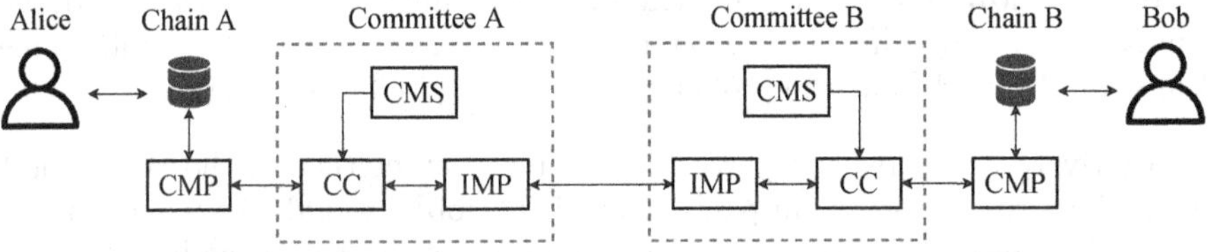

Fig. 1. Procedure of our universal cross-chain framework

5 Detailed Protocol

Notations. For a blockchain, we denote the total number of nodes as N, the total number of dishonest nodes as F, the number of nodes in each committee be n, and the maximum number of Byzantine nodes in one committee be f. It is worth noting that the data structure and the number of participants on two chains can be different, and the analysis for one chain can be trivially applied to the other by simply changing the above notations' concrete value. W.l.o.g., we will use common notations for both chains instead of notations with indices.

We denote δ_{i} as the maximum time of the chain message passing module. δ_{comm} as the maximum time of the committee consensus module. δ_{t} as the maximum time of the inter-chain message passing module. Besides, we add an index to δ_{i} and δ_{comm} in order to represent the value on a certain chain. For example, δ_{iB} and δ_{commB} represents the δ_{i} and δ_{comm} value on chain B. We denote Δ_{A} as the timeout that cccom_A waits for the result from cccom_B, and Δ_{B} as the timeout that cccom_B waits for the result from chain B.

Specifically, a cross-chain transaction consists of transaction id, target address, chain id of the target chain, and transaction amount. Besides, an extra field recording the specific information on the invoker's chain is needed, whose size may vary. See Appendix C for details.

5.1 Chain Message Passing Module

This module involves two functions, downloading transaction data from the blockchain to the committee members, and uploading transaction data in consensus from the committee members to the blockchain.

Since blockchains have their data propagation protocol, these two functions can be trivially realized. The former function can be realized if each committee member obtains transaction data from the blockchain, and the latter can be realized by sending transaction data and attaching members' signatures to the blockchain. Moreover, since we have assumed that our protocol runs under a synchronous network, both of the two functions can be satisfied with a known time interval δ_{i}. We illustrate this module in Algorithm 1.

Algorithm 1: Chain message passing

Input: State of local blockchain $\mathsf{state}_{\text{chain}}$, state of committee $\mathsf{state}_{\mathsf{cccom}}$
Output: New state of committee $\mathsf{state}'_{\mathsf{cccom}}$

1 $\{\mathsf{inc}_{\text{chain}}\} \leftarrow$ {new cross-chain txs generated in the local chain}
2 $\{\mathsf{inc}_{\mathsf{cccom}}\} \leftarrow$ {new transactions in cccom}
3 $\mathsf{state}'_{\text{chain}} \leftarrow \mathsf{state}_{\text{chain}} + \{\mathsf{inc}_{\mathsf{cccom}}\}$
4 Broadcast $\mathsf{state}'_{\text{chain}}$ to the local chain
5 $\mathsf{state}'_{\mathsf{cccom}} \leftarrow \mathsf{state}_{\mathsf{cccom}} + \{\mathsf{inc}_{\text{chain}}\}$
6 **return** $\mathsf{state}'_{\mathsf{cccom}}$

Specifically, $\mathsf{state}_{\text{chain}}$ is composed of intra-chain transactions, outwards transaction requests, results of outwards transactions, and committee information. $\mathsf{state}_{\mathsf{cccom}}$ consists of outwards requests collected from the current chain, inwards requests received from other chains, and results of all cross-chain transactions related to the current chain.

In the pseudo-code, we first obtain the new cross-chain transactions $\mathsf{inc}_{\text{chain}}$ from the local chain and $\mathsf{inc}_{\mathsf{cccom}}$ from committee cccom (Line 1–2). Then we update the state of local chain to $\mathsf{state}'_{\text{chain}}$ by adding $\mathsf{inc}_{\mathsf{cccom}}$ (Line 3–4). Finally, we update the state of the committee to $\mathsf{state}'_{\mathsf{cccom}}$ (Line 5).

5.2 Committee Consensus Module

Since the committee may have at most f Byzantine nodes, each node may has different local state. The module is used to synchronize the state within the committee. Specifically, the committee consensus module described in Algorithm 2 works under a synchronous network, for n nodes, and at most f of them are Byzantine nodes. After executing the protocol, the probability that the honest nodes do not obtain the same result within a known time δ_{comm} is negligible. It should also satisfy the two properties of permissioned consensus.

Each honest member of cccom runs a consensus algorithm and obtains state (Line 1), and updates his or her state to state (Line 3–4), while each Byzantine member updates the state to an arbitrary value (Line 5–6).

Algorithm 2: Committee consensus

Input: State $\mathsf{state}_1, \mathsf{state}_2, \ldots, \mathsf{state}_n$ of n committee members
Output: New state $\mathsf{state}'_1, \mathsf{state}'_2, \ldots, \mathsf{state}'_n$ of n committee members

```
1 state ← Consensus(state_1, state_2, ..., state_n)
2 for i ← 1 to n do
3 |   if node i is honest then
4 |   |   state'_i ← state
5 |   else
6 |   |   state'_i ← arbitrary value
7 |   end
8 end
9 return state'_1, state'_2, ..., state'_n
```

5.3 Inter-chain Message Passing Module

The module propagates messages from one committee to another in a reliable manner. A committee informs another committee of new cross-chain transactions and finished transactions through the module.

Algorithm 3: Inter-chain message passing

Input: Outwards message $\mathsf{Out}_{\mathsf{chain}}$ to be sent to committee on the target chain, and message $\mathsf{icm}_{\mathsf{chain}}$ from the target chain
Output: Inwards message $\mathsf{In}_{\mathsf{chain}}$

```
// Send messages to the target chain
{sender_chain} ← f + 1 senders randomly chosen from current committee
{sender_chain} broadcast Out_chain to committee on the target chain
// Receive messages icm_chain from the target chain
if no valid inter-chain message received yet and icm_chain is valid then
|   In_chain ← icm_chain
else
|   Ignore icm_chain
end
return In_chain
```

This consensus module works under a synchronous network. Suppose that $\mathsf{cccom}_{\mathrm{A}}$ wants to send a message $\mathsf{Out}_{\mathsf{chain}}$ to $\mathsf{cccom}_{\mathrm{B}}$. Both $\mathsf{cccom}_{\mathrm{A}}$ and $\mathsf{cccom}_{\mathrm{B}}$ have n members and at most f of them are Byzantine nodes. Then after executing the protocol, the probability that there exists some honest node that does not receive $\mathsf{Out}_{\mathsf{chain}}$ after a certain time δ_{t} is negligible. Before sending the message, the majority of the committee first generates multiple signatures of the message. After that, randomly chosen $f+1$ nodes will send the message to the destination committee. The destination committee will only preserve the message with the correct signature. The whole procedure is in Algorithm 3.

The first part of the pseudo-code demonstrates the process of message sending. The committee decides the senders randomly (Line 1), and the senders broadcast outwards messages to another committee (Line 2). The rest describes the process of message receiving. If the message $\mathsf{icm}_{\mathsf{chain}}$ from the target chain has not been received and $\mathsf{icm}_{\mathsf{chain}}$ is valid, the committee will save it as $\mathsf{In}_{\mathsf{chain}}$ (Line 3–4). Otherwise, it will discard $\mathsf{icm}_{\mathsf{chain}}$ (Line 5–6).

5.4 Committee Member Selection Module

The module is invoked by an old committee to construct a new committee. It is used in the term changing of the committee. This module takes N nodes as input, among which at most F nodes are Byzantine nodes. It randomly chooses n nodes as output, among which at most f_c are Byzantine nodes. The module satisfies the 4 properties of committee construction. See Algorithm 4 for details.

Algorithm 4: Committee member selection

Input: Candidate number N, committee size n, candidates $c_1, c_2 \ldots, c_N$, their tokens $t_1, t_2 \ldots, t_N$

Output: Committee members set cccom

1 **for** $i \leftarrow 1$ *to* N **do**
2 | $r_i \leftarrow \mathrm{VRF}(t_i)$
3 **end**
4 *sort*$\{c_i\}$ *according to* r_i
5 $\mathsf{cccom} \leftarrow \{c_1, c_2, \ldots, c_n\}$
6 Broadcast cccom to the target chain
7 **return** cccom

Firstly, each candidate generates the VRF value-based token (Line 1–3). When the deadline comes, the committee sorts the VRF values (Line 4) and picks up the candidates with the smallest n values as the new committee (Line 5). The committee will broadcast the result to the chain (Line 6) so that everyone can obtain and verify it.

The committee member selection is based on a public rule, and the candidates' information has been recorded on the chain. Therefore, any user on a chain can identify each committee independently, without the help of the old committee. On the other hand, to learn the ongoing committee over another chain, users need to keep listening to the chain. To reduce the cost, we let the old committee inform it of the block height of the data.

5.5 Pipeline Committee Rotation Method

To defend the bribery attacks, each cross-chain committee cannot work too long. Every publicly selected committee takes charge of the cross-chain transactions' confirmation for a certain period. To make full use of each committee's ability and achieve the smooth rotation, we provide a pipeline committee rotation method, as described in Fig. 2.

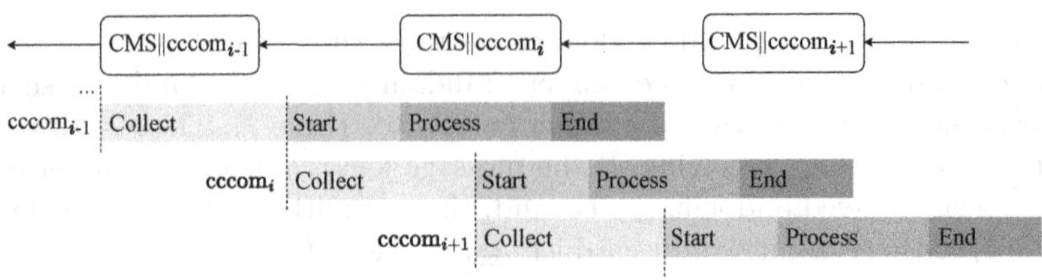

Fig. 2. Committee rotation

In detail, one committee's lifetime consists of 4 phases. The lengths of the four phases are predetermined and known by everyone.

- In *the collect phase*, the committee collects new cross-chain transactions from its own blockchain and from other chains' committees during this phase.
- In *the start phase*, if there exists at least one transaction to another chain, the committee informs committees on that chain. Otherwise, it will skip the rest of the process of that chain.
- In *the process phase*, the committee processes transactions by the committee consensus module.
- In *the end phase*, the committee balances their assets with the committees on other chains and then exits.

Before the end of one committee's collect phase, the next committee has been publicly generated. Once the former committee ends the collect phase, the next committee will immediately start the collect phase. The selection scheme forms a pipeline to make sure that there is one and only one committee receiving new transactions at any time.

5.6 Complete UCC Process

To finish this section, we take Fig. 1 as an example to illustrate the whole procedure of our universal cross-chain protocol UCC.

Firstly, $\mathsf{cccom}_\mathrm{A}$ run the CMS module to collect Alice's cross-chain requirement from chain A, and make a consensus with the CC module within time δ_{commA}. After that, $\mathsf{cccom}_\mathrm{A}$ run the ICM module to send the confirmed cross-chain transactions to $\mathsf{cccom}_\mathrm{B}$ within time δ_t.

Later, $\mathsf{cccom}_\mathrm{B}$ decide which inward transactions are successful by making a CC consensus, and then send them to $\mathsf{cccom}_\mathrm{A}$ through the ICM module.

To reply to Alice, $\mathsf{cccom}_\mathrm{A}$ will wait for at most Δ_A for $\mathsf{cccom}_\mathrm{B}$'s reply and run the CMS module again, otherwise refund a coins to Alice with the same module. Meanwhile, $\mathsf{cccom}_\mathrm{B}$ will only wait for Δ_B when transferring b coins to Bob, otherwise, abandon the transaction. Here $\Delta_\mathrm{A} > \Delta_\mathrm{B}$, and are set considering the maximum delay of the networks. To guarantee that the committee is not controlled by Byzantine nodes, the members of the committee will regularly be reelected through the CMS module.

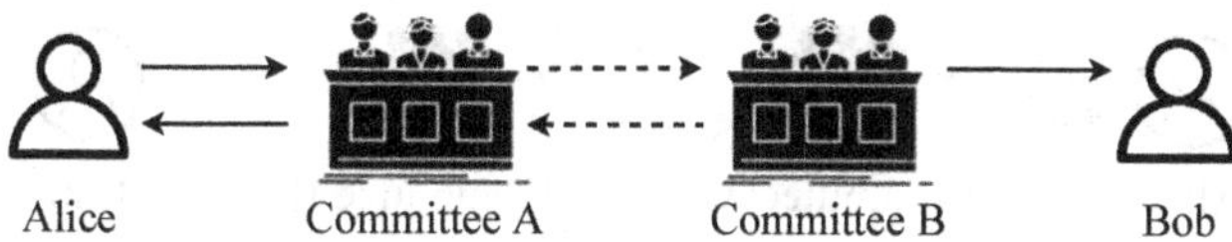

Fig. 3. Asset flow chart of UCC

6 Security Analysis

To analyze the security properties of UCC, we describe the asset flow chart as the Fig. 3. Intuitively, we will prove that the honest user will not lose money, which means if Alice launches a cross-chain transaction, it will either succeed or fail within a predetermined time-bound. In the first case, Alice's target account, (say, Bob), can get the transferred coins. In the latter case, Alice gets a refund.

Lemma 1. ***(Reliability of the committee)*** *Once a cross-chain requirement is recorded on a chain, then this requirement can get committed by a cross-chain committee of this chain.*

Proof. Via the chain message passing module, the cross-chain committees keep watching the underlying chain and downloading the fresh cross-chain requirements from it, and run the committee consensus module to generate the consensus results. Suppose that during one inner-committee consensus procedure, the initial result of an honest member is r_h, and the result of the consensus is r_c. We claim that $r_c = r_h$ always holds.

We prove this claim by contradiction. If $r_c \neq r_h$ then at least $f+1$ of the members have claimed that their initial result is r_c. Since there are at most f Byzantine nodes, there is at least one honest node that has the initial value r_c. However, from the consistency and liveness properties in the BFT consensus, each honest node in the committee agrees on the initial value r_h, which means one of the honest members claimed both r_h and r_c. This leads to the contradiction. Therefore, the honest members' consensus results must be the same.

Lemma 2. ***(Reliability of message sending)*** *A committed cross-chain requirement on one chain A can always reach the other chain B's cross-chain committee.*

Proof. Suppose that $\mathsf{cccom}_{\mathrm{A}}$ wants to send a committed cross-chain transaction tx to $\mathsf{cccom}_{\mathrm{B}}$, by utilizing the IMP module. We claim that even if only one honest node in $\mathsf{cccom}_{\mathrm{A}}$ sends the correct tx, all the nodes in $\mathsf{cccom}_{\mathrm{B}}$ will receive it. Otherwise, all the $f+1$ nodes randomly chosen fail to send the correct tx to all members in $\mathsf{cccom}_{\mathrm{B}}$. This is impossible because there are at most f Byzantine nodes in $\mathsf{cccom}_{\mathrm{A}}$, and at least one of the $f+1$ selected nodes behaves honestly.

Note that we have assumed that there exists an *authenticated channel* between $\mathsf{cccom}_{\mathrm{A}}$ and $\mathsf{cccom}_{\mathrm{B}}$, as long as there is one honest node sending the message correctly, the message will reach $\mathsf{cccom}_{\mathrm{B}}$.

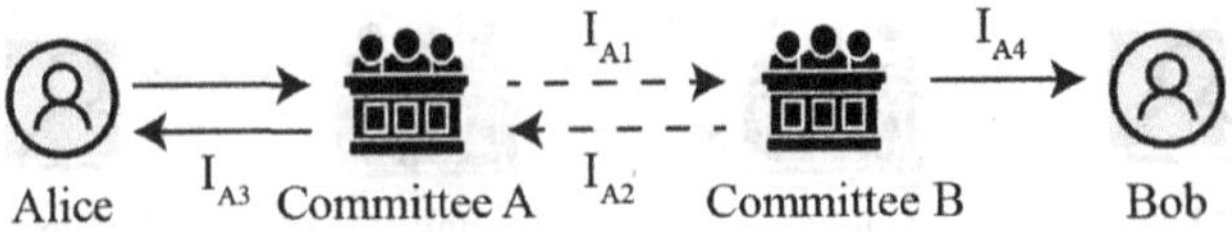

Fig. 4. Case I_A

Theorem 1. *Assume that the two chains, the committee consensus, and the committee construction, satisfy their security definitions respectively, then the proposed universal cross-chain protocol satisfies the atomicity in Definition 1.*

Proof. Recall we denote the event that Alice's asset decreases by a coins as I_A, and the event that Bob's asset increases by b coins as I_B. We will prove by contradiction. For atomicity, we need to prove the probability that only one of I_A and I_B happens is non-negligible. That is, each of the events that $I_A \wedge \neg I_B$ and $\neg I_A \wedge I_B$, happens with a negligible probability.

If the case is $I_A \wedge \neg I_B$, then we know that Alice has sent a coins along with the transaction message on-chain, while Bob does not receive b coins. These two steps are fixed so that we only need to consider the remaining part of the transaction process, which can be divided into 4 sub-cases, by analysis Fig. 4.

- Denote the incident that $\mathsf{cccom}_\mathrm{B}$ does not receive the transaction message from $\mathsf{cccom}_\mathrm{A}$ as I_{A_1}. In this case, either the transaction is not included in the consensus result of $\mathsf{cccom}_\mathrm{A}$, or the message is sent but fails to reach $\mathsf{cccom}_\mathrm{B}$. The former contradicts the Lemma 1, and the latter contradicts with the Lemma 2. Therefore, I_{A_1} happens with negligible probability.
- Denote the incident that $\mathsf{cccom}_\mathrm{A}$ does not receive success information from $\mathsf{cccom}_\mathrm{B}$ within Δ_A but does not refund Alice as I_{A_2}. Similar to the previous analysis, I_{A_2} is also impossible.
- Denote the incident that while receiving $\mathsf{cccom}_\mathrm{B}$'s success information, however, Alice does not get the refund of a coins as I_{A_3}. There can be two reasons. Firstly, $\mathsf{cccom}_\mathrm{A}$ still does not refund a coins to Alice, which contradicts the Lemma 1. Secondly, $\mathsf{cccom}_\mathrm{A}$ have refunded but chain A ignores the refunding transaction, which contradicts the security definition of the chain.
- Denote the incident that $\mathsf{cccom}_\mathrm{B}$ have sent assets to Bob, but chain B ignores the refunding transaction as I_{A_4}, which contradicts the security of the chain (Fig. 4).

It is not difficult to figure out that the three cases mentioned above have covered all the cases. Thus, $I_A \wedge \neg I_B = I_{A_1} \vee I_{A_2} \vee I_{A_3} \vee I_{A_4}$. Since I_{A_1}, I_{A_2}, I_{A_3} and I_{A_4} are all impossible, $I_A \wedge \neg I_B$ is also impossible.

If the case is $\neg I_A \wedge I_B$. In this case, Bob has received b coins. For Alice, there are two cases. First, Alice has not sent a coins to $\mathsf{cccom}_\mathrm{A}$ at all (NONE case). Secondly, Alice has sent a coins but gets refunded later (BOTH case). Furthermore, each case could be divided into two sub-cases (Fig. 5).

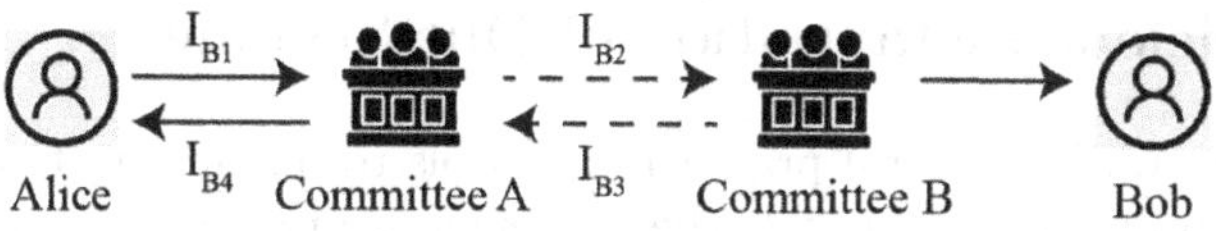

Alice I_{B1} Committee A I_{B2} Committee B Bob I_{B4} I_{B3}

Fig. 5. Case I_B

We first focus on the NONE cases.

- Denote the incident that $\mathsf{cccom}_\mathrm{A}$ forges Alice's transaction data and sends it to $\mathsf{cccom}_\mathrm{B}$ be I_{B_1}. This is impossible because this breaks the security of the underlying chain's signature algorithm.
- Denote the incident that $\mathsf{cccom}_\mathrm{B}$ transfers coins to Bob without receiving $\mathsf{cccom}_\mathrm{A}$'s transaction data be I_{B_2}. This is impossible because it contradicts Lemma 1.

Now let's analyze the BOTH cases.

- Denote the incident that $\mathsf{cccom}_\mathrm{A}$ does not receive success data from $\mathsf{cccom}_\mathrm{B}$ despite Bob obtaining b coins from $\mathsf{cccom}_\mathrm{B}$ be I_{B_3}. The reason is that either $\mathsf{cccom}_\mathrm{B}$ refuses to send the message or the message-sending process fails. The two cases contradict Lemma 1 and Lemma 2 respectively.
- Denote $\mathsf{cccom}_\mathrm{A}$ refunds despite receiving $\mathsf{cccom}_\mathrm{B}$'s success data in Δ_A be I_{B_4}. This indicates that $\mathsf{cccom}_\mathrm{A}$ has made a wrong decision, which contradicts Lemma 1.

We have $\neg I_A \wedge I_B = I_{B_1} \vee I_{B_2} \vee I_{B_3} \vee I_{B_4}$. Similarly, since I_{B_1}, I_{B_2}, I_{B_3} and I_{B_4} are all impossible, $\neg I_A \wedge I_B$ is impossible.

Theorem 2. *The proposed universal cross-chain protocol satisfies the termination in Definition 1.*

Proof. We assume that the transaction from Alice to Bob is generated at time t_A, and is completed at time t_B, and prove the time-interval is less than a predetermined time-bound t_L.

Denote the time bound for chain message passing module in $\mathsf{cccom}_\mathrm{A}$ and $\mathsf{cccom}_\mathrm{B}$ as δ_iA and δ_iB respectively, the time-bound for committee consensus module as δ_commA and δ_commB respectively, and the time-bound for inter-chain message passing module as δ_t.

If the transaction from Alice to Bob is successful, the total time is $t_s = \delta_\mathrm{iA} + \delta_\mathrm{commA} + 2\delta_\mathrm{t} + \delta_\mathrm{commB}$. Here we regard the transaction as a successful one when Bob receives b coins. For a successful transaction, the probability that $t_B - t_A > t_s$ is negligible.

If the transaction is unsuccessful, the total time is $t_f = 2\delta_\mathrm{iA} + \delta_\mathrm{commA} + \Delta_\mathrm{A}$. For an unsuccessful transaction, the probability that $t_B - t_A > t_f$ is negligible.

Denote $t_L = max\{t_s, t_f\}$, then no matter the cross-chain transaction succeeds or not, the probability that $t_B - t_A > t_L$ is negligible.

7 An Efficient Instantiation of Our Scheme

In this section, we use several practical protocols to instantiate the modules in our universal protocol and provide the implementation and evaluation results.

7.1 Detailed Instantiation of Each Module

In this section, we use hash puzzles and the VRF function to implement the committee member selection module, the intra-committee consensus in Rapidchain to implement the committee consensus module, and the IDA gossip protocol to implement the inter-chain message passing module. The detailed security analysis of each module is shown in Appendix B.

Committee Member Selection via the VRF Function. For the committee member selection module, we will use hash puzzles and the VRF function, inspired by the BABE consensus in Polkadot.

VRF (Verifiable Random Functions) function takes a tuple (s, sk) as input, where s is a random string, and sk is the secret key (the corresponding public key is pk). The function will give an output (d, π), where d is a random number generated by the function, and π is a proof. Anyone can verify whether d is a random number generated with s under pk if π is given.

In our solution, when the committee is about to be reelected, the n old committee members will collaboratively generate randomness r. Candidate nodes should solve a hash puzzle related to r and a predetermined difficulty parameter D. Suppose that the public key and secret key of candidate P_i are pk_i and sk_i respectively. P_i needs to enumerate possible random strings s_i and calculate $(d, \pi) = VRF(r||s_i, sk_i)$, until he finds a s_i such that $d < D$. After that, P_i will send (s_i, π_i) and s_i to the committee by constructing a "voting transaction", which contains (pk_i, r, s_i, π_i).

When the deadline for selection arrives, the committee members collect all the voting transactions related to r, and verify the validity of each voting transaction. After that, they will choose the nodes with the smallest d_i's to form the next committee. After applying the consensus protocol, the final list of the next committee members is determined.

Intra-committee Consensus in Rapidchain. For the committee consensus module, we use the intra-committee consensus protocol in Rapidchain. The protocol involves three steps.

- The leader gossips the hash value H of the message, with a proposed tag.
- When nodes receive H, they will gossip H along with an echo tag.
- If nodes see different versions of H, then the leader is malicious. They will reject it by gossiping a pending tag. If nodes receive $f + 1$ echoes and only one version of H, they accept it by gossiping H along with accepting tag and proof.

For pending messages, the next leader will propose a safe massage that does not conflict with previously accepted messages. Readers can refer to [2] for details.

Inter-chain Message Passing via IDA Gossip. For the inter-chain message passing module, we utilize the IDA gossip protocol proposed in Rapidchain, which is based on the information dispersal algorithm (IDA) introduced in [17, 19,20]. Denote M as the message to be sent from cccom_A to cccom_B, d is the number of neighbors in cccom_B, $\phi = \frac{f}{n}$ as the fraction of Byzantine nodes. Now a sender in cccom_A wants to send M to cccom_B.

The sender first divides M into $(1-\phi)\kappa$ chunks of equal size, obtaining $M_1, M_2, ..., M_{(1-\phi)\kappa}$, and generates additional $\phi\kappa$ parity chunks using an erasure code scheme [18]. Now, the sender has κ chunks $M_1, M_2, ..., M_\kappa$. Any honest node can reconstruct M with any $(1-\phi)\kappa$ of the κ chunks.

Next, the sender sends a unique set of $\frac{\kappa}{f}$ chunks (here we assume that κ is divisible by f) along with their Merkle proof to each of the d receivers in cccom_B. After receiving a new chunk, each receiver verifies the chunks with Merkel proof, forward valid new chunks to its neighbors, and so on. When a node receives $(1-\phi)\kappa$ chunks, it can reconstruct M.

Since our cross-chain messages are attached with a majority number of signatures signed by members of cccom_A, the sender cannot forge a wrong message. Using a distributed random algorithm, the members of cccom_A can choose a random node at a time as a sender initializing IDA gossip. By repeating c times, the probability that M is not propagated to all honest nodes in cccom_B will become negligible.

7.2 Simulation and Evaluation

We provide the communication overhead and the transaction delay analysis, then implement our scheme in Python 3.9, and run the experiment on Windows 10 with Intel G3260 CPU and 8GB memory.

Communication Overhead Analysis. For cross-chain transactions from chain A to chain B. Suppose that there are u transactions and n committee members, then the communication overheads in each procedure are listed in Table 2. See Appendix C for details.

Table 2. Communication overhead.

Phase	tx identity	Target address	chain identity	tx amount	Signature	Total
cccom_A consensus	-	-	-	-	-	Ignored
From cccom_A to cccom_B	8u	35u	2u	8u	20n	53u+20n
cccom_B consensus	8u	35u	2u	8u	-	53u
From cccom_B to cccom_A	8u	-	-	-	20n	8u+20n

Transaction Delay Analysis. The delay mentioned here refers to the user's perceived time. It starts when the user posts a transaction, and ends when the committee posts the result onto the chain. The election time can be ignored here since at any time, there is one and only one committee in charge of the chain, which is equivalent to the case that is one committee that is always working.

- **Block generation time.** We have collected the average block time in Bitcoin each day in the past years. We randomly choose some of the time data as our block time.
- **Committee consensus time.** For the committee consensus time, we simulate by adding a data sending time to a network delay. The network delay is chosen according to Rapidchain [2] when the committee size is 100. By dividing the total data size by the bandwidth, we obtain the data sending time. The bandwidth is set to 20 Mbps, the same as that in Rapidchain.
- **Inter-chain message passing time.** Similar to the consensus time, the message passing time is calculated by adding a data sending time to a network delay. The network delay here is set to 300ms, the same as that in Rapidchain.

Simulation Result. Here we estimate the $O(n^2)$ overhead by multiplying the message size to n^2, where n is the size of the committee. We also change the transaction number from 100 to 1000.

- For the simulation of the communication result, we change the committee size from 5 to 30. Figure 6 shows the result. We can see that the size of the committee should not be too large (e.g., no larger than 20), otherwise the cost will increase rapidly.
- We provide the simulation of the time delay in Fig. 7. Since the extra time spent in the cross-chain process is much less than the block time, the delay does not increase obviously when the number of transactions increases. For instance, when the transaction number is from 100 to 1000, the chain confirmation time is 300 s on average, and the cross-chain message passing and committee consensus time are around 0.9 s and 0.6 s respectively, which is low in comparison to the former.

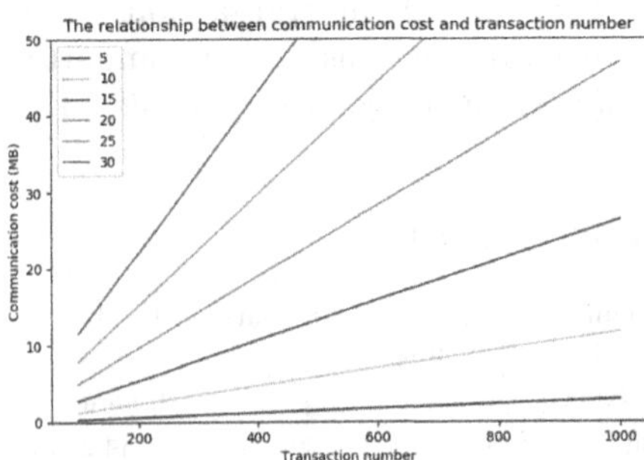

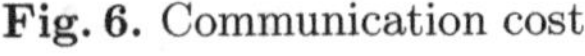
Fig. 6. Communication cost

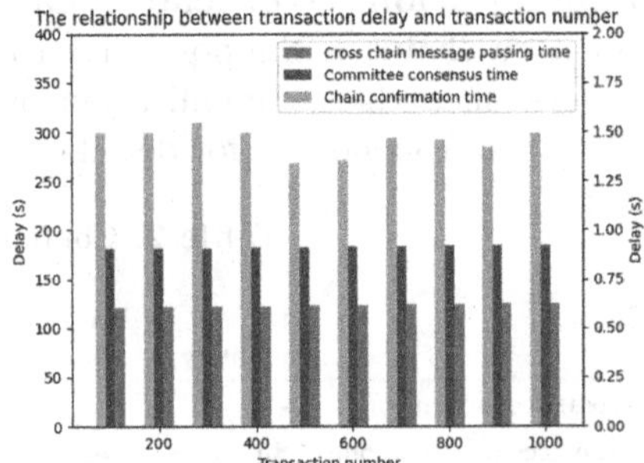

Fig. 7. Transaction delay

8 Discussion

It is worth noting that in the case of the cross-chain asset transfer, deposits are required from the committee to support the transfers of users between blockchains. In addition, a case-dependent settlement regulation between two committees may be necessary to balance their income and payout. In addition, incentives, such as the transaction fee, could be introduced to ensure that committee members behave honestly. Honest committee members can obtain transaction fees paid by the transaction invoker.

9 Conclusion

In this paper, we propose a universal cross-chain interoperation framework named UCC, by utilizing the cross-chain committees. To guarantee its security, we introduce the definitions of atomicity and termination and prove that UCC meets all these requirements. We also construct a practical scheme by applying some efficient protocols to instantiate each module of UCC. Then we evaluate the communication overhead and transaction delay with a simulation experiment, which justifies the feasibility of our scheme.

A Related definition

Definition 2. (Secure Committee Construction) For one run a secure committee construction protocol, the following properties need to be satisfied,

- **Termination** If at least $f+1$ honest nodes activate the protocol, and all messages among honest nodes arrive, then each honest node outputs a committee cccom within a pre-defined time.
- **Agreement** Any two honest nodes output the same cccom.
- **Validity** If any honest node outputs cccom, then the probability that (1) $|\mathsf{cccom}| = n$, (2) the probability of each candidate node $P_i \in \mathsf{cccom}$ is the same, (3) cccom contains at most f Byzantine nodes, is at least $1 - \epsilon$.
- **Unpredictability** Before an honest node innovates the election, the probability that the adversary predicts the result is at most $1/\binom{N}{n}$.

B Security Analysis of the Instantiation

In this part, we will analyze the security of each module in Sect. 7.1. We assume the adversary ratio is 1/3. That is, $F < N/3$.

Committee Member Selection Module. We will prove that when $F < N/3$, the probability that $f < n/2$ does not hold is negligible. The proof is inspired by Rapidchain [2]. Suppose there are X Byzantine nodes in the committee, then $Pr[X \geq \lfloor n/2 \rfloor] = \Sigma_{x=\lfloor n/2 \rfloor}^{n} \frac{\binom{F}{x}\binom{N-F}{n-x}}{\binom{N}{n}}$. When N and n are large enough, we can estimate the probability with a binomial distribution $Pr[X \geq \lfloor n/2 \rfloor] = \Sigma_{x=0}^{f} \binom{n}{x} (\frac{f}{n})^x (1 - \frac{f}{n})^x$. The value of this expression decreases exponentially when N and n increases. Thus, the security of this module is proved.

Committee Consensus Module. The intra-committee consensus protocol in Rapidchain achieves both safety and liveness if $f < n/2$ [2]. Here safety guarantees that all the honest nodes will obtain the correct value, and liveness guarantees that it can be completed within a bounded time.

Inter-chain Message Passing Module. The IDA gossip protocol in Rapidchain guarantees that the probability that all the honest nodes receive the correct message is at least 0.9 if the parameters are properly adjusted, and the time is bounded to a certain value δ_{IDA}. In our model, we perform IDA gossip k times. Therefore, the probability that there exist some honest nodes that do not receive the correct message is at most 0.1^k, a negligible value, with a bounded time.

C Communication Complexity Analysis

- When $\mathsf{cccom}_{\mathrm{A}}$ receives the transaction and make a consensus since every honest user can obtain the information from chain A and calculate the hash value according to a known rule, they are able to send only the hash value, which is a fixed small value that can be ignored.
- When the transaction is passed from $\mathsf{cccom}_{\mathrm{A}}$ to $\mathsf{cccom}_{\mathrm{B}}$, we assume that the message format is as follows. It has an 8-byte transaction id, 35-byte target address, 2-byte chain id, and 8-byte transaction amount. Thus, the size of one transaction is 53 bytes. Besides, we should add a $20n$-byte signature length. Thus, the total size is $53u + 20n$ bytes.
- When $\mathsf{cccom}_{\mathrm{B}}$ receives the transaction and makes a consensus, the signature is not included. Thus, the size is $53u$ bytes.
- When $\mathsf{cccom}_{\mathrm{B}}$ sends the message back to $\mathsf{cccom}_{\mathrm{A}}$, each transaction can be represented by 8-byte id. Thus, the total size is $8u + 20n$ bytes.
- Similarly, when $\mathsf{cccom}_{\mathrm{A}}$ makes a consensus for $\mathsf{cccom}_{\mathrm{B}}$'s response, the message size is $8u$ bytes.

References

1. Wood, G.: Polkadot: Vision for a heterogeneous multi-chain framework. In: White Paper, vol. 21 (2016)
2. Zamani, M., Movahedi, M., Raykova, M.: Rapidchain: scaling blockchain via full sharding. In: ACM CCS, pp. 931–948 (2018)
3. Thyagarajan, S.A., Malavolta, G., Moreno-Sánchez, P.: Universal atomic swaps: secure exchange of coins across all blockchains. In: S&P (2022)
4. Herlihy, M., Liskov, B., Shrira, L.: Cross-chain deals and adversarial commerce. VLDB J. **31**, 1–19 (2021)
5. Miller, A., et al.: Sprites and state channels: Payment networks that go faster than lightning. In: FC, pp. 508–526 (2019)
6. Guo, B., Lu, Z., Tang, Q., Xu, J., Zhang, Z.: Dumbo: faster asynchronous BFT protocols. In: ACM CCS, pp. 803–818 (2020)
7. Pass, R., Shi, E.: Hybrid consensus: efficient consensus in the permission less model. Cryptology ePrint Archive (2016)

8. Garay, J., Kiayias, A., Leonardos, N.: The bitcoin backbone protocol: analysis and applications. In: Oswald, E., Fischlin, M. (eds.) EUROCRYPT 2015. LNCS, vol. 9057, pp. 281–310. Springer, Heidelberg (2015). https://doi.org/10.1007/978-3-662-46803-6_10
9. Micali, S., Rabin, M., Vadhan, S.: Verifiable random functions. In: FOCS, pp. 120–130 (1999)
10. Canetti, R.: Security and composition of multiparty cryptographic protocols. J. Cryptol. **13**(1), 143–202 (2000)
11. Thyagarajan, S.A.K., et al.: Verifiable timed signatures made practical. In: ACM CCS, pp. 1733–1750 (2020)
12. Aumayr, L., et al.: Generalized bitcoin-compatible channels. IACR Cryptol. ePrint Arch. **2020**, 476 (2020)
13. Shadab, N., Houshmand, F., Lesani, M.: Cross-chain transactions. In: ICBC, pp. 1–9. IEEE (2020)
14. Buterin, V.: Chain interoperability. In: R3 Research Paper, vol. 9 (2016)
15. Hearn, M., Brown, R.G.: Corda: a distributed ledger. In: Corda Technical White Paper, vol. 2016 (2016)
16. Frauenthaler, P., Sigwart, M., Spanring, C., Sober, M., Schulte, S.: Eth relay: a cost-efficient relay for Ethereum-based blockchains. In: ICBC, pp. 204–213 (2020)
17. Rabin, M.O.: Efficient dispersal of information for security, load balancing, and fault tolerance. J. ACM **36**(2), 335–348 (1989)
18. Massey, J.: Review of 'theory and practice of error control codes' (Blahut, R. 1983). IEEE Trans. Inf. Theory **31**(4), 553–554 (1985)
19. Alon, N., Kaplan, H., Krivelevich, M., Malkhi, D., Stern, J.: Scalable secure storage when half the system is faulty. In: ICALP, pp. 576–587 (2000)
20. Alon, N., Kaplan, H., Krivelevich, M., Malkhi, D., Stern, J.: Addendum to scalable secure storage when half the system is faulty. Inf. Comput. **205**(7), 1114–1116 (2007)

Security for Critical Infrastructure

A Low-Cost and Cloud Native Solution for Security Orchestration, Automation, and Response

Juan Christian[1,2(✉)], Luis Paulino[2], and Alan Oliveira de Sá[3]

[1] Faculdade de Ciências, Universidade de Lisboa, 1749-016 Lisboa, Portugal
juan.christian@outlook.com
[2] OutSystems, Boston, Massachusetts 02210, USA
[3] LASIGE, Departamento de Informática, Faculdade de Ciências, Universidade de Lisboa, 1749-016 Lisboa, Portugal
alan@di.fc.ul.pt

Abstract. Information security is a must-have for any organization willing to stay relevant and grow, it plays an important role as a business enabler, be it from a regulatory or reputation perspective. Having people, process, and technology to solve the ever growing number of security incidents as fast as possible and with the least amount of impact is a challenge. The use of security orchestration, automation and response (SOAR) is a way to translate the manual procedures followed by the security analysts into automated actions, making the process faster and scalable while saving on human resources budget. This paper proposes a low-cost cloud native SOAR platform, presenting the underlying details of its design. The performance of the proposed solution is evaluated through real-world experiments performed in a large multinational enterprise. The results show that the solution decreases the duration of the tasks by an average of 99.02% while having an operating expense of less than $65/month.

Keywords: SOAR · Cloud computing · Serverless · Security · Orchestration · Automation · Incident response · State machine

1 Introduction

There are countless headlines [18] about security incidents that caused great damage to companies and their customers. It has become commonplace to see news of yet another cyber attack against private and public organizations. It is impossible to prevent all security incidents from happening, but when they happen, organizations want to solve them fast and keep the impacts low, this is one of the main reasons why they maintain a Security Operations Center (SOC).

A SOC is composed of various security professionals that are responsible for the detection, analysis, containment, eradication, and recovery of security incidents. They must react fast to the security incidents, but that is not always

C. Su et al. (Eds.): ISPEC 2022, LNCS 13620, pp. 115–139, 2022.
https://doi.org/10.1007/978-3-031-21280-2_7

possible due to many factors (e.g. lack of personnel, lack of expertise, SOC is not 24×7). To overcome that, various companies started enhancing their SOC with automation and orchestration capabilities delivered by SOAR solutions.

The term SOAR was coined by Gartner in 2017 in their research [17] "Innovation Insight for Security Orchestration, Automation and Response". It has since become a relevant topic in the information security field, but without clear and common definition as many security practitioners have their own definition of SOAR, as evidenced by C. Islam et al. [20]. The authors came up with their own definition during their analysis: "Security Orchestration is the planning, integration, cooperation, and coordination of the activities of security tools and experts to produce and automate required actions in response to any security incident across multiple technology paradigms".

A typical SOAR solution make use of built-in and custom integrations to orchestrate and automate the many tasks that would be manually executed by a security analyst during an incident response. The tasks are executed according to a preconfigured workflow that is strictly followed, so the outcome is predictable. Response times are also shortened as there is no human fatigue involved and the system is able to do repeated tasks indefinitely with the same accuracy and with a speed that is impossible for a human to achieve.

To the best of the authors' knowledge, the majority of the academic materials about SOAR systems focuses on theoretical work and/or experiments in controlled environments. Moreover, there is a need to promote the development of low-cost SOAR solutions as the commercial ones are very expensive, ranging from $10K to $40K per month (these values are extrapolated to avoid disclosing company's internal information) and in the rare cases where they provide a free version, it is inviable for production usage. In this context, the main contributions of this work are:

- it proposes a low-cost and cloud native SOAR solution;
- it fills the gap between the theory and practice by evaluating the performance of the proposed solution in the production environment of a large multinational company.

The remainder of this paper is organized as follows: Sect. 2 presents the related works around the security orchestration and automation topic. Section 3 presents the problem statement and the requirements considered for the developed system. Section 4 provides details about the proposed solution, including its architecture and the technologies used. Section 5 describes the use cases considered to validate and assess the solution and the practical results obtained with the proposed low-cost SOAR system, focusing on quantitative metrics. Finally, Sect. 6 brings the conclusions and discusses possible future works.

2 Related Works

There is a good number of articles related to security orchestration and automation, some focuses on the review of the state of the art as well as the conceptual and social part of the problem [19,20,23], others on the creation of frameworks and solutions [22,27], and finally, one discuss the implementation of security orchestration and automation in a real world scenario [25].

A critical analysis on the use of security automation and how it is not a one-size-fits-all solution to solve all the scalability issues of the information security field was made by W. Keith Edwards et al. [19]. The authors also suggested a definition of security automation for end-users along a spectrum of rigidity, which provides a basis for discussing three sources of limits in automation: situational and social dependencies, accommodation of end-user values, and user interface costs deriving from automation failures.

C. Islam et al. [20] identified and analyzed critical aspects of security orchestration solutions found in 95 papers. Their review tried to address three research questions: what is security orchestration; what challenges security orchestration intend to solve; and what types of solutions have been proposed. The authors identified the key functionalities provided by security orchestration solutions and listed their quality attributes.

Song Luo et al. [22], in turn, present a service-oriented approach to security orchestration for software-defined infrastructure that abstracts security controls as security services. Their approach interprets assets' security policies as service requirements.

Raydel Montesino et al. [23] analyzed three widely used information security standards and best practice guidelines, showing that about 30% of the security controls included in the ISO 27001 and the NIST Special Publication 800-53 can be automated by existing tools. The analysis has shown that no single tool exploits the full security control automation potential. Instead a combination of different tools is required to achieve the maximum automation degree.

Weija Wang et al. [27] presented a data driven Security Device Orchestration Framework (SDOF) for Software-Defined Security (SDS). In SDOF, they put forward uniform interfaces for security devices so that they could be orchestrated by software and their data could be collected and processed centrally.

A solution to orchestrate several information systems and automate the initial incident response was presented by Motoyuki Ohmori [25]. The Incident Tracking System (ITS) automatically locates and isolates a suspicious host, and sends an e-mail notification to the person in charge of handling the incident. The ITS can also identify or suggest a user of the suspicious host by network authentication logs or other service logs. The work reduced the time required for the initial incident response to automatically isolate a suspicious host to less than 40 s while a manual operation required more than 30 min, several hours or even several days in some cases.

In general terms, the related works confirm the need of orchestration and automation of security processes, and that having manual processes clearly defined is a necessary condition to a successful SOAR implementation. Apart from Motoyuki Ohmori's work, the other ones have a more theoretical approach that does not include real-world experimentation. The work presented here takes into consideration the insights provided by the related works to create a low-cost and cloud native SOAR solution that is implemented and evaluated in a real-world scenario.

3 Background and Problem Statement

Following project management best practices, and considering the typical needs of the personnel working in the SOC (see Table 1), it was defined a list of requirements for the low-cost SOAR system herein presented. A summarized list of the most important and relevant requirements is presented below:

- Serverless: the stakeholders want to avoid the operational and financial overhead of deploying and maintaining servers, so the solution must use serverless technologies such as AWS Lambda, Azure Functions, or Google Cloud Functions.
- Secure: the solution must implement secure coding practices as defined by relevant organizations such as OWASP [21] and NIST [24]. Additionally, cloud security best practices proposed by the selected cloud provider must be taken into consideration.
- Fast: The automated actions performed by the system must be, at least, ten times faster than the same action performed by the security analyst.
- Scalable: The system must be able to handle, at least, 10,000 security incidents/month. This number was intentionally extrapolated to avoid disclosing internal company metrics and to guarantee that the system is able to handle a very high volume of incidents.
- Cost-efficient: The system must be, at least, 1/10 of the price of a commercial SOAR product that delivers similar capabilities. All the costs must be operating expense (OpEx) and not capital expenditures (CapEx).

Table 1. Typical needs of SOC personnel

Role in SOC	Typical needs
Analyst	Spend less time doing repetitive and mundane tasks that could be automated, so it is possible to allocate more time to tasks that require critical-thinking and experience, and therefore, must be done by a human.
	Spend less time working on security incidents, so it is possible to have more time to participate in high-visibility and strategic security projects.
	Decrease the time it takes to solve security incidents, so it is possible to decrease the potential impacts to the company (e.g. financial, reputational, and operational).
Manager	Remove low-value and boring tasks from the analyst's daily routine, to improve the team morale and retention.
	Orchestrate and automate as many tasks as possible, to increase the SOC capacity while maintaining the same headcount.

The market for SOAR solutions is rather new when compared to more mainstream and mature markets like Security Information and Event Management (SIEM), Endpoint Protection, Network Security etc. There are multiple vendors with commercial off-the-shelf (COTS) products like Palo Alto, IBM, Splunk etc. These products have a high upfront cost as they demand lots of person-hour for planning, implementation, initial configuration, and training of the team. But, this initial cost usually pays off when the solution is properly set up and doing the job of multiple full-time equivalent (FTE) employees at lower costs and without worrying about sickness, fatigue etc.

There are also open-source tools like Apache Airflow and Luigi that are not considered SOAR products because their focus is not security and they lack many, if not all, built-in integrations with various security tools. Even so, they can be used as a SOAR if one decides to build all the security integrations necessary and make use of their orchestration and automation capabilities.

Finally, there are other ways to achieve similar results by leveraging the capabilities of managed cloud services. AWS has shown [26] that services like Step Functions and Lambda can orchestrate and automate various aspects of the incident response process. The same could be achieved by using equivalent services from other cloud providers such as Microsoft Azure and Google Cloud.

The goal of the SOAR system proposed in this work is to encompass the advantages of cloud services such as on-demand resources, competitive pricing, scalability, and high availability to create a system that is able to achieve all the project requirements in a timely fashion.

4 Architecture

This section is divided into 2 sub-sections: design and technology. The first focuses on presenting the system architecture and a brief overview of it. The second dives into the technologies used, their limits, costs, and the motivation behind their use.

4.1 Design

This paper proposes a SOAR platform that is serverless, secure, fast, scalable, and cost-efficient. As shown in Fig. 1, the system architecture includes many parties such as the code repository system, the SIEM system, and multiple AWS services. These parties are numbered and briefly described below and a more in-depth description is presented in sub-section 4.2.

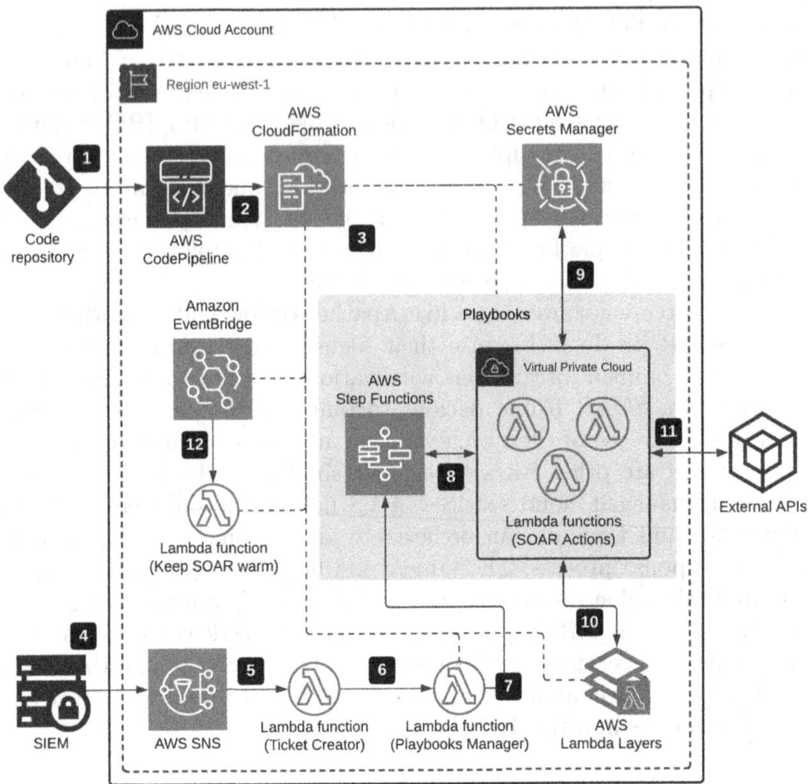

Fig. 1. SOAR platform architecture diagram

1. The source code and supporting files are hosted in a private repository in GitHub Cloud. There are 2 branches: dev (development) and main (production). Branch protection is activated for the main branch, so changes are only possible via pull requests (PRs) that must be analyzed and approved by the repository maintainers. When the PR is applied to the main branch, it automatically triggers the production pipeline in AWS CodePipeline.
2. The pipeline has 3 stages: source, build, and deploy. The source stage is triggered via the GitHub Cloud integration that was mentioned above. The build stage receives the code and supporting files from the source stage to perform the compilation and sends it to the next stage. In the final stage, deploy, AWS CloudFormation takes care of the deployment.
3. AWS CloudFormation create, update, or delete the resources according to the changes that were pushed. All the platform resources such as the Lambda functions, Lambda Layers, Step Functions, and many others are centrally managed by CloudFormation. The entire platform can be deployed and decommissioned with one-click. The dotted lines in the diagram connects the CloudFormation to all the resources it manages.
4. The SOAR platform is SIEM-agnostic, the only requirement is that the system is able to send messages to an SNS topic (all major SIEM vendors are

capable of doing that natively or via add-ons). For every new security incident alert, the system sends a message with the relevant data (e.g. username, URL, IP, hash etc.) to the pre-configured SNS topic.

5. The SNS topic receives the alert message and automatically triggers the Ticket Creator Lambda function and pass the message to it. This is a publish-subscribe messaging pattern where the SIEM is the publisher and the Lambda is the subscriber.
6. The Ticket Creator Lambda function creates the security incident ticket in the ticking system used by the organization. If the execution is successful, this function will trigger another one, the Playbooks Manager Lambda function, and pass the alert message to it.
7. The Playbooks Manager Lambda function triggers the execution of an AWS Step Function's state machine and pass the alert message to it, if there is one created for that given alert. The state machines are the automated playbooks. In case there is no automated playbook, the function logs the execution details (as it always does) and exits gracefully.
8. The automated playbooks are basically a collection of sequential and concurrent actions placed in a visual workflow that has logical capabilities (e.g. if-else, loops etc.). The playbook's original input is the alert message, but within the workflow the output of one action can be used as input for another one. An automated playbook may use one or more actions (e.g. check IP reputation, get user details, add a hash to the threat intel database etc.).
9. The actions are grouped into modules (e.g. the module AbuseIPDB has the actions check IP, check subnet, report IP etc.). Each module has one associated Secrets Manager object to securely store sensitive data such as username, password, API key etc. The actions have read-only access to their module's secret object to retrieve the necessary data during runtime.
10. The modules are Lambda layers that are imported into the Action Lambda functions. There are also other supporting Lambda layers such as the SOAR utils (utility code that is used by all actions) and the AWS Lambda Powertools [6].
11. The Action Lambda functions use the SOAR Virtual Private Cloud (VPC) with 2 static public IPs to interact with the Internet. By default, a Lambda interacts with the Internet using a random IP allocated by AWS during runtime, but this is not viable for the SOAR platform because some APIs require adding the IP to an allowlist and ultimately because using a VPC provides more control and isolation capabilities.
12. When talking about Lambda usage at scale, which is the case of this paper, cold start avoidance is a recurring topic [16]. To avoid cold start and to make the Action Lambda functions promptly available, there is a scheduled EventBridge rule that triggers the Keep SOAR warm Lambda function which then sends a heartbeat to all the SOAR Action Lambda functions to keep them cached within the AWS infrastructure.

It's important to note that the deployment, configuration, and usage of the SIEM system (item 4), the AWS SNS topic (item 5), and the Ticket Creator Lambda function (item 6) are out of the scope of this paper. These resources were already set up and in production prior to the SOAR platform project. They were included in the diagram for better understanding of the entire architecture, but they were not deployed nor configured by the author. Except for these 3 resources, all the other resources in the diagram were fully deployed and configured by the author.

4.2 Technology

The technologies used are mainly AWS services, but there is also the SIEM system (e.g. Azure Sentinel, IBM QRadar, Splunk etc.) and the code repository (e.g. Bitbucket, GitHub, GitLab etc.) which are important pieces of the solution.

A single company can own multiple AWS accounts at the same time and only pay for the deployed resources, this is usually the case for large companies with specific business and technical demands. This capability is achieved by using AWS Organizations [7]. The author considered a dedicated AWS account for the SOAR platform to avoid taking into consideration unpredictable usage patterns from other solutions that might be deployed into a multipurpose account. The service limits presented used the AWS's Service endpoints and quotas [15] reference page.

To calculate the costs of the solution the author considered a volume of 10K security incidents/month, intentionally extrapolating the number of security incidents to prove that the platform can scale while keeping the costs low. To avoid long-term commitment, the solution considered the on-demand pricing available in the AWS Pricing Calculator [14] and not the Savings Plans pricing as they require a 1- or 3-year commitment. The discounts provided by the AWS Free Tier were also intentionally avoided. Finally, the cost and availability of some services vary according to the AWS region, so the author used the region `eu-west-1` (Ireland, Europe) as reference. The total cost of the solution is presented in Table 2 and a more detailed pricing structure in presented in each sub-section.

Table 2. Total cost of the solution per month

Description	Cost/month
SIEM	–
AWS SNS	\$0.27
AWS Lambda	\$3.72
AWS Secrets manager	\$40.82
AWS Step functions	\$12.50
AWS CodePipeline	\$6.05
AWS CloudFormation	\$0.00
Code repository	–
TOTAL	\$63.36

Splunk Cloud. The SIEM system used in this project is the Splunk Cloud, it is a Software as a Service (SaaS) developed by the company Splunk. The company behind this project uses it to collect, search, and correlate logs from various sources in order to detect and alert on security incidents. Each alert can be configured to do one or more actions as a result of it being triggered, there are many built-in actions provided by Splunk itself (e.g. send an email, call a webhook etc.) and additional actions can be installed via add-ons or created by the customer.

For the security incident alerts, the SOC team uses a custom action provided by one of the installed add-ons, which sends the alert payload to an AWS SNS topic. This process has been in place before this project started and there was no need to change it to integrate with the SOAR platform, this part was included as-is in the architecture.

The alert payload contains data that is included by default such as time, title, description, and severity, but also alert specific data such as username, email, source IP, destination IP, hash, path etc., that can be present or not depending on the type of the alert. Regardless of the type, the payload size sits between 1 and 8 KB as it's just a plain text with delimiters to separate the data for the subsequent parsing.

The costs related to the SIEM are not considered in the platform's total cost, as having a SIEM is a pre-requisite for this project. Additionally, the platform has no hard dependencies on the SIEM system being used. The only data the platform needs from the SIEM is the alert payload that is delivered via SNS topic, and this capability is available in all the major SIEM systems, be it built-in or via official/supported add-ons.

AWS Simple Notification Service (SNS). This is a fully managed messaging service for both application-to-application (A2A) and application-to-person (A2P) communication. The A2A pub/sub functionality provides topics for high-throughput, push-based, many-to-many messaging between distributed systems, microservices, and event-driven serverless applications. [1]

As previously mentioned, Splunk Cloud sends the alert payload to a specific SNS topic. Every new message added to the topic triggers the Lambda subscriber which receives the alert payload and interacts with the company's ticketing system to create the ticket. The platform uses this setup to receive the alert payload that triggers the execution of the associated automated playbook.

There are some relevant service limits that the author took into consideration when designing the architecture, the main one being the 256 KB maximum payload size allowed by SNS. All the relevant limits are listed in Table 3.

AWS SNS pricing is competitive, they don't charge to deliver messages to Lambda subscribers, there are only data transfer costs as shown in Table 4. For cost reference, the author considered the maximum alert payload size of 256 KB, which is 32 times bigger than the biggest alert payload currently in production (8 KB), so the cost estimate errs on the side of caution. Even with the extrapolated payload size and the large numbers of messages, the SNS costs were just \$0.27/month.

Table 3. AWS SNS limits

Item	Limit	Comment
Standard topics/account	100K	The platform only needs 1 standard topic (the one that receives the alerts payload).
Subscriptions/std. topic	100M	The platform only needs 1 Lambda subscriber configured in the topic mentioned above.
Messages/second	9K	Each message is equivalent to one security incident and the author considered a high volume of 10K security incidents/month, which is still way below the limit. To reach this limit the company would have to have 9K security incidents/second, which is extremely unusual.
Payload size/message	256 KB	The majority of the alert payload sizes are between 1 and 3 KB, with some outliers going as high as 8 KB, which is still safely below the limit. As mentioned, the alert payloads are plain text with delimiters, so it is expected to have a small size

Table 4. AWS SNS costs

Description	Cost/month
10K messages to a Lambda subscriber (1 message is equivalent to 1 alert)	$0.00
3 GB outbound data transfer (256 KB * 10K messages = 2.56 GB, rounded upward to 3 GB)	$0.27
TOTAL	$0.27

AWS Lambda. This is a serverless, event-driven compute service that lets you run code for virtually any type of application or backend service without provisioning or managing servers. You can trigger Lambda from over 200 AWS services and software as a service (SaaS) applications, and only pay for what you use. AWS Lambda natively supports many programming languages like Python, Java, Node.js, C#, Go etc. [5]

The author created the platform using Python, but this is not a requirement as the logic behind the code can be easily implemented in any high-level programming language. An important feature that was also used is the AWS Lambda Layers [13], as they can store custom libraries and dependencies which are then imported into the main Lambda function, making the update and maintenance process easier and faster. The Lambda functions and Lambda Layers that were presented in the Fig. 1 are described below:

- Ticket Creator: this Lambda is triggered by the SNS topic to create the ticket in the SOC queue within the ticketing platform used by the company. Nothing was changed in the actual code, it works independently from the SOAR. On the other hand, the author did a simple configuration change in the Lambda settings to enable a Lambda Destination, so the Playbooks Manager Lambda can be triggered after this one is executed successfully.

- Playbooks Manager: this Lambda is responsible for receiving the alert payload from the Ticket Creator Lambda and running the automated playbook that is associated with that alert. There can be cases where this is triggered but there is no automated playbook for that specific alert, in such cases the Lambda will just log the attempt and finish silently as this is expected.
- SOAR Action: there is one SOAR Action Lambda function for each action (e.g. check an IP on AbuseIPDB, report an IP to the AbuseIPDB etc.). These actions work like building blocks to construct the automated playbooks. These functions are responsible for input validation and for calling the intended module to interact with the API.
- SOAR Module: there is one SOAR Module Lambda Layer for each system the platform integrates with (e.g. AbuseIPDB, VirusTotal, PhishTank etc.). The actual code that implements the logic for interacting with the APIs is in the modules, the actions are just callers.
- SOAR Utils: this Lambda Layer contains libraries and dependencies that are transversal to all Lambda functions.
- Keep SOAR warm: this Lambda function runs on a schedule (by default, it is every 3 min) and sends an asynchronous heartbeat to all the SOAR Action Lambda functions to keep them cached within the AWS infrastructure to avoid cold-start delays. The Amazon EventBridge rule that triggers this function has no cost, as it is using the default bus.
- AWS Lambda Powertools: this Lambda Layer was created and is maintained by AWS. It is a suite of utilities to ease adopting best practices such as tracing, structured logging, custom metrics, and more [6]. The platform uses it for logging, input validation, and parameters.

It's important to note that the communication between the platform and the APIs is encrypted using TLS 1.2 or higher to protect data in transit. To guarantee isolation and traceability, the platform's Lambda functions are inside a dedicated Amazon Virtual Private Cloud (VPC) and all the communications are initiated by the platform using its two dedicated public IPs. Also, like any service, the AWS Lambda has limits that were taken into consideration when designing the architecture. Table 5 shows the limits that are relevant to the platform.

Finally, estimating the Lambda costs was more complex than the other services as there are many variables involved. For cost reference, the author considered the 10K security incidents/month, an average of 30 actions/incident, and 100 modules with an average of 10 actions each. The average execution duration values were taken from the platform metrics for July 2022. The Lambda usage is described below and the costs are \$3.72/month as described in Table 6.

- Playbooks Manager
    - Executions (each security incident is 1 execution): 10K executions/month
    - Average execution duration: 11 milliseconds
- Keep SOAR warm
    - Executions (scheduled to run every 3 min): 14.6K executions/month
    - Average execution duration: 3 s

Table 5. AWS Lambda limits

Item	Limit	Comment
Execution timeout	15 min.	The configured value is 1 min. The fastest actions take less than a second to execute and the slowest ones take less than a minute. Actions that are intrinsically more time consuming (e.g. SSL/TLS site scan) are built using a job queue structure to avoid idling Lambda resources and hitting the timeout.
Concurrent executions	1K	The configured value is 1K. The actions are executed in a very short time span, so having 1K actions running at the same time is unlikely. This is a soft limit that can be increased to tens of thousands.
RAM	10 GB	The configured value is 512 MB. The actions are not resource intensive. Analysis were made using AWS's Lambda Power Tuning utility, which indicated that 512 MB is the sweet spot for balancing cost and performance.
Ephemeral storage	10 GB	The configured value is 512 MB. The actions do not save temporary files to the ephemeral storage, so this value was left as the minimum possible.
Environment variable size	4 KB	The actions use environment variables to store the execution log level (e.g. debug, info, warning etc.) and the Amazon Resource Name (ARN) of the Secrets Manager's object that is associated with that action. Considering the env vars set by AWS and the ones created by the SOAR, the final size is less than 1 KB.
Invocation payload size	256 KB	As mentioned, the biggest alert payload is just 8 KB and once this payload arrives at the automated playbook, each action receives only the data that is relevant to it and not the complete payload (e.g. AbuseIPDB's check IP only receives the IP).
Deployment package size	250 MB	Both the Lambda and the Lambda Layers deployment package sizes are way below this limit, the biggest one is around 3 MB (unzipped).
Attached Lambda Layers	5	This is the only concerning limit as the actions need 3 layers attached to the Lambda at all times: the AWS Lambda Powertools library, the SOAR utils library, and the SOAR module library. This leaves only 2 free slots. Unfortunately, this is a hard limit that can not be increased via request.

- SOAR Action (Keep SOAR warm calls)
  - Executions (14.6K heartbeat calls * 1K actions): 14.6M executions/month
  - Average execution duration: 1 millisecond
- SOAR Action (Playbook calls)

Table 6. AWS Lambda costs

Description	Cost/month
Playbooks manager	$0.00
Keep SOAR warm	$0.36
SOAR Action (Keep SOAR warm calls)	$3.04
SOAR Action (Playbook calls)	$0.32
TOTAL	$3.72

- Executions (10K security incidents/month * 30 actions each): 300K executions/month
- Average execution duration: 105 milliseconds

AWS Secrets Manager. This service securely stores applications, services, and IT resources secrets. It enables you to easily rotate, manage, and retrieve database credentials, API keys, and other secrets throughout their lifecycle. Users and applications retrieve secrets with a call to Secrets Manager API, eliminating the need to hardcode sensitive information in plain text. [8]

The platform needs to secure sensitive data such as usernames, API keys, and access tokens both in transit and at rest. Data security in transit was already discussed in the sub-section 4.2. Now, for data security at rest, the chosen solution was AWS Secrets Manager due to its usability and scalability. Each secret is a JSON with key-values for storing the data.

This service was publicly released in 2018, so it is a relatively new service offered by AWS. Before this, developers had only one option for storing secrets: the Systems Manager Parameter Store. Both services are very similar, but there are key differences that make the use of Secrets Manager more reasonable for storing and managing secrets, as presented in Table 7.

Table 7. AWS Secrets Manager vs Parameter Store (adapted)

	Secrets Manager	Parameter store (standard tier)
Encryption of data at rest	Supported	Supported
Automatic secret rotation	Supported	Not supported
Generate random secrets	Supported	Not supported
Secrets/region	500K	10K
Maximum secret size	64 KB	4 KB
Pricing	Paid	Free

There are many Secrets Manager limits and the ones related to API calls are quite restrictive when compared to other services. AWS recommend avoid calling

`PutSecretValue` or `UpdateSecret` at a sustained rate of more than once every 10 min to avoid facing issues related to secret versions limit [9]. In the case of the SOAR platform, the restrictive limits are not a problem as the architecture design took them into consideration and even at high load the platform is safely below the limits. The relevant limits are described in Table 8.

Table 8. AWS Secrets Manager limits

Item	Limit	Comment
Secrets/region	500K	Apart from the global secret that is shared by all the modules (e.g. platform name, version etc.), each module contains only 1 secret object.
Secret size	64 KB	The secrets are JSONs with key-values such as URL, username, password, user-agent etc. The biggest secret object in use is not even 1 KB in size.
`GetSecretValue` calls/sec	5K	The Lambda functions have a cache of the secrets that is updated just when necessary. Because of this setup, hitting this limit is unlikely.
`CreateSecret` calls/sec	50	The secrets are created in two moments: when the platform is first deployed and when a new module is deployed. In both cases, AWS CloudFormation handles the rate limiting transparently.
`UpdateSecret` calls/sec	50	The secrets are updated according to the necessity (e.g. API key rotation, username change etc.). Even considering an unlikely high-rate of daily secret updates of all the secrets, this limit would not be reached.
`DeleteSecret` calls/sec	50	The secrets are deleted in two moments: when a module is deleted and when the platform is decommissioned. In both cases, AWS CloudFormation handles the rate limiting transparently.

Even though Secrets Manager is paid while the Parameter Store is free, the benefits it offers outweighs the cost. The pricing model is simple: pay for the number of secrets stored/hour and the number of API calls. For reference, the author considered the same 100 modules as previously used, which translates to 100 stored secrets as each module has 1 dedicated secret object. Add to that the 2 secrets used by the Playbooks Manager and the SOAR Utils library, culminating in a total of 102 secrets that are stored 24×7.

As previously mentioned, the SOAR Action Lambda functions are cached via the Keep SOAR warm heartbeats and that cache includes the secret object to avoid a high volume of unnecessary calls to the Secrets Manager. On the other hand, this approach may cause sync issues if a secret is updated in the Secrets Manager (e.g. replace an API key) as the heartbeat calls do not include a secret refresh. To mitigate that, the platform has a cache invalidation mechanism to purge the cache of all the actions or just the ones related to a given module whenever necessary.

Considering the daily secret updates of all the secrets, we would have 102 API calls/day which added to the 102 secrets stored 24×7 ends up with a cost of $40.82/month as shown in Table 9.

Table 9. AWS Secrets Manager costs

Description	Cost/month
102 secrets	$40.80
3.1K API calls	$0.02
TOTAL	$40.82

The Secrets Manager's cost is by far the highest one when compared to all the other AWS services used by the platform, but data security at rest and secrets isolation are a must-have and using any other method for storing data such as Lambda environment variables or Parameter Store were not acceptable due to security, maintainability, and/or scalability concerns.

AWS Step Functions. This is a low-code, visual workflow service that developers use to build distributed applications, automate IT and business processes, and build data and machine learning pipelines using AWS services. Workflows manage failures, retries, parallelization, service integrations, and observability so developers can focus on higher-value business logic. [11]

There are two types of Step Functions workflows, Standard and Express, the main differences between them are presented in Table 10. Most importantly, the maximum duration of 5 min of the Express workflows made them inviable for the platform as there can be automated playbooks that needs to run for more than that, for example, a playbook that is waiting for the analyst's feedback to proceed with a given action.

The platform uses the Step Functions' state machines as automated playbooks in a 1:1 correspondence. These playbooks contains one or more SOAR Action Lambda functions to execute the actions the analyst would do during an incident response. The playbooks contains logical flows such as if-else, loops, sleep etc. and are able to make simple decisions. On the other hand, tasks that requires critical-thinking or are too complex to be automated are not included.

There are many Step Functions limits: state throttling, API action throttling, state machine executions, and task executions to name a few. First, all the limits related to the creation, update and deletion of the state machines are handled by AWS CloudFormation in a transparent way. Second, the limits that are relevant to the platform are presented in Table 11.

Table 10. AWS Step Functions: Standard vs Express [12]

	Standard	Express
Max duration	1 year	5 min
Execution start rate	2K/second	100K/second
State transition rate	4K/second	"nearly unlimited"
Pricing	Priced per transition. It is counted each time a step is completed	Priced by the number of executions, duration, and memory consumption

Table 11. AWS Standard Step Functions limits

Item	Limit	Comment
State machines/account	10K	Hitting this limit is unlikely as one security playbook is equivalent to one state machine, and the SOC team have less than 1K playbooks. This is a soft limit that can be increased to 23K.
States/state machine	10K	Roughly, each state represents a manual action that would be done by the analyst and there is no playbook that requires more than 50 actions. This is a soft limit that can be increased to tens of thousands.
Request size (header included)	1 MB	The alert payload is capped at 256 KB due to the SNS limit, leaving 768 KB for the header, which is plenty already. This is a hard limit.
Concurrent executions/region	1M	The 9K messages/second SNS limit would be a bottleneck long before the system reaches this limit. This is a soft limit that can be increased to millions.
Execution timeout	1 year	Most automated playbooks do not require human intervention so they finish in minutes, at most. For the ones that require, it is expected that an analyst will be available in minutes or hours. This is a hard limit.
Execution start rate	2K/sec.	To reach this limit, the platform would have to ingest 2K security incidents/second, which is unlikely. This is a soft limit that can be increased (the maximum value was not disclosed by AWS).
State transition rate	4K/sec.	This limit is relevant when the state machine has large scale concurrent loops. This is not the case of the automated playbooks, where even the biggest concurrent loops are in the hundreds transitions/second. This is a soft limit that can be increased (the maximum value was not disclosed by AWS).

The platform uses Standard Workflows so the costs estimative is straightforward. It's important to note that there is no cost for having a state machine, you are only charged when they are executed. Considering the 10K security incidents/month (that is 10K state machine executions/month) and an average of 50 state transitions/state machine, we have a cost of $12.50/month as described in Table 12.

Table 12. AWS Step Functions costs

Description	Cost/month
10K Standard Workflow requests	–
50 state transitions/workflow	–
TOTAL	$12.50

AWS CodePipeline. This is a fully managed continuous delivery service that automates release pipelines for fast and reliable application and infrastructure updates. It automates the build, test, and deploy phases of the release process every time there is a code change. [4]

The platform has 2 pipelines: production and development. Both pipelines have the same stages (Source, Build, and Deploy) and very similar configurations. In the Source stage, GitHub was configured as the action provider, it points to the SOAR platform code repository and automatically starts the pipeline when a source code change is detected. Each pipeline points to a different branch in the repository (development points to the dev branch and production points to the main branch).

In the Build stage, for each pipeline AWS CodeBuild compiles the source code and the CloudFormation template to create the package that is sent to the Deploy stage. A compute instance with 3 GB of RAM, 2 vCPU, and the operating system Amazon Linux 2 (the same one that is used by the Lambda functions) was configured for the build process, it was the cheapest one available and had plenty of compute power for the job. The build instance is managed by AWS, we do not have direct access to it nor need to worry about the operating system configuration and maintenance.

The build times are billed by the minute and were in most cases around 1 min, with some outliers going as high as 3 min. For cost reference, the author decided to err on the side of caution and considered the worst-case scenario and a high deployment rate of multiple deployments per day, even in the production environment, which is unlikely as new features are generally introduced in a weekly or monthly basis. The following usage pattern was considered:

- Development
  - Compute instance `general1.small` (3 GB RAM, 2 vCPU)
  - 180 builds/month
  - 3 min/build
- Production

- Compute instance `general1.small` (3 GB RAM, 2 vCPU)
- 90 builds/month
- 3 min/build

Finally, in the Deploy stage, the platform uses AWS CloudFormation to automatically create, update, and delete the resources, as described in detail in the sub-section 4.2.

AWS CodePipeline has limits for the number of pipelines, stages, actions, and webhooks by region, but they can be increased via request. The limits that are relevant to the platform are listed in Table 13.

Table 13. AWS CodePipeline limits

Item	Limit	Comment
Pipelines/region	1K	The solution was designed considering the use of 2 pipelines (dev and prod), but even with a more granular deployment model with dev, test, qa, stage, and prod, the platform would still be under the limit.
Webhooks/region (Source stage)	300	The GitHub action provider configured in the pipelines uses webhook for detecting source code changes. The above comment applies here as well, the platform is well below the limit.
CodeBuild timeout (Build stage)	8 h	It depends on the quantity of changes that were included in the pull request. The build times ranged from a few seconds for small hofixes, 2 min for adding a new module with multiple actions, and 5 min for a full platform build.
CloudFormation timeout (Deploy stage)	3 days	The CloudFormation deployment times ranged from 1 min for small hofixes, 2 min for adding a new module with multiple actions, and 9 min for a full platform deployment.

The costs related to the AWS CodePipeline are divided into 3 parts: the pipeline itself, the build process, and the deployment process. The deployment costs are not considered in this sub-section as they are discussed in the sub-section 4.2 AWS CloudFormation. Table 14 presents the costs, which are $6.05/month.

Table 14. AWS CodePipeline costs

Description	Cost/month
Development pipeline	$1.00
Production pipeline	$1.00
Development build time (180 builds, 3 min each)	$2.70
Production build time (90 builds, 3 min each)	$1.35
TOTAL	$6.05

AWS CloudFormation. This is an Infrastructure as code (IaC) service that allows the provisioning and management of resources in an orderly and predictable fashion. Developers can deploy and update compute, database, and many other resources in a simple, declarative style that abstracts away the complexity of specific resource APIs [2]. All the resources that compose the platform are created, updated, and deleted via AWS CloudFormation, there are no manual tasks involved in the deployment and decommissioning of the platform.

Regarding service costs, there is no additional charge for using AWS CloudFormation with resource providers in the following namespaces: `AWS::*`, `Alexa::*`, and `Custom::*`. In these cases, you only pay for the created resources the same as if you had created them manually [3]. For the SOAR platform, only resources in the namespace `AWS::*` were created, so the cost of using CloudFormation was zero.

Both the development and the production resources were deployed from the same AWS CloudFormation YAML template. A prefix is dynamically added to the resource names according to the environment and some resources are only created if a pre-defined condition is met as they are environment-specific. The template is divided into the following sections:

- Transform: this is where AWS CloudFormation macros are defined. The template uses AWS Serverless Application Model (SAM) [10].
- Parameters: this is where input values are configured. They are used during the stack creation and update process. The template has many parameters such as environment prefix, Python version, Lambda timeout etc.
- Conditions: they define the circumstances under which resources are created or configured. For example, the template has the condition `DevelopmentEnv` that defines that a resource must only be created if the parameter `EnvPrefix` is set to `DEV`.
- Resources: this is where the resources used by the SOAR platform are declared.

GitHub. This is a very popular a code hosting platform used by many individuals and companies for version control and collaboration. It offers free and paid products for storing and collaborating on code. Some products apply only to personal accounts, while other plans apply only to organization and enterprise accounts.

As in the SIEM system case, the costs related to GitHub subscriptions are not considered in the SOAR's total cost. Even more because a paid subscription is not needed, everything done on GitHub related to this project is available in the free plan.

The SOAR platform's code and supporting files are hosted on GitHub Cloud, under the account of the company where this project took place. The repository is private so even within the company only the SOC team is able to see it. The repository contains 2 branches (main and dev) and has branch protection enabled to block direct changes to the main branch, instead they are done via pull requests that are analysed and approved.

In order to make the SOAR platform scalable and modular, each integration with a given system (e.g. AbuseIPDB, VirusTotal, PhishTank etc.) is a self-contained module that has all the code necessary for it to work properly. Each module contains one or more actions to interact with the target system (e.g. the AbuseIPDB module has the `check_ip` action).

5 Results

This section is divided into 2 sub-sections: use cases and results. The first presents the use cases considered to validate and assess the solution, while the second presents the practical results obtained with the proposed low-cost SOAR system, focusing on quantitative metrics.

5.1 Use Cases

The author and the company's SOC team decided on the 11 manual playbooks that should be the first ones to have an automated version, based on multiples factors: feasibility of automation, number of occurrences/month, complexity of the playbook, complexity of the incident, and number of manual actions. The selected use cases are described below, in order of implementation.

Impossible Travel. This alert has the objective of detecting authentications being done in very far locations in a short time span, something impossible to be accomplished by taking into consideration the current transportation infrastructure. It's important to note that even with continuous fine-tuning of the alert itself, there are always some false-positives, even more in today's context with lots of employees working from different locations and using multiple virtual private networks (VPNs).

AWS EC2 Changes. The company has many AWS accounts under its control, each one of them with one or more AWS Elastic Compute Cloud (EC2) instances that run very important workloads. Changes to said instances must be justified and applied according to the company's maintenance window. This alert has the objective of detecting suspicious changes made to the EC2 instances (e.g. changes on network security groups, instance status, attached storage etc.).

AWS IAM Changes. This alert is similar to the one above, but focuses on identity security of the many AWS accounts owned by the company. This alert has the objective of detecting suspicious changes made on the AWS Identity and Access Management service (e.g. changes on users, groups, policies etc.).

Access to Credentials without Justification. The company has a standard operating procedure (SOP) for when an eligible employee need to access customers' infrastructure. Every access is made using an ephemeral credential with time-limited session, and the employee must provide a reason for the access, for example, a support ticket number. In the rare occasions where the reason is not valid (e.g. typo in the ticket number), the SOC team is triggered to investigate the situation.

New Digital Certificate Issued. The company has many domains under its responsibility and must ensure their security. There is monitoring in place to track the issuance of new digital certificates to all the owned domains. In the rare occasions where a Certificate Authority (CA) issues an illegitimate certificate, the SOC team is triggered to investigate the situation.

Possible SQL Injection. The company's main commercial product is intrinsically exposed to the Internet on port TCP 443 (HTTPS), so it is subject to attacks. This alert has the objective of detecting possible SQL injections against the product.

Login Brute Force Against the Company's Product. This alert has the objective of detecting login brute force attempts against the company's main commercial product. As previously mentioned, the product is intrinsically exposed to the Internet on port TCP 443 (HTTPS).

Login Brute Force Against an Internal System. This alert has the objective of detecting login brute force attempts against one of the systems the company uses internally. The system is not exposed to the Internet so a lower rate of occurrence is expected.

Login Brute Force Against an External System. This alert has the objective of detecting login brute force attempts against one of the systems the company uses. The system is intrinsically exposed to the Internet so a higher rate of occurrence is expected.

Partner Registered as Employee. Like many large enterprises, the company's workforce is composed of interns, employees, contractors, partners etc. During the on-board, the entity is assigned the necessary permissions according to their position in the company and the job requirements. The on-board process involves many teams and has some manual operations, hence it is prone to human-error. This alert has the objective of detecting inconsistencies in the employees directory.

Update Indicators of Compromise (IOCs) base. A common practice of SOC teams is sharing threat intelligence with partners and security networks. This use case is not related to a security incident alert, but rather a security process. Most of the security tools provide built-in capabilities to automatically collect IOCs (e.g. the firewall has a list of known botnet IPs). The issue is that there are many threat intel feeds that are not included in said tools and adding/updating the IOCs manually is a monotonous task, event with bulk import.

5.2 Performance Assessment

This project took place in a large multinational company with a 24×7 SOC team composed of analysts located in different continents and timezones. The SOAR solution was properly tested before being shipped to production. The experiments were conducted in the production environment with real-world security incidents. The system was deployed to production on July 1, 2022.

To avoid disclosing sensitive information, Table 15 presents the use cases in a randomized and anonymized way. It compares how many seconds a selected range of actions took to complete before and after implementing the solution. The presented values are not the time it takes to solve the incident, aka the mean time to resolve (MTTR), as there are other tasks executed during the incident response that are out of the scope of the SOAR solution. The range of the analysis was between 2022-07-01 00:00:00 UTC and 2022-08-13 23:59:59 UTC, inclusive.

Table 15. Manual vs Automated tasks duration per alert

Use Case	Manual tasks duration (s)	Automated tasks duration (s)	Decrease in duration
A	900	8	99.1%
B	780	11.5	98.5%
C	240	1.6	99.3%
D	1,560	6	99.6%
E	120	1.7	98.6%
F	1,020	6.2	99.4%
G	120	1.6	98.7%
H	120	1.7	98.6%
I	180	2.12	98.8%
J	1,080	7.2	99.3%
K	1,110	6.9	99.4%

The manual tasks duration considered the time an analyst took to execute a group of actions, for example: open the incident ticket, open and follow the manual playbook, access the AbuseIPDB site, enter the IP being investigated, collect the evidence, go back to the ticket to add the evidence. The author did not even took into consideration the delays that might occur during the execution of the tasks, such as lunch, coffee break, bathroom, meetings etc. These values are the best-case scenario.

The automated tasks duration considered the execution time of the automated playbooks for doing the same actions without human intervention. These values are accurate as they were obtained from the state machine's execution times and by doing a trimmed mean (TM) that ignores the 10% top and bottom values to exclude the outliers.

During the experiment, we had a total of 363 security incidents matching the use cases. The IOC use case, which is not related to incidents but rather a continuous threat intelligence process, ran more than 9K times. Considering the time range of the experiment, the number of incidents (the IOC use case was excluded), and the time saved by the SOAR solution, we have the following:

- Before: 4,550 min (75.84 h) of the analyst's time to execute the manual tasks
- After: The same tasks were executed by the SOAR in 31.2 min, without human intervention

The solution met all the defined requirements. As explained in the Sect. 4, it is serverless and secure, it is able to handle more than 10K security incidents/month, the automated actions are more than ten times faster than the manual ones, and the solution costs less than $65/month while the cheapest comparable commercial solution goes for at least $10K/month.

6 Conclusion

In this paper, we proposed a low-cost cloud native SOAR platform, presenting the underlying details of its design. The performance of the proposed solution was evaluated through real-world experiments performed in a large multinational company. The results show that the solution was able to decrease the duration of the tasks in an average of 99.02% while having an operating expense of less than $65/month.

It's important to note that it was not possible to automate all the actions in all the use cases, as some of them require critical-thinking, are too complex to automate, or the system does not provide an API. This is expected and reinforce what was observed in the academic materials [19,23], SOAR is not a silver bullet and one must not try to automate everything blindly.

As future work, the author plans to move from AWS CloudFormation to an Infrastructure as Code solution like Terraform, Chef, Ansible etc. to avoid cloud vendor lock-in and to make the SOAR solution cloud-agnostic.

Acknowledgements. This work was supported by FCT through the LASIGE Research Unit, ref. UIDB/00408/2020 and ref. UIDP/00408/2020, and by OutSystems, with a special mention to the Security Office team.

References

1. AWS: Amazon simple notification service. https://aws.amazon.com/sns/. Accessed 14 Aug 2022
2. AWS: Aws CloudFormation. https://aws.amazon.com/cloudformation/. Accessed 14 Aug 2022
3. AWS: Aws CloudFormation pricing. https://aws.amazon.com/cloudformation/pricing/. Accessed 14 Aug 2022
4. AWS: Aws CodePipeline. https://aws.amazon.com/codepipeline/. Accessed 14 Aug 2022
5. AWS: Aws lambda. https://aws.amazon.com/lambda/. Accessed 14 Aug 2022

6. AWS: Aws lambda powertools for python. https://awslabs.github.io/aws-lambda-powertools-python/latest/. Accessed 14 Aug 2022
7. AWS: Aws organizations. https://aws.amazon.com/organizations/. Accessed 14 Aug 2022
8. AWS: Aws secrets manager. https://aws.amazon.com/secrets-manager/. Accessed 14 Aug 2022
9. AWS: Aws secrets manager quotas. https://docs.aws.amazon.com/secretsmanager/latest/userguide/reference_limits.html. Accessed 14 Aug 2022
10. AWS: Aws serverless application model. https://aws.amazon.com/cloudformation/pricing/. Accessed 14 Aug 2022
11. AWS: Aws step functions. https://aws.amazon.com/step-functions/. Accessed 14 Aug 2022
12. AWS: Aws step functions standard vs. express workflows. https://docs.aws.amazon.com/step-functions/latest/dg/concepts-standard-vs-express.html. Accessed 14 Aug 2022
13. AWS: Creating and sharing lambda layers. https://docs.aws.amazon.com/lambda/latest/dg/configuration-layers.html. Accessed 14 Aug 2022
14. AWS: pricing calculator. https://calculator.aws/. Accessed 14 Aug 2022
15. AWS: service endpoints and quotas. https://docs.aws.amazon.com/general/latest/gr/aws-service-information.html. Accessed 14 Aug 2022
16. Beswick, J.: Operating lambda: performance optimization - part 1. https://aws.amazon.com/blogs/compute/operating-lambda-performance-optimization-part-1/. Accessed 14 Aug 2022
17. Neiva, C., et al.: Innovation insight for security orchestration, automation and response. https://www.gartner.com/en/documents/3834578/innovation-insight-for-security-orchestration-automation. Accessed 14 Aug 2022
18. McCandless, D., et al.: World's biggest data breaches & hacks. https://www.informationisbeautiful.net/visualizations/worlds-biggest-data-breaches-hacks/. Accessed 14 Aug 2022
19. Edwards, W.K., Poole, E.S., Stoll, J.: Security automation considered harmful? In: Proceedings of the 2007 Workshop on New Security Paradigms. NSPW 2007, pp.. 33–42. Association for Computing Machinery, New York, NY, USA (2008). https://doi.org/10.1145/1600176.1600182
20. Islam, C., Babar, M.A., Nepal, S.: A multi-vocal review of security orchestration. ACM Comput. Surv. **52**(2), 1–45 (2019). https://doi.org/10.1145/3305268
21. Turpin, K., et al.: Owasp secure coding practices-quick reference guide. https://owasp.org/www-project-secure-coding-practices-quick-reference-guide/migrated_content. Accessed 14 Aug 2022
22. Luo, S., Ben Salem, M.: Orchestration of software-defined security services. In: IEEE International Conference on Communications Workshops (ICC), pp. 436–441 (2016). DOI: https://doi.org/10.1109/ICCW.2016.7503826
23. Montesino, R., Fenz, S.: Information security automation: how far can we go? In: 2011 Sixth International Conference on Availability, Reliability and Security. pp. 280–285 (2011). DOI: https://doi.org/10.1109/ARES.2011.48
24. Souppaya , M., Scarfone, K., Dodson, D.: Sp 800–218, secure software development framework (ssdf). https://csrc.nist.gov/publications/detail/sp/800-218/final. Accessed 14 Aug 2022
25. Ohmori, M.: On automation and orchestration of an initial computer security incident response by introducing centralized incident tracking system. J. Inf. Process. **27**, 564–573 (2019). https://doi.org/10.2197/ipsjjip.27.564

26. Smith, B.: Orchestrating a security incident response with AWS step functions. https://aws.amazon.com/blogs/compute/orchestrating-a-security-incident-response-with-aws-step-functions/. Accessed 14 Aug 2022
27. Wang, W., Qiu, X., Sun, Li; Zhao, R.: A data driven orchestration framework in software defined security. In: IEEE International Conference on Communications Workshops (ICC), pp. 34–39 (2016). DOI: https://doi.org/10.1109/ICNIDC.2016.7974531

Protecting Cyber-Physical System Testbeds from Red-Teaming/Blue-Teaming Experiments Gone Awry

Md Rakibul Hasan Talukder(✉), Md Al Amin, and Indrajit Ray

Colorado State University, Fort Collins, CO 80523, USA
{rakibul.talukder,md.al_amin,indrajit.ray}@colostate.edu

Abstract. Many cyber-physical systems (CPS) are critical infrastructure. Security attacks on these critical systems can have catastrophic consequences, putting human lives at risk. Consequently, it is very important to pace CPS systems to red-teaming/blue teaming exercises to understand vulnerabilities and the progression/impact of cyber attacks on them. Since it is not always prudent to conduct such security exercises on live CPS, researchers use CPS testbeds to conduct security-related experiments. Often, such testbeds are very expensive. Since attack scripts used in red-teaming/blue-teaming exercises are, in the strictest sense of the term, malicious in nature, there is a need to protect the testbed itself from these attack experiments that have the potential to go awry. Moreover, when multiple experiments are conducted on the same testbed, there is a need to maintain isolation among these experiments so that no experiment can accidentally or maliciously affect/compromise others. In this work, we describe a novel security architecture and framework to ensure protection of security-related experiments on a CPS testbed and at the same time support secure communication services among simultaneously running experiments based on well-formulated access control policies.

Keywords: CPS · Testbed · Security experiment · Authorization · Isolation · Tuple space

1 Introduction

A Cyber-Physical System (CPS) consists of many individual units or systems and often is a critical infrastructure. Some example of such CPSs are power plants and distribution grids, gas transmission systems, traffic control systems, water treatment and supply systems, transportation systems, and others [2,10]. A single security vulnerability in CPS can lead to catastrophic consequences, which ultimately can cause considerable financial and business loss, human lives, suffering, and others [7,8]. Thus, it is paramount that CPSs are free from security

C. Su et al. (Eds.): ISPEC 2022, LNCS 13620, pp. 140–157, 2022.
https://doi.org/10.1007/978-3-031-21280-2_8

vulnerabilities. However, it is challenging to test a functioning CPS to identify security issues or weaknesses. This is because a live CPS cannot afford even a single error or mistake introduced while performing the testing; there is a real possibility of the testing process damaging the CPS. Consider, for example, a security experiment that needs the introduction of spoofed sensor measurements in the control network of a CPS to simulate an attack. Allowing this experiment to be conducted on a live system will cause it to malfunction. Unfortunately, the CPS can not be stopped or interrupted for this purpose. Moreover, such security testing needs to be done periodically since security threats are continuously evolving.

CPS testbeds play an important role for the security analysis of the CPS [14]. The testbed environment emulates the actual behaviors of the different CPS components and simulates their interactions. This allows researchers and engineers to identify security issues in the designed systems before deploying them in the real world and continuously update the knowledge with evolving threats. Since the testbed mimics existing systems' behaviors, it is essential to ensure that different experiments launched in the testbed environment reflect real-world behavior as closely as possible. This raises significant challenges in the design of the CPS testbed itself.

The CPS testbed provides an environment to conduct experiments to study the behaviors of the concerned systems. Researchers [6,11–13], have identified several requirements for testbeds to conduct CPS centric experiments. Fidelity, repeatability, scalability, adaptability, cost-effectiveness, measurement precision, diversity, and safe experiment execution are the major requirements. These requirements form the minimum set to conduct the CPS experiments effectively. However, these do not fully satisfy the requirements for cybersecurity-related experiments, those requirements are not enough to ensure the security of the security-oriented testbeds. Researchers also have to ensure that one experiment can not get data from another experiment without authorization (intentionally or unintentionally) [9]. Also, shared hardware resources can be an attack vector or data leakage platform.

For security centric experiments, it is important to ensure that one experimental process cannot go outside of its run-time memory. If this is allowed to happen, then it can cause unintended program execution or memory corruption of other infected experiments' memory and processes. This would ultimately produce erroneous results. Therefore, we must deploy individual experiments in isolated environments to confine operations and data inside the allocated working memory area. It may require different components of a sizeable cyber-physical system to be deployed as multiple experiments, and these experiments may need to share specific data among them. An experiment can utilize another experiment's data to complete a specific task. Although different units depend on each other to reflect the whole system's activities, ensuring safe communication to exchange information among the isolated components is necessary. It is impossible to provide a communication mechanism among isolated nodes using inter-process communication (IPC).

In this paper, we propose a novel communication design leveraging the tuple space model to provide inter-experiment data sharing where experiment nodes are deployed in isolated manner. The idea of classic tuple space is based on the Linda Programming Model [5]. Our proposed framework ensures the reliability of the whole system incorporating the mechanisms of isolation of the nodes, safe communication among experiments, and an authorization module with well formed access control policies. Specific contributions of out work are noted in the following.

- Identifying design requirements for security experiment-oriented testbed.
- Proposing a novel design of inter-experiment secure communication leveraging the concept of tuple space.
- Modeling access control system to allocate system resources for the experiments and approve inter- communication requests.

2 Threat Model Relevant for the CPS Testbed

Before delving into our contributions, we would like to explain the threats that a security-oriented testbed must guard against. Experiments perform various attacks on different simulated physical models of different devices in the testbed. If an attack goes beyond any experiment run-time environment, it causes severe damage to another experiment, like modifying configuration files, input data sets, output results, and others. The testbed threats can mainly be classified into two groups: *(i) outsider threats* and *(i) insider threats* and are discussed in the following.

2.1 Outsider Threats

A testbed is vulnerable to threats that are initiated from outside of it. Malicious actors from the outside world can exploit the testbed to compromise it and gain confidential information from it. Outside attackers can compromise the testbed by exploiting vulnerabilities in the testbed's hardware and software resources. In this work, we assume the testbed is secured from outside threats.

2.2 Insider Threats

Insider threats are originated within the testbed itself. Multiple experiment nodes share testbed resources like hardware, software, attack library module, network I/O, and other essential resources while deployed on the testbed and executed at the same time. Without any preventive mechanism, an experiment can access information from another experiment by unauthorized means and can push malicious data into another experiment's memory space. We classify testbed insider threats into three groups: *(i) confidentiality threats*, *(ii) integrity threats*, and *(iii) availability threats*.

Confidentiality Threats: Critical Cyber Physical Systems (CCPS) have many critical units to provide services. Since the testbed simulates the actual behaviors of those systems, it can hold notable data about those critical units and proprietary information about the system organization. If a malicious entity gains access of an experiment node, it may also obtain significant architectural information or system vulnerabilities. This reveal of system knowledge may help the malicious entity to plan a more sophisticated attack in the testbed. Moreover, malicious organizations can use that information to gain business profits and defeat competitors in business market competition.

Integrity Threats: An erroneous input data or process can introduce faulty results or add bias to the experiment results. An experiment can intentionally or unintentionally violate the data integrity of other experiments, if attack and data isolation are not maintained properly. As experiments share the same testbed resources, if a set of attacks goes beyond a component's memory scope, then an erroneous evaluation may take place.

Availability Threats: A malicious experiment can hold the computing resources intentionally for indefinite time period to make the service/resources unavailable for other experiments. In this scenario, other experiments remain in the waiting queue for log time because of resource shortage. Our current scope of proposed method does not deal with this kind of threat.

3 Overview of Our CPS Testbed Structure

As most CCPSs are distributed and networked, a testbed should imitate the functionalities of a distributed networked system. Otherwise, the threats related to any distributed networked system can not be explored while performing security experiments in the testbed. This is why, in order to provide a platform for message-passing capabilities among the nodes, a network event simulator is required. This simulator is also responsible for managing and distributing resources among the experiment nodes. A bunch of experimental nodes together build the whole structure of a cyber-physical system. Figure 1 illustrates different components of a testbed that we require. The major components are *(i) testbed controller*, *(ii) experiment server*, *(iii) virtualization of experiment nodes*, *(iv) experiment controller layer*, and *(v) experiment nodes*.

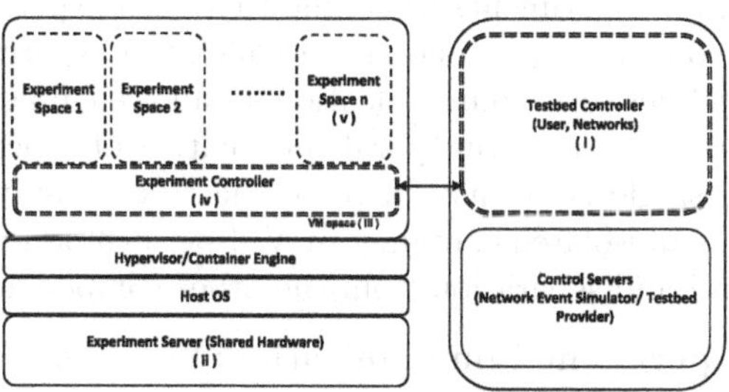

Fig. 1. Testbed structure.

The testbed controller (i) is responsible for managing resources for experiment nodes (v). It also provides services to allocate network address spaces for the experiment nodes as required by the experiment requirements. The controller has overall knowledge of the availability of resources, user space, node visualization, shell management, etc. It must be installed on a machine other than the experiment servers, allowing us to use resources in a request-response manner. This separation prevents experiment nodes from manipulating the control server's memory space. The system on which this controller is installed is known as the testbed control server.

Experiment servers(ii) provide the computing platform for experiment nodes. A single or multiple machines combined can provide the processing capability for experiment nodes. The number of experiments and connectivity among them is generally greater than the actual physical resources. Therefore, an abstraction of virtual machines (iii) and networking topology are supported based on containerization or hypervisor. One control node mapped to each owner of the experiment(s) will reside in the experiment control layer(iv). It is responsible for maintaining a gateway to the experiment space containing multiple nodes. A user, the experiment owner, can instantiate multiple nodes for the experiment. An experiment cannot have more than one owner. Experiment nodes are allocated resources from the experiment server(s). A hypervisor will run on the hardware of the experiment server to provide virtualization to the nodes.

4 Cybersecurity Centric Experiment Support in Testbed

There are some essential requirements for the testbed which play vital roles in providing a secure, efficient, and effective simulation environment and preventing improper experiment results. The most common requirements, identified by researchers [6,11–13], are *fidelity, repeatability, scalability, flexibility, cost-effectiveness, measurement accuracy, diversity, and safe execution of experiments.* In the following, we identify some essential cyber security-oriented testbed requirements in addition to the above-mentioned requirements. We also discuss their impact and influence on the testbed environment for conducting cybersecurity experiments in a safe manner.

Nodes and Experiments Isolation: To prevent unintended or malicious data exchange across experiments, an isolation mechanism is required to protect the data and process of an experiment. Assuming that each experiment has a single owner, this grants control over the nodes on which the experiment is executed. No inter-experiment network communication is allowed unless an authorized mechanism supports one. Moreover, parallel execution of processes (component functionality) on a single node may increase the risk of unintended influence. However, initializing an isolated container or VM per component can provide an extra layer of control and separation from the other components' functionality.

Secured Inter-Experiment Communication: Each experiment deployed on the testbed may represent a single component of an extensive system. Because separate units rely on one another to represent the activities of the entire system, it is necessary to ensure secure communication between the experiments. But before one experiment collaborates with another, a coordinated approval is necessary to make the collaboration secure. Moreover, the testbed must ensure the communication messages' confidentiality, integrity, and availability. Violation of these three aspects of security can compromise sensitive information or produce incorrect results. Since experiment outputs influence the real CCPS design, it would be vulnerable when erroneous results are considered to design and deploy the real system.

Attack Libraries: Users need to launch multiple attacks on different experiments based on the deployed system components in the testbed. Support of built-in attack libraries provides accessible interfaces to perform attack experiments. Distribution and execution of attack libraries can be done in three ways: *(i) scripts provided and run by the testbed, (ii) scripts pulled from third-party organizations*, and *(iii) scripts developed by the owner*. The best practice is that users don't need to write scripts or access third-party sources. Before adding attack scripts to the testbed, they must be tested and evaluated correctly to ensure their intended outputs. Also, the testbed must maintain attack script integrity once they are included in the testbed.

Monitoring Module and Attack Analytic: An experiment owner can spawn a dedicated monitoring node with predefined objectives. The monitoring module performs tasks to collect and analyze experiment activities. An attack analytic, a part of the monitoring module, generates insights for further actions with visualization and relevant reports from the collected data.

Experiment Checkpoints: Sometimes it is necessary to roll back experiments to a certain executed state so that users can review experimental decisions and reconfigure the setup. Experiment checkpoints are necessary to recover from wrong states caused by cybersecurity experiments [4]. They also provide a quick recovery option so that experiments become fault-tolerant.

Attack Confinement: Various security analyses are carried out across multiple experiments based on the deployed system components at different nodes. But security attack experiments may attempt to expose the component's security flaws. Attack scripts are executed with predetermined actions to observe their consequences on a predefined perimeter of the system. It is essential to protect the testbed to confine an attack and its effect to prevent intentional or unintentional damage to another experiment. So an attack can not go from one experiment run-time environment to another without proper authorization.

Experiment Data Confinement: Each experiment node has a different set of data, like configuration and design files, experiment results, attack scripts, etc., containing sensitive information about the system organization. Any data leakage event may compromise the sensitive information, which can cause many unwanted consequences. Moreover, data integrity is also essential to ensure that experiments generate correct results, which are considered while making design decisions in a real CCPS system to protect it from known and unknown security threats. However, data integrity may also be tampered with while data is shared and processed across experiments. Hence, the testbed needs to avoid these data leakage events where isolation can provide data confinement services.

5 Experiment Communication Model

Experiments are deployed as a combination of isolated nodes in the testbed. An isolated node of an experiment cannot communicate or share any data with other experiment nodes using the inter-process communication (IPC). But there are some scenarios where experiments need to exchange information to complete tasks. In this section, we identify and explain two types of communication required for our proposed security framework of communication in the testbed environment. They are: *(i) coordination communication* and *(ii) collaboration communication.*

Suppose, two experiments are active at the same time on the testbed and one experiment needs to access some data that another experiment contains. Any kind of communication that involves two nodes from different experiment is supported by the combined execution of coordination and collaboration communication. The coordination communication model (illustrated in Fig. 2) is occurred first to ensure the availability of resources, approval of the communication from etc. The actual intended communication or data sharing will not start before the coordination completes and the approval is received. Collaboration communication (illustrated in Fig. 3) starts when coordination is complete and nodes have received approval in the completed coordination process.

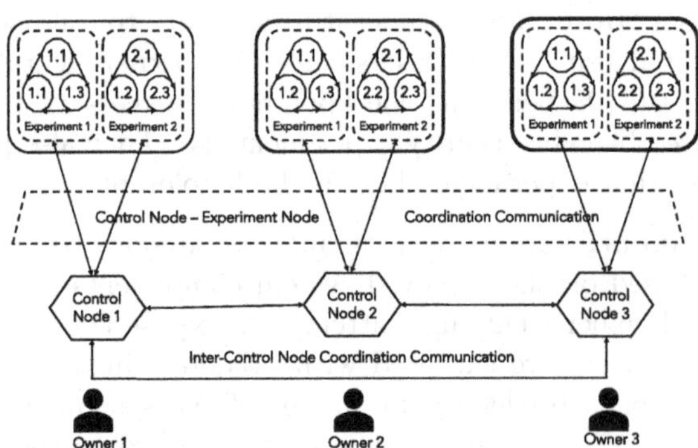

Fig. 2. Coordination communication.

Coordination Communication: A control node performs the main role in this communication model, where it sends predefined control messages to/from other experiment nodes. A control node acts as a coordinator on behalf of a user to initiate, manage, and terminate experiments in the testbed environment. A control node can send/receive coordination information (data access request, broadcast request, node summary, etc.) to/from the experiments it controls or the other control nodes. The control node also expects feedback if it sends messages to other control nodes or experiments. Figure 2 depicts the coordination communication model where two types of coordination communication may occur: (i) control-to-control, (ii) control-to/from-experiment. In coordination communication, no experiment data is shared. Coordination communication should occur first if two experiments need to collaborate (share data).

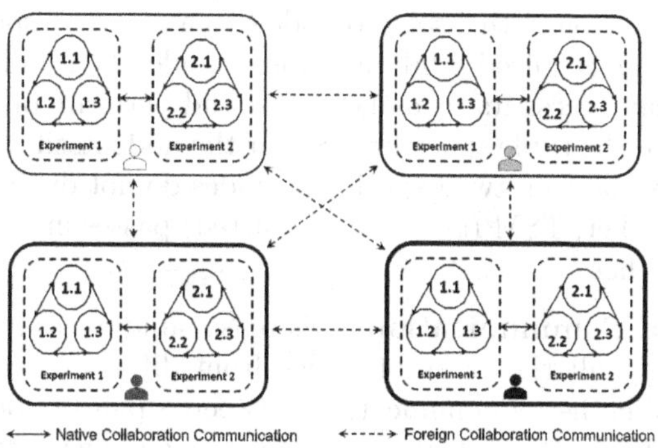

Fig. 3. Collaboration communication.

Collaboration Communication: The actual data transfer, labelled as collaboration of experiments, happens between two experiment nodes in this type of communication. No collaboration occurs without executing the coordination communication beforehand. In the collaboration communication, no control node is involved. The solid bi-directional arrows in Fig. 3 indicate this native collaboration where experiments under the same control collaborate (data transfer) with each other. In foreign collaboration communication (depicted in the Fig. 3 with dotted arrows), experiments from one control can communicate with experiments from another control node.

6 Overview of Experiment Execution on Testbed

In this work, we provide a system design for the testbed to provide control over communication among the experiments. Our proposed approach for inter-experiment communication leverages the technology of tuple space in an isolated environment. We assume that the testbed already has the facility of providing virtualization and isolation of nodes.

Experiment Initialization: When an owner wants to create experiments, a control node (allocating an isolated node) is instantiated first. A secure communication channel between a user and a control node is established to exchange necessary information. A control node is responsible for managing multiple experiment nodes for its owner. It passes a resources and privileges allocation request containing the necessary node configuration from the owner to the authorization module. After getting the approval, multiple isolated nodes are allocated with a defined networking topology among them. For each initialized node, a tuple space is initialized, which is required for future coordination or collaboration communication. Thus, an experiment is initialized in the testbed.

Inter-Experiment Secure Communication: When two nodes from different experiments (owned by the same or different user) need to communicate, secure communication via tuple space is used. A tuple space is a service that provides a dedicated memory region in the isolated node's local memory space to store data or remove data when required. Only a mapped node itself and the tuple space manager (TSM) can access its memory region and perform an action on it. All the operations with the tuple space by TSM or the node itself are assumed to be secured. In this mechanism, two experiment nodes do not directly communicate with each other; rather, TSM (assumed as trusted) passes information from one tuple space to another.

Authorization of Communication: It is reasonable to assume that the communication between all the pairs of nodes from different experiments is not allowed directly. Whether communication between a pair of nodes is allowed or not is defined by the access control policy. When one node needs to access information held by another one from a different experiment space, a communication request is sent to the authorization module via the control node. The approval decision is sent back to the control node after evaluating the predefined access control policy. The process of approving resource allocation undergoes the same approval procedure.

7 Inter-Experiment Secure Communications

Three types of communication channels are notably used in the testbed to fulfill the requirements of communication nature. Nodes from the same experiments communicate with each other via standard or specialized networking protocols without prior approval (called intra-experiment communication, illustrated as a dotted line in Fig. 4). Communication is performed using the IP address or hostname of the nodes.

The secured communication between the authorization module and any control node (illustrated as a solid arrow in Fig. 4) is another type of channel. The third type of communication is between two tuple spaces. Each node (experiment or control) is mapped with a tuple space (illustrated as a rectangular purple region attached to each node). The details of tuple space communication managed by a Tuple Space Manager (TSM) are described in Sect. 8. Figure 4 illustrates the step-by-step process of inter-experiment communication involving different channels and related components. The steps are explained in the following:

Send Data Access Request (DAR): The data requester node sends the request information to the control node of its own experiment space (we call it the requester control node) first, leveraging tuple space communication (step 1

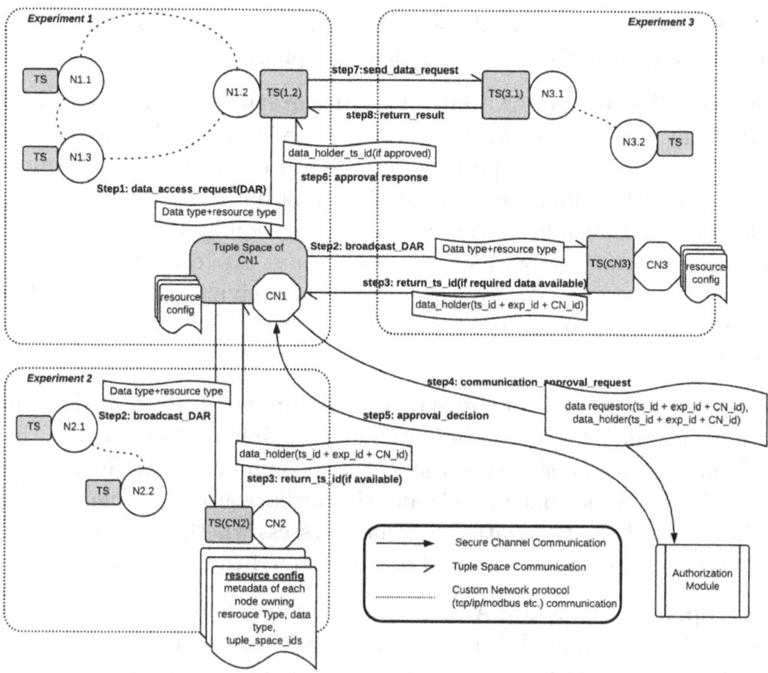

Fig. 4. Inter-experiment communication flow diagram.

from Fig. 4). The data requester does not know which node has the specific type of data that the requester wants. It only informs its own control node about the requirements of the specific data type. And in return, it only expects the identity of the data-holder tuple space so that it can start communication with it. No IP address or machine address of any node is disclosed in the whole communication process.

Broadcast DAR to Other Control Nodes: After receiving the DAR, the control node looks for the identity information of the requested data type from the past communication history that is stored in the *resource config*. A resource config file is maintained at every control node to provide necessary information about tuple space (TS) identities of experiment nodes it controls, experiment identities, mapping information between nodes and experiments, type of data each node holds, past communication history, TS identities of other control nodes, etc. This resource config file is updated from time to time if any event occurs at its own experiment spaces or other control nodes so that the config information remains consistent. Resource config files can also be updated when any previous approval decision is changed. If any approved active tuple space is found from the history as a data holder, no further approval is necessary. The TS id of the data holder is returned to the requester (go to step 6 as illustrated in Fig. 4). But if there is no history of prior approval of the same DAR, then a broadcast to all the other control nodes takes place (step 2 from Fig. 4). It relays the same message of DAR in this broadcasting phase.

Return Data/Resource Availability Information: After getting a broadcast DAR from any other control node, the receiving control node will look for the availability of the data type in its own resource config file. If there is any experiment node that holds the requested type of data, the corresponding control node will find that information in its resource config file and return the TS id of the data holder along with other information (experiment id, control node id, etc.) back to the requester control node. If a receiving control node finds no data availability of the requested type, 'NOT_AVAILABLE' is sent back (step 3 from Fig. 4).

Send Approval Request to the Authorization Module: Now the requester control node has the information (node TS id, experiment id, etc.) about the data requester and data holder. Using the secured communication channel already established between the control node and the authorization module, an approval request is sent to the authorization module to assess whether the requested data from the data holder can be accessed or not. (step 4 from Fig. 4).

Return Approval Decision: After receiving an approval request from a control node, the authorization module intends to check if the request complies with the access control policies. Details of the authorization module and access control can be found in Sect. 9. The approval decision is notified to the tuple space manager to update the *approved_communication_list*. Finally, the approval decision is sent back to the requester control node (step 5 from Fig. 4).

Return TS Id to Requester: Before passing the approval decision to the data requester node, the control node stores this information in the resource config file for future use. If the DAR is approved, the TS id of the data holder node is included in the approval response message. If the DAR is denied or data is not available, DENIED or NOT_AVAILABLE is included in the approval response message. No further communication takes place; this flow terminates here.

Send Data Request to Data Holder: If the DAR is approved, the awaited communication via tuple space takes place now. First, a data request message is passed from the requester to the holder via tuple space manager. This message includes the holder's TS id and data type.

Return Result to Data Requester: In response to the data request sent by the requester, the requested result is passed from the holder to the requester.

8 Testbed Tuple Space Design for Isolated Experiments

The tuple space model provides a mechanism which allows experiment nodes placed in an isolated environment share data without using any direct communication channel. In the following, we discuss the tuple space manager, tuple space operations, and tuple space transactions.

8.1 Tuple Space Manager-TSM

The TSM is a secured and trusted entity that performs data transfer operations from source tuple space to destination tuple space. A secured entity protects data from being modified or revealed to illegitimate subjects. Also, it does not analyze the tuple space content (called tuple) to disclose data to other entities or to learn more about data for itself. It needs to read a tuple from the sender tuple space and add it to the receiver tuple space. There is only one global TSM in the proposed security-oriented testbed. The TSM maintains an *approved_communication_list* that gets updated by the authorization module from time to time. The list is essential to crosscheck the authorization status of the incoming request to prevent malicious transactions.

8.2 Tuple Space Operation

The proposed framework supports three basic tuple space operations: *(i) write*, *(ii) take*, and *(iii) read* and described in the following.

Write(tuple): This operation provides the functionality to add a tuple within the mapped tuple space. It does not modify the tuple space contents. The sender node and the tuple space manager can execute this operation. The sender node uses this to add the tuple into the tuple space it owns. The TSM executes this operation by adding the tuple in the receiver node's tuple space.

Take(template tuple): This operation is called to execute an associative search for a tuple that matches the template. Once found, the tuple is deleted from the space and then returned to the tuple space owner's run-time memory. Only tuple space owners can use this function to remove tuples from their tuple space. The Tuple Space Manager cannot execute this operation because TSM does not have any rights to remove tuples from any tuple space.

Read(tuple): To read from the sender's tuple space, the TSM executes the read operation. This operation gets a tuple back from sender's tuple space to TSM's own memory space without removing from the source tuple space.

8.3 Tuple Space Transaction

This section provides the illustration (depicted in Fig. 5) of a tuple space transaction for communication between two isolated nodes. The tuple space manager is the main medium for passing contents(tuple) from sender tuple space to receiver tuple space. The TSM has access to all the tuple spaces whereas the nodes can access their respective ones.

There are two phases in communication: the request phase and the response phase. In the request phase, the sender node sends a message to the receiver node. In the response phase, the receiver node returns a message to the sender node. The returned response can be completely new information or serve as an acknowledgment for the tuple that has just been received. After sending the response message, the communication flow is terminated. Both request and

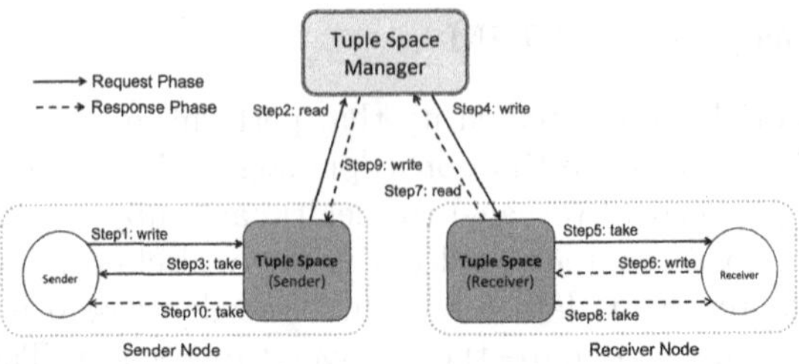

Fig. 5. Tuple space transaction.

response phase execute the same transaction process to share information which are depicted in the Fig. 5. If a node acts as sender in request phase then it is receiver in the response phase and vice versa.

9 Authorization Module (AM)

The authorization Module's entire structure and functionalities are explored and illustrated in this section, including the necessary examples. The resources and privilege allocation method are discussed to construct an isolated space for each experiment.

9.1 Experiment Resources and Operations

We need to define the resources required and the operations performed by the experiments. The authorization module acts as a reference monitor to control the operations of resources requested by the nodes. An experiment needs multiple hardware and software resources with different privileges to perform operations to complete the scheduled tasks. The control node is responsible for identifying and releasing both resources before an experiment. Some of the resources required by the experimental nodes to complete experiments are network topology configurations, internal memory, disk space, simulated physical models, attack libraries, PLC program control code, proprietary information, snapshots, loggers, status logs, tracers, experimental results, and others.

The experiments in this model perform three operations: *(i) read operation*, *(i) write operation*, and *(i) execute operation*. The *read operation* accesses various files and resources, such as configuration files, input data, programs, and so on. Experiments use *write operation* to write output results, modify configuration files, adjust input parameters, and so on. Finally, the *execute operation* allows experiments to run various attack scripts, simulated physical models, and other processes.

9.2 Resources and Privileges Allocation

A control node (CN) determines an experiment's required resources and privileges. After selecting the needed resources and rights, CN securely sends the list to the authorization module. In Algorithm 1, the details of resource and privilege allocation processes are given. Both the control node and the authorization module ensure that no experiment is given root permission or excessive resources and rights than required. In addition, the control node can terminate an experiment node after the simulation is completed.

Algorithm 1: Resources and privileges allocation

```
Input  : A list of resources (R) and privileges (P), and experiment id m.
Output: IsolatedNode for the experiment m under control node i.
Initialization:
R ← {R_1, R_2, R_3, ........R_r},
P ← {P_1, P_2, P_3, ........P_p};
CN_i → AM;
AM checks resources' availability and verify resources and privileges legitimacy
  for the CN;
if resource available then
    AM executes required OS command with R and P;
    IsolatedNode_{i,m} is deployed;
    AM returns a success message to CN with contained id;
else
    AM returns an error message to CN;
end if
```

9.3 Relationship Between Control Node, Experiments, and Subjects

The distinction between control nodes, experiments, and subjects is fundamental to the authorization module of this work. The relationship between control node, experiments, and subjects is depicted in Fig. 6. Usually, each node can perform three operations in the testbed, but in data sharing, only read operation is permitted. The other two operations, write and execute, are not allowed for data sharing.

Control Node: Every user has one control node, which acts as a single identity in the testbed environment. An authorized organization has only one control node but multiple control nodes. Violation of this requirement is often the cause of security violations in the proposed system.

Experiments: Each control node may have several experiments associated with it. On the other hand, one experiment must not be mapped to more than one control unit. Therefore, each experiment associated with the control node gains different resources and privileges based on its functionalities.

Subjects: A subject is a program in the system being executed. An experiment can generally spawn several subjects, but each subject is associated with only one experiment. A subject runs with all the privileges of its associated experiment.

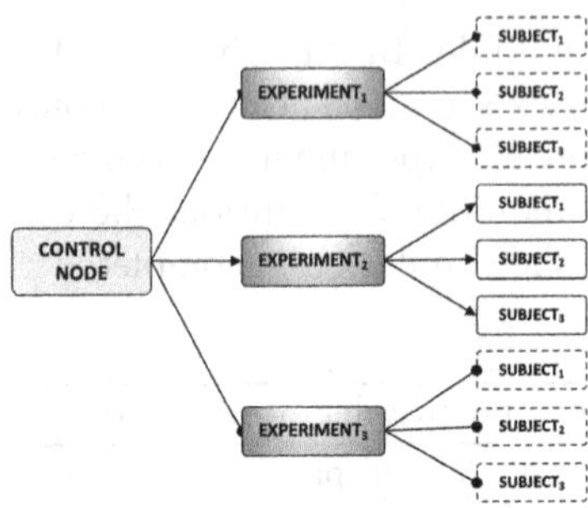

Fig. 6. Relationship between control node, experiments, and subjects.

9.4 Object Classification

To maintain data security and privacy, we classify objects(data) into three main categories. The object classes are the conflict of interest class, agreement class, and open class.

Conflict of Interest Class: The member objects of this type of class are in a conflict of interest and cannot be shared among their owner.

Agreement Class: Objects labelled with this class are in an agreement and can be shared among the agreement signing parties.

Open Class: Object data tagged with open class is for all. Any control node can send requests to get the data.

9.5 Control Node Identification

Each control node is labeled as a member of the conflict of interest class and the agreement class. The authorization module considers the control node's identity when making a data-sharing decision where the sender and receiver are from different control nodes. Experiments or subjects are not considered. Because experiment nodes from the same control node can share information without regard to security or policy constraints. We avoid experiments or subjects while the access control module approves data sharing to prevent this situation. When a control node is in a conflict of interest class or not in the agreement class, it will not receive data from that class's members.

9.6 Security Policy

In this section, we present some access control policies to ensure inter-experiment communication and testbed security and privacy. There are mainly two, native owner and foreign owner, communication scenarios.

Native Owner: In this case, we describe data sharing among various experiments when they are all from the same control node. Every node does not need to access data from every node. Experiment nodes must ensure data confidentiality. There are two principles when sharing data among experiments or subjects. Both principles are noted in the following.

Principle 1: *An experiment or a subject can not read data from other experiments or subjects if it violates the confidentiality of the data.*

Principle 2: *An experiment or a subject can read data from other experiments or subjects if they do not violate Principle 1.*

Foreign Owner: When there is a data-sharing request where the requester and data holder are from different control nodes, in this case, data sharing can be done if there is no conflict of interest among the experiments. If there is a conflict of interest, the authorization module must not approve data sharing. The conflict of interest issue is raised when the requester and the data holder are from the same conflict of interest class. Data sharing is also possible if there is an agreement between the requester and the data holder. Any control node can access the open class data. A control node puts in a request on behalf of its experiments and subjects. The authorization module depends on the object class and requester control node identity to make the decision. In the following, there are three principles for each type of object.

Principle 3: *A control node can read an object if they are not in the same conflict of interest class.*

Principle 4: *A control node can read an object if they are in the same agreement class.*

Principle 5: *A control node can read any object if objects are in the open class.*

10 Related Works

The Linux Policy Machine is proposed by [3] as the centralized reference monitor to provide secure inter-component communication in an isolated environment. In addition, they introduce tuple space to facilitate communication mechanisms for the isolated components. They may require regulated and secure access to system resources and the ability to collaborate and coordinate with one another. [9] propose an architecture, ISAAC, for performing security experiments on a testbed for smart grid systems. It's a cross-domain, re-configurable, and distributed framework that simulates data from power generation in operations. It allows researchers to develop, test, evaluate, and validate holistic cyber-physical security techniques for cyber-physical systems and the Smart Grid. [1] utilize simulation data from the Internet Scale Event and Attack Generation Environment (ISEAGE) to characterize the system architecture of a security testbed for PowerCyber developed at Iowa State University. [12] present EPIC framework that can accurately assess the effects of cyber-attacks on the cyber and physical dimensions of networked critical infrastructures (NCIs), such as power plants.

11 Conclusion and Future Directions

This paper identifies some requirements for cyber security-oriented testbeds to ensure the security of the testbed while carrying out various security experiments. Our designed communication mechanism using tuple space in context with isolated experiments provides desired protection against threats. We also recognize the significance of data sharing among organizations while avoiding conflicts of interest and protecting proprietary information. Our designed authorization module and access control policy prevent unauthorized access to data and communication.

In future, we will consider the TSM not trusted. Cryptographic algorithms or zero-trust-based solutions may come into use in that scenario. We will also detect availability threats based on testbed resource consumption and run time.

Acknowledgements. This work was supported in part through funding from the US Department of Energy under CID #DE-NE0008986, the US National Science Foundation under grant #1822118, the industry partners AMI, NIST, Cyber Risk Research, Statnett, New Push and ARL of the NSF IUCRC Center for Cybersecurity Analytics and Automation, and the Colorado State University. Any opinions, finding, and conclusions or recommendations expressed in this material are those of the authors and do not necessarily reflect the views of the DOE, the NSF, the industry partners, the University, or any other federal agencies.

References

1. Ashok, A., Hahn, A., Govindarasu, M.: A cyber-physical security testbed for smart grid: system architecture and studies. In: Proceedings of the Seventh Annual Workshop on Cyber Security and Information Intelligence Research, pp. 1–1 (2011)
2. Banerjee, A., Venkatasubramanian, K.K., Mukherjee, T., Gupta, S.K.S.: Ensuring safety, security, and sustainability of mission-critical cyber-physical systems. Proc. IEEE **100**(1), 283–299 (2011)
3. Belyaev, K., Ray, I.: Component-oriented access control for deployment of application services in containerized environments. In: Foresti, S., Persiano, G. (eds.) CANS 2016. LNCS, vol. 10052, pp. 383–399. Springer, Cham (2016). https://doi.org/10.1007/978-3-319-48965-0_23
4. Burtsev, A., Radhakrishnan, P., Hibler, M., Lepreau, J.: Transparent checkpoints of closed distributed systems in emulab. In: Proceedings of the 4th ACM European Conference on Computer Systems, pp. 173–186 (2009)
5. Carriero, N., Gelernter, D.: Linda in context. Commun. ACM **32**(4), 444–458 (1989)
6. Holm, H., Karresand, M., Vidström, A., Westring, E.: A survey of industrial control system testbeds. In: Buchegger, S., Dam, M. (eds.) Nordic Conference on Secure IT Systems, LNSC, vol. 9417, pp. 11–26. Springer, Cham (2015). https://doi.org/10.1007/978-3-319-26502-5_2
7. Kim, S., Heo, G., Zio, E., Shin, J., Song, J.G.: Cyber attack taxonomy for digital environment in nuclear power plants. Nuclear Eng. Technol. **52**(5), 995–1001 (2020)
8. Line, M.B., Tøndel, I.A., Jaatun, M.G.: Cyber security challenges in smart grids. In: 2011 2nd IEEE Pes International Conference and Exhibition on Innovative Smart Grid Technologies, pp. 1–8. IEEE (2011)
9. Oyewumi, I.A., et al.: ISAAC: the idaho cps smart grid cybersecurity testbed. In: 2019 IEEE Texas Power and Energy Conference (TPEC), pp. 1–6. IEEE (2019)
10. Shi, J., Wan, J., Yan, H., Suo, H.: A survey of cyber-physical systems. In: 2011 International Conference on Wireless Communications and Signal Processing (WCSP), pp. 1–6. IEEE (2011)

11. Siaterlis, C., Garcia, A.P., Genge, B.: On the use of emulab testbeds for scientifically rigorous experiments. IEEE Commun. Surv. Tutorials **15**(2), 929–942 (2012)
12. Siaterlis, C., Genge, B., Hohenadel, M.: Epic: a testbed for scientifically rigorous cyber-physical security experimentation. IEEE Trans. Emerging Top. Comput. **1**(2), 319–330 (2013)
13. Smadi, A.A., Ajao, B.T., Johnson, B.K., Lei, H., Chakhchoukh, Y., Al-Haija, Q.A.: A comprehensive survey on cyber-physical smart grid testbed architectures: requirements and challenges. Electronics **10**(9), 1043 (2021)
14. Sridhar, S., Hahn, A., Govindarasu, M.: Cyber-physical system security for the electric power grid. Proc. IEEE **100**(1), 210–224 (2011)

IoT Security

Robust Anomaly Detection via Radio Fingerprinting in LoRa-Enabled IIoT

Subir Halder(✉) and Thomas Newe

CONFIRM Centre and University of Limerick, Limerick, Ireland
{subir.halder,thomas.newe}@ul.ie

Abstract. Long Range (LoRa) communications are gaining popularity in the Industrial Internet of Things (IIoT) domain due to their large coverage and high energy efficiency. However, LoRa-enabled IIoT networks are susceptible to cyberattacks mainly due to their wide transmission window and freely operated frequency band. This has led to several categories of cyberattacks. However, existing intrusion detection systems are inefficient in detecting compromised device due to the dense deployment and heterogeneous devices. This work introduces Hawk, a distributed anomaly detection system for detecting compromised devices in LoRa-enabled IIoT. Hawk first measures a device-type specific physical layer feature, Carrier Frequency Offset (CFO) and then leverages the CFO for fingerprinting the device and consequently detecting anomalous deviations in the CFO behavior, potentially caused by adversaries. To aggregate the device-type specific CFO behavior profile efficiently, Hawk uses federated learning. To the best of our knowledge, Hawk is the first to use a federated learning method for anomaly-based intrusion detection in LoRa-enabled IIoT. We perform extensive experiments on a real-world dataset collected using 60 LoRa devices, primarily to assess the effectiveness of Hawk against passive attacks. The results show that Hawk improves the detection accuracy by 8% and reduces the storage overhead by 40% than the state-of-the-art solutions.

Keywords: Anomaly detection · Carrier frequency offset · Federated learning · Industrial IoT · LoRa communication

1 Introduction

The growing adoption of Industrial Internet of Things (IIoT) coupled with Internet, cloud computing and machine learning into the smart manufacturing space has changed all aspects of the production process. For instance, smart manufacturing applications that integrate smart switches, thermostats, robots and cloud manufacturers to monitor and interact with production systems to improve productivity, delivery, reduced labor and energy costs. While smart manufacturing and logistics have equally adopted IIoT, significant concerns have increased about the security and privacy of digitally augmented manufacturing spaces.

C. Su et al. (Eds.): ISPEC 2022, LNCS 13620, pp. 161–178, 2022.
https://doi.org/10.1007/978-3-031-21280-2_9

Particularly, due to the weak security protection capability of IIoT devices, several attack surfaces and complex application environments, smart manufacturing spaces are exposed to cyberattacks [1]. Once an IIoT device is under attack, it might force causing chaos in the supply chain and even affecting the safety of human beings. Hence, as a precaution for future production process failure and safety of human beings, early cyberattack detection is of significant importance.

In the IIoT setting, it is expected that several hundreds of low-power IIoT devices will provide service for a span of typically five to ten years without or limited maintenance. To support these requirements, Low-Power Wide-Area Networks (LPWANs) have been developed. Among all available LPWANs, Long Range (LoRa) communication [2] is widely used as it is an open-source technology in the physical layer, robust in the unlicensed sub-GHz Industrial band and offers noise free, fading resilient and long range communication. However, LoRa-enabled IIoT is vulnerable to cyberattacks as it uses a wider transmission window than conventional wireless techniques, e.g., WiFi, which gives sufficient time for an adversary to launch passive attacks, e.g., Denial of Service (DoS).

To defend against cyberattacks, several security schemes use cryptographic mechanisms like message authentication code [3] and encryption technique [4] in LoRa-enabled networks. Although cryptographic mechanisms are successful to authenticate, it is possible for an adversary to apply reverse engineering for retrieving security keys. Hence, as an alternative to existing cryptographic solutions, Intrusion Detection Systems (IDSs) leveraging radio fingerprinting have recently received significant attention. Radio fingerprinting uses the device-specific signal imperfections introduced by the radio frequency circuitry in the physical layer to obtain a *fingerprint* of the IIoT device, which is intrinsic to the analogue device and cannot be imitated by the adversaries. These imperfections include Carrier Frequency Offset (CFO), In-phase and Quadrature (IQ) imbalance, and power amplifier non-linearity, among others. One of the major benefits of radio fingerprinting based IDS is that it offers security without generating computational overhead on the IIoT devices. This primarily motivates us to design an IDS by leveraging radio fingerprinting in LoRa-enabled IIoT.

In recent years, numerous IDSs were proposed [5,6] by leveraging radio fingerprinting in IIoT. Note that designed IIoT devices have a well-defined and stable radio signature. However, the feature of radio signature changes considerably when an IIoT device is compromised [7]. Therefore, extracting the feature is the most critical aspect of radio fingerprinting based IDS. Recently, several handcrafted features have been assumed including IQ imbalance [8], time-frequency statistics [9] and CFO [10], while designing IDS. However, most of these IDSs exhibit a high false alarm rate and often need manual modification, making it unsuitable in practice [11]. Further, training a model characterizing normal device behavior is aggravated in the IIoT setting as there are hundreds of IIoT devices, which makes it challenging to detect anomalous behavior that deviates from normal behavior. In this context, we argue that Federated Learning (FL) is a suitable tool for distributed training of Machine Learning (ML) model and subsequent detection of anomalous behavior. In FL, every local node uses its locally collected data to train a local model and sends the local model to a central aggregator node. The central aggregator node aggregates the received local models into a global model using a federated average algorithm, and then transmits back the global model to the local nodes. As the local node does not send raw data to the central aggregator node, FL gives us significant privacy benefit [12]. This is specifically critical in IIoT if behavioral data of IIoT devices are compromised, adversaries can profile the production and operational related data of the manufacturing company, hence potentially violating privacy.

Contributions. We present Hawk, a distributed IDS for detecting compromised devices in LoRa-enabled IIoT. Hawk exploits hardware imperfections of IIoT devices, where signals sent by such hardware produce offset in frequency at the receiver and measure fine-grained CFOs of transmitting devices, which are then used to fingerprint the devices. The rationale behind CFO is that it is more reliant on the hardware behavior than channel behavior [13], making it more reliable for IIoT scenarios. The contributions of this work are as follows:

- To the best of our knowledge, we are the first to present a comprehensive analysis of CFO-based IDS for LoRa-enabled IIoT. Based on our analysis, we design a scalable radio fingerprinting framework based on a deep metric learning-powered CFO extractor.
- We propose Hawk, a novel distributed anomaly-based IDS, which builds device-type specific detection models based on the devices' normal CFO behavior for detecting the adversary. Hawk is the first to apply FL for aggregating anomaly-detection profiles for detecting the adversary in LoRa-enabled IIoT.
- We perform extensive experiments on a real-world LoRa-enabled IIoT *Deployment* dataset [10]. The results show that Hawk achieves the highest detection accuracy of 97.36% while enjoying the least system complexity and the lowest training time.

Organization. We organize the rest of the paper as follows. Section 2 reviews the related work. In Sect. 3, we present the system model. Section 4 describes the detail design of Hawk. In Sect. 5, we evaluate the performance of Hawk and compare them to the state-of-the-art. Finally, Sect. 6 concludes this work.

2 Related Work

Nowadays, intrusion detection in IIoT have attracted significant interest from academia and industrial domains. We present here some works more relevant in our context.

Machine Learning-Based IDS. In the recent past, significant achievements have been made in cyberattack detection by designing numerous approaches using radio fingerprinting coupled with ML. For example, many radio fingerprinting based IDSs [14,15] have been proposed using Support Vector Machine (SVM). To detect malicious application(s) or malware within an IoT environment, a threat hunting model has been designed using multikernel SVM in [14].

The authors use a meta-heuristic feature selection technique to extract optimum features and minimize computational overhead. Wang et al. [15] proposed SLoRa, a lightweight benign device detection scheme using SVM. SLoRa uses two radio fingerprinting features, i.e., CFO and link signature, to identify a benign device. A novel device fingerprinting technique has been designed to identify LoRa devices in [10] by exploiting spectrogram and Convolutional Neural Network (CNN). To detect intrusion in IIoT, Huong et al. [16] designed an IDS based on FL architecture. The proposed IDS uses a hybrid model, a combination of Variational Autoencoder (VAE) and Long-Short Term Memory (LSTM), to improve detection accuracy.

Traffic Classification. To improve anomaly detection, Yan et al. [5] proposed a hinge classification algorithm based on mini-batch gradient descent. The experimental results show that the proposed solution improved the training efficiency and accuracy of the model. Dong et al. [18] examined the privacy leakage issue by evaluating network traffic in complex and realistic IoT networks. The result reveals that by utilizing the temporal relationships between packets of individual devices, one can reliably identify the device. Perdisci et al. [17] designed IoTFinder, an IoT device identification system by fingerprinting DNS traffic. Unlike earlier works, as a promising security approach, traditional fixed rule based method has been developed for malicious traffic detection technique in [19]. Abdel-Basset et al. [6] designed a deep learning model to identify intrusions from network traffic. The model learns the local representations of network traffic using local Gated Recurrent Units (GRUs). Lu et al. [20] introduced a deep belief network based cyberattack detection scheme for industrial system. They used an evolutionary algorithm to automatically tune the adjustable parameters of the deep belief network. A locality-sensitive hash function has been used to generate traffic signature and subsequent device fingerprinting in [21]. The experimental results show that the proposed approach improves the detection accuracy significantly.

Difference from Existing Works. Our work differs from the aforementioned works in several ways. First, we use CFO as a device-type specific radio fingerprint to identify a specific benign device. Second, our designed IDS performs dynamic detection of any unknown cyberattacks that deviate from the normal behavior of the IIoT device, as it only models normal network traffic. Third, we use GRU, which can be learned utilizing a small amount of training data, allowing Hawk to be trained faster, and work in almost real-time anomaly detection in live network traffic. Last but not the least, we perform experiments on real-world *Deployment* dataset collected using LoRa devices, whereas, most of the previous works used non-LoRa devices.

3 System Overview

This section briefly discusses the models used in Hawk. Particularly, Sect. 3.1 presents the system model. Section 3.2 introduces the threat model. Finally, we present the assumptions in Sect. 3.3.

3.1 System Model

This work assumes a smart manufacturing environment, where hundreds of heterogeneous IIoT devices are connected through a LoRa network, as shown in Fig. 1. Hawk is based on training a model with CFOs in an IIoT device's communication flows and identifying abnormal CFOs caused by the adversary that are inconsistent with the normal communications of the IIoT device in question. We use an FL approach to train the detection model for anomaly detection. The Hawk system comprises of two main modules, namely, local security service and remote security service. To adopt the FL approach, the local security service locally trains the anomaly detection model, which it sends to the remote security service, who aggregates them to a global detection model and disseminates this global detection model back to the local security service. The major functionalities of the two modules are as follows.

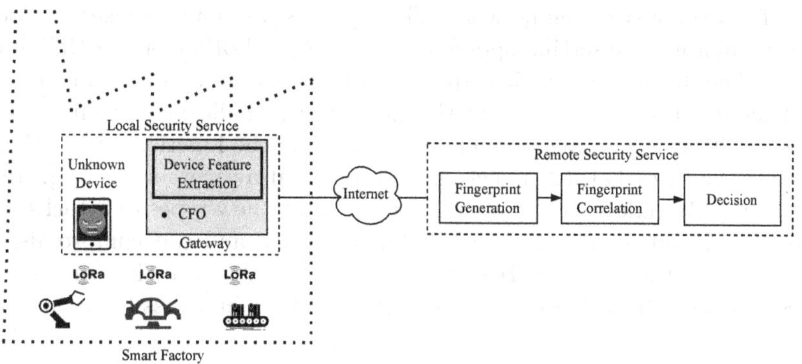

Fig. 1. The Hawk system model.

Local Security Service. It monitors the IIoT devices and performs anomaly detection to identify compromised IIoT devices. In Hawk, the local security service acts as a local access point to the Internet, to which the IIoT devices are connected through the LoRa network. It consists of a anomaly detection component. Once a new IIoT device is connected to the network, the local security service obtains a radio fingerprint to uniquely identify the IIoT device. The anomaly detection component observes the communications of IIoT devices and detects any deviation in normal communication behavior that is potentially caused by an adversary.

Remote Security Service. It aggregates the IIoT device-type specific anomaly detection model trained by the local security service in the system. In Hawk, remote security service can be a service provider, e.g., Google, Microsoft, Amazon. Once a new IIoT device is found in the local network, the local security service identifies its device-type specific radio fingerprint and retrieves the subsequent anomaly detection model for this specific IIoT device from the remote security service. Additionally, the remote security service aggregates and updates the device-type specific radio fingerprinting anomaly detection models provided by the local security service.

In Hawk, we train the anomaly detection model iteratively to gradually improve the accuracy of the detection model, as additional training data becomes available. We can perform this repetitive training procedure either regularly or until the global detection model attains a certain level of convergence, e.g., the detection model does not improve considerably anymore. We discuss more details about the FL approach in Sect. 4.2.

3.2 Threat Model

The primary goal of Hawk is to detect passive attacks on IIoT devices so that the incident response team can take suitable countermeasure, e.g., by thwarting the targeted devices from being compromized or separating compromized devices from the rest of the network. This work assumes an attacker (insider or outsider) capable of inserting spoofed devices into a LoRa-enabled IIoT infrastructure. The illegitimate devices spoof real IIoT devices and try to gain access to restricted services of the network and perform malicious activities. These malicious activities may include: (1) compromising the functionality of the system (e.g., DoS attacks), (2) injecting false physical measurements (e.g., replay attack), and (3) building the conditions to facilitate new types of attacks in the future. We do not assume insiders that have access and can compromise real devices used in the network. However, we consider that attackers use spoofed devices that imitate real IIoT system operations to gain access to the network.

3.3 Assumption

In this work, we assume that an adversary can compromise one or more devices in different local networks under a local security service. We also assume that a compromised device can inject arbitrary traffic in the LoRa network. Furthermore, we assume that an adversary has complete knowledge of the operations and parameters of the Hawk. However, an adversary cannot compromise Hawk. As the local security service is the device implementing security in the smart manufacturing environment, we assume that an adversary cannot compromise the local security service.

4 Hawk Design

This section presents the technical details about Hawk.

4.1 IIoT Device's Radio Fingerprinting Features

LoRa-enabled IIoT device uses Chirp Spread Spectrum (CSS) modulation in physical layer, which employs linear chirps for communication. Note that the frequency increases or decreases linearly with time in CSS modulation. In this work, we utilize the preamble part of LoRa packets to obtain fine-grain CFO estimation. Let $u[nT_s]$ and $y[nT_s]$ be the transmitted baseband signal and the received baseband signal in digital form, respectively, where n is the number of samples and T_s is the sampling interval. We can mathematically express the basic chirp of $y[nT_s]$ as:

$$y[nT_s] = u[nT_s]e^{j2\pi f_{tx}t}e^{-j2\pi f_{rx}nT_s} = u[nT_s]e^{j2\pi \Delta f nT_s},$$

where f_{tx} and f_{rx} are the carrier frequencies of transmitting and receiving IIoT devices, respectively, and $\Delta f = f_{tx} - f_{rx}$ is the CFO. In LoRa, the ideal instantaneous frequency of baseband signal $u[nT_s]$ increases linearly from $-\frac{B}{2}$ to $\frac{B}{2}$ due to CSS modulation, where B is the channel bandwidth. However, in presence of Δf, the actual instantaneous frequency of $u[nT_s]$, $f[nT_s]$ become:

$$f[nT_s] = -\frac{B}{2} + \Delta f + \frac{B}{T}nT_s,$$

where T is the symbol duration. Due to linearity of $f[nT_s]$, our course-grain estimation of Δf is as follows:

$$\Delta f_{cg} = \frac{1}{L}\sum_{n=0}^{L-1} f[nT_s] = \frac{1}{L}\sum_{n=0}^{L-1} f[nT_s], \tag{1}$$

where L is the symbol length, which is defined as:

$$L = \frac{T}{T_s} = \frac{2^\alpha}{BT_s},$$

where α is the spreading factor ($7 \leq \alpha \leq 12$). Based on the estimated Δf_{cg}, we can derive the compensated baseband signal as follows:

$$y'[nT_s] = y[nT_s]e^{-j2\pi\Delta f_{cg}t} = y[nT_s]e^{-j2\pi\Delta f_{cg}nT_s}. \tag{2}$$

Note that the estimated Δf_{cg} in Eq. (1) contains residual frequency offset, which must be derived to achieve fine-grain CFO. We employ the repeating property of preambles [10] to determine fine-grain CFO, Δf_{fg}. Based on the repeating property of preambles, we estimate Δf_{fg} as:

$$\Delta f_{fg} = -\frac{1}{2\pi T_s L}\angle\left(\sum_{n=0}^{L-1} y'[nT_s]\cdot y'^*[(n+L)T_s]\right), \tag{3}$$

where $\angle\cdot$ provides the angle of the variable and $(\cdot)^*$ signifies conjugation. Since the phase of a signal can be ranged from $-\pi$ to π, the range of Δf_{fg} can be estimated using Eq. (3) as follows:

$$|\Delta f_{fg}| < \frac{\pi}{2\pi T_s L} = \frac{B}{2^{\alpha+1}}.$$

Note that during LoRa transmission in a typical setting of $\alpha = 7$ and $B = 125$ kHz, the frequency drift of the oscillator is within ±488.3 Hz [10]. In contrast, the frequency drift of the oscillator becomes nearly 8.68 kHZ for a carrier frequency of 868 MHz [22], which is significantly higher than 488.3 Hz. Considering this oscillator behavior, we must use coarse-grain estimation before fine-grain estimation to reduce the residual offset. Therefore, using Eqs. (1) and (3), our overall estimated CFO is:

$$\begin{aligned}\Delta \widehat{f} &= \Delta f_{cg} + \Delta f_{fg} \\ &= \frac{1}{L}\sum_{n=0}^{L-1} f[nT_s] - \frac{1}{2\pi T_s L}\angle\left(\sum_{n=0}^{L-1} y'[nT_s]\cdot y'^{*}[(n+L)T_s]\right). \end{aligned} \tag{4}$$

4.2 Model Training Approach

We train the GRU model using signals collected at numerous local security services, by monitoring IIoT devices within a LoRa-enabled IIoT network. Specifically, each local security service monitors the IIoT devices to training its anomaly detection model in a LoRa-enabled IIoT network. We use FL to achieve distributed learning of models. The rationale behind FL approach is that it is a privacy-preserving and communication efficient approach. Most importantly, in smart manufacturing scenarios, the FL approach is suitable as: (i) data is highly distributed in nature, and (ii) different LoRa-enabled IIoT networks contribute distinct amounts of data. Note that the availability of training data at every local security service depends on the duration that an IIoT device has been in the network, and the number of interactions between the IIoT device and local security service, which varies among networks.

Figure 2 illustrates the FL process used in Hawk. In Step ❶, each local security service having connected devices of a specific type receives a detection profile for this type from the remote security service. So, the remote security service sends the initial GRU model to the local security service. At the beginning of Hawk, initial GRU model is random, otherwise it is already trained via numerous rounds of the following process. In Step ❷, the local security service trains the local GRU model using individual CFO of the device. Once the training is completed, the local security service generates the local GRU model parameter updates, and send them to the remote security service in Step ❸. In Step ❹, the remote security service aggregates all the received local GRU models to enhance the global GRU model, following the process as defined in Definition 1. Finally, in Step ❺, the remote security service sends the updated global GRU model to the local security service. The local security service then used the updated global GRU model to detect anomaly.

Definition 1 (Global Model Aggregation). Given m participating IIoT devices with their associated model weights $\omega_1, \cdots, \omega_m$ trained by the corresponding number of CFO samples $\Delta\widehat{f}_1, \cdots, \Delta\widehat{f}_m$. We define the global model G, which aggregates the local models as follows:

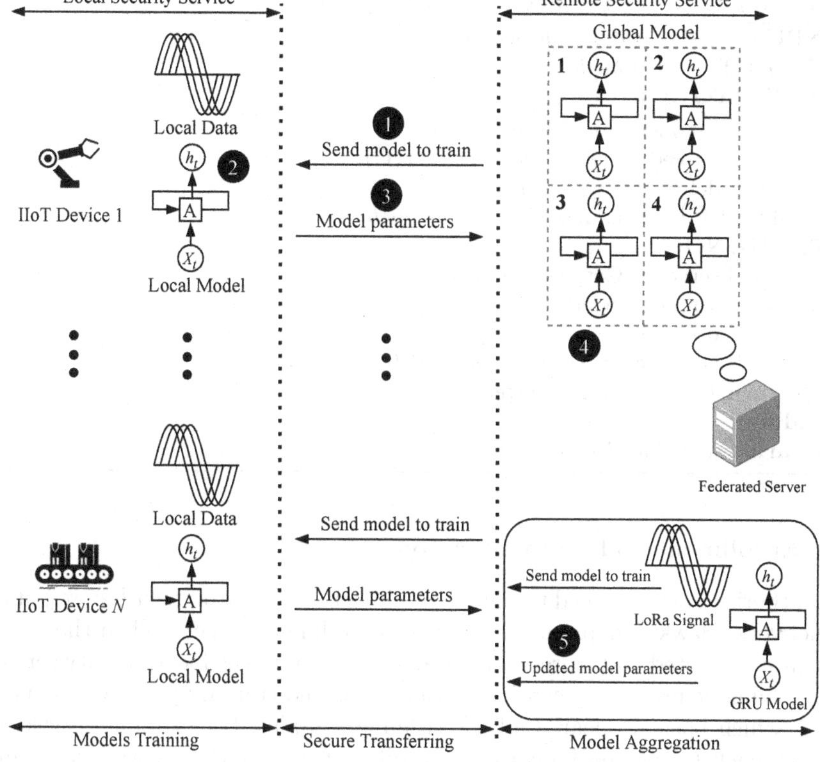

Fig. 2. Overview of model training approach.

$$G = \sum_{j=1}^{m} \frac{\Delta \widehat{f_j}}{\Delta \widehat{f_{ac}}} \omega_j,$$

where $\Delta \widehat{f_{ac}} = \sum_{j=1}^{m} \Delta \widehat{f_j}$.

FL Training. We propose Algorithm 1 to train GRU model. In Algorithm 1, m is the number of participating IIoT devices, nT_s is the data samples, Y is the dataset of IIoT devices and G is the trained global model. At the initializing phase, both global and local models parameters are initialized to use them in the training procedure. The primary objective of Algorithm 1 is to find a global GRU model based on local models trained at the local security service. This reduces the communication overheads by limiting unnecessary sending of the number of updates to the local security Service. In Hawk, the training only needs to be performed once as the trained model can extract the unique fingerprint from newly joined (out-of-library) devices. The training devices are not essentially the same devices as the ones for enrollment and authentication.

Algorithm 1. Model Training using Federated Learning

INPUT: Pre-trained and device's data
OUTPUT: Global model
INITIALIZING:

Pre-trained model $\rightarrow$ Federated server
Parameter = Federated server (m, nT_s, Y, G)
Global model = Set (w, F, m)
Local model = Global model (Set (*parameters*))

TRAINING:

Federated server = Get *(Global model)*
Federated server $\rightarrow$ Send *(Local model)*
for $i = 1$ to m **do**
    Each IIoT device = Train *(Local model)*
    return *Local model parameters*
end for
return *Updated model parameters*

4.3 Enrollment and Authentication

The authorized devices need to send several packets for enrollment before joining the network. Hawk first preprocesses these enrollment packets. Then the fingerprints are extracted and stored in a database located in the local security service. The enrollment procedure can be considered as the training phase of the GRU model, which basically learns all the training samples. For example, Hawk collects 100 packets from each device for enrollment. Our authentication procedure consists of two parts, namely, anomaly detection and device-type classification. The anomaly detection decides whether the device is authorized (previously enrolled) or not. In contrast, the device-type classification further determines its type. Once a device is successfully authenticated, it is allowed administrative access to the network (or, local security service).

4.4 Anomaly Detection

By determining $\Delta\widehat{f}$ from observation of carrier frequencies, we can fingerprint transmitter IIoT devices. We exploit this in designing Hawk, a CFO-based IDS for LoRa-enabled IIoT. To determine anomaly in $\Delta\widehat{f}$, we process signals in batches of N (e.g., 10) and compute the CFO in the k-th signal using Eq. (4) as $\Delta\widehat{f}_{k-N}, \Delta\widehat{f}_{k-(N-1)}, \cdots, \Delta\widehat{f}_{k-1}$. We then pre-trained a model using GRU. Particularly, the GRU model calculates a probability estimate p_k for each CFO $\Delta\widehat{f}_k$ based on the batch of N signals following the approach as demonstrated in [23]. The rationale behind using GRU is that it is computationally less intensive and provides similar accuracy as other RNN methods. Finally, we evaluate the sequence of probability estimates, i.e., $p_1, p_2, \cdots, p_k$ to determine potential anomalies. Specifically, if the occurrence probability p_k of $\Delta\widehat{f}_k$ falls below a detection threshold, we conclude that the CFO sequence is deemed anomalous and an alarm is generated.

Detection Process. As mentioned earlier, our intrusion detection approach is based on estimating the anomaly occurrence probability by observing an individual signal given the batch of received signals. The motivation behind this approach is the recent observation in the work [10] that LoRa-enabled IIoT device communications follow specific characteristic patterns. Communication signal generated by adversary or IIoT malware, however, does not follow these patterns and can hence be detected. In Hawk, the detection model first calculates an occurrence probability p_k of $\Delta\widehat{f}_k$ given the batches of N signals $< \Delta\widehat{f}_{k-N}, \Delta\widehat{f}_{k-(N-1)}, \cdots, \Delta\widehat{f}_{k-1} >$ as follows:

$$p_k = P\left(\Delta\widehat{f}_k | < \Delta\widehat{f}_{k-N}, \Delta\widehat{f}_{k-(N-1)}, \cdots, \Delta\widehat{f}_{k-1} >\right). \tag{5}$$

In Eq. (5), parameter N is a property of the used GRU model and signifies the length of the history, i.e., the number of CFOs that the GRU model considers while calculating the probability estimate. To detect an anomaly and subsequent generation of an alarm, we define the anomalous signals as follows.

Definition 2 (Anomalous signals). Baseband signal $y_k[nT_s]$ mapped to CFO $\Delta\widehat{f}_k$ is anomalous, if its occurrence probability p_k is below a detection threshold δ, i.e., $p_k < \delta$.

We conducted an extensive experimental analysis of the probability estimates given by device-type specific detection models for both malicious and benign traffic for the datasets illustrated in Sect. 5. We found that $\delta = 0.014$ provides a significant difference between benign and malicious traffic for IIoT devices. This motivates us to set $\delta = 0.014$ for distinguishing benign and malicious traffic. Note that triggering an alarm signal each time a malicious signal is monitored would lead to several false positive detections. The increase in false positive detections will further intensify as a benign signal might contain noise that is not included by the GRU model, resulting in low occurrence probability estimation. Therefore, to avoid triggering a false alarm, Hawk generates an alarm signal only in the case where a significant number of signals in a batch of consecutive signals are anomalous. We define the anomaly triggering condition as follows.

Definition 3 (Anomaly triggering condition). Given a batch of N consecutive signals $Y = (y_1[nT_s], \cdots, y_N[nT_s])$ and their corresponding CFOs $F = (\Delta\widehat{f}_1, \cdots, \Delta\widehat{f}_N)$, we generate an alarm signal, if the fraction of anomalous signals in Y is more than an anomaly generating threshold γ, i.e., $\frac{|\{\Delta\widehat{f}_k \in F | p_k < \delta\}|}{N} > \gamma$.

We propose an intrusion detection approach to identify anomaly by the RNN classifier in Algorithm 2. We initially build a model for all N IIoT devices based on CFO, $\widehat{f}_k$. We then estimate the occurrence probability p_k and anomaly generating threshold γ during the classification stage. Finally, we generate an intrusion alarm once the fraction of anomalous signals in Y is more than an anomaly generating threshold γ.

5 Experimental Evaluation

This section first introduces the implementation of Hawk, followed by the detailed performance evaluation.

Algorithm 2. Anomaly detection

INPUT: Y, G, F, γ
OUTPUT: Intrusion alarm

for $k = 1$ to N **do**
  Calculate p_k
  if $\frac{|\{\Delta \widehat{f}_k \in F | p_k < \delta\}|}{N} > \gamma$ **then**
    return Intrusion
  else
    return $\neg$ Intrusion
  end if
end for

5.1 Experimental Setup and Dataset

Dataset. We use a real-world *Deployment* dataset [10], which was generated from 60 LoRa-enabled IIoT devices of four models, i.e., Pycom LoPy4 (D1–D45), mbed SX1261 shield (D46–D50), Pycom FiPy (D51–D55) and Dragino SX1276 shield (D56–D60). For each device, 3000 packets were collected by setting the transmission interval as 1 s in an indoor environment with LOS between the device and the receiver. During data collection, the receiver (i.e., local security service) was a USRP N210 Software Defined Radio (SDR) and configured with $\alpha = 7$, $B = 125$ kHz, carrier frequency 868.1 MHz and sampling rate 1 MS/s. The *Deployment* dataset contains 26 sub-datasets, each of which is an Hierarchical Data Format version 5 (HDF5) file. Each HDF5 file consists of a number of LoRa packets (IQ samples of preamble part) and respective device indexes. The preamble part of LoRa signals in the dataset contains 8,192 IQ samples. To avoid the processing of complex numbers by the FL model, IQ data samples have been divided into I (real part) and Q (imaginary part) branches. Hence, the input dimension of the FL model in Hawk is 2×8192.

Model Training. We trained our learning model using 1000 packets from each of D1-D40. We used Adam as the model optimizer and set the initial learning rate as 0.001. The learning rate decays every time the validation loss does not decrease for 10 epochs with a drop factor of 0.3. We chose the number of epochs that each IIoT device trains its local model as 15 and set the number of communication rounds between devices and local security service as 4. Hence, the local models are trained with 60 epochs. We set the mini-batch size to 32 and the L_2 regularization factor as 0.0001. The model training stops once the maximum 60 epochs are achieved. We implemented the learning model using Keras. For device enrollment before joining the system, we extracted 100 packets from each device. Additionally, we extracted 100 packets from each device for authentication. In Hawk, the learning model only needs to be trained once. However, enrollment and authentication have been performed several times to evaluate system performance.

Baseline. We compare Hawk with two baselines: LLink [15] and Hybrid [16]. LLink used link signature for fingerprinting devices and SVM model for anomaly detection. In contrast, Hybrid follow unsupervised learning and require no labelled data. Unless specified otherwise, we use the same parameter values during implementing baselines as mentioned in [15] and [16].

5.2 Evaluation Metrics

We compare the performance of the trained model predictions with real labels based on the following metrics: True Positive (TP), False Positive (FP), True Negative (TN) and False Negative (FN). TP and TN denote the number of instances, where the ML model has predicted match with real labels. Whereas, FP and FN calculate the number of cases, where the ML model has predicted erroneous values. Additionally, we measured Hawk and compared the results against the baseline approaches using the following metrics: Accuracy, Precision, Recall and F1-Score [16].

5.3 Federated Learning Setup

We use PySyft deep learning framework for FL feature and GRUs as our ML neural network. We further use PyTorch deep learning framework to implement the non-FL deep learning framework. For chosen devices, we generate virtual instances using PySyft, and to simulate the central FL server, we create a dedicated instance to enable sharing of trained model parameters between the local FL model and the global FL server. Note that the local FL model for each device-type and the global FL server are trained in the local security service and remote security service, respectively. During FL implementation, we use Mini – Batch Aggregation [12] for the interaction between the local and global FL models. We set the local mini-batch size to 20. In Hawk, ML model consists of six layers: an input layer, four hidden layers (contain 128 neurons each) and an output layer. The size of the input layer is the same as the number of network traffic features in the training data. The size of the output layer is the same as the number of classes of network traffic in the training data.

5.4 Performance Evaluation

Efficiency of FL. We first study the appropriate value for the anomaly triggering threshold γ in Hawk. To perform this study, we consider the trained model as described in Sect. 5.1. Whereas we obtain 500 packets from each of D46-D60 as malicious samples. To chose a suitable value of γ, we perform a series of classification experiments by varying γ and measure two vital metrics from the Receiver Operating Characteristic (ROC) curve, namely, the Area Under the ROC (AUROC) and the Equal Error Rate (EER). Note that the ROC curve plots True Positive Rate (TPR) against False Positive Rate (FPR). We calculate TPR and FPR using our dataset for a fixed batch size of 32, where $TPR = \frac{TP}{TP+FN}$ and $FPR = \frac{FP}{FP+TN}$. Figure 3 shows that AUROC is rapidly increasing initially against γ. We notice that the AUROC plot is almost completely plateaued after $\gamma = 0.48$. This signifies that the classification result does

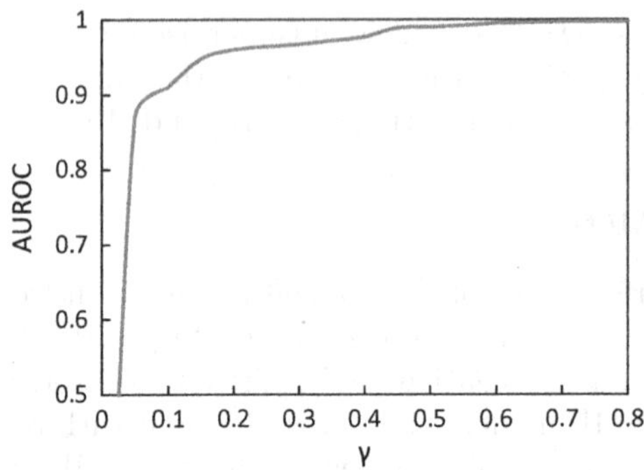

Fig. 3. AUROC under varying γ and $\delta = 0.014$.

not deviate after $\gamma = 0.48$. We measure the AUROC and EER from the plot as 0.923 and 0.025, respectively. Thus, we chose $\gamma = 0.5$. Following a similar approach, we determined $\delta = 0.014$.

Performance of Models. We use accuracy, precision, recall, and F1-score to evaluate the performance of the various decision models. While measuring the performance, we consider the three intruder set of devices as follows:

- *Intruder Set 1 [Known Devices].* D1–D20 are devices present during our model training. Thus, these devices are used to measure the performance of our training model on known malicious devices, which already had access to the network but gets compromised.
- *Intruder Set 2 [Unknown Devices, same manufacturer].* D41–D45 are devices with the same device model, i.e., Pycom LoPy4 but did not participate during our model training. We utilized these devices to validate the performance of our model on unknown malicious devices.
- *Intruder Set 3 [Unknown Devices, distinct manufacturers].* D46–D60 are devices produced by distinct manufacturers, whose hardware specifications are different from training devices D1–D40. Detecting unknown malicious devices from distinct manufactures is the most challenging scenario.

Figure 4 show that our proposed Hawk has the highest detection accuracy, precision, recall, and F1-score irrespective of the intruder sets. About the performance of ML models, GRU outperforms SVM and VAE-LSTM. Specifically, the classification performance of Hawk is 10%$\sim$15% and 6%$\sim$8% higher than LLink and Hybrid, respectively, for Intruder Set 1. We also notice similar performance improvement in Hawk compared to LLink and Hybrid for both Intruder Set 2 and 3. This is because Hawk inherits the intrusion detection advantages of GRU, which combines the advantages of both spatial learning and sequential learning. The plots show that there is a significant performance gap between Hawk, LLink and Hybrid on the Intruder Set 3. It is due to the hardware specifications of

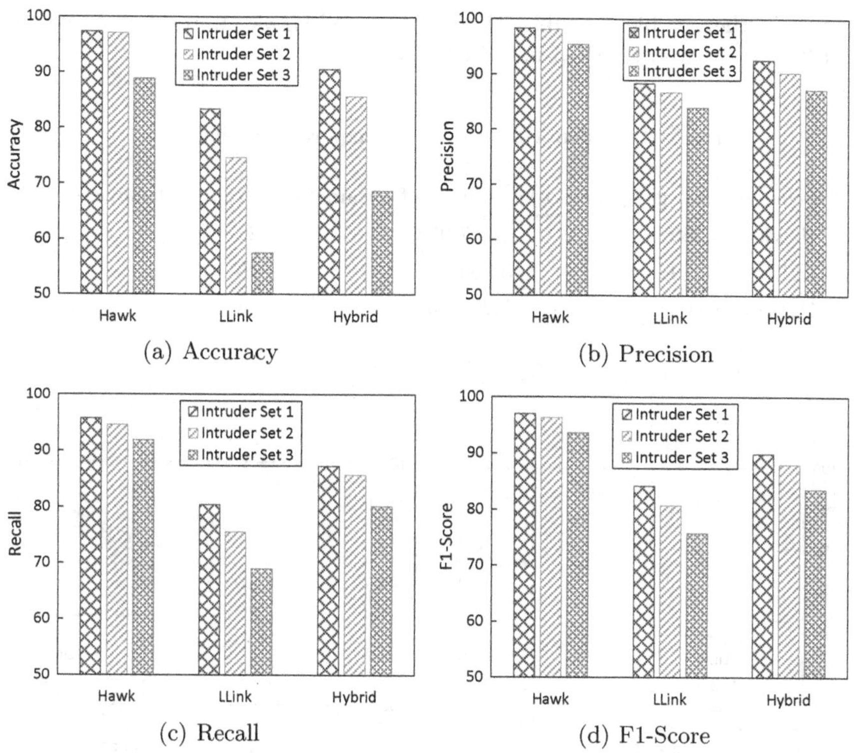

(a) Accuracy

(b) Precision

(c) Recall

(d) F1-Score

Fig. 4. Comparison of detection models based on the training dataset.

D46-D60 are significantly different from the training devices (LoPy4). We also notice that SVM and VAE-LSTM exhibit comparable performance. It is because VAE-LSTM is more time-consuming, as the gating mechanism it uses requires long-term computation. Moreover, SVM has lower performance than GRU and VAE-LSTM as it suffers from poor feature extraction capability.

System Complexity and Training Time. Here, we measure the system complexity and time required to train the ML models. To measure the system complexity, we use storage space and amount of parameters. Table 1 shows that Hawk requires the least amount of parameters, and the trained ML model takes less storage space. Particularly, in Hawk, the trained ML model needs 37.98% and 57.70% less storage space compared to LLink and Hybrid, respectively. Likewise, Hawk improves the amount of parameters by 51.49% and 69.20% compared to LLink and Hybrid, respectively. In summary, the results indicate that radio fingerprint based system is less complex and requires few parameters, which ultimately helps to reduce the authentication time of the IDS.

The training time is another crucial parameter for measuring the performance of a ML model. In Table 1, we notice that the GRU-based Hawk needs 27 mins for training, which is only a trisect of the VAE-LSTM-based Hybrid scheme. Further, Table 1 exhibits that GRU-based Hawk improves training time by 41.30% compared to SVM-based LLink.

Table 1. System complexity and required training time

Scheme	Storage space (kb)	Amount of parameters	Training time (min)
Hawk	6,352	1,627,073	27
LLink	10,244	3,354,719	46
Hybrid	15,018	5,283,557	94

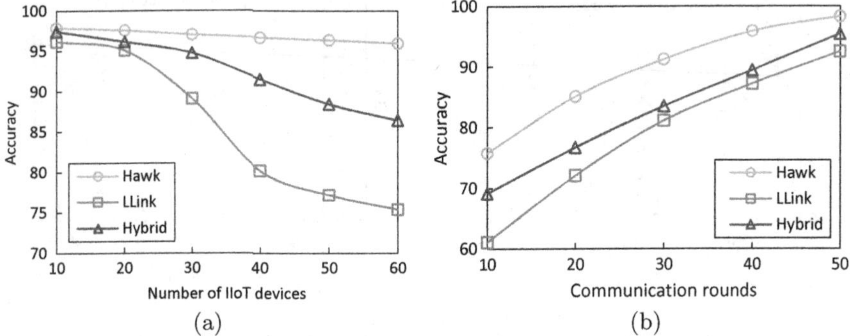

Fig. 5. Detection accuracy (a) Under varying number of IIoT devices, (b) Under varying communication round.

The Effect of Number of IIoT Devices on Models. We plot the classification accuracy by varying the number of IIoT devices in Fig. 5(a). The plot reveals that an increase in the number of IIoT devices adversely affect the performance of LLink and Hybrid. The possible reason is that the increasing number of devices bring more updated parameters, creating more overheads for the server to execute simultaneous model parameter aggregation. Additionally, these overheads can influence the upload of critical device parameters, decreasing the accuracy of the global model. In contrast, Hawk determines γ and δ judiciously, which potentially reduces the number of participating devices. In this way, Hawk updates the ML model, ensuring model training reliability.

Communication Efficiency. We here measure the learning speed of the FL algorithm used in Hawk via communication rounds. We also compare the classification accuracy of the learning algorithms used in LLink and Hybrid under varying number of communication rounds and the same is plotted in Figure 5(b). The plot shows that Hawk achieves superior performance and quickest learning speed under the same communication round. Alternatively, Hawk needs fewer communication rounds than LLink and Hybrid to achieve model convergence. In summary, Hawk improves the classification accuracy by 11.36% and 9.52% than LLink and Hybrid, respectively.

6 Conclusion

In this paper, we introduce Hawk, a distributed anomaly detection system that utilizes CFO of radio signature to enable robust malicious device detection. The radio signature enables Hawk to achieve both high detection accuracy and low system complexity. We design a novel technique by making full use of LoRa's communication mechanism to estimate fine-grained CFOs for fingerprinting IIoT device, which ensures robust detection and thwarts attackers from evading detection. Hawk then leverages the derived fingerprints to construct a baseline of device's normal CFO behavior using FL. Hawk learns anomaly detection models autonomously using data captured by 60 LoRa devices of four models and a USRP N210 SDR as the receiver. Extensive experiments show that Hawk achieves better intrusion detection accuracy, efficiency and robustness than two state-of-the-art realizations. Particularly, Hawk achieves 97.46% accuracy and 98.27% precision using 6,352 kb storage space and 27 min training time.

In the future, we design Hawk to defend against active attacks. The challenge of dealing with passive attacks, e.g., eavesdropping, information leakage remains an open problem.

Acknowledgment. This work has received funding from the European Union's Horizon 2020 research and innovation programme under the Marie Skłodowska-Curie grant agreement No. 847577; and a research grant from Science Foundation Ireland (SFI) under Grant Number 16/RC/3918 (Ireland's European Structural and Investment Funds Programmes and the European Regional Development Fund 2014–2020).

References

1. Figueroa-Lorenzo, S., Añorga, J., Arrizabalaga, S.: A survey of IIoT protocols: a measure of vulnerability risk analysis based on CVSS. ACM Comput. Surv. **53**(2), 1–53 (2020)
2. Sundaram, J.P.S., Du, W., Zhao, Z.: A survey on loRa networking: research problems, current solutions, and open issues. IEEE Commun. Surv. Tutorials **22**(1), 371–388 (2019)
3. Heeger, D., Plusquellic, J.: Analysis of IoT authentication over LoRa. In: 16th International Proceedings on DCOSS, pp. 458–465. IEEE, California, USA (2020)
4. Chen, D., et al.: Privacy-preserving encrypted traffic inspection with symmetric cryptographic techniques in IoT. IEEE Internet Things J. 1–15 (2022)
5. Yan, X., Xu, Y., Xing, X., Cui, B., Guo, Z., Guo, T.: Trustworthy network anomaly detection based on an adaptive learning rate and momentum in IIoT. IEEE Trans. Indust. Inf. **16**(9), 6182–6192 (2020)
6. Abdel-Basset, M., Chang, V., Hawash, H., Chakrabortty, R.K., Ryan, M.: Deep-ifs: intrusion detection approach for IIoT traffic in fog environment. IEEE Trans. Indust. Inf. **17**(11), 7704–7715 (2021)

7. Babun, L., Aksu, H., Uluagac, A.S.: CPS device-class identification via behavioral fingerprinting: from theory to practice. IEEE Trans. Inf. Forensics Secur. **16**, 2413–2428 (2021)
8. Zhang, J., Woods, R., Sandell, M., Valkama, M., Marshall, A., Cavallaro, J.: Radio frequency fingerprint identification for narrowband systems, modelling and classification. IEEE Trans. Inf. Forensics Secur. **16**, 3974–3987 (2021)
9. Ren, Z., Ren, P., Zhang, T.: Deep RF device fingerprinting by semi-supervised learning with meta pseudo time-frequency labels. In: Proceedings on IEEE WCNC, pp. 2369–2374. IEEE, California, USA (2022)
10. Shen, G., Zhang, J., Marshall, A., Cavallaro, J.: Towards scalable and channel-robust radio frequency fingerprint identification for LoRa. IEEE Trans. Inf. Forensics Secur. **17**, 774–787 (2022)
11. Xie, R., et al.: A generalizable model-and-data driven approach for open-set RFF authentication. IEEE Trans. Inf. Forensics Secur. **16**, 4435–4450 (2021)
12. Rey, V., Sánchez, P.M.S., Celdrán, A.H., Bovet, G.: Federated learning for malware detection in IoT devices. Comput. Networks **204** (2022)
13. Hou, W., Wang, X., Chouinard, J.-Y., Refaey, A.: Physical layer authentication for mobile systems with time-varying carrier frequency offsets. IEEE Trans. Commun. **62**(5), 1658–1667 (2014)
14. Haddadpajouh, H., Mohtadi, A., Dehghantanaha, A., Karimipour, H., Lin, X., Choo, K.-K.R.: A multi-kernel and meta-heuristic feature selection approach for IoT malware threat hunting in the edge layer. IEEE Internet Things J. **8**(6), 4540–4547 (2021)
15. Heeger, D., Plusquellic, J.: Slora: towards secure LoRa communications with fine-grained physical layer features. In: 18th International Proceedings on SenSys, pp. 258–270. ACM, Yokohama, Japan (2020)
16. Huong, T., et al.: Detecting cyberattacks using anomaly detection in industrial control systems: a federated learning approach. Comput. Indust. **132** (2021)
17. Perdisci, R., Papastergiou, T., Alrawi, O., Antonakakis, M.: Iotfinder: efficient large-scale identification of IoT devices via passive DNS traffic analysis. In: 5th International Proceedings on EuroS&P, pp. 474–489. IEEE, Genova, Italy (2020)
18. Dong, S., Li, Z., Tang, D., Chen, J., Sun, M., Zhang, K.: Your smart home can't keep a secret: towards automated fingerprinting of IoT traffic. In: 15th International Proceedings on AsiaCCS, pp. 47–59. ACM, Taipei, Taiwan (2020)
19. Haugerud, H., Tran, H.N., Aitsaadi, N., Yazidi, A.: A dynamic and scalable parallel network intrusion detection system using intelligent rule ordering and network function virtualization. Future Gener. Comput. Syst. **124**, 254–267 (2021)
20. Lu, K.-D., Zeng, G.-Q., Luo, X., Weng, J., Luo, W., Wu, Y.: Evolutionary deep belief network for cyber-attack detection in industrial automation and control system. IEEE Trans. Indust. Inf. **17**(11), 7618–7627 (2021)
21. Charyyev, B., Gunes, M.H.: Locality-sensitive IoT network traffic fingerprinting for device identification. IEEE Internet Things J. **8**(3), 1272–1281 (2021)
22. LoRa Modulation Crystal Oscillator Guidance, AN1200.14, Rev 2, July 2017. https://lora-developers.semtech.com/library/product-documents/. Accessed 6 May 2021
23. Nguyen, T.D., Marchal, S., Miettinen, M., Fereidooni, H., Asokan, N., Sadeghi, A.-R.: DIoT: a federated self-learning anomaly detection system for IoT. In: 39th International Proceedings on IEEE ICDCS, pp. 756–767. IEEE, Dallas, USA (2019)

A New Scalable Mutual Authentication in Fog-Edge Drone Swarm Environment

Kyusuk Han[1(✉)], Eiman Al Nuaimi[1], Shamma Al Blooshi[1], Rafail Psiakis[1], and Chan Yeob Yeun[2]

[1] Technology Innovation Institute, Adu Dhabi, UAE
{kyusuk.han,eiman.alnuaimi,shamma.alblooshi,rafail.psiakis}@tii.ae
[2] C2PS, EECS Department, Khalifa University, Abu Dhabi, UAE
chan.yeun@ku.ac.ae

Abstract. A drone swarm is a preferable way in deploying drones for large-scale missions. In establishing drone swarms, secure communication between a fog drone and several edge drones is essential to mutually authenticate each other. Although many research works proposed the designs of mutual authentications, none of them meets the adequate security for the drone swarm environments, requiring either involvement of the ground station during the authentication process or expensive PKI-based crypto operations. Only a few works proposed more lightweight authentication, however, they are still vulnerable to key compromises in addition to the limited flexibility and scalability. In this work, we propose an efficient and scalable authentication protocol for fog-edge drone swarm environments, enabling mutual authentication between fog and edges without involving the ground station. We also show the design can leverage various hardware-assisted security functions. Protocol evaluations show security requirements satisfaction while achieving 14–20 times less computation overhead as compared to PKI-based models.

Keywords: UAV · Drone Swarm · Fog-Edge · Authentication · PUF

1 Introduction

Unmanned Aerial vehicles (UAV) and more specifically drones are emerging in our modern cyber-physical environment, being used in various domains such as public safety, surveillance, and monitoring of industrial, agricultural, infrastructural facilities, telecommunications, and others [9]. Missions of large-scale demand multiple drones operating together, forming groups. Controlling those groups of drones requires efficient handling, thus 'swarming' is considered, as the management of each drone by the ground station would be complicated with the number of drones in the same mission.

For establishing secure communication in a swarm, mutual authentication among drones is one of the most important requirements, to avoid a man-in-the-middle attack. Authentication models exist for the fog-IoT environment,

C. Su et al. (Eds.): ISPEC 2022, LNCS 13620, pp. 179–196, 2022.
https://doi.org/10.1007/978-3-031-21280-2_10

however, many of them require the involvement of a ground station [7,11,18, 19], which could be a problem as certain environments may not guarantee the connectivity to the ground station. Employing PKI-based approaches [1–3,16], bringing substantial computation overhead, especially when a fog drone needs to authenticate hundreds of edge drones within swarms. Some techniques propose lightweight authentication for resource-constrained drone platforms [12]. The authors introduced a reputation model for immediate authentication decisions. However, since the protocol uses shared secret values to generate keys, once the key is exfiltrated, anyone can generate the shared key between certain entities.

Therefore, our main motivation in this paper is to provide low-cost mutual authentication in fog-edge drone swarm environments without the involvement of the ground station during the authentication process, while aiming for optimal efficiency by minimizing the use of the public key-based cryptography. Also, we provide a scalable and flexible design that is resilient against key compromises by design, and which can also leverage various hardware-assisted security functions, such as Physical Unclonable Functions (PUFs).

Our contributions are finally summarized as follows:

- Our protocol provides mutual authentication in the fog-edge drone swarm environments, efficiently preventing man-in-the-middle attacks and replay attacks on both sides.
- It effectively manages the drone compromise, providing forward and backward secrecy on the swarm management by limiting the impact only to the compromised drone or swarm.
- It doesn't require the involvement of the ground station during the authentication processes.
- Keys are automatically revoked and become invalid when the drone swarm mission is over. So key management can be done efficiently.
- In evaluating the protocol, 14–20 times better computational efficiency was observed, compared to the PKI-based design.
- It flexibly supports heterogeneous swarm configuration leveraging various types of hardware-assisted security functions including PUFs. (Refer to Appendix A).

The remainder of this paper is organized as follows. In the beginning, we discuss the drone swarm characteristics in Sect. 2. After that, we present the novel idea of efficient drone-to-drone authentication in the swarm environment in Sect. 3. Next, we present the evaluation of the proposed protocol in Sect. 4 and the related work in Sect. 5. We conclude this paper in Sect. 6. The use cases of hardware-assisted security including PUFs are presented Appendix A.

2 Characteristics of Drone Swarm Environment

In this section, we discuss the security issues in the Fog-Edge drone swarm environment.

2.1 Drone Swarm Environments

Let a number of drones are deployed into a certain region for a large-scale mission. In this case, controlling individual drones in the same way controlling a single drone could be complicated, grouping those multiple drones for the same mission into a drone 'swarm', and managing the swarm by setting a leading drone and delegating the management of all other drones in the swarm to the leading drone as *Fog-IoT* models (refer to Appendix 5) are considerable.

Similar to the Fog-IoT model, let us call the leading drone as *Fog Drone*, and the other drones in the swarm as *Edge Drones.* As depicted in Fig. 1, (a) the ground station has a direct channel only to the fog drone, while (b) other edge drones are interconnected over the mesh network channels within the swarm, and communicate to the ground station only through the fog drone.

Note that the fog drone's roles are more for the management of the swarm by controlling the multiple individual edge drones, in contrast to edge drones, who perform only specific operations and mostly only communicate to the fog drone or other nearby edge drones.

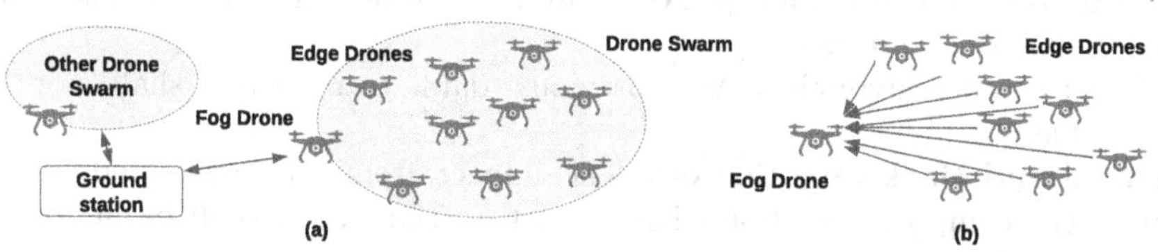

Fig. 1. (a) Ground station only communicates to fog drone in the drone swarm (b) Edge drones only communicate to fog drone

2.2 Security Issues in Fog-Edge Drone Swarm Environments

When drones are sent to the mission field, they first establish the communication as the operation phases in [8]. Here, an attacker around the field could try to attack the drones, for example, he/she tries to impersonate either the fog drone or edge drones to intercept the information or compromise the swarm. To prevent such attacks, all drones establish secure communication channels.

To avoid the man-in-the-middle attack, the mutual authentication processes between fog drones and edge drones need to be done. Since the communication and computation overheads become the burden more in fog drones than edge drones, achieving the efficiency of the authentication process is critical. As the attack can eavesdrop on the communication over the wireless channel, preventing a replay attack is also required.

Moreover, since the drone is flying out of the reach of the ground station, the attacker may physically capture and even disclose all information about the drone. In such a case, although the disclosure of the information in the current mission would be inevitable, however, attacker shall not know the previous secrets or future secrets from the exposure.

Some situations (e.g., desert areas) may not guarantee communication between the ground station and the fog drone. In such an environment, the authentication process should be able to be performed only between the fog drone and the edge drones.

Also, a drone swarm consists of hundreds of drones and the changing of the drone groups is very frequent. As this is a huge burden to the key management, an efficient way of key revocation is required.

Finally, as a fog drone could communicate to hundreds of edge drones, reducing the overhead in the authentication process for the fog drone is required.

2.3 Design Requirements

We define the following security requirements for the fog-edge drone swarm environment.

Man-in-the-middle-attack prevention Fog drone and edge drone shall authenticate each other.

Replay attack prevention Any previous data transmitted shall not be reusable.

Forward and Backward Secrecy The impact from any exfiltrated secrets from the compromised drone The impact on the swarm shall be limited to the current session.

Offline-authentication Each drone should authenticate the other without the involvement of the ground station.

Efficient key revocation The protocol should provide an efficient way to revoke the key.

Also, the overhead to the fog drone should be minimized.

3 Proposed Design

In this section, we propose a new scalable and efficient mutual authentication between fog and edges in establishing the drone swarm.

3.1 Protocol Overview

We have the following entities for the drone swarm authentication scenarios.

- Ground station **GS**, manages one or multiple drone swarms for missions.
- Fog drone, *fd*, communicates to **GS** on behalf of all drones in the swarm.
- Edge drone, *ed*, only communicates to the fog drone and other edge drones.
- a swarm, **S**, is a temporal group consisting of a fd and *ed*s for a mission. It is disbanded when the mission is over, either completed or aborted.

Our drone swarm authentication protocol consists of the following two phases.

- **Preparation Phase (PP)**: In this stage, **GS** collects edge drones and a fog drone to build a swarm before the mission starts. During the preparation phase, we assume that the communications between the ground station and the drones are protected. We describe the details in Sect. 3.2.
- **Authentication Phase (AP)**: In this stage, edge drones and the fog drone in the swarm are set to fly and mutually authenticate to establish secure channels. We describe the detail in Sect. 3.3. Note that **GS** does not involve in this phase.

3.2 Preparation Phase

Let a ground station **GS** build a an i-th swarm, S_i for a large scale mission. **GS** first collects n number of edge drones $ed_{i,j}$, where $1 \leq j \leq n$ for S_i. **GS** also collects a fog drone fd_i, to manage S_i. Once drones are collected, **GS** performs the following:

PP.1 **GS** selects a random challenge C_i for S_i.
PP.2 **GS** then sends C_i and S_i to each edge drone $ed_{i,j}$, $1 \leq j \leq n$.

Once $ed_{i,j}$, for $1 \leq j \leq n$, receives C_i, it performs the following:

PP.3 Each edge drone $ed_{i,j}$ uses C_i as the input and generates the output $R_{i,j}$, where $R_{i,j} = F_{i,j}(C_i)$. $F_{i,j}(X)$ denotes the function that generates an output upon the input X. The detailed scenario of the function is discussed in Appendix A.
PP.4 Each drone returns $R_{i,j}$ to **GS**, and stores S_i.

Then, **GS** performs the following:

PP.5 **GS** generates $dk_{i,j}$ per drone $ed_{i,j}$, where $dk_{i,j} = KDF(S_i||fd_i|| ed_{i,j}||R_{i,j})$. $KDF(X)$ denotes the key generation function with input X, and $X||Y$ denotes the concatenation of X and Y.
PP.6 **GS** then generates the drone list DL_i, where $DL_i = \{fd_i, ed_{i,j}, dk_{i,j}|1 \leq j \leq n\}$.
PP.7 **GS** deploys S_i, C_i, and DL_i to the fog drone.

We assume the communication between **GS** and drones are done in a protected environment. The overall sequences are depicted in Fig. 2.

Public Key Provisioning for Hybrid Authentication. For the hybrid authentication case that edge drones are capable of public-key cryptography operations, fd_i generates the public key pair (pk_{fd_i}, sk_{fd_i}), where pk_{fd_i} denotes the public key and sk_{fd_i} denotes the private key. fd_i provides pk_{fd_i} to GS. Then GS deploys the pk_{fd_i}, certified by GS, to each edge drone $ed_{i,j}$.

The hybrid authentication case is described as Case 2 in Sect. 3.3.

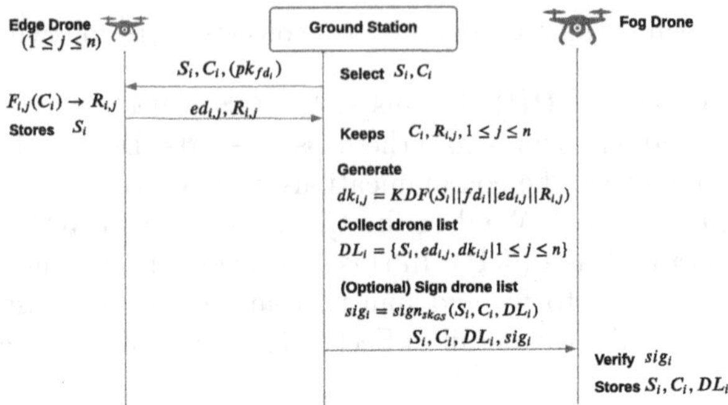

Fig. 2. Swarm secret establishment in preparation phase

3.3 Authentication Phase

When drones are deployed into the mission, they immediately start the establishment of the swarm S_i as the '*Ingress*' stage in [8]. In this stage, the fog drone and edge drones exchange the *challenge* and *responses* to mutually authenticate each other through the temporally established mesh network. We present two cases: using only symmetric cryptographic operations (Case 1) and a hybrid approach that uses digital signatures together (Case 2).

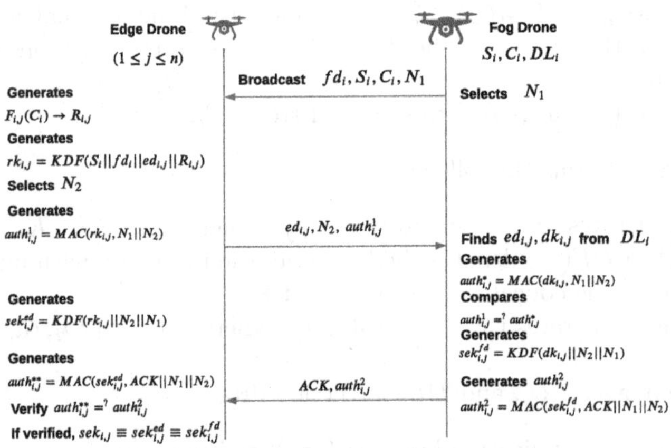

Fig. 3. Authentication phase (Case 1): Fog drone and edge drones perform mutual authentication only with symmetric cryptographic operation

Case 1: Using Only Symmetric Cryptographic Operation. Let a fog drone fd_i initiate the establishment of S_i. The fog drone fd_i performs the following:

AP.1 fd_i first randomly selects a nonce N_1.
AP.2 fd_i then broadcasts S_i, fd_i, and C_i with N_1 over the mesh network (line 2 in Fig. 1).

Once the edge drone $ed_{i,j}$ in the field, for $1 \leq j \leq n$, receives S_i, C_i and N_1 from fd_i, it performs following:

AP.3 $ed_{i,j}$ generates a mission secret $rk_{i,j}$, where $rk_{i,j} = KDF(S_i||fd_i||ed_{i,j}||R_{i,j})$. $R_{i,j}$ is obtained by using $F_{i,j}$, $R_{i,j} = F_{i,j}(C_i)$ as same as **PP.3**.
AP.4 $ed_{i,j}$ randomly selects nonce N_2 and generates $auth^1_{i,j}$, where $auth^1_{i,j} = MAC(rk_{i,j}, N_1||N_2)$. $MAC(K, M)$ denotes the message authentication code or keyed hash function of the message M using the key K.
AP.5 $ed_{i,j}$ responds it's ID $ed_{i,j}$, N_2 and $auth^1_{i,j}$ to Fog Drone.

Whenever the fog drone fd_i receives the response from each $ed_{i,j}$, it performs following:

AP.6 fd_i finds $dk_{i,j}$ associated to $ed_{i,j}$ from DL_i, and generates $auth^*_{i,j}$, where $auth^*_{i,j} = MAC(dk_{i,j}, N_1||N_2)$, then compare $auth_{i,j}$ to $auth^*_{i,j}$. If both are equivalent, fd_i authenticates $ed_{i,j}$. Note that $dk_{i,j} \equiv rk_{i,j}$.
AP.7 fd_i then generates a session key $sek^{fd}_{i,j}$, where $sek^{fd}_{i,j} = KDF(dk_{i,j}|| N_2||N_1)$. where $KDF(X)$ denotes the key derivation function using the input X.
AP.8 fd_i generates confirmation message ACK and $auth^2_{i,j}$, where $auth^2_{i,j} = MAC(sek^{fd}_{i,j}, ACK||N_1||N_2)$.
AP.9 fd_i sends ACK and $auth^2_{i,j}$ to the edge drone $ed_{i,j}$.

In receiving ACK and $auth^2_{i,j}$, each edge drone $ed_{i,j}$ performs following:

AP.10 $ed_{i,j}$ generates $sek^{ed}_{i,j}$ using N_1 and N_2, where $sek^{ed}_{i,j} = KDF(rk_{i,j}|| N_2||N_1)$.
AP.11 $ed_{i,j}$ generates $auth^{**}$ using $sek^{ed}_{i,j}$, where $auth^{**}_{i,j} = MAC(sek^{ed}_{i,j}, ACK||N_1 \ ||N_2)$. If $auth^2_{i,j}$ and $auth^{**}_{i,j}$ are equivalent, $ed_{i,j}$ authenticates fd_i.

For all edge drone $ed_{i,j}$ in the swarm S_i, $1 \leq j \leq n$ completed **AP.11**, each individual edge drone and fog drone are mutually authenticated, and established authenticated session key $sek_{i,j}$ between each $ed_{i,j}$ and fd_i, where $sek_{i,j} \equiv sek^{fd}_{i,j} \equiv sek^{ed}_{i,j}$.

Case 2: Hybrid Authentication Using Digital Signature. We also design the case that only the fog drone uses the digital signature in broadcasting the challenge message to edge drones. While most steps are the same as Case 1, Case 2 has the following modifications.

At first, instead of **AP.2**, Fog drone fd_i performs following in sending the challenge:

AP.2-1 fd_i generates Signature sig_i of S_i, C_i and N_1 using the private key sk_{fd_i}, where $sig_i = sign(sk_{fd_i}, S_i||C_i||N_1)$. $sign(K, M)$ denotes signing M using the private key K.
AP.2-2 fd_i then broadcasts S_i, fd_i, C_i, N_1, along with sig_i.

For the edge drone receiving the message from fd_i, it performs the following instead of **AP.3**:

AP.3-1 $ed_{i,j}$ verify sig_i using the fd_i's public key pk_{fd_i}.
AP.3-2 For the valid sig_i, $ed_{i,j}$ generates $rk_{i,j}$ as **AP.3**.

Since fd_i is authenticated by $ed_{i,j}$ at these steps, by performing **AP.6**, each edge drone $ed_{i,j}$ and fd_i can be mutually authenticated. Therefore, the remaining steps, from **AP.7** to **AP.11**, are optionally performed to generate the shared session key $sek_{i,j}$ between the edge drone and the fog drone. Figure 4 depicts the overall step sequences of Case 2.

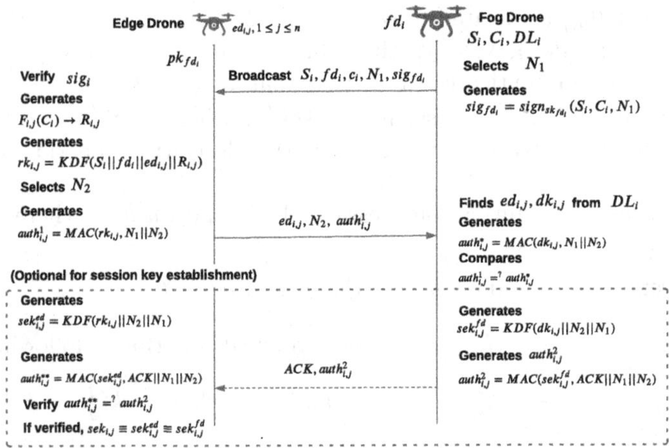

Fig. 4. Authentication phase (Case 2): Fog drone and edge drones perform mutual authentication with both asymmetric and symmetric cryptographic operation

3.4 Additional Processes

Once the fog drone and edge drones are mutually authenticated and the session keys are established, additional processes such as group key establishment or authentication among edge drones can be performed. Although our primary focus is the authentication between fog drones and individual edge drones during the swarm establishment, we discuss the brief ideas of such additional processes and leave them as our future work.

Group Key Establishment. Since the fog drone already shares the secret with the individual edge drone, the fog drone can randomly select a common group key GK_i and distribute it to the edge drone individually using the secure channel with the session key $sek_{i,j}$.

Authentication Between Edge and Edge. Edge drones may broadcast the beacon message periodically to detect the drone nearby. Once any neighbor drone is detected, two drones may not share the secret initially. However, since each edge drone already established the secure channel with the fog drone, the fog drone takes the role to interconnect each other as a general symmetric key management model such as Kerberos.

Message Authentication Between Edge and Ground Station. The ground station and edge drones may need to exchange the messages, such as configuration data, or sensing data. Since the communication could be done through the fog drone, it is important to check the authenticity of the data and whether the data is not modified by the fog drone. Such a process can be done either with another symmetric key shared between the ground station and edge drone or the digital signature signed by the ground station.

3.5 Authentication in Scalable Scenarios

Our protocol can be applied for various scalable scenarios, not limited to the single fog drone in a single swarm.

Authentication with Multiple Fog Drones in the Swarm. The failure of the fog drone may result in the disconnection of the channel between the swarm and the ground station since only the fog drone communicates to the ground station. Thus, to increase the robustness against such a situation, deploying multiple fog drones in the swarm could be considered.

Let **GS** generate the swarm secrets for θ number of fog drones in Swarm S_i. For fd_i^k, where $1 \leq k \leq \theta$, instead of **PP.5**, **GS** performs following:

PP.5-F For $1 \leq k \leq \theta$, **GS** generates $dk_{i,j}^k$, where $dk_{i,j}^k = KDF(S_i||fd_i^k||ed_{i,j}||R_{i,j})$.

i and j denote the swarm's number and edge drone's number respectively, as in Sect. 3.2. Figure 5 (a) depicts an example scenario that two fog drones $fd_{i,1}$ and $fd_{i,2}$ are leading the swarm S_i. In this case, **GS** generates two secrets $dk_{i,j}^1$ for $fd_{i,1}$ and $dk_{i,j}^2$ for $fd_{i,2}$, where $dk_{i,j}^1 = KDF(S_i||fd_i^1||ed_{i,j}||R_{i,j})$, and $dk_{i,j}^2 = KDF(S_i||fd_i^2||ed_{i,j}||R_{i,j})$. Note that the same $R_{i,j}$ is used to generate the different $dk_{i,j}^k$.

GS also performs following substituted steps instead of **PP.6** and **PP.7**.

PP.6-F **GS** generates the drone list DL_i^k, where $DL_i^k = \{fd_i^k, ed_{i,j}, dk_{i,j}^k | 1 \leq j \leq n, 1 \leq k \leq \theta\}$. θ denotes the number of fog drones in the same swarm.

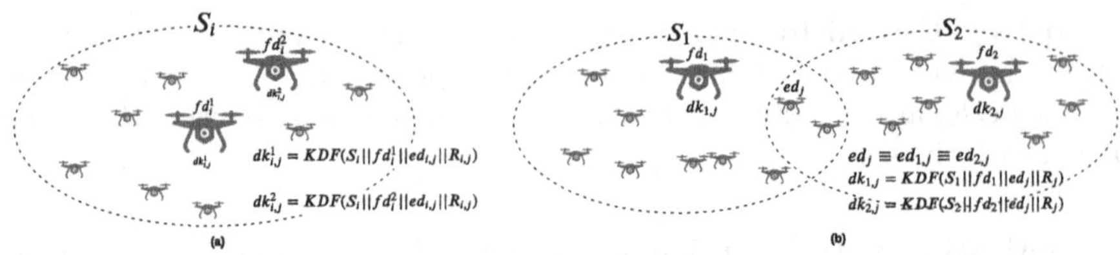

Fig. 5. (a) Multiple fog drones in the swarm (b) Edge drones join multiple swarms

PP.7-F **GS** deploys S_i, C_i, and DL_i^k to the fog drone fd_i^k.

The authentication phase (**AP**) can be performed with no modification.

Authentication of Drones in Multiple Swarms. Upon the size of the mission and area, even deploying multiple swarms could be considered. In this scenario, several edge drones may need to join multiple swarms adaptively, as depicted in Fig. 5(b).

Let **GS** set the edge drones to participate to multiple swarms. Instead of **PP.1** and **PP.2**, **GS** performs following:

PP.1-S **GS** selects a random challenge C for S_i, where $1 \leq i \leq z$. z denotes the number of swarms. Note that the same challenge C can be used for multiple swarms.

PP.2-S **GS** then sends C and S_i to each drone ed_j, $1 \leq j \leq n$ and $1 \leq i \leq z$. n denotes the number of the edge drone, and z denotes the number of the swarm. Note that we omitted i in the challenge and edge drone's ID.

Each edge drone keeps assigned S_i, $1 \leq i \leq z$ and uses them during the authentication phase. Once the mission is over, the edge drone removes all S_i. Note that C is never stored in the edge drone.

4 Evaluation

We evaluate our proposed protocol with security analysis in Sect. 4.1 and performance analysis by implementation in Sect. 4.2.

4.1 Security Analysis

Man-In-The-Middle Attack Prevention. Let a third-party attacker *Adv* try to impersonate an edge drone $ed_{i,j}$ in the swarm S_i. *Adv* has to able to generate a fake $auth_{i,j}^{Adv}$ without the knowledge of $rk_{i,j}$ in **AP.5**. For this case, the probability that *Adv* generates a valid $auth_{i,j}^{Adv}$, where $auth_{i,j}^{Adv} \equiv auth_{i,j}^1$, is not higher than the probability that the *Adv* randomly choose one.

Also, let *Adv* try to impersonate the fog drone. *Adv* also need to generate $auth_{i,j}^{Adv}$, where $auth_{i,j}^{Adv} \equiv auth_{i,j}^2$ without knowledge of $sek_{i,j}$ **AP.9**. For this case, the probability that Adv generates a valid $auth_{i,j}^{Adv}$, where $auth_{i,j}^{Adv} \equiv auth_{i,j}^2$, is not higher than the probability that the Adv randomly choose one.

For Case 2, Adv has to generate the fake signature sig^{Adv} without knowing the private key sk_{fd_i} to impersonate the fog drone in step **AP.2-1**. The probability that $sig^{Adv} \equiv sig_i$ is the same as Adv break RSA or ECC. Also, Adv may impersonate an edge drone by compromising the message authentication code in **AP.9**, which is already shown above.

Replay Attack Prevention. A third-party attacker Adv may try to reuse the values captured during the authentication process. For Case 1, Adv first captures the broadcast message fd_i, S_i, C_i, and N_1 in **AP.2**. Replaying this message without modification only results in the edge drone regenerating the $rk_{i,j}$ at most, although Adv has no advantage from this. Adv then also captures $ed_{i,j}$, N_2, and $auth_{i,j}^1$ from **AP.5**, and replay with these information. However, without the knowledge of $rk_{i,j}$, Adv has no control of $auth_{i,j}^1$, thus the replay fails. The probability of success that Adv makes the fog drone fd_i believes $auth_{i,j}^1$ with the attacker's fake identity ed^{Adv} is not higher than the probability of success that Adv generates the collision of the cryptographic hash function. Adv also captures ACK and $auth_{i,j}^2$ and replay it. However, The probability of success that another edge drone accepts $auth_{i,j}^2$ that Adv replayed is not higher than the probability of success that Adv finds the collision of the cryptographic hash function. Thus, we show our protocol prevents the replay attack.

Forward Secrecy. Assume that the attacker Adv captures either an edge drone or a fog drone, and completely discloses all secrets inside.

Attacker Captures Edge Drone. The attacker Adv uses a captured challenge C_i to generate the response $R_{i,j}$. Then, Adv may try to generate $rk_{i+1,j}$ using the swarm ID $S_i + 1$ and the fog drone's ID fd_{i+1}, however, those parameters are no longer valid in other swarm S_{i+1}, since the other fog drone, fd_{i+1} would not know the equivalent $dk_{i+1,j}$ in DL_{i+1}, Adv's attempt to be authenticated as the same edge drone ID $ed_{i,j}$ fails. Instead, Adv may try to impersonate other ID $ed_{i+1,j}$, whose can be caught during **AP.5**. However, in this case using $R_{i,j}$ is meaningless, thus the probability of success that Adv is authenticated and establish the session key in other swarm S_{i+1} is not higher than one that Adv randomly selects a value rk^{Adv}, where $rk^{Adv} \equiv rk_{i+1,j}$.

Attacker Captures Fog Drone. Let Adv capture a fog drone fd_1 of a Swarm S_1 and knows all secrets inside, and Adv tries to impersonate edge drones in a new swarm S_{i+1}.

However, The probability of success that Adv generates new $auth_{i+1,j}^2$ with old $dk_{i,j}$ is the same as the probability that Adv randomly selects dk^{Adv}, where $dk^{Adv} \equiv dk_{i+1,j}$.

In contrast, *Adv* may try to impersonate other fog drone fd_i^2 in the same swarm S_i, with knowledge of fd_i^1. *Adv* needs to replicate DL_i^2 with DL_i^1. However, the probability that *Adv* finds DL_i^2, where $DL_i^1 \equiv DL_i^2$ is not higher that the probability that *Adv* randomly chooses DL^{Adv}. Therefore, our protocol achieves forward secrecy.

Backward Secrecy. We also analyze that our protocol provides backward secrecy when the drones are compromised.

Compromised Edge Drone. Once *Adv* compromises the edge drone $ed_{i,j}$, then *Adv* can know the $R_{i,j}$ from the challenge C_i. Assuming *Adv* can also capture all previous public information of **AP.2**, **AP.6**, *Adv* may know all previous secrets. However, in practice, knowing all information in the previous mission that $ed_{i,j}$ joined is not easy, and all information is destructed once the mission is over. For example, nonce N_1 and N_2 are only not stored, even in **GS**. Although perfect backward secrecy may not be achieved, partial protection is available in the real scenario.

Thus, although *Adv* may break S_i by compromising the fog drone as a single point of the failure, we show the impact is limited to the current mission, and not influential to either past or future missions.

Compromised Fog Drone. Since S_i expires after the mission, all $dk_{i,j}$ become invalid after the mission. Fog drone erases any expired information after the mission, thus any disclosed $dk_{i,j}$ could only reveal the information within the mission of S_i, not from S_{i-1}.

Offline-Authentication. Once drones are put in the mission and grouping the swarm, the ground station does not involve in the mutual authentication process, as depicted in both Fig. 3, and Fig. 4. Also, the session key establishment and the group key establishment are performed without the involvement of **GS**.

Key Revocation. Since the secret $dk_{i,j}$ and $rk_{i,j}$ use S_i as the input, the secret becomes invalid once the mission is over. The fog drone simply renew the secret $dk_{i,j}$ with drone list DL_{i+1} when before the next mission S_{i+1}. The edge drone also generates $rk_{i+1,j}$ in joining the new mission S_{i+1}.

4.2 Performance Evaluation

We evaluated the performance of our protocol by first analyzing the computation overhead by design, then analyzing it with the implementation.

Table 1. (a) Computation overhead (b) Measured computation time on fog drone

Case	Step	Fog Drone	Edge Drone
Case 1	AP.6	$n \times$ H	$1 \times$ H
	AP.7	$n \times$ H	$1 \times$ H
	AP.8	$n \times$ H	$1 \times$ H
Case 2	AP.2-1	$1 \times$ S	$1 \times$ V
	AP.6	$n \times$ H	$1 \times$ H
	AP.7	$n \times$ H	($1 \times$ H)
	AP.8	$n \times$ H	($1 \times$ H)
Signature Only	*Challenge*	$1 \times$ S	$1 \times$ V
	Response	$n \times$ V	$1 \times$ S

(a)

Step	Number of Edge drones	Case 1	Case 2	Signature Only	Number of Edge drones	Case 1	Case 2	Signature Only
AP.2-1	1	N/A	646.639	645.583	100	N/A	646.639	645.583
AP.6		0.437	0.4280	13.5486		43.750	42.796	1354.860
AP.7		0.091	(Omitted)	N/A		9.060	(Omitted)	N/A
AP.8		0.412	(Omitted)	N/A		41.220	(Omitted)	N/A
AP.2-1	10	N/A	646.639	645.583	200	N/A	646.639	645.583
AP.6		4.375	4.280	135.486		87.500	85.592	2709.720
AP.7		0.906	(Omitted)	N/A		18.120	(Omitted)	N/A
AP.8		4.122	(Omitted)	N/A		82.445	(Omitted)	N/A
AP.2-1	50	N/A	646.639	645.583	300	N/A	646.639	645.583
AP.6		21.874	21.398	677.431		131.249	128.388	4064.580
AP.7		4.530	(Omitted)	N/A		27.180	(Omitted)	N/A
AP.8		20.61	(Omitted)	N/A		123.668	(Omitted)	N/A

(Unit: milliseconds)

(b)

Computation Overhead by Design. We analyzed the number of operations to evaluate the computation overhead by design.

Since the most overhead during the authentication occurs when the fog drone is receiving and handling the responses from multiple edge drones, evaluated the computation overhead during the following steps:

- Verification of the response from the edge drone, in **AP.6**
- Session key generation, in **AP.7**
- Generation of the authenticated confirmation, in **AP.8**

Additionally, the computation overhead of signature generation and verification are also evaluated as follows:

- Generation of signature of the fog drone, as **AP.2-1**.
- Verification of signatures of edge drones, only in *Signature Only* case.

Symbols used in Table 1 denote the operations. **H** denotes the operation of cryptographic hash functions such as *KDF* and *MAC*. **S** denotes the operation of signing the signature and **V** denotes the operation of verifying the signature.

The result is depicted in Table 1(a). The table shows the total computation overheads of Case 1 is 3**H**, while the ones of Case 2 is 1**S** + n**H**, when only the overhead of mutual authentication is measured. For Case 2, 2**H** for generating the authenticated session key is optional. Since it is trivial that the computation overhead of **H** operation is much less than the overhead of **V** operation, both Case 1 and 2 show more huge efficiency than the signature-based design that requires 1**S**+n**V** for the mutual authentication. Note that asymmetric crypto operations only case is simplified from signature-based models such as [1].

Evaluation by Simulation. We then implement the simulation environment to evaluate the protocol in the computation times.

Implementation. We first design the evaluation setup as Fig. 6(a). A fog drone is on a *Raspberry PI 4*, with *Ubuntu 20.04* and the edge drone swarm is on *Intel i9* system. Both devices are connected over the WiFi.

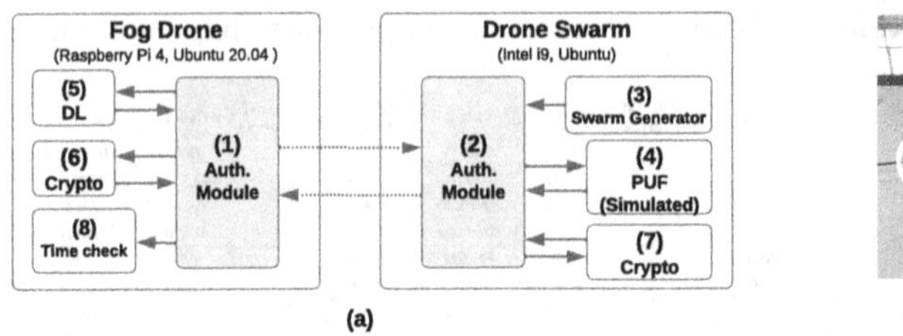

Fig. 6. Implementation scenario comprising of a fog drone and edge drones

On each side, (1) and (2), in Fig. 6(a), performs the overall protocol in Fog drone and edge drone simultaneously. The swarm generator, (3), selects the number of edge drones. PUF, (4), provides the pre-computed response assuming the output generated by the function $F_{i,j}$ with the input C_i, since the scope of the evaluation is focused on the fog drone side. The drone list DL containing the swarm secrets for fog drones is managed separately as (5), and called when the mutual authentication is in progress. Cryptography functions (6) and (7) were implemented with Python; The Python Standard Library's Cryptographic Services and PyCryptodome. Once the computation from **AP.6** to **AP.8** are done, the computation time is checked in (8).

Note that we assume the initial secrets DL is already established during the preparation phase, which is not the scope of this evaluation.

(1) and (2) perform three scenarios as discussed in Sect. 4.2. In addition to our two models, we implemented a mutual authentication protocol by exchanging the digital signature, which is a simplified model of existing protocols such as [1].

Cryptography Model Setup. As for the cryptographic functions, (6), we deployed two parts. For MAC and KDF on the edge drone and the fog drone, we chose HMAC-SHA512 as the algorithm. For the digital signature implementation, we deployed the RSA algorithm for signing and verification of the signature, and the key size of 4096 bits is used. We omitted other algorithms such as ECDSA in this evaluation as the digital signature is only for comparison purposes.

Evaluation Results. Based on the setup in Sect. 4.2, we measured the time, (8) in Fig. 6(a), to complete the authentication of all edge drones at the fog drone side. Table 1(a) shows the computation of three scenarios with different numbers of edge drones in a swarm, and The graphs in Fig. 7 show the comparison among different scenarios.

For the case of a single edge drone in Case 1, the total computation overhead of the symmetric only scenario is approximately 0.67 milliseconds to complete **AP.6**, **AP.7** and **AP.8**, which is approximately 20 times faster than the signature-only scenario. Note that the latter case doesn't include the time to establish the session key.

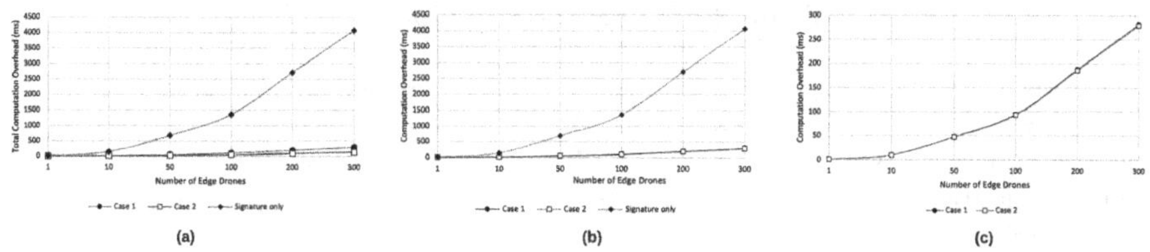

Fig. 7. Comparison of computation time for: (a) Mutual authentication only (b) Mutual authentication with the key agreement (c) Between Case 1 and Case 2

The signature generation in fog drone (**AP.2-1**) shows approximately 646.64 ms, however, it is generated only once, and at the beginning of the protocol. The RSA key generations in both Case 2 (hybrid case) and asymmetric only cases are approximately equivalent.

In contrast, the computation time for **AP.6** of Case 2 shows approximately 0.43 millisecond which is almost equivalent to the symmetric key-only scenario. Moreover, at this point, the fog drone and edge drones are mutually authenticated. The remaining steps including **AP.7** and **AP.8** can be optionally performed to generate the session key and exchange the confirmation message, which is not the authentication purpose and only to confirm that the session key is generated.

As the number of edge drones in a swarm increases, the difference in computation overhead between the proposed models (Case 1 and 2) and using asymmetric cryptography increases. As depicted in Table 1(b), the total overhead of our proposed model shows that it is approximately 14 times faster than the *signature-only* case.

Although the communication overhead is not explicitly measured, however, we can still see the hybrid design has the least overhead by reducing the 1 step for fog drone authentication, which is required in case 1. We leave the evaluation in the actual environment as future work.

4.3 Comparison

Table 2 shows the comparison of our proposed design with previous work. We discuss the detailed description of previous works in Appendix 5.

5 Related Work

We explore the related work including the generic Fog-IoT environments and the Fog-Edge drone environments. Several protocols for drone environments such as [7,11,18,19] are not suitable for the fog-edge swarm model, as they require communication between the ground station and the individual drone. PKI-based models [6,15] for Fog-IoT and [1,16] for drone environments could enable direct mutual authentication, however, they require a lot of performance overheads. The shared key-based models [10,12] could enhance the efficiency,

Table 2. Comparison of protocols

Requirements	[7] drone auth	[10] fog-edge	[5] PUF based fog-edge	[1] Proxy signature	Proposed
Offline Authentication		X	X	X	X
Mutual Authentication	X	X	X	X	X
Replay attack prevention	X	X	X	X	X
Forward Secrecy		X	X		X
Backward Secrecy					Fog drone
Automated Revocation					X
Scalability		X		X	X
Flexibility					X

however, require more complicated key management including key provisioning and revocation. To deal with threats that try compromising shared keys, some researchers focused on hardware-assisted methods such as PUF-based techniques [4,5]. Some research works [9,14] employed PUFs for the mutual authentication of drones. However, these protocols require the involvement of the authentication service, which owns Challenge-Response Pairs (CRPs), where the communication between the ground station and the drones may not be guaranteed. Our protocol addresses this limitation and enables lightweight mutual authentication between Fog and Edge drones, independent from the server, ensuring seamless authentication without communication with the server. Also, Our protocol can leverage hardware-assisted methods including PUF for drone authentication as described in Appendix A.

6 Conclusion and Future Work

In this paper, we proposed the scalable mutual authentication protocol between fog drones and edge drones in establishing a fog-edge drone swarm environment. We showed that our designs effectively protect against attacks such as man-in-the-middle attacks and replay attacks. Our designs have resiliency against compromise by providing forward and backward secrecy, and by providing an efficient key revocation process, which is adequately suitable for fog-edge drone swarm environments. We also showed that our protocol efficiently performs the mutual authentication and key agreement with hundreds of edge drones, 14–20 times more efficient than previous models, and can leverage various hardware-assisted security functions including PUFs, to increase the security strength of cryptographic assets used in real-world scenarios. In future work, we will provide more various drone swarm security management including group key agreement and authentications among edges in real environments.

A Response Generation in PP.3

We briefly show how the $F_{i,j}$ in **PP.3** can work in such varied environments. Note that the transactions between hardware-protected security environments

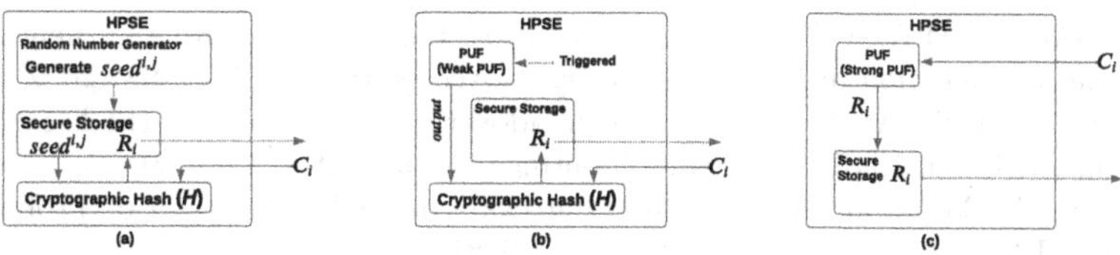

Fig. 8. (a) Response generation in generic edge drone, (b) Response generation in edge drone with weak PUF, (c) Response generation in edge drone with strong PUF

(HPSE) [17] and outside are protected as the assumption in the preparation phase (**PP**). $H(X)$ denotes a cryptographic hash function with an input X.

A.1 Response Generation in Generic Edge Drone

As depicted in Fig. 8(a), the edge drone generates a random unique value $seed_{i,j}$ using the random number generator and securely stores it in the secure storage.

Once C_i is received, $ed_{i,j}$ performs following.

$$F_{i,j}(C_i) : H(C_i||seed_{i,j}) \rightarrow R_{i,j}.$$

Response $R_{i,j}$ is stored within the HPSE and not disclosed to any other entity but only to the valid ground station.

A.2 Response Generation in Edge Drone with PUF

We focus on PUFs in two categories; *weak* and *strong* PUFs. That strength depends on the number of challenge-response pairs (CRPs) that can be generated from a single device. For more detail, please refer to [13].

Since *weak* PUF generates the constant *output* all the time, as depicted in Fig. 8(b), $F_{i,j}$ generates $R_{i,j}$ as following:

$$F_{i,j}(C_i) : H(C_i||PUF(output)) \rightarrow R_{i,j}$$

In contrast, as the *strong* PUF could generate CRPs without limitation, as depicted in Fig. 8(c), $F_{i,j}$ generates $R_{i,j}$ as following:

$$F_{i,j}(C_i) : PUF_{i,j}(C_i) \rightarrow R_{i,j}$$

References

1. Abdel-Malek, M.A., et al.: A proxy Signature-Based drone authentication in 5G D2D networks. In: 2021 IEEE 93rd Vehicular Technology Conference (VTC2021-Spring), pp. 1–7 (2021). www.ieeexplore.ieee.org

2. Abdel-Malek, M.A., et al.: A proxy Signature-Based swarm drone authentication with leader selection in 5G networks. IEEE Access **10**, 57485–57498 (2022)
3. Aydin, Y., et al.: Authentication and handover challenges and methods for drone swarms. IEEE J. Radio Frequency Identification **6**, 220–228 (2022)
4. Barbareschi, M., et al.: A PUF-based hardware mutual authentication protocol. J. Parallel Distrib. Comput. **119**, 107–120 (2018)
5. Barbareschi, M., et al.: PUF-enabled authentication-as-a-service in fog-IoT systems. In: 2019 IEEE 28th International Conference on Enabling Technologies: Infrastructure for Collaborative Enterprises (WETICE), pp. 58–63 (2019)
6. Ben Amor, A., et al.: A privacy-preserving authentication scheme in an edge-fog environment. In: 2017 IEEE/ACS 14th International Conference on Computer Systems and Applications (AICCSA), pp. 1225–1231 (Oct 2017)
7. Cho, G., et al.: SENTINEL: a secure and efficient authentication framework for unmanned aerial vehicles. NATO Adv. Sci. Inst. Ser. E Appl. Sci. **10**(9), 3149 (2020)
8. Chung, T.H., et al.: Live-fly, large-scale field experimentation for large numbers of fixed-wing UAVs. In: 2016 IEEE International Conference on Robotics and Automation (ICRA), pp. 1255–1262 (2016)
9. Gope, P., Sikdar, B.: An efficient privacy-preserving authenticated key agreement scheme for edge-assisted internet of drones. IEEE Trans. Vehicul. Technol. **69**(11), 13621–13630 (2020). https://doi.org/10.1109/TVT.2020.3018778
10. Ibrahim, M.H.: Octopus: an edge-fog mutual authentication scheme. IJ Network Secur. **18**(6), 1089–1101 (2016)
11. Jan, S.U., Khan, H.U.: Identity and aggregate signature-based authentication protocol for IoD deployment military drone. IEEE Access **9**, 130247–130263 (2021)
12. Khanh, T.D., et al.: TRA: effective authentication mechanism for swarms of unmanned aerial vehicles. In: 2020 IEEE Symposium Series on Computational Intelligence (SSCI), pp. 1852–1858 (2020)
13. McGrath, T., et al.: A PUF taxonomy. Appl. Phys. Rev. **6**(1),(2019)
14. Pal, V., A et al.: PUF based secure framework for hardware and software security of drones. In: 2020 Asian Hardware Oriented Security and Trust Symposium (AsianHOST), pp. 01–06 (2020)
15. Pardeshi, M.S., Yuan, S.M.: SMAP Fog/Edge: a secure mutual authentication protocol for Fog/Edge. IEEE Access **7**, 101327–101335 (2019)
16. Semal, B., et al.: A certificateless group authenticated key agreement protocol for secure communication in untrusted UAV networks. In: 2018 IEEE/AIAA 37th Digital Avionics Systems Conference, pp. 1–8 (2018)
17. Society of Automotive Engineers International: SAE J3101 - Hardware Protected Security for Ground Vehicles. Technical Report J3101, SAE (2020)
18. Tanveer, M., et al.: LAKE-IoD: lightweight authenticated key exchange protocol for the internet of drone environment. IEEE Access **8**, 155645–155659 (2020)
19. Tanveer, M., et al.: RAMP-IoD: a robust authenticated key management protocol for the internet of drones. IEEE Internet Things J. 1–1 (2021)

Sparse Attack on Skeleton-Based Human Action Recognition for Internet of Video Things Systems

Yinqin Huang[1(✉)], Cheng Dai[2], and Wei-Che Chien[3]

[1] University of Electronic Science and Technology of China, Chengdu, China
hyinq@hotmail.com

[2] Sichuan University, Chengdu, China
daicheng@scu.edu.cn

[3] National Dong Hwa University, Taipei, Taiwan
wcc@gms.ndhu.edu.tw

Abstract. Action recognition is widely used in industry like human-computer interaction and intelligent monitoring. But in the circumstance of deep model being threatened by adversarial attack, the robustness of skeleton base action recognition, which is widely concerned for its better performance, has not been widely discussed. Recently, the robustness of existing HAR models have been questioned for their vulnerability to adversarial attacks. However, Previous attacks introduce unnecessary perturbations which heavily increase the deviation between adversarial sample and origin sample. Base on solving this problem, this article proposes a sparse attack method with dynamic attention which generates adversarial samples with lower deviation and without a drop of attack success rate. Firstly, we develop spatial temporal consistency loss to preserve not only spatial integrity between reference sample and adversarial sample, but also temporal coherence between consecutive frames across adversarial sample. Then, we develop an interaction-based perturbation contribution analyze method to discard unnecessary perturbations. Finally, we design a dynamic attention approach to tilt the perturbations towards some joints that have higher dynamics which can decrease overall deviations. By attacks, our method contributes to discover potential causes of model fragility and provides material in adversarial training which will increase the robustness of HAR models.

Keywords: System robustness · Adversarial attack · Skeleton action recognition · Spatial-temporal · Graph convolutional neural networks

1 Introduction

Skeleton-based human action recognition has been developed as a hot research field in Internet of video things systems. In recent years, with the development of artificial intelligence, deep learning has been widely used in most recognition

C. Su et al. (Eds.): ISPEC 2022, LNCS 13620, pp. 197–212, 2022.
https://doi.org/10.1007/978-3-031-21280-2_11

tasks such as classification or segmentatio. However, as the development of deep learning, deep models has been proven to be vulnerable to carefully designed data perturbations, this problem will lead the poor robustness of the model, which will bring the great challenge in real applications particularly in the areas of safety and security [1]. Therefore, how to increase the robustness of deep model has been widely studied in recent years.

While the adversarial attack has been widely researched across different modality, but the time-series data has been explored only by several works [2,3]. In this work, we explore a special type of time-series data, skeleton motions. In Human Activity Recognition (HAR), skeleton based methods have been showing superior performance under varying view angles and complicated background which have attracted much attention in computer vision community [4] for its background independence. With this physical robustness of skeleton data, techniques of deep learning including convolutional neural networks, recurrent neural networks and graph convolutional neural networks have been applied to this new data representation and achieved high recognition accuracy [5].

However, there are researches [6] in adversarial attack have revealed the vulnerability of deep learning models and skeleton data also can't immune to the threat of adversarial attack [7]. Therefore, the robustness of skeleton-based classifiers under adversarial attack has recently drawn attention [8,9].

Different from attacking static data (e.g. images, texts), physical features of skeleton motion bring new challenges which increases the difficulty of a successful attack. One of the challenges to attack skeleton data is that is has much less domain of freedom (Dofs) whose significance to a successful attack has been proved [10]. This problem manifests as low redundance in skeleton which restricts the possible attacks within a smaller subspace. Another major challenge is that every joint, counterpart of pixels in image, is semantic relevant which is significantly different from images in which background pixels are always included. This means a tiny alteration on single joint will appears as tic on body, such unnatural jerk will be easily detected by human and processed with well designed algorithms.

Existing works [8,9] conquer these challenges and achieve high attack success rate by adopting a generative architecture along with multiple physical constrains. However, these works adopt bone length constrain which keeps the length of each bone the same as it in the original sample. This constrain has an intrinsic problem which will lead to the perturbation being propagated to all joints in the process of iteration and result in unnecessary perturbations are introduced into adversarial samples.

Basing on solving these problems we develop an iterative scheme to solve this problem and generate ideal adversarial skeleton sequence, see Fig. 1. To solve the problem caused by bone length constrain, we firstly deprecate this constrain and develop a new Spatial-Temporal Consistency loss to preserve not only spatial integrity between reference sample and adversarial sample, but also temporal coherence between consecutive frames across adversarial sample's frames. By removing the inner spatial constrains within a frame, the perturbations will

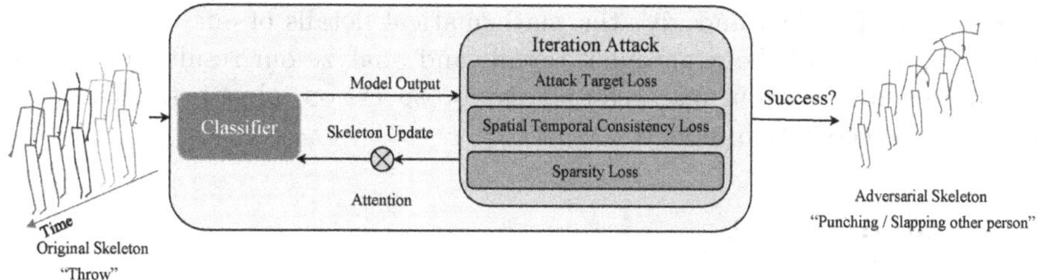

Fig. 1. The overall architecture of out model, the attack loss consists of three parts. Adversarial sample will be updated iteratively untill classifier gives a wrong label while obeying some constraints.

spread only across time during iterations. And for the neighborhood frames, the perturbations are restricted by spatial consistency loss of this frame. This design guarantees the perturbations will not propagate but spread evenly across frames. Then, perturbations on all joints will be examined by an interaction based pruning module to determine whether it contributes positively to the target function, and the updates on perturbation units with negative contributions will be set to 0. This module reduce unnecessary perturbations which is accumulated during the iterations. Last but not least, we design an dynamic attention with consistency and distance mask to tune the perturbations on different joints. This mask base on the intrinsic property of human that neighborhood joints have similar motion patterns in both spatial and temporal.

Over architecture perspective, for a given skeleton action, our method iteratively optimize the adversarial noise in small steps to minimize the attack target loss while satisfying spatial-temporal consistency loss to keep the imperceptibility. The derivatives of these two loss, calculated from back propagation, will be multiplied with attention vector which is calculated from the original skeleton. After that, perturbation units with negative contribution will be set to 0 by interaction analyze.

Analogous to image adversarial attacks, we validate our method in different attack modes namely *untargeted*, *random* and *hardest*. In untargeted mode, we allow fooled output to be any other label but not the real label. This type of attack always get semantic similar output, so we introduce random mode, in which we randomly assign a target label to test whether our method can fool the classifier to give an semantic dissimilar output. And in hardest mode, we specially assign the minimal confidence label of classifier's output on original data to get the extreme performance. Except for lower deviation without drop of attack success rates in attacking state-of-art skeleton action recognition models on HDM05 [11] and NTU [12] datasets, our method also shows high cross model transferability by attack an "unseen" model with adversarial skeleton generated from another.

The rest of this article is organized as follows. Related works about skeleton action recognition and adversarial attack are reviewed in Sect. 2. In Sect. 3, we formulate the problem and give the mathematical details of our method. And in Sect. 4, we detail the experiment details and analyze our results. Finally in Sect. 5 we summarize our research and give prospects on robustness of skeleton based action recognition models.

2 Related Works

2.1 Skeleton Based Action Recognition

Action recognition is significant for dealing human involved affairs for its rich connotation about what is happening and how they are feeling. A wide range of applications including surveillance system, human-computer interaction even car autopilot will benefits from precise action recognition.

Since skeleton data is formed as time series, RNN based methods [13,14], which has been proven an efficient way to handle sequential data are employed. However, the weakness of spatial modeling ability makes generally less competitive performance of RNN based methods. Meanwhile, convolutional neural networks are also applied to skeleton data for its efficiency in learning high level information. To migrate from image based tasks to skeleton based tasks, researches like [15,16] represent skeleton sequences as pseudo-image which allows image classification models to handle the skeleton data.

Human skeleton captured by devices like Microsoft Kinect [17] or extracted from video clips by motion estimation methods like OpenPose [18] resembles a graph, therefore, the graph convolutional networks (GCNs) can be applied to this non-Euclidean data to extract temporal-spatial relevance. Sijie and Yuanjun [19] constructed the first GCN based spatial temporal graph convolutional networks(ST-GCN) in which joints as vertexes and bones and connections across frames as edges. Following that, Maosen and Siheng [20] proposed the Action-Structural Graph Convolutional Networks(AS-GCN) which could not only give the classification results but make prediction on next poses using multi-task learning strategies. More recently, Pengfei and Cuiling [21] introduce semantic information into GCN model, by encoding the frame index and joint name into one-hot code and then incorporating into model training SGN reaches the best performance with an order of magnitude smaller model size.

2.2 Adversarial Attack

Recent breakthrough in computer vision has been imported into security-critical systems including autonomous cars, access identification, and face recognition with massive deployments. While reaches high recognition performance, recent works [6,22] show that deep models are easily fooled by delicately designed adversarial samples so that give wrong outputs. Under such atmosphere, abundant investigation [23] has been done on varies data including image, video and graphs.

In the domain of action recognition, Zhikai and Lingxi [24] attack the video based action recognition models by appending adversarial frames which contain semantic irrelevant information like caption shows "Thanks for watching" to original video clips and reaches high success rates in attacking six state-of-the-art video classification networks with high transferability. Jaehui and Jun-Hyuk [25] pay attention to the structural vulnerability of deep learning-based action recognition models against the adversarial attack using the one frame attack that adds an inconspicuous perturbation to only a single frame of a given video clip.

For skeleton data, Deepak and Chetan [26] reveal that the skeleton data, which they name it "Achilles' Heel", is more "vulnerable" under adversarial attack in multi-modal action recognition which involves other modal data including RGB video and depth map. On skeleton data, Jian and Naveed [9] proposed Constrained Iterative Attack for Skeleton Actions (CIASA) which perturbs joint locations in an action sequence while keep the keep the temporal coherence, spatial integrity and the anthropomorphic plausibility of the skeletons. CIASA shows that it is possible to attack state-of-art model by perturbing a part of joints with high confidence. He and Feixiang [8] proposed Skeletal Motion Action Recognition Attack (SMART) with a novel perceptual loss which keeps the attack imperceptibility. To quantify how distinct adversarial samples are from natural samples, SMART takes motion dynamics (derivatives) and bone length into consideration, and experiments show that it can reach high fool rate with low alteration rate. Yunfeng and Tianjia [27] developed the first black box attack on skeleton data by formulating a constrained optimization problem aiming to find a adversarial sample while still on the data manifold. Success of BASAR reveal that skeletal motion is a real-world example where on-manifold adversarial samples not only exist but are rather common which raises a serious concern for human activity recognition solutions as these on-manifold adversarial samples are implementable.

3 Method

3.1 Adversarial Attack Problem Formulation

Given a skeleton sequence $\mathbf{x} \in \mathbb{R}^{T \times N \times C}$ with T frames, in which $x^t \in \mathbb{R}^{N \times C}$ is the 3D coordinates ($C = 3$) of N joints at t-th frame, and a trained classifier $f_\theta(\mathbf{x}) : \mathbf{x} \to \mathbb{R}^k$ which gives a right classification result $y \in \mathbb{R}^k$ from k action classes. As usual, $\theta \in \mathbb{R}^p$ is the set of model parameters, we will not write θ in the following narration for convenience, since they will not change under the circumstance of adversarial attack. For a neural network, $f(\mathbf{x}) = \arg\max_i Z(\mathbf{x})_i = y$, where $Z(\mathbf{x})$ is the output of softmax function. Our goal, formulated in Eq. (1), then is to find a $\mathbf{x}'$ that classifier gives a wrong output y' while close to $\mathbf{x}$ under a certain distance metric $L(\cdot)$.

$$\begin{aligned} \min \quad & L(\mathbf{x}, \mathbf{x}') \\ \text{s.t.} \quad & f(\mathbf{x}') \neq f(\mathbf{x}) \text{ and } \mathbf{x}' \in [0,1]^{N \times C} \end{aligned} \tag{1}$$

However, Eq. (1) is difficult to solve due to the highly non-linearity of neural network models, it can be relaxed into following objective [28]:

$$\min_{\mathbf{x}'} L = \beta L_c(y, y') + (1-\beta) L(\mathbf{x}, \mathbf{x}') \tag{2}$$

where β is the weight balancing between two goals of adversarial attack: wrong classification result and perturbation imperceptibility. Practically, we choose minus cross-entropy as the $L_c(\cdot)$ to measure how far the model output and origin label are. For distance metric $L(\mathbf{x}, \mathbf{x}')$ will be explained later in Sect. 3.2.

Algorithm 1. Overview of our method

Input: Original sample $\mathbf{x}$, label y, classifier $f(\cdot)$, step size ϵ, attack target weight β and max epochs E.

INITIALIZE perturbations $\Delta \leftarrow \mathbf{0}$
Calculate dynamic attention A_d.
for $i = 1, ..., E$ **do**
  $\mathbf{x}' = \mathbf{x} + \Delta$
  $y' = f(\mathbf{x}')$
  if $y' \neq y$ **then**
    break
  end if
  $L_c = -\text{CrossEntropy}(Z(\mathbf{x}), y)$
  Calculate perceptual distance L_d with Eq. (4)
  $d = \frac{\mathrm{d}\beta L_c + (1-\beta) L_d}{\mathrm{d}\Delta}$
  Calculate perturbation contribution E with Eq. (10).
  $c = \frac{\mathrm{d}E}{\mathrm{d}\Delta}$.
  for joint j in all joints **do**
    if $c_j \leq 0$ **then**
      Set $d_j = 0$
    end if
  end for
  $\Delta = \Delta - \epsilon d$
end for

3.2 Perceptual Distance Metric

In adversarial attack to image classification models, there are three widely-used distance metrics in the literature for generating adversarial examples, all of them are L_p norms. In skeleton data, their physical meaning are as follow:

1. l_0 norm measures the number of coordinates in an adversarial skeleton sample that not equal to its counterpart in original one.
2. l_2 norm measures the Euclidean distance (root-mean-square) between $\mathbf{x}$ and $\mathbf{x}'$. l_2 norm was used in the initial adversarial example work [29].
3. l_∞ norm measures the maximum change to any coordinates which calculated as follow:

$$\|x_t - x_t'\|_\infty = \max\left(\left|x_t^1 - x_t^{1'}\right|, \ldots, \left|x_t^n - x_t^{n'}\right|\right) \tag{3}$$

l_∞ norm can be interpret as that each coordinates is allowed to change by up to a limit. Exist literature [30] argue that l_∞ is the optimal distance metric in image adversarial attack while the number of coordinates that allowed to alter is not restricted.

In skeleton adversarial attack, intuitively, we choose a combination of l_2 and l_∞ as the base distance metric since we want a small summation of perturbation while no conspicuous change on single joint. Except the similarity constrains, there are researches [31,32] in human action animation generation argue that inherent spatial and temporal dynamics play important roles in similarity judgement of human. Hence, we propose the following spatial-temporal dynamic similarity loss to avoid two problems: *(a)* drastic velocity and acceleration changes across frames; *(b)* perceptible difference comparing with reference sample.

$$L_d = \sum_{i=1}^{T} w_1 d(\mathbf{x}^i, \mathbf{x'}^i) + w_2 d(\mathbf{x'}^{i-1}, \mathbf{x'}^i) \tag{4}$$

$d(\cdot)$ in Eq. (4) calculate the difference of velocity and acceleration between two given samples with following equation:

$$d(\mathbf{x}, \mathbf{x}') = \sum_{i=1}^{T} w_v + w_a \tag{5}$$

Dynamic Attention. Since human prone to put more attention on high dynamic zones while identifying an action from another, we want to give more aggressive adversarial alteration on joints with higher dynamics across the frames. However, to alleviate drastic inconsistency on bone length, such attention weight on same part of body should be the same. To this ends, we use function mapped weight generator, formulated in Eq. (6), to calculate an attention vector in which element is the weight on corresponding joint.

$$w_j = \exp(\text{argrank}(\text{Var}(G\mathbf{x}))) \tag{6}$$

The whole body of 25 joints, HDM05 [11] as the example, are divided into 5 parts including two upper limbs, two lower limbs and spine with head.To implement the dynamic attention generator, we first calculate the mean of sum variance along the time for all joints in a group and then use a function to map the rank of dynamic level to weight. All the weight are normalized by l_2 norm to keep the convexity of loss function.

3.3 Sparsity Loss

Before works like SMART [8] and CIASA [9] contains a hard constrain called "Bone length Loss" which aims to keep the adversarial sample to have the same bone length with the original one.

$$l_{bl} = \|Bl(q) - Bl(\hat{q})\|_2^2 = \frac{1}{M} \sum_{i=1}^{M} \|Bl(q_i) - Bl(\hat{q}_i)\|_2^2 \tag{7}$$

However, such loss will cause cascaded alteration aggregation which means tiny alteration on a certain joint will cause changes on its neighborhood joints. To illustrate the flaw of bone length loss, we conducted a experiment whose result is shown in Fig. 2. To find out how an unconstrained bone length loss affect the adversarial sample, this experiment only use the bone length loss and give the adversarial sample a tiny starter noise and calculate the sum changes and run 10 iterations, the result shows that noise on single joint will spread to other joints which will damage the overall attack result.

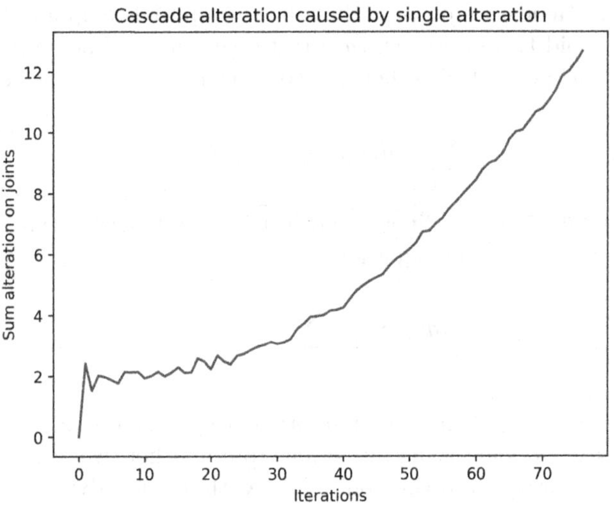

Fig. 2. To extend the cascade aggregation of alteration, we conducted this experiment which only use the bone length loos and give starter adversarial sample a small change on one joint. The result shows that the changes on one joints will spread to other joints by bone length loss if there is no any other constrains.

To alleviate such phenomenon, we abandoned the bone length loss and proposed the sparsity loss which punishes the unnecessary perturbation incases between joints. In this part, we use interaction, a term in game theory developed from Shapley Value [33] and proposed by Michel and Marc [34], to measure the contribution of a perturbation unit to the goal that fool the classifier. Shapley value on a joint is calculated by Eq. (8):

$$\varphi_i(v) = \sum_{S \subseteq N \setminus \{i\}} \frac{|S|!(n - |S| - 1)!}{n!}(v(S \cup \{i\}) - v(S)) \tag{8}$$

where N is the total number of joints and the sum extends over all subsets S of N not containing joint i and $v(\cdot)$ is a replaceable score function depending on attack strategy. The formula can be interpreted as follows: imagine the coalition being formed another joint at a time, with each joint demanding their contribution

$v(S \cup \{i\}) - v(S)$ as a fair compensation, and then for each joint take the average of this contribution over the possible different permutations in which the coalition can be formed.

Intuitively, perturbations do not appear on a joint independently, for example, perturbations on same the limb will have similar action pattern. According to work [34] and [31], the interaction between perturbation units i and j is defined by Eq. (9):

$$I_{ij}(\delta) = \varphi\left(S_{ij} \mid \Omega'\right) - \left[\varphi(i \mid \Omega \backslash \{j\}) + \varphi(j \mid \Omega \backslash \{i\})\right] \tag{9}$$

where $\varphi(i \mid \Omega \backslash \{j\})$ is the individual contribution of i which defined as the Sharply Value of i on collection without j. Equation (9) can be interpreted as the contribution change of unit i when the unit j exists w.r.t the case when the unit j is absent. Numerically, a positive interaction means the unit cooperate with each other while a negative interaction means the unit conflict with each other. However, calculate the combination is computational unacceptable thus we calculate the average interaction of joints which formulated as follow:

$$\mathbb{E}_{i,j}\left[I_{ij}(\delta)\right] = \frac{1}{n-1}\mathbb{E}_i[v(\Omega) - v(\Omega \backslash \{i\}) - v(\{i\}) + v(\emptyset)] \tag{10}$$

where $v(\Omega)$ is the score all joints are perturbed, $v(\Omega \backslash \{i\})$ is the score only joint i is not perturbed, $v(\{i\})$ is the score only joint i is perturbed and $v(\emptyset)$ is the score that no joint is perturbed. Since Sharply Value is reflexive ($I_{ij} = I_{ji}$), we can choose an arbitrary i.

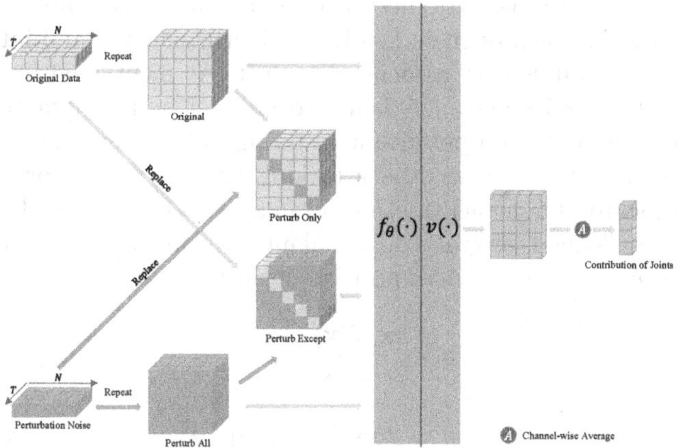

Fig. 3. Sparsity loss is calculated form four composited mini batch and

For the implementation of sparsity loss, shown in Fig. 3, we composite 4 mini batch whose batch size is the number of joints including origin sample ($\{\emptyset\}$), perturb all ($\{\Omega\}$), perturb one ($\{j\}$) and perturb except ($\{\Omega \backslash j\}$). Then the output are calculated by score function $v(\cdot)$ and calculate the average get the final loss value.

To suit different attack tasks, score function $v(\cdot)$ is alterable. For untargeted attack, the score is max value of z minus second largest value of z which suit our attack goal that decrease the classifier's confidence on right label, the max value of model output while haven't success attack), and increase the confidence on second largest value for efficiency.

$$v(z) = \max(z) - \text{second}(z) \tag{11}$$

And for targeted attack the score function are formulated as the increment of classifier's confidence on the target class.

4 Experiments

We validate our method in different modes on standard skeleton action datasets. We also test the transferability of adversarial sample generated from our method.

4.1 Dataset and Evaluation Metrics

HDM05 [11] is a MoCap (motion capture) dataset. It contains more than three hours of systematically recorded and well-documented motion capture data in the C3D as well as in the ASF/AMC data format. HDM05 contains almost 2,337 sequences with 130 motion classes performed by 5 different actors. **NTU-RGB-D** [12] is a large-scale dataset contains 56,880 samples of 60 action classes collected from 40 subjects. All these actions are recorded under 17 different scene conditions and each of them has RGB, depth, skeleton and infra-red data captured by Microsoft Kinect associated with it. As mentioned in [8], another widely used dataset **Kinectics** [35] is not covered for its low data quality which contains too much noise and perform as jittering in the origin data.

To adversarial attack tasks, the attacking success rate s, or fool rate, is the major indicator for attack method evaluations, but for further probe on our method we defined several additional metrics including average position deviation d, average absolute max positive deviation d_m:

$$s = \frac{|\mathbf{x}, f(\mathbf{x}) \neq y|}{|\mathbf{x}|} \tag{12}$$

$$d = \frac{1}{N}\sum_{j=1}^{N} ||\mathbf{x} - \mathbf{x}'||_2 \tag{13}$$

$$d_m = ||\mathbf{x} - \mathbf{x}'||_\infty \tag{14}$$

where N is the number of samples that classifier can't give a right classification.

4.2 Untargeted Attack

We first conduct the untargeted attack on NTU and HDM05 dataset. The numerical result of our method on untargeted attack is shown in Table 1. We achieved high success rate across different models with varying datasets which shows the generalize-ability. As we can see, the success rate of our method achieved state-of-art performance recorded by SMART in 2021 which remains higher than 95% on all test protocols. Except for hight attack success rate, our method also have kept a reasonably small perturbation value whose max deviation on all coordinates is 0.004. Similar as SMART, highest confusion is found between *walk_leftLC* (walk sideways, to the left, feet cross over alternately front/back) and *walk_right* on HDM05 attacking ST-GCN. It is common that original label and after-attack label have similar semantics, but there are also semantic deviated pairs like *grab* and *sit_down*.

Table 1. Success rate of untargeted attack on HDM05 and NTU

	HDM05			NTU_{XS}		
Method$n$Models	ST-GCN	AS-GCN	SGN	ST-GCN	2S-AGCN	SGN
SMART [8]	99	99	98	100	97	99
CIASA [9]	n	n	n	95	96	n
Ours	98	99	98	100	96	99

To extend the effectiveness of dynamic attention, we conduct the controlled experiment by setting the dynamic attention on all joints to $\frac{1}{N}$ in which N is the number of joints, so that all joints have the same weights. The result is shown in Fig. 4, in which adversarial sample generated with dynamic attention shows less alteration comparing with such without dynamic attention. By employ dynamic

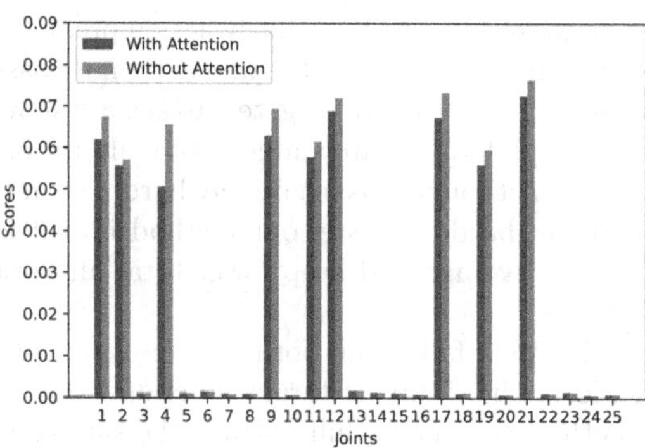

Fig. 4. A sample from action class *elbow_to_knee* is fooled to *kickRF*. Adversarial sample generated with dynamic attention shows less alteration on main joints overall.

attention, there are samples are fooled to different classes. For example, a sample form original class *walk_leftLC*, a lower limb movements, is fooled to a upper limb movements *throwFR* without dynamic attention, but fooled to *walk_left* after adding dynamic attention. Such example proved that dynamic attention can give the semantic information to guide the attack model to find adversarial sample semantically near the original sample.

Table 2. Deviation metrics attacking ST-GCN on HDM05

Method$n$Metrics	d	d_m
SMART	0.0028	6.3513
Ours	0.0074	**0.8338**

Except state-of-art attack success rate, our method shows superior performance in controlling unnecessary alteration which will potentially rise the risk of being perceived. We calculated two metrics Eq. (13) and Eq. (14) which measure the deviation between original skeleton and adversarial sample to estimate the ability to control unnecessary perturbations. The numerical results are shown in Table 2, in which sum deviation is much less than SMART, though max deviation on joints greater.

To understanding the perturbation on skeletons and show the perceptual similarity of a successful attack in Fig. 5. For every three attack tasks, we all choose "hand waving" as the target action. The red label on right is the label that classifier are fooled to. In untargeted attack (Top), the "hand waving" is fooled to a semantically close action "punching" comparing to which in targeted.

4.3 Targeted Attack

We use our method and SMART to perform targeted attack on HDM05 to compare the performance. To get equal conditions, we predefined the targeted classes before attack. Except the random mode, we setup another mode named hardest mode in which we specify the least-likely action prediction of the classifier as the target label implying that the most challenging misclassification target is chosen to launch attacks. The results of targeted attack are shown in Table 3, and we get a comparatively high fooling rate and low total alteration on both random mode and hardest mode. Although it is intuitively harder than untargeted attack in both random mode an hardest mode, our method is still able to success in more than 90% cases on average and keep lower total alteration comparing to other methods.

We analyze samples that failed for both method, and plot the fail attack matrix of them in Fig. 6, the y axis is target label and the x axis is the original label. Neither method can successfully attack the sample with target "walk backward". In mode hardest, SMART failed in all 82 attacks whose target label is "walk backward", and our method failed in 14 of them which shows great improvements in handling the attacks that contains little semantic relevance.

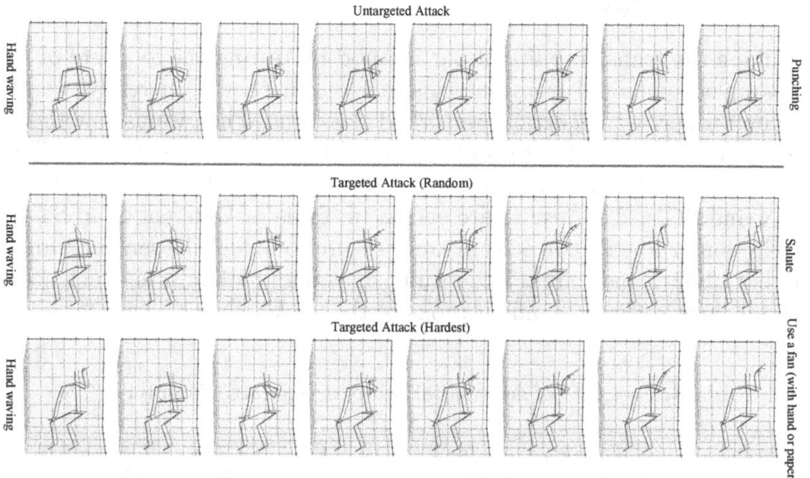

Fig. 5. Visual of adversarial sample (in red) and the original skeleton (in blue) generated from ST-GCN on NTU dataset. Top: Untargeted attack. Mid: Targeted attack with random assigned labels. Bottom: Targetted attack with most different semantics. (Color figure online)

Table 3. Success rate of targeted attack on HDM05 (Random/Hardest)

Method/Metric	Success rate	d	d_m
SMART	77.32/70.43	20.32/28.44	0.02/0.03
Ours	**93.17/83.12**	**13.91/17.23**	0.09/0.14

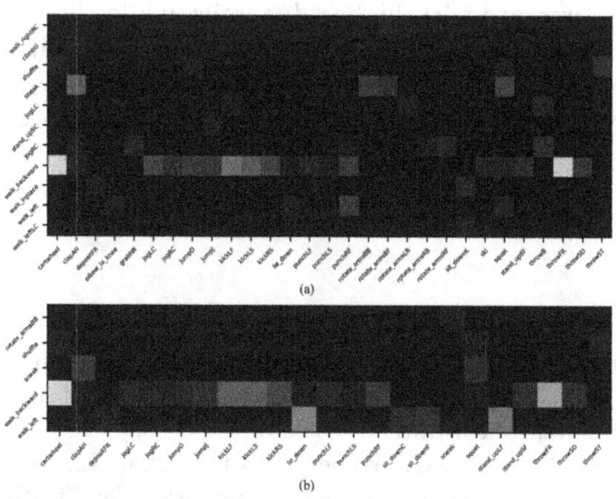

Fig. 6. (a) The fail pairs of SMART which failed in 29 original classes and 11 target classes, the hardest target class is *walk_backward*. (b) The fail pairs of **Ours** which failed in 11 original classes and 3 target classes, the hardest target class is *walk_backward*.

4.4 Transferability

We examine the transferability of our method by testing the fool rate of adversarial samples generated from one classifier on another. Concretely, we attack skeleton classifier A to generate perturbed skeletons. Then we use another classifier B to classify these skeletons and examine the fooling rate. We use ST-GCN as the classifier to generated the adversarial sample on NTU to attack AS-GCN, 2S-GCN and SGN. The results are shown in Table 4. Different from ST-GCN, 2s-AGCN constructed a two stream architecture to model the semantic information in both bones and joints. The results show high fooling rate which achieved 90% in all three different configurations of the 2s-AGCN.

Table 4. Fool rate of adversarial samples generated from ST-GCN

Classifier	Js-GCN	Bs-GCN	2S-GCN
Fooling rate	98.21%	97.12%	96.48%

5 Conclusion

In this paper, we reveal the alteration explosion problem caused by bone length constrain which will damage the quality of generated adversarial samples and present a novel sparse attack method which substitute the spatial temporal consistency constrain for bone length constrain. Meanwhile, in order to further reduce unnecessary perturbations, we design a perturbation pruning strategy base on interaction analyze. Besides, for a trait of human that one is prone to put his attention on zones with higher dynamics while they are identifying an action from another we use dynamic attention to attack joints are more active. Experiments on widely used datasets and trending models prove the superiority of our method. Numerically, we keep the state-of-art attack success rate while decrease the sum alteration by a large margin.

References

1. Wang, X., Li, J., Kuang, X., Tan, Y.-A., Li, J.: The security of machine learning in an adversarial setting: a survey. J. Parallel Distrib. Comput. **130**, 12–23 (2019)
2. Karim, F., Majumdar, S., Darabi, H.: Adversarial attacks on time series. IEEE Trans. Pattern Anal. Mach. Intell. 1 (2020)
3. Ismail Fawaz, H., Forestier, G., Weber, J., Idoumghar, L., Muller, P.-A.: Adversarial attacks on deep neural networks for time series classification. In: 2019 International Joint Conference on Neural Networks (IJCNN), pp. 1–8 (2019)
4. Nie, Q., Wang, J., Wang, X., Liu, Y.: View-invariant human action recognition based on a 3D Bio-constrained skeleton model. IEEE Trans. Image Process. **28**, 3959–3972 (2019)

5. Ahmad, T., Jin, L., Zhang, X., Lai, S., Tang, G., Lin, L.: Graph convolutional neural network for human action recognition: a comprehensive survey. IEEE Trans. Artif. Intell. **2**, 128–145 (2021)
6. Huang, X., et al.: A survey of safety and trustworthiness of deep neural networks: verification, testing, adversarial attack and defence, and interpretability. Comput. Sci. Rev. **37** (2020)
7. Bai, X., Yang, M., Liu, Z.: On the robustness of skeleton detection against adversarial attacks. Neural Netw. **132**, 416–427 (2020)
8. Wang, H., et al.: Understanding the robustness of skeleton-based action recognition under adversarial attack. In: Proceedings of the IEEE International Conference on Computer Vision, pp. 14656–14665 (2021)
9. Liu, J., Akhtar, N., Mian, A.: Adversarial attack on skeleton-based human action recognition. In: IEEE Transactions on Neural Networks and Learning Systems, pp. 1–14 (2020)
10. Tramèr, F., Kurakin, A., Papernot, N., Goodfellow, I., Boneh, D., McDaniel, P.: Ensemble adversarial training: attacks and defenses. In: Proceedings of the International Conference on Learning Representations (2018)
11. Müller, M., Röder, T., Clausen, M., Eberhardt, B., Krüger, B., Weber, A.: Documentation Mocap Database HDM05. Technical Report CG-2007-2 (2007)
12. Shahroudy, A., Liu, J., Ng, T.-T., Wang, G.: NTU RGB+D: a large scale dataset for 3D human activity analysis. In: Proceedings of the IEEE Conference on Computer Vision and Pattern Recognition, pp. 1010–1019 (2016)
13. Li, W., Wen, L., Chang, M.-C., Nam Lim, S., Lyu, S.: Adaptive RNN tree for large-scale human action recognition. In: Proceedings of the IEEE International Conference on Computer Vision, pp. 1444–1452 (2017)
14. Liu, J., Shahroudy, A., Xu, D., Kot, A.C., Wang, G.: Skeleton-based action recognition using spatio-temporal LSTM network with trust gates. IEEE Trans. Pattern Anal. Mach. Intell. **40**, 3007–3021 (2017)
15. Li, B., He, M., Dai, Y., Cheng, X., Chen, Y.: 3d skeleton based action recognition by video-domain translation-scale invariant mapping and multi-scale dilated CNN. Multimed. Tools Appl. **77**, 22901–22921 (2018)
16. Zhu, A., et al.: Exploring a rich spatial-temporal dependent relational model for skeleton-based action recognition by bidirectional LSTM-CNN. Neurocomputing **414**, 90–100 (2020)
17. Zhang, Z.: Microsoft kinect sensor and its effect. IEEE Multimed. **19**, 4–10 (2012)
18. Cao, Z., Hidalgo, G., Simon, T., Wei, S.-E., Sheikh, Y.: OpenPose: realtime multi-person 2D pose estimation using part affinity fields. IEEE Trans. Pattern Anal. Mach. Intell. **43**, 172–186 (2021)
19. Yan, S., Xiong, Y., Lin, D.: Spatial temporal graph convolutional networks for skeleton-based action recognition. In: Proceedings of the AAAI Conference on Artificial Intelligence (2018)
20. Li, M., Chen, S., Chen, X., Zhang, Y., Wang, Y., Tian, Q.: Actional-structural graph convolutional networks for skeleton-based action recognition. In: Proceedings of the IEEE International Conference on Computer Vision, pp. 3590–3598 (2019)
21. Zhang, P., Lan, C., Zeng, W. Xing, J., Xue, J., Zheng, N.: Semantics-guided neural networks for efficient skeleton-based human action recognition. In: Proceedings of the IEEE International Conference on Computer Vision, pp. 1112–1121 (2020)
22. Li, J., Liu, Y., Chen, T., Xiao, Z., Li, Z., Wang, J.: Adversarial attacks and defenses on cyber-physical systems: a survey. IEEE Internet Things J. **7**, 5103–5115 (2020)
23. Nowroozi, E., Dehghantanha, A., Parizi, R.M., Choo, K.-K.R.: A survey of machine learning techniques in adversarial image forensics. Comput. Secur. **100** (2021)

24. Chen, Z., Xie, L., Pang, S., He, Y., Tian, Q.: Appending adversarial frames for universal video attack. In: Proceedings of the IEEE Conference on Application of Computer Vision, pp. 3199–3208 (2021)
25. Hwang, J., Kim, J.-H., Choi, J.-H. Lee, J.-S.: Just one moment: structural vulnerability of deep action recognition against one frame attack. In: Proceedings of the IEEE International Conference on Computer Vision, pp. 7668–7676 (2021)
26. Kumar, D., Kumar, C., Seah, C.W., Xia, S., Shao, M.: Finding achilles' heel: adversarial attack on multi-modal action recognition. In: ACM International Conference on Multimedia, pp. 3829–3837 (2020)
27. Diao, Y., Shao, T., Yang, Y.-L., Zhou, K., Wang, H.: BASAR: black-box attack on skeletal action recognition. In: Proceedings of the IEEE International Conference on Computer Vision, pp. 7597–7607 (2021)
28. Carlini, N., Wagner, D.: Towards evaluating the robustness of neural networks. In: IEEE Symposium on Security and Privacy, pp. 39–57 (2017)
29. Szegedy, C., et al.: Intriguing properties of neural networks. In: Proceedings of the International Conference on Learning Representations (2014)
30. Hazan, T., Papandreou, G., Tarlow, D.: Adversarial perturbations of deep neural networks. In Perturbations, Optimization, and Statistics, pp. 311–342 (2017)
31. Mirzaei, M.S., Meshgi, K., Frigo, E., Nishida, T.: Animgan: a spatiotemporally-conditioned generative adversarial network for character animation. In: Proceedings of the IEEE International Conference on Intelligent Control and Information Processing, pp. 2286–2290 (2020)
32. Yan, X., et al.: MT-VAE: learning motion transformations to generate multimodal human dynamics. In: European Conference on Computer Vision, pp. 265–281 (2018)
33. Shapley, L.S.: 17. A value for n-person games. Contribut. Theory Games **2**, 307–318 (2016)
34. Grabisch, M., Roubens, M.: An axiomatic approach to the concept of interaction among players in cooperative games. Int. J. Game Theory **28**, 547–565 (1999)
35. Kay, W., et al.: The Kinetics Human Action Video Dataset. ArXiv:1705.06950 Cs (2017)

LMGROUP: A Lightweight Multicast Group Key Management for IoT Networks

Pegah Nikbakht Bideh(✉)

Electrical and Information Technology Department, Lund University, Lund, Sweden
pegah.nikbakht_bideh@eit.lth.se

Abstract. Due to limitations of IoT networks, including limited bandwidth, memory, battery, etc., secure multicast group communication has gained more attention, and to enable that, a group key establishment scheme is required to share the secret key among the group members. The current group key establishment protocols were mostly designed for Wireless Sensor Networks, requiring device interaction, high computation costs, or high storage on the device side. To address these drawbacks, in this paper we design LMGROUP, a lightweight and multicast group key establishment protocol for IoT networks, that is based on Elliptic Curve Integrated Encryption Scheme and HMAC verification and does not require device interaction. We also suggest an algorithm for unpredictable group member selection. Our experimental result of implementing LMGROUP indicates it has low storage, low computation, and low communication costs. Furthermore, the formal security verification indicates LMGROUP is secure and robust against different attacks.

Keywords: IoT · Group key establishment · Key management

1 Introduction

IoT networks have several challenges; one of the challenges is that the majority of devices are resource constrained, which means that they have limited memory, battery, power, and limited computational resources. In IoT networks, bandwidth is another challenge [1,2] since increasing the number of devices also makes the bandwidth and communication resources limited. Due to these limitations, multicast group communication has become more favorable in IoT networks since sending multicast messages to a group of devices is more efficient than sending unicast messages and overloading the network with multiple messages. Multicast group communication is particularly important, where software updates or patches are required to be sent to a group of devices simultaneously.

In order to enable multicast secure group communication, a group key needs to be established in advance. Various group key establishment methods have been proposed, which will be described in detail in Sect. 2. Most of these schemes have been designed for WSN (Wireless Sensor Network), which do not take the characteristics of IoT environments into account. The designed schemes for

C. Su et al. (Eds.): ISPEC 2022, LNCS 13620, pp. 213–230, 2022.
https://doi.org/10.1007/978-3-031-21280-2_12

WSN require interaction between group members to get access to the shared key. In such solutions, many nodes participate in the computations, and this results in unnecessary intensive cryptographic operations, and additional packet forwarding overhead [3]. Device interaction is hard to achieve in IoT networks where devices have the least communication. Examples of such networks in smart cities or smart homes are where different sensors are placed in different places to gather information about temperature, air pollution, etc. These sensors gather data and send aggregated data periodically (in a unicast way) to a central server for further analysis, and device-to-device communication is less likely.

The central server then should be able to send control commands or updates/upgrades and patches to the sensors in a multicast way. These commands and updates should not be broadcasted to all IoT sensors for availability reasons since if any unexpected error happens, it can affect the availability of the whole network. As a result, the central server needs to group the IoT devices and decides on group membership; this can be done manually by the administrator or automatically to make the group membership less predictable to attackers. In this paper, we first suggest an automatic algorithm for unpredictable group member selection. After the selection of group members, a group key needs to be established to the group members. These group keys need to be renewed frequently due to changes in the group membership to provide forward secrecy. For that, we then design LMGROUP, a new lightweight multicast group key management scheme that can work efficiently in small to large networks. LMGROUP does not have the problems of other group key establishment schemes for WSN, including interactions between group members or heavy procedures on constrained devices. We implement LMGROUP, and the experiments indicate it has efficient memory usage, communication, and computation costs. The experiments also show the scalability of LMGROUP. Finally, the formal security verification indicates our multicast scheme is secure against different attacks, such as replay attacks. Our main contributions are:

- We suggest an algorithm for unpredictable group member selection.
- We design a new lightweight and multicast group key management scheme based on hybrid cryptography.
- We implement LMGROUP and indicate it is scalable and has efficient memory usage, communication, and computation costs.
- We formally verify LMGROUP and indicate it is secure against different attacks.

The rest of this paper is organized as follows: in Sect. 2, the related work on group key establishment methods for WSN and IoT networks is presented. In Sect. 3, the details of LMGROUP, including the suggested group member selection algorithm and our designed scheme, are described. Implementation details are presented in Sect. 4. Performance evaluation and formal security verification are described in Sect. 5 and 6. Finally the paper is concluded in Sect. 7.

2 Related Work

Various Group Key Management (GKM) methods had been proposed for WSNs and IoT networks and were extensively reviewed in [4–6], in the case of the used cryptography method, they are divided into three categories: symmetric, asymmetric, and hybrid. In the case of key establishment authority, these methods can be divided into centralized and distributed methods [4]. Centralized methods are mostly applicable to networks with static topology, while distributed approaches are more suitable for dynamic networks where nodes have high levels of mobility and can join and leave the network quite often. Our work focuses on centralized schemes, and we do not review distributed schemes here. Among the reviewed schemes in [4], the most lightweight centralized approaches applicable to static small to large networks are: LKH [7], S2RP [8], TKH [9], and LEAP [10].

LKH (Logical Key Hierarchy) is a multicast rekeying approach for WSNs. In LKH the nodes are divided into subgroups based on a logical hierarchy and a symmetric key is assigned to each leaf node. LKH has a reasonable communication cost in most WSN networks since only the existing members in the subgroup receive the rekeying messages. However, each member of the group needs to maintain the keys from the leaf to the root node path, which causes additional storage and computation cost on the node's side [7]. S2RP (Secure and Scalable Rekeying Protocol) is similar to LKH with almost the same performance results, but instead, it has added security to authenticate the rekeying messages through the use of a one-way hash function [8].

TKH (Topological Key Hierarchy) is another variant of LKH in which the logical key tree is mapped to the physical topology of the nodes in the network (key tree); this further reduces the communication cost of total rekeying messages. In TKH, based on the routing tree, the key tree can be constructed; the nodes attach to a parent node until they reach the group controller (sink node). Although TKH reduces the storage overhead on the node side, it does not provide any key authentication mechanism.

In LEAP (Localized Encryption and Authentication Protocol), four types of keys are established to the nodes, including an individual key, a pairwise key, a cluster key, and a global key. This scheme has low computation, communication, and storage overhead, but for broadcast authentication, it relies on μTESLA [11] which requires synchronization between nodes, but the node synchronization is heavy, and it is hard to achieve in IoT or WSN networks.

Another lightweight and decentralized group key establishment for IoT was proposed in [5]. This scheme is also based on a logical hierarchy with one Key Distribution Center (KDC) and several Sub Key Distribution Centers (SKDCs) that can be used to avoid the single point of failure problem in centralized-based schemes discussed above. Same as LKH based schemes, each device needs to store the keys from the leaf to the parent path. Again, this scheme can have high storage costs on the device side, which depend on the subgroup size.

As mentioned above, the problems of Key Tree Hierarchy-based key establishment methods are high storage, high computation costs, and inability to provide key authentication mechanisms or requirement of time synchronization, which makes them non-practical to use for IoT networks. Most of these methods depend on the contribution of members of the same group, which is difficult to handle in IoT networks, especially in networks where IoT nodes do not interact with each other.

Other than key tree-based methods, there are a variety of non-interactive key agreement protocols [12–16] applicable to WSNs or IoT networks. For IoT networks, a secure group key establishment based on Elliptic Curve Cryptographic (ECC) operations was proposed in [12]. This work has high computation cost since the key establishment requires one signing and one signature verification on the IoT unit side.

In [15], two lightweight protocols based on ECC operations were proposed, which was an improvement of the schemes proposed in [13,14]. The protocols provide authenticity, confidentiality, and integrity. However, they are vulnerable to replay attacks [16], and they have high computational costs (especially protocol 1, which requires two signature verifications on the IoT unit side), which make them non-applicable to IoT environments. As an improvement of [15], the authors in [16] proposed a new key establishment protocol based on the Identity-Based Credentials (IBC) mechanism and ECC operations, which is resistant to replay attacks. In this scheme, they have used HMAC verification instead of signature verification which is more applicable to IoT devices than heavy signature-based operations. Although this scheme has a lower computation cost in comparison to protocols in [15], it has higher communication costs due to the increased number of transferred messages. Also, it does not consider multicast communication and group key sharing.

Considering the problems of Key Tree Hierarchy-based methods, we address these problems and suggested a scheme, LMGROUP, that does not require time synchronization, has low storage (it does not require storing all the keys from the leaves to the root) and has low communication and computation overhead. LMGROUP is a multicast authenticated key establishment mechanism with hybrid cryptography. In LMGROUP we consider the advantages of the protocol in [16] including HMAC verification and replay protection; we modified the second protocol presented in [15], protocol 2, and proposed a new scheme that applies to IoT networks. LMGROUP will be explained in detail in Sect. 3.

3 Scenario and Scheme

In this section, first, we provide the assumptions about the IoT network and the use case in which the proposed scheme is most suitable, and then we present the details of LMGROUP scheme.

3.1 Assumptions

In our network, we assume two types of nodes: resource-rich nodes and constrained IoT nodes. Resource-rich nodes do not have limited storage and processing capabilities, and they can be used to perform heavy operations and are used to manage different groups of IoT nodes. Resource-rich nodes are referred to as servers throughout this paper. We assume to have a fault-tolerant centralized architecture with redundant servers available in the network. To avoid a single point of failure having redundant servers is required. We assume a network scenario in which IoT devices are stable or have low mobility. Devices can join or leave the network for any reason, e.g., physical maintenance operations, adding new devices, or removing old ones from the network. Examples of such use case scenarios are in smart buildings with smart lights or smart doors where the devices have fixed positions.

In our use case networks, device interaction is not possible. We consider that the devices will not contribute in any way to the group key establishment. In these network scenarios, since there are usually many devices available, to keep the bandwidth as low as possible, the group key establishment is preferred to be done in a multicasted way. If during multicast group key establishment, one of the group members fails to receive or update the group key in its next contact with the server, it can retrieve the group key in a unicast way.

We assume that each device has owned a symmetric master key denoted by k_m, this key is provisioned by the network administrator in the setup phase, and the k_m keys are also stored with each device identity securely on the server. Later, in the bootstrapping step, k_m is used to extract a session key, k_s, based on a key derivation function to establish a secure session with the server. We assume that the server decides on the group members, and the devices themselves can not decide which group they want to belong to. The devices can belong to multiple groups at the same time, but messages encrypted with one group key can not be decrypted with another key.

3.2 Network Scenario

In our network scenario, after the bootstrapping phase, the devices send their aggregated data encrypted with k_s keys back to the server periodically based on defined time intervals. Then after receiving an acknowledgment from the server, the devices go to sleep mode to reduce the energy consumption. The server needs to decide which devices should to be grouped; our suggested algorithm to decide on the group members will be described below in Sect. 3.3. After deciding on the group members, the server will piggyback a hint along with the acknowledgment of the previous message to the IoT device. This hint carries information about the new group *ID*, and it can be used as the seed of the key derivation function on the IoT unit side to extract an authentication key which is further going to be used to authenticate the group key establishment messages. The required communication between IoT devices and the server to derive the group authentication key is depicted in Fig. 1. After receiving the new group *ID* by the IoT devices inside the group, they use it to derive the key K^*, which is the authentication key. The authentication key will be used during the group key establishment phase to protect the authenticity of multicast messages.

Other than the new group *ID*, the wake-up time should also be sent to the IoT devices so they can wake up at the defined time to receive the multicast group key establishment messages. To avoid heavy time synchronization procedure on IoT unit sides, instead of sending the wake-up time, the server sends two other parameters to the devices: T and a window frame. T defines the number of seconds that the device needs to wake up after receiving the acknowledgment, and the window frame (which depends on the network latency, delay, etc., will be defined by the network administrator), defines the window frame in which the device should be active. As an example, if T is 6000 and the window frame is 60, then the device needs to be active from 5940 until 6060 seconds after receiving the acknowledgment.

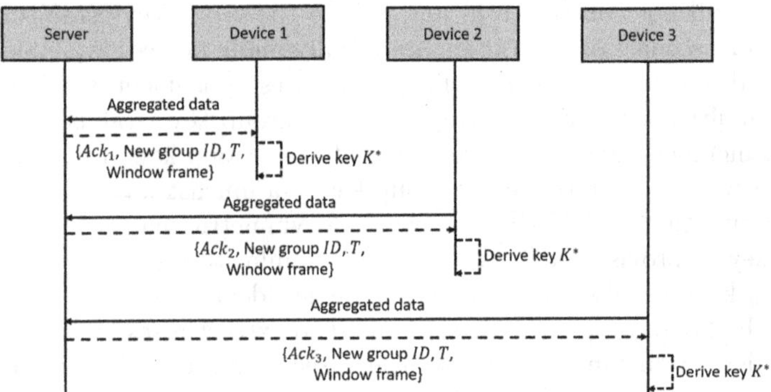

Fig. 1. Communication between the server and three IoT devices in the same group to derive authentication key

3.3 Group Member Selection

In WSN or IoT networks with more mobility, the nodes themselves can join or leave the groups based on different factors, e.g., signal strength, distance, etc. There have been some methods suggested for group member selection [17] or cluster head selection [18,19] in WSN. These algorithms do not apply to our use case scenario or, in general, to the networks where nodes are stable and cannot choose the grouping themselves; thus, we suggest an algorithm for group member selection that the server in our scheme can use.

The network administrator registers available IoT devices in the network to the central server (and redundant servers). On the device registration, information, including device identity number, device master secret, device public key, and device criticality level, will be stored on the server. The network administrator will decide the device's criticality level, depending on how critical the device's role is in the network. For example, in the case of smart doors in a hospital, the main entrance door has the highest criticality while the sub-doors have lower criticalities. We have considered three levels of criticality: low, medium, and high. These levels will be used for group member selection.

The group member selection should not be predictable by an outsider attacker; otherwise, the devices targeted for multicast group keying or update can become a target of DoS (Denial Of Service) attacks. Our suggested group member selection algorithm selects devices based on criticality levels and makes sure not all critical devices are in the same group. The algorithm works as follows:

Algorithm 1. Group member selection algorithm

Require: n, the number of group members, N, the total number of registered devices H, M, and $L \geq 0$ are the number of devices with high to low criticality, respectively, such that $H + M + L = N$.

$G_c \leftarrow \frac{N}{n}$,

$H' \leftarrow \lfloor \frac{H}{G_c} \rfloor$, $M' \leftarrow \lfloor \frac{M}{G_c} \rfloor$, $L' \leftarrow \lfloor \frac{L}{G_c} \rfloor$, (The remaining members will be added to the groups later by the administrator.)

$i \leftarrow 0$,

while $i < G_c$ **do**

  $G[i] \leftarrow$ Take random members from H, M, L with the size of H', M', and L', respectively.

  $i \leftarrow i + 1$

end while

Return the groups, $G[i]$s.

As it can be seen in Algorithm 1, based on the number of available devices with different criticality levels, the members of a group will be formed randomly. If new devices join the network, they will get group membership in the next round of the algorithm. If a device leaves the network due to maintenance or replacement, the group will continue with previous members until the next round of running the algorithm. Leaving a group to join another group is not possible by the device since the server only does the grouping process. The network administrator decides how often the group member selection algorithm should happen.

3.4 Designed Scheme

As mentioned earlier in Sect. 2, two lightweight key establishment protocols based on ECC operations were proposed in [15], and an improved version of them was proposed in [16]. The second protocol presented in [15], protocol 2, and the improved protocol presented in [16] are the basis of our scheme. In order to better understand our designed scheme, here, we first briefly explain these two protocols and then we suggest our scheme.

Basis of LMGROUP. Protocol 2 [15] uses ECIES or Elliptic Curve Integrated Encryption Scheme algorithm to establish a shared secret among the group members. In this scheme, an initiator (I) with several responders U_js in the network is considered, and the initiator determines the group members. The random r

is generated by *I*, then R is calculated as $R = rG$ (G is the base point as in ECDH). Then for each group member EC points S_js are computed by the initiator, $S_j = d_i Q_j$ + R, and Q_j represents the public key of the group members. The point $S_j = (x_i, y_j)$ will be encoded to another point (u_i, v_i) by calculating the hash over the point values. Then the encoded points will be XORed, and the results will be concatenated to make the set P. The group's secret key, k, is then the hash value over the XORed values of u_i. The *Auth* value is calculated as $Auth = h(k\|R\|P)$. The multicast message that will be sent to the group members includes: *Auth, C, R, U, P*, in which C is the counter value and U contains identities of all group members. Finally, a digital signature will be added to the message, and the message will be broadcasted to all sensor nodes in the network. Each receiver first checks if its identity is included in the U part of the message; if yes, it verifies the signature and the counter value. If the verification is successful it computes u_j using R and its private key as: $S_j = d_j Q_i$ + R. The node will encode the point, and finally, the values of the encoded point will be used to derive the group key. After that, the node verifies the authenticity of the key by checking if *Auth* is equal to $h(k\|R\|P)$. Finally, the recipient nodes will send an acknowledgment to the initiator to finish the handshake.

The problems of the above scheme are listed below:

- It is not protected against replay attacks;
- It requires heavy signature verification on the IoT unit side;
- The first message needs to be broadcasted to all sensor nodes in the network; this can cause many extra checking by IoT devices not belonging to the same group and can further cause extra overhead to the whole network.

In [16], the authors proposed a key management scheme that is quite similar to the work explained above [15]. In [16] HMAC verification is used instead of signature verification which makes it more energy efficient in comparison to [15]. In [16], replay attack protection is considered, but the scheme only works in a unicasted way, and it can not be used for group key management. The other problem of the scheme [16] is that, although it has lower computation overhead than the work presented in [15], it causes higher communication overhead.

LMGROUP. In our designed scheme, we take the advantages of these two protocols [15,16] including multicast and ECIES based operations for group key sharing from protocol [15] and HMAC verification instead of heavy signature verification for authenticity from protocol [16]. We design LMGROUP that is lightweight in case of communication, computation, and storage overhead. We also suggest a replay protection mechanism and a group member selection technique so that the messages are not required to be sent to all devices in the network and can be sent to the target devices in the beginning. We describe the details of LMGROUP here.

The operation flow of our designed scheme is depicted in Fig. 2. After deciding about the group members and pre-establishment of the authentication key K^*

to group members by the server, as can be seen in Fig. 2, the operation flow of LMGROUP, which starts on the server side, is as follows:

- The server selects a random r and computes $R = rG$, in which G is the base point as in ECDH, and based on the number of group members in the range of *1 to* n, the point $S_j = dQ_j + R = (x_i, y_j)$ will be calculated, where d is the private key of the server and Q_j is the public key of group members.
- A unique random session *ID* will then be generated by the server that is used to protect against replay attacks.
- For each member of the group, $\overline{x_j} = \{\oplus_{i \neq j} x_i\} \oplus y_j$ will be calculated and then the set $Se = (\overline{x_1}, ..., \overline{x_n})$ will be formed, and the group key is calculated as $k = h(\oplus_i x_i)$ which is the hash over XOR values of x_i.
- The authentication value is calculated as $Auth = h(k \| R \| Se)$.
- The HMAC will be calculated over the fields of $\{ID, Auth, R, Se\}$ with the use of the authentication key K^* and it will be sent along with $\{ID, Auth, R, Se\}$ to all group members.

Then the flow continues on the device side:

- The group members upon receiving the message, first verify the HMAC, then each recipient device uses R and its own private key d_j to construct the point $S_j = d_j Q + R = (x_j, y_j)$.
- Then, the device extracts its own $\overline{x_j}$ from the received set Se, and then it can derive the group key as $k = h(\overline{x_j} \oplus x_j \oplus y_j)$, $\overline{x_j}$ contains other x and y_j value, therefore the similar values of y_j will be removed from the calculation and only all x values will be XORed as expected.
- After key derivation, the $Auth$ should be checked if it is equal to $h(k \| R \| Se)$ or not. If $Auth$ is valid then an acknowledgment will be calculated as $Ack_j = h(k \| ID \| Q_j)$, in which k is the extracted group key, *ID* is the received session *ID* by the device and Q_j is the device public key.
- The acknowledgment along with device *ID* (device identity number) will be sent back to the server.

The flow is then finalized on the server side:

- The server uses the group key and device public key Q_j to verify the acknowledgment. On a successful verification, the authenticity of the derived group key by the device is verified.

4 Implementation

We have implemented LMGROUP on a real testbed setup. For the implementation, we have used ESP32-S2[1] a popular IoT development board representing IoT devices (the implemented code for device side and server side is available[2]). ESP32-S2 is a low power and single-core Wi-Fi Microcontroller SoC with

[1] https://www.espressif.com/en/products/socs/esp32-s2.
[2] https://github.com/pegahnikbakht/Multi-key-share.

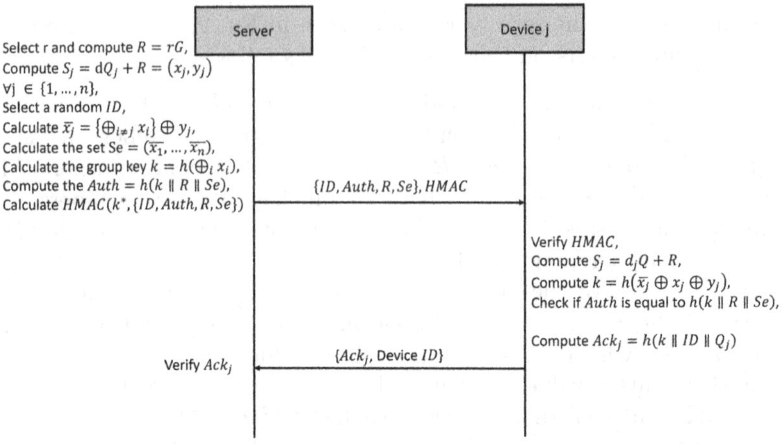

Fig. 2. Operation flow between server and a sample device in LMGROUP

high performance and a rich set of IO capabilities. ESP32-S2 has cryptographic hardware accelerators for enhanced performance, and it integrates a rich set of peripherals with different programmable GPIOs that can be configured to provide USB OTG, LCD interface, UART, and other common functionalities. In our implementation, to annotate measurements, we have used UART interface. In our measurements, we used Otii Arc[3] device as a power analyzer to record and measure real-time currents and voltages using UART logs.

We have used SHA256 for the hash function, and for HMAC, we have used HMAC-SHA256. For the hash function, we have used hardware acceleration on ESP32-S2. On the IoT device side, for the ECC point addition and multiplication, we have used the Mbed TLS library.

4.1 Testbed and Environmental Setup

Our testbed consists of 10 ESP32-S2 boards, and 7 out of these 10 boards are grouped by the server to receive the group key. After the server decides the group members, it calculates: S_j, $\overline{x_j}$ (j in range of 1 to 7), Se, k. $Auth$ and HMAC (as explained in Sect. 3.4). The calculation of these values can be done at any time between the time the group members have been decided until the time the devices wake up, based on the server workload during this time. During the specified wake-up time window, the devices wake up and wait to receive the group key information from the server. Our testbed setup and further communications between the server and IoT devices are depicted in Fig. 3. As shown in Fig. 3, the multicast group key message will be sent to all of the grouped devices by the server. After receiving, verifying the message, and extracting the group key, the devices will send back an acknowledgment to the server. Whenever the server

[3] https://www.qoitech.com/otii/.

receives the acknowledgment from all members, the group key is established and can be used for further communications. The server has a specified timeout for receiving the acknowledgments from all group members; if the server does not receive the acknowledgment from any of the group members, it will send the group key information again to those members in a unicast way later.

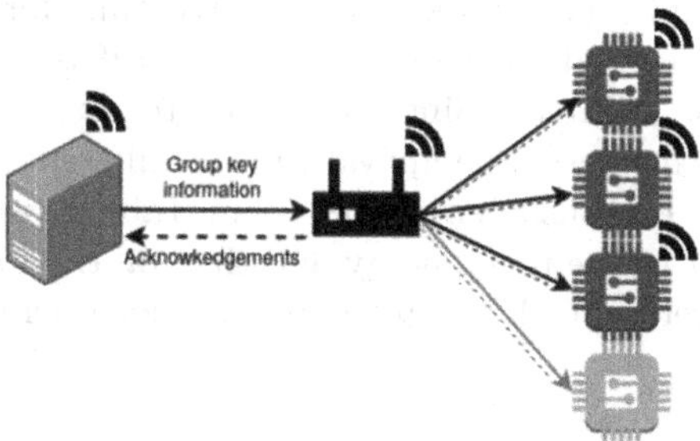

Fig. 3. Testbed setup for LMGROUP

5 Performance Evaluation

In order to show the efficiency of our group key establishment scheme, we measure the communication, computation, and storage overhead of our scheme.

5.1 Communication and Computation Cost

In order to calculate the communication overhead, the number of transferred bytes between the server and IoT devices during the group key establishment has been calculated; in the calculations, the number of bytes in the acknowledgment is also included. The number of bytes in the first message from server to the devices are $145 + 32 * n$ (n is the number of devices inside the group), which consists of 16 bytes of *ID*, 32 bytes of HMAC, 32 bytes of *Auth*, 64 bytes of *R*, and $32 * n$ bytes of *Se* which depends to the number of group members n. The response back from the device includes an acknowledgment (32 bytes) and a *Device ID* (12 bytes) which is in total 44 bytes. Therefore the total number of transmitted bytes between the server and the devices are $189 + 32 * n$.

In order to compute the computation overhead on the device side, the energy consumption and the time was measured from the time the device receives the group key information from the server until it sends back the acknowledgment. We have done the measurements using two different elliptic curves with the same security level, Secp256r1 (prime field curve) and Secp256k1 (Koblitz curve). The total time elapsed for the key establishment on the server was also measured, which is the time from when the key establishment message was sent until all acknowledgments from the devices in the multicast group have been received and verified. The results of computation overhead are indicated in Table 1. As can be seen, a single EC point addition and multiplication of Secp256r1 consumes more energy and requires more time than Secp256k1 since prime field curves are a few bits stronger than Koblitz curves [20]. Therefore, using the prime field curve Secp256r1 for the group key establishment would require more time and energy on both the device and server sides. The required time for single acknowledge verification does not depend on the curve type, and it is almost equal for both curves, as can be seen in Table 1. Since Secp256r1 requires more processing time on the device side, it increases the arrival time of different acknowledgments as well as the total key establishment time. From Table 1, we can also conclude that the greatest part of the used energy and time on the IoT side is due to the ECC operations; therefore the hash and MAC function operations are considered negligible.

Table 1. Computation overhead of LMGROUP with two different curves

Curve		Energy (μwh)	Time (ms)
Secp256k1	Total key establishment (IoT side)	32.0809	405.7857
	Total key establishment (Server side)	–	570.3442
	Single Ack verification (Server side)	–	0.1129
	Time between arriving Acks (Server side)	–	0.8210
	Singel EC point addition and multiplication	25.6172	321.3448
Secp256r1	Total key establishment (IoT side)	39.0281	494.0000
	Total key establishment (Server side)	–	692.0681
	Single Ack verification (Server side)	–	0.1226
	Time between arriving Acks (Server side)	–	1.3483
	Singel EC point addition and multiplication	33.5333	414.1000

According to the measured values in Table 1, we tried to calculate how long the whole key establishment time (from the time the server sends the key establishment message until it receives and verifies all the acknowledgments from the group members) takes on the server side for larger group sizes. The results for different group sizes are depicted in Fig. 4. As can be seen, the key establishment time increases by increasing the group size, and for large group sizes (larger than 100), this increase is more noticeable. Although the key establishment time for larger group sizes increases but for instance, this increase for a group of 448 nodes is still less than a second; hence LMGROUP is scalable to large-size networks as well. Note that based on the latency threshold in the network [21], appropriate group size should be selected. As mentioned earlier curve Secp256k1 has better performance than Secp256r1 as can be seen in Fig. 4.

We have also compared the computation and communication overhead of LMGROUP to the schemes presented in [15,16], and the results are depicted in Table 2. Different operations are indicated as follows: *PM* for ECC point multiplications, *PA* for point addition, *h* for hash function operation, *SV* for signature

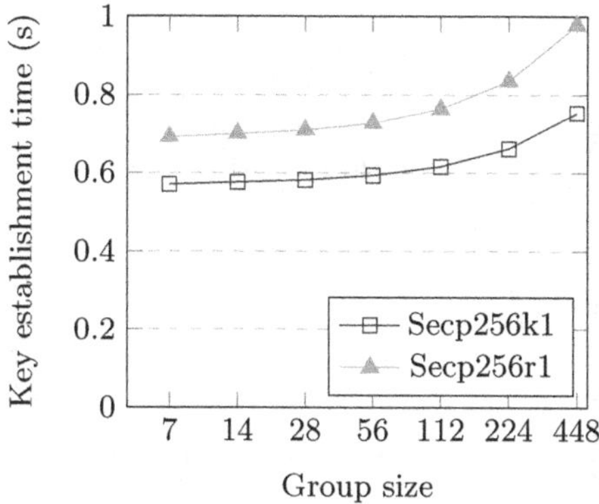

Fig. 4. Total key establishment time of LMGROUP for different group sizes

verification, *HM* for HMAC operation, *MM* for modular multiplication, *SE* for symmetric encryption, and *SD* for symmetric decryption. As the hash function and HMAC operations are negligible, we can conclude from Table 2 that the protocols presented in [15,16] obviously have more computation overhead than LMGROUP due to heavy signature verification operation and also more ECC or modular operations in schemes [15,16], respectively. In scheme, [15], the authors have originally used the curve Secp160r1, which has less byte overhead than Secp256r1 or Secp256k1 (the curves used in LMGROUP), for the scheme [15] to be comparable with our scheme, we have also considered a curve with 256 bit modulus in [15]. The results of the communication overhead comparison are also indicated in Table 2.

Table 2. Communication and computation overhead comparison of LMGROUP with the protocols presented in [15,16]

	LMGROUP	Protocol [15]	Protocol [16]
Computation overhead (number of operations)	PM + PA + 3h + HM	PM + PA + 5h + SV	2PM + 2MM+ h+2HM+SE+SD
Communication overhead (number of bytes)	$189 + 32 * n$	$146 + 18 * n$	$128 * n$

Considering the communication overhead represented in Table 2, we calculate the communication overhead for different values of n or the group size, and the results are depicted in Fig. 5. As can be seen, LMGROUP has slightly higher overhead than the protocol [15] and this is due to the fact that in scheme [15] SHA128 was used as the hash function which generates 16 bytes lower overhead than SHA256 which was used in LMGROUP. The protocol [16] is not a multicast protocol, and as can be seen, it has the highest byte overhead; increasing the group size will cause a significant increase in its communication overhead.

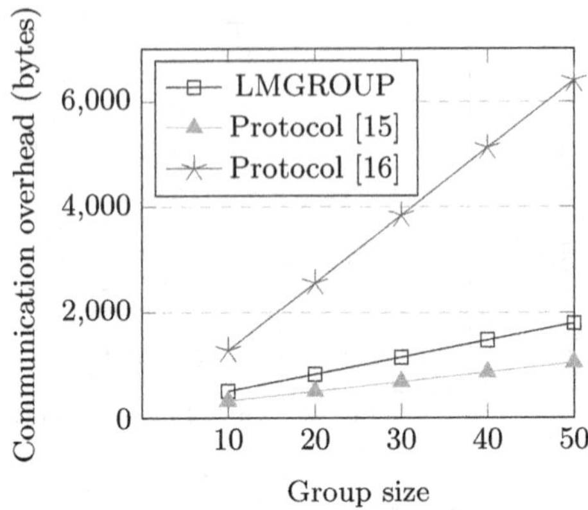

Fig. 5. Communication overhead comparison of LMGROUP with protocols [15,16]

5.2 Storage Overhead

In LMGROUP the following information needs to be stored on the device side: the public key of the server, the device private and public keys, the device *ID*, and some other variables regarding the used ECC curve. We measured the memory footprints of our multicast key establishment scheme using ESP32-S2, and the results are shown in Table 3. DRAM specifies the RAM usage, which is assigned to zero and non-zero values at the program's startup. IRAM indicates the total executable code which is executed from IRAM, and D/IRAM specifies the total size of DRAM and IRAM together. Flash code specifies the total size of executable code which is executed from the flash cache or IROM. Flash rodata, on the other hand, indicates the total size of read-only data that is loaded from the flash cache or DROM. Finally, the total image size indicates the estimated total binary file size of the program, which includes the whole size of all used memory types. As indicated in Table 3, the RAM and ROM usage of LMGROUP are reasonable on the IoT device side. Considering the limitations of resource-constrained devices, LMGROUP is applicable to be used in such devices.

Table 3. Memory footprints of LMGROUP

	D/IRAM(B)	Flash code(B)	Flash rodata(B)	Total image size(B)
LMGROUP	110855	467427	102736	681018

6 Formal Security Verification

In order to formally verify the security properties of LMGROUP, we have used ProVerif [22]. ProVerif uses Dolev-Yao model [23] for the adversary model, and it can be used to verify the security properties of cryptographic protocols formally. Applied pi calculus [24] is used in ProVerif as the modeling language. In our protocol modeling, we start with the declaration phase, where different protocol components, including variables, functions, and channels, are declared. We used different types in our ProVerif model to declare the type of variables, such as key, nonce (used for session *ID*), point (used for ECC point), and bitstring. The term [private] in front of some variable definitions indicates that those variables are not known by the attacker. Our modeled protocol using ProVerif is also available[4].

The main functions used in the modeling of our key establishment scheme are hash function, ECC point multiplication and addition, MAC, and XOR; these functions are modeled as follows:

```
fun hash(bitstring):bitstring.
fun mul(bitstring,bitstring):bitstring.
fun add(bitstring,point):point.
fun mac(key,nonce,bitstring,point,bitstring) : bitstring.
fun xor(bitstring,bitstring):bitstring.
```

The functions can have different input and output types; as an example, the MAC function takes five inputs of type key, nonce, bitstring, point, and bitstring, and it generates an output of type bitstring.

After declaring variables and functions, we defined different queries; these queries are used to check whether the protocol has specific security properties or not. We verified security properties, including secrecy, authentication, and correspondence, through different queries. These security properties can protect against various attacks, including 1) Man in The Middle attack, 2) Replay and Impersonation attacks, and 3) Denial Of Service attack. The queries used to verify the secrecy properties to protect against these attacks are described below.

6.1 Man in The Middle Attack Protection

Man in The Middle Attack (MITM) can be protected through secrecy property. To verify secrecy, we have used the following queries:

```
query attacker ( da ).
query attacker ( db ).
```

In our ProVerif model, we modeled two devices, Device A and B, modeled as *Da* and *Db*, and a server modeled as *S*. In the above queries, *da* and *db* represent the private keys of devices A and B, and the queries check whether the attacker can gain any knowledge about the private keys of those devices or not. ProVerif verification results indicate that the above queries are successfully verified, and the attacker can not get access to the private keys (*da* and *db*) and can not access the information required to generate the group key.

[4] https://github.com/pegahnikbakht/Multi-key-share/.

6.2 Replay and Impersonation Attacks Protection

We have used correspondence property to verify protection against replay and impersonation attacks. To prove correspondence, we have used these queries:

```
query a:bitstring,b:nonce,c:bitstring,d:point,e:bitstring;
event(termDevice(a,b,c,d,e))==>event(initserver(a,b,c,d,e)).

query a:bitstring,b:bitstring;
event(termserver(a,b))==>event(initDevice(a,b)).
```

As it can be seen, four different events are used in the above queries: *initDevice* and *termDevice* refer to initiating and terminating the device, respectively, and *initserver* and *termserver* refer to initiating and terminating the server. The inputs of the events in the first query represent HMAC, *Session ID*, *Auth*, *R*, and *Se* and the inputs of events in the second query are device *ID* and acknowledgement. The above queries are satisfied if for each occurrence of the event *termDevice*, there is a previous execution of *initserver*, and also if for each occurrence of *termserver* there is a previous execution of *initDevice*. These correspondence relations protect against replay and impersonation attacks. The above queries are successfully verified in ProVerif.

6.3 Denial of Service Attack Protection

To protect against DoS attacks, we have used the authentication property; if all of the messages are authenticated in the protocol, then it can protect against DoS attacks; we have used *HMAC* verification to verify the authenticity of the messages in LMGROUP. To prove the authentication, again, the correspondence assertion (the relationships between the execution of events) is used in ProVerif, and the same queries used in Sect. 6.2 are used to verify the authentication property. ProVerif has already verified the correspondence successfully.

7 Conclusion

In this paper, we propose LMGROUP a lightweight and multicast group key establishment scheme for IoT networks. In LMGROUP the IoT devices do not need to interact with each other to gain the shared key; instead, a central server is used to select the group members and send the group information to the members (having some redundant servers is preferred to avoid a single point of failure). In this paper, we suggest an unpredictable group member selection algorithm based on the criticality level (which is decided by the network administrator) of the devices in the network. LMGROUP uses ECIES based operations to share the group key and uses HMAC verification instead of heavy signature verification to authenticate the group key establishment messages. The evaluation result of implementing LMGROUP on a real testbed setup indicates it is lightweight and scalable and can be used in small to large-size networks. The results also indicate that LMGROUP has low storage, communication, and computation costs. Furthermore, we formally verify LMGROUP and prove it is secure and robust against different attacks, including replay and DoS attacks.

Acknowledgment. This work was financially supported by the Wallenberg AI, Autonomous Systems and Software Program (WASP).

References

1. Samuel, S.S.: A review of connectivity challenges in IoT-smart home. In: 2016 3rd MEC International Conference on Big Data and Smart City (ICBDSC), pp. 1–4. IEEE (2016)
2. Chen, Y., Kunz, T.: Performance evaluation of IoT protocols under a constrained wireless access network. In 2016 International Conference on Selected Topics in Mobile & Wireless Networking (MoWNeT), pp. 1–7. IEEE (2016)
3. Kim, J.Y., Hu, W., Shafagh, H., Jha, S.: Seda: secure over-the-air code dissemination protocol for the internet of things. IEEE Trans. Depend. Secur. Comput. **15**(6), 1041–1054 (2016)
4. Cheikhrouhou, O.: Secure group communication in wireless sensor networks: a survey. J. Netw. Comput. Appl. **61**, 115–132 (2016)
5. Dammak, M., Senouci, S.M., Messous, M.A., Elhdhili, M.H., Gransart, C.: Decentralized lightweight group key management for dynamic access control in IoT environments. IEEE Trans. Netw. Serv. Manag. **17**(3), 1742–1757 (2020)
6. Piccoli, A., Pahl, M.O., Wüstrich, L.: Group key management in constrained IoT settings. In: 2020 IEEE Symposium on Computers and Communications (ISCC), pp. 1–6. IEEE (2020)
7. Wong, C.K., Gouda, M., Lam, S.S.: Secure group communications using key graphs. IEEE/ACM Trans. Netw. **8**(1), 16–30 (2000)
8. Dini, G., Savino, I.M.: S2rp: a secure and scalable rekeying protocol for wireless sensor networks. In: 2006 IEEE International Conference on Mobile Ad Hoc and Sensor Systems, pp. 457–466. IEEE (2006)
9. Son, J.-H., Lee, J.-S., Seo, S.-W.: Topological key hierarchy for energy-efficient group key management in wireless sensor networks. Wirel. Pers. Commun. **52**(2), 359–382 (2010)
10. Zhu, S., Setia, S., Jajodia, S.: Leap+ efficient security mechanisms for large-scale distributed sensor networks. ACM Trans. Sens. Netw. (TOSN) **2**(4), 500–528 (2006)
11. Perrig, A., Canetti, R., Tygar, J.D., Song, D.: The tesla broadcast authentication protocol. Rsa Cryptobytes **5**(2), 2–13 (2002)
12. Ferrari, N., Gebremichael, T., Jennehag, U., Gidlund, M.: Lightweight group-key establishment protocol for IoT devices: Implementation and performance analyses. In: 2018 Fifth International Conference on Internet of Things: Systems, Management and Security, pp. 31–37. IEEE (2018)
13. Harn, L., Lin, C.: Authenticated group key transfer protocol based on secret sharing. IEEE Trans. Comput. **59**(6), 842–846 (2010)
14. Lee, C.-Y., Wang, Z.-H., Harn, L., Chang, C.-C.: Secure key transfer protocol based on secret sharing for group communications. IEICE Trans Inf. Syst. **94**(11), 2069–2076 (2011)
15. Porambage, P., Braeken, A., Schmitt, C., Gurtov, A., Ylianttila, M., Stiller, B.: Group key establishment for enabling secure multicast communication in wireless sensor networks deployed for iot applications. IEEE Access **3**, 1503–1511 (2015)

16. Sani, A.S., Yuan, D., Yeoh, P.L., Bao, W., Chen, S., Vucetic, B.: A lightweight security and privacy-enhancing key establishment for internet of things applications. In: 2018 IEEE International Conference on Communications (ICC), pp. 1–6. IEEE (2018)
17. Fatemeh, K., Johnsen, E.B., Owe, O., Balasingham, I.: Group selection by nodes in wireless sensor networks using coalitional game theory. In 2011 16th IEEE International Conference on Engineering of Complex Computer Systems, pp. 253–262. IEEE (2011)
18. Behera, T.M., et al.: Residual energy-based cluster-head selection in WSNS for IoT application. IEEE Internet Things J. **6**(3), 5132–5139 (2019)
19. Hamzeloei, F., Dermany, M.K.: A topsis based cluster head selection for wireless sensor network. Procedia Comput. Sci.**98**, 8–15 (2016)
20. Bjoernsen, K.: Koblitz curves and its practical uses in bitcoin security. order (ε (GF (2k) **2**(1), 7 (2009)
21. Raptis, T.P., Passarella, A., Conti, M.: Performance analysis of latency-aware data management in industrial IoT networks. Sensors **18**(8), 2611 (2018)
22. Blanchet, B., Smyth, B., Cheval, V., Sylvestre, M.:. Proverif 2.00: automatic cryptographic protocol verifier, user manual and tutorial. Version from, pp. 05–16 (2018)
23. Dolev, D., Yao, A.C.:. On the security of public key protocols. In: Proceedings of the 22nd Annual Symposium on Foundations of Computer Science, SFCS 2081, pp. 350–357, Washington, DC, USA, 1981. IEEE Computer Society (1981)
24. Ryan, M.D., Smyth, B.: Applied pi calculus. In: Formal Models and Techniques for Analyzing Security Protocols, pp. 112–142. Ios Press (2011)

Software Security

Using API Calls for Sequence-Pattern Feature Mining-Based Malware Detection

Gheorghe Balan[1(✉)], Dragoş Teodor Gavriluţ[1], and Henri Luchian[2]

[1] Faculty of Computer Science IaŞi, Bitdefender Labs, "Al.I. Cuza" University, Iasi, Romania
{gbalan,dgavrilut}@bitdefender.com
[2] Faculty of Computer Science Iaşi, "Al. I. Cuza" University, Iasi, Romania

Abstract. This paper presents an ANN-based approach to malware detection focused on sequence-pattern feature mining. Some prevalent malware families (Emotet, Trickbot) try to deceive detection algorithms by automatically changing their file format with each attack campaign; consequently, detection based on features derived directly from the content of a suspected file can be avoided by this type of polymorphic malware. However, while a given malware can easily be changed in terms of its static characteristics, the same cannot be said for the behavioural it exhibits. This paper focuses on building ANN models using behaviour features related to OS API calls sequences that can improve malware detection. Our experiments with Feed Forward Neural Networks having as input such features (obtained via emulators) show that this is a promising approach against polymorphic malware families, well-suited for real-world applications.

Keywords: Neural networks · Feature-mining · API calls · Emulators · Malware · Emotet family detection · Trickbot family detection · Behavioral features

1 Introduction

Artificial neural networks are intensively used in various anti-malware approaches; some of these approaches remain rather theoretical, due to excessive resource requirements (e.g., training time). This paper is focused on conceiving a practical anti-malware approach based on FF-NNs[1] within a feasible resource usage.

Security Landscape. Malware and security products co-evolve as in a prey-predator game. While malware aims towards avoiding detection, security products focus lies in improving their classification models. Detection technology has evolved from simple detection (hash based), to pattern searching, behavior analysis and machine learning. On the other hand, malware creators, take advantage

[1] Feed-forward neural networks.

C. Su et al. (Eds.): ISPEC 2022, LNCS 13620, pp. 233–251, 2022.
https://doi.org/10.1007/978-3-031-21280-2_13

of a set of constraints that security products have (e.g., the difference between detection and protection, update/maintenance time, etc) to avoid detection.

Detection vs. Protection. In a detection-based scenario, a security product works asynchronously allowing a malware to run, while analysing it. This is well-suited if the ultimate target is to provide visibility into how malware behaves. Products such as EDR[2], XDR[3], SIEM[4] or services such as MDR[5] illustrate the concept of detection. Their main functionality consists in analyzing, detecting and deciding on the response. One important advantage for these products is that analytic resources and time constraints are not an issue (e.g., you don't need to identify an attack immediately, you can use time-expensive algorithms, etc). While these technologies provide great insights in terms of malware identification and possible remediation solutions, there are certain type of attacks that cannot be addressed in this way; ransomware and data ex-filtration techniques are such examples where even if you understand the attack prior a security breach, you can not do anything about it (e.g. once your documents have been stolen you can not "un-stole" them).

On the other hand, protection technologies analyze a potential attack before it happens (e.g., analyse a process before it gets executed). The main advantage of this approach is that if an attack is identified at this stage, the security product can block it (without any need of system remediation). The downsides, are that this solution come at the cost of impairing the OS-performance (e.g. each process that is about to be executed is analysed before it starts, each written file is scanned before allowing other processes to access it, etc). As a consequence, there are certain limitations related to machine learning models performance.

Polymorphic Malware. One common technique malware creators use to avoid detection is code obfuscation/packing [23]. However, these techniques only change the file appearance (e.g. number of sections, code entropy, strings, etc) but not its behaviour. Since an application is considered to be malicious if it **behaves** malevolently, detection approaches based on this fact are very effective in identifying new malware. As an example, a ransomware[6] follows 3 steps:

- search for private documents
- encrypt them
- ask for a ransom in exchange for the decryption key

While the file format of a ransomware can be changed easily, its behaviour should remain the same (e.g. a ransomware that lacks the ability to encrypt file is not a ransomware anymore). Ultimately, a malware behaviour is a direct result of the sequences of API-calls that it employs during its execution. These sequences can be monitored by a security product in two ways:

[2] Endpoint Detection and Response.
[3] eXtended Detection and Response.
[4] Secrity Information and Event Management.
[5] Managed Detection and Response.
[6] https://en.wikipedia.org/wiki/Ransomware.

- via dynamically hooking APIs and logging their calls; this technique is usually used in detection scenarios, where a malware is allowed to be executed, but its actions (API calls) are logged and analysed
- through the use of emulators; this technique is used by protection technologies and implies some sort of code emulation that produces simulated responses for API calls while analysing them (such as [11])

In this paper we focus towards building a machine learning classifier that uses features derived for sequences of API calls. This approach is effective in detecting polymorphic malware families (such as Trickbot or Emotet).

The rest of the paper is organized as follows: Sect. 2 summarises similar work done in the field, Sect. 3 describes the problem in the frame of the current threat security landscape, Sect. 4 presents the API-calls sequences based neural approach in solving it, Sect. 5 gives the results and the last section discusses some conclusions drawn from this research.

2 Related Work

The detection of polymorphic malware received growing attention in the last decade. Such malware modifies its directly identifiable features, while preserving its disruptive behaviour and effects. Madhu K. Shankarapani et al. [27] proposed two algorithms, SAVE and MEDiC, for detecting polymorphic malware. Features based on API calls and Assembly opcodes are suggested to improve detection rate on obfuscated malware, over traditional approaches. However, careful tuning is in order, given the sensitivity of the two algorithms to the choice of the parameter value (threshold).

An interesting approach based on building the API call graph and using an LCS algorithm is reported in [13] to achieve a high detection rate and close to 0% false-positives; however, tests on real-world applications are not reported.

In [19], a more complex system using an LCS algorithm among other techniques, was used for building a signature-based system. Nevertheless, since such systems are easily evaded by attackers, this would rather work as a method for detecting already known malware variants rather than as a proactive way to detect yet-unknown real-world malware.

Lately, malware emulation and ANNs are combined in security solutions: the indicators/features obtained through malware emulation are used as input for a malware-detecting neural network. Microsoft conducted a series of experiments described in [24] and [8]; various hybrid models are tested, which combine ESN, RNN, LSTM, GRU with a higher-level classifier. The lowest score was achieved by a RNN model with a true positive rate (TPR) of 60% (nearly 2% false positives (FP)) while the highest score was achieved by the LSTM model which scored nearly 80% TPR while preserving the same FP rate.

A similar study - [25] - focuses on the parameters of the API calls. The best model, XGBoost, had an accuracy of 96.7% on a 5-fold cross-validation and 99.4% on a 10-fold cross-validation. However, this method raises concerns regarding time complexity.

Detection of Windows-targeted malware by studying the API call structure is presented, in 2020, by Eslam Amer et al. [3,4]. This Markov-chain approach uses a heuristic for identifying and clustering malicious files; the reported detection accuracy is 0.990, with a false positive rate of 0.010. However, the time needed to train, run and maintain such a system likely makes this solution unsuitable for real-world applications.

Such anti-malware solutions, integrating emulation and API-call sequences with various machine learning techniques, lack proven real-world efficiency and the quality of their results depends on the performance of the technique used for feature mining [1,33].

CHIH-TA LIN et al. in [22] report some of the most promising results. By using a hefty 5-step system based on n-grams, SVMs and dimension-reducing algorithms (PCA, KPCA), an effective classification of 4,288 samples from 9 malware families is achieved. However, this method is likely to become time-inefficient when tackling polymorphic malware: such malware reduces the high-performance lifetime of complex machine learning detection solutions to merely six months [32], hence the need to constantly retrain the anti-malware system - which makes it less attractive.

As shown in [26] through a comparison between different feature mining techniques, the use of opcodes and features extracted from the binary files format, enhance the accuracy and speed of malware detection. However, this improvement comes with a significant increase of the false-positive rate. Reducing the rate of FP's requires alternative methods. A promising direction in this respect is the use of API-call based features; the malware evolution (towards becoming more profitable, harder to detect, with enhanced obfuscation techniques and automation) points to such an approach as each evolution target mentioned above requires extensive use of API calls. Very good results using automatically-mined features based on API call sequences are presented in [12,20,30].

To conclude, some of the anti-polymorphic-malware solutions summarised above, while showing remarkable classification results, are inefficient in practice, because of one or more of the following: the time needed for training / maintaining the anti-malware solution, the false positive rate, the overall resource needs. Obviously, the environment used for developing a cyber-security solution - in particular, the ANN-based one described below - has limited capacities, but a huge number of files (mostly clean ones) to be processed. Hence, the challenge to identify a low number of classification-wise efficient NN inputs (features), in order to keep a low memory footprint. Before designing the NN, a balanced feature mining method is in order, for both properly describing the dataset, and keeping within a moderate training time limit.

3 Problem Description

The evolution of malware industry is largely accountable for the way security measures are developed to counteract the attacks. A comprehensive study of this evolution [29] shows that nowadays the old fashioned ways to detect malware through static analysis are merely obsolete, hence the necessity of a dynamic analysis. However, this may impair performance, which makes hybrid analysis (a combination of both static and dynamic analysis) a more practical approach. The inefficiency of machine learning models based on statically extracted features is discussed in [5], followed up by [6]. The results in the first paper were just a beginning good enough to make a point, while the improved version of the paper convincingly strengthens this point.

We illustrate the relative weakness of static features in Table 1 which summarizes such static features in the wild: similarity between benign files and malware is self-evident.

Table 1. A comparison in terms of common static features

Feature	Malware file	Benign file
Family/Name	DarkKomet[a]	HDSCtrl.exe[b]
Hash (md5)	707d4a225237425bb60718dd0b914cba	35e7c32027c094e64d96f44bf41489da
Location	VirusTotal[c]	HDSentinel Site[d]
Packer	UPX	UPX
Size	258048 bytes	262536 bytes
Nr. of Section	3	3
First Section File Size	0	0
Second Section Entropy	7.924	7.928
File Entropy	7.89	7.87
Entrypoint section	UPX1	UPX1
Address of entrypoint	0 × 3DD10 (last 10% of the file)	0 × 398F0 (last 10% of the file)
Company Name	Microsoft Corp.	H.D.S. Hungary
Internal Name	MSRSAAPP	HDSentinel
File Version	1, 0, 0, 1	6.0.1.0
PDB	Not present	Not present

[a] A recent version (First Submission on VT: 2022-05-21 14:10:52 UTC) of https://en.wikipedia.org/wiki/DarkComet

[b] A component of Hard Disk Sentinel, hdsctrl.exe which may be downloaded from https://www.hdsentinel.com/download.php

[c] https://www.virustotal.com/gui/file/707d4a225237425bb60718dd0b914cba.

[d] https://www.hdsentinel.com/download.php.

This paper investigates further the above mentioned point of view and suggests a practical way for dynamic features mining, with an eye to making the detection model more effective.

3.1 Emulators

Static emulation simulates the functionality of an operation system without actually providing it: assembly code is fully emulated and an API call only triggers a virtual response, with no actual action. A virtual file system is also emulated in order to keep track of various system changes during the emulation.

A static emulation system requires far less memory and disk space and is faster than a virtual machine. Since API calls are only emulated, most of them just return a value and save a state in an internal execution environment[7].

Emulators do come with some limitations:

- Reaching a preset maximum number of assembly instructions causes the emulation to stop; this is a requirement for the On-Access blocking scenario where files under emulation-based scrutiny are locked, hence an overly long emulation process impairs the performance of the OS.
- Not all OS-APIs can be correctly emulated (that is, keeping their behavior consistent with the API parameters).
- Not all assembly instructions are correctly emulated (more complex instructions sets - such as SSE2, SSE3, SSE4, MMX, AVX[8]) - may be incorrectly identified, in which case the emulation usually stops.
- Threads (and in particular synchronization objects: mutex, semaphore, etc) and exceptions are harder to simulate
- Third-party libraries that normally exist in the OS cannot be emulated if they are not present in the virtual environment

Because of the limitations above, emulators are often deceived by malware families [23], through tricks such as:

- large loops (containing nothing malicious) that cause the emulator to reach the maximum number of emulated assembly instructions
- rare assembly instructions (e.g. SSE4 instruction set)
- a rarely used API from OS

Despite their limitations, emulators make a most valuable tool for identifying features for malware detection, among which:

- all *APIs called* from the file under scrutiny, with their parameters (which is instrumental in detecting *polymorphic malware*)
- statistics related to the assembly instructions used by that file (particularly useful for identifying *obfuscation techniques*)
- behavioural information on that file (e.g.: if the file under scrutiny is connecting to an URL and tries to download and save its content to a local file, followed by the execution of the downloaded file, a *download behavior feature* can be set).

4 The Proposed Approach

4.1 Features Derived From API Calls vs Static Features

Until relatively recently [14,29], malware detection largely used static characteristics of files (size, structure, strings, entry point, etc) as the main source

[7] There are some exceptions (e.g. APIs used for memory operations, such as: VirtualAlloc / VirtualFree, etc).

[8] https://www.intel.com/content/www/us/en/support/articles/000005779/processors.html.

for classification features. There is however the possibility for a malware to be adjusted by changing its appearance and hence its set of static features. In particular, the usage of a packer can make some of the static features indistinguishable from those of benign file.

One way to respond to this challenge is to use API calls as features. An API call used in an attack cannot be obliterated: it will be executed at some point. On the other hand, obtaining such features is a complex task; it requires either emulation or a virtual environment, hence it is not an attractive choice when large amounts of files have to be processed.

This observation is described in [2,13,20,28] where authors show that API Calls are a viable solution in increasing detection accuracy and lowering the number of false positives.

4.2 API Calls vs Sequences of API Calls

While an API call can be relevant in itself, the behavior of a binary file is fully illustrated through its sequences of API calls. Consider a ransomware; there are three behavior traits a ransomware must have:

1. it is searching for private documents that are valuable for the potential victim
2. it encrypts the files found in the previous step
3. it asks for ransom (decryption key in exchange for some sort of financial gain)

Consequently, there are some OS specific APIs that a ransomware has to use: FindFirstFile[9]/FindNextFile(See footnote 9) (or similar) to enumerate/search for relevant files, CreateFile/WriteFile (or similar) to modify an existing file and to create a ransom note. A crucial question is then: a ransomware which does not use such sequences of APIs is still a ransomware? The answer is obviously NO. No matter how much the code may be morphed, the ransomware still has to perform the sequence of three steps above, hence use the API Calls. Similar ideas are reported in [3,4,19,30].

4.3 The Architecture of Our Solution

Our study was made on a dataset of over 1.6 million files, with a realistic ratio of 1:100 malware vs benign, carefully balanced for pragmatic detection solutions[10]. By contrast, the papers mentioned in Sect. 4.2 report results obtained on data which is less relevant for practical solutions from the viewpoint of total number of files and malware/benign ratio: [3] tested their solution on 700 malicious samples and 300 clean ones, [4] - 25000 malicious, 21000 clean, [19] - 26 clean, 6918 malicious, [30] - 120 malicious, 150 clean. Another concern may arise when

[9] https://docs.microsoft.com/en-us/windows/win32/api/fileapi/nf-fileapi-findfirstfilea.

[10] In practice, the number of clean files is larger than malicious ones, hence the necessity of using a properly balanced dataset from the viewpoint of the malicious vs clean ratio.

testing the practicality of their solution in term of utilised resources. Most of the above papers are trying to analyse API Calls sequences using algorithms based on Markov Chain, DNA Sequencing, Words Embedding Correlations, NGrams which are requiring huge resources (such as time); these approaches are less responsive to API Calls obfuscation [15]. We focused our research on identifying malicious behavior through features derived from sequences of two API Calls, forward-fed to a neural network[11].

To empirically prove the effectiveness of this approach we undertook a three-step procedure:

1. The feature mining process:
   - using an emulator to extract the list of API calls for a given binary
   - identifying **relevant pattern sequences** of API calls that are likely to reflect a malicious behavior
   - filtering existing pattern sequences using **various metrics** (F_1, F_2)
2. Collect large sets of polymorphic malware and benign files. For each file run the feature mining process and extract relevant behavior features and record them in the database.
3. Train and evaluate the results of a feed-forward neural network classifier which uses the database obtained in the previous step.

5 Feature Mining

While both an emulator and a virtual machine can be used to safely extract a list of API Calls, for the purpose of this study we have used an emulator. The main reason for this choice was the practical protection requirements: we focused on identifying a method to use behaviour features in an On-Access blocking scenario. Since this type of scenario cannot allow an execution to run for more than a couple of seconds, a virtual machine is not practical. Annex 1 discusses pros and cons related to emulators and their ability to extract meaningful behavioural features. The rest of this chapter is organized in the following way:

1. a definition of what an API pattern-sequence feature is and some metrics we can use to compare two such features
2. identify the optimal set of API pattern-sequences features (in terms of size and detection rate)
3. generate a set of behavioral features from the set of API pattern-sequence features obtained in the previous step.
4. apply a dimension reduction algorithms of the behavior feature list to obtain a reduced feature set with similar detection rate but better performance in terms of testing

[11] Tests against three or four API Calls sequences showed no improvement over two API Calls, especially due to obfuscation techniques.

5.1 Feature Definition and Feature Metrics

Any pair of consecutive APIs is a potential feature; our detection model uses only features of this type. However, the huge number of potential features (in the range of millions) is not feasible. Therefore, we define a feature selection process which ends up with roughly 300 features. As an ANN input each selected feature is boolean, with 0 meaning "the respective sequence of APIs is not identified during emulation" and the opposite for 1. In the sequel we describe in some detail **our feature selection algorithm**.

For a given feature **j**, consider the following:

- $MP_j = |\bigcup_{i=1}^{|D|} D_i|$, **with** $D_i.label = malware$ **and** $D_i.Feat_j = true$
- $BP_j = |\bigcup_{i=1}^{|D|} D_i|$, **with** $D_i.label = benign$ **and** $D_i.Feat_j = true$
- $BN_j = |\bigcup_{i=1}^{|D|} D_i|$, **with** $D_i.label = benign$ **and** $D_i.Feat_j = false$
- D_i - the i-th entry from the dataset

Using these values we can compute the following metrics:

- $ABS_j = |MP_j - BP_j|$,
- $F1_j = \dfrac{2 * MP_j}{2 * MP_j + BN_j + BP_j}$
- $F2_j = \dfrac{5 * MP_i}{5 * MP_j + 4 * BN_j + BP_j}$

5.2 Optimal API Pattern-Sequences Features

As previously mentioned, an API pattern-sequence feature is the expression of API call A followed by API call B. An emulator identifies multiple API calls, hence the possible combinations between two consecutive API calls can reach a very high number (e.g. for 2000 different API possible API calls, the total number of possible API pattern-sequences features will be $2000^2 = 4$ millions). Due to the obfuscation techniques and randomisation of the order of API calls used by malware creators, the length of the pattern is set to two. Using a bigger number will not provide sufficient generality for the detection model.

As mentioned before, we focused on building a model that could run in a blocking scenario, one of its main constraints being that testing speed should be appropriate for this type of usage. Consequently, the number of feature that we can use in such a model should be relatively low. With this in mind we performed the following steps to identify the optimal set of API pattern-sequences features:

1. For each sample extract the sequence of API calls using an emulator
2. Create a list of all possible previously described API pattern-sequences features which are found across the entire dataset

3. Sort that list using the three previously mentioned metrics: F_1, F_2 and ABS
4. Train a model over a database of files using the first 25/50/75 ... features from the sorted list from the previous step. Figures 1, 2, 3 shows how Sensitivity, Specificity, F1 score and F2 score evolves during training performed on a small portion of dataset.

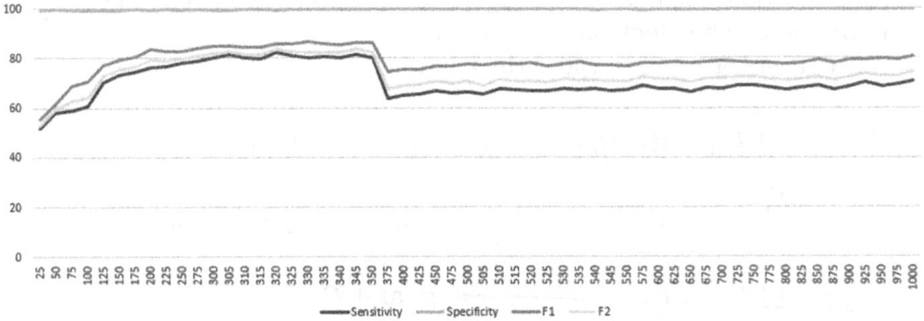

Fig. 1. ROC curve ABS (x - nr. of features, y - metrics)

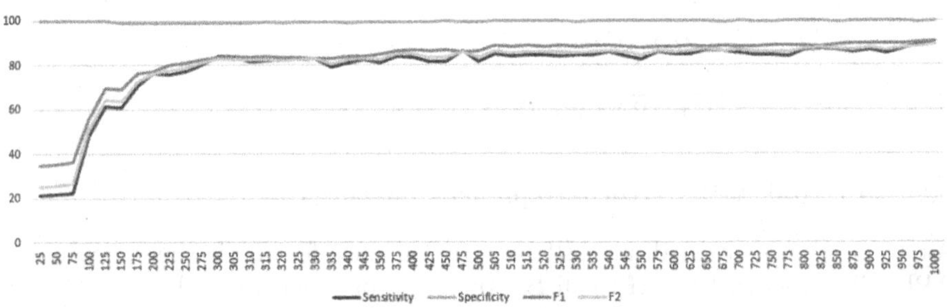

Fig. 2. ROC curve F1 (x - nr. of features, y - metrics)

Some cap points may be observed around (300, 320) - especially for ABS and (500, 525) - for F1 and F2. With that in mind, we tested the resulted models against the entire database. We decided to use ABS-300 as the results were similar in terms of accuracy with F1/F2 500/525 but with a significant less features used and a good sensitivity (Table 2).

5.3 Behavior Features

We define a behavior feature a feature that reflects the possibility that two API pattern-sequence features are triggered during one execution (irrespective of their order). To obtain a behavior feature we use a method already empirically

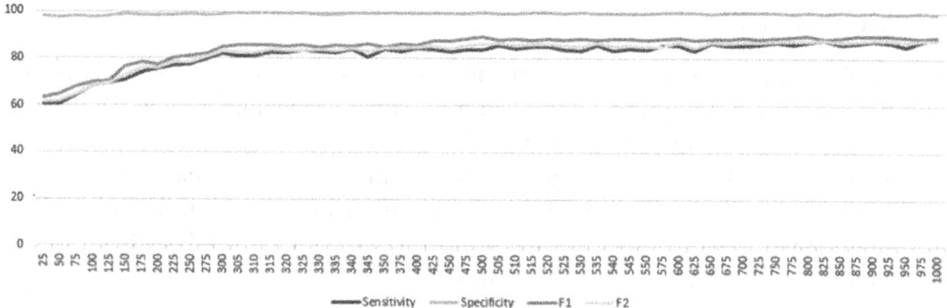

Fig. 3. ROC curve F2 (x - nr. of features, y - metrics)

Table 2. Feature-selection steps - testing results

Model	Features number	Accuracy	Sensitivity	Specificity
F2	500	99.46	84.34	99.59
F2	525	99.37	84.83	99.49
F1	525	99.33	84.12	99.45
F1	520	99.27	84.33	99.40
ABS	**300**	**99.23**	**77.44**	**99.41**
ABS	520	99.21	67.08	99.47
ABS	500	99.19	67.06	99.46
ABS	320	99.14	80.30	99.30
F2	520	99.06	85.52	99.17
F2	320	99.00	81.15	99.15
F1	500	98.96	81.44	99.11
ABS	525	98.96	67.09	99.22
F2	300	98.90	81.92	99.04
F1	300	98.53	81.72	98.67
F1	320	98.42	82.22	98.55

proven to enhance the accuracy and the FP-rate in malicious code analysis [9, 16, 18]. If we denote by AC the set of all pairs of API pattern-sequence features, we build the Cartesian product $AC \times AC$; the result is a list of all possible combinations between two API pattern-sequence features.

As some combination of API pattern-sequence features are not possible (e.g. you can not delete a file twice) we have remove all such combinations that were not observed in our database. To simply put it, if none of the files that we have in the database exhibit a given behavior, we would remove that behavior from the list of behavior features.

5.4 Selection Phase

As explained in previous sections, using a small set of feature is essential for building a practical model to be used in a blocking scenario. As such we divided a way to reduce the number of features from the previous.

We conceived Algorithm 1 a generic technique for feature selection that can be performed with various parameters and feature ranking scores (F1, F2, ABS). We define three feature selection techniques (that can be used with all of the above mentioned ranking scores) as follows:

Algorithm 1. Feature selection algorithm

```
function COMPUTE(M, B, F, RankingFunction, Position, MinFeat)
    Result ← ∅
    repeat
        for i = 1 → |F| do
            F_i.score ← RankingFunction(F_i, M, B)
        end for
        F ← Sort(F, descendent)
        Mal ← ∅
        for i = 1 → |M| do
            if F_Position ∈ M_i.Features and |M_i.Features| > MinFeat then
                Mal ← Mal ⋃ M_i
            end if
        end for
        M ← M \ Mal
        Benign ← ∅
        for i = 1 → |B| do
            if F_Position ∈ B_i.Features and |B_i.Features| > MinFeat then
                Benign ← Benign ⋃ B_i
            end if
        end for
        B ← B \ Benign
        Result ← Result ⋃ F_Position
        F ← F \ F_Position
    until |M ⋃ B| = 0
    return Result
end function
```

M the training set of malware files, [B] the training set of benign files
F the list of features
RankingFunction One of F_1, F_2 or ABS
Position Index of the feature that will be selected
MinFeat a minimum number of features required for any file to be removed

1. *feature-selection-highest* is Algorithm 1 with *Position* parameter set to 1 and $MinFeat$ parameter set to 0. While each of the three functions ranks the

features according to certain characteristics, any chosen score may, however, lead to a non-optimal ranking (w.r.t. the subsequent classification); the next variant of the algorithm builds a less-biased feature list, while preserving some properties provided by the scoring function.

2. *feature-selection-middle-x*, is the same as Algorithm 1, this time with parameter *Position* set to one of the following values: 5, 10, 15. Parameter *MinFeat* stays at 0. Reducing the overall number of features is the main concern; however, it is also important to make sure that for each selected file a minimal number of features will be considered by the classifier. To this end, the same algorithm 1 is used, this time changing the *MinFeat* parameter in order to enforce a minimal number of features per file.
3. *feature-selection-adaptable-x* For our experiment the following values were used for the *MinFeat* parameter: 1, 2, 3, 4, 5, 6 and 392 (this last value is actually the standard deviation of the number of the features identified in each sample). *Position* parameter is set to 1.

6 Models and Validation Methodology

The above analysis was necessary for designing our classifier - a forward-feed neural network with 1024 input nodes, 4 hidden layers of 512, 256, 256 and 128 neurons respectively; all of the hidden layers having *ReLu* as activation function. The reasons for all these design choices are discussed below.

Function-wise: compared to *Sigmoid* and *TanH*, *ReLu* solves the problem of vanishing gradients, having also a better time performance. Moreover, of the state-of-the-art activation functions, *ReLu* has been proven to provide the best trade-off between training time and accuracy & FP for a large set of detection problems [34] and [7].

Architecture-wise: The input layer has the size of the feature space and depends on the training that is conducted, while the output layer is of size 1 with *Sigmoid* as the activation function. The Sigmoid function fits best this model, since binary classification is in order (the output can be other malicious or benign).

Having at most 1024 neural inputs allows the control of the depth of emulation in the real-time analysis. A comparatively large number of neurons in hidden layers is needed, since the FF-NN should be able to tackle complex combinations of API sequences, in order to detect shape-changing malicious files. Obviously, the quality of the ANN design and ultimately the performance of the ANN are strongly dependent on the quality of the sequence-mining process.

In terms of scaling to large problem instances, the Adam optimiser is known to be both accurate including FP rates and time-wise efficient [21]. This strongly supports the usage of *Binary Cross-Entropy* as loss function.

Regarding the number of batches and iterations, the FF-NN's are trained in batches of size 50, since - due to the huge amount of data - online training is ineffective. Taking into account that Adam runs the risk of over-fitting, a lower number of iterations is appropriate: for the feature mining techniques presented above, 10 iterations generally lead to balanced results.

Methodology Our validation methodology consists in the following steps:

1. split the file database into two smaller databases (one for training and one for validation)
2. we applied the feature mining process described in Sect. 5 over the training database and obtain several behaviour feature sets according to different variations of Algorithm 1 (*feature-selection-highest*, *feature-selection-middle-x* and *feature-selection-adaptable-x*)
3. we train a model using 3-fold cross-validation for each behaviour feature set obtained in the previous step; 3-fold cross-validation has been chosen in order to have a larger validation set and to address over-fitting and generalization concerns.
4. the resulted models were validated over the validation database obtained in the first step

7 Databases

The initial *file-database* contained 13,332 malicious binaries of Emotet family (various versions known either as Emotet, Dridex or Trickbot), collected in February 2021, and 1,614,668 benign files collected over a period of 5 years (2016-2021).

Analysing these files, we identified a list of 2198 unique API Calls (top eight libraries that export most APIs can be observed in Table 3).

Table 3. First eight API libraries ordered by number of extracted APIs

Library name	No. extracted API functions	Library name	No. extracted API functions
kernel32	650	user32	439
advapi32	231	gdi32	172
shlwapi	124	msvbvm60	108
shell32	57	oleaut32	56

As previously explained, the first step in our methodology was to split the initial file database into two smaller databases (one for training and one for validation). Taking into account related work[12] performed on early stages of malware detection [9,10,16,17,31], we concluded that there are empirical evidence that a suitable *malicious to benign* ratio is 1:10. Consequently, we created the training dataset (further denoted as *file-training-database*) to contain 5000 randomly selected malicious files and 50000 benign ones. The validation dataset consists in the rest of the files: 8,156 malicious files and 1,564,669 benign one. The ratio of the malicious to benign samples found in the validation dataset tends to mimic a real-world environment where is most important to keep a low false positive.

On the training dataset (*final-training-database*), we performed the feature mining procedures described in Sect. 5.1 and Sect. 5.2 and obtain a new database

[12] Compatible with ours in terms of data format and goal.

with a total of 300 API sequence pattern features. Applying Sect. 5.3 resulted initially in 45,150 pairs of behavioral features; after removing impossible combinations, the number of behavioral features went down to 26,726.

Finally, we applied variations of Algorithm 1 (*feature-selection-highest*, *feature-selection-middle-x* and *feature-selection-adaptable-x*) and obtained several features sets with sizes between 69 and 634 features (Table 4) according to various parameters used in Algorithm 1.

Table 4. Min/max number of features per algorithm

Algorithm	ABS	F1	F2
feature-selection-highest	8 sets (min 70, max 224)	8 sets (min 84, max 441)	8 sets (min 69, max 299)
feature-selection-middle-x	3 sets (min 92, max 105)	3 sets (min 87, max 95)	3 sets (min 76, max 91)
feature-selection-adaptable-x	7 sets (min 229, max 634)	7 sets (min 239, max 621)	7 sets (min 228, max 606)

8 Experimental Results

This section focus on validating the models resulted by applying the metodology described in Sect. 6 over the databases resulted in the final step of Sect. 7.

Selecting only the first feature (*feature-selection-highest*) lead to an Accuracy of 98.78% for ABS ranking (with a Sensitivity[13] of 68.77% and Specificity[14] 99.03%), 98.35% for F_1 (Se 80.69%, Sp 98.5%) and 98.97% for F_2 (Se 77.66, Sp 99.15%). Those results were obtained using only 70 features (ABS), 84 features (F_1) and 69 features (F_2), respectively.

For each selected feature, the next 1, 2, 3, 4, 9, 14, 19 features were added without additionally removing the files that had those additional features set (as their best feature is not necessarily among them). The results are given in Table 5 where NF is the total number of selected features previously described.

The $F_2 - 2$ method led to the highest accuracy. Moreover, the majority of the results show a significant improvement of the method, offering a trade-off between the number of total selected features, Accuracy, Sensitivity and Specificity. Therefore, this method (*feature-selection-highest*) better fits the dataset.

By applying *feature-selection-middle-x*, we observed that using values {5, 10, 15} for x the obtained results were similar to *feature-selection-highest*, but with a significant reduced number of total features (Table 6).

The best result in terms of accuracy and specificity were obtained by *feature-selection-adaptable-x*, with x in {1, 2, 3, 4, 5, 6, 392}; the results are listed in Table 7.

---

[13] The percentage of malicious files correctly classified out of the total number of malicious files.

[14] The percentage of benign files correctly classified out of the total number of benign files.

Table 5. Feature-selection-highest - validation results

Method	NF	Total feats	Acc	Se	Sp	–	Method	NF	Total feats	Acc	Se	Sp
F_2	2	89	99.2	76.19	99.39	–	ABS	4	110	98.83	70.42	99.07
F_1	15	364	99.18	76.64	99.37	–	ABS	3	97	98.82	70.98	99.05
F_2	4	119	99.16	73.31	99.38	–	ABS	5	121	98.82	69.91	99.06
F_1	4	158	99.09	79.28	99.25	–	ABS	15	194	98.81	69.47	99.05
F_1	10	274	99.07	78.73	99.24	–	ABS	2	81	98.79	69.2	99.03
F_1	3	141	99.05	79.19	99.21	–	ABS	1	70	98.78	68.77	99.03
F_2	5	134	99.05	77.57	99.23	–	F_1	2	116	98.78	80.56	98.93
F_1	5	177	**99.03**	**79.79**	**99.19**	–	ABS	20	224	98.75	70.63	98.99
F_2	10	201	99.0	79.07	99.17	–	ABS	10	162	98.72	71.21	98.95
F_2	1	69	98.97	77.66	99.15	–	F_2	20	299	98.64	80.26	98.79
F_1	20	441	98.96	79.62	99.12	–	F_2	15	256	98.52	81.49	98.66
F_2	3	106	98.85	79.8	99.01	–	F_1	1	84	98.35	80.69	98.5

Table 6. Feature-selection-middle-x - validation results

Method	X	Total feats	Acc	Se	Sp	–	Method	X	Total feats	Acc	Se	Sp
ABS	10	92	98.97	71.29	99.2	–	F_1	15	87	98.8	71.73	99.02
F_2	15	87	98.9	65.38	99.17	–	F_2	5	76	98.78	71.05	99.01
ABS	5	95	98.89	72.62	99.11	–	F_1	10	94	98.55	75.02	98.74
ABS	15	105	98.88	70.9	99.11	–	F_1	5	95	98.47	78.97	98.64
F_2	10	91	98.8	73.05	99.01	–	–	–	–	–	–	–

Table 7. Feature-selection-adaptable-x - validation results

Method	X	Total feats	Acc	Se	Sp	–	Method	X	Total feats	Acc	Se	Sp
F_2	1	228	99.32	66.32	99.59	–	F_2	3	230	99.0	78.79	99.16
F_1	**3**	**241**	**99.16**	**79.47**	**99.32**	–	ABS	1	229	98.95	72.59	99.17
F_2	2	229	99.16	78.55	99.33	–	ABS	5	233	98.95	71.89	99.18
F_2	4	231	99.16	78.29	99.33	–	F_1	1	239	98.93	79.85	99.09
F_1	4	242	99.14	79.42	99.3	–	F_2	5	232	98.9	80.11	99.06
F_1	392	621	99.11	78.27	99.29	–	F_1	6	244	98.88	80.29	99.03
ABS	392	634	99.1	78.28	99.27	–	F_2	392	606	98.87	79.34	99.03
F_1	5	243	99.07	79.8	99.22	–	ABS	3	231	98.84	73.37	99.05
F_1	2	240	99.06	79.76	99.22	–	ABS	2	230	98.78	73.87	98.98
F_2	6	233	99.02	79.34	99.18	–	ABS	4	232	98.74	73.73	98.95
ABS	6	234	98.51	73.19	98.72	–	–	–	–	–	–	–

9 Conclusions and Future Work

The detection approach using a FF-NN classifier based on API-call input leads to very good results on polymorphic malware, in terms of both accuracy and FP rate. The results reported above suggest that the combination algorithm-method *feature-selection-adaptable-f1-3* is the best balanced for practical purposes[15] in terms of detection, false positive rate, number of used features and validation time complexity. We underline that the techniques described in this paper are designed for Windows native binaries.

This approach allows building a fast classifier that can be used in blocking scenario (including emulation, feature mining and testing the model). From a practical point of view, this is relevant if a security solution focuses on building a protection mechanism against polymorphic malware. However, this approach is directly dependent on the specifications of the implemented emulator. For example, in case of large loops, rare assembly instructions or rarely used API from OS a weak emulator may be tricked. Hence the list of resulted APIs may be affected as well as the obtained verdict.

We plan to extend this technique beyond native executable for VM based languages such as Java or C-Sharp and scripts that are used by malicious actors (powershell, javascript, etc). In all of these cases, the algorithms are similar with the specificity that identifying the final APIs that are called differs for various languages.

References

1. Ahmadi, M., Ulyanov, D., Semenov, S., Trofimov, M., Giacinto, G.: Novel feature extraction, selection and fusion for effective malware family classification. In: Proceedings of the Sixth ACM Conference on Data and Application Security and Privacy, pp. 183–194 (2016). https://doi.org/10.1145/2857705.2857713
2. Alazab, M., Venkatraman, S., Watters, P.: Towards understanding malware behaviour by the extraction of API calls. In: 2010 Second Cybercrime and Trustworthy Computing Workshop, pp. 52–59 (2010). https://doi.org/10.1109/CTC.2010.8
3. Amer, E., El-Sappagh, S., Hu, J.: Contextual identification of windows malware through semantic interpretation of API call sequence. Appl. Sci. **10**(21), 7673 (10 2020). https://doi.org/10.3390/app10217673
4. Amer, E., Zelinka, I.: A dynamic windows malware detection and prediction method based on contextual understanding of API call sequence. Comput. Secur. **92**, 101760 (2020). https://doi.org/10.1016/j.cose.2020.101760
5. Anderson, H.: Evading Machine Learning Malware Detection (2017)
6. Anderson, H., Kharkar, A., Filar, B., Evans, D., Roth, P.: Learning to evade static PE machine learning malware models via reinforcement learning (2018)
7. Apicella, A., Donnarumma, F., Isgró, F., Prevete, R.: A survey on modern trainable activation functions. Neural Netw. **138**, 14–32 (2021). https://doi.org/10.1016/j.neunet.2021.01.026
8. Athiwaratkun, B., Stokes, J.: Malware classification with LSTM and GRU language models and a character-level cnn. In: 2017 IEEE International Conference on Acoustics, Speech and Signal Processing (ICASSP), pp. 2482–2486 (2017). https://doi.org/10.1109/ICASSP.2017.7952603

[15] A practical score is computed: (10*Specificity+Sensitivity)/11.

9. Balan, G., Popescu, A.: Detecting java compiled malware using machine learning techniques. In: 2018 20th International Symposium on Symbolic and Numeric Algorithms for Scientific Computing (SYNASC), pp. 435–439 (2018). https://doi.org/10.1109/SYNASC.2018.00073
10. Bucevschi, A., Balan, G., Prelipcean, D.B.: Preventing file-less attacks with machine learning techniques. In: 2019 21st International Symposium on Symbolic and Numeric Algorithms for Scientific Computing (SYNASC), pp. 248–252 (2019). https://doi.org/10.1109/SYNASC49474.2019.00042
11. Chen, W., Wang, Z., Chen, D.: An emulator for executing IA-32 applications on arm-based systems. J. Comput. **5**(7), 1133–1141 (2010). https://doi.org/10.4304/jcp.5.7.1133-1141
12. Choi, S., Bae, J., Lee, C., Kim, Y., Kim, J.: Attention-based automated feature extraction for malware analysis. Sensors **20**(10), 2893 (2020). https://doi.org/10.3390/s20102893
13. Elhadi, A., Maarof, M., Barry, B.: Improving the detection of malware behaviour using simplified data dependent API call graph. Int. J. Secur. Appl. **7**, 29–42 (2013). https://doi.org/10.14257/ijsia.2013.7.5.03
14. Elhadi, A., Maarof, M., Hamza Osman, A.: Malware detection based on hybrid signature behaviour application programming interface call graph. Am. J. Appl. Sci. **9**, 283–288 (2012)
15. Fadadu, F., Handa, A., Kumar, N., Shukla, S.K.: Evading API call sequence based malware classifiers. In: Zhou, J., Luo, X., Shen, Q., Xu, Z. (eds.) ICICS 2019. LNCS, vol. 11999, pp. 18–33. Springer, Cham (2020). https://doi.org/10.1007/978-3-030-41579-2_2
16. Gavriluţ, D., Benchea, R., Vatamanu, C.: Optimized zero false positives perceptron training for malware detection. In: 2012 14th International Symposium on Symbolic and Numeric Algorithms for Scientific Computing, pp. 247–253 (2012).https://doi.org/10.1109/SYNASC.2012.34
17. Gavriluţ, D., Cimpoesu, M., Anton, D., Ciortuz, L.: Malware detection using machine learning (2009). In: 2009 International Multiconference on Computer Science and Information Technology, pp. 735–741. https://doi.org/10.1109/IMCSIT.2009.5352759
18. Gavriluţ, D., Cimpoesu, M., Anton, D., Ciortuz, L.: Malware detection using perceptrons and support vector machines. In: 2009 Computation World: Future Computing, Service Computation, Cognitive, Adaptive, Content, Patterns, pp. 283–288 (2009). https://doi.org/10.1109/ComputationWorld.2009.85
19. Ki, Y., Kim, E., Kim, H.K.: A novel approach to detect malware based on API call sequence analysis. Int. J. Distrib. Sens. Netw. 1–9 (2015). https://doi.org/10.1155/2015/659101
20. Kim, H., Kim, J., Kim, Y., Kim, I., Kim, K.J., Kim, H.: Improvement of malware detection and classification using API call sequence alignment and visualization. Cluster Comput. **22**(1), 921–929 (2017). https://doi.org/10.1007/s10586-017-1110-2
21. Kingma, D., Ba, J.: Adam: a method for stochastic optimization. In: International Conference on Learning Representations (2014)
22. Lin, C.T., Wang, N.J., Xiao, H., Eckert, C.: Feature selection and extraction for malware classification. J. Inf. Sci. Eng. **31**(3), 965–992 (2015)
23. Liţă, C.V., Cosovan, D., Gavriluţ, D.: Anti-emulation trends in modern packers: a survey on the evolution of anti-emulation techniques in UPA packers. J. Comput. Virol. Hacking Tech. **14**(2), 107–126 (2017). https://doi.org/10.1007/s11416-017-0291-9

24. Pascanu, R., Stokes, J., Sanossian, H., Marinescu, M., Thomas, A.: Malware classification with recurrent networks. In: 2015 IEEE International Conference on Acoustics, Speech and Signal Processing (ICASSP), pp. 1916–1920 (2015). https://doi.org/10.1109/ICASSP.2015.7178304
25. Rabadi, D., Teo, S.: Advanced windows methods on malware detection and classification. In: Annual Computer Security Applications Conference, pp. 54–68 (2020). https://doi.org/10.1145/3427228.3427242
26. Ranveer, S., Hiray, S.: Comparative analysis of feature extraction methods of malware detection. Int. J. Comput. Appl. **120**, 1–7 (2015). https://doi.org/10.5120/21220-3960
27. Shankarapani, M., Ramamoorthy, S., Movva, R., Mukkamala, S.: Malware detection using assembly and API call sequences. J. Comput. Virol. **7**, 107–119 (2011). https://doi.org/10.1007/s11416-010-0141-5
28. Sundarkumar, G., Vadlamani, R., Nwogu, I., Govindaraju, V.: Malware detection via API calls, topic models and machine learning. In: 2015 IEEE International Conference on Automation Science and Engineering (CASE), pp. 1212–1217 (2015). https://doi.org/10.1109/CoASE.2015.7294263
29. Tahir, R.: A study on malware and malware detection techniques. Int. J. Educ. Manag. Eng. **8**, 20–30 (2018). https://doi.org/10.5815/ijeme.2018.02.03
30. Uppal, D., Sinha, R., Mehra, V., Jain, V.: Malware detection and classification based on extraction of API sequences. In: 2014 International Conference on Advances in Computing, Communications and Informatics (ICACCI), pp. 2337–2342 (2014). https://doi.org/10.1109/ICACCI.2014.6968547
31. Vitel, S., Balan, G., Prelipcean, D.B.: Improving detection of malicious office documents using one-side classifiers. In: 2019 21st International Symposium on Symbolic and Numeric Algorithms for Scientific Computing (SYNASC), pp. 243–247 (09 2019). https://doi.org/10.1109/SYNASC49474.2019.00041
32. Xu, K., Li, Y., Deng, R., Chen, K., Xu, J.: Droidevolver: self-evolving android malware detection system. In: 2019 IEEE European Symposium on Security and Privacy (EuroS&P), pp. 47–62 (2019). https://doi.org/10.1109/EuroSP.2019.00014
33. Zuech, R., Khoshgoftaar, T.: A survey on feature selection for intrusion detection. In: Proceedings of the 21st ISSAT International Conference on Reliability and Quality in Design, pp. 150–155 (2015)
34. Štursa, D., Doležel, P.: Comparison of ReLU and linear saturated activation functions in neural network for universal approximation. In: 2019 22nd International Conference on Process Control (PC19) pp. 146–151 (2019). https://doi.org/10.1109/PC.2019.8815057

Evaluating the Possibility of Evasion Attacks to Machine Learning-Based Models for Malicious PowerShell Detection

Yuki Mezawa(✉) and Mamoru Mimura

National Defense Academy of Japan, Yokosuka, Japan
{em60014,mim}@nda.ac.jp

Abstract. In cyber attacks, PowerShell has become a convenient tool for attackers. A previous study proposed a classification method for PowerShell scripts that combines natural language processing (NLP) techniques and machine learning models. Although it has been pointed out that the accuracy of machine learning is degraded by adversarial input, no evaluation has been reported for PowerShell classification. In this study, we evaluated the possibility of evasion attacks to the machine learning-based model for malicious PowerShell detection. In addition to Bag-of-Words, Latent Semantic Indexing (LSI), and Support Vector Machine (SVM), we combined Doc2Vec, RandomForest, and XGBoost with the previous models. As a result, we confirmed that evasion attacks are possible in PowerShell. In particular, the models using Doc2Vec decreased the recall rate by 0.78 at maximum. The effect mainly depends on the NLP technique, and there was almost no difference in any machine learning models with LSI.

Keywords: PowerShell · Latent semantic indexing · Doc2Vec · XGBoost

1 Introduction

Fileless malware attacks, which are difficult to detect by conventional antivirus software, are on the rise. It has been reported that the number of fileless malware attacks increased about tenfold in 2020 compared to the previous year [16]. Fileless malware differs from common malware in that the executable file is not stored on disk. Fileless malware calls an application by script or other means and executes it in memory as a process. Since data in memory is generally lost when power is turned off, traces of fileless malware are also unlikely to remain. In addition, since no executable files exist, it is difficult to detect fileless malware. Fileless malware often uses PowerShell, a regular Windows tool, for its operation. As a previous study on the detection of such malicious PowerShell, a method based on dynamic analysis combines with traditional natural language

C. Su et al. (Eds.): ISPEC 2022, LNCS 13620, pp. 252–267, 2022.
https://doi.org/10.1007/978-3-031-21280-2_14

processing (NLP) techniques and convolutional neural networks has been proposed [5]. In addition, a detection method based on static analysis combines with machine learning models has also been proposed, focusing on NLP techniques [12,14]. Although such methods using machine learning models can be expected to detect unknown samples, it is pointed out that the classification accuracy may be degraded by adversarial inputs assuming the mechanism [2]. Although the methods proposed in previous studies [12,14] may be affected in the same way, it is difficult to say that sufficient evaluation has been conducted. Previous studies on evasion of machine learning models have been conducted on PDF (Portable Document Format), PortableExecutable (PE), Android, VBA macros, etc. [1,4,11,19]. However, no evaluation of malicious PowerShell detection models has been reported.

In this study, we test an evasion method against the malicious PowerShell detection method based on word-level machine learning models [12], and confirm whether the detection rate decreases. In this detection method, a language model is constructed by dividing PowerShell scripts into words, and malicious PowerShell scripts are detected by linguistic features such as the frequency of occurrence of specific words. We attempt to evade malicious scripts by inserting words that frequently appear in benign scripts [19]. In addition, to compare the effects of combining NLP techniques and machine learning models, we add Doc2Vec as a NLP technique and RandomForest and XGBoost as machine learning models. To the best of our knowledge, this is the first attempt to validate NLP techniques including Doc2Vec against multiple machine learning models.

This paper provides the following contributions:

1. This study shows that evasive attacks against machine learning models are possible against malicious PowerShell scripts while maintaining their functionality by adding features of benign samples.
2. As a NLP technique, we newly apply the evasion method by adding features of benign samples to Doc2Vec, and evaluate its effectiveness.
3. As a machine learning model, we apply the evasion method to RandomForest and XGBoost to classify the samples, and evaluate its effectiveness.
4. We confirm that the model using Doc2Vec is more susceptible to evasion attacks than the models using Bag-of-Words (BoW) and Latent Semantic Indexing (LSI), and its recall rate is reduced by as much as 0.78.
5. We confirm that the effect of evasion attacks depends on the NLP technique, and that LSI shows little difference among the machine learning models.

The structure of this paper is shown below. Section 2 introduces related research and Sect. 3 introduces related techniques used in this study. Section 4 describes the evaluation method, and Sect. 5 describes the evaluation experiment and its results. Section 6 produces some considerations. Finally, we conclude this paper.

2 Related Work

2.1 Deobfuscation Malicious PowerShell Scripts

Malware is often obfuscated to prevent analysis. This is true for malicious PowerShell scripts as well. Several methods have been proposed to deobfuscate PowerShell scripts.

A representative study is the development of PowerDrive [15] by Ugarte et al. In their experiments, Ugarte et al. correctly analyzed 4642 out of 4828 malicious scripts collected from security vendors and VirusTotal. The 186 scripts that failed to be analyzed used APIs belonging to the .NET language that could not be deobfuscated by PowerDrive. PowerDrive enables more efficient deobfuscation of the source code required for static analysis of malicious PowerShell scripts. Jeff White used regular expressions to deobfuscate malicious PowerShell scripts and showed the results of behavior analysis [17]. Liu et al. also proposed an deobfuscation method using regular expressions, and proposed the method as a model called PSDEM [10]. Li et al. proposed a lightweight deobfuscation method focusing on the subtrees of Abstract Syntax Trees (ASTs) [9]. Their method requires less than 0.5 s for average deobfuscation, and improves the similarity between the obfuscated script and the original from 0.5% to about 80%. These studies are aimed at deobfuscating malicious PowerShell scripts. In this study, we focus on the detection of malicious PowerShell scripts themselves.

2.2 Detection of Malicious PowerShell

In order to detect malicious PowerShell, several methods using machine learning models have been proposed. Hendler et al. proposed a method for detecting malicious PowerShells using deep neural networks [5]. It is a combination of deep learning architecture and traditional NLP, using 4-CNN and 3-grams. Hendler et al. also proposed a method for detecting malicious PowerShells using contextual embedding of words [6]. This method extracts obfuscated PowerShell tokens based on Anti-Malware Scan Interface (AMSI) supplied by Microsoft Corporation and uses contextual word embedding (Word2Vec and FastText), Token-Char, Convolution Neural Network (CNN), and Recurrent Neural Network (RNN). Rusak et al. proposed a method that combines AST and deep learning to detect malicious PowerShell [13]. It is a detection method that uses structural information of the code instead of text-based information. In this method, Base64-encoded scripts and commands are decoded and converted to ASTs as preprocessing, and then the root of each AST node is constructed based on the corpus of PowerShell scripts. Jeff White analyzed 4100 malicious PowerShells and classified them into 27 groups [18]. Through this analysis, he was able to determine what targets the malicious PowerShells were attacking and how they were attacking them. Based on these studies, Tajiri et al. proposed a detection method for malicious PowerShells using a word-based language model with static analysis only [12,14]. This method generates a word-based language model from the source code using LSI, a kind of NLP techniques, and uses machine learning to classify unknown PowerShell scripts. In their experiments, they achieved a recall rate of 0.98 using samples available on GitHub. Fang et al. proposed a method to detect malicious PowerShell by combining multiple features [3]. This method combines features extracted at the character level, the function level, and the AST level with semantic features extracted from FastText, and achieves an accuracy of 0.9776 in experiments. However, this method does not support obfuscated PowerShell scripts, and requires prior deobfuscation.

As described above, previous studies have proposed several malicious PowerShell detection methods that combine NLP and machine learning or deep learning [5,6,12–14]. Simultaneously, methods for deobfuscating PowerShell scripts have also been studied, and detection methods using static analysis combined with these methods have achieved a high reproduction rate. However, it is difficult to say that the robustness of the detection method has been sufficiently evaluated because it does not assume the case where an attacker is aware of the existence of the detection method and tries to evade it. In this study, we assume that an attacker is aware of the detection methods and tries to evade them.

2.3 Evading Machine Learning Models

For detection methods using machine learning models, the threat of attacks that evade detection has been pointed out. Maiorca et al. proposed a method to evade PDF malware detection by machine learning using generative adversarial networks (GANs), and showed a high detection evasion rate against the targeted detection methods [11]. Chen et al. proposed a method to evade detection methods for malware in PE format using CNNs [1]. In this study, they evaded detection by adding the source code to the PE file, and also showed how to counter the attack by adversarial learning and pre-detection of adversarial samples. Grosse et al. showed that Android malware can evade detection by dynamic analysis while maintaining the functionality of the malware by adding code with the characteristics of a benign application [4]. Yamamoto et al. showed that by adding benign VBA macro features to VBA malware, it is possible to evade detection by machine learning models while maintaining the functionality of the malware [19]. In this study, they tested an evasion attack against a VBA malware detection model that combines NLP techniques, BoW and LSI, with a machine learning model, Support Vector Machine (SVM). As an evasion technique, they insert word-level features obtained from benign macros into VBA malware. In this evaluation, the recall rate of the model using BoW is reduced to 1.5% of the reference rate, and the recall rate of the model using LSI is reduced by 73%.

Thus, the threat of evasion attacks against malware detection methods such as PDF, PE, Android, and VBA macros has been pointed out. However, the threat of evasion attacks against malicious PowerShell detection models has not been reported to date. As in the cases of Android malware and VBA malware, we can assume that attacks that add benign script features to the source code are also possible for PowerShell scripts. Therefore, in this study, we examine the possibility that an attacker can evade the detection model of malicious PowerShell using machine learning.

3 Related Technique

In this section, we describe the NLP techniques and machine learning models used in this study. Since both of them have a significant impact on the classification accuracy, it is necessary to compare their combinations in order to ascertain the impact of the evasion methods. In addition, to evaluate the possibility of evasion attacks, it is necessary to actually apply the evasion method to the proposed malicious PowerShell detection method. Since the detection method proposed by Tajiri et al. [12,14] is the target of this study, we use the same NLP technique and machine learning model as in their work. These are BoW, Doc2Vec, and LSI as NLP techniques, and SVM, RandomForest, and XGBoost as machine learning models. Each of these NLP techniques and machine learning models has different properties, which are useful for evaluating the impact of evasion methods.

3.1 NLP Technique

Bag-of-Words (BoW) is a vector representation of a document based only on the frequency of occurrence of words. The order of each word is not taken into account. Let w denote a word and n denote the frequency of occurrence corresponding to w, then document d can be expressed as (1).

$$d = [(w_1, n_{w_1}), (w_2, n_{w_2}), (w_3, n_{w_3}), ..., (w_j, n_{w_j})] \tag{1}$$

Based on this equation (1), if we omit the word w by fixing the position of n, we can express d as a number. The document-word relationship, which represents the number of occurrences of a word in each document $\hat{d_i}$, can then be represented by the vector in Eq. (2).

$$\hat{d_i} = (n_{w_1}, n_{w_2}, n_{w_3}, ..., n_{w_j}) \tag{2}$$

By using BoW, each document can be converted into a vector of a fixed number of dimensions with a unique number of words.

Doc2Vec is one of the implementations of Paragraph Vector [8] proposed by Le et al. The Paragraph Vector is an extension of word2vec, a model for generating feature vectors of words proposed by Mikolov et al. The Paragraph Vector generates feature vectors of documents instead of words. Since Paragraph Vector has no limitation on the length of input sentences, the process does not need to be modified according to the length of input. By comparing the generated feature vectors, it is possible to calculate the similarity between documents and classify them.

Latent Semantic Indexing (LSI) can analyze the relevance between documents and words contained in documents. LSI applies singular value decomposition to the feature vectors obtained by BoW and other methods to analyze the relevance. Based on the relevance obtained by LSI, documents and words can be classified. In BoW, the number of dimensions increases in proportion to the number of words, and the computational complexity increases accordingly. However, LSI compresses the dimensionality to a low level by singular value decomposition, thus reducing the computational complexity while maintaining the features of the documents.

3.2 Machine Learning Technique

SVM is a type of pattern recognition model that uses supervised learning, and it is used for classification and regression problems. SVM obtains a decision boundary based on the idea of finding a hyperplane that maximizes the distance from each data point, called margin maximization. Using the obtained decision boundary, SVM discriminates each data point.

RandomForest is a typical method of ensemble learning that improves on bagging by using decision trees as weak learners. RandomForest is an algorithm that generates a large number of decision trees by random sampling and determines the predictions by majority voting.

XGBoost is a type of ensemble learning that combines decision trees and gradient boosting. XGBoost is scalable and can handle large scale data. XGBoost is also an algorithm that can deal with sparse data with many missing values and zeros.

4 Evaluation Method

In this section, we describe an evaluation method for evasion attacks against the malicious PowerShell detection method based on word-level machine learning models [12].

4.1 Outline

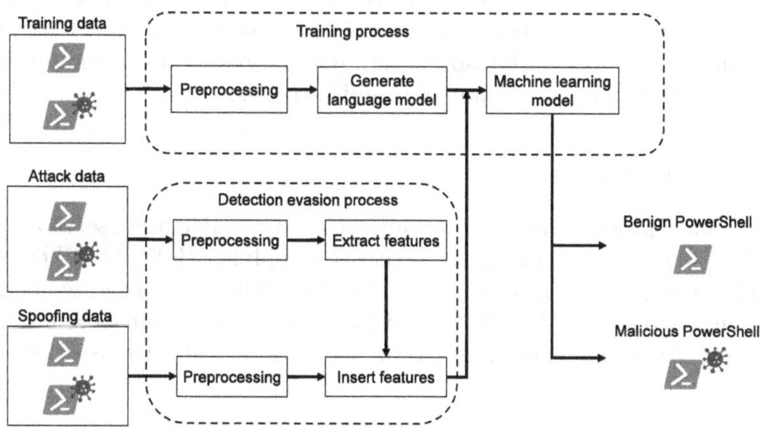

Fig. 1. Overview of the evaluation method.

The evaluation method is divided into two main parts: the training process and the detection evasion process. The datasets include training data, spoofing data, and attack data, and each dataset contains samples of both benign and malicious PowerShells. The training data is used to train the machine learning model that serves as the classifier, the spoofing data is used to apply evasion techniques to the malicious PowerShell, and the attack data is used to extract the word-level features of the benign PowerShell. Figure 1 shows the relationship between each process and dataset. First, each process preprocesses the data by deobfuscation, data cleansing, and Partitioning. Second, a training process is used to train a machine learning model that serves as a classifier. Following the training process, the detection evasion process is executed to generate spoofed data with word-level features of benign PowerShell. Finally, we classify the spoofed data and ascertain the recall rate of the classification.

The sample $x^*$of the malicious PowerShell that evades the machine learning model F generated by our method can be expressed by Eq. (3).

$$x^* = x + \delta_{y_a} \; s.t. \; F(y_t) = F(x + \delta_{y_a}) \tag{3}$$

Here, x represents the normal malicious PowerShell, y represents the benign PowerShell, and δ_y represents the features of the benign PowerShell. Also, t represents the training data and a represents the attack data. In this study, we assume that the attacker is aware of the existence of the machine learning model and has access to the training data. Therefore, $y_a = y_t$.

The details of each procedure will be described in the following sections.

4.2 Preprocessing

In preprocessing, each data is subjected to deobfuscation, data cleansing, and sharing. Each process is performed using regular expressions. In the deobfuscation, the obfuscated part is extracted by matching, and then unified to lower case, Base64 encoding is replaced, and the line is broken at the end character. In data cleansing, commenting out, URLs, IP addresses, and multi-byte characters are each replaced so that they can be used as one of the features. Partitioning splits strings by symbols (whitespace, terminators, parentheses, and operators) that serve as boundaries for commands and variables.

4.3 Training Process

In the training process, we train machine learning models that serve as classifiers. First, language models are generated by applying BoW, Doc2Vec or LSI NLP techniques to the preprocessed training data. Then, the generated language model is input to the SVM, XGBoost, or RandomForest machine learning model and trained. The trained machine learning model is then able to classify samples.

4.4 Detection Evasion Process

In the detection evasion process, an evasion method is applied to the spoofed data. The procedure is shown in Algorithm 1. X_a and Y_a are word groups that frequently occur in malicious and benign PowerShells in the attack data, respectively. First, from the difference between X_a and Y_a, we extract δ_{Y_a}, a set of words that frequently occur only in benign PowerShell. From the extracted word group δ_{Y_a}, one word δ_{y_a} is randomly selected and inserted into the malicious PowerShell x of the spoofed data. Simply inserting δ_{y_a} violates PowerShell syntax and adversely affects the behavior of malicious PowerShell. As a solution, when inserting δ_{y_a}, we use a method or property g in combination that does not affect the behavior of malicious PowerShell, such as case conversion or character count. The method or property g used here is randomly selected from the list G prepared in advance for each word to be inserted. An example of the changes in the source code due to insertion is shown in Fig. 2. In this example, the words "hello" and "error" are inserted while following PowerShell syntax by combining capitalization or character count. In this study, the number of insertions k is varied in the range of 0 to 500 times, and the change in the recall rate is measured. After all insertions are completed, the spoofed data is input into the machine learning model for classification.

Algorithm 1. Detection Evasion Process

Require: $X_a = \{w_{x_a n}\}$, $Y_a = \{w_{y_a n}\}$, k, $G = \{g_n\}$
  $\delta_{Y_a} = Y_a - X_a$
  while Number of adds $< k$ **do**
    $\delta_{y_a} = \text{random } \delta_{Y_a}$
    $g = \text{random } G$
    $x^* = x + \delta_{y_a} + g$
  end while
  return x^*

```
$num = (Get-ChildItem -Recurse).count;
$length = 0;
Get-ChildItem -Recurse | ForEach-Object
{ $length += $_.Length };
Write-Host "File count = $num File size = $length"
```

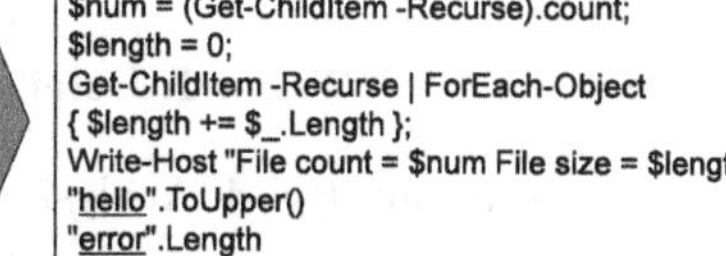

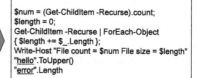

Fig. 2. Example of source code changes due to insertion.

5 Experiment

5.1 Dataset

In this study, we used the same dataset to compare the detection rate with previous studies [12]. The dataset was created from PowerShell scripts collected from HybridAnalysis (589 scripts), PowerShell scripts collected from AnyRun (355 scripts), and benign PowerShell scripts obtained from github (5000 scripts). The collection period is between January 2019 and March 2020. From HybridAnalysis, the sample information was retrieved four times a day using the public API, and the publicly available PowerShell samples were obtained. From AnyRun, we searched for samples that contained the .ps extension and obtained the samples manually. From github, we first searched all repositories containing PowerShell and downloaded the top 1000. Then, we extracted files that contained the .ps extension and used all of them as samples. Thus, we collected samples from multiple sources over a long period of time, and the samples have a certain degree of comprehensiveness. Malicious PowerShell scripts are not recognized as a threat by some antivirus software. From the samples collected by HybridAnalysis and AnyRun, we assigned a malicious label to samples that were judged to be a threat by at least two of the five major vendors (Kaspersky, McAfee, Microsoft, Symantec, and TrendMicro) at the time of collection. We assigned a benign label to the samples for which zero vendors judged them to be malicious. Samples that did not fall into either of these categories were excluded. The samples collected from github were used as benign PowerShell samples only if there were zero vendors that were judged to be malicious.

Following the sample collection, we divided the dataset into time series. The reason for this is that only known samples can be used to train the machine learning model in the case of actual malicious PowerShell detection. The samples collected from HybridAnalysis and AnyRun were divided before and after June and July 2019 based on the date of submission. The samples from before June were used as known samples for training and attack data, and the samples from after July were used as unknown samples for spoofing data. The sample collected from github was randomly divided into two parts, and one part was used for training data and attack data, and the other part was used for spoofing data. The details of the datasets used are shown in Table 1.

Table 1. Details of the datasets

AnyRun, HybridAnalysis			Github
Dataset type	Malicious	Benign	Benign
Training & Attack data	309	232	4901
Spoofing data	171	92	

5.2 Experiment Contents

In our experiments, we varied the number of insertions into the spoofed data from 0 to 500 times. We then classified the spoofed data into each models and measured the recall rate of malicious PowerShells. The datasets collected in this study all consist of benign and malicious PowerShell with a imbalanced sample size. Training a machine learning model on imbalanced data will significantly reduce the classification accuracy for minority groups [7]. As a countermeasure, we conducted experiments after undersampling the benign PowerShells in the training data. The undersampling was performed by randomly selecting the same number of malicious PowerShells from all benign PowerShells in the training data. Therefore, different training data were used for each trial, and the results varied. In order to eliminate variations in the results, 10 trials were conducted in the measurement, and the average value was used as the result.

Undersampling is not necessary if the number of benign PowerShells and malicious PowerShells is balanced in the training data. Since undersampling is omitted when balanced training data are used, it is not included in the evaluation method in this study, but is part of the experimental content. A balanced training data can be prepared for the actual operation of the detection model. Therefore, this study has achieved practical accuracy. Note that undersampling is not applied to the spoofed data. This is because the probability of encountering a malicious PowerShell script is much lower than that of a benign one when assuming actual operation.

The experimental environment is shown in Table 2. .The libraries used for the implementation of the NLP techniques and machine learning models are shown in Table 3.

Table 2. Experimental environment

CPU	Core i7-9700K 3.60 GHz
Memory	64 GB
OS	Windows10 Home
Programming language	Python3.7.7

Table 3. Main Python libraries used for experiments

NLP	Bag-of-Words	gensim -3.8.3
	Doc2Vec	
	LSI	
Machine learning	SVM	sickit-learn -0.23.2
	RandomForest	
	XGBoost	xgboost -1.2.0

5.3 Result

In this section, we confirm the effectiveness of the evaluation method. Figure 3 shows the results of each model using BoW as the NLP techniques. The vertical axis of graph is the value of the recall rate of malicious PowerShell classified by each model, and the horizontal axis is the number of insertions of the evaluation method. In this study, we focus on the recall rate of malicious PowerShells because we want to evaluate the degree of influence of evasion attacks on the detection of malicious PowerShells. From Fig. 3, we confirmed that the models using BoW as the NLP techniques were the least affected by insertion. In particular, the classifier combined with XGBoost had a recall rate of 0.76 when 500 features were added. However, when no insertions were made, the recall rate was 0.96, a 21% decrease in performance. Figure 4 shows the results of each model using Doc2Vec as the NLP techniques. The recall rate of each model that used Doc2Vec as the NLP techniques decreased significantly after 10 insertions. In particular, the model combined with RandomForest almost halved the recall rate from 0.77 to 0.39 after 10 insertions. Figure 5 shows the results of each model using LSI as the NLP techniques. From Fig. 5, we confirmed that the models using LSI as a NLP techniques shows almost the same change regardless of the combined machine learning model.

Among all the combinations of NLP techniques and machine learning models, the model with the lowest recall rate after 500 insertions was the combination of Doc2Vec and XGBoost. The recall rate decreased by about 0.78 from the case without the insertion process.

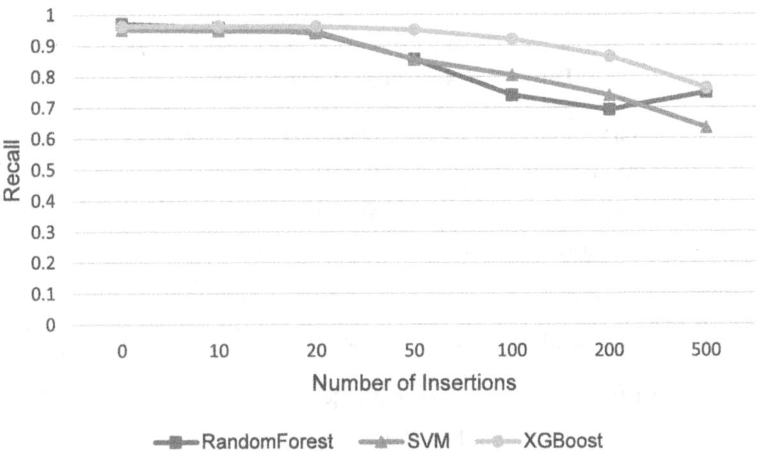

Fig. 3. The recall rate of the models using BoW.

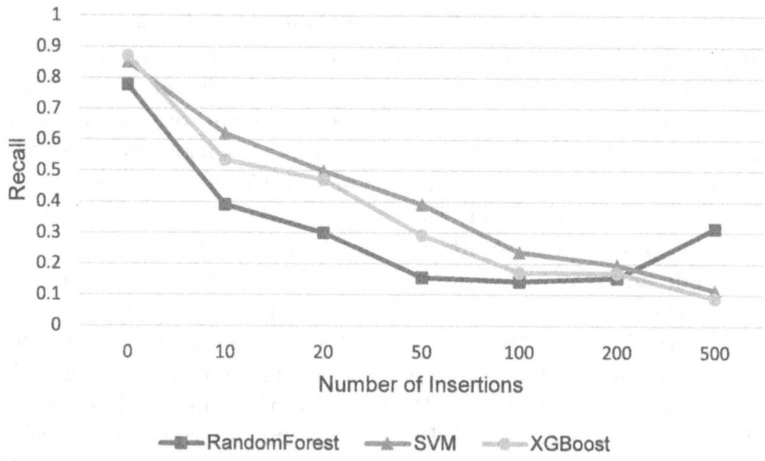

Fig. 4. The recall rate of the models using D2V.

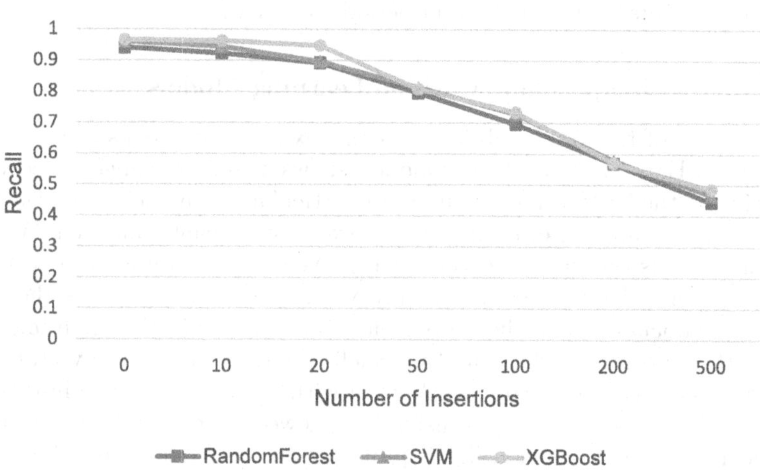

Fig. 5. The recall rate of the models using LSI.

6 Discussion

6.1 Possibility of Evasion Attack

As a result of our experiments, we confirmed that all combinations of NLP techniques and machine learning models showed a decrease in the recall rate. All the models that used Doc2Vec and LSI as well as NLP techniques eventually had a recall rate below 0.5. This means that more than half of the malicious PowerShells were missed, which is not practical. The model using BoW shows a smaller decrease in the recall rate, and the model combined with XGBoost shows a recall rate of about 0.76. However, this also means that 1/4 of the malicious PowerShells are missed. In addition, since the recall rate was 0.96

before the insertion, we believe that the reliability of the detection model is not sufficient. Furthermore, from the change in the graph in Fig. 3 if we add more insertions, the recall rate may decrease further. Therefore, the evaluation method that was effective in evading the detection of Android malware and VBA malware is also effective in evading the detection of malicious PowerShell. Thus, we believe that evasion attacks against the machine learning model for malicious PowerShell detection can occur. However, in the case of a small number of words and function types used for insertion, many of the same words may appear in the source code and may be considered a new feature of malicious PowerShell.

Although the attack data used in this experiment is older than the spoofed data, we observed a decrease in the recall rate. This may indicate that the attacker does not necessarily need to extract the elements of the benign PowerShell script from the latest dataset. We speculate that this is related to the way benign PowerShell scripts are used. Benign PowerShell scripts are generally used for task automation and configuration management. Since the needs for PowerShell scripts are considered to be stable, we assume that the characteristics of PowerShell scripts change little from period to period.

6.2 NLP Techniques and Machine Learning Models

A comparison of the graphs obtained in this experiment reveals some interesting features. Each of the evaluated models shows a similar change in recall rate depending on the NLP techniques used. In particular, the models using Doc2Vec, which is a newly applied evasion method, are all significantly affected. We speculate that this is due to the feature of Doc2Vec to generate feature vectors of documents. In order to generate feature vectors, Doc2Vec predicts the words between the document and the words before and after it. In this experiment, we inserted the features of a benign PowerShell script, so the feature vector of the entire document changed significantly even with a small amount of insertion.

On the other hand, the model using LSI showed almost no difference among the machine learning models. This is probably due to the feature of LSI, which uses singular value decomposition to generate feature vectors that focus on the relationship between documents and words. Singular value decomposition eliminates elements that do not contribute much to the determination of a document, and concentrates only on the important elements. Since the feature vectors generated by this process are optimal for all the machine learning models, we believe that the differences among the machine learning models are no longer recognized. This suggests that the impact of the evaluation method depends on the NLP technique.

6.3 Research Ethics

Previous studies [5,13,15] have used large datasets, which were collected independently by security vendors. In general, it is difficult to obtain such a dataset from security vendors. In this study, we use all the PowerShell samples that are publicly available. In addition, libraries such as gensim and scikit-learn, which were used to implement NLP techniques and machine learning models, are also available free of charge. Therefore, it is easy to build an environment similar to the one used in this study, and we believe that our study has reproducibility.

6.4 Limitations

In this study, although we conducted experiments using the same number of samples as in previous studies [12], the number of samples of malicious PowerShell is not necessarily sufficient. This is because we collected malicious PowerShell samples from freely available malware distribution sites in order to ensure reproducibility. If the number of samples used in the experiments can be increased, the accuracy of the evaluation can be improved. In this study, we also focused on maintaining the behavior of the malicious PowerShell script during evasion attacks. Theoretically, we believe that the malicious PowerShell script maintains its behavior, but because we could not prepare a sandbox for evaluation, we were not able to actually execute the PowerShell script for evaluation.

7 Conclusion

In this study, we showed that it is possible to perform evasion attacks against machine learning models by adding features of benign samples to malicious PowerShell scripts, while maintaining their functionality. We also applied the evasion method to Doc2Vec, and classified samples against RandomForest and XGBoost to evaluate its effectiveness. Since this is the first study to evaluate the effectiveness of these evasion methods, we have provided new insights into evasion attacks against machine learning models. As a result of the evaluation experiments, we confirmed that the model using Doc2Vec is more susceptible to evasion attacks than the other models. In particular, the model combining Doc2Vec and XGBoost showed a recall rate decrease of about 0.78 due to evasion attacks. The model combining BoW and XGBoost showed the smallest impact from evasion attacks, but the recall rate was decreased by about 21% compared to normal. We also confirmed that the impact of evasion attacks depends on the NLP techniques, and that LSI shows little difference among machine learning models.

Future work includes the evaluation of the application of other NLP techniques and machine learning models. Many methods have been devised for both, and the combinations of NLP techniques and machine learning models that we have tested are only a few of them. By combining other NLP techniques and machine learning models, we may be able to find a method that is robust to the evasion attacks we have examined.

Acknowledgments. This work was supported by JSPS KAKENHI Grant Number 21K11898.

References

1. Chen, B., Ren, Z., Yu, C., Hussain, I., Liu, J.: Adversarial examples for cnn-based malware detectors. IEEE Access **7**, 54360–54371 (2019). https://doi.org/10.1109/ACCESS.2019.2913439
2. Chen, S., Xue, M., Fan, L., Hao, S., Xu, L., Zhu, H., Li, B.: Automated poisoning attacks and defenses in malware detection systems: An adversarial machine learning approach. Comput. Secur. **73**, 326–344 (2018). https://doi.org/10.1016/j.cose.2017.11.007
3. Fang, Y., Zhou, X., Huang, C.: Effective method for detecting malicious powershell scripts based on hybrid features. Neurocomputing **448**, 30–39 (2021). https://doi.org/10.1016/j.neucom.2021.03.117
4. Grosse, K., Papernot, N., Manoharan, P., Backes, M., McDaniel, P.: Adversarial examples for malware detection. In: Foley, S.N., Gollmann, D., Snekkenes, E. (eds.) ESORICS 2017. LNCS, vol. 10493, pp. 62–79. Springer, Cham (2017). https://doi.org/10.1007/978-3-319-66399-9_4
5. Hendler, D., Kels, S., Rubin, A.: Detecting malicious powershell commands using deep neural networks. In: Kim, J., Ahn, G., Kim, S., Kim, Y., López, J., Kim, T. (eds.) Proceedings of the 2018 on Asia Conference on Computer and Communications Security, AsiaCCS 2018, Incheon, Republic of Korea, 04–08 June 2018, pp. 187–197. ACM (2018). https://doi.org/10.1145/3196494.3196511
6. Hendler, D., Kels, S., Rubin, A.: Amsi-based detection of malicious powershell code using contextual embeddings. In: Sun, H., Shieh, S., Gu, G., Ateniese, G. (eds.) ASIA CCS 2020: The 15th ACM Asia Conference on Computer and Communications Security, Taipei, Taiwan, 5–9 October 2020, pp. 679–693. ACM (2020). https://doi.org/10.1145/3320269.3384742
7. Japkowicz, N.: The class imbalance problem: significance and strategies. In: Proceedings of the 2000 International Conference on Artificial Intelligence (ICAI), pp. 111–117 (2000)
8. Le, Q.V., Mikolov, T.: Distributed representations of sentences and documents. In: Proceedings of the 31th International Conference on Machine Learning, ICML 2014, Beijing, China, 21–26 June 2014, JMLR Workshop and Conference Proceedings, vol. 32, pp. 1188–1196. JMLR.org (2014). https://proceedings.mlr.press/v32/le14.html
9. Li, Z., Chen, Q.A., Xiong, C., Chen, Y., Zhu, T., Yang, H.: Effective and lightweight deobfuscation and semantic-aware attack detection for powershell scripts. In: Cavallaro, L., Kinder, J., Wang, X., Katz, J. (eds.) Proceedings of the 2019 ACM SIGSAC Conference on Computer and Communications Security, CCS 2019, London, UK, 11–15 November 2019, pp. 1831–1847. ACM (2019). https://doi.org/10.1145/3319535.3363187
10. Liu, C., Xia, B., Yu, M., Liu, Y.: PSDEM: a feasible de-obfuscation method for malicious powershell detection. In: 2018 IEEE Symposium on Computers and Communications, ISCC 2018, Natal, Brazil, 25–28 June 2018, pp. 825–831. IEEE (2018). https://doi.org/10.1109/ISCC.2018.8538691
11. Maiorca, D., Biggio, B., Giacinto, G.: Towards adversarial malware detection: Lessons learned from pdf-based attacks. ACM Comput. Surv. **52**(4), 78:1–78:36 (2019). https://doi.org/10.1145/3332184
12. Mimura, M., Tajiri, Y.: Static detection of malicious powershell based on word embeddings. Internet Things **15**, 100404 (2021). https://www.sciencedirect.com/science/article/pii/S2542660521000482

13. Rusak, G., Al-Dujaili, A., O'Reilly, U.: Ast-based deep learning for detecting malicious powershell. In: Lie, D., Mannan, M., Backes, M., Wang, X. (eds.) Proceedings of the 2018 ACM SIGSAC Conference on Computer and Communications Security, CCS 2018, Toronto, ON, Canada, 15–19 October 2018, pp. 2276–2278. ACM (2018). https://doi.org/10.1145/3243734.3278496
14. Tajiri, Y., Mimura, M.: Detection of malicious powershell using word-level language models. In: Aoki, K., Kanaoka, A. (eds.) IWSEC 2020. LNCS, vol. 12231, pp. 39–56. Springer, Cham (2020). https://doi.org/10.1007/978-3-030-58208-1_3
15. Ugarte, D., Maiorca, D., Cara, F., Giacinto, G.: PowerDrive: accurate de-obfuscation and analysis of powershell malware. In: Perdisci, R., Maurice, C., Giacinto, G., Almgren, M. (eds.) DIMVA 2019. LNCS, vol. 11543, pp. 240–259. Springer, Cham (2019). https://doi.org/10.1007/978-3-030-22038-9_12
16. WatchGuard Technologies: Internet Security Report - Q4 2020 (2021). https://www.watchguard.com/wgrd-resource-center/security-report-q4-2020. Accessed 21 July 2021
17. White, J.: Practical behavioral profiling of powershell scripts through static analysis (part 1). https://unit42.paloaltonetworks.com/practical-behavioral-profiling-of-powershell-scripts-through-static-analysis-part-1/. Accessed 20 Aug 2021
18. White, J.: Pulling back the curtains on encodedcommand powershell attacks. https://unit42.paloaltonetworks.com/unit42-pulling-back-the-curtains-on-encodedcommand-powershell-attacks/. Accessed 20 Aug 2021
19. Yamamoto, R., Mimura, M.: On the possibility of evasion attacks with macro malware. In: Ranganathan, G., Fernando, X., Shi, F., El Allioui, Y. (eds.) Soft Computing for Security Applications. AISC, vol. 1397, pp. 43–59. Springer, Singapore (2022). https://doi.org/10.1007/978-981-16-5301-8_4

Detect Compiler Inserted Run-time Security Checks in Binary Software

Koyel Pramanick(✉) and Prasad A. Kulkarni(✉)

EECS, University of Kansas, Lawrence, KS, USA
{koyel_pramanick25,prasadk}@ku.edu

Abstract. Our goal in this work is to develop a mechanism to determine the presence of targeted compiler-based or automated rules-based run-time security checks in any given binary. Our generalized approach relies on several key insights. First, instructions added by automated checks likely follow just one or only a few fixed patterns or templates at every insertion point. Second, any security check will guard some *interesting* or vulnerable program structure, like return addresses, indirect jumps/calls, etc., and the placement of the security check will inform about the nature of the check. By contrast, we would not expect ordinary user code to follow any single pattern at every such interesting program location. Our technique to detect automated security checks in binary code does not rely on known code signatures that can change depending on the language, the compiler, and the security check. We implement and evaluate our technique, and present our results, observations, and challenges in this work.

Keywords: Program binary · Security check · Automated security assessment

1 Introduction

Most software available to ordinary customers are shipped *without* any quality control indicators or metrics regarding the security and reliability properties of that software. Likewise, software are often shipped and distributed in their binary form without access to the original source code, which makes it especially challenging for customers to independently verify their security properties. End-users have limited means and few accessible tools to validate binary software security. This state of security validation for software customers persists even as the number of reported vulnerabilities have been increasing in number and severity for many years [11] and software vulnerabilities have been found to cause many disastrous real-world attacks [10,37].

To mitigate this concerning state of affairs for deployed software, researchers have developed techniques that identify and trigger potential vulnerabilities in

C. Su et al. (Eds.): ISPEC 2022, LNCS 13620, pp. 268–286, 2022.
https://doi.org/10.1007/978-3-031-21280-2_15

software binaries without availability of source code or debug symbol information [4,6,26]. However, even when applied, these tools may not find all the vulnerabilities present in that software. Attackers can exploit these software vulnerabilities to compromise user systems and expose sensitive customer data.

Unfortunately, there is considerably little prior work on automatically identifying provisions employed by the software developer and present in the binary software to detect and prevent such attacks even when software vulnerabilities are exploited. Many such provisions to thwart software attacks are available to developers, including techniques to detect and prevent all memory attacks [21], that use stack canaries to detect some buffer overflows [7], and to prevent control-flow attacks [1], etc. To be most effective, rather than being applied manually and in an ad-hoc manner by the software developer, such security techniques must be applied automatically and systematically by a tool like the compiler during the software build process. The knowledge that the given software is protected from attacks, even in the presence of software bugs, can relieve customers and increase their confidence and comfort to use the software.

In this work we explore and develop a generalized technique to identify security checks inserted by compilers and other automated tools in binary software. Our techniques do not depend on knowledge of the source programming language, or the compiler used to insert the check, or (the signature of) the specific security check implemented. Rather, our techniques to detect security checks in binaries employ insights that we expect (and aim to verify in this work) are typical to most such checks that are inserted by automated tools, like compilers. Our experiments in this paper focus on memory-related attacks and vulnerabilities, which are dominant is binary code built from memory unsafe languages, like C/C++ [32].

Our approach employs the following unique insights to detect security checks in binaries. We hypothesize that security checks applied by automated tools will be inserted at *code sites* just before the *interesting* or vulnerable code construct they are designed to protect, like return addresses, indirect calls/jumps, and array/buffer references. We also reason that the code inserted by any specific automated security check will display a similar instruction pattern or a few sets of patterns across its multiple deployment code sites. For the class of memory-related attacks we study in this work, we also speculate that the security checks will *validate* the vulnerable memory address that must be protected. Finally, we hypothesize that, by contrast, code that is built without the security check will not typically contain any uniform code pattern across the multiple potential deployment code sites in the binary.

Our novel technique then uses these insights to identify compiler-inserted security checks in any given arbitrary binary software by following these general steps: (a) employ a reverse engineering tool (Ghidra [22], in this work) to detect the potential deployment sites in the given binary (also called *interesting* instructions or constructs in this work) for any specific security check, (b) fetch and dump disassembled code blocks around the interesting program points, (c) process the dumped instruction traces to normalize constants, register numbers, labels, etc., and (d) validate and find common instruction patterns across collected traces. Our technique uses the presence of common instruction sequences/patterns across traces to deduce the likelihood of compiler checks to protect against attacks related to that code construct.

Thus, our primary contribution in this work is the conception, development, and detailed assessment of a novel and all-inclusive technique to determine the presence of security checks inserted by automatic tools in binary software. Our work has the potential to benefit the customers and end-users of software that can now independently verify certain security aspects of the binary program without relying on information (that is mostly not) provided by the software developer.

The remainder of this paper is organized as follows. We describe background information and related works in Sect. 2. We present our experimental and benchmark configuration in Sect. 3. We explain the insights for this work in Sect. 4. We describe our technique in Sect. 5. We present our experimental results and observations in Sect. 6. Finally, we discuss avenues for future work and state our conclusions in Sects. 7 and 8, respectively.

2 Background and Related Works

Code bugs and missing safety oversight for vulnerable code constructs are widespread [23], especially in software built using memory and type unsafe languages, like C/C++. *Memory corruption errors* have consistently ranked in the top three most dangerous software weaknesses [9]. Memory bugs can be exploited to alter the program behavior and take over program control [32], and launch many critical software attacks [8,36]. While memory-safe language alternatives are available, C/C++ remain popular[1] due to the large amount of existing legacy code, and low-level features of these languages that are desired by performance and memory critical systems.

Modern compilers provide a number of security checks to protect software and end-users from attacks that target such code vulnerabilities. Many checks are applied completely statically or at compile-time. For example, most compilers use *warnings* to indicate some potential code bugs to developers. Likewise, static analyzers can also provide algorithms to perform deeper syntactic and semantic analysis of the code to find more complex coding bugs without running the program[2]. By contrast, some security checks require run-time support and add instrumentation code in the binary to detect problems during execution. Such security checks are called *run-time checks*. In this work we focus on run-time checks that may be inserted by compile-time tools in the binary object files or executables.

For ordinary users, it is typically up to the software developers to enable (static or run-time) security checks for their software. Moreover, in most cases the software companies do not indicate whether their products were built with

[1] https://www.tiobe.com/tiobe-index/.

[2] https://clang-analyzer.llvm.org/.

security checks enabled. There is also currently no way (to our knowledge) for end-users to independently determine or verify the presence of security measures in the software they own or use. Knowing this information will be useful for end-users to select the appropriate software product and use it more confidently.

To our knowledge, this is first work that aims to develop an automated algorithm to identify the presence of any general run-time security check in the distributed binary software. Related to our present work is prior research in binary analysis methods to address security issues, including code vulnerability detection [4,26], malware identification [2,35], and code similarity analysis.

Vulnerability detection attempts to find exploitable bugs in the binary using static binary analysis [12,14], symbolic execution [5,6], or run-time analysis [27,31] Detecting and eliminating vulnerable code from binaries will deny attackers the opportunities to compromise software, and thus protect end-user systems and data. In this respect, our work shares a similar goal with these approaches. However, our directions differ considerably. Our work is based on the assumption that vulnerability detection systems cannot detect all vulnerabilities in the binary. Indeed, none of the existing approaches claim to find all code vulnerabilities. Therefore, security checks will remain relevant, and their presence in binaries can provide end-users the assurance that their system and data will still be protected if any (remaining) vulnerabilities are exploited.

Common malware detection software, including virus scanners [3,33], employ signature based methods that identify unique strings or byte patterns in the binary code [15,30]. Signature based methods cannot protect against advanced malware that employ obfuscation, or polymorphic and metamorphic malware variants that can change their code, signatures, or other identifiable patterns to evade detection [25]. Signature based methods to detect the presence of a few known security checks in binary programs have also been developed [19], and suffer from similar issues regarding generality. To avoid a similar limitation, we do not employ signature-based methods in this work. Also different from our work, the malware detection methods rely on prior knowledge that the analyzed software is malicious and the techniques need to detect patterns that the malware is specifically attempting to hide.

Somewhat related to our current work is research in code similarity analysis that attempts to determine if distinct code regions or software are derived from the same code base [12,13,18,24]. However, research in code similarity analysis needs to address a vastly different set of challenges to identify similar codes when their representations are expected to be significantly different due to variations in, for example, hardware architectures and compiler configurations. Instead, our goal is to identify security checks inserted by automated tools that we expect will exhibit similar code patterns.

3 Evaluation Framework

In this section we describe our experimental configuration and the benchmarks used for this work. To evaluate our hypothesis and approach, we design a controlled experiment by selecting a fixed set of compiler inserted security checks in the Clang/LLVM tool-chain [28] that we can explicitly enable or disable. The first column in Table 1 lists the three security checks that we use for our experiments in this work. These are: (a) the stack canary check, *Stackguard* [20], (b) the *Control Flow Integrity (CFI)* protection [34], and (c) a fast memory error detector, *AddressSanitizer (Adsan)* [29]. The final two columns in Fig. 1 show the Clang/LLVM flags we use to explicitly enable or disable the respective security check. Additionally, all benchmarks were compiled with optimizations (-O2) ON.

Table 1. Clang/LLVM security checks and flags to enable/disable each check

Sec. check	Enable flag	Disable flag
Stackguard	-fstack-protector-all	-fno-stack-protector
CFI	-flto -fsanitize=cfi fvisibility=default	-flto
Adsan	-fsanitize=address -fno-omit-frame-pointer	-fno-omit-frame-pointer

We employ twelve C/C++ programs from the SPEC cpu2006 benchmark suite for experimentation [17]. Binaries are generated for the x86-64-Linux platform. We expect our observations from this work to extend generally to other compilers, programs, and platforms.

Static analysis on the binary executables is conducted by extending the Ghidra reverse engineering framework [22]. Scripts to extend Ghidra's functionality are written in Python.

4 Insight

Code to check for program safety and security conditions may be added by the human developers or by automated tools, like the compiler. Our approach to detect security checks in binary code is guided by a few key principles and insights. We hypothesize that security checks inserted by automated algorithms follow a small number of well-defined rules with regards to when and where they are inserted and the actual instructions used at the instrumentation points, which can enable us to detect their presence in binaries. Firstly, security checks will be placed close to the actual code construct that is being protected. For example, checks to detect memory-related errors are likely to be placed just before the code that references the vulnerable memory address. Conversely, the location of the security check code can reveal the purpose of the security check. Secondly, the inserted security check code will follow a single pattern or one from a small number of code templates/patterns. Thirdly, we expect the inserted security check code to perform some operation on the protected memory address and/or test it for correctness. Finally, the inserted code will likely accomplish a task that is orthogonal or different than the primary program logic.

To verify these hypotheses we first conducted a small manual study with a few security checks inserted by standard C/C++ compilers, like GNU GCC [16] and LLVM [28], to prevent common memory corruption attacks. Figure 1 shows (portions of) the security check code inserted by three different protection mechanisms in the Clang/LLVM compiler. Figure 1(a) shows the pattern for the security check code inserted by Clang's stack canary check [20], Fig. 1(b) and Fig. 1(c) show two code patterns used by the control-flow integrity protection [34], and Fig. 1(d) shows one of the instruction patterns used by the *AddressSanitizer* memory error detector [29].

```
mov %rax, (gbl_can_addr)
mov %rax, (%rax)
cmp %rax, (%rbp - lcl_can_off)
jnz L1
...
L1:
Call <stack_chk_fail>
```

(a) Stackguard check pattern

```
mov %rax, (ind_call_addr)
mov %rcx, chk_addr_imm
cmp %rax, %rcx
jz L1
ud2
...
L1:
call %rax
```

(b) CFI check pattern – 1

```
mov %rbx, (ind_call_addr)
mov %rax, chk_addr_imm
mov %rcx, %rbx
sub %rcx, %rax
mov %rax, %rcx
shr %rax, 0x3
shl %rcx, 0x3d
or  %rax, %rcx
cmp %rax, const_imm
jbe L1
UD2
...
L1:
call %rbx
```

(c) CFI check pattern – 2

```
mov %rax, %rdi
shr %rax, 0x3
mov %al, (%rax+const)
test %al, %al
jnz L2
L1:
reference to (%rdi)
...
L2:
mov %ecx, %edi
and %cl, 0x7
add %cl, 0x3
cmp %cl, %al
jl  L1
call <asan_chk_fail>
...
```

(d) AddressSanitizer check pattern

Fig. 1. Portions of security check code inserted by different security mechanisms built into the Clang/LLVM compiler (determined by manual code analysis)

We find that the instrumentation codes added by these three security techniques largely support our key insights that we presented earlier. By design, we do not attempt to decipher the logic of the checks, but only look for common instruction patterns. We observe specific instructions added by each security check immediately prior to the protected memory address dereference. For instance, with *Stackguard*, the instrumentation code is inserted in the (function prologue and) epilogue before the *return* instruction. With CFI, the security check is inserted before the indirect branch and indirect call instructions. All the security check codes we studied also perform a *compare-branch* to either the original (protected) program code on success, or the exception checking code on failure.

This manual study also revealed several factors the can complicate automated analysis to detect security checks patterns in binaries. Even when the instruction patterns are consistent, register and constant operands vary from one instance of the check to another. The security check is not added at every point of interest, but only when deemed necessary by the compiler to limit run-time overhead. Many security checks, including *CFI* and *AddressSanitizer*, may introduce multiple code patterns for different cases. Compiler optimizations may intersperse the instruction pattern with (unrelated) program instructions and make them harder to detect. We employ these observations to develop our algorithm to automatically detect security check code patterns in binaries.

We only perform this manual identification of security check patterns to confirm our hypothesis. Our technique described and evaluated in the remainder of the paper does not rely on any manual work, and attempts to ***automatically*** identify all targeted security checks and corresponding instruction patterns, when present in the binary.

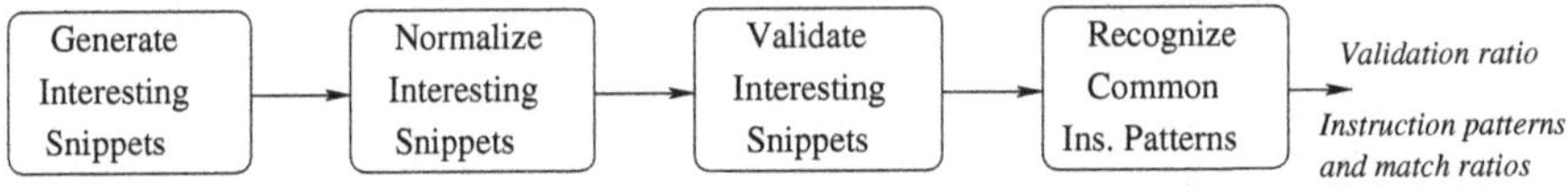

Fig. 2. Approach to detect compiler-inserted security checks in binary code

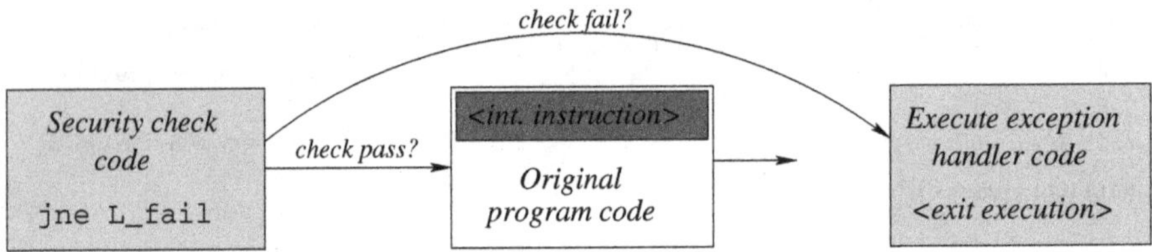

Fig. 3. Typical code structure when a security check is inserted before the interesting code construct in binaries

5 Technique to Detect Security Checks in Binaries

In this section we explain our approach to automatically detect compiler-inserted security checks in the binary code. A signature based method that *manually* collects and stores each security check pattern, and later attempts to detect the signatures in a given binary to identify enabled security checks is plausible. However, this method is tedious and intrinsically limited to only the collected instruction signatures and harder to generalize to different languages, compilers, and checks. We therefore propose a method to *automatically* determine the security checks without any a prior knowledge of known signature patterns.

Figure 2 illustrates our automatic technique to detect compiler-inserted security checks in binary object/executable files. We employ the observations and insights explained in the previous section to guide our approach. We explain each step of our technique in the remainder of this section.

5.1 Generate *Interesting* Code Snippets

The first step of our technique uses Ghidra to statically analyze the given binary and locate the memory operands, or code constructs, or instructions of interest. For the security checks against memory corruption attacks we selected for this work, our Ghidra scripts find (a) the *return* instruction for the (*stackguard*) checks to prevent control-flow hijacking by overflowing the 'return' address, (b) the *indirect branch/call* instruction for the (*CFI*) checks related to confirming control-flow integrity, and (c) any memory *address dereference* for the (*Address-Sanitizer*) checks attempting to detect other memory errors, like out-of-bound memory access.

Algorithm 1: Validation of the code snippet

```
Input: Vulnerable memory address
Input: Original block containing the interesting instruction, srcBlk
predBlk ← getPredecessorBlock(srcBlk) ;
if predBlk == Null then  return False
NormInsList ← Concatenate(predBlk, srcBlk) ;
InsList ← Reverse(NormInsList) ;
intOperList ← Vulnerable memory address ;
validated ← False ;
foreach ins ∈ InsList do
    if ins is Compare/test instruction then
        cmpOperList ← getOperands(ins) ;
        if cmpOperList contains operand from intOperList then
            validated ← True ;
            return ;
        end
        break ;
    end
    else
        dstOper ← getDestinationOperands(ins) ;
        srcOper ← getSourceOperands(ins) ;
        if intOperList contains operand from dstOper then
            delete(intOperList, dstOper) ;
            append(intOperList, srcOper) ;
        end
    end
end
foreach remaining ins ∈ InsList do
    dstOper ← getDestinationOperands(ins) ;
    srcOper ← getSourceOperands(ins) ;
    if cmpOperList contains dstOper then
        if intOperList contains any srcOper then
            validated ← True ;
            return ;
        end
        delete(cmpOperList, dstOper) ;
        append(cmpOperList, srcOper) ;
    end
end
return False ;
```

We hypothesize that the security check instructions are typically placed just before the *interesting* code and contain a compare-branch construct. The typical code structure is illustrated in Fig. 3, where the nodes are basic blocks and edges represent the control-flow between blocks. The *instruction* that is highlighted in red indicates the interesting code construct that is detected by our Ghidra based scripts for each security check. When an interesting code construct is located in the binary, we suppose the security check code to be present (at the bottom) of the *predecessor* block, and the exception code that is reached when the security check condition fails to be placed in the *other successor* block. If the security check is successful, the original program instructions are executed, but if the check fails, then the exception condition is reached.

Then, our Ghidra script concatenates the instructions in the predecessor and 'other successor' blocks to form the *interesting code snippet* for that instance of the interesting code construct. We refer to them as *'instances'*. Similarly, our analysis will find and output all the interesting code snippets in the binary for further analysis.

5.2 *Normalize* Interesting Code Snippets

Next, we generalize the instruction operands that can vary between the different occurrences of the same security check. We call this process *normalization* of the code snippets, and it is done to make it easier for automated algorithms to find common patterns in the code snippets extracted in the previous step.

We experimented with different modes of aggressiveness in this phase. The most aggressive mode eliminates all instruction operands and only keeps the opcodes in the code snippets. We settled on a less aggressive mode that maintains most of the operand context information to better balance the two objectives of reducing false positive matches while still enabling detection of similar instruction patterns. We make the following changes to the instruction operands during the normalization phase: (a) delete address offsets, (b) generalize all register names, except the stack pointer (%rsp) and the base pointer (%rbp) registers that are used to access local variables on the *stack*, (c) generalize the different JUMP statements (like JNE, JZ, JGE, etc.), (d) remove most constants and immediate operands, and (e) replace distinct label names with a constant string.

5.3 *Validate* Interesting Code Snippets

In our next optional step, we statically analyze the code snippet using another key insight of this work. Specifically, we hypothesize that, for the memory corruption attacks selected in this work, the security check codes will perform some computation on and/or comparison with the vulnerable memory address to confirm that it is not corrupted. We call this step the *validation* of the code snippet. We can see from Fig. 1 that this insight is true for all the security check mechanisms employed in this work. We expect a higher likelihood of validations when the security check is enabled (in the compiler) compared to code snippets collected from binaries with the security check flags disabled.

Algorithm 1 describes the high-level steps performed during the validation process. The validation check is performed over all the code in the block containing the interesting instruction and its predecessor block. The algorithm first checks if the protected memory address or a value derived from it (dependent) is used directly in a comparison statement. If not, then the algorithm checks if the operands used in the comparison statement are derived from the protected memory address or its dependents. If true, then the algorithm declares the memory address to be *validated*.

Algorithm 2: Pattern Recognition using String Compare

```
Input: Instances of Interesting Snippets
Input: Count of the instructions ⟶ N(1≤ N ≤ 10)
Let I_d ⟶ Set of interesting snippets;
Let M ⟶ Set of instruction patterns of length N;
Let Count ⟶ Set of count of matched patterns of length N;
Let LeftOut ⟶ Set of instances containing the most matched instructions of length N;
Let InsCount ⟶ Count of the total number of instances;
foreach n ∈ N (10 ⟶ 3) do
    compare ← 0;
    foreach i ∈ I_d do
        foreach j ∈ I_d do
            M_i ← last n instructions of i not in LeftOut;
            if Last n instructions of i == Last n instructions of j then
                count_i ← count_i + 1
            end
        end
    end
    ratio ← count[index(maximum(count))]/InsCount;
    if ratio > compare then
        Final ← M.index(maximum(count));
        M.emptyList();
        Count.emptyList();
        n ← n-1;
        compare ← ratio;
    end
    else
        n ← 10;
        LeftOut ← instances whose last n instructions are identical to final;
    end
end
```

5.4 Recognize Common Instruction Patterns

After generating, normalizing and validating the code snippets, our next task is to detect common instruction patterns over all snippets. We expect a single or a small number of dominating instruction patterns when a security check is enabled, and no single instruction pattern to dominate, otherwise. We experimented with several different pattern matching algorithms to find one that best differentiates the two categories of binaries. We describe two such algorithms in this section.

Pattern Matching Using Simple String Comparison

Algorithm 2 explains our first pattern matching algorithm. Each iteration of this algorithm uses a simple string comparison over the *last 'N'* ($(3 \leq \text{N} \geq 10)$ instructions of all (unmatched) instances of interesting code snippets to find the *longest* string (sequence of instructions) that has the *highest* number of matches. The *match ratio* is computed for this string by dividing the number of code snippets it matched by the total number of interesting code snippets. Then, all the code snippets that contain this longest string are removed from consideration, and the next iteration of this algorithm is performed to find the next longest string (sequence of instructions) with the highest number of matches among the remaining code snippets. This process is repeated until the algorithm cannot find any string with at least two matches.

This algorithm is simple and fast, yet can automatically vary the pattern length ('N') across its successive iterations to find successive longest strings of matches. However, it may not work well when instruction patterns are hindered by code reordering and other compiler optimizations. Next, we describe an algorithm to overcome this limitation.

Algorithm 3: Pattern Recognition using Longest Common subsequence

Input: Instances of Interesting Snippets

Let $I_d \longrightarrow$ Set of the last 15 instructions of each instance of interesting snippets;
Let LCS $\longrightarrow$ Set of longest common subsequences between instance i and all the other instances till n(i)$\leq$ n(I_d) , where *n(X)*$\longrightarrow$ Count of instructions in X;
Let Y $\longrightarrow$ Nested list of set of largest subsequences for each instance i;
Let Eqclasses $\longrightarrow$ Final list of equivalence classes i;
foreach $i \in I_d$ **do**
    foreach $j \in I_d$ **do**
        LCS $\leftarrow$ FindLongestCommonSubsequence(i,j);
    end
    Y $\leftarrow$ FindSetOfLargestSubsequences(LCS);
end
foreach $Y_s \in Y$ **do**
    Eqclasses $\leftarrow$ FindEquivanceClasses(Y_s)
end

FindEquivalenceClass(a)
currentString $\leftarrow$ a;
foreach *equalString* $\in$ *Eqclasses* **do**
    if *Levenshtein.ratio(currentString,equalString)* $\leq$ *0.9 found FALSE* **then**
        Eqclasses $\leftarrow$ currentString;
    end
end
return eqclasses

Using Longest Common Subsequence Algorithm

Our next approach uses the longest common subsequence (LCS) algorithm to find potentially non-sequential common instruction patterns across code snippets. Algorithm 3 explains the main steps in this technique. The algorithm is given the set of the last *15 instructions* of all code snippets collected by Ghidra for the targeted vulnerability protection (I_d). Following our hypotheses for the *interesting snippets generation*, the security check codes, if present, should be observed at the end of the interesting code snippet.

The technique begins the first iteration by using the standard LCS algorithm to compare the first code snippet ($N = 0$) with all other code snippets ($1 \leq N \leq I_d$) to generate ($N-1$) LCS strings. It then finds the (set of) LCS string(s) with the maximum length. There could be more than one *longest* distinct LCS string. The first *longest* LCS string is put into a new *equivalence class*. Each successive longest LCS string is compared with all pre-existing equivalence classes using the Levenshtein's distance formula.[3] If the Levenshtein distance ratio is greater than 0.9, then this longest LCS string is considered to be part of the same equivalence class, and the *hit-count* of the equivalence class is incremented by one. If this longest LCS string does not match any existing equivalence class, then a new class for this LCS string is created.

Successive iterations of this algorithm repeat this process for all the other code snippets in the set. Finally, for each equivalence class, we compute the *match ratio*, which is its hit-count divided by the total hit-count over all equivalence classes for that benchmark. The set of equivalence classes is sorted using this "match ratio" metric to output the set of dominating instruction patterns.

6 Experimental Results and Observations

In this section we present the results of experiments we conducted using the framework, approach and benchmarks described earlier. First, we only present the results with the two pattern matching algorithms in Sects. 6.1 and 6.2, respectively. Then, we discuss our overall observations in Sect. 6.3.

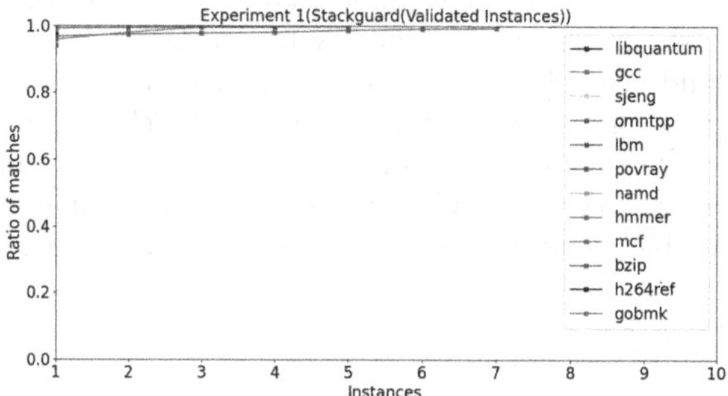

Fig. 4. Results using the simple string comparison algorithm for Stackguard.

[3] The Levenshtein distance is a string metric for measuring the difference between two sequences. Levenshtein distance between two words is the minimum number of single-character edits required to change one word into the other. An "edit" is defined by either an insertion, a deletion, or a replacement of a character.

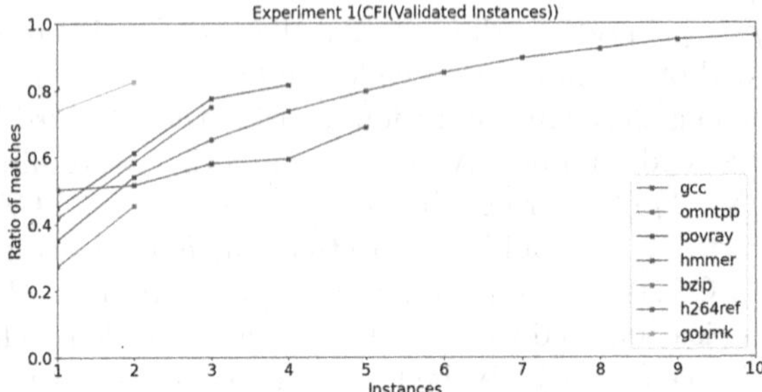

Fig. 5. Results using the simple string comparison algorithm for CFI.

6.1 Results with the Simple String Comparison Algorithm

We first present results with our approach using the simple string comparison algorithm for pattern matching. Figures 4 and 5 plot the sorted cumulative *match ratio* for each benchmark with the Stackguard and CFI security check enabled, respectively. In both these cases, our address validation check was very effective at eliminating almost all code snippets for most benchmarks when the respective security check was turned OFF. For the few code snippets that remained for some benchmarks after validation, there were no dominant code patterns detected. Therefore, we do not plot the corresponding (blank) graphs with the Stackguard and CFI checks turned OFF.

Also, for the CFI check in Fig. 5, we only plot results for seven of the eleven total benchmarks. The remaining 4 benchmarks generate very few code snippets (typically, less than 5), almost none of which are validated. Wherever fewer code constructs are generated, the curves stop after the few instances present. We manually looked at these cases and found that the compiler did not apply the CFI check for these cases even with the flag turned ON.

Figures 6(a) and 6(b) plot the sorted cumulative *match ratio* over the validated code snippets for *AddressSanitizer* with the check turned ON and OFF, respectively. We note that we have currently implemented a simplistic Ghidra-based binary analysis script for AddressSanitizer. Rather than only detecting the potentially vulnerable memory dereferences (vectors and pointers), our script is

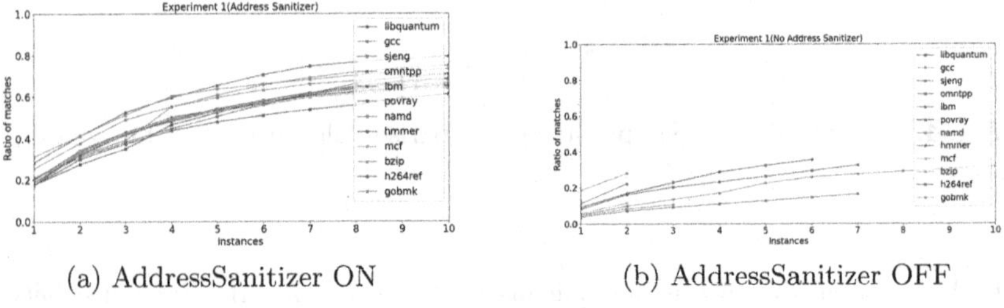

(a) AddressSanitizer ON (b) AddressSanitizer OFF

Fig. 6. Results using the simple string comparison algorithm for the AddressSanitizer security check enabled and disabled.

overly aggressive and currently detects all memory dereferences (even scalars) in the binary as opportunities for protection. We then rely on the validation algorithm to eliminate many of the spurious instances. Even then, we are left with a significant number of code snippets to analyze even with the AddressSanitizer security check turned OFF.

6.2 Results with the LCS Pattern Matching Algorithm

In this section we present the results of experiments that use the LCS algorithm for pattern matching. Similar to the previous section, Figs. 7 and 8 plot the sorted cumulative *match ratio* for each benchmark with the Stackguard and CFI security check enabled, respectively, and using the LCS algorithm. Likewise, Figs. 9(a) and 9(b) plot the sorted cumulative *match ratio* over the validated code snippets for *AddressSanitizer* with the check turned ON and OFF, respectively.

6.3 Observations

We can make a number of important observations from our experimental results. First, for the automated run-time security checks we study in this work, the combination of the validation and pattern matching components of our technique can clearly indicate when and which security check is enabled or disabled.

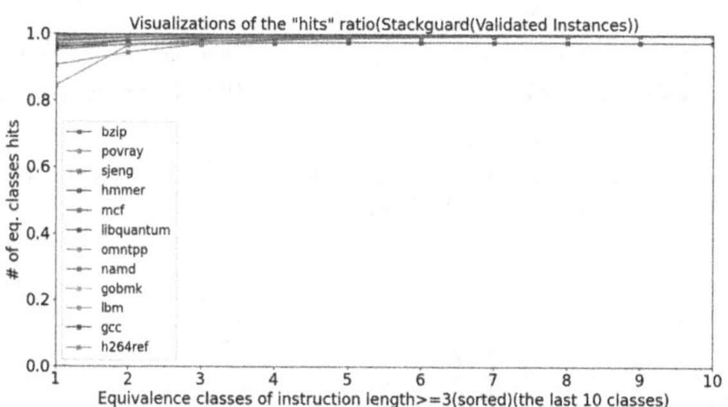

Fig. 7. Cumulative match ratio of top ten equi. classes with *Stackguard* ON

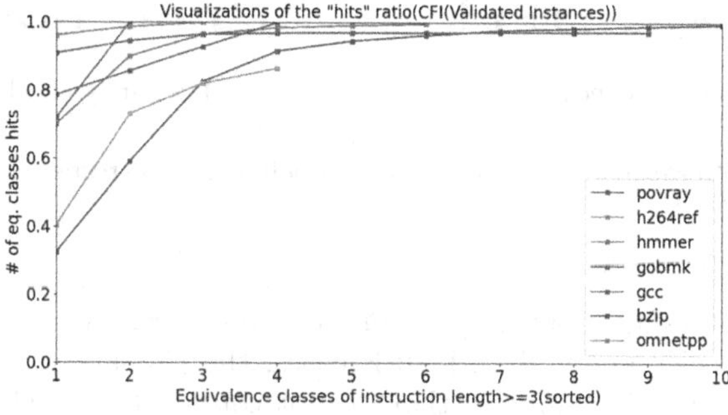

Fig. 8. Cumulative match ratio of the top ten equi. classes with *CFI* ON

We find that both our pattern matching algorithms obtain results that show a starkly different trajectory of the graph for each benchmark when the respective security check is ON, as compared to when the check is OFF. Even so, the LCS algorithm appears to be more adept at finding the common instruction patterns. Thus, while both algorithms perform well for Stackguard (Figs. 4 and 7), the LCS algorithm detects pattern matches more efficiently for the CFI and AddressSanitizer checks (Figs. 5 and 8, and Figs. 6(a) and 9(a)).

However, the greater adeptness of LCS can also sometimes be a disadvantage. Thus, we find that the LCS algorithm produces a few false positives in the *AddressSanitizer* OFF case (Fig. 9(b)) for *bzip* and *povray*). We analyzed the *bzip* benchmark and found that there is indeed a high-frequency pattern that is produced by a set of three frequently used macros. While compiler optimizations sufficiently interleave this pattern with other instructions in several cases to hide it from the simpler string comparison algorithm, the LCS algorithm finds it even when the instructions in the pattern are not consecutive.

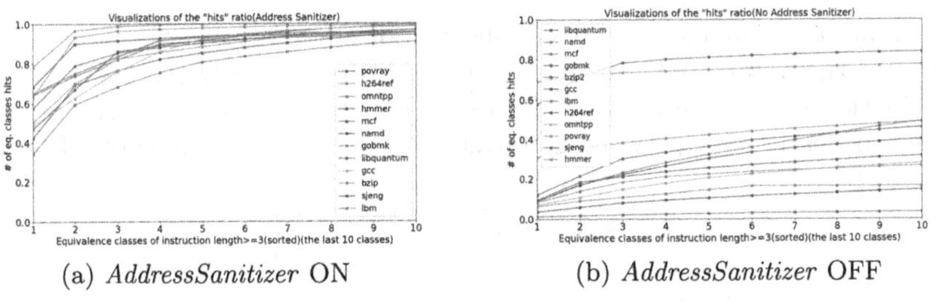

(a) *AddressSanitizer* ON (b) *AddressSanitizer* OFF

Fig. 9. Cumulative match ratio of the top ten equivalence classes with the *AddressSanitizer* flags turned ON and OFF, respectively.

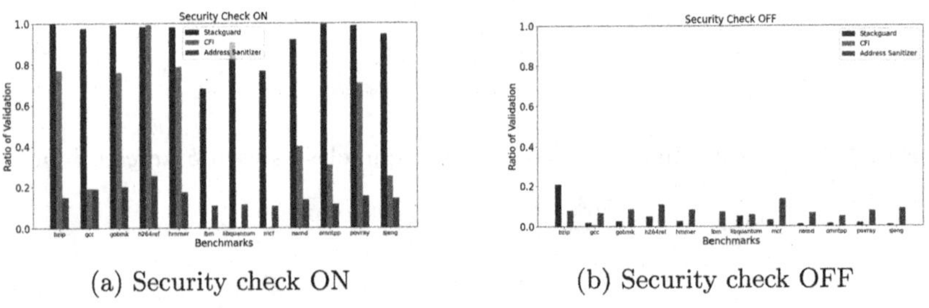

(a) Security check ON (b) Security check OFF

Fig. 10. Validation ratio of interesting code snippets when the respective security check is either ON or OFF

Second, the *validation* algorithm can effectively weed out the spurious code snippets. For stackguard and CFI OFF cases, the validation algorithm eliminates most of the code snippets (that do not contain the check) from further analysis. Figures 10(a) and (b) illustrate the validation ratio when each security check is either ON or OFF, respectively. The validation ratio is computed by dividing the number of validated code snippets by the total number of interesting code snippets generated by the Ghidra script for each security check. Assuming that our hypothesis that a security check should *test* the protected/vulnerable memory address is correct, a low validation ratio in the security check OFF case correctly indicates that no code is inserted at interesting points in the binary.

Third, the validation algorithm is consistently low in the AddressSanitizer ON case. This effect is due to the simplistic binary analysis (Ghidra) script we developed for this check, as was mentioned earlier. Improving this script to correctly locate only the vulnerable code locations is part of our future work.

Fourth, we find that the most common security patterns found by our algorithms in the security check ON cases closely match the expected patterns from the manual study in Sect. 4.

Fifth, we observed several cases where there are fewer interesting code constructs detected and interesting code snippets generated in the security check OFF case, compared to when the security check is ON. This discrepancy happens for two reasons. First, enabling the security check sometimes requires the compiler/linker to create or link additional code and functions in the binary. Our Ghidra script can then detect additional interesting code locations in the binary generated with the security check ON. Second, in some cases, especially when the security check is OFF, no interesting snippet may be generated at an interesting code location, if the code layout does not match that illustrated earlier in Fig. 3.

7 Future Work

There are several avenues for future work. First, one limitation of our approach that is based on finding common instruction patterns over multiple code snippets is that a very small number of instances could generate results that produce misleading conclusions. Our current approach benefits from having a sizeable number of instances of each interesting code construct to detect patterns. We plan to address this limitation in future work by also developing some other indicators for detecting security checks. Second, we hypothesize that compiler-added security checks will perform tasks that are orthogonal to the primary function of the program. But, we do not yet apply and use this hypothesis. We plan to implement this measure in our future techniques. Third, we plan to improve our validation algorithm to eliminate even more spurious code snippets and improve pattern identification. Likewise, we will also develop and evaluate other pattern recognition algorithms. Finally, we would like to develop a more comprehensive metric to rate the security properties of any arbitrary binary.

8 Conclusion

Our goal in this work is to develop a generalized technique to detect compiler-based run-time security checks in any given binary. We develop several hypothesis regarding the properties of such security checks in binary code. We then devise a detailed mechanism that employs these hypothesis to achieve our goal, and conduct a comprehensive evaluation. Overall, we find that our technique is able to largely achieve our goal and in doing so, validates and confirms our hypotheses. Thus, security checks indeed appear to be consistently inserted immediately before the dereference of the protected memory address and contain a compare-branch sequence, which we use for our code snippet extraction. Likewise, we can deduce that the inserted security check code follows a small number of regular templates. Overall, our technique detects consistent instruction patterns much more regularly in the code snippets extracted when the security checks are ON, compared to when the checks are OFF. Our technique in almost all cases can correctly deduce if the respective security check is present in the binary. We expect our work will greatly benefit automated and independent security analysis of binary code for end-users when source code is unavailable.

References

1. Abadi, M., Budiu, M., Erlingsson, U., Ligatti, J.: Control-flow integrity principles, implementations, and applications. ACM Trans. Inf. Syst. Secur. **13**(1) (2009)
2. Abijah Roseline, S., Geetha, S.: A comprehensive survey of tools and techniques mitigating computer and mobile malware attacks. Comput. Electr. Eng. **92**, 107143 (2021)
3. Aycock, J.: Computer Viruses and Malware (Advances in Information Security). Springer, Heidelberg (2006). https://doi.org/10.1007/0-387-34188-9
4. Brooks, T.N.: Survey of automated vulnerability detection and exploit generation techniques in cyber reasoning systems. In: Arai, K., Kapoor, S., Bhatia, R. (eds.) SAI 2018. AISC, vol. 857, pp. 1083–1102. Springer, Cham (2019). https://doi.org/10.1007/978-3-030-01177-2_79
5. Cadar, C., Dunbar, D., Engler, D.R., et al.: Klee: unassisted and automatic generation of high-coverage tests for complex systems programs. In: OSDI, vol. 8, pp. 209–224 (2008)
6. Cha, S.K., Avgerinos, T., Rebert, A., Brumley, D.: Unleashing mayhem on binary code. In: Proceedings of the 2012 IEEE Symposium on Security and Privacy, SP 2012, pp. 380–394. IEEE Computer Society, USA (2012)
7. Cowan, C., et al.: StackGuard: automatic adaptive detection and prevention of Buffer-Overflow Attacks. In: Proceedings of the 7th Conference on USENIX Security Symposium, SSYM 1998, vol. 7, pp. 5 (1998)
8. CVE: A buffer overflow vulnerability in whatsapp voip stack (2019). https://www.cvedetails.com/cve/CVE-2019-3568/
9. CWE: CWE Top 25 Most Dangerous Software Weaknesses (2022). https://cwe.mitre.org/top25/archive/2021/2021_cwe_top25.html
10. Cybersecurity, U., Agency, I.S.: Top routinely exploited vulnerabilities (2021). https://www.cisa.gov/uscert/ncas/alerts/aa21-209a
11. Database, N.N.V.: Cvss severity distribution over time (2021). https://nvd.nist.gov/general/visualizations/vulnerability-visualizations/cvss-severity-distribution-over-time
12. Eschweiler, S., Yakdan, K., Gerhards-Padilla, E.: discovre: efficient cross-architecture identification of bugs in binary code. In: NDSS, vol. 52, pp. 58–79 (2016)

13. Feng, Q., Zhou, R., Xu, C., Cheng, Y., Testa, B., Yin, H.: Scalable graph-based bug search for firmware images. In: Proceedings of the 2016 ACM SIGSAC Conference on Computer and Communications Security, pp. 480–491 (2016)
14. Gao, D., Reiter, M.K., Song, D.: BinHunt: automatically finding semantic differences in binary programs. In: Chen, L., Ryan, M.D., Wang, G. (eds.) ICICS 2008. LNCS, vol. 5308, pp. 238–255. Springer, Heidelberg (2008). https://doi.org/10.1007/978-3-540-88625-9_16
15. Griffin, K., Schneider, S., Hu, X., Chiueh, T.: Automatic generation of string signatures for malware detection. In: Kirda, E., Jha, S., Balzarotti, D. (eds.) RAID 2009. LNCS, vol. 5758, pp. 101–120. Springer, Heidelberg (2009). https://doi.org/10.1007/978-3-642-04342-0_6
16. Griffith, A.: GCC: The Complete Reference, 1st edn. McGraw-Hill Inc., USA (2002)
17. Henning, J.L.: Spec cpu2006 benchmark descriptions. SIGARCH Comput. Arch. News **34**(4), 1–17 (2006)
18. Hu, Y., Zhang, Y., Li, J., Gu, D.: Binary code clone detection across architectures and compiling configurations. In: 2017 IEEE/ACM 25th International Conference on Program Comprehension (ICPC), pp. 88–98 (2017)
19. Kamathe, G.: Identify security properties on linux using checksec (2021). https://opensource.com/article/21/6/linux-checksec
20. Kuznetsov, V., Szekeres, L., Payer, M., Candea, G., Sekar, R., Song, D.: Code-Pointer integrity. In: 11th USENIX Symposium on Operating Systems Design and Implementation, Broomfield, CO, pp. 147–163 (2014)
21. Nagarakatte, S., Zhao, J., Martin, M.M., Zdancewic, S.: Softbound: highly compatible and complete spatial memory safety for c. In: Proceedings of the 30th ACM SIGPLAN Conference on Programming Language Design and Implementation, pp. 245–258 (2009)
22. National Security Agency ghidra, N.: Ghidra (2019). https://www.nsa.gov/resources/everyone/ghidra/
23. NIST: National Vulnerability Database (2022). https://nvd.nist.gov/general/visualizations/vulnerability-visualizations/cvss-severity-distribution-over-time
24. Pewny, J., Garmany, B., Gawlik, R., Rossow, C., Holz, T.: Cross-architecture bug search in binary executables. In: 2015 IEEE Symposium on Security and Privacy, pp. 709–724. IEEE (2015)
25. Preda, M.D., Christodorescu, M., Jha, S., Debray, S.: A semantics-based approach to malware detection. ACM Trans. Program. Lang. Syst. **30**(5) (2008)
26. Qasem, A., Shirani, P., Debbabi, M., Wang, L., Lebel, B., Agba, B.L.: Automatic vulnerability detection in embedded devices and firmware: Survey and layered taxonomies. ACM Comput. Surv. **54**(2) (2021)
27. Rebert, A., et al.: Optimizing seed selection for fuzzing. In: 23rd USENIX Security Symposium (USENIX Security 2014), pp. 861–875 (2014)
28. Sarda, S., Pandey, M.: LLVM Essentials. Packt Publishing, Birmingham (2015)
29. Serebryany, K., Bruening, D., Potapenko, A., Vyukov, D.: Addresssanitizer: a fast address sanity checker. In: USENIX ATC 2012 (2012)
30. Shabtai, A., Menahem, E., Elovici, Y.: F-sign: automatic, function-based signature generation for malware. IEEE Trans. Syst. Man Cybern. Part C (Appl. Rev.) **41**(4), 494–508 (2011)
31. Stephens, N., et al.: Driller: augmenting fuzzing through selective symbolic execution. In: NDSS, vol. 16, pp. 1–16 (2016)
32. Szekeres, L., Payer, M., Wei, T., Song, D.: Sok: eternal war in memory. In: IEEE Symposium on Security and Privacy, SP 2013, pp. 48–62 (2013)

33. Szor, P.: The Art of Computer Virus Research and Defense. Addison-Wesley Professional, Boston (2005)
34. Tice, C., et al.: Enforcing forward-edge control-flow integrity in GCC & LLVM. In: 23rd USENIX Security Symposium (USENIX Security 2014), pp. 941–955. USENIX Association, San Diego (2014)
35. Ucci, D., Aniello, L., Baldoni, R.: Survey of machine learning techniques for malware analysis. Comput. Secur. **81**, 123–147 (2019)
36. Wheeler, D.A.: Preventing heartbleed. IEEE Comput. **47**(8), 80–83 (2014). https://doi.org/10.1109/MC.2014.217
37. Wired: The reaper iot botnet has already infected a million networks (2017). https://www.wired.com/story/reaper-iot-botnet-infected-million-networks/

Detection of MSOffice-Embedded Malware: Feature Mining and Short- vs. Long-Term Performance

Silviu Viţel[1,2](✉), Marilena Lupaşcu[1,2], Dragoş Teodor Gavriluţ[1,2], and Henri Luchian[1]

[1] Faculty of Computer Science, "Al.I. Cuza" University, Iaşi, Romania
svitel@bitdefender.com
[2] Bitdefender Labs, Iaşi, Romania
http://info.uaic.ro, http://www.bitdefender.com

Abstract. This paper presents a study on the detection performance of MSOffice-embedded malware; the detection models were trained and tested using a very large database of malicious and benign MSOffice documents (1.8 million files), collected over a long period of time (1995–2021). The time-wise comprehensive database allowed us to shed a light on *perishability* (evolution of feature relevance) and detection performance of anti-malware classifiers. For the latter, we look into *proactivity* (short-term detection efficiency against future malware) and *endurance* (long-term detection robustness); aspects of the co-evolution of malware and security products are also discussed.

Along the various training and testing timewidths available in the database, our experiments indicate that, on average, neural networks reach higher levels of accuracy in MSOffice-embedded malware detection, while Random Forest achieves lower false-positive rates.

Keywords: MSOffice-embedded (VBA) malware detection · Machine learning · Feature mining · Spear-phishing · Neural networks · Random forest · Classifier proactivity · Classifier endurance

1 Introduction

Email-based attacks (e.g., spear-phishing) are one of the widely used methods by cyber-criminals; such attacks target enterprises/organizations and, to some extent, individual computer users. While email-security solutions have improved over the last decade, there are still filetypes (Office documents with macros) for which malware detection continues to be a challenging task. In the sequel, we use interchangeably "malware embedded in MSOffice documents", "macro virus", "VBA malware", "VBA malicious code".

1.1 Context

The extensive fair use of document exchange through email communication in most organisations favours malware infiltration via Office files. A modest level of

C. Su et al. (Eds.): ISPEC 2022, LNCS 13620, pp. 287–305, 2022.
https://doi.org/10.1007/978-3-031-21280-2_16

cybersecurity-compliant behaviour may increase the risk for such attacks, mostly in departments where opening Office documents (CVs, invoices, etc.) is a must. Nowadays, macro VBA malicious code is delivered almost exclusively through email vectors.

Cyber-security developers strive to improve their detection mechanisms against macro viruses, while cyber-attackers seek ever new detection-eluding techniques. The latter rely on obfuscating the VBA code with an eye towards making ineffective simple approaches such as syntactic pattern-matching detection mechanisms.

1.2 Goal and Structure of the Paper

This paper focuses on timewise robustness of detection models (neural networks and Random Forest) used in macro virus detection. Proactivity and time-resilience of the trained detection models are studied, based on a thorough feature mining and classifier selection process. It is worth mentioning that the data set covers comprehensively the bi-decennial history of macro viruses; it provides the factual support for tracing an evolution line of both macro viruses and the respective anti-malware detection tools. The current paper is a first step in this direction.

2 Study Methodology

2.1 Feature Mining

In order to establish a base set of macro relevant features, a large number of samples were analyzed. Before elaborating on feature mining itself, a key aspect is in order: *feature perishability.* Malware evolves, trying new ways of evading detection; therefore, the set of active features in malware files changes continuously. A file feature f may appear/become active (hence, potentially useful for detection too) at time t_1 and disappear from malware files at time t_2. Given a file feature f, we call *feature perishability of* f the variation over time of the frequency of f in malware files. A frequent pattern is an overall decrease over time of the presence of a given feature (hence, the term *perishability*); however, sequences of higher and lower frequencies may also occur.

There exist open-source tools that can be used to process information from Office documents. For this study, we have used olevba[1] for extracting the VBA code. After extracting each VBA script, we generated a VBA lexer using the antlr4 library[2]. The code was split into tokens which were grouped according to their type, as shown in Fig. 1.

The feature mining process resulted in the definition of 61 features. These were determined using the tokens extracted when parsing the VBA script. In order to obtain features which give an accurate description of the macro

[1] https://github.com/decalage2/oletools/wiki/olevba.
[2] https://www.antlr.org/.

Table 1. Features obtained from VBA macros

Feature type	Feature name	Example
Generic	VBA specific keywords	*Sub, Function, If, Dim, While*
	Arithmetic operations	+, −, *, /, =, <, >
Obfuscation-related	Random variables Random function names	*fsdwiueinet, 234inp44fff*
	Indentations count	
	String operations Concatenations count	*s = "E" & "M" & "P"* *tmm1 = Environ ("T" & s)*
	Random comments count	
	Unused variables count	
Behavioural	*Shell* function call counts	
	On Error Resume Next statement	

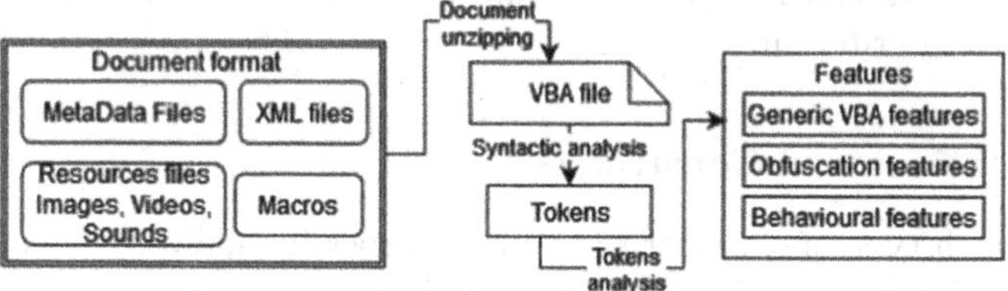

Fig. 1. Feature mining flow

contained in MSOffice documents, three different views on the VBA code were enforced: generic (6 features), behavioural (dynamic - 26 features) and obfuscation-related (29 features). Consequently, we defined three types of features:

- generic VBA features, reflecting a statistical characteristic (e.g., how many functions are defined, length of code etc.);
- features related to the obfuscation techniques used by attackers[3];
- behavioural features, defining VBA specific runtime characteristics.

Some of these features are summarized in Table 1. It is worth mentioning that, while the FPR (especially in the case of RF) has very good levels, the TPR in our experiments are less competitive; this is due to the fact that we focused on the time-wise relevance of the feature set (in relation to the classifiers' endurance) and not on optimizing the feature set towards optimal detection.

2.2 Classifiers: Selection and Design

A comparison of the performance of various classifiers in detecting malicious executables [20] concluded that Random Forest and a feed-forward neural network

[3] Code obfuscation is the intended modification of the original code aimed at making it unreadable/unparsable, without altering its functionality.

produced the best values for TPR and FPR, with the latter having the fastest detection time. A study on the detection of malicious Windows executables [2] also found as best performing classifiers a feed-forward neural network and a Random Forest model. Similar results had been obtained on detection models for files written in languages similar to VBA, namely VBS files [30].

Considering the concordant results mentioned above, we decided to use for this study the following two machine learning classifiers: a feed-forward neural network and Random Forest. The neural network has three hidden layers, each one containing 300 neurons with ReLU as activation function (both the vanishing gradient problem and the time performance [28] were considered). The output of the network is a probability of maliciousness obtained through a Sigmoid activation. Since our feature matrix is sparse, the network was trained using the Adam optimizer. Because the problem is a binary classification task, Binary Cross-Entropy was chosen as the loss function.

As for the Random Forest, it generates 200 decision trees, with information gain as splitting criterion.

2.3 Limitations and Constraints

Deciding which type of classifier to train for a specific malware detection task is a key element to success. The focus of the classification process sets the overall goal (minimizing FPs and/or increasing specificity etc.) within a specific set of constraints, e.g., related to training, running and updating time. For this study, the choice of classifiers was guided by the following concerns:

- **memory footprint:** sophisticated classification models are impractical since they generate high traffic costs for each update;
- **classification speed:** additional pre-processing may increase the classifier's time complexity, if run in a file-blocking scenario. For example, if the on-access driver intercepts an attempt to open a file, it suspends the execution thread which tries to read that file until the scanning result is available; if the classifier labels the file as malicious, access will be denied. A slow classifier would further magnify this delay up to a point where visible performance delays of the OS are perceived by the user.
- **generalization:** the classifier should be able to identify new variants of VBA-based malware, beyond the training examples.

3 Data Collection

The database used in this study (we call it D) consists of 1.750.013 MSOffice files collected between 1995 and 2021; in D, each file was assigned a timestamp indicating the moment when it was first encountered in the wild[4] Out of these, 905.526 are malicious files and 844.487 are benign (clean); all clean and malicious files contain VBA code. Table 2 shows the distribution of files over the 26 years. In

[4] See "in-the-wild" description from http://www.wildlist.org/CurrentList.txt.

recent years, the risk of an attack through macro VBA malware has increased[5] However, "document inertia" preserves the usefulness of older benign files in VBA-based malware detection; older benign MSO documents do not evolve, while binary benign files do[6]. Moreover, while new documents may be constantly created, they are often based on old templates, leading to a similar set of features. Consequently, all available benign files should be used for devising a new macro VBA malware detection model.

Table 2. Number of files in database D, per year and label

Year(s)	1995–2008	2009	2010	2011	2012	2013	2014
Benign files	16080	18263	33205	30971	53001	19361	17424
Malicious files	0	24	150	196	977	2111	3253
Year(s)	2015	2016	2017	2018	2019	2020	2021 (Feb)
Benign files	15532	34653	198377	143754	131708	117227	14931
Malicious files	14697	224411	174757	118280	119968	235007	11695

Unbalanced as it may seem, the yearly ratio between benign and malicious files in the database D reflects accurately the real-world developments over time. The discrepancy between the number of benign and malicious samples prior to 2014 is due to a dormant phase of VBA macro threats. In 2014, a resurgence of macro malware was noticeable [9]: malicious documents were used as infection vectors for various types of threats; the effectiveness of social engineering techniques[7] paved the way to this approach[8].

In database D, the increase in the numbers of malicious files in 2015–2016 is due to a surge of macro-based malware[9] illustrated by the Donoff family (it introduced a new technique to make malicious documents look legitimate[10]). The shift of ransomware families towards document infection vectors[11] may have also contributed to the above-mentioned dynamics.

The number of VBA malicious files from 2020 in D (twice as many as the benign ones), reflects real-world trends during the pandemics[12], as a result of the extensive use of electronic communication (in particular, MSOffice documents).

[5] https://www.ncsc.gov.uk/guidance/macro-security-for-microsoft-office.

[6] The Operating System/application updates may change the entire set of binaries.

[7] Despite the fact that Microsoft introduced security measures aimed at preventing the execution of malicious macros, attackers often managed to convince unsuspecting users to open infected documents, by disguising their origin or describing the enabling of macros as a necessary step to access a document's data.

[8] https://nakedsecurity.sophos.com/2014/09/17/vba-injectors/.

[9] https://threatpost.com/microsoft-extends-malicious-macro-protection-to-office-2013/121618/.

[10] https://isssource.com/macro-malware-on-way-back/.

[11] https://www.securityweek.com/locky-variant-osiris-distributed-excel-documents.

[12] https://www.f-secure.com/en/press/p/covid-19-spam-phishing-emails-plagued-users-in-first-half-of-2.

Table 3 shows the distribution of malware files in D according to their Office type; macro code is almost exclusive to Excel and Word documents. Moreover, mostly Excel and Word files use the older document format (DOC, XLS), while comparatively fewer PowerPoint files act similarly. Attackers take into consideration the fact that older document types have a wider scope, with newer MSOffice versions being backwards compatible. Excel and Word documents are extensively used in Accounting, Human Resources and Legal departments; from an attacker's point of view, these Excel and Word files are more likely to appear legitimate to a potential victim. This confirms that the lower percentage of Powerpoint files in D reflects the real-world landscape. Building such a large database constituted a significant part of our work and included multiple steps:

- collecting samples and assigning them to a specific period of time when they were first encountered (this process required searching several databases such as VirusTotal for sample information);
- we tried to make sure that the database is representative in terms of Microsoft Office formats (DOC, XLS, PPT etc.);
- handling embedded documents (for example, extracting them from various email formats);
- sample validation (making sure that the sample is valid);
- classification of each collected sample (benign or malicious);
- build a multi-tenant feature extraction process.

Table 3. Distribution of malicious MSOffice files in D, by type of document

DOC	DOCX	XLS	XLSX	PPT(X)
43%	11%	31%	13%	2%

4 Feature Perishability

At any given moment, a specific set of file features is best suited for malware detection. As suggested in Sect. 2, this (optimal) set varies over time. Figure 2 illustrates *feature perishability* for 8 out of the 61 features, in terms of frequency (as a percentage) in malicious files. A feature emerges at a certain moment, has a relatively high frequency for some time and then diminishes its frequency in subsequent years (eventually "perishing"), while new features arise and become frequent in malicious files. There are features having a more complex behaviour: their frequency in malicious files has sequences of (longer) ups and/or (longer) downs over the years; even in such cases, the global pattern illustrates an overall increase followed by an overall decrease. The dynamics of feature frequencies over time is an illustration of the co-evolution between, on one hand, detection methods and on the other hand, malware evasion techniques.

Figure 3 presents the overall[13] frequencies (as percentages) of the 61 features, for all benign and malware files, respectively. The figure shows that none of the 61 features is sufficient by itself for identifying malicious VBA code.

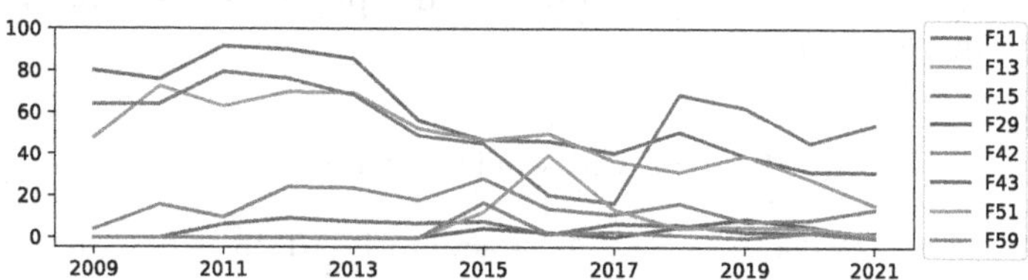

Fig. 2. Feature perishability for 8 of the 61 features

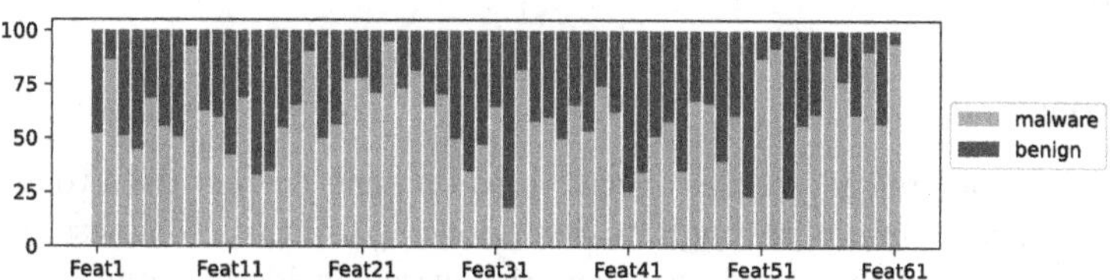

Fig. 3. The ratio #benign vs. #malware files in D which share each of the 61 features. Note that the sum #benign + #malware is different for each feature.

5 Experiments and Results

In order to evaluate MSOffice-embedded malware detection from the viewpoint of short vs. long-term performance, we conducted three different experiments:

1. **Time-insensitive accuracy** of detection models: training and testing on D as a time-amorphous database;
2. **Proactivity**: tracking the performance of classifiers in successive time slots;
3. **Classifier endurance**: various scenarios were considered, falling into one of two categories: a) training on all the documents available at a specific moment and testing on files having timestamps subsequent to that moment or b) training on documents from a time interval close to and preceding the testing one.

5.1 Time-Insensitive Accuracy

In the first set of experiments, the performances of the ANN classifier and of the Random Forest classifier were evaluated via 3-fold cross-validation; the entire database D was used and timestamps (see Sect. 3) were ignored. Experiments

[13] In the whole database D, ignoring the time stamps.

under this scenario rated how fit each classifier is for generalization if timestamps are ignored. Table 4 lists the results of cross-validation. The accuracy, TPR and FPR values indicate promising generalization potential for both classifiers, but with different optimisation focuses. The neural network model is better in the detection rate, while the random forest model produces a significantly lower number of false positives.

Table 4. Cross-validation results

Model	Accuracy	FPR	TPR
Neural network	98.10%	0.84%	97.12%
Random Forest	96.65%	0.13%	93.49%

5.2 Proactivity

Proactivity is the ability of a classifier trained on past/current data to anticipate emerging malware threats through its detection capabilities. To assess the proactivity of the selected classifiers, two scenarios were considered: *long-term trained proactivity* and *short-term trained proactivity*; in each of the two scenarios, two time granularities where considered: yearly and monthly.

Algorithm 1 describes the way proactivity metrics are computed. Depending on the configuration of parameters, either scenario (short-term and long-term) can be illustrated. For the long-term scenario, the *delta* parameter is always ∞: all files with timestamps preceding a given date **t** are used for training. January 2015 was chosen as the first test year/month, in order to have a relevant number of both clean and malicious files in the training set; the last test year/month was February 2021.

The results of the *long-term trained proactivity* experiment are given in Table 5. Results in Tables 4 - 3-fold cross-validation - and Table 5 - long-term trained proactivity - show similar trends, even though the level of performance differs depending on granularity. The one-year granularity models are to a lesser extent successful in responding to changes in VBA-based malicious tactics, which results in a significant proportion of new attacks not being detected. On the other hand, the one-month granularity produces models which better adapt to malware changes (higher detection rate). Again, the neural network model is better with respect to the detection rate, while the Random Forest classifier produces fewer false positives. It is worth noticing that granularity does not significantly influence the FPR for Random Forest. This is indicative of the main goal the attackers have in mind: to avoid detection; FPR is less likely to be their concern.

For the second scenario the training interval was set to two years for the yearly granularity and three months for the monthly one. This training scheme tests the idea that more recent changes in malware are the most relevant ones in training detection models. A comparison between the results in Tables 5 and 6

Algorithm 1. Long/Short-term proactivity compute algorithm

```
function GetDB(D, after, before)
    newDB ← ∅
    for i = 1 → |D| do
        if D_i.TimeStamp ≥ after and D_i.TimeStamp < before then
            newDB ← newDB ⋃ D_i
        end if
    end for
    return newDB
end function

function ComputeProactivity(D, algorithm, step, delta)
    epochs ← 0
    metrics ← (ACC = 0, TPR = 0, FPR = 0)
    for t = Jan.2015 → Feb.2021, with t ← t + step do
        start = max(0, t − delta)
        trainDB ← GetDB(D, start, t)
        model ← algorithm.Train(trainDB)
        db ← GetDB(D, t, t + step)
        metrics ← metrics + model.Test(db)
        epochs ← epochs + 1
    end for
    return metrics.ACC/epochs, metrics.FPR/epochs, metrics.TPR/epochs
end function
```

metrics a structure that contains the values for accuracy, FPR and TPR

delta a backwards timespan for the training database. A value of ∞ (infinite) means the entire database from the first record until moment t will be used for testing.

model.Test a method in the model that returns a structure of type metrics with values that reflect how the model behaves on a specific database.

suggests that this idea is valid, leading to resource saving in the training process, since fewer files need to be used.

The *short-term trained proactivity* results are listed in Table 6. These results highlight the fact that malware evolves in small steps; if the detection model does not follow closely this sequence of small steps, the detection rate may drop significantly. Further confirming the results above, granularity proves to be instrumental for the training/maintenance of a detection model. However, as compared against the previous scenario, the number of false positives increases irrespective of the classifier at hand. In general, legitimate applications (benign files) may impair the FPR rate because: a) they do not display a counter-detection oriented trend and b) they are hugely diverse. Thc long-term scenario leads to better FPR rates because a long-term perspective allows for a more comprehensive coverage of the specificity of benign-files, improving the trained classifiers.

Table 5. Long-term trained proactivity results

Model	Update granularity	Accuracy	FPR	TPR	ComputeProactivity Parameters
Neural network	1 year	88.62%	1.05%	79.37%	(D, ANN, 1 year, ∞)
Neural network	1 month	94.76%	0.98%	91.13%	(D, ANN, 1 month, ∞)
Random Forest	1 year	82.05%	0.18%	69.85%	(D, RF, 1 year, ∞)
Random Forest	1 month	93.80%	0.16%	88.76%	(D, RF, 1 month, ∞)

Table 6. Short-term trained proactivity results

Model	Update granularity	Accuracy	FPR	TPR	ComputeProactivity Parameters
Neural network	1 year	88.19%	1.53%	78.39%	(D, ANN, 1 year, 2 years)
Neural network	1 month	93.92%	1.92%	90.35%	(D, ANN, 1 month, 3 months)
Random Forest	1 year	91.41%	0.39%	84.77%	(D, RF, 1 year, 2 years)
Random Forest	1 month	94.90%	0.46%	90.61%	(D, RF, 1 month, 3 months)

5.3 Classifier Endurance

Next we tested the endurance of our detection models, as a generalization of the *long-term trained proactivity* scenario. Namely, we used the *long-term trained proactivity* scenario, with yearly granularity, to evaluate how detection and FP rates of the ANN and RF models vary over longer periods of time. The experiment is described by Algorithm 2; parameter **start** varies between 2014 and 2020. Figures 4, 5, 6 and 7 show the evolution of TPR and FPR for the neural network model and the Random Forest one.

Algorithm 2. Classifier endurance

function COMPUTEENDURANCE($D, algorithm, start$)
  $metrics \leftarrow \emptyset$
  $trainDB \leftarrow GetDB(D, 0, start)$
  $model \leftarrow algorithm.Train(trainDB)$
  for $t = start \rightarrow 2020$, **with** $t \leftarrow t + 1year$ **do**
    $db \leftarrow GetDB(D, t, t + 1year)$
    $metrics \leftarrow metrics \bigcup \{model.Test(db)\}$
  end for
  return $metrics$
end function

metrics a list of metrics (accuracy, FPR and TPR) computed with the same model over several years
GetDB A function described in Algorithm 1

Intuitively, classifiers should exhibit a performance degradation in terms of TPR and FPR as the time-span between the last training year and the evaluation year increases. With respect to FPR, our experiments confirm this intuition for both classifiers. For the ANN model, the FPR is constantly higher than the RF FPR. For the ANN, the evolution of FPR (Fig. 5) has a relatively stable (though high) level whenever the training set covers a time-span beyond a certain threshold (timestamps $\leq$ 2016). As for the RF classifiers (Fig. 7), all the FPR rates are lower by nearly one order of magnitude compared to ANN; nevertheless, the FPR increases as the test years are further from the last training year. Detection-wise, despite initial decreases of TPR, each ANN (Fig. 4) and each RF (Fig. 6) classifiers have one or two rebounds in TPR performance in years relatively distant from the last training year. This behaviour suggests that older files may be useful for training a new detection classifier: new malware families might use techniques similar to older ones, easily identifiable by detection models whose training set included relevant older files. This indicates an increased feature-relevance time span and a slowed down feature perishability process.

Focusing on further details of TPR evolution, a certain volatility is obvious. However, some classifiers exhibit periods of stability: the model with $\mathbf{t} = \mathbf{2016}$ (green segment) does not drop below its initial TPR value in the case of the ANN, while RF models with $\mathbf{t} \in \{2015, 2016, 2018\}$ show a stable TPR for 1 or 2 years after the initial test year. The detection rate does not reach desirable levels in these cases.

In a pragmatic view, the above mentioned evolution of TPR and FPR is further confirmation that a long-term use of a given classifier has to be thoroughly controlled and adjusted.

Even with a relatively small feature set (61 features in all), the FPR results are very good. As for TPR, the overall lower level of performance is due to the fact that the feature set is focused on obfuscation (presumably with a lower performance on non-obfuscated malware). On the other hand, most of our experiments focus on using test files with timestamps beyond the training files - as opposed to cross-validation, where test files are "contemporary" with training files.

To summarize, our experiments indicate that:

- from a detection point of view (TPR), the ANN classifiers display a more robust performance level;
- the RF models reach the best FPR performance; they also show a slower degradation of FPR performance in successive years;

6 Related Work

We review the existing literature on macro viruses following two concerns: code obfuscation analysis and machine learning algorithms for malicious-VBA detection. Consequently, this section covers:

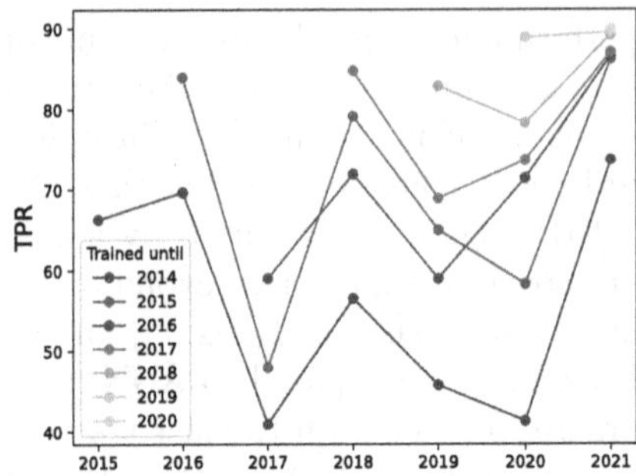

Fig. 4. TPR evolution in the Time-Resilience scenario - Neural Network model (Color figure online)

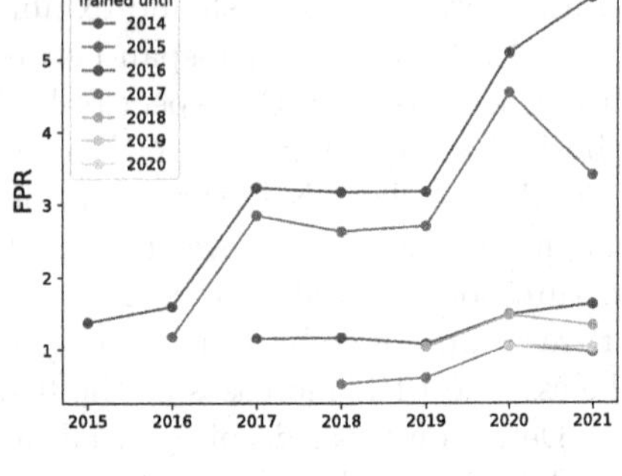

Fig. 5. FPR evolution in the Time-Resilience scenario - Neural Network model (Color figure online)

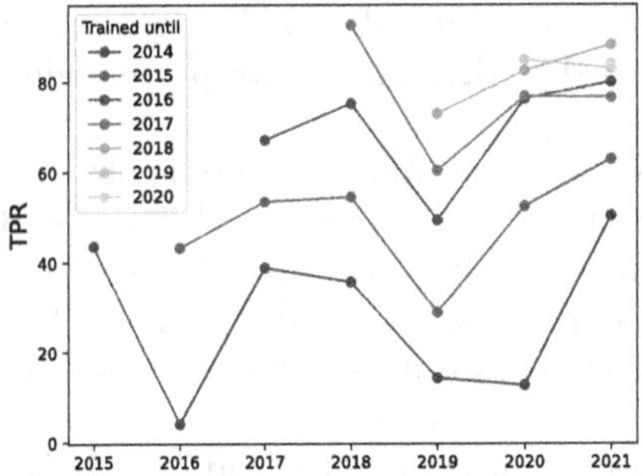

Fig. 6. TPR evolution in the Time-Resilience scenario - Random Forest model (Color figure online)

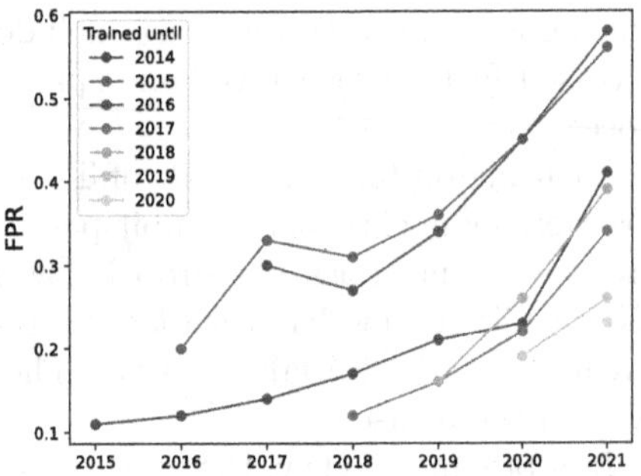

Fig. 7. FPR evolution in the Time-Resilience scenario - Random Forest model (Color figure online)

- generic techniques for code obfuscation;
- specific aspects of VBA code obfuscation;
- machine learning approaches for detecting malicious VBA macro code.

6.1 Generic Techniques for Code Obfuscation

Several obfuscation techniques implemented in various programming languages are categorized and described in [6–8,32].

In [32] six of the most common obfuscation techniques for binary code are discussed: dead-code insertion, register reassignment, subroutine reordering, instruction substitution, code transposition and code integration.

A classification of the obfuscation techniques used in Java files is presented in [6]. The two classification criteria are: the type of information that is targeted (lexical or data structure) and the kind of operation that is performed on the respective information.

Other classifications for Java obfuscation are given in [7] and [8]. The authors consider 35 obfuscation algorithms which are labeled according to the type of transformation that they perform: layout, control, data, preventive, splitting, merging, reordering and miscellaneous.

6.2 VBA Code Obfuscation Specific Aspects

As discussed above, implementations of general obfuscation techniques in various programming languages have been studied extensively; however, when it comes to obfuscation techniques for VBA code, there is a less substantial literature. The two most noticeable analyses are [12] and [1].

In [12], features describing various techniques of VBA code obfuscation are mined: random obfuscation, split obfuscation, encoding obfuscation and logic obfuscation; 15 features across these four categories are thus obtained. Subsequently, five machine learning classifiers were trained (Support Vector Machines (SVM), Random Forests (RF), multi-layer perceptrons (MLP), linear discriminant analysis and naive Bayes). RF models are reported to have reached the best precision; the MLP had the best accuracy and recall[14].

In [1], the authors report on the best-performing VBA-related features with respect to the detection rate: the average variable assignment length, the count of variables, the count of integer and string variables, macro keys, the number of consecutive mathematical operations and the upper case/lower case ratio in variable declarations. Among the several classifiers under that study, Random Forest is again reported to have had the best performance.

6.3 Machine Learning Techniques for Detecting Malicious VBA Code

Regarding the detection of malware in MSOffice documents through machine learning techniques, various approaches have been proposed with respect to feature engineering and classifier choice: 1) VBA macro-based detection, 2) P-code detection, 3) feature engineering through NLP, 4) code-agnostic systems and 5) hybrid systems which merge some of 1) - 4).

Macro-Based Detection. There are several code-based detection methods which aim to classify documents by using features extracted from the VBA code, focused mainly on describing obfuscation. In [25], the authors introduce obfuscation-feature mining for macro malware detection, by means of the Ole-File and OleVBA tools; thus they built a vector of 45 binary features. Using this feature vector, four classifiers (Neural Network, SVM, Decision Tree and Random Forest) were trained and tested; SVM reached the highest detection accuracy - 93%. A similar approach can also be found in [12] and [1].

P-code Detection. The VBA P-code is a compiled version of the VBA code which consists of a set of custom assembly instructions[15]. These assembly

---

[14] Precision = TP/(TP + FP); recall = TP/(TP + FN), where: TP - true positive; FP - false positive; FN - false negative.

[15] https://en.wikipedia.org/wiki/Pcode_machine#Microsoft_PCode.

instructions are used in several studies as features for document classification systems. In this regard, [3] used a frequency measure of instruction n-grams combined with a KNN classifier. On a small dataset of 40 malicious and 118 benign samples with a 90%–10% train-test split, they reached an overall accuracy of 96.3%. In [10], the same method of p-code instruction processing is used, but, in addition to this, the authors introduce code-specific features and experiments with a wider range of classifiers. A stratified 10 fold cross validation experiment including 4181 p-code samples showed that the Random Forest classifier had the best performance in terms of accuracy (98.86%) and precision (0.95).

Feature Engineering Through NLP. In [19], the authors devise a natural language processing tool for analysing VBA macros. Features are obtained by means of various language processing techniques, such as TF[16], TF-IDF[17], BoW[18] and Doc2Vec. Features thus identified are subsequently submitted to classifiers (SVM, RF, and MLP). The method was assessed by training the classifiers on a dataset from 2015 and testing them on a dataset from 2016; they reach an accuracy of 89% on new malware families and an F-score of 0.93 using MLP with Doc2Vec. This method is further investigated in [17]. Two new elements are introduced: LSI[19] for feature mining and a classifier based on a convolutional neural network; in this new frame, the F-score was improved up to 0.99, using SVM and Doc2Vec. Another language processing method for the detection of malicious macro code, SCDV[20], is introduced in [16]. In cross-validation testing, SCDV is shown to be a better performer, but is surpassed by Doc2Vec in a time series scenario. Doc2Vec model is also used in [18] in order to enhance small training sets. In this research, fake samples are generated by adding random noise to the extracted feature vectors. The results show that the fake samples improved the detection rate. Another NLP approach to macro code detection is presented in [23]. This uses an obfuscation-focused Word2Vec processing procedure for feature mining, combined with a Random Forest classifier. In the context of a classification task involving 6053 samples, this system achieved 82.65% accuracy.

Code-Agnostic Systems. Many systems designed to detect malicious Office documents use other features than the ones that can be derived from macro code. ALDOCX approach to feature mining was proposed in [21]; it uses document characteristics derived from file metadata. A method called "SFEM" is used to search for relevant features by analyzing the paths of files inside the ZIP archive representing an Office document. "SFEM" is presented extensively in another paper [5] by the same author. The features thus identified were provided to several classifiers, while an Active Learning component continuously updates the detection model. On a set of 327 malicious files and 16484 benign files, ALDOCX achieved the best results with SVM: 99.67% accuracy, 93.34% TPR and 0.19% FPR.

[16] Term Frequency.
[17] Term Frequency - Inverse Document Frequency.
[18] Bag of Words.
[19] Latent Semantic Indexing.
[20] Sparse Composite Document Vectors.

The detection of the social engineering component of an Office-based attack is assessed in [4]. The proposed system processes images embedded in documents and flag a malicious file if an image is found in a previously established database or if the image contains a text that tries to trick the user into enabling macros. This system achieved an accuracy, precision and recall of 99.5%, 0.93 and 0.98 respectively, on a small test set consisting of 890 benign files and 159 malicious ones. A technique similar to the previously mentioned p-code processing is presented in [24]. The authors use statistical measures over the raw bytes of a document, such as n-gram histograms and pair these measures with a deep neural network and decision trees. These classifiers where evaluated in a time-series experiment on over 5 million samples and achieved an AUC[21] > 0.99. Another byte-level processing method is used in [31] in order to construct an image from an Office document. This study investigates the performance of three CNN classifiers (Le-Net5, AlexNet and VGG) on the image representation of 201 files, 105 malicious and 96 benign. In this setting, VGG achieves the best average accuracy of 94.09%.

Hybrid Systems. Many studies merge various components of the aforementioned systems. In [15], multiple static analysis techniques are merged, such as structural analysis (similar to SFEM) and VBA keyword analysis. When paired with a Random Forest classifier, this feature mining method can achieve an average recall of 0.97 and FPR of 1.4% for MS-DOC documents and 0.97 recall and 0.7% FPR for Office documents using the OOXML format.

In [14], the authors indicate that a hybrid solution, combining static and dynamic analysis techniques, is more suitable to detect malicious documents. Their conclusion is that there are some weaknesses that make either of these two methods incomplete if used in isolation. This is also the conclusion of [13], which combines VBA-specific features and dynamic ones, such as opened processes or DNS calls. In their experiments involving a 10-fold cross-validation procedure over 18307 files (2736 benign, 15571 malicious), MLP and Random Forest models are the best performers, with an average precision of 0.99 and average recall of 0.97. A similar approach is also used for the detection of malicious PDF documents [29] by analyzing the input file, reconstructing the logic structure and extracting the JavaScript code that is executed in an instrumented interpreter, which can detect embedded shellcode[22]. In [33], the authors propose a two-layer feature mining system based on a tree representation of the Office document format and a custom intermediate language in which the VBA code is translated. Using this document representation method and multiple machine learning classifiers (Linear SVM, RBF SVM, Decision Tree, Random Forest, AdaBoost and Logistic Regression), they achieve an average accuracy of 98.52%, 0.98 precision and 0.98 recall in an experiment over a dataset consisting of 1000 malicious documents and 1000 benign ones. Dynamic analysis is also used in [11] in order to detect malware shellcode. After extracting the shellcode from the documents, it

[21] Area Under the ROC Curve.

[22] https://en.wikipedia.org/wiki/Shellcode.

is executed using an emulator and some features are identified: self-modifying code, API calls and access to the Process Environment Block.

Other security studies focus on Microsoft Office vulnerability detection. Systems like the ones described in [26,27] and [22] are often used to identify potential vulnerabilities and shellcodes (that may lead to features) in Microsoft documents.

7 Conclusions and Future Work

It is our hope that the Conclusions presented below generalize safely, since our training and testing data is likely to illustrate accurately the real-world battlefield VBA-based malware vs. detection models, in several respects: the very large dimension of the database of files (1.8 million), all of which contain VBA code; the realistic ratio between benign files and malware; the 25-year timespan of the database. By contrast, the Related Work, as discussed in Sect. 6, used mostly relatively small datasets, while the presence of VBA code in all training/testing files is not always confirmed [24].

The use of a large database of malicious and benign files collected over more than a decade (with clean files actually spanning over more than two decades), allowed us to get some insights into how VBA-based malware evolves.

Here are some of our conclusions:

- Malware (co-)evolves largely as a reaction to what security products are doing and is also driven by its own new goals. Therefore, better detection systems require regular updates at all levels. Indeed, the results of our endurance experiments show that regularly updated classifiers improve their detection performance. These results also point to *feature perishability*: the set of detection-relevant file features changes as malware evolves, which enforces the need to include a feature mining step in each classifier update/ maintenance phase. As for time granularity, the proactivity experiments indicate that small/frequent retraining steps lead to higher accuracy and lower FPR than larger ones.
- *Feature perishability* strongly influences the feature mining process. As the experiments show, there are not only cases of constant decrease of a feature's relevance, but also cases where a decrease is followed by an important increase (see feature F15 in Fig. 2). Since the detection relevance of each feature fluctuates over time, feature mining and validation should be a continuous process.
- A reasonable level of TPR can be reached using a relatively small set of malware files provided that they are recent. Our experiments show that very large training sets in the long-term trained proactivity experiment (Table 5) lead to only slightly better performance compared to more modest sized training sets in the short-term trained proactivity experiment (Table 6).
- Older benign files lower the FPR. While using only recent benign files may increase the detection rate, older benign files are most useful in reducing the FPR. Indeed, our experiments show that short-term trained proactivity FPR

values are well above (i.e., worse) those of the long-term trained proactivity - see Tables 5 and 6.
- No obfuscation-based feature can detect VBA malware files by itself (Fig. 3). Therefore, such features have to be combined in sets of features (possibly including other types of features).
- As mentioned in Sect. 2.2, the overall choice of classifiers directs towards ANN and RF [2,20,30]. Our experiments show that the training scheme and main detection goal decide which of the two classifiers should be chosen. In short-term training, the RF model is superior in both TPR and FPR. In long term training, if avoiding false positives is the main target, then an RF model is in order, while if the detection rate is the more important goal, then an ANN would be recommended. Our experiments (Table 5 and Table 6) strongly support these choices.

Our future study concerns will be threefold:

- Feature mining in a controlled virtual environment. More sensitive features can be defined if one interprets, instead of the intent, the actual dynamic run-time behaviour of a document.
- Further speedup of the feature mining process may result from NLP techniques for identifying classification-relevant features from VBA macros.
- We plan to further investigate the proactivity and endurance of various classifiers and also the non-monotone dynamics of "feature perishability". Comprehensive testing involving files covering the years 2021/2022 will be the first step in this direction.

References

1. Aboud, E., O'Brien, D.: Detection of malicious VBA macros using machine learning methods (2018)
2. Azeez, N.A., Odufuwa, O.E., Misra, S., Oluranti, J., Damaševičius, R.: Windows PE malware detection using ensemble learning. Informatics **8**(1) (2021)
3. Bearden, R., Lo, D.C.T.: Automated Microsoft office macro malware detection using machine learning. In: 2017 IEEE International Conference on Big Data (2017)
4. Casino, F., Totosis, N., Apostolopoulos, T., Lykousas, N., Patsakis, C.: Analysis and correlation of visual evidence in campaigns of malicious office documents (2021)
5. Cohen, A., Nissim, N., Rokach, L., Elovici, Y.: SFEM: structural feature extraction methodology for the detection of malicious office documents using machine learning methods. Expert Syst. Appl. **63** (2016)
6. Collberg, C., Thomborson, C.: A taxonomy of obfuscating transformations (1997)
7. Ertaul, L., Venkatesh, S.: JHide-a tool kit for code obfuscation. In: IASTED Conference on Software Engineering and Applications, pp. 133–138 (2004)
8. Ertaul, L., Venkatesh, S.: Novel obfuscation algorithms for software security. In: Proceedings of the 2005 International Conference on Software Engineering Research and Practice, SERP, vol. 5. Citeseer (2005)
9. Gabor, S.: VBA is not dead! Virus Bulletin (2014). https://www.virusbulletin.com/virusbulletin/2014/07/vba-not-dead

10. Huneault-Leblanc, S., Talhi, C.: P-code based classification to detect malicious VBA macro. In: 2020 International Symposium on Networks, Computers and Communications (ISNCC), pp. 1–6. IEEE (2020)
11. Iwamoto, K., Wasaki, K.: A method for shellcode extraction from malicious document files using entropy and emulation (2015)
12. Kim, S., Hong, S., Oh, J., Lee, H.: Obfuscated VBA macro detection using machine learning. In: DSN, pp. 490–501. IEEE Computer Society (2018)
13. Koutsokostas, V., et al.: Invoice# 31415 attached: automated analysis of malicious Microsoft office documents. Comput. Secur. **114**, 102582 (2022)
14. Li, W., Stolfo, S., Stavrou, A., Androulaki, E., Keromytis, A.: A study of malcode-bearing documents (2007)
15. Lu, X., Wang, F., Shu, Z.: Malicious word document detection based on multi-view features learning, pp. 1–6 (2019). https://doi.org/10.1109/ICCCN.2019.8846940
16. Mimura, M.: Using sparse composite document vectors to classify VBA macros. In: Liu, J.K., Huang, X. (eds.) NSS 2019. LNCS, vol. 11928, pp. 714–720. Springer, Cham (2019). https://doi.org/10.1007/978-3-030-36938-5_46
17. Mimura, M.: An improved method of detecting macro malware on an imbalanced dataset. IEEE Access **8**, 204709–204717 (2020)
18. Mimura, M.: Using fake text vectors to improve the sensitivity of minority class for macro malware detection (2020)
19. Mimura, M., Miura, H.: Detecting unseen malicious VBA macros with NLP techniques. J. Inf. Process. **27**, 555–563 (2019)
20. Moubarak, J., Feghali, T.: Comparing machine learning techniques for malware detection. In: ICISSP (2020)
21. Nissim, N., Cohen, A., Elovici, Y.: ALDOCX: detection of unknown malicious Microsoft office documents using designated active learning methods based on new structural feature extraction methodology (2016)
22. Otsubo, Y.: O-checker: detection of malicious documents through deviation from file format specifications (2016)
23. Ravi, V., Gururaj, S., Vedamurthy, H., Nirmala, M.: Analysing corpus of office documents for macro-based attacks using machine learning (2022)
24. Rudd, E.M., Harang, R.E., Saxe, J.: MEADE: towards a malicious email attachment detection engine. CoRR abs/1804.08162 (2018)
25. De los Santos, S., Torres, J.: Macro malware detection using machine learning techniques-a new approach. In: ICISSP, pp. 295–302 (2017)
26. Schreck, T., Berger, S., Göbel, J.: BISSAM: automatic vulnerability identification of office documents (2012)
27. Smutz, C., Stavrou, A.: Preventing exploits in Microsoft office documents through content randomization (2015)
28. Szandała, T.: Review and comparison of commonly used activation functions for deep neural networks. In: Bhoi, A.K., Mallick, P.K., Liu, C.-M., Balas, V.E. (eds.) Bio-inspired Neurocomputing. SCI, vol. 903, pp. 203–224. Springer, Singapore (2021). https://doi.org/10.1007/978-981-15-5495-7_11
29. Tzermias, Z., Sykiotakis, G., Polychronakis, M., Markatos, E.: Combining static and dynamic analysis for the detection of malicious documents (2011)
30. Wael, D., Sayed, S.G., Abdelbaki, N.: Enhanced approach to detect malicious VBScript files based on data mining techniques. In: Shakshuki, E.M., Yasar, A.U.H. (eds.) EUSPN/ICTH. Procedia Computer Science, vol. 141, pp. 552–558 (2018)

31. Yang, S., Chen, W., Li, S., Xu, Q.: Approach using transforming structural data into image for detection of malicious MS-doc files based on deep learning models. In: 2019 Asia-Pacific Signal and Information Processing Association Annual Summit and Conference (APSIPA ASC), pp. 28–32 (2019)
32. You, I., Yim, K.: Malware obfuscation techniques: a brief survey. In: 2010 International Conference on Broadband, Wireless Computing, Communication and Applications, pp. 297–300. IEEE (2010)
33. Yu, M., et al.: A unified malicious documents detection model based on two layers of abstraction (2019)

PriApp-Install: Learning User Privacy Preferences on Mobile Apps' Installation

Ha Xuan Son(✉), Barbara Carminati, and Elena Ferrari

University of Insubria, Varese, Italy
{sha,barbara.carminati,elena.ferrari}@uninsubria.it

Abstract. It is undeniable that smartphones play a vital role in our lives, as their applications (apps) can be used to access various services anytime and anywhere. Despite the benefits provided by mobile apps, there are risks connected to the release of personal and sensitive data. Understanding the potential privacy risks of installing an app based on its description or privacy policy could be challenging, especially for non-skilled users. In this paper, to assist users in their app selection process, we propose PriApp-Install, a privacy-aware app installation recommendation system. It leverages semi-supervised learning to learn individual privacy preferences w.r.t mobile app installation. Learning is done based on a rich set of features modelling both the app behavior w.r.t. personal data consumption and the benefits a user can get in installing the app. We tested four learning strategies on a real dataset by exploiting three participant groups: security and privacy experts, IT workers, and crowd workers. The obtained results show the effectiveness of our proposal.

Keywords: Mobile apps · Privacy preferences and policies · Static analysis · Semi-supervised learning

1 Introduction

Nowadays, smartphones are an integral part of our lives, and, as a result, we heavily rely on them and their apps. Several apps exist to support us in almost all our activities, whether these activities are related to our digital life, social life, real-life or working time. The result is that, on average, users install from 20 to 60 apps on their mobile devices.[1] This trend has relevant advantages: users benefit from different services almost everywhere. However, apps may collect sensitive information about users (e.g., users' profiles and habits) and their devices (e.g., locations), which may not be all needed for the app's execution.

To mitigate privacy risks, different privacy laws have been approved to limit service providers' requests for unnecessary information, such as GDPR[2] for the European countries. Also, mobile platforms have started to care more about

[1] https://www.statista.com/statistics/267309/number-of-apps-on-mobile-phones/.
[2] https://eur-lex.europa.eu/eli/reg/2016/679/oj.

C. Su et al. (Eds.): ISPEC 2022, LNCS 13620, pp. 306–323, 2022.
https://doi.org/10.1007/978-3-031-21280-2_17

individual privacy. For example, Android OS introduced the `permission` and `permission group` principle, by which developers can indicate the type and scope of collected data, and apps have to request such permissions from end-users before getting access to sensitive resources.[3] These efforts reduce the set of permissions required by apps to some extent [25], but users are still largely unaware of the privacy implications of some permissions they grant to apps.

For this reason, several approaches have recently been proposed to develop recommendation systems supporting users in making more privacy-aware decisions on app installation. However, most of them (a) assign a risk score to target apps and (b) suggest not installing apps with a high-risk score. Therefore, their main focus is the definition of the risk score metric. For instance, some approaches suggest determining the risk by comparing the app's requested permissions with the app's description [3,23]. Other studies focus on static analysis of the app's code to capture the app's behavior w.r.t personal data collection (see Sect. 6 for more details).

However, we envision these approaches not fully supporting end-users in the app installation process. Focusing only on the risk of an app w.r.t personal data consumption, they ignore other relevant factors to be considered when installing an app. First, the possible risk must be compared with the benefits that an app can bring to a specific user. For instance, a user may decide to install a risky medical app since it collects sensitive information because it is essential for him/her as it monitors a disease he/she suffers. The other important aspect is that privacy is subjective by nature, so one-size-fits-all solutions do not work properly. Users might have different opinions w.r.t. the installation of apps with the same risk level.

To cope with all these issues, this paper proposes PriApp-Install, a tool whose goal is to learn user preferences on app installation to suggest whether to install a new app or not.[4] Learning exploits three main dimensions: the app's behavior w.r.t. personal data usage; the benefits that installing the app could bring to target users; and the sharing of collected personal information with third parties. All this information is collected through (a) the app market, (b) the static analysis of the app's code, and (c) the analysis of the app's privacy policy.

To balance users' effort and the prediction quality, we opt for semi-supervised learning [20]. In particular, we have experimentally tested four different learning strategies over the selected features, and we show that, among different semi-supervised approaches, the ones that better fit the considered scenario are those based on ensemble learning [12]. We also show that semi-supervised learning provides better accuracy than supervised approaches (i.e., random forest, linear regression, and SVM) even with a small training dataset.

We have tested our learning approaches with three different groups of participants. First, we considered the feedback of 51 cybersecurity and privacy experts (S&P experts) who work in academic institutions. We then collected feedback from 90 IT workers, i.e., junior and senior developers in industrial institutions

[3] https://developer.android.com/guide/topics/permissions/overview.

[4] Implementation is available at https://github.com/SonHaXuan/PriApp-Install.

from different countries. Finally, we used a crowd-sourcing platform to have a more significant (i.e., 300 participants), more balanced (i.e., gender, ages), and more heterogeneous (i.e., different nationalities and education levels) dataset. The obtained results show that around 94.51% of S&P experts, 86.39% of IT workers, and 80.69% of crowd workers were satisfied with the app installation decisions suggested by our tool.

The remainder of this paper is organized as follows. Section 2 describes the overall architecture of PriApp-Install. Sections 3 and 4 present the adopted learning approaches and dataset, respectively. The evaluation and related work are presented in Sects. 5 and 6, respectively. Section 7 concludes the paper. Finally, the appendix includes information about the adopted metrics.

2 Overall Architecture

PriApp-Install aims at assisting users in deciding whether to install an Android app or not. The decision is mainly based on the privacy risks related to the information collected and shared with third parties and the benefits the users might get from the app. Moreover, in developing our tool, we acknowledge that users might have different perceptions of privacy risks implied by apps' data collection [8], or more in general of privacy, as well as, on possible benefits. To consider this subjective dimension, PriApp-Install leverages semi-supervised learning to build a classifier for predicting app installation decisions based on users' feedback.

The learning process relies on a rich set of features describing different aspects of the target app relevant to the decision process. First of all, thanks to the information available in app store,[5] we obtain some *app's basic information*, including the app's name, developers' name, app's category, app's description, and so on.

Additionally, we consider the *app's privacy policy* to collect other relevant information. In particular, we parse the privacy policy to determine the declared purposes for data collection and third-party usage. We focus on these information because they are always present in the analyzed apps' privacy policies. In contrast, other information, such as the retention period (i.e., for how long the server stores the data), is present only in a few apps' privacy policies. However, this publicly available app's information is not sufficient for users to fully understand the app's behavior w.r.t personal data consumption. To overcome this limitation, PriApp-Install also considers the *app's source code* to determine which data is collected by an app.

In particular, in this paper, we leverage on the static analysis tool developed in [15] to model and capture the API usage w.r.t. the collection of personal data. [15] models the app's behavior w.r.t personal data collection through the definition of the *app's signature* which is generated through the static analysis of the app's source code. In particular, given a data type *dt* and an app *app*, [15] models

[5] Android app store: https://play.google.com/store/apps.

its behavior w.r.t. collection of data of type dt as an array $sign_{app}^{dt}$, containing an element for each specific API able to retrieve a data of dt's type. $sign_{app}^{dt}$'s elements have value 1, if the corresponding API is present in *app*'s source code; 0, otherwise. [15] focuses on seven types of personal data, namely: user location (e.g., city, country), media (e.g., users' image, video, audio), connection (e.g., activity on Bluetooth, NFC), hardware (e.g., camera, USB devices), telephony (e.g., contacts info, phone number), user profile (e.g., gender, name), and health & fitness (e.g., heart rate, body fat). Therefore, the app's signature consists of seven arrays $sign_{app}^{dt}$, one for each of the considered data type dt.

By analyzing 30 permissions with significant security/privacy impact, provided by Google[6], [15] has determined 66 potentially dangerous APIs that collect data of the above-mentioned data types.[7] The app signature is therefore an array of 66 elements, corresponding to: $sign_{app}^{Loc}$ (6), $sign_{app}^{Med}$ (24), $sign_{app}^{Con}$ (13), $sign_{app}^{Har}$ (8), $sign_{app}^{Tel}$ (8), $sign_{app}^{U\_P}$ (2), and $sign_{app}^{H\&F}$ (5).

Example 1. Let us consider the Google Fit: Activity Tracking app signature ($sign_{G\_F}$). For simplicity, we will focus on the Location data type only. Its corresponding array $sign_{G\_F}^{Loc}$ in $sign_{G\_F}$ can be defined as follow:[8] $sign_{G\_F}^{Loc} = 100000$, where the first element has value "1", representing that the android.location API is used in the app code; whereas, the other elements' value is "0" (i.e., 5 elements), since the corresponding APIs are not used in the app code.

Therefore, we model an app as a set of features extracted by its *basic information* provided in the app market, *source code* analysis, and *privacy policy*, as the following definition states.

Table 1. *App*'s dimensions and corresponding fields

Dimension	Collection process	App's features
Basic information	Crawled from the app market	*an*, *dn*, *cat*
Data consumption behavior	App's signature, determined via the static analysis tool proposed in [15]	*sign*
Privacy policy	Data collection purposes and third party usages, extracted by exploiting [22]	*pp*, 3*pt*

Definition 1. ***App's features:*** *Given an app, we model its features as a tuple* $(an, dn, cat, sign, pp, 3pt)$, *where: an is the app's name; dn is the developer's name; cat is the app's category; sign is the app's signature; whereas pp and 3pt model the data collection purposes and third-party usages, respectively, as stated in the app's privacy policy. pp is defined as a set of pairs, each one denoting a purpose and the corresponding collected data.*[9] *Finally, 3pt is a set of triples,*

[6] https://developer.android.com/reference/android/Manifest.permission.

[7] We presented the APIs list and dangerous permissions at https://bit.ly/3qm5VT4.

[8] Arrays for the other personal data types can be similarly defined.

[9] *pp* contains *not_specified* if the policy does not specify any purpose.

each one denoting the third party name, the corresponding shared data and the sharing purpose.[10]

Table 1 summarizes the considered dimensions, the corresponding app's features and the way we collect them.

Example 2. Let us consider Google Fit: Activity Tracking app and let $sign_{G\_F}$ be its app signature, defined similarly to its location component $sign^{Loc}_{G\_F}$ given in Example 1. According to Definition 1, its features are modelled as follow:

$GoogleFit$=(Google Fit: Activity Tracking, Google LLC, Health&Fitness, $sign_{G\_F}$, {(analysis, user profile), (marketing, $not\_specified$), (maintenance, {loc- ation, user profile})}, {(ads, Google Ads, $not\_specified$)}).

To learn user judgment w.r.t apps' installation, we build a labeled training dataset *LApp*, by asking users to assign a judgment (label) for each *app* in the training set. This judgment indicates whether the user wants to install the corresponding app or not, based on its features (see Definition 1). If the user finds the provided information insufficient, he/she may decline to respond. The corresponding labels are therefore: Yes (Y), No (N), and Maybe (M). We used *LApp* to test different learning approaches described in the next section.

3 Learning Approaches

Literature offers several learning approaches that could be used for our goal. However, as mentioned in Sect. 2, we opt for semi-supervised learning [20], which has the advantage of achieving good accuracy with a small labeled training set (see Subsect. 5.3). It allows us not to require users to label many apps since this would negatively impact the usability and acceptability of our solution. To select the best semi-supervised learning approach, we test four different learning strategies with different complexity (the results are reported in Sect. 5). These four strategies are described in the following sections.

3.1 Naive and Category-Based Prediction Models

As learning algorithm we exploit the Expectation-maximization (EM) algorithm [2]. EM is an iterative method to find maximum likelihood or maximum a posteriori (MAP) estimates of θ parameters[11] in statistical models, where the model depends on unobserved latent variables. The EM algorithm alternates between an expectation (E) and a maximization (M) steps. The first step computes the maximum likelihood estimation for θ, quantified by the log-likelihood of all the items, based on the current estimation for θ parameters. In the second step, the algorithm updates θ to maximize the likelihood. In our case, the first step trains a classifier with only the available labeled apps and uses the classifier to

[10] If shared data are not specified in the privacy policy, $3pt$ is set to $not\_specified$.

[11] θ parameters aim at optimizing the label probability.

assign probabilistically weighted class labels to each target app, by calculating the expectation of the missing class labels. The algorithm, then, trains a new classifier using all the apps (i.e., both the labeled and pseudo-labeled apps).

Our baseline is a naive approach that considers all *app*'s features (i.e., $an, dn, cat, sign, pp, 3pt$) to predict the pseudo-labels of the target apps.

The second approach, i.e., category-based, takes in consideration that apps belonging to the same category might have similar behavior (in terms of required personal data). At this aim, the category-based approach groups all apps with the same category to build the classifier pseudo-labeling the target apps.

Algorithm 1. EM($LApp$, $UApp$)

```
1: input: the set of labeled apps LApp, the set of unlabeled apps UApp.
2: output: labels for UApp.
3: for each app_i ∈ UApp do
4:    θ = EM(LApp);
5:    Calculate log-likelihood L(θ);
6:    convergence = false;
7:    Dataset = LApp ∪ {app_i};
8:    while convergence==false do
9:       E-step: Estimate likehood on Dataset based on θ parameter values;
10:      M-step: Update θ parameter values;
11:      Calculate new log-likelihood L(θ_new);
12:      if |L(θ_new) - L(θ)| ≤ ε then
13:         convergence=true;
14:         lab_{app_i} = argmax_θ(p(app_i, lab_{app_i}|θ)p(θ));
15:         UApp = UApp - {app_i};
16:         LApp = LApp ∪ {(app_i, lab_{app_i})};
17:      else
18:         L(θ) = L(θ_new);
19:      end if
20:   end while
21: end for
22: return LApp;
```

Algorithm 1 describes how the pseudo-labels of each app in the unlabeled dataset are generated using the EM algorithm. This algorithm is used both for naive and category-based approaches. In the case of the naive approach, Algorithm 1 receives as *LApp* all apps. In contrast, in the case of category-based, we pass to Algorithm 1 only apps with the same category. The algorithm is thus re-executed for each category, obtaining a different prediction model.

Algorithm 1 executes EM to estimate the θ parameters using only the labeled dataset, i.e., *LApp*, and the pseudo-labeled apps from the previous iteration (see line 4). Line 5 calculates the initial value of the log-likelihood $L(\theta)$. The expectation step calculates the membership probability for each app and each label (i.e., yes, no, maybe) (line 9). In the maximization step, parameters are optimized for each label based on the current membership probability (line 10). The expectation and maximization phases are iterated until log-likelihood does not change (i.e., the difference between values of log-likelihood computed in two subsequent iterations is less than a value ϵ (see line 12)). Then, the pseudo-label returned for each app (app_i) is associated with the highest membership probability (line 14).[12] Algorithm 1 repeatedly labels the unlabeled apps in *UApp* until this set is empty (the for-loop from line 3 to line 21). Finally, it returns *LApp*, including the original labeled apps and the pseudo-labeled ones (line 22).

3.2 Simple and Advanced Ensemble-Based Prediction Models

The first two approaches benefit from being efficient in terms of time required for building the prediction model [19]. However, they do not exploit the correlations that might exist among the considered features, which can affect the accuracy during label prediction [9]. We believe that different combinations of apps' features might impact the prediction models, and thus the app installation decisions. For instance, prior studies have found that knowledge of the data collection purposes (i.e., *pp*), as well as third party usages (i.e., *3pt*), can increase user awareness when installing an app [7,21].

For these reasons, we further apply two ensemble-based algorithms with the aim of better capturing user behavior w.r.t app's installation. Ensemble-based learning combines a group of sub-classifiers to create a more robust prediction model [11]. In practice, we use ensemble learning to define prediction models on the app's features subsets. Then, we combine the most confident one.

Table 2. Classifiers for the simple (Sim) and advanced (Adv) ensemble-based approach

	Classifier 1 features	Classifier 2 features	Classifier 3 features
Sim	*an*, *dn*, *cat*	*sign*	*pp*, *3pt*
Adv	*an*, *dn*, *cat*, *sign*	*sign*, *pp*, *3pt*	*pp*, *3pt*, *an*, *dn*, *cat*

Algorithm 2 implements the simple ensemble-based approach. It exploits the app's features corresponding to each app's dimension to define a different classifier (line 3). In particular, as reported in the first row of Table 2, the first classifier is built only on *an*, *dn*, and *cat* features; the second on the *sign* feature; and the third on *pp* and *3pt* features.

Once the classifiers have been built, given a target app (app_i), the `Ensemble` algorithm identifies to which label app_i most likely belongs to by using the bagging method [12] (see lines 6–11). Bagging is an effective method for ensemble learning, where the final label is assigned by computing the average of membership probabilities returned by the obtained classifiers (line 12). Algorithm 2 repeatedly labels the unlabeled apps in *UApp* until *UApp* is empty (the for-loop from lines 4 to 15). Finally, the algorithm returns *LApp*, including the original labeled apps and the pseudo-labeled apps (line 16).

[12] `argmax` is used for finding the label (i.e., Y, N, MB) with the highest probability.

Algorithm 2. Simple_Ensemble($LApp$, $UApp$)

input: labeled apps $LApp$, unlabeled apps $UApp$.
output: labels for $UApp$.
Let $dimension = \{(\text{an,dn,cat}), \text{sign}, (\text{pp,3pt})\}$
for each $app_i \in UApp$ **do**
    $\theta_{ens} = \text{EM}(LApp)$;
    for $X \in dimension$ **do**
        Let $LApp_X$ be the projection of $LApp$ on X;
        Let app_{i_X} be the projection of app_i on X;
        $\theta_X = \text{EM}(LApp_X, app_{i_X})$;
        $\theta_{ens} = \theta_{ens} \cup \theta_X$;
    end for
    $lab_{app_i} = argmax_{\theta_{ens}}(p(app_i, lab_{app_i}|\theta_{ens})\ p(\theta_{ens}))$;
    $UApp = UApp - \{app_i\}$;
    $LApp = LApp \cup \{(app_i, lab_{app_i})\}$;
end for
return $LApp$;

Implementation of the advanced ensemble-based approach is similar to that of the simple ensemble-based one (Algorithm 2), being the only difference the app's features used to build the classifiers, which are those reported in the second row of Table 2. In particular, in the advanced ensemble-based learning, we build three classifiers exploiting correlations among features belonging to different dimensions. Indeed, users might have different opinions on apps by considering features of different dimensions simultaneously. As an example, Lin et al. [6] found that users are not willing to install dictionary apps since they access their locations (i.e., data collection). However, when users realize that this data is needed to compute location-based trending words (i.e., purpose), they are fine to install them. As such, we believe that features of different dimensions should be combined together. Therefore, in the advanced ensemble-based approach we design each classifier to combine two out of the three dimensions. For instance, the first classifier is built by considering features belonging to the first and second dimension, namely an, dn, cat, and $sign$, whereas the second classifier combines features belonging to the second and third dimension (see the second row of Table 2). Figure 1 describes the architecture of PriApp-Install and the supported learning strategies.

4 Dataset

To generate the app dataset to test our learning strategies, we selected a list of the most-downloaded apps from 15 popular categories. Table 3 reports the considered categories. In total, we crawled 32,856 apps in Feb. 2021. We crawled app's basic information from the app market, namely app's name, developer's name, and category. Also, we downloaded the APK files of the selected apps.

To generate the app's signature, we first leveraged decompiler reverse engineering to obtain the Java code from the corresponding APK (see Fig. 1). Among

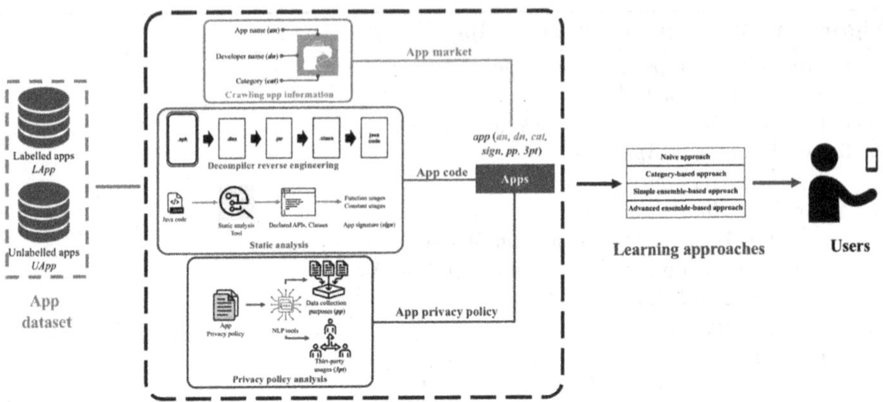

Fig. 1. PriApp-Install architecture

Table 3. App dataset (i.e., #apps in Java code and Privacy policy)

Category	Java code	Privacy policy	Category	Java code	Privacy policy	Category	Java code	Privacy policy
Beauty	1311	1061	Food & Drink	2115	1515	Shopping	2087	1537
Business	2258	1568	Health & Fitness	1546	1167	Social	1506	1158
Education	2249	1782	Maps & Navigation	1606	1240	Sports	1655	1303
Entertainment	1838	1407	Medical	1733	1232	Tools	1799	1387
Finance	2225	1747	Music & Audio	1425	1203	Travel & Local	1857	1513

the 32,856 crawled apps, we successfully decompiled 27,210 of them (about 82.82%).[13] Then, we applied the static analysis approach in [15] to collect the APIs usage for the seven considered data types (i.e., 66 APIs), namely location, media, connection, hardware, telephony, user profile, and health & fitness. To determine if a declared API is exploited by an app, we checked whether the functions/constants of the target API are used in the app's source code.

To minimize the amount of information that participants to our experiments must check, we show only the information on API usage for each target app (66 APIs), rather than information on classes (nearly 1.4K classes) or functions/constants usage (more than 13.6K functions/constants).[14]

Finally, to analyze privacy policies to determine data collection purposes and third-party usage, we exploited the natural language processing (NLP) tool defined by Wilson et al. in [22]. Among all 27,210 decompiled apps, we successfully collected privacy policies of 20,820 apps (approximately 76.52%). For data collection purposes (i.e., component *pp* of Definition 1), we considered the 18 most popular ones, such as Profiling, Analysis, Statistical, Advertisements, Maintenance. We also determined the corresponding collected data (by restrict-

[13] Failure to decompile was primarily due to code obfuscation.

[14] On average, in our dataset, an app uses 6 APIs, 48 classes, and 238 functions/constants to collect personal data.

ing our analysis to the seven personal data types) for each purpose mentioned in the app's privacy policy. Additionally, we captured the third-party usage (i.e., component *3pt* of Definition 1) by extracting from the privacy policy the name of the third party with which data are shared, the corresponding usage purposes, and collected data. For usage purposes, we considered the five most common ones (i.e., Payment, Delivery, Marketing, Advertisement, and Analysis).

5 Experiments

We carried out several experiments to evaluate the effectiveness of the proposed learning approaches in capturing users' preferences regarding app's installation.

5.1 Experiments Setting

In our experiments, users have been involved both to label the training set and evaluate if a prediction model has correctly labeled a target app. For this purpose, we developed a web application through which participants label the training apps in the learning phase (i.e., training dataset), and give their feedback on the labels generated by the prediction models in the testing phase (i.e., test dataset). During the learning phase, participants are asked to associate a decision (i.e., Y, N, M) with ten apps that belong to two categories, randomly selected from the 15 categories in Table 3 (i.e., five apps/category). For each app, we show its features (those listed in Definition 1), namely: app's name, developer's name, category, its signature, data collection purposes, and third-party usages.

Once the labeling phase is terminated, the collected training dataset is elaborated by the learning algorithms illustrated in Sect. 3. To evaluate the learning strategies, the web application shows 16 new apps to the experiment's participants to build the test dataset for the four proposed approaches (i.e., four target apps/approaches). For each target app, the participants give feedback on the labels, i.e., agree (Y) or disagree (N) - and in case of disagreement, they provide the correct label. Finally, the web application asks the participants whether they are satisfied with the labels assigned by the four approaches. The participant can answer with yes, no, or maybe.

In the survey, we set a timer to track how long participants spend in evaluating an app. Reading basic app information takes on average 26 s, whereas participants spend approx. 46 s to (a) check information regarding API usages (i.e., app's signature) and privacy policy (i.e., third party usage, and data collection purposes) and (b) answer the proposed questions. The total average time to complete the survey is therefore approximately 30 min for 26 apps (i.e., 11 and 19 min for the training and test phase, respectively).

5.2 Participants

We selected three groups of participants to evaluate our prediction models' accuracy and app installation suggestions.

The first group includes S&P experts who work in academic institutions. For the recruitment process, we send the invitation email to the members of different S&P research groups. Specifically, we collected feedback from 51 S&P experts in different countries (e.g., USA, Italy, Switzerland, Germany, Belgium, Greece, Vietnam, Morocco). Participants have an average age of 28.9 (from 24 to 42). 84.31% of them were male (43 participants). Among the 51 participants, 14 are lecturers/professors, whereas the others are Ph.D. students and post-docs.

The participants in the first group have a strong background in security and privacy. However, not all of them work on software or mobile development. Therefore, to check if this background impacts the results, IT workers were selected as the second group to assess the predictions of our models. We collected high-quality feedback from 90 IT workers, junior and senior developers in industrial institutions from different countries (e.g., France, Singapore, Vietnam, Taiwan, Australia). IT workers have an average age of 29.6 (between 23 and 38). Among these participants, 18.88% (17 participants) were female. For the geographical distribution, 86.67% are working in Asian countries (78 participants), whereas the remaining participants are working in European countries (10 participants - 11.11%) and Australia (2 participants - 2.22%).

The third group aims at ensuring a good number of participants from different regions, nationalities, ages, and educational levels. At this purpose, we used the Microworkers crowdsourcing platform[15] for the enrollment of participants (called workers). To achieve diversity in evaluating the prediction models, we selected participants from five different regions. The regions are Latin America (e.g., Brazil, Argentina, Venezuela), USA - Western (e.g., USA, Canada, Australia), Western Europe (e.g., Italy, Spain, France), Eastern Europe (e.g., Poland, Greece, Hungary), Asia & Africa (e.g., Singapore, Vietnam, Ethiopia). For each geographic area, we try to balance gender, nationalities, ages, and educational levels. Specifically, we received 60 feedback per geographic area - a total of 300 participants - 157 - of them 52.33% were male. The participants came from 81 countries (e.g., UK, Italy, India, Spain, Portugal, USA), with an average age of 28.2, being the oldest worker 48, and the youngest 18. Also, they have different educational levels (e.g., student, bachelor) and backgrounds (e.g., accountant, teacher, manager). Moreover, nearly 60% of the participants reported to have a bachelor's degree or equivalent, whereas 10% of them had a master's degree or a Ph.D. The workers were given $1.5 for each successful feedback.

As the proposed approach depends on the participants' input on the training and testing datasets, we removed low-quality feedback. We use three characteristics to detect low-quality feedback: time to complete the survey, the number of labelled apps, and the workers corresponding answers. Therefore, we measured how much time a user devotes to give feedback for an app. If it was less than a desirable time (1 min/app), we suspect that the participant did not read the app's information carefully; thus, his/her feedback was removed from the dataset. As we want to analyze the accuracy and satisfaction level for all four approaches, participants' feedback was considered only when they have evaluated

[15] https://www.microworkers.com/.

all 26 apps. Finally, we removed feedback from participants that gave a unique label to all apps (e.g., Maybe for all the 26 apps). In total, we removed 45 low-quality feedback from 8 experts, 7 IT workers, and 30 crowd workers.

5.3 Evaluation

To evaluate the effectiveness of the proposed learning approaches, we measure the accuracy, precision, recall and F1 (see Appendix A for more details).

In the first experiment, we compare the accuracy of the proposed prediction models, namely naive, category-based, simple ensemble-based, and advanced ensemble-based. In the second experiment, we compare the accuracy obtained by our semi-supervised approaches with the ones obtained through traditional supervised learning techniques (i.e., Linear Regression, Random Forest, and SVM).

Prediction Models' Accuracy. In this experiment, we test the accuracy of PriApp-Install prediction models in labelling target apps. As shown in Fig. 2, around 72.22%, 76.72% and 78.27% of S&P experts, **crowd workers**, and IT workers' choices in labeling app installation are correctly predicted by the naive prediction model, respectively. It is the lowest accuracy of the four prediction models. Whereas, simple ensemble-based and advanced ensemble-based have the highest accuracy, with around 89.22% and 92.89% for S&P experts, 86.24% and 84.79% for crowd workers, and 86.29% and 84.21% for IT workers. For the remaining models, approximately 78.04%, 79.63%, and 80.04% of the labeling predictions done by the category-based model are made correctly for crowd workers, S&P experts, and IT workers, respectively. This experiment shows that the performance of both ensemble approaches is better than those of the other approaches. In particular, the ensemble-based approaches capture the app installation behavior of S&P experts with outstanding accuracy (about 90%). It highlights that relationships among elements of an app play a vital role in the participants' decisions.

Satisfaction Level. For this experiment, the web application showed participants a set of apps with the labels generated by our prediction models and asked them if they were satisfied with the model decisions. In the testing phase, 16 target apps and corresponding predictions were presented to participants (4 apps for each approach, randomly presented to the participants).

As shown in Fig. 3, around 66.67% of S&P experts, 62.80% of crowd workers, and 77.84% of IT workers are satisfied with the decisions taken using the naive prediction model, and this represents the lowest satisfaction level of the four prediction models; whereas around 73.15%, 79.63%, and 81.13% are fine with the decisions taken using the category-based prediction model. The highest satisfaction levels are obtained with the ensemble-based prediction models. Specifically, the satisfaction level of the decisions taken by advanced ensemble-based model

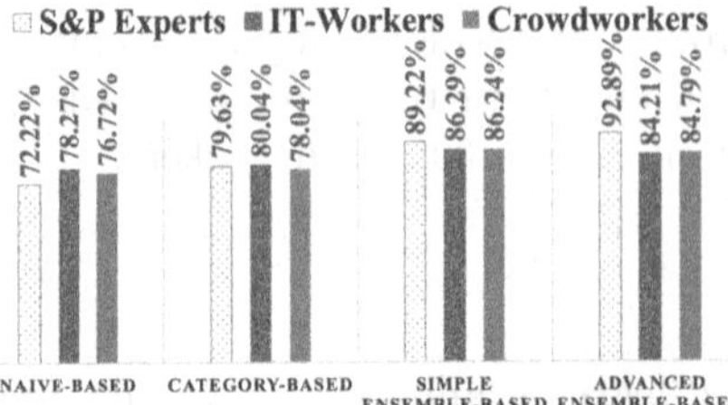

Fig. 2. Four prediction models' accuracy

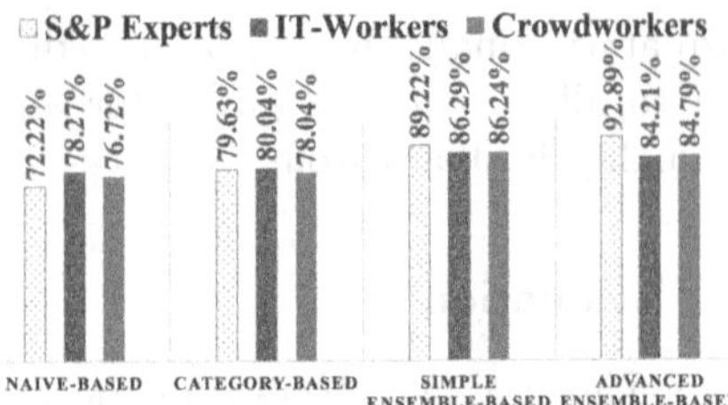

Fig. 3. Participants satisfaction level

ranges from 80.69% (crowd workers) to 94.51% (S&P experts); whereas, the satisfaction level of the simple ensemble-based model ranges from 80.16% (crowd workers) to 93.46% (S&P experts). This experiment further confirms that ensemble approaches outperform the others.

The difference between the two ensemble-based approaches is that if the simple ensemble-based approach considers essential relationships among the app's features of the same type, the advanced ensemble-based approach considers a combination of dimensions. These relationships may affect the app installation decision of the participants. Indeed, some participants' feedback points out that combining the app's fields (which is exploited by the ensemble-based prediction models) is essential for predicting the labels of target apps. For instance, **Expert 27**: *"I will install the app if it does not collect my location ... the collected data is used for healthcare purposes"*; **Crowd 181**: *"I don't want to use apps that collect too much personal information and share it with third parties..."*; or **IT-worker 31**: *"... In the same app's category, I only install the app in the same app's category if I know the collected data and its purposes ..."*.

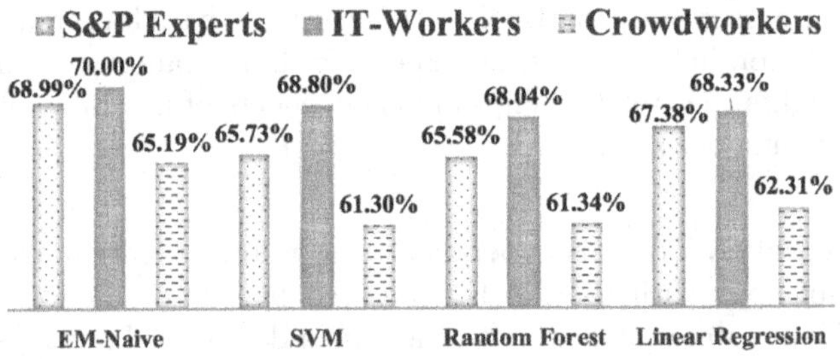

Fig. 4. Accuracy of the EM-based naive prediction models vs SVM, Random Forest, and Linear Regression

Supervised vs. Semi-supervised Learning. As mentioned in Sect. 3, we select semi-supervised EM as our learning approach, because we aim at reducing participant burden on the training dataset. Nevertheless, we also tested the performance of hard clustering supervised machine learning techniques. For this purpose, we compare the accuracy of our EM-based naive prediction model against three supervised hard-clustering algorithms, namely Linear Regression, Random Forest, and SVM. We use the naive prediction model to compare since it is the weakest among the four proposed models. The naive approach exploits all app's features to define the prediction model. Figure 4 shows the results, with a training dataset consisting of 6 apps and a testing dataset of 16 apps. We randomly selected 6 training apps instead of 10 since we would like to analyze the performance given a small training dataset. The results show that the performance of our naive prediction model is the highest for the three participant groups (see Fig. 4). Moreover, the accuracy of the three supervised hard-clustering prediction models is less than that of the naive prediction model because these models need more extensive training datasets for the prediction process. This motivates us to use semi-supervised rather than supervised learning.

Table 4. Comparison of the four prediction models for the test dataset

		Naive prediction model			Category-based prediction model			Simple ensemble-based prediction model			Advanced ensemble-based prediction model		
		Y (%)	N (%)	M (%)	Y (%)	N (%)	M (%)	Y (%)	N (%)	M (%)	Y (%)	N (%)	M (%)
S&P experts (N = 51)	Precision	63.38	82.61	71.05	78.79	81.54	78.82	92.31	86.49	88.46	94.53	86.36	94.87
	Recall	90.00	60.00	76.06	69.33	85.48	84.81	83.72	96.97	88.46	95.28	95.00	84.09
	F1	74.38	69.51	73.46	73.76	83.47	81.71	87.81	91.43	88.46	94.90	90.48	89.16
IT workers (N = 90)	Precision	83.33	67.54	84.19	75.48	85.50	80.00	91.18	89.10	76.92	81.11	87.50	91.22
	Recall	75.43	81.91	78.17	81.25	75.68	82.76	81.58	89.10	90.10	94.81	68.86	74.29
	F1	79.19	74.94	81.07	78.26	80.29	81.36	86.11	89.10	83.33	87.45	77.06	81.89
Crowd workers (N = 300)	Precision	79.12	74.59	76.43	74.61	80.70	79.04	87.35	84.02	87.23	85.06	81.73	86.00
	Recall	82.42	71.65	76.43	78.28	76.35	79.34	86.54	88.26	83.25	94.05	66.93	73.71
	F1	80.74	73.09	76.43	76.40	78.46	79.19	86.94	86.13	85.19	89.33	73.59	79.38

F1 Measure. Finally, we measure the F_1 score for each label (Y, N, M) in the test datasets (see Table 4). F_1 score considers both the precision and the recall aspects (see Table 6 in Appendix A). Our analysis proves that both ensemble-based approaches work better than naive and category-based for the test dataset. It means that combining multiple aspects/classifiers helps predict participants' app installation decisions better for both participants with and without a security/privacy background.

From our experiments, we obtain an accuracy for the three participant groups ranging between 86.24% and 92.89%. We believe that this is acceptable since we strike a balance between the user burden and the prediction quality. However, we plan to improve our tool by testing alternative prediction models, especially for less skilled participants.

When a user decides to install Pri-App Install on his/her smartphone, it takes approx 11 min to train the tool (with 10 sample apps) in such a way that it learns the privacy preferences of the user w.r.t the app's installation. This training phase, although time-consuming, is done only once when the tool is installed.

6 Related Work

Literature offers several proposals for app recommendation. For instance, some papers propose tools to determine if target apps are benign based on over-privileged apps' detection. As an example, Taylor et al. [17,18] propose a contextual permission analysis tool, called SecuRank, which allow users to detect if any of their installed apps could be replaced with functionally similar apps that collect less sensitive data. By running SecuRank on the app market, they found that up to 50% of privacy-breaching apps could be replaced with more privacy-preserving apps.

Exploiting the same approach, Tingmin et al. [23] introduces the PERSCRIPTION platform that aims to replace the app's description with a new personalized one based on users' preferences on security concerns and linguistic preferences. More precisely, to model user's security concerns, given a target app, PERSCRIPTION asks user to label as grant/deny all app's default permissions. Additionally, to generate the personalised description w.r.t. linguistic preferences, PERSCRIPTION classifies users into distinct personalities based on their behaviors. Specifically, they considered five personality traits models [4], (e.g., Extraversion, Agreeableness, Conscientiousness, Neuroticism, and Openness) to bridge between the users' mobile behaviours (i.e., app adoption) and linguistic preferences. To each personality a set of preferred words (linguistic preference) is associated. The final app's description is then generated by using proper words, based on users personality and highlighting risky permissions.

Zhiqiang et al. [24] proposes the FideDroid framework that predicts permissions needed by an app by analyzing its description. After that, FideDroid compares the inferred permissions with those marked as suspicious and unnecessary by determining whether the predicted permissions from the app's description are used in the app's code. Moreover, Huseyin et al. [1] proposes a model, called Attention, to discover inconsistencies between the app's descriptions and the requested permissions, by leveraging on recurrent neural networks (RNNs) [5].

However, all the above-mentioned approaches: (a) only estimate the risk of installing an app without considering the possible benefits; and (b) only consider the app's requested permissions that do not accurately describe the actual behavior of an app w.r.t. the consumption of personal data. Indeed, many studies (e.g., [10]) have shown that apps could actually exploit more permissions than what they provide in the app market.

Other approaches take this issue into account by leveraging on app's code analysis. For instance, Zhang et al. [26] develops a cloud-based system, called Privet, that logs app's behavior w.r.t resources' usage (e.g., CPU, memory) and personal data collection (e.g., location, media). For dangerous API usages, Zhuo et al. [13] exploits static analysis to generate a graph representation of the data flow among API classes and possibly personal data collection. These graphs are trained on a set of malicious and benign apps. The two graphs are then compared to determine the set of dangerous APIs. Son et al. [15,16] leverage an app's static analysis to model an app's behavior w.r.t data collection on the basis of APIs, classes, functions, and constant usage. They measure an app's risk level by quantifying how much the app's behaviour diverges from the behavior of most apps in the same category.

Although those approaches show some similarities with our proposal, in that we also leverage on static analysis to have a more precise assessment of the app's collected personal data (that we borrow from [15]), all these approaches only estimate the privacy risk connected to a target app. In contrast, the goal of our proposal is not to propose yet another privacy risk measure for mobile apps. Rather, we design a tool that learns from end users their preferences w.r.t app's installation. This tool can complement the risk analysis performed by the above mentioned approaches. Learning takes into account not only the privacy risk of an app (in terms of personal data it consumes and share with third parties), but also the benefits an app can provide (in terms of delivered service), as well as the subjective aptitude that each user might have towards privacy.

7 Conclusion

This paper proposed PriApp-Install, a tool to guide users in selecting the apps to install on their smartphones based on their subjective assessment of utility and privacy risks. PriApp-Install leverages semi-supervised learning and a rich set of features to determine user privacy preferences on app's installation. We have experimentally tested our learning approaches by using feedback from different set of participants (i.e., security and privacy experts, IT workers, and crowd workers). The experimental results for ensemble-based approaches are promising. In the future, we plan to perform a more extensive experimental evaluation. We also plan to test more sophisticated learning strategies, such as those combining semi-supervised classification with deep learning. This combination may increase performance by, at the same time, not requiring a considerable amount of resources, time, and effort. Finally, we plan to extend the current approach to be adopted in the Personal Data Storage (PDS) [14] architecture, where users can store and control access to their personal data.

Acknowledgments. This work has received funding from RAIS (Real-time analytics for the Internet of Sports), Marie Skłodowska-Curie Innovative Training Networks (ITN), under grant agreement No 813162 and from CONCORDIA, (Cybersecurity Competence Network) supported by H2020 Research and Innovation program under grant agreement No 830927. The content of this paper reflects only the authors' view and the Agency and the Commission are not responsible for any use that may be made of the information it contains.

Appendix A: Metrics

We use conventional measures to measure the effectiveness of the proposed learning approaches. In particular, since we have classes with three labels (Y, N, and M), we exploit a 3×3 confusion matrix, see Table 5, where columns represent predicted labels, rows possible actual value and cells denote error value (E) or true positive value (TP). From the confusion matrix, we define the evaluation metrics given in Table 6.

Table 5. Confusion matrix

	Predicted value: Y	Predicted value: N	Predicted value: M
Actual value: Y	TP_Y	$E_{Y,N}$	$E_{Y,M}$
Actual value: N	$E_{N,Y}$	TP_N	$E_{N,M}$
Actual value: M	$E_{M,Y}$	$E_{M,N}$	TP_M

Table 6. Metrics definition

$Accuracy$	$(TP_Y + TP_N + TP_M)/\#samples$
Pre_X	$TP_X/(TP_X + E_{N,X} + E_{M,X})$
Re_X	$TP_X/(TP_X + E_{X,N} + E_{X,M})$
$F1_X$	$2{*}\ (Pre_X * Re_X)/(Pre_X + Re_X)$
	where $X \in \{Y, N, M\}$

References

1. Alecakir, H., Can, B., Sen, S.: Attention: there is an inconsistency between Android permissions and application metadata! Int. J. Inf. Secur. **20**, 797–815 (2021)
2. Borman, S.: The expectation maximization algorithm-a short tutorial. Submitted for Publication **41** (2004)
3. Feng, Y., et al.: AC-Net: assessing the consistency of description and permission in Android apps. IEEE Access **7**, 57829–57842 (2019)
4. John, O.P., Srivastava, S., et al.: The Big-Five Trait Taxonomy: History, Measurement, and Theoretical Perspectives, vol. 2. University of California Berkeley (1999)
5. Jones, K.S., et al.: Readings in Information Retrieval. Morgan Kaufmann (1997)
6. Lin, J., et al.: Expectation and purpose: understanding users' mental models of mobile app privacy through crowdsourcing. In: Proceedings of the 2012 ACM Conference on Ubiquitous Computing, pp. 501–510 (2012)
7. Martin, K., Shilton, K.: Putting mobile application privacy in context: an empirical study of user privacy expectations for mobile devices. Inf. Soc. **32**(3), 200–216 (2016)
8. Nguyen, T.T., et al.: Measuring user perception for detecting unexpected access to sensitive resource in mobile apps. In: Proceedings of the 2021 ACM Asia Conference on Computer and Communications Security, pp. 578–592 (2021)
9. Nigam, K., Ghani, R.: Analyzing the effectiveness and applicability of co-training. In: Proceedings of the Ninth International Conference on Information and Knowledge Management, pp. 86–93 (2000)
10. Olukoya, O., et al.: Security-oriented view of app behaviour using textual descriptions and user-granted permission requests. Comput. Secur. **89** (2020)
11. Polikar, R.: Ensemble based systems in decision making. IEEE Circuits Syst. Mag. **6**(3), 21–45 (2006)
12. Polikar, R.: Ensemble learning. In: Zhang, C., Ma, Y. (eds.) Ensemble Machine Learning, pp. 1–34. Springer, Boston (2012). https://doi.org/10.1007/978-1-4419-9326-7_1

13. Singh, A.K., et al.: Experimental analysis of Android malware detection based on combinations of permissions and API-calls. J. Comput. Virol. Hacking Tech. **15**, 209–218 (2019)
14. Singh, B.C., Carminati, B., Ferrari, E.: Privacy-aware personal data storage (P-PDS): learning how to protect user privacy from external applications. IEEE Trans. Dependable Secure Comput. **18**, 889–903 (2019)
15. Son, H.X., Carminati, B., Ferrari, E.: A risk assessment mechanism for Android apps. In: 2021 IEEE International Conference on Smart Internet of Things (SmartIoT), pp. 237–244. IEEE (2021)
16. Son, H.X., Carminati, B., Ferrari, E.: A risk estimation mechanism for Android apps based on hybrid analysis. Data Sci. Eng. **7**, 242–252 (2022)
17. Taylor, V.F., Martinovic, I.: SecuRank: starving permission-hungry apps using contextual permission analysis. In: Workshop on Security and Privacy in Smartphones and Mobile Devices, pp. 43–52 (2016)
18. Taylor, V.F., et al.: There are many apps for that: quantifying the availability of privacy-preserving apps. In: ACM Conference on Security and Privacy in Wireless and Mobile Networks, pp. 247–252 (2017)
19. Triguero, I., García, S., Herrera, F.: Self-labeled techniques for semi-supervised learning: taxonomy, software and empirical study. Knowl. Inf. Syst. **42**(2), 245–284 (2015)
20. Van Engelen, J.E., Hoos, H.H.: A survey on semi-supervised learning. Mach. Learn. **109**(2), 373–440 (2020)
21. Van Kleek, M., et al.: Better the devil you know: exposing the data sharing practices of smartphone apps. In: Proceedings of the 2017 CHI Conference on Human Factors in Computing Systems, pp. 5208–5220 (2017)
22. Wilson, S., et al.: The creation and analysis of a website privacy policy corpus. In: Proceedings of the 54th Annual Meeting of the Association for Computational Linguistics, pp. 1330–1340 (2016)
23. Wu, T., et al.: Catering to your concerns: automatic generation of personalised security-centric descriptions for Android apps. ACM Trans. Cyber-Phys. Syst. **3**(4), 1–21 (2019)
24. Wu, Z., et al.: Enhancing fidelity of description in Android apps with category-based common permissions. IEEE Access **9**, 105493–105505 (2021)
25. Xiao, J., et al.: An Android application risk evaluation framework based on minimum permission set identification. J. Syst. Softw. **163** (2020)
26. Zhang, L.L., et al.: Characterizing privacy risks of mobile apps with sensitivity analysis. IEEE Trans. Mob. Comput. **17**(2), 279–292 (2017)

Network and Web Security

BADPASS: Bots Taking ADvantage of Proxy as a Service

Elisa Chiapponi[1](✉), Marc Dacier[2], Olivier Thonnard[3], Mohamed Fangar[3], and Vincent Rigal[3]

[1] EURECOM, Biot, France
elisa.chiapponi@eurecom.fr
[2] RC3, CEMSE - KAUST, Thuwal, Kingdom of Saudi Arabia
marc.dacier@kaust.edu.sa
[3] Amadeus IT Group, Sophia Antipolis, France
{olivier.thonnard,mohamed.fangar,vincent.rigal}@amadeus.com

Abstract. Web scraping bots are now using so-called Residential IP Proxy (RESIP) services to defeat state-of-the-art commercial bot countermeasures. RESIP providers promise their customers to give them access to tens of millions of residential IP addresses, which belong to legitimate users. They dramatically complicate the task of the existing anti-bot solutions and give the upper hand to the malicious actors. New specific detection methods are needed to identify and stop scrapers from taking advantage of these parties. This work, thanks to a 4 months-long experiment, validates the feasibility, soundness, and practicality of a detection method based on network measurements. This technique enables contacted servers to identify whether an incoming request comes directly from a client device or if it has been proxied through another device.

Keywords: Web scraping · Residential IP Proxy · RESIP · Round trip time measurement · TLS · Security · Bots

1 Introduction

Nowadays, websites in different domains, such as e-commerce, ticketing, and social media, are engaged in a persistent fight against subtle but damaging actors: scraping bots. They produce a significant amount of traffic towards these websites producing large financial losses, as explained in recent works [16,23].

Lately, scrapers behind these bots have started to take advantage of IP addresses from Residential IP Proxy (RESIP) providers, as explained in [18]. RESIP providers announce to have access to tens of millions of devices belonging to real users. These device IPs[1] can be used as exit points of requests.

This situation is problematic for scraped websites because these IPs addresses belong to legitimate users. Online companies are reluctant to block traffic from

[1] In the rest of the paper, we will use IP and IP address interchangeably.

C. Su et al. (Eds.): ISPEC 2022, LNCS 13620, pp. 327–344, 2022.
https://doi.org/10.1007/978-3-031-21280-2_18

IP addresses that could come from potential customers. As a result, more and more scrapers can perpetuate their activities without being stopped.

To limit the actions of scrapers taking advantage of RESIP services, it is important to find new techniques to distinguish whether or not a connection is proxied through a device or comes directly from it. Very recently, some attempts were made to leverage the behavioral differences between the two types of connections by using machine learning [37]. Differently from it, we propose a RESIP detection method based on the evaluation of the Round Trip Time (RTT) difference of the TLS and TCP packets exchanges.

Our intuition is based on a difference at the transport layer among direct and proxied connections. In the second case, two distinct TCP sessions are built (scraper-RESIP and RESIP-target server). In a direct connection, only one TCP session is created (scraper-server). On the other hand, only one TLS session is put in place in both scenarios. In proxied connections, TLS packets are just forwarded by the RESIP and TLS is end-to-end between scraper and server, as in direct connections.

This difference is reflected on the RTT at TCP and TLS layers. The RTT gives us information on the distance[2] between the sender and the receiver. In case of a proxied connection, the sender of the TCP packets differs from the sender of the TLS ones, creating discrepancies between the two RTT values. In a direct connection, the two values are similar. We exploit this aspect to design our detection method.

Our idea, simple and straightforward in theory, could not work in practice if the typical variations of the TCP RTT were of the same order of magnitude of the differences between the TLS RTT and the TCP RTT. This is why we have run a long and thorough experiment to assess the feasibility of the approach. In this work, we show the successful results we have obtained.

The contributions of this paper are twofold:

- We propose a novel server-side proxy detection technique based on the evaluation of the RTT difference between TCP and TLS RTT values.
- We provide experimental results demonstrating the feasibility, reliability, and practicality of this solution, based on the results of a 4 months-long measurement campaign.

Our paper is structured as follows. Section 2 illustrates the state of the art regarding scraping bots and RESIP services as well as RTT based proxy detection methods. Section 3 describes the experimental infrastructure, the detection method and the details of the campaign. Section 4 provides obtained results while Sect. 5 discusses the stability and practicality of the method. Section 6 concludes the paper and offers thoughts for future work.

[2] To be exact, the RTT is a measure of time, from which we can infer an approximation of the distance [20,26,32].

2 State of the Art

2.1 Scraping Bots Exploiting RESIP Services

Existing anti-bot solutions leverage several different techniques to detect bots [13,14]. In the past years, RESIP companies have emerged and scrapers have started using them for their activities. In [27], Li et al. show that more than half of the bot IP addresses they collected with their honeypots belong to residential networks. As explained in [16], current detection techniques struggle in blocking bots using such IPs.

In 2020, Mi et al. proposed the first comprehensive study of RESIP services [28]. They created an infiltration framework to study 5 RESIP providers and their IPs. Our infrastructure is similar to theirs, but it is used differently: we take network measurements of the connections and we use them to validate a new detection method.

The dataset provided by Mi et al. has been used for subsequent studies [17, 21], focused on geo-localization and reputation of IP addresses. Yang et al. [39], recently investigated Chinese RESIP services and their IP addresses. Chiapponi et al. [15] performed a mathematical analysis of IP addresses hypothesized to belong to RESIP providers, examining the repetitions of IP addresses. Study and detection of software used in devices to enroll them as RESIP GATEWAYs have been investigated in recent publications [29,34].

Very recently, a blog post from the anti-bot company DataDome [37], proposed a new ML based approach to identify RESIP connections. They claim that RESIP IPs exhibit a different behavior compared to residential IPs used only by humans, even when the IPs are shared by the two categories. Thanks to an infrastructure similar to ours, they collect RESIP IPs. Every time they detect one of these IPs sending them requests, the ML model checks if the request exhibits RESIP behavior. This approach, differently from ours based on network measurements, is intriguing and might prove to be effective. However, their blog post only offers a high-level overview of the behavioral features used. Furthermore accuracy, false positive and false negative values are not provided.

2.2 Proxy Detection Based on RTT

Our detection method relies on the comparison of the TCP and TLS RTT, measured between packets that are exchanged within a TLS session. To the best of our knowledge, we are the first ones to have implemented this technique and to have conducted a thorough measurement campaign to assess its feasibility.

Using some form of RTT measurement for proxy detection has been proposed before, though. For instance, Hoogstraaten [22] suggests that comparing the RTT of the application layer and the transport layer could potentially indicate the presence of a proxy. He advises to calculate the application RTT by retrieving consecutive elements from the server (e.g. HTML page and associate image) using HTTP. As far as we know, this technique was not implemented and this approach is different from the one we propose. Indeed, this method requires changes in the application code and only works if some specific assumptions hold (no caching in the proxy, no parallel requests to retrieve both objects, etc.). Our technique, on the other hand, does not require any modification of the original server code because it leverages the exchanges that normally take place in a TLS connection.

In another blog post [24], the author suggests a proxy detection based only on the measurement of the TLS RTT (ignoring the TCP RTT) which could, possibly, work thanks to an implementation issue in chromium-based browsers. His technique takes advantage of JavaScript code running at the client-side. The code queries 5 times both 127.0.0.1 and 0.0.0.0 with HTTPS. In the case of direct connections, the RTT of the two connections are comparable. When the connection is proxied, there should be a relevant difference between the two measurements. This technique is different from ours for various reasons. Our detection method does not require any code running at the client-side, is independent from the client application or operating system, and is solely based on measurements obtained at the server-side. No additional URL needs to be queried and the comparison of RTT values is performed between the TCP and TLS RTTs of a single connection.

Other works leverage similar approaches. In [38], a RTT at the application layer is calculated by fetching an HTTP object that cannot be cached. A patent [35] performs the detection with the comparison of the RTTs obtained when fetching a cached and a non cached object. Our approach, in contrast to the described ones, works completely at the server-side, does not require fetching any object and uses the more stable TCP and TLS RTTs as opposed to the ones at the application layer.

In summary, previous works have considered using some form of RTT measurement to detect proxied connections. However, they all require either modification of the server code and/or some JavaScript to be executed on the client-side. Our proposal, in contrast, is exclusively based on passive measurement made at the server-side, which does not need to be modified in any way. Furthermore, contrary to our work, none of the previous works compares the TCP RTT to the TLS one.

3 Setup and Methodology

3.1 Infrastructure

The goal of our experiments is to validate a detection technique for scrapers using RESIP services. To achieve this result, we have created an infrastructure that reproduces the real-world conditions scrapers experience when using such services. RESIP infrastructures are merely instruments in the hands of scrapers. Scrapers cannot access their internal parts and change their functioning, they can just rent the provided service using a well-defined API. Similarly, RESIP providers take advantage of real people devices that they cannot access directly. Thus, they cannot alter their hardware and they can only use application-level features. These constraints create a fixed environment in which scrapers have to send their requests. Our infrastructure reproduces these conditions and enables

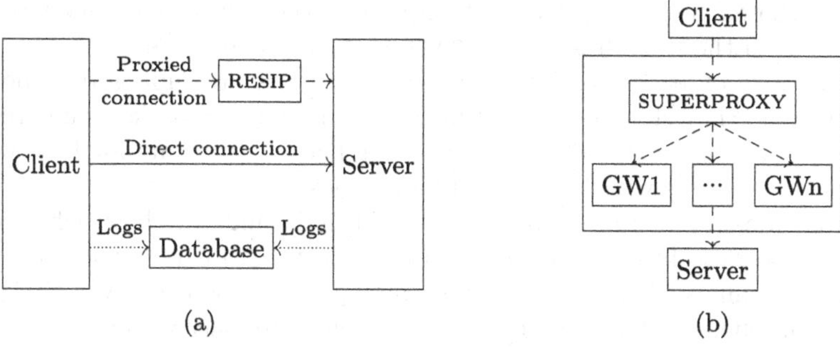

Fig. 1. Infrastructure schema (a) and internal structure of RESIP (b)

us to perform network measurements that are representative of those observed in real-world scraping traffic carried out through RESIP proxies.

As shown in Fig. 1a, our infrastructure includes: a client sending requests to a target server, a target server, a RESIP provider, and a database.

The client, which represents the scraper, sends requests either directly to the server (Direct connection) or through a RESIP provider (Proxied connection) of which we purchased the services. On the other side of the connection, the server analyses each received query at the application and network layers. The client and the server locally produce logs and send them to a database where they are aggregated and processed.

22 machines and 4 RESIP providers constitute the core of the infrastructure. Section 3.2 discusses the examined RESIP services. Configuration, location, and roles of our clients and servers are explained in Sect. 3.3. Section 3.4 and Sect. 3.5 outline the performed network measurements and the detection technique. Section 3.6 describes the timeline and data storage of the experiment.

3.2 RESIP Providers

Thanks to the information provided by analysts and companies working against scraping bots as well as online blogs devoted to web scraping activities, we have identified 4 RESIP providers widely used by scrapers: Bright Data [3], Oxylabs [6], Proxyrack [8], and Smartproxy [10].

The four services offer different packages and options. We subscribed to each of them to have 40 GB (Bright Data) and 50 GB (the other providers) of (incoming+outgoing) traffic per month proxied through residential IP addresses.

The details about the internal implementation of RESIP services are not known. From the information available on their websites, the four providers appear to have a similar architecture. As displayed in Fig. 1b, the client sends the HTTP/HTTPS request to the SUPERPROXY, through an HTTP CONNECT. The SUPERPROXY forwards the request to one of the residential GATEWAYs (GW1,..., GWn). It is not known if there are other machines in between these two parties. The chosen GATEWAY sends the request to the server. The server receives a request with the IP address of the GATEWAY as source address.

In the case of HTTPS connections, RESIP services are supposed to perform SSL tunneling: they should not decrypt and re-encrypt the packets they receive. They act as a circuit GATEWAY by forwarding packets back and forth between 2 distinct TCP sessions while changing IP addresses.

We have experimentally confirmed that this is, indeed, their behavior. To do so, we have established a connection through the 4 RESIP services to one of our servers configured to never send any ACK packet. The three-way handshake between our client and SUPERPROXY always completes successfully, whereas the one between GATEWAY and server does not. This confirms that two distinct TCP connections are created. Then, we have checked if the request sent by the client and the one received by the server have the same encryption and that the Session ID is the same in the "ClientHello" and "ServerHello" messages of the TLS protocol. This check has given us a positive result, confirming that the session is not decrypted and re-encrypted by the proxy.

3.3 Clients and Servers

Each of our machines plays both the roles of client and server described in Fig. 1a. In this way, we maximize the number of different client-server paths covered in our experiment. To avoid any possible geographical or vendor bias, our clients and servers are spread all over the world and are rented from two different suppliers: we use 16 machines from Amazon Lightsail and 6 from Azure. We host two machines in each of the following locations: India, Australia, Japan, Germany, Ireland, Canada, USA (Virginia and Oregon), South Africa, United Arab Emirates, and Brazil. The last three locations correspond to the machines acquired from Azure.

We have implemented both client and server algorithms in Python3. The server has been built thanks to the ThreadingHTTPServer and BaseHTTPRequestHandle of the library http.server [4]. We have modified the source code to insert a timeout for connections not completing the TCP handshake. For the client, the library urllib [11] is used both to perform direct and proxied connections.

The client algorithm consists of an infinite loop. According to the speed set in the configuration file, queries are sent to each server in the experiment. Each machine is queried five times, with one direct connection and four proxied ones, one per provider. The query is performed with an HTTPS GET.

To communicate the IP address of the client to the server as well as information on the RESIP provider used, we encode it into the requested URL. We assign a unique numeric code to each machine, from 01 to 22. We also assign a numeric code to each RESIP provider, from 1 to 4. Direct connections have code 0. Every time we need to perform a request, we obtain a random sequence of 5 digits. We XOR this random sequence with the concatenation of client, proxy, and server codes. The final URL is the concatenation of the XORED and the random values.

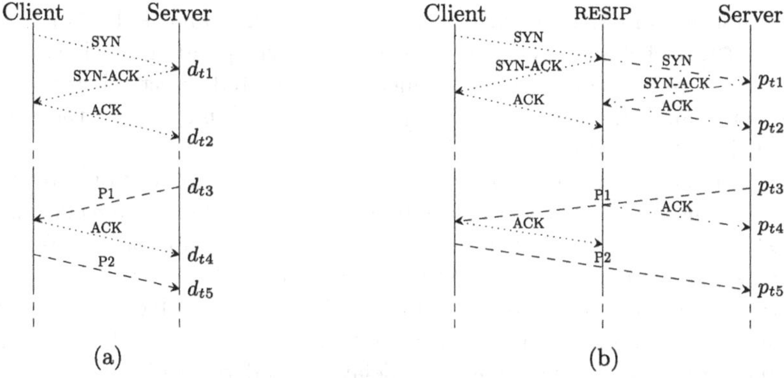

Fig. 2. TCP and TLS packet exchanges used in the detection technique for a) direct and b) proxied connections.

The server algorithm keeps listening for new incoming HTTPS connections on port 443. At launch time, an option can be used to specify if the server uses TLS1.2 or TLS1.3. Every time a new HTTPS GET request arrives, the URL is studied to check if it is part of the experiment (as opposed to, e.g. a scanner or a crawler) and to retrieve the client, proxy, and server codes. Requests not passing the check are answered with an error page. Otherwise, a simple page is delivered.

3.4 Network Measurements

In each machine, a sniffer is put in place to collect network measurements. The sniffer parses each incoming packet to port 443. It is implemented in Python3, thanks to the library PyShark [25]. It is restarted every hour for the stability of the code and to avoid increasing memory consumption. Information about packets is saved in a structure representing the corresponding stream.

For each incoming stream, we use the RTT to measure how far from each other[3] the parties taking part in the communication are. The explanation of these measurements is illustrated by the schema in Fig. 2. Figure 2a shows the packets in the TCP (on top) and the TLS (on the bottom) exchanges that we use for detection in case of direct connection. Dotted lines represent TCP packets, dashed lines the TLS ones. Figure 2b presents the same exchanges in the case of proxied connection. Dotted lines represent TCP packets between the client and RESIP, dash-dotted lines stand for TCP packets between RESIP and server, and dashed lines show the TLS connections. d_{tx} and p_{tx} represent the timestamp measurements of the sending/arrival of a packet at the server for direct (d_{tx}) and proxied (p_{tx}) connections.

[3] For sake of concision, we take the liberty of using the expression "measure of distance" instead of "approximation of the measure of distance" when referring to the RTT in the rest of the paper.

The first measurement we take is the TCP RTT. This value is the RTT between the SYN-ACK packet sent by the server and the corresponding received ACK. In case of direct connection, the TCP connection is created directly between client and server. Thus, the TCP RTT (d_{t2}-d_{t1} in Fig. 2a) is a measure of the distance between these two parties.

By contrast, in a proxied connection, two distinct TCP connections are created (Sect. 3.2). One connection takes place between client and SUPERPROXY, and one between GATEWAY and server. In this scenario, the TCP RTT (p_{t2}-p_{t1} in Fig. 2b) represents the distance between GATEWAY and server.

Network delays can increase the RTT value of the first TCP exchange, both in direct and proxied connections. In this case, the measured TCP RTT is the sum of the real RTT of the exchange plus the delay. To understand how this delay can influence our analysis, we collect the RTT for all packets sent by the server. We calculate statistics of these values that we use in Sect. 4 to discuss the variability of the TCP RTT within a given connection.

Secondly, we compute the TLS RTT. This value corresponds to the RTT of the TLS layer. The TLS protocol is end-to-end between client and server both in case of direct and proxied connection. Thus, this metric should give us the measure of the distance between client and server in all scenarios.

To obtain the TLS RTT, we consider two packets, P1 and P2. P1 contains a server TLS record after which the server does not send any other TLS records before receiving a specific TLS answer, as per the protocol. P2 is the packet containing the client TLS record that allows the continuation of the protocol. Any couple of TLS packets that satisfy these conditions can be considered.

As explained in Sect. 3.1, the RESIP architecture can be considered fixed for our scenario. Thus, the only variables that can influence the choice of P1 and P2 are the server and client implementations. Our detection method is server-side and we assume anyone recreating this experiment will have full access and knowledge of the server implementation. In the TLS connection, the server decides which information is needed for the client to complete the connection e.g. accepting the cipher proposed by the client or deciding if client authentication is required. In such conditions, we expect to be able to anticipate all the possible exchanges between client and server to find a couple of packets and cover possible corner cases. For these reasons, having full control over the client in our experiment, contrary to the real-world case, does not constitute a bias.

In our setup, we have a generic HTTP server, which does not require any client authentication and accepts common encryption ciphers. We expect this to be a common scenario for scraped websites that need to be accessed by the largest possible number of clients. In these conditions, we can identify P1 and P2 among the first TLS packets. This is an added value because it enables us to perform detection before any application content is delivered to the client.

Hereafter, we focus on the TLS records we use to perform our measurement. We refer to [31] for an accurate and detailed description of TLS.

Depending on the version of TLS, we use different TLS records to identify P1 and P2. For TLS1.2, the RFC 5246 [19] states that, after sending the "ServerHelloDone" TLS message, the server waits for a client response. We recognize P1 as the packet containing the TLS record encapsulating this message.

After the "ServerHelloDone" message, the client needs to continue the communication. The first TLS message sent by the client must be the "ClientKeyExchange", according to the RFC [19]. We identify P2 as the packet whose TLS record contains this TLS message.

In TLS1.3, if the server agrees on the cipher chosen by the client, it sends the "ServerHello" TLS message. Since the server has already obtained the client-side information for encryption, subsequent data in the message is encrypted. We choose P1 as the packet whose TLS record contains the last encrypted server data sent after the "ServerHello" message.

As explained in Appendix D of RFC 8446 [33], TLS1.3 implementations include a dummy "change_cipher_spec" TLS record to guarantee backward compatibility for middleboxes. This record is sent by the client before its encrypted handshake flight if the client does not offer early data and it does not send a second "ClientHello" message. In our implementation, the server imposes these conditions and thus "change_cipher_spec" TLS record is the first client TLS record sent upon reception of the "ServerHello" TLS message. We identify P2 as the packet containing this record.

We define the TLS RTT as the difference between the sending of P1 and the arrival of P2 at the server. As shown in Fig, 2, this corresponds to the difference d_{t5}-d_{t3} in the case of direct connection and p_{t5}-p_{t3} in the case of proxied one[4].

3.5 The Detection Method

In this section, we present our approach for detecting connections passing through RESIP services. The method is based on the study of RTT measurements.

As described in Sect. 3.4, for each incoming connection, the server collects the TCP RTT and the TLS RTT. As previously discussed, these two metrics give us measures of distances. TCP RTT informs about the distance between client and server, for direct connections. In the case of a proxied connection, this value represents the distance between a RESIP GATEWAY and a server. TLS RTT represents the distance between a client and a server in both scenarios.

Our intuition is that the TLS RTT is similar to the TCP RTT in the case of a direct connection. On the contrary, we expect a difference between the two values for a proxied one. When a proxy is used, the TLS RTT represents the sum

[4] The reader may wonder why we are not using the arrival of the ACK packet of P1 as the second point of measurement (d_{t4} and d_{t4}, in Fig. 2). In case of proxied connection, there are two distinct TCP connections (client-SUPERPROXY and GATEWAY-server, as explained in Sect. 3.2). The ACK packet is created by the kernel and it is sent at the arrival of P1 at the GATEWAY, without synchronization with the client-SUPERPROXY TCP connection. Hence, the difference p_{t5}-p_{t4} represents the distance between GATEWAY and server and not the one between client and server.

of the distances between the parties plus the increased distance imposed by the traversal of the RESIP infrastructure, starting from a, possibly, far away gateway.

Indeed, in the RESIP setup, the connection passes through, at least[5], two more points (SUPERPROXY and GATEWAY), before arriving at the destination. In this scenario, the total distance is the sum of the distances client-SUPERPROXY, SUPERPROXY-GATEWAY, and GATEWAY-server. Depending on the geo-localization of the client, SUPERPROXY, GATEWAY, and server, packets could take a much longer route to arrive at the destination, with respect to a direct connection.

We define RTT *difference* as the difference between the TLS RTT and the TCP RTT. If this value is systematically, constantly, and significantly higher for proxied connections than direct ones, it offers to the server a mean to know if an incoming connection comes through such proxy or not, and to act accordingly if deemed appropriate.

3.6 Timeline and Data Storage

The experiment was started at 15:00 UTC +0 on 12/01/2022. In this work, we will study only the connections performed till 01/05/2022 at 15:00 UTC +0. Thus, the total number of examined days is 110.

Every day at 00:00 UTC +0, each server is restarted and switches from TLS1.2 to TLS1.3 and vice versa. In this way, we obtain the same amount of data for both protocols.

Initially, only 16 machines from Amazon were part of the experiment. Considering all machines, 10.88 requests/second were sent/received and each RESIP provider was processing 2.18 requests/second. We used these rates to remain below the limits imposed on us by our RESIP subscriptions. On 24/01/2022 at 19:00 UTC +0, we added 6 machines from Azure to our pool. At first, we kept the same rates per client/server. Hence, the rate was 14.96 requests/second and the ratio per RESIP provider was 2.99 requests/second. On 25/01/2022 at 16:00 UTC +0, Bright Data stopped our access to their network and ended our subscription. More details on the motivation for this choice are provided in Appendix A. Since it was not possible to restore this service, on 02/02/2022, we eliminated it from our experiment. We adjusted the rates accordingly and since then, 9.90 requests/second were sent/received for the rest of the experiment. Each RESIP provider processed 2.48 requests/second.

On 07/03/2022 at 00:00 UTC +0, we started collecting more network information to study the variability of our measurements. For each connection, we measure the RTT of all the TCP exchanges.

Occasionally, some machines were restarted by the cloud providers and this resulted in losses of data. We also had some brief synchronization issues, caused by using one port for both TLS1.2 and TLS1.3 server program and switching among them at midnight. Fortunately, this has been an extremely rare event. It

[5] The internal implementations of RESIP services are not known.

has happened, on average, only 1.6 times per machine over the 110 days, with an average loss of only 0.17% of the traffic per machine.

We have created a database with POSTGRESQL [7] to gather the data from the experiment. In the database, we keep a unique record for each connection. This record includes information collected at the client and the server as well as the network measurements.

For each connection, we save the epoch of the client request and the difference between the epoch of the server request and this value, the URL of the connection, the code of the used RESIP, client IP and port, SUPERPROXY IP and port, GATEWAY IP and port, server IP and port. Moreover, we gather the TCP version, TCP RTT, and TLS RTT. We calculate the minimum and maximum RTT of all the TCP packets exchanges and their corresponding positions in the stream.

In total, our clients have generated close to 98M connections but, as explained before, some observed connections were incomplete. Client requests sent when some servers were down only exist in the client-side logs (around 4M). Similarly, some requests are made to our servers from other machines than our clients (e.g. from scanners and crawlers) and, for those, we have no matching record in the client logs (around 200K). Moreover, the sniffer program restarts every hour, and incoming connections arriving at the moment of the switch could have incomplete RTT measurements. We only create a record in our database for connections that exist both in the client and server logs and for which we have no missing field. In other words, we ignore connections for which we have no measurement from the sniffer logs. As a result, we use 95% of the total amount of connections started by the clients which sums up to 92,712,461 connections.

4 Results

In Fig. 3 we show the RTT *differences* for each proxy and for direct connections. To better visualize the RTT *differences* of the majority of the connections, we consider different ranges. 97% of direct connections have an RTT *difference* value lower or equal than 20ms. We use the range [0,20]ms for the x-axis. For proxied connections, we consider instead the RTT differences in the range [0,2000] ms, which amounts to the same percentage of connections.

We can see how for direct connections (Fig. 3e), the difference is always close to zero. In the RESIP plots (Figs. 3a–3d), instead, we can see how the difference varies for proxied connections. It is very important to note that the maximum value of the RTT *difference* (x-axis) in Fig. 3e is 100 times smaller than the ones in the other graphs. The maximum values on the y-axis is at least 3 orders of magnitude larger for direct connections than for the proxied ones. Yet, the total amount of connections has similar values for each proxied and the direct scenario[6]. These results clearly show that direct and proxied connections have dramatically different distributions of RTT *differences*.

6 Except for Bright Data for which we have less traffic due to the early end of the service, as explained in Appendix A.

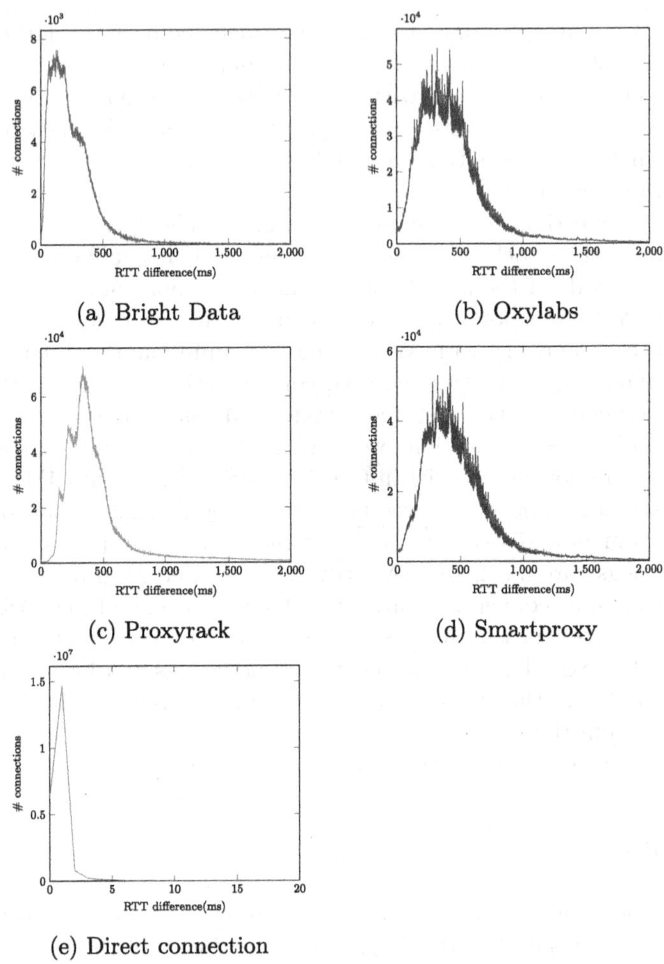

Fig. 3. RTT *difference* of the connections, divided among RESIP and direct ones

Our approach determines if a connection passes through a RESIP provider from the measurement of the RTT *difference*. This measurement is conducted on packets sent and received on the Internet. Thus, network delays could, possibly, negatively impact our approach.

In our experiment, we see connections with negative values for the RTT *difference*. The percentage of the total amount of connections per provider is 2.9%, 0.9%, 1.8%, 0.2%, 1.4%, respectively for direct connections, Bright Data, Oxylabs, Proxyrack and Smartproxy. A negative value of RTT *difference* occurs when the TCP RTT is higher than the TLS RTT. This happens when the SYN-ACK and/or the ACK packets of the TCP connection are delayed but the subsequent packets in the TCP connections are not. Thus, the TLS handshake packets are not delayed.

Similarly, it can also happen that only the TLS packets are delayed while the initial TCP ones are not. In this case, the RTT *difference* increases. This case is visually shown by the long tails of the distributions in Fig. 3. We note that, in the case of proxied connections, the packets participating in the TLS handshake have a longer "journey" than the ones used to compute the TCP RTT. Indeed, the packets travel from the client, through SUPERPROXY and GATEWAY, to the server whereas the latter only travel between GATEWAY and server. Hence, it is more likely to observe *an increase* of the RTT *difference* caused by temporary network congestion rather than *a decrease.* Our experimental results confirm this.

Fortunately, the above-mentioned situations, as reflected by the data of our experiment, are rare. To better understand how the variability of the network could influence our technique, we have studied the variation of the RTT values per connection.

For 56 days, we have collected the RTT of each TCP packet sent by the server and the corresponding ACK. For each connection, we identify the minimum value of RTT and its position within the stream as well as the maximum RTT value and its corresponding position.

For our proxy detection technique to work, the ideal case is to have the minimum RTT in the first exchange and/or to have low variability of its value throughout the connection. Our method could work taking as TCP RTT a RTT value of later exchanges (e.g. the minimum one of an entire connection). However, in this scenario, it would not enable us to detect the RESIP proxy at the very beginning of the connection (to possibly block it).

We have studied the network metrics collected in 45,902,917 connections. The minimum RTT is found in the first exchange in 56% of the connections but, fortunately, the variability is low (relatively to our use case). More than half of the connections (53%) present a difference between the maximum and minimum RTT lower or equal to 50 ms.

We have chosen this value to empirically have a threshold above which we categorize the connections as proxied. After experimenting with different values, we found this to be the best threshold. Beyond being higher than more than half of TCP variations, it induces low values for the False Positive (FPR)[7] and False Negative (FNR)[8] rates. Indeed choosing this threshold we obtain a FPR of 0.04% and a FNR of 1.93%. The corresponding accuracy is 99.01%.

In 29% of the connections, the first RTT is the maximum one among all the exchanges. Despite that, the RTT *difference* shows relevant differences in the case of proxied connections. Let us consider the very unlucky case where all first RTTs would have the highest observed value of that connection. If we compute the RTT *difference* with this value and we choose 50ms as the threshold, we obtain a FPR of 0.01%, a FNR of 9.68%, and an accuracy value of 92.78%. Naturally, the percentage of false negatives increases with respect to our previous results (1.93%), but the accuracy remains high, even in this worst-case scenario.

---

[7] Direct connections flagged as RESIP over the total amount of direct connections.

[8] RESIP connections flagged as direct over the total amount of RESIP connections.

These results show that our technique is robust and can confidently detect RESIP connections even in very unlikely worst-case situations.

For each connection, as explained in Sect. 3.6, we collect the GATEWAY IP address. Studying their distribution per provider with Hilbert Curves [30], we have discovered that they are not uniformly distributed around the world. Naturally, we could fear that this influences the RTT *difference* values calculation. More specifically, we could wonder if the connections between clients and servers that are both in a location in which there is a high number of GATEWAYs of a specific provider could result in a small RTT *difference*. In such scenario, indeed, the added distance by the RESIP infrastructure could be small.

Based on our observations, Bright Data has the majority of its GATEWAYs in ARIN [2] and RIPE [9]. We have checked the RTT *differences* for the connections of this provider from our clients in Virginia to our servers in the same location. Oxylabs and Smartproxy GATEWAYs are mainly registered in LACNIC [5]. We have studied the RTT *difference* distributions between our machines in Brazil. For Proxyrack, whose IPs are mostly registered in AFRINIC [1], we have examined the RTT *differences* between clients and servers in South Africa.

The distributions of the above-mentioned combinations are in line with the other distributions of the same providers. Considering our threshold (50 ms), the FNR value for these combinations is even lower than the one for all the connections (FNR = 0.78%). This data confirms the idea that the detection of RESIP based on the RTT *difference* is a possible and viable method, even when clients, servers, and GATEWAYs are geographically close to each other.

5 Discussion

We propose a new method based on the measurement of the RTT to detect connections coming from RESIP providers. Our results show that this approach is feasible and robust.

The difference between the measurements in case of direct and proxied connections is substantial. 97% of the direct connections have an RTT *difference* lower than 20 ms. In the same interval of RTT *difference* ([0,20] ms), Bright Data, Oxylabs, Proxyrack and Smartproxy connections accounts for, respectively, the 0.6%, 0.4%, 0.05% and 0.3% of the total. Moreover, the accuracy of our method remains high even in conditions of network delays.

Our technique can be easily implemented to protect existing servers because it applies to all connections using TLS1.2 or TLS1.3. Nowadays, more than 79% of websites use HTTPS connections and this percentage grows every year [12]. Thus, we can use our method in the majority of the Internet transactions.

Furthermore, our approach does not need any change in the existing software of the server. The measurement can be done outside the server with a sniffer, as we did in our setup.

Our technique does not detect only connections passing through RESIP services. It recognizes all the tunnel techniques that break the TCP connection between client and server. An example of this is SSH forwarding. Both local and remote forwarding do not provide end-to-end TCP connections and are thus detected with our method.

Generally, secure tunneling solutions do not break TCP, but leverage encapsulation. Tunneling providers guaranteeing anonymization typically use Network Address Translation (NAT) and IPSEC. This technique is nowadays really popular and widely used both in private and commercial networks. Neither NAT devices nor IPSEC, however, do break the TCP connection. Hence, requests passing through a VPN or a NAT device are not classified as proxied by our technique. There are methods, however, to detect these tunnels, such as the ones based on the Maximum Transmission Unit (MTU) analysis [22,36]. It is thus not a convenient solution for RESIP providers to switch to it, in order to avoid our detection.

A widely deployed defense for companies is the Web Application Firewall (WAF). WAFS need to break TLS to study the application content and assess if the communication is allowed to continue. Thus, if a client is behind a WAF, both TCP and TLS between client and server are broken and we see comparable TCP RTT and TLS RTT measurements. These connections are not declared as proxied by our method.

The reader could wonder if RESIP providers could break TLS, as WAF do, to avoid detection through the study of the RTT *difference*. This scenario is technically feasible but, in our opinion, unlikely to occur. Indeed, to do this, the proxy has to establish a TLS connection with the client and another one with our server. If the TLS session with the client terminates at the SUPERPROXY, an additional TLS connection has to be created between SUPERPROXY and GATEWAY. This implies that i) the client has to accept a root certificate that enables the SUPERPROXY or the GATEWAY (depending on where the first TLS session ends) to impersonate any server in the world, ii) the GATEWAY devices are now capable of decrypting (and thus monitoring or modifying) the exchanges between the clients and the servers, iii) the GATEWAY must handle two distinct TLS connections and decrypt/re-encrypt in both directions.

It is improbable that RESIP customers would let a third company observe and possibly modify contents of communications that should normally be encrypted between them and the server. Retrieved content could be modified and this could damage their web scraping activity.

RESIP providers leverage home devices, mobile phones, etc. which they do not own and on which they do not have full control. Furthermore, they must consume as few resources as possible to remain invisible to the owner of these devices. Users accept (consciously or not) to run RESIP software on their machines in moments in which they do not need them (e.g. when they are not using them and they are being charged). The additional burden of having to manage 2 distinct TLS sessions plus the decryption/re-encryption in both of them is likely to be a deterrent for devices' owners.

To be able to impersonate any possible end server, the proxy would have to establish certificates on the fly and to push them to the GATEWAY. Moreover, the client would have to accept the root certificate that would make this possible. While technically feasible, this adds a level of complexity and latency that would hurt the RESIP business and would be a major threat to the client once this root certificate is installed.

For all these reasons, we think breaking TLS would be difficult to implement in the RESIP infrastructure. If RESIP providers were to do that, we could still measure the RTT to the end client by serving HTML pages containing objects that the client would need to request to us. By measuring the time between the sending of the page to the client and the arrival of the request we would have a pretty good approximation of the RTT (objects need to be defined in a way that caching by the proxy would not be possible). Injecting objects for the sake of identifying proxies, as proposed in past work [22,24,35,38], could be leveraged for this. Defeating that scenario would require running a browser-like application on the GATEWAY itself which, for the reasons explained above, would increase even more the complexity of RESIP systems.

The reader could now also wonder whether RESIP providers could just produce delays at the TCP level to evade our detection method. This is not a feasible approach. RESIP providers do not own the devices used to proxy out the requests. They simply leverage them at the application level only. They cannot alter the connection settings of the device and/or do kernel level modifications to increase the TCP RTT.

Another point to raise is that an unexpectedly high delay caused by the certificate validation at the client side could increase the number of false positives. This scenario happens in case the server certificate is not signed by a known trusted party, requiring the client to fetch information online to establish a successful certificate chain. In this scenario, since we have full knowledge of the server, we expect to be able to anticipate this and account that all the real clients will have a somehow fixed delay. The chosen threshold can be then modulated to consider this delay. Moreover, we do not expect this situation to happen often. Scraped websites want to be largely accessed and, thus, use certificates that are widely trusted by their clients.

6 Conclusion and Future Works

In this paper, we provide a new sound method to detect proxied connections through the comparison of the TLS and TCP RTT of a single connection. We show that the method is easy to deploy and stable in case of network delays. We explain how it would be difficult for scrapers behind RESIP to evade it.

The next steps will consist in deploying this detection technique in front of servers suffering from scrapers using RESIP services. This will enable us to assess the real-world effectiveness of the proposed solution.

A Bright Data End of Subscription

In our experiment, we legitimately bought 4 RESIP services to test their infrastructures. Subscriptions were made and paid online. Three out of four providers gave us access to the pool of residential IPs upon payment.

On the other hand, Bright Data did not enable us to use the residential IPs directly after the payment. They asked us to participate in a recorded interview in which we had to explain the motivations of our work and how we wanted to use their infrastructure. We communicated to them that we wanted to test our client and server machines with their infrastructure. The scope was a project we were developing with a third party that did not want to be named at the time. We told them that we would simply perform requests from our client to our server machines, as we did.

However, 13 days after the beginning of the experiment, they paused our subscription telling us that our scenario (targeting our own machines) could "expose their users IPs, which can become a privacy issue". They told us that we would need to disclose additional information about what we were doing and whom we were working with. Since we did not accept to do so, they completely stopped the subscription and they refunded it.

References

1. AFRINIC. https://afrinic.net/
2. ARIN. https://www.arin.net/
3. Bright Data. https://brightdata.com/
4. http.server. https://github.com/python/cpython/blob/3.10/Lib/http/server.py/
5. LACNIC. https://www.lacnic.net/
6. Oxylabs. https://oxylabs.io/
7. POSTGRESQL. https://www.postgresql.org/
8. Proxyrack. https://www.proxyrack.com/
9. RIPE. https://www.ripe.net
10. Smartproxy. https://smartproxy.com/
11. urllib. https://github.com/python/cpython/tree/3.10/Lib/urllib/
12. Usage statistics of Default protocol https for websites. https://w3techs.com/technologies/details/ce-httpsdefault
13. Azad, B.A., Starov, O., Laperdrix, P., Nikiforakis, N.: Web runner 2049: evaluating third-party anti-bot services. In: Proceedings of DIMVA 2020 (2020)
14. Carielli, S., DeMartine, A.: The Forrester New Wave^{TM}: Bot Management, Q1 2020. Technical report, Forrester (2020)
15. Chiapponi, E., Dacier, M., Catakoglu, O., Thonnard, O., Todisco, O.: Scraping airlines bots: insights obtained studying honeypot data. Int. J. Cyber Foren. Adv. Threat Invest. **2**(1), 3–28 (2021)
16. Chiapponi, E., Dacier, M., Thonnard, O., Fangar, M., Mattsson, M., Rigal, V.: An industrial perspective on web scraping characteristics and open issues. In: 2022 52nd Annual IEEE/IFIP International Conference on Dependable Systems and Networks - Supplemental Volume (DSN-S), pp. 5–8 (2022)
17. Choi, J., et al.: Understanding the proxy ecosystem: a comparative analysis of residential and open proxies on the internet. IEEE Access **8**, 111368–111380 (2020)
18. DataDome: Bot IP addresses: 1/3 of bad bots use residential IPs. Here's how to stop them (2022) https://datadome.co/bot-management-protection/one-third-bad-bots-using-residential-ip-addresses/
19. Dierks, T., Rescorla, E.: The Transport Layer Security (TLS) Protocol Version 1.2. RFC 5246, RFC Editor (2008). https://www.rfc-editor.org/rfc/rfc5246.txt, https://www.rfc-editor.org/rfc/rfc5246.txt

20. Gueye, B., Ziviani, A., Crovella, M., Fdida, S.: Constraint-based geolocation of internet hosts. IEEE/ACM Trans. Networking **14**(6), 1219–1232 (2006)
21. Hanzawa, A., Kikuchi, H.: Analysis on malicious residential hosts activities exploited by residential IP proxy services. In: Information Security Applications, pp. 349–361. Springer International Publishing (2020). https://doi.org/10.1007/978-3-030-65299-9_26
22. Hoogstraaten, H.: Evaluating server-side internet proxy detection methods (Msc Thesis) (2018)
23. Imperva: Bad Bot Report 2021. Technical report, Imperva (2021)
24. incolumitas: Is this a valid method to detect Proxies? (2021). https://incolumitas.com/2021/11/26/is-this-a-valid-method-to-detect-proxies/
25. KiwiNet: pyshark. https://github.com/KimiNewt/pyshark
26. Landa, R., Clegg, R.G., Araujo, J.T., Mykoniati, E., Griffin, D., Rio, M.: Measuring the relationships between internet geography and RTT. In: 2013 22nd International Conference on Computer Communication and Networks (ICCCN), pp. 1–7 (2013)
27. Li, X., Azad, B.A., Rahmati, A., Nikiforakis, N.: Good bot, bad bot: characterizing automated browsing activity. In: 2021 IEEE Symposium on Security and Privacy (SP), pp. 1589–1605 (2021)
28. Mi, X., et al.: Resident evil: understanding residential IP proxy as a dark service. In: 2019 IEEE Symposium on Security and Privacy (SP), pp. 1185–1201 (2019)
29. Mi, X., Tang, S., Li, Z., Liao, X., Qian, F., Wang, X.: Your phone is my proxy: detecting and understanding mobile proxy networks. In: Proceedings of NDSS 2021 (2021)
30. Munroe, R.: Map of the Internet (2006). https://xkcd.com/195/
31. Oppliger, R.: SSL and Tls: Theory and Practice, 2nd edn. Second Edition. Artech House Inc, USA (2016)
32. Percacci, R., Vespignani, A.: Scale-free behavior of the Internet global performance. Eur. Phys. J. B - Condensed Matter Complex Syst. **32**(4), 411–414 (2003)
33. Rescorla, E.: The Transport Layer Security (TLS) Protocol Version 1.3. RFC 8446, RFC Editor (2018)
34. Tosun, A., De Donno, M., Dragoni, N., Fafoutis, X.: RESIP host detection: identification of malicious residential IP proxy flows. In: 2021 IEEE International Conference on Consumer Electronics (ICCE), pp. 1–6 (2021)
35. Turgeman, A., Lehmann, Y., Azizi, Y., Novick, I.: Detection of proxy server, United States Patent US10069837B2 (2019). https://patents.google.com/patent/US10069837B2
36. ValdikSS: Detecting VPN (and its configuration!) and proxy users on the server side (2015). https://medium.com/@ValdikSS/detecting-vpn-and-its-configuration-and-proxy-users-on-the-server-side-1bcc59742413
37. Vastel, A.: How to Use Machine Learning to Detect Residential Proxies (2022). https://datadome.co/bot-management-protection/how-to-use-machine-learning-to-detect-residential-proxies/#ML-collecting-dataset
38. Webb, A.T., Reddy, A.L.N.: Finding proxy users at the service using anomaly detection. In: 2016 IEEE Conference on Communications and Network Security (CNS), pp. 82–90 (2016)
39. Yang, M., et al.: An extensive study of residential proxies in China. In: Proceedings of the 2022 ACM SIGSAC Conference on Computer and Communications Security (2022)

A CNN-Based Semi-supervised Learning Approach for the Detection of SS7 Attacks

Orhan Ermis[1(✉)], Christophe Feltus[1], Qiang Tang[1], Hoang Trang[2], Alexandre De Oliveira[2], Cu D. Nguyen[2], and Alain Hirtzig[2]

[1] LIST, Esch-sur-Alzette, Luxembourg
{orhan.ermis,christophe.feltus,qiang.tang}@list.lu
[2] Cyberforce Department, POST, Luxembourg, Luxembourg
{hoang.trang,alexandre.deoliveira,cu.nguyen,alain.hirtzig}@post.lu

Abstract. Over the years many standards were defined to solve the security vulnerabilities of the Signalling Systems No:7 (SS7) protocol. Yet, it still suffers from many security issues that make it vulnerable to attacks such as the disclosure of subscribers' location, fraud, interception of calls or SMS messages. Several security measures employ rule-based solutions for the detection of attacks in telecom core networks. However, they become ineffective when an attacker deploys sophisticated attacks that are not easily detected by filtering mechanisms. One particular solution to overcome those attacks is to use supervised machine learning solutions since they have demonstrated their ability to achieve promising results to detect anomalies in various applications. Nonetheless, they generally need to be trained with a large set of labeled data that cannot be obtained from the telecom operators due to the excessive resource allocation and cost of labeling the network traffic. Therefore, in this work, we propose an innovative approach based on semi-supervised learning, which combines the use of labeled and unlabelled data to train a particular model for the detection of SS7 attacks in telecom core networks. Our approach adapts the Convolutional Neural Network (CNN)-based semi-supervised learning scheme in [26] and an improved version of the feature engineering in [10] together with the hyperparameter optimization. Experiment results show that the proposed approach achieves up to 100% accuracy on both the real world and simulated datasets, respectively.

Keywords: Signalling system No:7 · Telecom core network security · Semi-supervised learning · Convolutional Neural Networks · Autoencoder neural networks

1 Introduction

In telecommunication, signaling protocols are used for organizing signaling exchange among communication endpoints and switching systems. Signaling

C. Su et al. (Eds.): ISPEC 2022, LNCS 13620, pp. 345–363, 2022.
https://doi.org/10.1007/978-3-031-21280-2_19

Security No:7 (SS7) is the signaling protocol used in 2G and 3G networks. Since it was initially designed for public switched telephone networks (PSTN), SS7 is vulnerable to security attacks such as the disclosure of IMSI (International Mobile Subscriber Identity), location of the subscriber, disruption of subscriber's availability, interception of calls and SMS messages, etc. [22,29]. Rule-based mechanisms can be used for detecting some of those attacks but they become dysfunctional if the attacker uses signaling messages that seem legitimate. In general, this situation arises when the signaling messages are directed to the home network of subscribers while they are in a visiting network. The idea is therefore to use more intelligent approaches than rule-based mechanisms that benefit from the statistics derived from historical records of subscribers.

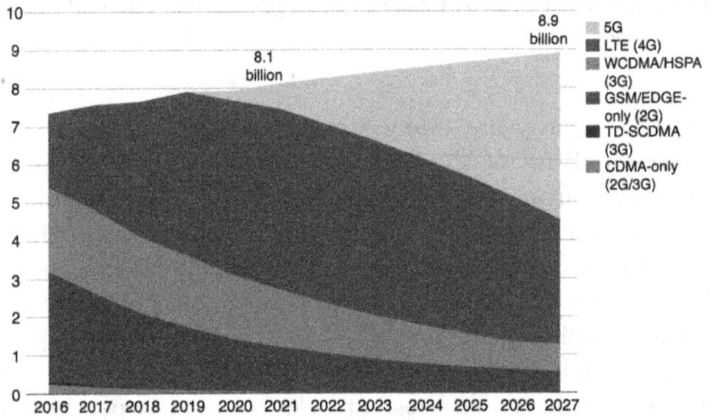

Fig. 1. Mobile subscribers (in billions) by technology 2016–2027 (expected) (https://tinyurl.com/4wze6un5)

In 5G, network signaling forms part of the transactions in the Control Plane, together with other activities such as network function communications. The transmission of signaling messages is carried through standard HTTP2 protocols [28]. While 5G is gradually being deployed and 4G has covered most of the population, the earlier generations (2G and 3G) are still in the place as illustrated in Fig. 1. In fact, for a variety of reasons, these legacy systems are expected to exist for many years to come, and they raise serious cybersecurity concerns about the security of signaling protocols. Consequently, a potential risk exists that attackers exploit the vulnerabilities in the legacy systems [19] and launch downgrade attacks to bypass the security mechanisms in 4G and 5G. Additionally, as described in [14], because the legacy systems and therefore the SS7 protocol is used for the roaming between countries, SS7 attacks such as location tracking, call/SMS interception, fraud, DoS, spoofing are also potential threats for 5G Core Networks.

Machine learning (ML) has become an effective tool to detect malicious attacks associated with Internet applications. Particularly, Deep Neural Networks (DNN) have demonstrated promising results in terms of the accuracy for various scenarios, such as classification of network traffic [26]. This motivates us to explore DNN for detecting cyber attacks against the legacy signaling protocols. Additionally, as introduced in [18], attacks that target the security of the 4G Diameter signaling protocol follow similar patterns to SS7 attacks. Therefore, in this work, we are not only aiming at mitigating the threats against the SS7 core network but also, we are planning to extend our work for countermeasure mechanisms of 4G and 5G signaling systems.

1.1 Our Contribution

Detection of signaling attacks in SS7 core networks is a challenging issue when the signaling messages of subscribers in the visiting network are directed to the home network. These attacks are known as the most challenging attacks in the literature [10,11] because they cannot be easily detected by the filtering-based countermeasure mechanisms. Solutions that employ the statistics derived from subscribers' historical records provide promising results to overcome this issue [10,12,24,29]. However, they are not able to effectively detect the aforementioned SS7 attacks. Therefore, in this work, we propose an innovative SS7 attack detection scheme that relies on semi-supervised learning and benefits from the existing works in the literature. Our contributions in this work are as follows:

- We adapt the network traffic classification scheme that uses a Convolutional Neural Network (CNN)-based semi-supervised learning scheme in [26] for the detection of SS7 attacks in telecom core networks:
  - We have improved the feature engineering in [10] to obtain a refined subset of features using well-known feature selection techniques.
  - We have optimized the model hyperparameters to tailor them for the detection of SS7 attacks.
- To evaluate the performance of our approach, we have conducted our experiments on the real-world (private) dataset and simulated dataset. Experiment results show that our scheme achieves the best performance for the detection of attacks when compared with the existing works in the domain.

1.2 Organisation

The organization of the paper is as follows. In Sect. 2, we overview the main functions of the SS7 protocol and its security vulnerabilities. Section 3 revisits Autoencoder-based attack detection for SS7 based on [10]. In Sect. 4, we survey CNN-based semi-supervised learning approaches for anomaly detection and we present our improvements on the scheme from [26]. Section 5 presents our experimental results using private and simulated datasets. Finally, Sect. 6 concludes the paper.

2 SS7 Protocol and Its Security Vulnerabilities

2.1 SS7 Overview

SS7 is a signaling protocol that is used in 2G (GSM) and 3G (UMTS/CDMA) mobile networks [4] that was first developed as the signaling systems of telephone and telegraph networks. Later, the International Telecommunication Union - Telecommunication Standardization Sector (ITU-T) recommended using SS7 as the family of signaling systems among core network elements of telecommunications [1]. The Signaling Transport (SIGTRAN) protocol was proposed by IETF [27] as a complementary protocol for SS7 to support the transfer over IP networks. With SIGTRAN, SS7 messages are wrapped to be transferred to the lower layers and IP networks together with the use of the Stream Control Transmission Protocol (SCTP) [11]. In Fig. 2, an overview of the SS7 core network is illustrated together with the fundamental entities. Short descriptions and the functionalities of those entities are given below:

- **HLR:** *Home Location Register* HLR is the main entities to store subscribers' information in 2G and 3G networks.
- **SGSN:** *Serving GPRS Support Node.* This node is responsible for transferring the geolocation-related packets to or from the network.
- **STP:** *Signalling Transfer Point.* This entity is responsible for the routing operations in the SS7 core network.
- **MSC:** *Mobile Switching Center.* In SS7 networks, MSC is the core entity of the network that enables the data and voice transfer between the subscriber and the core network. MSC is connected with the other entities in the core network (i.e., HLR, VLR, SMSC, etc.)
- **VLR:** *Visiting Location Register.* This entity is a database that contains information about the subscribers to reduce the MSC's queries in the telecom networks when they are in the visiting network.
- **SMSC:** *Short Message Service Center.* This entity is responsible for all operations related to receiving, storing, routing, and forwarding SMS messages.
- **SBC:** *Session Border Control.* SBC is included in SS7 together with Voice-over-IP (VoIP) to include additional security measures against attacks (i.e., distributed denial of service (DDoS), toll fraud, service theft, etc.) [20].
- **MGW:** *Media Gateway.* This entity is mainly used for enabling VoIP networks to connect PSTN and mobile networks.

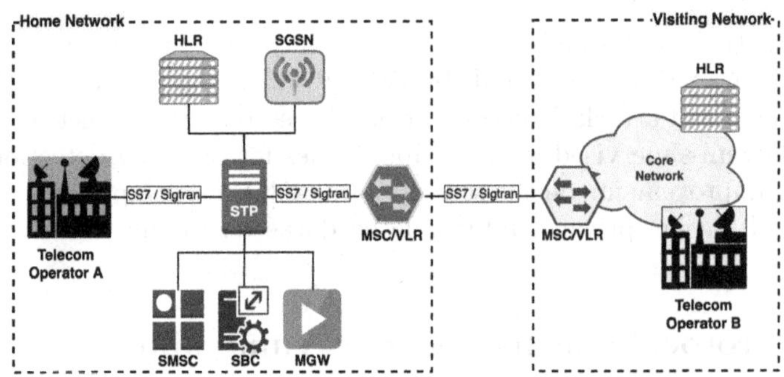

Fig. 2. SS7 overview

2.2 Security Vulnerabilities in SS7 Networks

The study in [25] analyzes the location tracking attacks in different procedures of SS7 networks such as the call setup messages, SMS procedures, etc. Traditionally, SS7 attacks range from theft of service up to denial of service (DoS) [6]; or rerouting/intercepting the call traffic [29] but these attacks also occur due to cross-protocol communication (e.g., between SS7 and Diameter). For instance, in [23], Puzankof et al. describe how an attacker can benefit from vulnerabilities from various generations of signaling protocols to achieve attacks (e.g., man-in-the-middle) in the era of 5G networks. The thesis in [16] provides a detailed overview of SS7 attacks and overviews the tools for running simulations on telecommunication networks. Additionally, [29] surveys the vulnerabilities of SS7 core networks. Referring to GSMA IR.82 [2,10,11], SS7 core network messages are categorized as follows:

- **Category 1 (Cat. 1):** Messages in this category are transmitted inside the home network.
- **Category 2 (Cat. 2):** Messages in this category are transmitted from the home network to the visiting network.
- **Category 3 (Cat. 3):** Messages in this category are transmitted from the visiting network to the home network.

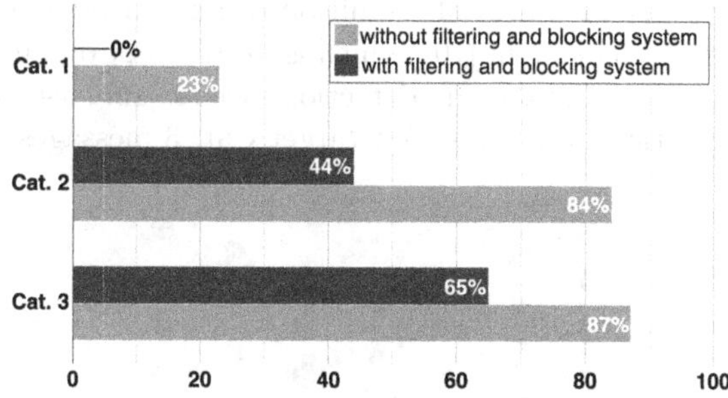

Fig. 3. Percentage of successful attacks against SS7 with respect to message categories based on the presence of a filtering-based defense mechanism (Credit: [22])

The report of Positive Technologies in [22] illustrates the effect of using filtering and blocking systems based on the message category breakdown for the detection of SS7 attacks (Fig. 3). For attacks that use Cat. 1 messages, the success rate is 23% if there is no filtering and blocking system employed. Filtering and blocking systems can detect all attacks that use Cat. 1 messages. For Cat. 2 messages, the success rate is 84% without using a filtering-based detection mechanism, and using traffic filters can reduce this success rate to 44%. Finally, for Cat. 3 messages, using filtering and blocking systems are not as effective as using traffic filters for Cat. 1 or Cat. 2 messages. Traffic filters of Cat. 3 messages can only reduce the success rate of attacks from 87% to 65%. According to the same report of Positive technologies, the reason behind the ineffective detection performance of traffic filters for Cat. 3 messages is that in both Cat. 1 and Cat. 2 messages, the originating nodes of the messages are in the home network. Therefore, telecom service providers can easily determine whether the originating node is legitimate or not. However, in Cat. 3 messages, the originating nodes (i.e., MSC/VLRs) are in the visiting network which means they are the nodes of another telecom service provider(s) and information about the legitimacy of those nodes should be continuously provided by visiting network(s) to home network to keep the list of traffic filters up to date. Otherwise, traffic filters in the home network may mistakenly block some nodes in the visiting networks, and hence, roaming[1] subscribers become unreachable due to the network disruption. Because of this, using traffic filters is a less preferred approach for the detection of attacks that use Cat. 3 messages. Nonetheless, Cat. 3 messages open the widest threat surface for the core networks since attackers may deploy various attacks such as SMS/call interception, denial of service for subscribers and network, fraud, etc. One particular solution to detect such kinds of attacks is to analyze the historical records of subscribers by employing intelligent techniques such as solutions based on ML as in [10,11,13], which is also our main motivation for this study.

3 Autoencoder-Based SS7 Attack Detection

In this section, we first give a brief definition of autoencoder neural networks. Then, we overview the scheme in [10], which is, to the best of our knowledge, the first study that proposes an anomaly detection mechanism based on a real-world dataset for the detection of attacks that target Cat. 3 messages.

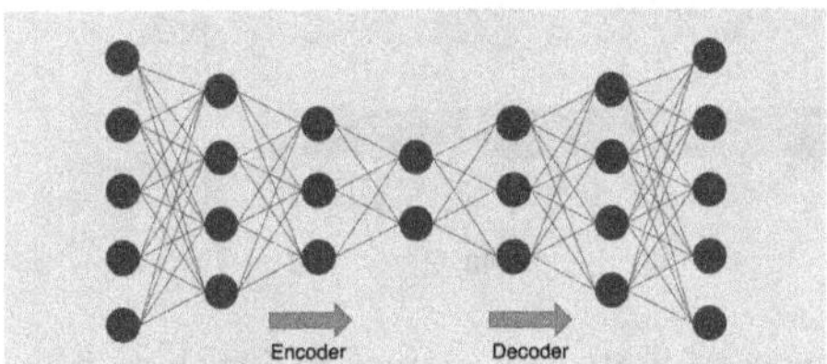

Fig. 4. Example autoencoder architecture (https://www.mygreatlearning.com/blog/autoencoder/)

3.1 Autoencoder Neural Networks

Autoencoder is one of the unsupervised learning techniques based on neural networks [8]. The architecture of the autoencoder consists of two parts, namely the encoder and the decoder as illustrated in Fig. 4. The encoder learns the discriminating characteristics of a dataset while reducing the dimensions of the input

[1] a subscriber is outside of the range of its service provider's home network (in the visiting network).

data into a low-dimension latent space. The decoder, on the other hand, tries to reconstruct the data from the encoding while minimizing the reconstruction error. One particular use of autoencoders is the detection of anomalies in a given dataset [3]. The idea is therefore to train the autoencoder with the normal inputs and observe the reconstruction error for the abnormal inputs by relying on the fact that abnormal inputs have higher reconstruction errors than the normal ones. By using this observation a threshold can be employed to discriminate between normal and abnormal inputs.

3.2 Autoencoder-Based Solution for SS7 Attack Detection [10]

In this section, we re-visit the scheme proposed by Hoang in [10] (we call this scheme as Hoang's scheme in the rest of the paper) as illustrated in Fig. 5. First, we summarize the details of the exploratory analysis of Hoang's real-world dataset that is collected by POST (the Luxembourgish telecommunications service provider) for two days of the period including national and international traffic for more than 500 roaming partners. The goal of this preliminary analysis is to explore some new details about the statistics of call flows[2] in the collected data. In short, it has been detected that the majority of the call flows are update location *(updateLocation/updateGPRSLocation)* and authentication *(SendAuthenticationInfo-SAI)* call flows. Since SAI call flows are executed just before update location call flows, the number of these call flows needs to be increased proportionally per subscriber. Therefore, for any subscriber, if there exists any inconsistency between the number of update location and the number of SAI call flows, this can be the result of an attack, specifically the SMS interception attacks as illustrated in Fig. 6. In such attacks, the attacker tries to register himself as the legitimate MSC/VLR of the victim subscriber to HLR using *updateLocation* call flow. Once the attacker is registered as the legitimate MSC/VLR of the subscriber, HLR of the home network always replies *Send-Routing-Info for SMS messages* requests with the information of the attacker. Consequently, the messages will be forwarded to the attacker instead of the MSC/VLR of the victim subscriber. Therefore, in this work, we focus on the detection of SMS interception attacks using *updateLocation* call flows. One particular way to detect these attacks is to extract statistics from the location update events of subscribers for a period of time to use them for finding the inconsistencies in the location of subscribers. Therefore, in the feature engineering phase of Hoang's scheme, traffic features are transformed into a new form to expand the analysis using update location events, SAI call flows, subscriber-oriented historical events, etc. as given in Fig. 6:

Hoang's Real-World Dataset: This dataset consists of the real-world SS7 traffic collected from the core network of an European telecom operator for two days period. In total, the dataset contains 11.173.593 unlabelled and 62 labeled instances. There exist 43 features in the dataset and they are categorized

[2] The *call flow* is the name of the process (voice call/data call) that is routed by the network to a mobile device.

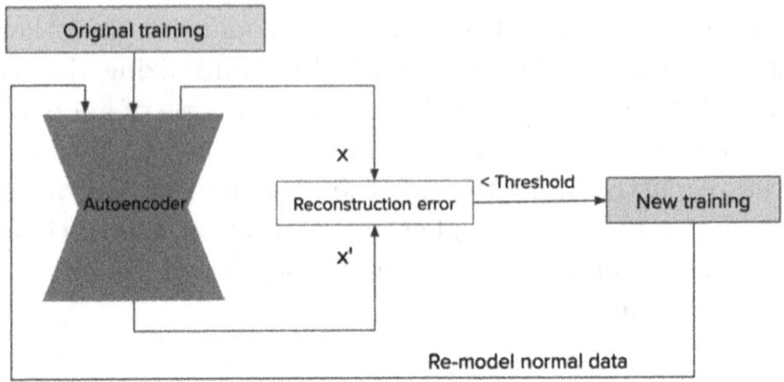

Fig. 5. Autoencoder-based SS7 attack detection scheme (Credit: [10])

under four groups, namely the current *updateLocation* events *(Group 1)*, historical *updateLocation* events of a subscriber *(Group 2)* in last m minutes, last two *updateLocation* of the same IMSI *(Group 3)* in last m minutes and finally, the historical events of the same Global Title (GT) in last m minutes *Group 4* (see Appendix A for detailed explanations of features).

Hoang's One-Time Dataset: This dataset consists of instantly collected 100 labeled records from the same network. The data set has the same set of features as the real-world dataset. As its name indicates, Hoang's one-time dataset was used for the performance evaluation of Hoang's scheme only.

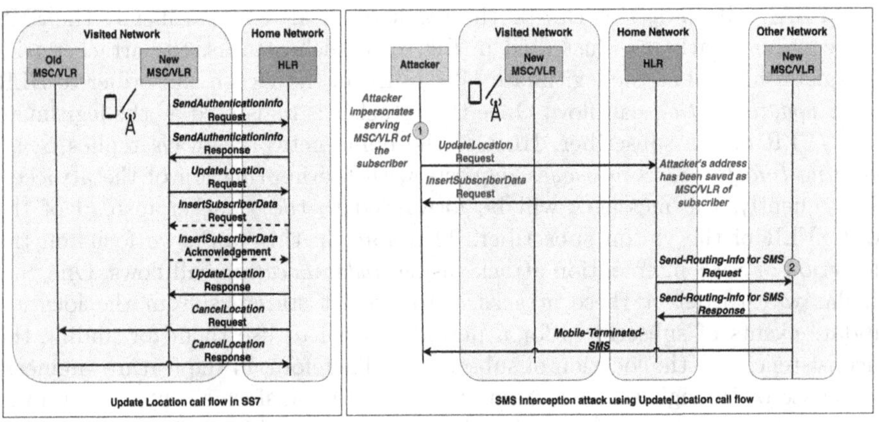

Fig. 6. The *updateLocation* call flow in the SS7 protocol and SMS interception attack using update location (inspired from [10])

For the training of an autoencoder model and the optimization of hyperparameters of the model, unlabelled records in the dataset are used. Since the attack traffic instances have higher reconstruction errors, a threshold-based approach is used for discriminating attack traffic from the normal one. Later, the trained model and its hyperparameters are optimized via the labeled instances of the dataset under three categories:

- **Autoencoder hyperparameters:** Those hyperparameters consist of the number of hidden layers at each layer, the number of hidden nodes per layer, the scaling factor of the autoencoder and finally, the activation functions (ReLU, tanh).
- **Mini-batch gradient descent hyperparameters:** loss function, batch size, learning rate and regularization.
- **System hyperparameters:** The number of running iterations and the threshold to discriminate attack traffic from the normal one based on the reconstruction error.

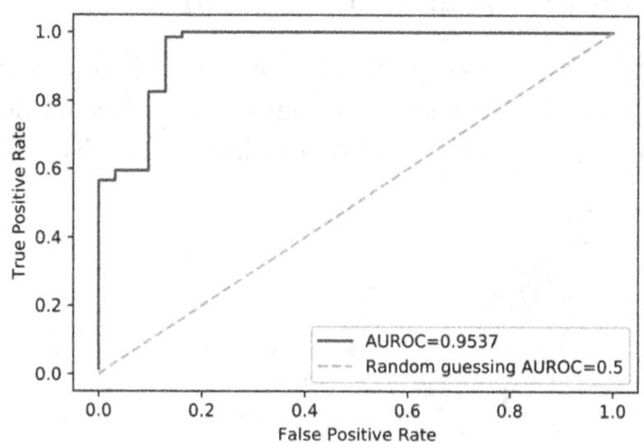

Fig. 7. The ROC curve and AUROC value of the top 100 detected events [10]

For the validation of Hoang's scheme, the one-time dataset was used. According to the experiments, the scheme achieves 69% accuracy and 69% precision. Furthermore, Fig. 7 shows the Receiver Operating Characteristic curve (ROC) and Area Under ROC curve (AUROC). As a consequence, using autoencoder neural networks is one of the effective approaches for detecting anomalies, particularly for semi-supervised learning problems. However, as it was explained in [10], the proposed scheme is not able to detect some of the attack patterns. Experiments show that 31 events out of 100 events from the one-time data set are set as false positive (legitimate events are labeled as attack events) due to the short duration between two consecutive update location events. However, these events were performed by trusted Global Titles (GTs, which are addresses used for routing messages within SS7) and they cannot be categorized as anomalies. Additional mechanisms can be adapted to handle such exceptional situations but then, we may need to detect all potential exceptions, which cannot be practical in real-life scenarios. Therefore, an ideal solution must be able to learn attack patterns and normal events together with exceptional situations. To this end, we consider using another well-known assumption, which is using a CNN-based solution for semi-supervised learning. Hence, we adopt the scheme in [26] for the detection of SS7 attacks.

4 CNN-Based Semi-supervised Learning for Attack Detection

In this section, we first overview Convolutional Neural Networks (CNNs), and then, we discuss why it is important to use CNN-based semi-supervised learning solutions for the detection of SS7 attacks in telecom core networks. Later, we introduce our improvements on [26] for SS7 attack detection.

4.1 Recap of Convolutional Neural Networks

Convolutional Neural Networks (CNNs) is a type of neural network, which is generally used for the classification of images [13]. CNN models can be formed using different combinations of the following layers (see Fig. 8 for the example):

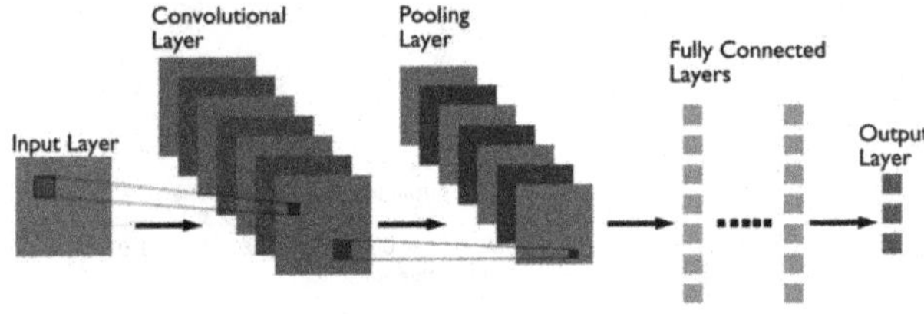

Fig. 8. Example CNN architecture (https://tinyurl.com/3v57sx3e)

- **Convolution layer (Conv.):** In this layer, a kernel or a set of kernels is applied on the input to extract specific features.
- **Pooling layer (Pool)** (max pooling, average pooling, etc.) helps to reduce the number of parameters to make it easy to manage for the computations in the further layers
- **Activation layer** (ReLU, sigmoid, tanh, etc.): This layer is used for controlling the learning process of the model.
- **Fully-Connected layer (FC)** is used for obtaining the correlation between the outputs of the previous layer and the inputs of next layer or output classes if the fully-connected layer is the last layer.

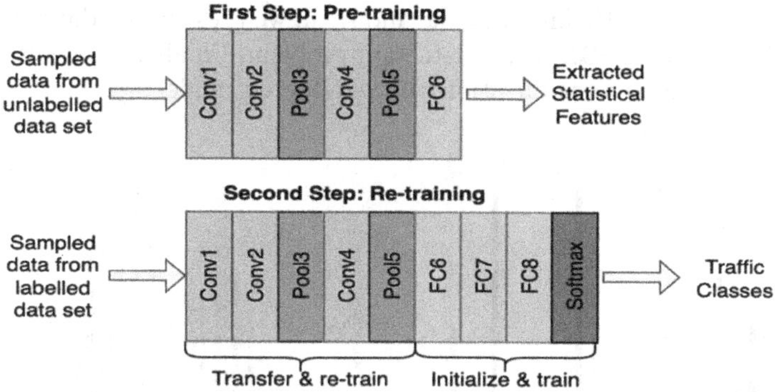

Fig. 9. The semi-supervised steps and model architecture (Credit: [26])

4.2 Recap of CNN-Based Semi-supervised Learning

As we explained in the previous section, using an autoencoder-based mechanism may yield high positive rate for some exceptional situations. Therefore, using CNN classifiers [5,21,26] provide more accurate results due to their shift-invariant property, which means a CNN classifier can detect patterns even if they are present in the different features of the input. In [5], a scheme for the detection of anomalies in Software Defined Networks (SDN) for the detection of Distributed Denial of Service (DDoS) attacks is proposed, where the network traffic is first processed by employing Continuous Wavelet Transform to obtain appropriate inputs for the CNN classifier. Experimental results show that the scheme can be a good candidate for the detection of DDoS attacks in SDN. However, the scheme cannot be directly applied to the problem of detecting attacks in the SS7 network since the SS7 network traffic has different characteristics such as the geographical locations of subscribers in two consequent update location events. The work in [21] proposes a federated semi-supervised learning approach to train a CNN traffic classifier with the collaboration of multiple servers. The proposed approach achieves 97.81% accuracy in traffic classification.

Another study in [26] also proposes a novel scheme based on a CNN model for the network traffic classification up to 98.99% accuracy. The training process of the scheme operates in two steps. In the first step, the pre-training process is executed to extract statistical features from the unlabelled dataset. Later, the model is re-trained with the labeled dataset as illustrated in Fig. 9. Therefore, in this work, we aim to benefit from the shift-invariant property by adopting CNN classifiers such as the scheme in [26], and by employing the improved version of feature engineering from Hoang's scheme.

4.3 Our CNN-Based Semi-supervised Learning Solution

In this subsection, we present our CNN-based semi-supervised learning scheme for the detection of SS7 attacks. We first introduce an improved version of the feature engineering of Hoang's scheme and then, we present an adaptation of the scheme in [26] for the SS7 attack detection problem. Finally, we give the details of our hyperparameter optimization on the adapted model.

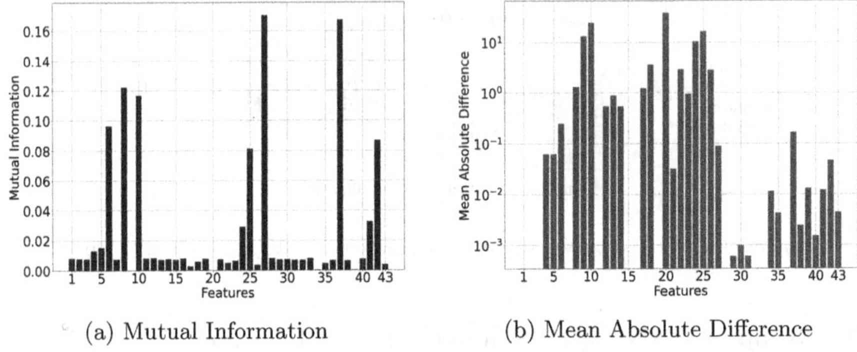

(a) Mutual Information

(b) Mean Absolute Difference

Fig. 10. Mutual information and mean absolute difference results on labelled real world dataset.

Feature Selection

In this section, we present our improvements based on the feature engineering methodology of Hoang's scheme. According to the original version of the methodology, there exist 43 different features for analyzing the mobility management records of each subscriber as it is explained in the previous section. However, from our initial investigations, we observe that some of these features mostly have the same value and hence, the same variance value for both the attack and normal subscriber records. Therefore, they have no or very little effect on the detection rate. To this end, we employ mutual information (MI) (Fig. 10a) to investigate the correlation between features and corresponding labels and mean absolute difference (MAD) (Fig. 10b) to analyze the features concerning their distance to the average mean. Consequently, 31 features are selected from 43 features as the intersection of features that have positive values. More formally, let $\mathcal{F}$ and $\mathcal{F}'$ be the old and new feature sets, respectively. $\mathcal{F}' = \{MI(f)\}_1^{|\mathcal{F}|} \cap \{MAD(f)\}_1^{|\mathcal{F}|}$, where $f \in \mathcal{F}$.

Adaptation of the Scheme in [26] for SS7 Attack Detection

The scheme in [26] is designed for the classification of the network traffic. The CNN classifier in the scheme is a multi-class classifier. Since there exist only two classes in our problem as *attack* and *normal*, we have updated the output layer accordingly. Based on our feature selection approach, we have 31 features as the input. Hence, we have updated the number of neurons in the input layer and the corresponding layers of the architecture. The original version of the CNN architecture and the final version of the architecture is given in Table 1.

Table 1. The original and updated CNN architectures

	Original architecture		New architecture	
	# of Neurons	Kernel size	# of Neurons	Kernel size
Conv1	32	5	31	5
Conv2	32	5	31	5
Pool1	–	3	–	3
Conv3	64	3	62	3
Pool2	–	3	–	3
FC1	256	–	62	–
FC2	128	–	124	–
FC3	128	–	124	

Hyperparameter Optimisation

Our preliminary experimental results on Hoang's real-world data set have shown that the initial version of the model achieves 68% accuracy and 90% average precision, which is higher than Hoang's scheme in terms of precision and almost similar in terms of accuracy. Note that the study in [10] uses the 62 labeled records for fine-tuning the model and a one-time dataset with 100 records for the test but in our case, because of the lack of this one-time dataset, we have empirically selected 45 labeled records for retraining phase and 17 labeled records for tests. Given that the adopted scheme is not optimized for the SS7 attack detection problem, to improve the results that we have obtained in the preliminary experimental results, we have applied the following optimizations for the model hyperparameters based on accuracy and the average precision of the model:

- **Number of hidden layers:** We have used different numbers of hidden layers between 1 and 5 for our experiments. Using 3 hidden layers provides the best results.
- **Number of hidden neurons:** We have tried different numbers of neurons, $[10, 25]$, and according to our metrics, 15 hidden neurons has the best values.
- **Activation function:** To optimize activation function, we have tried well-known activation functions: Rectifying Linear Unit (ReLU) [7], Leaky ReLU [15], sigmoid [9], hyperbolic tangent function (tanh) [17]. Among these activation functions, ReLU achieves the best performance.
- **Learning rate and number of iterations:** We have also considered the optimization of the learning rate of the network in our experiments and we ran experiments for the learning rate that spans from 0.1 to 0,00001 in our experiments. We have obtained 0,001 and 0,0001 for the learning rates of pre-training and re-training, respectively. For the number of iterations, we have tried number of iterations from 100 to 500 and the optimum results have been produced with 200 iterations for pre-training and re-training phases.

5 Experiments

5.1 Results on the Real World Dataset

Table 2. Results of our scheme on the real world dataset

Metric	Min	Avg	Max
Accuracy (%)	31	88	100
Precision (%)	76	96	100
Recall (%)	10	73	100
F1 (%)	18	81	100

Our results on Hoang's real-world dataset are given in Table 2. During our experiments, unlabelled records of Hoang's real-world dataset are used for the pre-training phase. For the re-train phase, 62 labeled records are divided as 45 and 17 records for training and test purposes, respectively. Since we have a very limited amount of labeled instances, we prefer to use a random sampling approach in our tests so that all the records in train and test subsets are selected in different combinations. We have repeated our experiments 100 times. Experimental results obtained from our scheme using the labeled dataset of the Hoang's Real-World dataset and Hoang's scheme using Hoang's one-time data set are as follows:

- Our scheme achieves 88% (from 68%) accuracy on the average using less amount of labeled data, which is pretty higher than the accuracy of the scheme in [10] (69%).
- Additionally, with the optimized hyperparameters, our scheme achieves 96% average precision which is higher than the precision of Hoang's scheme (69%) and our preliminary results (90%).

Our experimental results show that with the optimized hyperparameter values our scheme achieves better results even with less amount of labeled training data when compared with Hoang's scheme. We believe we can improve our results if we use more labeled data for the re-training phase. Finally, Fig. 11 shows the receiving operating characteristics (ROC) curve based on the best detection performance of our scheme.

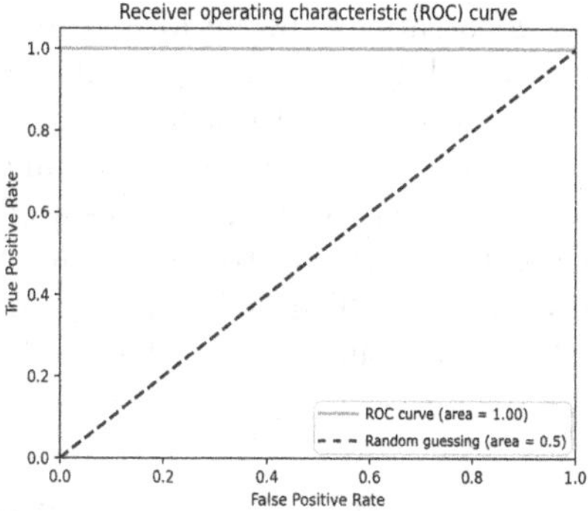

Fig. 11. ROC curve for the best detection performance of CNN-based Semi-supervised learning approach

5.2 Results on the Simulated Dataset

In order to evaluate and compare the performance our scheme, we have employed JSS7 attack simulator in [11] to generate a synthetic dataset. Details of the simulated dataset are as given below:

Simulated Dataset: This dataset is obtained by using the JSS7 attack simulator [11]. We run our experiments for 20 subscribers. The simulator generates 66.969 procedures and 183 of them are attack procedures based on location tracking with ProvideSubscriberInfo and AnyTimeInterrogation events and SMS interception. However, ProvideSubscriberInfo and AnyTimeInterrogation events are not related to Cat. 3 messages. Therefore, we have only consider SMS interception attacks which contain 4.642 update location events of subscribers. Additionally, JSS7 attack simulator deploys attacks for only one subscriber in the network, which is called the VIP subscriber. The traffic generated for the rest of the subscribers does not contain any attack and this traffic can be considered normal traffic. Therefore, we divided the records dataset into 85 labeled records coming from the VIP subscriber and 4557 unlabelled records coming from normal subscribers. Later, we have used the feature engineering from Hoang's Feature Engineering for extracting 43 features from the simulated records. Finally, we have selected 31 features among 43 features based on our Feature Selection approach. Performance evaluations for our scheme and Hoang's one are as shown in Table 3 and ROC curves are illustrated in Fig. 12 based on the results of maximum detection performances. As expected, our scheme achieves better performance than Hoang's scheme on the simulated dataset for the detection of SS7 attacks. Additionally, we have extended our performance results compared with other studies in the literature. The study in [29] compares the various machine learning techniques (K-means, Seasonal Hybrid Extreme Studentized Deviate - SHESD, Pattern Recognition Artificial Neural Network - PRANN, and Generalized Regression Artificial Neural Network - GRANN) and a rule-based approach. Although the dataset used in the experiments in [29] is different from ours, again we may have ideas about the performance of approaches that are used for the detection of attacks. Experiment results in the study show that K-means and SHESD have the best detection rate with 100%, and rule-based, PRANN, and GRANN approaches have 98.8%, 99.5%, and 99.75%, respectively. On the other hand, for the average precision, schemes used in [29] do not present efficient results. GRANN is the most effective technique in [29] in terms of the average precision value of 72.4% which is lower than our scheme (95%) and Hoang's scheme (89%). Therefore, our scheme achieves the best performance for the detection of SS7 attacks.

Table 3. Comparison of detection performances for our scheme and Hoang's scheme on the simulated dataset

	Hoang's scheme			Our scheme		
	Min	Max	Average	Min	Max	Average
Accuracy	64%	94%	83%	88%	100%	95%
Precision	50%	100%	89%	67%	100%	94%
Recall	16%	85%	60%	67%	100%	93%
F1	25%	90%	70%	67%	100%	93%

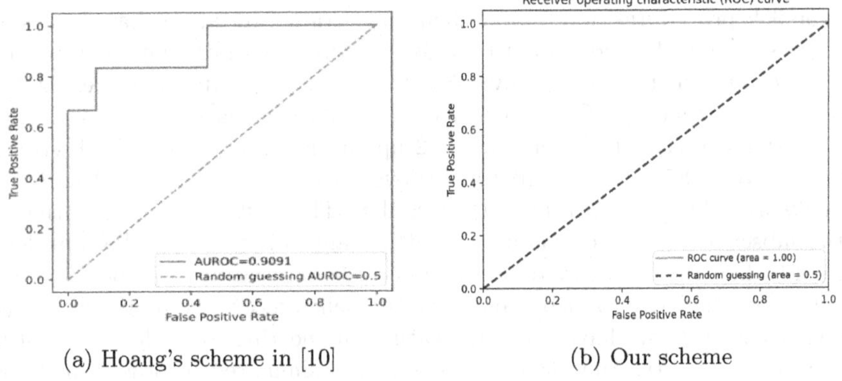

(a) Hoang's scheme in [10]

(b) Our scheme

Fig. 12. ROC Curves on the simulated dataset.

6 Conclusion and the Future Work

In this work, we have proposed an innovative attack classifier, specifically designed for the detection of SMS interception attacks that employs *updateLocation* call flows, in SS7 core network traffic. To this end, we have employed the CNN-based semi-supervised learning approach proposed by Rezaei et al. [26] as the classifier and have combined the adopted scheme with the improved version of the feature engineering in [10]. Moreover, we have applied hyperparameter optimization to improve the detection rate of the model. This improved model has been validated based on two datasets, namely the real-world dataset and the simulated dataset. Experiment results show that our scheme can achieve 99% accuracy for the real-world dataset and 100% accuracy for the simulated one.

Because the attack patterns of SS7 and Diameter are similar [18], we are planning to extend our work for 4G core networks. Additionally, our another future research direction is to improve our solution for the detection of other attacks that target Cat. 3 messages. Furthermore, investigation of the potential use of our findings in 5G core network security is another future research direction.

Acknowledgement. This work is supported by Luxembourg Ministery of the Economy under the scope of Secure5GeXP project.

Appendix A

Table 4. List of features in the real-world dataset [10]

Feature	Group	Description
f_ossn_others	1	Checks whether the transmitted update location (updateLocation/updateGprsLocation) messages is sent by HLR or SGSN.
f_velocity_is_ greater_than_1000	2	Checks the velocity of the subscriber whether the velocity is >1000 km/h between two last update location messages
f_count_unique_ country_previous_ul	2	This feature checks the number of unique countries visited based on the update location messages of the same IMSI in last m minutes
f_count_gap_ok_sai _and_all_lu	3	This feature keeps the difference between number of Send Authentication Info (SAI) messages and update location messages
f_one_cggt_multi_ cdgt_psi	3	This feature keeps checks the historical events and tries to find if one GT sent multiple PSI events to multiple GTs or not
f_count_ok_X_ between2lu	3	This feature counts number of successful X events[a]
f_frequent_ok_X_ between2lu	3	This feature keeps the frequency of X events
f_same_cggt_is_ hlr_ossn	4	By using SSN, the feature checks whether the same calling GT is acting as HLR in last m minutes
f_same_cggt_is_ hlr_oc	4	By using operation code, the feature checks whether the same calling GT is acting as HLR in last m minutes
f_same_cggt_is_ gmlc_ossn	4	By using SSN, the feature checks whether the same calling GT is acting as GMLC in last m minutes
f_same_cggt_is_ gmlc_oc	4	By using operation code, the feature checks whether the same calling GT is acting as GMLC in last m minutes

[a] Cancel-Location (CL), Delete Subscriber Data (DSD), Insert-Subscriber-Data (ISD), Mobile-Originated-SMS (MO-ForwardSM), Mobile-Terminated-SMS (MT-ForwardSM), Provide-Roaming-Number (PRN), Provide-Subscriber-Info (PSI), Purge-Mobile-Subscriber (PurgeMS), Send-Authentication-Info (SAI), Service-Indicator (SI), Send-Routing-Info (SRI), Update-Location (UL), Update-Location-GPRS (ULGPRS), Send-Routing-Info-for-SMS message (SRI-SM), Unrestricted-Supplementary-Service-Data (USSD)

References

1. Itu-t recommendation q.700 (03/1993) introduction to ccitt signalling system no. 7. online (1993)
2. GSM Association. IR.82 SS7 Security Network Implementation Guidelines v5. https://www.gsma.com/security/resources/ir-82-ss7-security-network-implementation-guidelines-v5-0/ (2016)
3. An, J., Cho, S.: Variational autoencoder based anomaly detection using reconstruction probability. Spec. Lect. IE **2**(1), 1–18 (2015)
4. Dryburgh, L., Hewett, J.: Signaling System No. 7 (SS7/C7): Protocol, Architecture, and Applications. Cisco Press (2003)
5. Fouladi, R.F., Ermiş, O., Anarim, E.: A novel approach for distributed denial of service defense using continuous wavelet transform and convolutional neural network for software-defined network. Comput. Secur. **112**, 102524 (2022)
6. Ghannam, R., Sharevski, F., Chung, A.: User-targeted denial-of-service attacks in LTE mobile networks. In: 2018 14th International Conference on Wireless and Mobile Computing, Networking and Communications (WiMob), pp. 1–8. IEEE (2018)
7. Glorot, X., Bordes, A., Bengio, Y.: Deep sparse rectifier neural networks. In: Gordon, G., Dunson, D., Dudík, M. (eds.) Proceedings of the Fourteenth International Conference on Artificial Intelligence and Statistics, vol. 15, pp. 315–323 (2011)
8. Goodfellow, I., Bengio, Y., Courville, A.: Deep Learning. MIT Press, Cambridge (2016)
9. Han, J., Moraga, C.: The influence of the sigmoid function parameters on the speed of backpropagation learning. In: Mira, J., Sandoval, F. (eds.) From Natural to Artificial Neural Computation, pp. 195–201 (1995)
10. Hoang, T.H.T.: Improving Security in Telecom Networks with Deep Learning Based Anomaly Detection. Master's thesis, Faculty of Science, Technology and Communication, Université du Luxembourg (2021)
11. Jensen, K.: Improving SS7 Security Using Machine Learning Techniques. Master's thesis, Norwegian University of Science and Technology (2016)
12. Jensen, K., Nguyen, H.T., Do, T.V., Arnes, A.: A big data analytics approach to combat telecommunication vulnerabilities. Cluster Computing (2017)
13. Khan, A., Sohail, A., Zahoora, U., Qureshi, A.S.: A survey of the recent architectures of deep convolutional neural networks. Artif. Intell. Rev. **53**(8), 5455–5516 (2020). https://doi.org/10.1007/s10462-020-09825-6
14. Kim, H.: 5G core network security issues and attack classification from network protocol perspective. J. Internet Serv. Inf. Secur. **10**, 1–15 (2020)
15. Maas, A.L., Hannun, A.Y., Ng, A.Y.: Rectifier nonlinearities improve neural network acoustic models. In: ICML Workshop on Deep Learning for Audio, Speech and Language Processing (2013)
16. Magklaris, E.: Attacks on SS7. Master's thesis, University of Piraeus (2019)
17. Malfliet, W.: The tanh method: a tool for solving certain classes of nonlinear evolution and wave equations. J. Comput. Appl. Math. **164**, 529–541 (2004)
18. Mashukov, S.: Diameter security: an auditor's viewpoint. J. ICT Stand. **5**, 53–68 (2017)
19. Metzler, J.: Security Implications of 5G Networks. https://cltc.berkeley.edu/wp-content/uploads/2020/09/Security_Implications_5G.pdf. Accessed 22 Mar 2022
20. Penfield, B., Hautakorpi, J., Bhatia, M., Hawrylyshen, A., Camarillo, G.: Requirements from Session Initiation Protocol (SIP) Session Border Control (SBC) Deployments. RFC 5853 (2010). https://www.rfc-editor.org/info/rfc5853

21. Peng, Y., He, M., Wang, Y.: A federated semi-supervised learning approach for network traffic classification. arXiv preprint arXiv:2107.03933 (2021)
22. Positive Technologies: SS7 Vulnerabilities and Attack Exposure Report. Online (2018)
23. Puzankov, S.: Stealthy SS7 attacks. J. ICT Stand. 39–52 (2017)
24. Qasim, T., Durad, M.H., Khan, A., Nazir, F., Qasim, T.: Detection of signaling system 7 attack in network function virtualization using machine learning. In: 2018 15th International Bhurban Conference on Applied Sciences and Technology (IBCAST), pp. 484–488 (2018)
25. Rao, S.P., Oliver, I., Holtmanns, S., Aura, T.: We know where you are! In: 2016 8th International Conference on Cyber Conflict (CyCon), pp. 277–293 (2016)
26. Rezaei, S., Liu, X.: How to achieve high classification accuracy with just a few labels: a semi-supervised approach using sampled packets. CoRR abs/1812.09761 (2018). arxiv:1812.09761
27. Sharp, C., et al.: Signalling transport protocol. IETF - Online (1999)
28. Tang, Q., Ermis, O., Nguyen, C.D., Oliveira, A.D., Hirtzig, A.: A systematic analysis of 5g networks with a focus on 5g core security. IEEE Access **10**, 18298–18319 (2022)
29. Ullah, K., Rashid, I., Afzal, H., Iqbal, M.M.W., Bangash, Y.A., Abbas, H.: SS7 vulnerabilities-a survey and implementation of machine learning vs rule based filtering for detection of SS7 network attacks. IEEE Commun. Surv. Tutorials **22**(2), 1337–1371 (2020)

Federated Intrusion Detection on Non-IID Data for IIoT Networks Using Generative Adversarial Networks and Reinforcement Learning

Nguyen Huu Quyen[1,2], Phan The Duy[1,2(✉)], Nguyen Chi Vy[1,2(✉)], Do Thi Thu Hien[1,2(✉)], and Van-Hau Pham[1,2(✉)]

[1] Information Security Laboratory,
University of Information Technology, Ho Chi Minh city, Vietnam
{18521321,18521681}@gm.uit.edu.vn,
{duypt,hiendtt,haupv}@uit.edu.vn
[2] Vietnam National University, Ho Chi Minh city, Vietnam

Abstract. Federated learning (FL) has become the promising approach for building collaborative intrusion detection systems (IDS) as providing privacy guaranteeing among data holders. Nevertheless, the non-independent and identically distributed (Non-IID) data in real-world scenarios negatively impacts the performance of aggregated models from training client updates. To this end, in this paper, we introduce Generative Adversarial Networks (GANs) and Reinforcement Learning (RL) approach for federated IDS that can deal with Non-IID data among organizational networks. More specifically, the imbalanced state between data classes is tackled by GAN-based data augmentation, while RL provides better performance in the client choosing process for federated IDS model training. Finally, the experimental results on Kitsune dataset indicate that our work can help to set up the collaboration between data holders for building more effective IDS to deploy in practice with distinguished data distribution.

Keywords: Federated learning (FL) · Reinforcement learning (RL) · Intrusion detection system (ids) · Generative Adversarial Networks (GANs) · Cyberattack

1 Introduction

Federated learning has been considered as a privacy preserving-machine learning solution in the era of data breach and privacy leakage [12]. Sharing this same trend, cybersecurity is one of the most potential fields for adopting federated learning (FL) to form the federation of learned and shared model through training participants [3,8]. For example, there are many works that utilize FL to benefit the contribution from the cybersecurity community without raw data sharing. Such approaches can be mentioned including malicious URL detection [10],

C. Su et al. (Eds.): ISPEC 2022, LNCS 13620, pp. 364–381, 2022.
https://doi.org/10.1007/978-3-031-21280-2_20

threat hunting [1,23], intrusion detection system (IDS) [2,4,6,11,21], anomaly data detection [15,26,27], and malware detection [9,19,20].

Nonetheless, FL is suffered from many security and privacy threats [16]. Of such problems, FL usually encounters non-independent and identically distributed (Non-IID) data in real-world scenarios, where it cannot achieve high performance [5]. If training data on local devices is Non-IID data, it gives worse performance for the global model than centralized training models due to the non-robust aggregation algorithms [28]. To tackle this issue, some works use a data-based approach, including data sharing and data augmentation to modify the distributions in clients. Therein, Generative Adversarial Networks (GANs) are considered potential solutions to create and supplement the data in minor classes. Instead of centralizing the data for training GAN, when balancing Non-IID data, all participants in the FL process need to balance their raw data by themselves before training to avoid sharing the data which will violate the main principle of FL of keeping private data locally. However, training GAN in all participants will take a lot of cost and time, bringing low effectiveness to FL model performance. Besides, also aiming to solve Non-IID data, reinforcement learning (RL) is utilized as an experience-driven method to select the training clients to participate in each training round to reduce the bias in Non-IID data for speeding up the model convergence [22]. However, by the experiments in [22], their results proved that RL-integrated FL would take a lot of communication rounds to reach the target performance if only focusing on selecting a group of clients which is desired to give the high performance of the global model in next round without balancing raw data of clients. And to address these problems, we first give a comprehensive empirical analysis of the impact of Non-IID data on the FL model. Then, to tackle the problem of Non-IID data in FL-based IDS, we introduce 3 measures using GAN, RL, and RL with GAN in the FL process to experiment, evaluate and find the best solution.

The main contributions of this paper in comparison to previous relevant studies are summarized as follows:

- First, we re-evaluate the FedIDS model, a CNNGRU-based deep learning model proposed in [21], on the scenario of Non-IID data training to explore the influence of Non-IID data on the performance of FL-based IDS on the real-world network intrusion dataset.
- Second, we investigate two alternative methods to reduce the influence of Non-IID data on FL scheme, including GANs and RL. Specifically, data distribution of clients is balanced by GAN-based augmentation data, while RL is adopted to dynamically choose the best group of clients for model aggregation. Consequently, we point out the limitations in terms of training efficiency of 2 measures on federated IDSs.
- Finally, this work introduce a new approach for FL-based IDS scheme on Non-IID data using RL with GAN to improve disadvantages of 2 disjoint methods mentioned above. The quality of the models, the data contribution from each participant, and the performance of the global model also are enhanced by balancing data for a chosen group of clients before aggregating the global model.

The remainder of this paper is organized as follows. Section 2 gives an overview of related studies, which motivate us to conduct this research. In Sect. 3, the methodology and detailed workflow of our proposed system is described. The implementation and experiments are presented in Sect. 4. Finally, we conclude the paper in Sect. 5.

2 Related Work

In this section, we briefly review deep learning model, Non-IID data problem and the proposed countermeasure to solve this problem which are associated with federated learning-based intrusion detection methods.

Recently, with many studies being researched and evaluated, FL algorithm has proven its effectiveness in many fields. Especially, in the fields of IDS, many IDSs have gained the desired performance when applied FL in these systems. As in [17], to automatically detect threats for IoT devices, Nguyen Duc Thien et al. proposed a machine learning model for a FL-based intrusion detection system (IDS). This solution is located at the security gateways of each network whose computers participate in the training process. Similarly, Nguyen Chi Vy et al. [21] have developed a deep learning model combined with FL to build an IDS to defend poisoning attack in the context of Industrial Internet of Things (IIoT). Besides that, Beibei Li et al. proposed DeepFed [11], a federated learning scheme for IDS in industrial cyber-physical systems (CPSs), which conducts collaboratively training a deep learning model on each security agents. The model is structured with a combination of convolutional neural networks (CNN) and gated recurrent units (GRUs). This approach helps multiple industrial CPSs to build a comprehensive intrusion detection model and ensure data privacy of involved organizations. Moreover, to increase the training efficiency of the model in collaborative learning (FL), Nguyen Gia Tri et al. [18] proposed DeepMonitor method for monitoring network traffic, used for IoT devices in Software-defined network (SDN). Along with that, the authors also introduce an algorithm called Double Deep Q-network (DDQN) to improve the training performance of the model in this programmable network architecture. But in reality, the collecting data process of all parties is completely independent, it is difficult to ensure that all parties have Independent and Identically Distributed (IID) data. But, in their work, they have yet to make a specified evaluation of how the model performs when training in the context of Non-IID data. So, when training on Non-IID data, these FL-based IDS also do not avoid the same problem of FL algorithm causing the negative impact on the performance of global model. As in [25], Pengqian Yu et al. has illustrated that the performance of global model has reduced when training with Non-IID data with these state-of-the-art aggregation functions such as FedAvg, FedProx,... And to deal with this problem, they proposed Fed+ which is a class of methods for federated learning.

Overall, to address the negative influence of heterogeneous data (Non-IID) on the performance of FL models, Hangyu et al. [28] conducted a survey to analyze in detail the effect of heterogeneous data (Non-IID) on collaborative learning (FL) models. The results have shown that the performance of the training models heterogeneously converges due to imbalanced data (Non-IID) and the synthesized model on the server experiences slow and ineffective convergence. And upon taking deep into the data distribution, a method to handle the imbalanced data distribution (Non-IID) has been proposed, by input data-based and individual data-based (Personalization Methods) approaches. And several works attempt to adopt FL in many applications, whereas a few studies investigate how Non-IID data can affect the global FL-based model and find countermeasure to defend. Recently, Hao Wang et al. [22] proposed the FAVOR method, which aims to optimize the performance of the model training using reinforcement learning (RL) for heterogeneous datasets (Non-IID). The proposed method based on Deep Q-Learning gives the capability to select a set of devices with good performance in each training loop, which can promise better performance in later training rounds at the synthesized model. With the same goal, Pravin Chandran et al. [7] take the idea from the divide-and-conquer algorithm to design their solution to help FL to overcome the problem when the data is not uniform (Non-IID). Furthermore, another work by the research group of Ryo Yonetani [24] attempted to apply Generative adversarial networks (GAN) to build ML models on heterogeneous data (Non-IID). In their study, they try to figure out a distribution that deals with all the classes to which the input data can belong, while keeping the data hierarchical in each client's storage. Although these studies have found out some countermeasures for FL algorithm when training with Non-IID data, they seem only focus on image datasets and still do not work with another kind of datasets such as text, voice and also network attacks.

3 Methodology

This section gives the overview of our FL strategy for making a collaboration between different parties to build a more robust IDS without leaking raw data. After that, we introduce a countermeasure which outperforms existing methods for tackling the problem of Non-IID data in the context of FL-based IDS.

3.1 Federated Learning

In this part, we introduce the FL scheme for training IDS which consists of one global server and many collaborating machines, as shown in Fig. 1.

- The server is responsible for aggregating local models from each collaborative machine to build the global model. Then, the updated global model will be transmitted to the collaborators to continue training and improving the global model. Note that, the server is built on a trust infrastructure to provide the reliability for involved networks.
- The collaborators take the duty of locally training on its raw data and sending the trained parameters up to the global server. These parameters are the weight of the collaborator's training model. A collaborator is a training server representing for IDS builder in each network joined in the FL scheme.

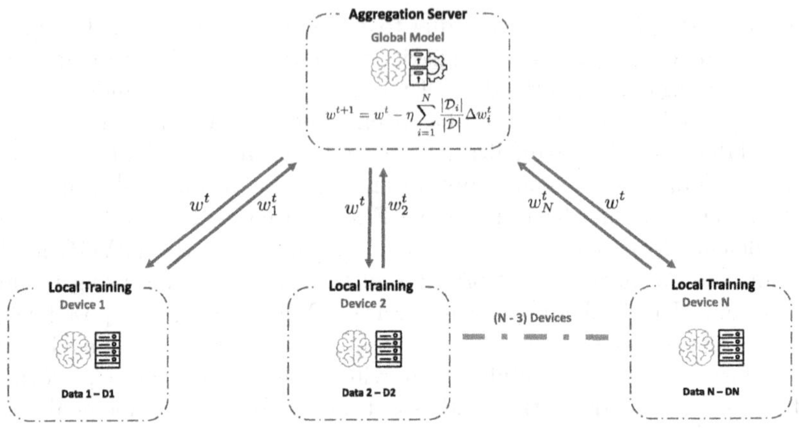

Fig. 1. The architecture of federated learning.

The workflow of this model can be summarized as follows:

- First, the server sends the weight and gradient of a pre-trained model or a generated model randomly to the collaborators.
- Based on the set of parameters received from the server, the collaborating machines proceed with training using the amount of data in each one. In this method, $\mathcal{D}_i$ is the dataset at the ith collaborator and Δw_i^t is the difference between the parameters after the training at i^{th} collaborator and the global weight w^t.
- The set of weights Δw_i^t and the size of the dataset are sent to the server when the collaborator finishes its training process.
- The new model's weights are calculated using Eq. (1).
- Finally, the server sends the updated model to collaborating machines for continuous usage, evaluation, and training.

To establish the aggregate formula at the server, we assume that there are N machines participating in collaboration during the training phase. Moreover, only the case in which the server receives models from all N machines is considered, and those models are used to aggregate and update the new model. More specifics, the aggregation formula is calculated as in Eq. (1).

$$w^{t+1} = w^t - \eta \sum_{i=1}^{N} \frac{|\mathcal{D}_i|}{|\mathcal{D}|} \Delta w_i^t \tag{1}$$

In which, w^{t+1} is the set of weights in the new model in the global server, $|\mathcal{D}|$ is the total size data of N collaborators and is calculated as in Eq. (2).

$$|\mathcal{D}| = \sum_{i=1}^{N} |\mathcal{D}_i| \tag{2}$$

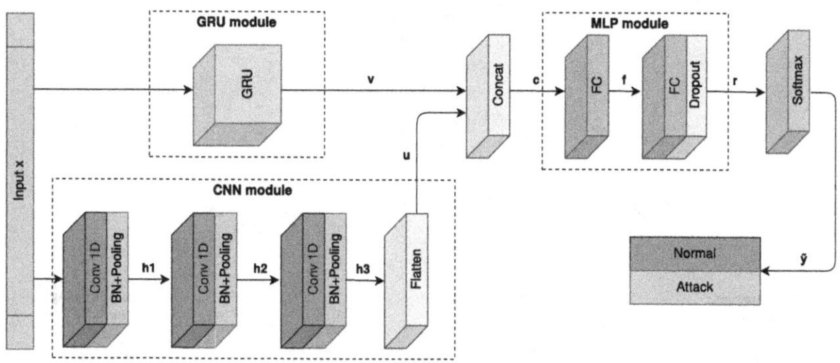

Fig. 2. The architecture of CNNGRU model for attack detection.

3.2 Training Detection Model on Collaborative Machines

In this study, training models of all collaborative machines are built based on Fed-IDS architecture, which is a CNNGRU model proposed in [21]. In this model, data is passed through CNN and GRU modules simultaneously. As depicted in Fig. 2, the input x contains features that indicate whether it is an attack or not. When passing through GRU, x is extracted into the features as sequential information with timestamp and turned into v as in Eq. (3).

$$v = GRU(x) \tag{3}$$

In Eq. (4), when x comes to CNN module, it goes through 3 Convolutional blocks, each of which includes a Convolutional 1D layer, a Batch Normalization layer, and a Pooling layer. The last layer in CNN is the Flatten layer.

$$u = CNN(x) \tag{4}$$

The Concat layer concatenates the result u and v from GRU model and CNN model, as in Eq. (5).

$$c = Concat(u, v) \tag{5}$$

Then, the result c passes through the MLP module consisting of 2 Fully Connected layers and a Dropout layer to avoid over-fitting as shown in Eq. (6).

$$r = MLP(c) \tag{6}$$

Eventually, the result r is sent through the Softmax layer to form the probability, $\widetilde{y}$ as in Eq. (7).

$$\widetilde{y} = Softmax(r) \tag{7}$$

The objective of this model is to optimize the cross-entropy loss function between the output vector $\widetilde{y}$ and the vector y which contains the actual value of traffic label.

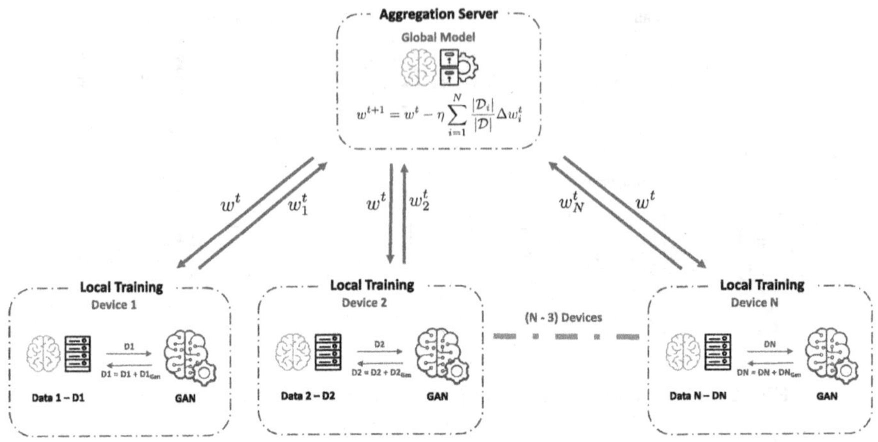

Fig. 3. The scheme of FL with GAN in training attack detection model.

3.3 FL with GAN for Non-IID Data

In this strategy, we use Generative Adversarial Networks (GAN) to balance the Non-IID data before feeding it to FL training, as shown in Fig. 3. Therein, Conditional GAN is used to generate more data for classes which has a small amount in the training data. To generate numerous artificial data aiming to balance Non-IID data, we design a GAN architecture, which is shown in Fig. 4. It consists of 2 main neural networks: Generator G and Discriminator D. The Discriminator D is responsible for distinguishing between the actual data and the data generated by the Generator G. Meanwhile, the Generator G performs the task of crafting new data to bypass the recognition of the Discriminator D.

The generator G is built based on CNN module including three convolutional blocks of $GenConvBlock_1$, $GenConvBlock_2$ and $GenConvBlock_3$ and a $Flatten$ layer Eq. (8). The input value of this component is the label y of the desired new data to be generated, combined with a random noise vector z.

$$\begin{aligned} g_1 &= GenConvBlock_1(z + y) \\ g_2 &= GenConvBlock_2(g_1) \\ g_3 &= GenConvBlock_3(g_2) \\ g_4 &= Flatten(g_3) \end{aligned} \tag{8}$$

Then the value of g_4 is passed through in Fully Connected Eq. (9) to generate new fake data of the same size as the real data.

$$x_{gen} = GenFC(g_4) \tag{9}$$

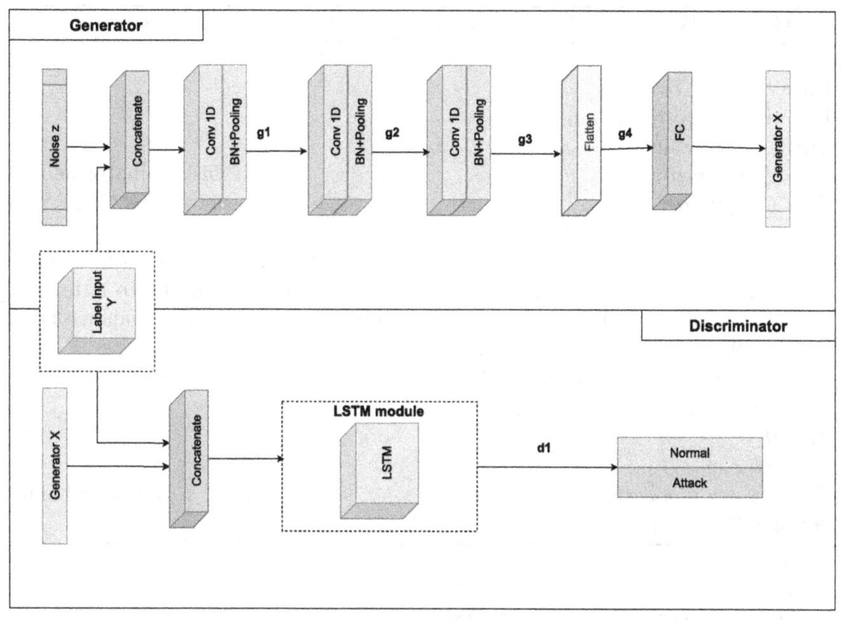

Fig. 4. The CGAN data generation structure.

In short, the generator G will take a random noise vector z and generate the data x_{gen} as shown in Eq. (10).

$$x_{gen} = G(z|y) \tag{10}$$

Meanwhile, in the proposed GAN structure, we utilize Long Sort Term Memory networks (LSTM) to build the Discriminator D. The output of Generator G, which is x_{gen}, is passed as the input of LSTM module Eq. (11), and vector output d_1 will show that x_{gen} is Attack or Normal.

$$d_1 = LSTM(x_{gen}) \tag{11}$$

$$\begin{aligned} min_G\ max_D\ V(D,G) = E_{x \sim p_{data}(x)}[\log D(x|y)] \\ + E_{z \sim p_z(z)}[\log (1 - D(G(z|y))] \end{aligned} \tag{12}$$

Finally, the generated data $G(z|y)$ from the Generator G is checked by the Discriminator D by $(G(z|y))$ whether the new data is different from the training data. The goal of GAN training is shown in Eq. (12) of $V(D,G)$, where the loss of the Generator G will gradually approach the minimum and the loss of the Discriminator D will gradually approach the maximum. And algorithm Algorithm (1) describes the training scheme of CGAN for crafting new data records to balance data $\mathcal{D}$.

Algorithm 1. Balancing Non-IID data using Conditional GANs

Input:
Data training $\mathcal{D}$;
List of noise vector $\mathcal{Z}_{noise}$;
Output: Data balanced $\mathcal{D}_{balanced}$
$D \Leftarrow Discriminator()$ ▷ Init Discriminator as LSTM
$G \Leftarrow Generator()$ ▷ Init Generator as CNN module
Training G and D with $\mathcal{D}$
$\mathcal{D}^{y_0} \Leftarrow \mathcal{D}[y = 0]$ ▷ Init data belong to Normal label
$\mathcal{D}^{y_1} \Leftarrow \mathcal{D}[y = 1]$ ▷ In it data belong to Attack label
if $|\mathcal{D}^{y_0}| - |\mathcal{D}^{y_1}| \leq 0$ **then** ▷ Init conditioning label-$\mathcal{Y}$ to balance Data $\mathcal{D}$
    $\mathcal{Y} \Leftarrow 0$
else
    $\mathcal{Y} \Leftarrow 1$
end if
$\mathcal{X} \Leftarrow G(\mathcal{Z}_{noise}|\mathcal{Y})$
$\mathcal{D}_{balanced} \Leftarrow Concat(\mathcal{D}, \mathcal{X})$ ▷ Init data balanced
return $\mathcal{D}_{balanced}$

3.4 FL with RL for Non-IID Data

Reinforcement Learning (RL) is the learning process of an agent that acts in corresponding to the environment to maximize its rewards. The recent success of RL [13] comes from the capability that RL agents learn from the interaction with a dynamic environment. As shown in Fig. 5, to converge to the target accuracy for FL as quickly as possible, we formulate device selection for FL as a deep reinforcement learning (DRL) problem. To train the DRL agent, we access the Double Deep Q-learning Network (DDQN) in RL agent.

Markov Decision Process (MDP) Model. To apply RL into FL process, we model per-round FL process as an MDP, specify constraints reflecting concerns for practice detecting and build the environment to simulate real-world intrusion detection systems. And MDP model of IDS is described as follows:

- State $s_t = [w_t, w_t^{(1)}, ..., w_t^{(N)}]$: is a vector including weights of global model w_t after round t, and $w_t^{(1)}, ..., w_t^{(N)}$ are model weights of the N devices, respectively.
- Given a state, the DRL agent takes an action a to select a subset of devices that perform local training and update the global model. And action $a = \{1, 2, ..., N\}$: is a vector of N devices that perform local training and update the global model, and where $a = i$ means that device i is selected to participate in FL.

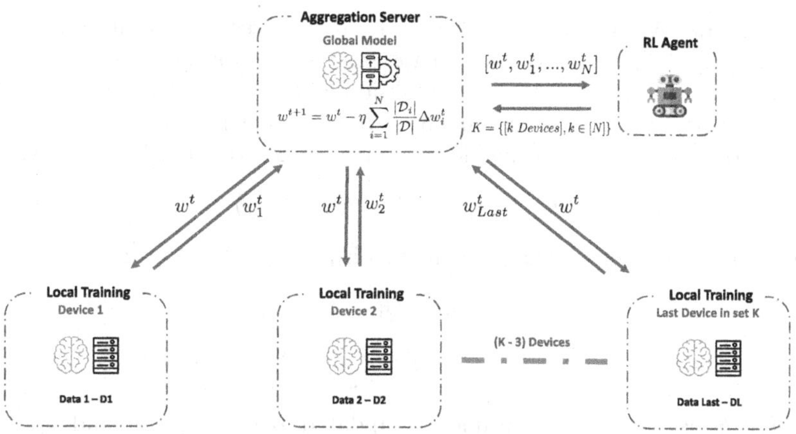

Fig. 5. The architecture of federated learning with RL.

– And reward r which is observed as Eq. (13) is a function of the test accuracy achieved by the global model. In r function, w_t is the testing accuracy value of global model on validation dataset after round t, Ω is the target accuracy, and Ξ is a positive constant that ensures that r_t grows exponentially with the testing accuracy w_t. Furthermore, to promote the training process, reward r value has been reduced 1 unit because the more rounds it takes, the less cumulative reward the agent will receive. Because of $0 \leq w_t \leq \Omega \leq 1$, reward r will be valid in range $(-1, 0]$.

$$r_t = \Xi^{w_t - \Omega} - 1 \tag{13}$$

And the agent is trained to maximize the expectation of the cumulative discounted reward given by Eq. (14)

$$R = \sum_{t=1}^{T} \gamma^{t-1} r_t \tag{14}$$

where $\gamma \in (0, 1]$ is a factor discounting future rewards.

– The optimal action-value function $Q^*(s_t, a)$ which shown in Eq. (15) estimates the expected reward of taking an action a at state s_t. In particular, the agent is trained by selecting only one out of N devices to participate in FL per round based on DDQN, while in testing and application the agent will sample a batch of top-K devices to participate in FL. To deal with this issue, in round t, the DQN agent will compute action-value for all N devices (actions). Each action-value indicates the maximum expected return that the agent can get by selecting a particular device (action) a at state s_t. Then, we select the K devices, each corresponding to a different device (action) a, that lead to the top-K values of $Q^*(s_t, a)$.

$$Q^*(s_t, a) = E\{r_{t+1} + \gamma \max_{a'} Q^*(s_{t+1}, a')\} \tag{15}$$

Training the Agent with DDQN. In RL process, to train the agent in optimizing $Q(s_t, a)$ to the optimal action-value function $Q^*(s_t, a)$, we use the DDQN. To initialize the states, several random device selections are fed into the FL training process. And based on Eq. (16), the agent is trained to generate an action a to select a device to participate in the next round of FL process.

$$l_t(\theta_t) = (Y_t^{DoubleQ} - Q(s_t, a; \theta_t))^2 \tag{16}$$

and the target at round t which defined as Eq. (17) is $Y_t^{DoubleQ}$:

$$\begin{aligned} Y_t^{DoubleQ} &= r_t + \gamma \max_a Q(s_{t+1}, a; \theta_t) \\ &= r_t + \gamma Q(s_t, \arg\max_a Q(s_t, a; \theta_t); \theta_t'), \end{aligned} \tag{17}$$

where θ_t is the online parameters updated per time step and θ_t' is the frozen parameters to add stability to action-value estimation. Then, to minimize $l_t(\theta_t)$, the action-value function $Q(s_{t+1}, a; \theta_t)$ is updated by gradient descent as Eq. (18).

$$\theta_{t+1} = \theta_t + \alpha(Y_t^{DoubleQ} - Q(s_t, a; \theta_t))\nabla\theta_t Q(s_t, a; \theta_t), \tag{18}$$

where α is the learning rate.

Algorithm 2. Clients selection using RL

Input:
Vector including weights of global model and model of all devices $s = [w, w^{(1)}, ..., w^{(N)}]$;
Vector including actions $a = 1, 2, ..., N$;
Output: List K devices selected $a_{Selected}$
$Q_a = [\,]$ ▷ Init list action-value of all actions
for each $(\mathcal{A}, i) \in$ **a do**
  Calculate action-value $Q(s, \mathcal{A})$
  Q_a.**add**($\{value : Q(s, \mathcal{A}), action : \mathcal{A}\}$)
end for
sort($Q_a, 'value'$) ▷ Sort list action-value by value
$a_{Selected} = Q_a[\,:K]$ ▷ Get Top-K from list action-value
return $a_{Selected}$

3.5 RL and GAN-Integrated FL for Non-IID Data

In this part, we introduce the GAN-based data augmentation approach in association with RL to take advantages of using GAN and RL in solving Non-IID data problem. In this strategy, we have 2 main parts as shown in Fig. 6:

- An agent RL is trained with DDQN as Part. 3.4 above to intelligently choose group of devices, which is desired to bring the highest performance after aggregation task at the server.
- These selected devices utilize GAN as Part. 3.3 above to balance training data before feeding data into training FL process.

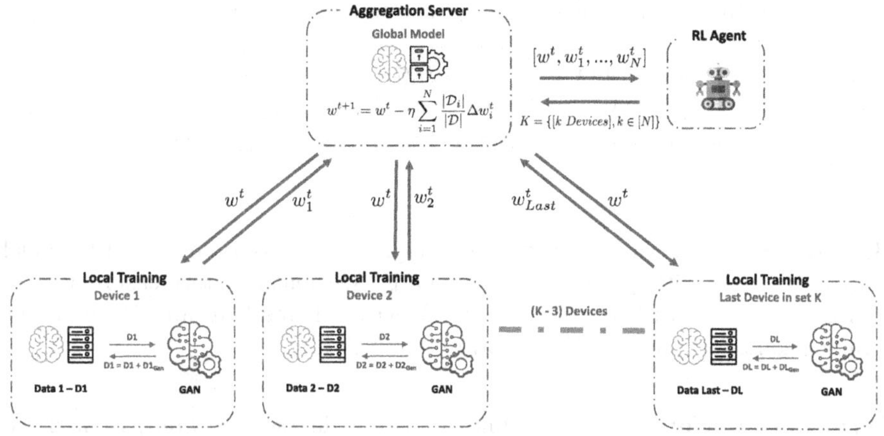

Fig. 6. The architecture of federated learning with RL combination with GAN.

4 Experimental Evaluation

In this section, our experiments focus on evaluating the performance of FL model using 2 proposed methods to resolve the problem of Non-IID data. And the first, we give data resource description and partitioning. Then, we focus on experimental settings, including the environmental settings, baseline studies, and performance metrics. Finally, we carry out a series of experiments to compare the performance of FL model with countermeasures on Non-IID data including GAN method, RL method, and RL combination with GAN method.

4.1 Data Preprocessing

In this experimental testing, we utilize Kitsune Network Attack Datasets [14], a collection of 9 network attack datasets captured from an IP-based commercial surveillance system or a network of IoT devices. Each dataset contains millions of network packets and different cyberattacks. In this data resource, all collected records were labeled by two type states, including: Normal and Attack. Therein, each piece of records contains 115 features and 1 label column.

We assess the performance of FL model on Fuzzing sub-dataset as one of unbalanced datasets in Kitsune datasets consisting of 1,811,356 samples labeled Normal and 432,783 samples labeled Attack. In our experiments, we divide datasets into two parts as described in Table 1.

4.2 Experimental Settings

Environmental Setup. We implemented FL model as a federated learning algorithm by using the TensorFlow framework. The designed CNN-GRU model is implemented using Keras. Our experiments are conducted on Google Colab Pro with the Intel Xeon Processor CPU 2 cores 2.3 GHz and the Tesla T4 GPU with 27 GB RAM.

Table 1. The number of samples in training and testing data.

Dataset	Train		Test		Total
	Attack	Normal	Attack	Normal	
Fuzzing	302948	1681521	129835	129835	2244139

Baseline Studies. In this work, we compare the performance of FL model on Non-IID data with 4 scenarios including FL without countermeasure against Non-IID data, FL with GAN method, FL with RL method, and FL with the combination of RL and GAN method respectively.

Performance Metrics. We use four metrics as follows: *Accuracy* is the ratio of all correct predictions for all records in test dataset; *Precision* is the ratio of correct predictions having attack label and total predictions belong to attack class; *Recall* is the correct predictions having attack label over the sum of correct predictions having attack label and misclassified belong to normal class; and *F1-score* is calculated by taking harmonic mean of precision and recall.

4.3 Evaluation Result

In our experiments, we investigate different levels of Non-IID data to evaluate the efficiency of 3 methods on FedIDS model. We define R is the ratio of records labeled Attack over Normal. In these experiments, we choose $R = 0.75, 0.5, 0.25$ for three different levels of Non-IID. In each scenario, all parties will have the same level of Non-IID R in training process to compare the performance of FedIDS model in 4 experiments including FL without solving the Non-IID problem, FL with GAN, FL with RL and FL with RL-GAN. Furthermore, to evaluate our method as close to reality, we also evaluate our model with the ratio $R = R^*$ which is a combination of three levels Non-IID as mentioned above and IID in data training of all parties. In the scenario of R^*, all parties will be separated into 4 groups with the same number of members, corresponding to $R = 0.75, 0.5, 0.25$, and 1. Notably, all experiments are conducted under condition of training FedIDS model on Non-IID data with 20 agents participating in FL process. Furthermore, these agents will be trained in a limit of 100 communication rounds to compare the performance of all countermeasures relied on the number of training rounds for the model to converge. Additionally, the training agents are desired to achieve the target test-accuracy, which is the pre-defined goal of a global model obtaining the values of all 4 metrics above 96%.

To figure out RL's superior performance over conventional selections based solely on the accuracy value of all clients, we made a comparison between RL and Top-5 countermeasure. In Top-5 countermeasure, we will select top of 5 clients, which have the highest accuracy, to aggregate the global model in the

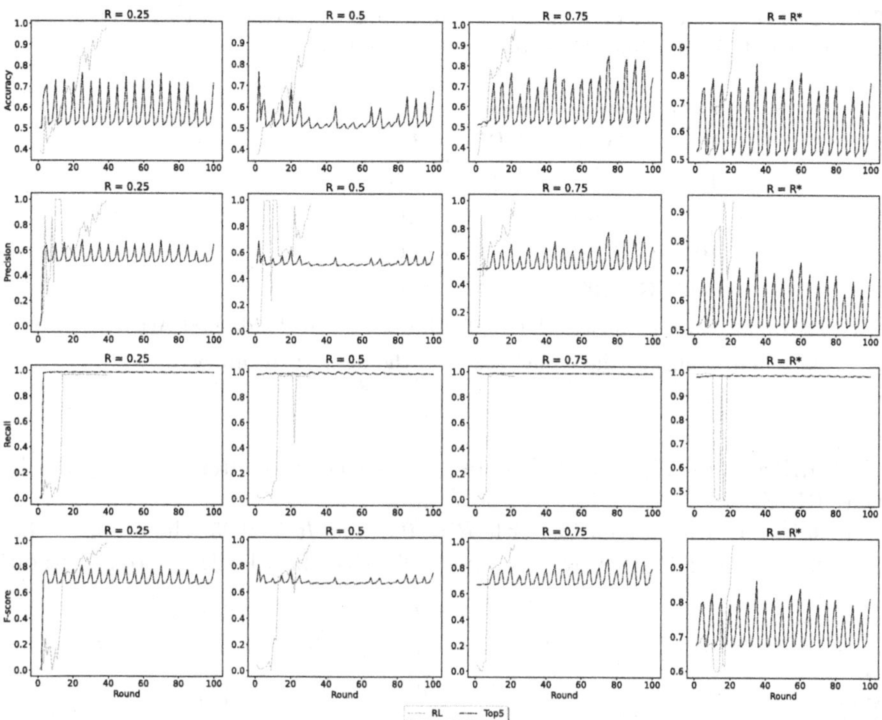

Fig. 7. Performance of IDS model on different levels of Non-IID data for comparison between RL and Top-5 countermeasures.

aggregation server. As results shown in Fig. 7, we can easily see that Top-5 through 100 rounds still does not reach the accuracy of the target test, whereas RL takes less than 50 rounds to achieve the target test-accuracy in 4 Non-IID levels. These results demonstrated that RL countermeasure has worked better than Top-5 in all 4 levels of Non-IID.

Results of 3 Countermeasures. The numerical results shown in Table 2 and Fig. 8 illustrate the performance of FL models, in terms of the accuracy, precision, recall and F-score, under the four different levels of Non-IID data $R = 0.25, 0.5, 0.75$, and R^* respectively. It can be easily seen that without solving Non-IID data problem, the test-accuracy of detection model is still not reached at 96% even though trained through 100 rounds. Also, the performance of the Fed-IDS model when applying three types of measures using GAN, RL and RL-GAN had obvious effects, which greatly reduced the number of communication rounds during FL training and also achieved high test-accuracy, precision, recall and F-score value. Specifically, in the scenario of the ratio $R = 0.75$, the global model's test-accuracy has reached 98.81% after 8 rounds when using GAN. Meanwhile, the model achieves accuracy greater than 98% after 22 rounds in case of using

Table 2. The number of communication rounds to reach a target accuracy on different levels of Non-IID with 3 methods solving Non-IID data.

Ratio R	Method solving Non-IID data.			
	Non	GAN	RL	RL-GAN
0.75	100(NG)	8(G)	22(G)	7(G)
0.5	100(NG)	20(G)	31(G)	7(G)
0.25	100(NG)	23(G)	46(G)	8(G)
R^*	100(NG)	100(NG)	22(G)	3(G)

NG (Not Gained) means the model did not reach the desired Accuracy.

G (Gained) means the model achieved the desired Accuracy.

RL. FedIDS model also reaches the target test-accuracy after only 7 rounds by using RL-GAN.

Besides, in other scenarios with $R = 0.5$ and $R = 0.25$, three approaches for tackling Non-IID data are also more effective than FedIDS model without

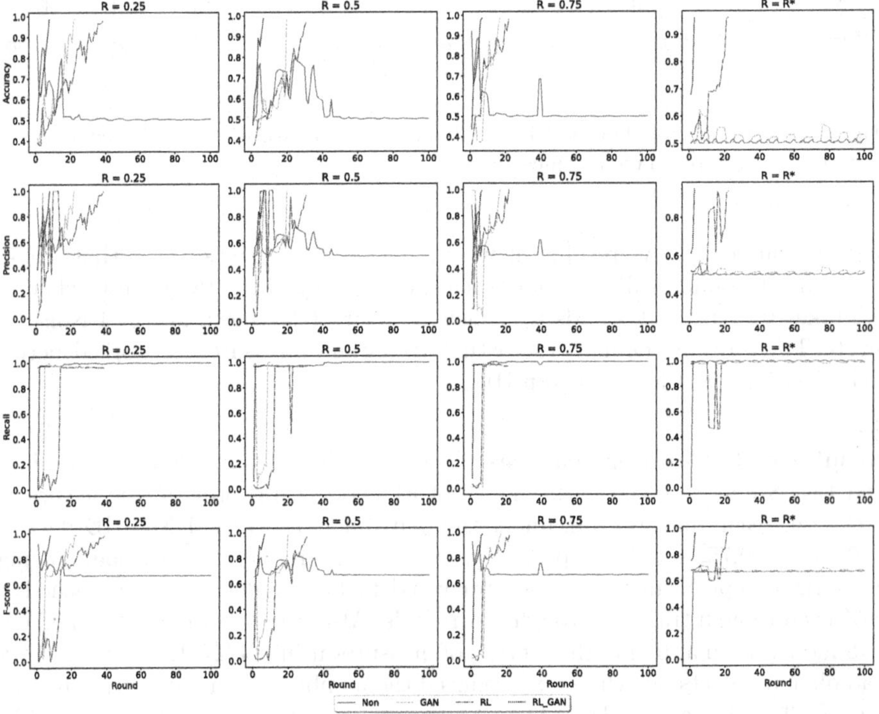

Fig. 8. Performance of IDS model on different levels of Non-IID data with 3 methods.

countermeasure. With $R = 0.5$, RL-GAN approach has achieved target test-accuracy with only 7 rounds, faster than RL and GAN approach with rounds of 31 and 20 respectively. With $R = 0.25$, RL-GAN approach still achieves target test-accuracy after only 8 rounds, which is faster than RL and GAN approach with rounds of 46 and 23 respectively. Finally, in the scenario $R = R^*$, RL-GAN and RL have achieved the target test-accuracy after 3 and 22 rounds respectively, while GAN through 100 rounds still does not reach the target. It is clear that Fed-IDS model with 3 different approaches can resolve the problems of Non-IID data. Specifically, with the required communication rounds for training FL-based IDS model to reach the target accuracy in above experiments, RL-GAN approach has proved itself more effective in training FL model on Non-IID data than other approaches of standalone adoption of RL or GAN.

5 Conclusion

Non-IID data is one of the major problems in adopting FL scheme for training collaborative ML-based models, leading to non-convergence in model aggregation with poor performance. It is also true in the context of collaborative intrusion detection systems, where the training data of participants is difficult to share the same distribution. To end this problem, we introduce the GAN-based approach in association with RL to mitigate the negative impacts of Non-IID data on training clients. The experimental results on different datasets show that the performance of FL-based IDS model increases with augmented data by GANs. Also, the RL agent learn from trial-and-error experiences gives a better strategy of choosing clients for global model aggregation in the IIoT context. Eventually, the combination of GAN and RL in FL-based IDS can help resolve the problem of heterogeneous data in distributed clients in the IIoT context. In the future, we intend to explore the Differential Privacy and Homomorphic Encryption for privacy-enhanced model aggregation and poisoning attack-resistance in the context of federated IIoT intrusion detection.

Acknowledgement. This research is funded by the University of Information Technology - Vietnam National University Ho Chi Minh City under grant number D1-2022-46.

Phan The Duy was funded by Vingroup JSC and supported by the Domestic Master, PhD Scholarship Programme of Vingroup Innovation Foundation (VINIF), Institute of Big Data, code VINIF.2021.TS.152.

References

1. Abdel-Basset, M., Hawash, H., Sallam, K.: Federated threat-hunting approach for microservice-based industrial cyber-physical system. IEEE Trans. Ind. Inform. **18**(3), 1905–1917 (2022)
2. Abdel-Basset, M., Moustafa, N., Hawash, H., Razzak, I., Sallam, K.M., Elkomy, O.M.: Federated intrusion detection in blockchain-based smart transportation systems. IEEE Trans. Intell. Transp. Syst. **23**(3), 2523–2537 (2022)

3. Alazab, M., RM, S.P., Parimala, P., Maddikunta, P.K.R., Gadekallu, T.R., Pham, Q.V.: Federated learning for cybersecurity: concepts, challenges, and future directions. IEEE Trans. Ind. Inform. **18**(5), 3501–3509 (2022)
4. Attota, D.C., Mothukuri, V., Parizi, R.M., Pouriyeh, S.: An ensemble multi-view federated learning intrusion detection for IoT. IEEE Access **9**, 117734–117745 (2021)
5. Bouacida, N., Mohapatra, P.: Vulnerabilities in federated learning. IEEE Access **9**, 63229–63249 (2021)
6. Campos, E.M., et al.: Evaluating federated learning for intrusion detection in internet of things: review and challenges. Comput. Netw. **203**, 108661 (2022)
7. Chandran, P., Bhat, R., Chakravarthi, A., Chandar, S.: Weight divergence driven divide-and-conquer approach for optimal federated learning from non-IID data (2021)
8. Ghimire, B., Rawat, D.B.: Recent advances on federated learning for cybersecurity and cybersecurity for federated learning for internet of things. IEEE Internet Things J. (2022)
9. Hsu, R.H., et al.: A privacy-preserving federated learning system for android malware detection based on edge computing. In: 2020 15th Asia Joint Conference on Information Security (AsiaJCIS), pp. 128–136 (2020)
10. Khramtsova, E., Hammerschmidt, C., Lagraa, S., State, R.: Federated learning for cyber security: SOC collaboration for malicious URL detection. In: 2020 IEEE 40th International Conference on Distributed Computing Systems (ICDCS), pp. 1316–1321 (2020)
11. Li, B., Wu, Y., Song, J., Lu, R., Li, T., Zhao, L.: DeepFed: federated deep learning for intrusion detection in industrial cyber-physical systems. IEEE Trans. Ind. Inform. **17**(8), 5615–5624 (2021)
12. Li, Q., et al.: A survey on federated learning systems: vision, hype and reality for data privacy and protection. IEEE Trans. Knowl. Data Eng. (2021)
13. Mao, H., Alizadeh, M., Menache, I., Kandula, S.: Resource management with deep reinforcement learning. In: Proceedings of the 15th ACM Workshop on Hot Topics in Networks, pp. 50–56. HotNets 2016. Association for Computing Machinery, New York, NY, USA (2016)
14. Mirsky, Y., Doitshman, T., Elovici, Y., Shabtai, A.: Kitsune: an ensemble of autoencoders for online network intrusion detection. In: The Network and Distributed System Security Symposium (NDSS) 2018 (2018)
15. Mothukuri, V., Khare, P., Parizi, R.M., Pouriyeh, S., Dehghantanha, A., Srivastava, G.: Federated-learning-based anomaly detection for IoT security attacks. IEEE Internet Things J. **9**(4), 2545–2554 (2022)
16. Mothukuri, V., Parizi, R.M., Pouriyeh, S., Huang, Y., Dehghantanha, A., Srivastava, G.: A survey on security and privacy of federated learning. Future Gener. Comput. Syst. **115**, 619–640 (2021)
17. Nguyen, T.D., Marchal, S., Miettinen, M., Fereidooni, H., Asokan, N., Sadeghi, A.R.: Dïot: a federated self-learning anomaly detection system for IoT. In: 2019 IEEE 39th International Conference on Distributed Computing Systems (ICDCS), pp. 756–767 (2019)
18. Nguyen, T.G., Phan, T.V., Hoang, D.T., Nguyen, T.N., So-In, C.: Federated deep reinforcement learning for traffic monitoring in SDN-based IoT networks. IEEE Trans. Cogn. Commun. Netw. **7**(4), 1048–1065 (2021)
19. Rey, V., Sánchez Sánchez, P.M., Huertas Celdrán, A., Bovet, G.: Federated learning for malware detection in IoT devices. Comput. Netw. **204**, 108693 (2022)

20. Taheri, R., Shojafar, M., Alazab, M., Tafazolli, R.: FED-IIoT: a robust federated malware detection architecture in industrial IoT. IEEE Trans. Ind. Inform. **17**(12), 8442–8452 (2021)
21. Vy, N.C., Quyen, N.H., Duy, P.T., Pham, V.H.: Federated learning-based intrusion detection in the context of IIoT networks: poisoning attack and defense. In: Yang, M., Chen, C., Liu, Y. (eds.) Network and System Security, pp. 131–147. Springer International Publishing, Cham (2021). https://doi.org/10.1007/978-3-030-92708-0_8
22. Wang, H., Kaplan, Z., Niu, D., Li, B.: Optimizing federated learning on non-iid data with reinforcement learning. In: IEEE INFOCOM 2020 - IEEE Conference on Computer Communications, pp. 1698–1707 (2020)
23. Yazdinejad, A., Dehghantanha, A., Parizi, R.M., Hammoudeh, M., Karimipour, H., Srivastava, G.: Block hunter: federated learning for cyber threat hunting in blockchain-based IIoT networks. IEEE Trans. Ind. Inform. (2022)
24. Yonetani, R., Takahashi, T., Hashimoto, A., Ushiku, Y.: Decentralized learning of generative adversarial networks from non-iid data (2019)
25. Yu, P., Wynter, L., Lim, S.H.: Fed+: A family of fusion algorithms for federated learning. arXiv:2009.06303 (2020)
26. Zhang, T., Gao, L., He, C., Zhang, M., Krishnamachari, B., Avestimehr, S.: Federated learning for internet of things: applications, challenges, and opportunities (2021). https://doi.org/10.48550/ARXIV.2111.07494, arxiv:2111.07494
27. Zhang, W., et al.: Blockchain-based federated learning for device failure detection in industrial IoT. IEEE Internet Things J. **8**(7), 5926–5937 (2021)
28. Zhu, H., Xu, J., Liu, S., Jin, Y.: Federated learning on non-IID data: a survey. Neurocomputing **465**, 371–390 (2021)

Preventing Adversarial Attacks Against Deep Learning-Based Intrusion Detection System

Xuan-Ha Nguyen[1,2], Xuan-Duong Nguyen[1,2], and Kim-Hung Le[1,2](✉)

[1] University of Information Technology, Ho Chi Minh City, Vietnam
{hanx,hunglk}@uit.edu.vn, 18520212@gm.uit.edu.vn
[2] Vietnam National University, Ho Chi Minh City, Vietnam

Abstract. Deep learning (DL) applications in network intrusion detection systems (NIDS) are increasingly popular in protecting IoT networks against cyber threats. However, these systems are threatened by adversarial attacks that can evade detection and disrupt the network. Preventing such attacks is highly challenging due to their variation and the resource-constrained nature of IoT devices. Therefore, in this paper, we first evaluate the impact of adversarial attacks on a novel DL-based NIDS designed for IoT networks. Then, we propose an adversarial detector powered by a light gradient boosted algorithm against adversarial attacks. The superiority of our proposal is to detect several types of adversarial attacks with high accuracy while ensuring low additional latency. The evaluation results on practical datasets show that our model effectively detects adversarial attacks, with an overall F-score of 99.66% and much higher than that of its competitors.

Keywords: Adversarial attack detection · Network intrusion detection system · Machine learning

1 Introduction

With the exponential growth of the Internet, the accumulated frequency and severity of cyber-attacks on modern networks have been notably increasing and gaining more attention from both academia and industry. The attack that may shut down the oil networks of the largest American oil supplier in May 2021 is just one example of the many emerging threats [1]. This led to an increased need for defense solutions to protect critical system components against cyber-attacks. Therefore, the network-based intrusion detection system, a straightforward and high-performance solution, is widely deployed on Internet gateways to monitor and identify suspicious network patterns transmitted over the network, generating alerts if these patterns are detected.

The early generations of NIDSs were designed on the basis of the security rules and characteristics of attacks provided by security experts. These systems

C. Su et al. (Eds.): ISPEC 2022, LNCS 13620, pp. 382–396, 2022.
https://doi.org/10.1007/978-3-031-21280-2_21

aim to prevent well-known attacks from the past; however, several weaknesses are revealed in the modern complex network environment where novel and complex attacks frequently emerge, making traditional NIDSs hardly adapt to emerging zero-day attacks. Furthermore, they are ineffective in monitoring and comparing complex traffic with large-scale attack datasets, especially in edge computing systems with resources-constrained devices [2]. Motivated by these limitations, the modern generation of NIDS aims to use anomaly or hybrid techniques, which create a model from the characteristic of a typical network and detect anomaly points based on the difference with normal points. These new techniques are superior to traditional approaches due to their ability to detect unknown attacks. They typically employ machine learning algorithms such as K-Nearest neighbor (KNN) [3,4], Random Forest (RF) [5,6], and Support Vector Machine (SVM) [7]. However, the success of deep learning (DL) in many fields has recently facilitated researchers to develop NIDS based on deep learning algorithms. Several state-of-the-art deep learning-based NIDSs can distinguish normal and abnormal network activities with higher performance and less constraint [8–10]. Therefore, this research direction draws more attention and shows potential for anomaly detection in networks.

Despite its success in various fields, deep learning has been shown to be vulnerable to adversarial attacks that have successfully targeted DL models in various domains recently [11]. In particular, in network security, there have been novel studies about attacking DL-based NIDSs [12,13]. However, their detection performance is severely affected by the imperceptible perturbation of the input data generated by adversarial attacks. These attacks are also potential threats that attackers exploit to bypass existing DL-based NIDS [11]. Therefore, the main purpose of this paper is to improve the robustness of DL-based NIDS against adversarial attacks by proposing an effective adversarial detector based on the light gradient boosted machine model. Our contributions are listed below.

- We propose an adversarial detector placed before NIDSs to prevent adversarial attacks. The proposed detector employs a light gradient boosted machine algorithm to enhance not only detection accuracy but also processing speed, limiting the effect on network latency.
- We evaluated the impact of adversarial attacks on DL-based NIDS in the context of edge computing.
- We comprehensively evaluated and compared our proposal with its competitors on CICIDS2017, a popular IDS dataset.

The remainder of this paper is presented as follows. Section 2 first introduces some research on adversarial attacks against machine learning models in general and Dl-based NIDSs in detail. Then, Sect. 3 denotes the notation and related background knowledge. Next, Sect. 4 presents an overview of the adversarial attack and our solution. Subsequently, Sect. 5 presents evaluated datasets, evaluation metrics, and the results of our experiment. Finally, Sect. 6 summarizes our work.

2 Related Works

In recent decades, accompanied by the explosive growth of DL models is the appearance of adversarial attacks, which can cause the DL model to make a wrong prediction. Realizing this weakness of the DL model, there have been studies on the level of influence and defensive measures to minimize the impact of adversarial attacks on DL models. Research [11] synthesizes and presents an overview of leading research on adversarial attack techniques against deep learning and defensive strategies. The study investigates the application of adversarial attack techniques in real-world industrial contexts, explains some of the most recently studied defense techniques, and comments on open issues for future research.

Due to the emergence of adversarial threats, the development of ML protectors against adversarial attacks has attracted attention. Existing research in this area can be divided into three main groups according to the approach. The first is a collection of studies that use data preprocessing techniques, such as feature engineering and feature selection [14–16]. These studies stem from the need to handle spammers on social networks, a problem related to adversarial sample processing. These techniques help build more accurate ML models and partially limit the impact of adversarial attacks. However, they cannot cope with the evolution of today's adversarial attack techniques. The second research group approaches the problem through the lens of game theory, in which both adversary and detector play a game to deceive each other [17–19]. Recent studies in this direction focus on the application of Generative Adversarial Networks (GANs) [20,21]. The weakness of this approach is that the modeling process is too diverse when faced with many types of ML models. The third research group focuses on preserving Deep Neuron Network (DNN) models by using gradient methods or their variations [22,23]. Many techniques have been researched, such as defensive distillation [24] or adversarial retraining [25–27].

In the cyber-security domain, particularly in the design of NIDSs, the study [28] and [29] evaluated the effectiveness of several machine learning and ANN models in detecting adversarial samples. The study evaluates five algorithms for detecting adversarial attacks generated from four adversarial attack techniques. The results are auspicious, with a detection rate of adversarial samples of up to 99%. The studies [12] and [13] investigated the effect of adversarial attack techniques on anomaly-based NIDS. They tested several machine learning models with adversarial samples generated from different adversarial attack techniques and network datasets. The results show that the attack techniques work well when causing high misclassification rates in anomaly-based NIDS. These researches highlight the vulnerability of anomaly-based NIDS in the face of adversarial attacks and propose the need for research on safeguards for NIDS. In the study [30], the authors developed the Hydra toolkit to evaluate the influence of adversarial attack techniques on anomaly-based NIDS models. Research using Neptune, an anomaly-based NIDS, as a target for attacks from Hydra. Experimental results show that with just a small change in features, many classifiers completely fail to detect SYN Flood attacks.

In a narrower study, study [31] designs a novel adversarial attack against NIDS operating in IoT environments. The study proposes two new techniques to extract the black-box model from a small amount of data and to evaluate the impact of data features to find critical ones. Therefore, the proposed technique successfully bypassed one of the state-of-the-art NIDS-Kitsune, achieving an average attack success rate of 94.31% though it only needs to change a tiny number of bytes in packets. Shuang Zhao et al., in study [32] proposed an advanced GAN-based attack model called attackGAN. This new method can generate an adversarial attack that can efficiently overcome the back-box IDS while maintaining network traffic functionality. The NSL-KDD dataset experiments prove that attackGAN achieved a better attack success rate and a higher Evade increase rate than other adversarial attack techniques.

3 Preliminaries

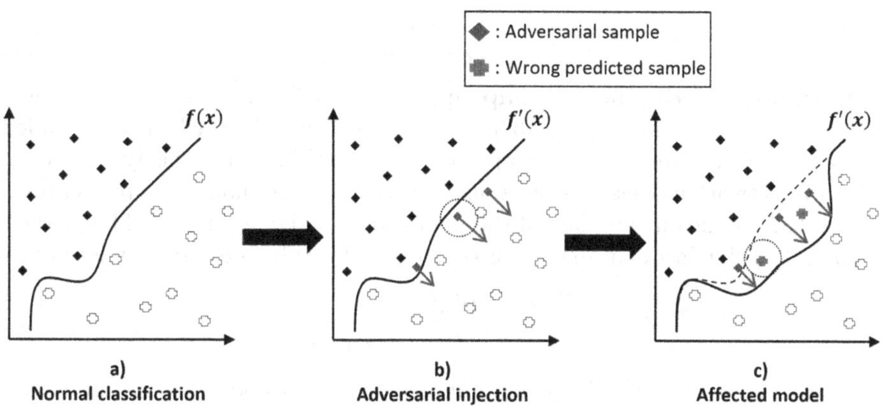

Fig. 1. The effect of adversarial attacks on model performance.

In this section, we first introduce the notation and background definitions of the relative techniques used in this paper. Specifically, let denote the dataset without adversaries as $\{X \in \mathbb{R}^{N*M}, y \in \mathbb{N}^N\}$, where N presents the number of samples and M is the dataset feature dimensions. The vector $x_i = X[i,:](1 \leqslant i \leqslant N)$ is a data sample with label y_i, in which x_{ij} $(1 \leqslant j \leqslant M)$ presents the jth feature of sample x_i. Our primary goal is to build an adversarial detector $f(x)$ to filter adversaries before they can affect the targeted model. Let x^{adv} be the adversarial sample created by perturbing the origin sample x. Therefore, $\epsilon = \Delta x = x^{adv} - x$ represents the perturbation added to the origin samples. We use $X^{adv} \in \mathbb{R}^{N'*M}$ to present the adversarial dataset, in which mixed non-adversarial and adversarial samples.

An adversarial attack often attempts to skew the prediction results of a target machine learning model. Figure 1 better describes the process of an adversarial attack. A classification model usually attempts to construct a function $f(x)$ to distinguish between labels. However, when adversaries appear (red nodes in phase b) of Fig. 1), they affect the function $f(x)$, causing misclassification. As a result, the effectiveness of the classifier is reduced when more samples are misclassified (blue nodes). In practice, an adversarial attack can poison the model during the training process to degrade performance or avoid being detected by the classifier in executed mode. In our experimental setup, we focus only on the latter strategy. To evaluate the impact of adversarial attacks on NIDS, we used the four techniques mentioned below to attack the targeted model.

- **Fast Gradient Sign Method** Goodfellow et al. [27] introduced an untargeted attack method called Fast Gradient Sign Method (FGSM) to generate adversarial examples by adding a small perturbation. In essence, FGSM computes the loss function gradient $l(x_i, y_i)$ of the detection model. Then, according to the direction of the gradients, FSGM adds the meaningful noise to the original samples, which maximizes the magnitude of the loss function but does not exceed a ϵ value. Clearly, the FGSM algorithm creates an adversary as follows:
$$x_i^{adv} = x_i + \epsilon * sign(\nabla_x l(x_i, y_i)) \tag{1}$$
- **Jacobian-based saliency map approach (JSMA)** Based on the Jacobian matrix, the authors in [33] proposed a targeted attack method called the Jacobian-based saliency map approach (JSMA), which easily fools deep neural network models. The Jacobian matrix describes how the input features could affect the output class of the model for an original sample. The method computes the Jacobian matrix of the neuron layer before the softmax layer:
$$\nabla\theta(x) = \frac{\partial\theta(x)}{\partial x} = \left[\frac{\partial\theta_v(x)}{\partial x_u}\right]_{u\in[1,..,L_{in}],v\in[1,..,L_{out}]} \tag{2}$$
where L_{in}, L_{out} respectively the number of hidden nodes on the input and output layer; u, v respectively the index for the x features and the $\theta(x)$ output player. Based on these values, JSMA attempts to define an adversarial saliency map $M(x; y')$ and perturb the feature $x[u]$ with $\|M(x; y')\|_\infty$ to have a significant impact on the output of the targeted classifier.
- **DeepFool** Moosavi-Dezfooli et al. [34] proposed a new approach to generate minimal noise to fool a model into deciding that it belongs to a wrong label. The algorithm shows that for an affine binary classifier $f(x) = \theta^\top x + \beta$, where θ and β, respectively, present the weight and bias of the model, then the minimal noise necessary to change the sample class x_0 is the distance from x_0 to the boundary hyperplane $\mathcal{F} = \{x : f(x) = 0\}$, which is $\frac{-f(x_0)}{\|\theta\|_2^2}\theta$. For a general binary classifier, DeepFool iteratively calculates the noise ϵ:
$$\underset{\epsilon}{\operatorname{argmin}} \|\epsilon\|_2 \text{ subject to } f(x') + \nabla f(x')^\top \epsilon = 0 \tag{3}$$
This process runs until $f(x') \neq f(x)$, and the final noise is finally calculated by the sum of ϵ. In practice, the final noise is multiplied by a small constant to certainly reach the other side of the boundary.

- **Carlini and Wagner attack (CW)** Carlini and Wagner [35] proposed a powerful approach based on deep learning, namely the C&W attack. By modifying the objective function that opts for gradient optimization, adversarial examples can be generated accurately using the robustness of different measured perturbations, such as $L0$, $L2$, and L_∞. CW generates adversarial noise ϵ by optimizing the objective function as follows:

$$\min_{\epsilon} D(x, x+\epsilon) + C \cdot L_{cw}(x+\epsilon) \text{ subject to } x+\epsilon \in [0,1] \tag{4}$$

where $D(,)$ denotes $\left\|x - x^{adv}\right\|^2$; C presents a constant and $L_{cw}(x+\epsilon)$ is the adversarial loss function, which satisfies $L_{cw}(x+\epsilon) \leq 0$ if only the prediction of the model is the target attack class. In practice, the loss function L_{cw} can be formulated as follows:

$$L_{cw} = \max\left(Z\left(\boldsymbol{x}^{\text{adv}}\right)_k - \max_{i \neq k} Z\left(\boldsymbol{x}^{\text{adv}}\right)_i, 0\right) \tag{5}$$

4 Our Proposal

This section presents an overview of the anomaly-based adversarial detector approach. First, we present the system diagram and introduce the background of adversarial attack techniques. Then, describe how to design a machine learning model for the detector model.

4.1 Overview

Our proposal is designed to detect and remove adversarial samples before reaching the NIDS attack detection model. To archive that, we integrate our detector into the NIDS data processing flow and place it before the central processing component, behind the preprocessing constituents. To better illustrate the main data processing flow, Fig. 2 provides an overview of the composition of the proposed detector in a NIDS:

- **Preprocessing Data & Features Extraction Components** are the two data preprocessing parts of the NIDS system. They are migrated in front of the Adversarial Detection Components but retain the original design and functionality. Raw mixed data is processed to generate valuable features that describe the current state of the network. Then they are passed to the adversarial detection module for processing instead of being passed directly to the NIDS model.
- **The Adversarial Detection Component** is the main processing block that we propose. This block is responsible for detecting adversarial samples and discarding them before reaching the main NIDS processing block. Valuable features are analyzed to find adversarial samples, and nonadversarial samples are transferred to the NIDS model for further processing.

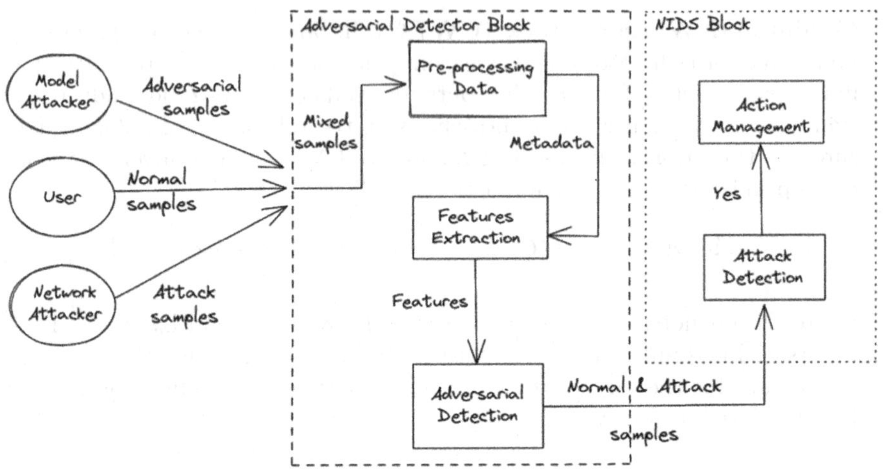

Fig. 2. The overview of our proposal.

- **Attack Detection & Action Manager Component** are the two main processing parts of NIDS, which detect network attacks and send alerts to the administrator. Our proposal does not change the design and operation of these two blocks.

Designing an adversarial detector before the NIDS models offers significant advantages over previous techniques: (1) Performance: Detects and removes adversarial samples accurately without affecting NIDS performance (2) Flexibility: easily integrates with NIDS against various types of adversarial attacks without retraining NIDS models. Take the adversarial retraining technique as an example. This technique is a kind of augmented data that retrains the NIDS model with adversarial samples. This method can be used successfully with some specific attacks, but it is ineffective against others. It also affects the effectiveness of NIDS when dealing with more complex data. Furthermore, attackers can change adversarial techniques to bypass NIDS.

Therefore, a separate detector that focuses on adversarial attacks is a better strategy when it performs more efficiently against various adversarial attacks. Reducing the number of labels that the NIDS model has to deal with, hence enhancing the NIDS performance. Also, it is hard to create adversarial samples that fool both the adversarial detector and the NIDS model in time.

4.2 Adversarial Detection Method

We define the necessary criteria for an adversarial detector model as follows to effectively protect NIDS from adversarial attacks. First, the detector must be able to accurately detect a variety of attack techniques and minimize the false positive rate. Second, the detector must have a fast processing speed to avoid affecting the overall performance of the system in the IoT context. To satisfy those criteria, we proposed to use an ensemble algorithm - light gradient boosted machine (LightGBM) [36] - for the adversarial detector.

LightGBM is a boosted version of the Gradient Boosting Decision Tree (GBDT) algorithm. The basic idea of the algorithm is to combine many weak models into strong ones, and this design allows us to take advantage of the fast learning ability of weak models and optimize performance when combining multiple models. First, due to the sparsity of the feature space of the network data, we operate the Exclusive Feature Bundling (EFB) technique to minimize the number of features. This preliminary stage guarantees that mutually exclusive features that appeared in the dataset are merged into the smallest number of features to reduce memory computation. After that, the algorithm performs iterations to optimize the target decision tree. In this stage, we invoked Gradient-based One-Side Sampling (GOSS) to reduce the training-time computation. Based on the values of gradients, we focused on a set of large-gradient samples to minimize the loss function and keep the influence of the small-gradient sample, aiming not to significantly change the distribution of data. First, we compute the gradients and sort them in descending order according to the absolute values. Afterward, we selected the top $\alpha \times 100\%$ samples and randomly selected $\beta \times 100\%$ samples from the rest of the dataset. The information gain score is calculated by combining all $\alpha \times 100\%$ samples and a normalized sum of the gradients of $\beta \times 100\%$ samples by multiplicating a constant $\frac{1-a}{b}$. We generate a new decision tree and update the target function based on the information gain score. Algorithm 1 better describes the LightGBM algorithm.

To optimize the algorithm's performance, we need to choose appropriate hyperparameters. In our experience, we notice these parameters that considerably impact the tuning results (e.g., maximum leaves node for base learners, the number of boosted trees that require training). They affect accuracy and execution speed and limit the possibility of overfitting. To optimize hyperparameters effectively, we use Bayesian search based on the Bayes Theorem to guide the search to reach optimized hyperparameters quickly [37,38]. In this problem, the priority is to optimize the value of an unknown function f at a sample point.

$$x = \arg\max_{x \in S} f(x) \tag{6}$$

where S denotes the search space of x. Unlike other search methods, the main idea of Bayesian search is to optimize parameter selection by combining the prior distribution of the function $f(x)$ with the current sample to acquire the posterior value. Next, the posterior value is used to determine whether the $f(x)$ function is optimized according to the acquisition function u. Then, the function u finds the next combination of samples.

Algorithm 2 clearly presents the Bayesian search algorithm, where $D_i = \{x_i, y_i\}$ represents the training dataset consisting of the i distribution of the function f. Specifically, it focuses on optimizing the acquisition function u (line 2) and updating the objective function f (lines 3 and 4). During the searching process, the objective function is updated on the basis of the input data. This process is repeated continuously until the u function is optimized or reaches its

Algorithm 1: The LightGBM algorithm

Input: Training dataset $T = \{(x_i, y_i) \mid x_i \in \mathbb{R}, y_i \in \{0,1\}\}_{i=1}^{N}$
Output: Predicted function $\hat{y}$
Hyperparameter: Γ : total iterations; $\mathcal{L}$: loss function; α : sampling ratio of large gradient data; β : sampling ratio of small gradient data;

`/* EFB technique */`
Merge mutually exclusive feature of $x_i, i = \{1 \dots N\}$
$\hat{y}_0(x) = 0$
for $t \leftarrow 1$ **to** Γ **do**
    `/* GOSS technique */`
    $\Delta = \left\{ \frac{\delta \mathcal{L}(y_i, \hat{y}(x_i))}{\delta \hat{y}(x_i)} \mid \hat{y}(x) = \hat{y}_{t-1}(x) \right\}_{i=1}^{N}$
    $N_\alpha = \alpha \times N; N_\beta = \beta \times N$
    $sorted\_x = Sorted(x, |\Delta|)$ `// Descending sort x according` $|\Delta|$ `values`
    $A = sorted\_x[1 : N_\alpha]$ `// Select top` N_α `samples`
    $B = RandomSelect(sorted\_x[N_\alpha + 1 : N], N_\beta)$ `// Randomly select` N_β `samples from the rest`
    $V_j(d) = \frac{1}{n} \left(\frac{(\sum_{x_i \in A_l} |\Delta|_i + \frac{1-a}{b} \sum_{x_i \in B_l} |\Delta|_i)^2}{n_l^j(d)} + \frac{(\sum_{x_i \in A_r} |\Delta|_i + \frac{1-a}{b} \sum_{x_i \in B_r} |\Delta|_i)^2}{n_r^j(d)} \right)$
    `// The variance gain of splitting feature` j `at point` d `(`A_l`,` A_r`,` B_l `and` B_r `are parts of A and B respectively).`
    $T' = A + B$
    $\hat{y}_t(x)' \leftarrow T'$ `// Generate a new decision tree based on set` T'
    $\hat{y}_t(x) = \hat{y}_t(x)' + \hat{y}_{t-1}(x)$
end

Algorithm 2: The Bayesian Search algorithm.

for $i = 1,2...$ **do**
    Determine x_i by optimizing the acquisition function u:

$$x_i = \arg\max_x u(x \mid D_{i-1})$$

    Sample the objective function f: $y_i = f(x_i)$
    Update data $D_i = \{D_{i-1}),(x_i,y_i)\}$ and update function f
end

maximum iterations. It should be noted that Bayesian Search takes advantage of both exploration (sampling from an unreliable area) and exploitation (sampling from a high-value area). So, it can help simplify the sampling process and improve performance even with multiple local maxima [38].

5 Evaluation

5.1 Evaluation Dataset and Metrics

In our experiment, we select the detection model from the study [8], which applies a deep learning model deployed to edge devices as the target model for adversarial attacks. We reuse the model pre-trained on the packet-based CICIDS2017 dataset and use a subset for further research experiments. It should be noted that our proposed methodologies can be generalized for the applications of other machine learning models. The adversarial samples generated from attacks, introduced in Sect. 3, are mixed with the original samples to create a new dataset. The training pipeline follows Sect. 4.2 when the LightGBM model is first tuned to select the best hyperparameters and then trained/tested with the train/test set.

According to adversarial attacks benchmarks, an attack performs better if the lower the difference in the adversarial sample and the lower accuracy of the targeted model. Therefore, to evaluate adversarial attack techniques, we use the $L2 - norm$ index to calculate the error level of the adversarial samples and to calculate the accuracy index of the targeted model when processing adversarial samples. The formula for the $L2 - norm$ score is presented as follows:

$$L2 = \frac{\sum_{i=1}^{N} x_i}{N} \tag{7}$$

$$|x_i| = \sqrt{\sum_{k=1}^{M} |x_{i,k}|^2} \tag{8}$$

where X_i is the $L2 - norm$ value of each sample in the data set of N samples; $L2$ is the average $L2 - norm$ value of the data set. Formula 8 describes how to calculate X_i of a sample of M features. In addition to that, the accuracy index is defined as the ratio of correctly predicted samples among all samples examined.

5.2 Experimental Results and Discussion

The Impact of Adversarial Attacks on the Target Model: The results in Table 1 show the impact of adversarial attacks on the target model and the effectiveness of our defense method. In more detail, the CW attack has the best ability to fool the target model by reducing the accuracy from 99.74% to 0.14%. The DeepFool attack is less efficient than the CW attack in terms of accuracy (1.48% compared to 0.14%), but it exceeds the $L2$ score by 0.88 compared to 40.37. The low $L2$ score means that Deepfool only needs to change very little original data while archiving a high impact on the NIDS model. Both FGSM and JSMA attacks have a relatively good ability to attack the targeted model when the accuracy is reduced to approximately 23%. However, the FGSM attack requires a considerable change from the original data ($L2 = 3912.82$), which is a challenge to apply in practice. In general, the experimental results show that adversarial

Table 1. The performance of the target model before and after being attacked with and without our defense method.

	Before attack	After attack				After Filter
		CW	DeepFool	FGSM	JSMA	
L2	x	40.37	0.88	3912.82	3.78	x
Accuracy (%)	99.74	0.14	1.48	23.63	23.48	98.67

attacks can effectively bypass the NIDS model. Therefore, it is necessary to protect NIDS by applying our adversarial detector. Our proposal proved to be superior in limiting the impact of these attacks when recovering the accuracy of the NIDS model to 98.67%, close to the pre-attack accuracy of 99.74%.

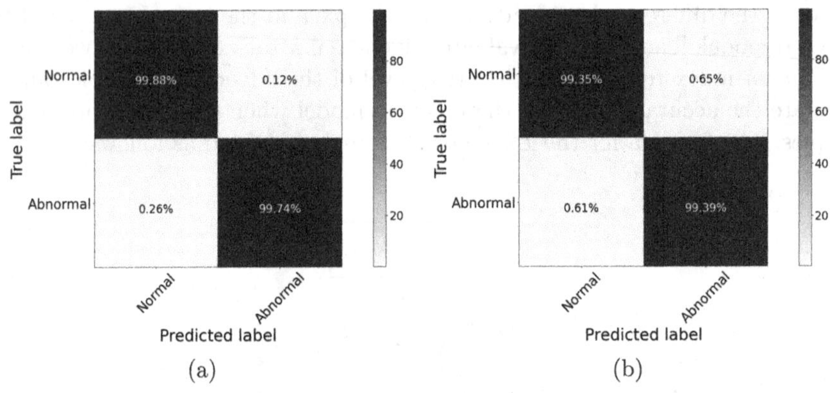

Fig. 3. The defense performance of our proposal: (a) The confusion matrix of the target model before being attacked by adversarial samples; (b) The confusion matrix of the target model after filtering adversarial samples using our proposal

The Defense Performance Against Adversarial Attacks: Figure 3 shows the results of the NIDS model before suffering adversarial attacks and when protected by our adversarial detector. We can see that the NIDS model is not significantly affected by adversarial attacks. This means that the detection performance is well recovered. In detail, the false alarm rate increased from 0.12% to 0.65%; the true positive rate decreased slightly from 99.74% to 99.39%. These results again prove the superiority of our proposal in terms of defending against adversarial attacks. Furthermore, Fig. 4 shows the results of our proposed adversarial detector as a confusion matrix. Our proposed model achieves outstanding results when accurately detecting 99.54% of attack samples, and the false alert rate (or fall positive rate) is minimized to 0.75%. These indicators show that the model effectively minimizes the impact of adversarial attacks on the NIDS model. We also note that our proposal consumes low computational resources.

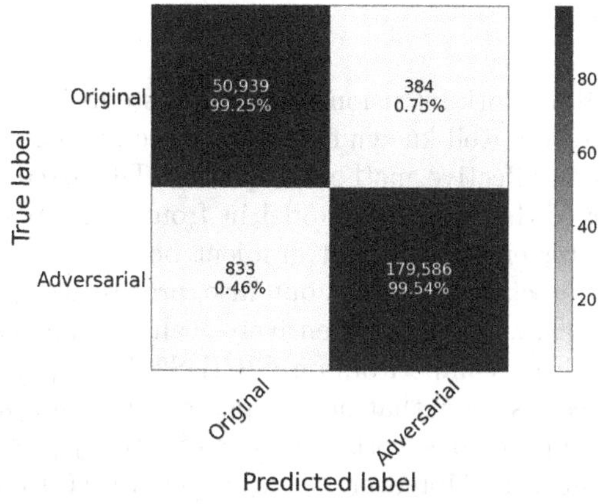

Fig. 4. The confusion matrix of detecting adversarial attacks using our proposal.

With the default setup of the Colab environment, our model uses up to 48.95% CPU and 171 MB of RAM. The experimental results show that the proposed model operates effectively with low resource consumption.

Table 2. Comparing the defense performance between our proposal and its competitors.

Model	Accuracy	Precision	Recall	Fallout	F1 score	Training time	Inference time
Our proposal	99.47	99.79	99.54	0.75	99.66	0.62	0.40
GP-based [39]	84.64	84.85	97.76	61.46	90.83	4300.73	0.51
ANN-based [28]	x	99.00	85.00	x	91.00	x	x
NN-based [28]	x	99.00	91.00	x	95.00	x	x
Random forest [28]	x	99.00	91.00	x	95.00	x	x
AdaBoost [28]	x	99.00	88.00	x	93.00	x	x
SVM [28]	x	99.00	93.00	x	96.00	x	x

Baseline Comparison: Table 2 presents the comparison between our proposed method and related works. We can see that our proposal offers the best accuracy of 99.47% and the lowest false positive rate of 0.75%. It ensures that there is no bottleneck when filtering adversarial samples. To compare with our results, we re-experiment the [39] study, using the Gaussian Process Regression (GP-based) model, and reuse the results from the [28] study. The GP-based model reaches a high recall (97.76% compared to 99.54% of ours), but the fallout is extremely high (61.46% compared to 0.75% of ours). The results from [28] are superior to the GP-based model but do not surpass our proposal. They have 99% precision and 88–93% recall (compared to our 99.79% and 99.54%). However, they did not present other metrics such as accuracy, fallout, or train/test time for comparison. Generally, the results show that our study has had better compared indicators.

6 Conclusion

Deep learning-based network intrusion detection systems have been widely used in recent years to prevent well-known cyber-attacks on modern networks. In this paper, we propose an effective method to protect DL-based NIDS by placing an additional layer of the ensemble model in front of it to filter adversarials. The proposed detector employs a light gradient boosted machine algorithm to enhance not only detection accuracy but also processing speed, limiting the effect on network latency. We comprehensively evaluated and compared our proposed algorithm with its competitors on CICIDS2017, a popular IDS dataset. The experimental results show that our proposed algorithms achieve F-score of 99.66%, higher than in previous works, and can effectively protect the DL model against adversarial attacks. Moreover, the false alert rate (or fall positive rate) is minimized at 0.75%. In future work, we will design another method and detector to classify multi-adversary attacks and evaluate them in a more comprehensive experiment.

Acknowledgment. This research was supported by The VNUHCM-University of Information Technology's Scientific Research Support Fund

References

1. Hobbs, A.: The colonial pipeline hack: exposing vulnerabilities in us cybersecurity. In: SAGE Business Cases. SAGE Publications, SAGE Business Cases Originals (2021)
2. Eskandari, M., Janjua, Z.H., Vecchio, M., Antonelli, F.: Passban IDS: an intelligent anomaly-based intrusion detection system for IoT edge devices. IEEE Internet Things J. **7**(8), 6882–6897 (2020)
3. Wazirali, R.: An improved intrusion detection system based on KNN hyperparameter tuning and cross-validation. Arab. J. Sci. Eng. **45**(12), 10859–10873 (2020)
4. Tran, B-S., Ho, T-H., Do, T-X., Le, K-H.: Empirical performance evaluation of machine learning based DDoS attack detections. In: Recent Advances in Internet of Things and Machine Learning, pp. 283–299. Springer (2022). https://doi.org/10.1007/978-3-030-90119-6_23
5. Resende, P.A.A., Drummond, A.C.: A survey of random forest based methods for intrusion detection systems. ACM Comput. Surv. (CSUR) **51**(3), 1–36 (2018)
6. Nguyen, D-T., Ho, X-N., Le, K-H.: MidSiot: a multistage intrusion detection system for internet of things. Wirel. Commun. Mob. Comput. (2022)
7. Ahmad, I., Basheri, M., Iqbal, M.J., Rahim, A.: Performance comparison of support vector machine, random forest, and extreme learning machine for intrusion detection. IEEE Access **6**, 33789–33795 (2018)
8. Nguyen, X.-H., Nguyen, X.-D., Huynh, H.-H., Le, K.-H.: Realguard: a lightweight network intrusion detection system for IoT gateways. Sensors **22**(2), 432 (2022)
9. Sun, P., et al.: Dl-IDS: extracting features using CNN-LSTM hybrid network for intrusion detection system. Secur. Commun. Netw. (2020)
10. Le, K.-H., Nguyen, M.-H., Tran, T.-D., Tran, N.-D.: IMIDS: an intelligent intrusion detection system against cyber threats in IoT. Electronics **11**(4), 524 (2022)

11. Ren, K., Zheng, T., Qin, Z., Liu, X.: Adversarial attacks and defenses in deep learning. Engineering **6**(3), 346–360 (2020)
12. Pacheco, Y., Sun, W.: Adversarial machine learning: a comparative study on contemporary intrusion detection datasets. In: ICISSP, pp. 160–171 (2021)
13. Alhajjar, E., Maxwell, P., Bastian, N.: Adversarial machine learning in network intrusion detection systems. Expert Syst. Appl. **186**, 115782 (2021)
14. Castillo, C., Mendoza, M., Poblete, B.: Information credibility on Twitter. In Proceedings of the 20th International Conference on World Wide Web, pp. 675–684 (2011)
15. Lee, K., Eoff, B., Caverlee, J.: Seven months with the devils: a long-term study of content polluters on twitter. In: Proceedings of the International AAAI Conference on Web and Social Media, vol. 5, pp. 185–192 (2011)
16. Yang, C., Harkreader, R.C., Gu, G.: Die free or live hard? Empirical evaluation and new design for fighting evolving twitter spammers. In: International Workshop on Recent Advances in Intrusion Detection, pp. 318–337. Springer (2011). https://doi.org/10.1007/978-3-642-23644-0_17
17. Alfeld, S., Zhu, X., Barford, P.: Explicit defense actions against test-set attacks. In: Thirty-First AAAI Conference on Artificial Intelligence (2017)
18. Brückner, M., Kanzow, C., Scheffer, T.: Static prediction games for adversarial learning problems. J. Mach. Learn. Res. **13**(1), 2617–2654 (2012)
19. Dalvi, N., Domingos, P., Sanghai, S., Verma, D.: Adversarial classification. In: Proceedings of the Tenth ACM SIGKDD International Conference on Knowledge Discovery and Data Mining, pp. 99–108 (2004)
20. Li, D., Chen, D., Jin, B., Shi, L., Goh, J., Ng, S-K.: MAD-GAN: multivariate anomaly detection for time series data with generative adversarial networks. In: International Conference on Artificial Neural Networks, pp. 703–716. Springer (2019). https://doi.org/10.1007/978-3-030-30490-4_56
21. Ghafoorian, M., Nugteren, C., Baka, N., Booij, O., Hofmann, M.: EL-GAN: embedding loss driven generative adversarial networks for lane detection. In: Proceedings of the European Conference on Computer Vision (ECCV) Workshops (2018)
22. Kurakin, A., Goodfellow, I.J., Bengio, S.: Adversarial examples in the physical world. In: Artificial Intelligence Safety and Security, pp. 99–112. Chapman and Hall/CRC (2018)
23. Liu, Y., Chen, X., Liu, C., Song, D.: Delving into transferable adversarial examples and black-box attacks. arXiv preprint arXiv:1611.02770, 2016
24. Papernot, N., McDaniel, P., Wu, X., Jha, S., Swami, A.: Distillation as a defense to adversarial perturbations against deep neural networks. In: 2016 IEEE Symposium on Security and Privacy (SP), pp. 582–597. IEEE (2016)
25. Li, B., Vorobeychik, Y., Chen, X.: A general retraining framework for scalable adversarial classification. arXiv preprint arXiv:1604.02606 (2016)
26. Grosse, K., Manoharan, P., Papernot, N., Backes, M., McDaniel, P.: On the (statistical) detection of adversarial examples. arXiv preprint arXiv:1702.06280 (2017)
27. Goodfellow, I.J., Shlens, J., Szegedy, C.: Explaining and harnessing adversarial examples. arXiv preprint arXiv:1412.6572 (2014)
28. Pawlicki, M., Choraś, M., Kozik, R.: Defending network intrusion detection systems against adversarial evasion attacks. Future Gener. Comput. Syst. **110**, 148–154 (2020)
29. Vu, A-H., Nguyen-Khac, M-Q., Do, X-T., Le, K-H.: A real-time evaluation framework for machine learning-based ids. In: Recent Advances in Internet of Things and Machine Learning, pp. 317–329. Springer (2022). https://doi.org/10.1007/978-3-030-90119-6_25

30. Aiken, J., Scott-Hayward, S.: Investigating adversarial attacks against network intrusion detection systems in SDNs. In: 2019 IEEE Conference on Network Function Virtualization and Software Defined Networks (NFV-SDN), pp. 1–7. IEEE (2019)
31. Qiu, H., Dong, T., Zhang, T., Jialiang, L., Memmi, G., Qiu, M.: Adversarial attacks against network intrusion detection in IoT systems. IEEE Internet Things J. **8**(13), 10327–10335 (2020)
32. Zhao, S., Li, J., Wang, J., Zhang, Z., Zhu, L., Zhang, Y.: attackGAN: adversarial attack against black-box ids using generative adversarial networks. Procedia Comput. Sci. **187**, 128–133 (2021)
33. Papernot, N., McDaniel, P., Jha, S., Fredrikson, M., Celik, Z.B., Swami, A.: The limitations of deep learning in adversarial settings. In: 2016 IEEE European Symposium on Security and Privacy (EuroS&P), pp. 372–387. IEEE (2016)
34. Moosavi-Dezfooli, S-M., Fawzi, A., Frossard, P.: DeepFool: a simple and accurate method to fool deep neural networks. In: Proceedings of the IEEE Conference on Computer Vision and Pattern Recognition, pp. 2574–2582 (2016)
35. Carlini, N., Wagner, D.: Towards evaluating the robustness of neural networks. In: 2017 IEEE Symposium on Security and Privacy (SP), pp. 39–57. IEEE (2017)
36. Ke, G., et al.: LightGBM: a highly efficient gradient boosting decision tree. Adv. Neural Inf. Process. Syst. **30** (2017)
37. Pelikan, M., Goldberg, D.E., Cantú-Paz, E., et al.: Boa: the Bayesian optimization algorithm. In: Proceedings of the Genetic and Evolutionary Computation Conference GECCO-99, vol. 1, pp. 525–532. Citeseer (1999)
38. Jia, W., Chen, X.-Y., Zhang, H., Xiong, L.-D., Lei, H., Deng, S.-H.: Hyperparameter optimization for machine learning models based on Bayesian optimization. J. Electron. Sci. Technol. **17**(1), 26–40 (2019)
39. Lee, S., et al.: Adversarial detection with gaussian process regression-based detector. KSII Trans. Internet Inf. Syst. (TIIS) **13**(8), 4285–4299 (2019)

Detection of Adversarial Examples Based on the Neurons Distribution

Jiang-Yi Zeng(✉), Chi-Yuan Chen, and Hsin-Hung Cho

Department of Computer Science and Information Engineering, National Ilan University, Yilan, Taiwan
r1043002@ems.niu.edu.tw, chiyuan.chen@ieee.org, hhcho@niu.edu.tw

Abstract. Deep neural network has very good achievements in the detection, identification, and prediction of various fields because deep learning models can efficiently learn the features of various fields. However, a recent attack called adversarial examples can interfere with feature extract of deep learning models by producing data that is similar to real data but completely different. We found that although the output examples are indistinguishable to the naked eye, the activation state of neurons is completely different. Based on this observation, we used the probability distribution model to count the activation of neurons and successfully detected the attack of adversarial examples.

Keywords: Adversarial examples · Artificial intelligence security · Probability distribution

1 Introduction

In recent years, deep neural networks (DNNs) have become tools for progress in various industries, such as face recognition [1], intrusion-detection systems (IDS) [2], natural disaster prediction [3], autonomous vehicles [4], precision medicine [5], and so on. Although there are great differences in various fields, for DNNs, the input is only digital data, and at best the encoding or format is different. DNNs can strengthen decisive features from cluttered features and weaken insignificant features through various feature extraction methods [7]. These methods include principal components analysis (PCA), linear discriminant analysis (LDA), t-distributed stochastic neighbor embedding (t-SNE), locally linear embedding (LLE), autoencoder, and others [6,8]. Each method has its own advantages and disadvantages, and there are areas of expertise. In image and image recognition, convolution is often used as a tool for feature extraction, which is also known as convolutional neural networks (CNNs). CNNs are very good at enhancing the continuity between image pixels [9]. For example, edges, curvature and noise are very common features that require a continuous relationship.

However, even though DNN is so powerful, it is not completely without weaknesses. In recent years, there have been attacks called adversarial examples (AE) that can interfere with the feature learning of DNNs [10]. It mainly tricks DNNs

C. Su et al. (Eds.): ISPEC 2022, LNCS 13620, pp. 397–405, 2022.
https://doi.org/10.1007/978-3-031-21280-2_22

by generating a data that the naked eye cannot discern the difference, but is substantially different. DNNs will be misled into believing that false examples are real instead, and models will collapse so that artificial Intelligence (AI) will not be able to help the field to which it belongs. Therefore, this issue is regarded as one of the most important topics in the field of AI security.

In general, AE often occurs in unsound DNN models. DNNs that are not regularized enough, the data are not diverse enough, or the amount of data is not large enough may fall into a situation of overfitting. Overfitting means that some features are overlearned and unable to accept the representation of other features [11]. If these overlearn features are wrong, the entire model will deviate farther and farther from the real data. In short, the generalization ability of the model will be very low, making the ability to understand unknown data much less.. However, since the model already has the problem of insufficient generalization, it is even more impossible to detect errors. AE originally generated error data that is very similar to the original data to achieve the purpose of deception, even if manual inspection is very difficult. The process of generating a model for DNNs is actually about finding the optimal combination of weight permutations between neurons and neurons. These neurons will have different activation states for images of different noise features. Based on this observation, we tried to find out AE by the activation state of neurons.

This paper is organized as follows. In Sect. 2, we will briefly introduce AE and the used probability distribution. In Sect. 3, we will explain the methodological architecture proposed in this study. Section 4 will give the results of our experiments and the analysis. Finally, we will conclude the proposed method and give future research directions.

2 Related Works

2.1 Adversarial Examples

AE is an attack method that makes the DNN model misjudge. The main means is to make small changes in the input data of the DNN so that the changed data will not be detected by the naked eye, but in fact at the output layer it is a different result [12]. This small change is physically very simple, consisting of reversing the minimum value of the loss function, raising the gradient to the point where the classifier thinks the loss value is too large and the image belongs to another classification. However, the degree of this change needs to be within a threshold value as shown in Eq. (1), otherwise the resulting image will be easily recognized by the manager [10].

$$D(X^{AE}, X^{Origin}) = \sqrt{\sum_{i=1}^{n} (X_i^{AE} - X_i^{Origin})^2} \tag{1}$$

where X^{AE} is AE and X^{Origin} is the original example. $D(X^{AE}, X^{Origin})$ is the vector distance within the n-dimensions.

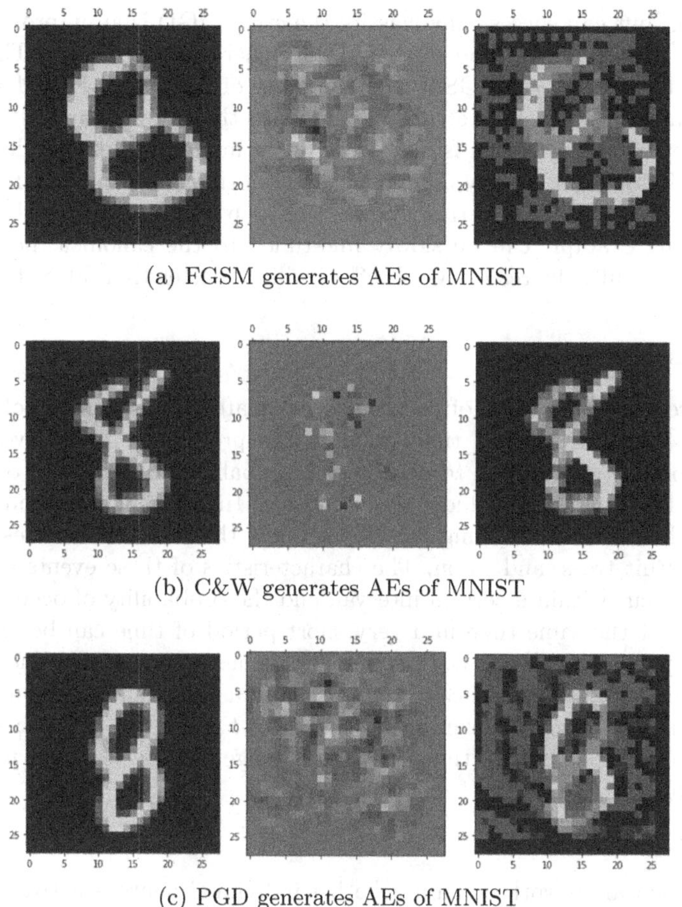

(a) FGSM generates AEs of MNIST

(b) C&W generates AEs of MNIST

(c) PGD generates AEs of MNIST

Fig. 1. Common adversarial example attack generation algorithms

Common AEs are Fast Gradient Sign Method (FGSM) [13], Carlini & Wagner(C&W) [14], and Projected Gradient Descent (PGD) [15], all of which can add some noise to the original diagram to cause the resulting diagram to look like the original category, but will cause a classification error, as shown in Fig. 1. Figure 1(a)–(c) are the simple examples of MNIST conducted through three methods. FGSM recognized 8 as 2, C&W recognized 8 as 5 and PGD recognized 8 as 6. FGSM is an extremely fast AEs attack algorithm. It produces examples by maximizing the loss function along the gradient as much as possible. This gradient-based attack generator can successfully and quickly generate AE as long as the error can be within a certain range. C&W is an optimization-based AE generation algorithm. In simple terms, it tries to control various hyperparameters, confidence parameters, etc., by observing the loss value between the output and the input to find a high-quality example with small perturbation and small error, but can successfully classify the error. PGD is an improved version of FGSM, so it is also a gradient-based AE generation algorithm. The biggest difference between it and FGSM is the number of iterations. FGSM will make the loss value in place at one time. This is also the reason why FGSM is very fast. However, this approach is limited to linear models, otherwise the AE generated by FGSM will be very different from the original example and cannot be effectively deceived. PGD narrows down each step to solve this problem so that the resulting example can be slowly fine-tuned to the canonical perturbation range. As a result, the resulting AE effect will be better than FGSM.

2.2 Poisson Distribution

The Poisson distribution is often used to calculate the probability of an event occurring T times per unit time, such as the probability of an event occurring randomly T times, and to observe the probability distribution of different numbers [16]. Examples include: the number of times students spend on cooperatives, the number of typing errors per hour, the number of times the fruit falls from fruit trees, and so on. The characteristics of these events are mainly that they occur within a certain interval, and the probability of occurring more than twice at the same time in a very short period of time can be ignored. In non-overlapping time intervals, the number of times events occur is independent. The probability of an event occurring only once in a very short period of time is proportional to time, as shown in Eq. (2). where t refers to the number of times an event occurs per unit of time, with an average of μ occurrences per unit of time, as follows:

$$P(T = t) = \frac{\mu^t}{t!}e^{-\mu} \tag{2}$$

In the neural network domain, whether individual neurons activate depends on the model's knowledge of the characteristics of the input data. That is to say, each different amount of data will cause different indicators such as the number and degree of activation in the neuron. This study treats each activation as an independent event, so we were able to use The Poisson distribution as an important parameter for assessing whether the data is an AE.

3 Proposed Method

During the training phase of DNN, the data is transmitted from the input layer to each neuron, and the feature information is exchanged and extracted, and finally the neural network generated at the output layer predicts the result. However, because each neuron perceives the characteristics of the data differently, the weights vary from neuron to neuron. As a simple example, we can find that certain links have low weights, which means that the neuron does not have an impact on downstream neurons and does not contribute to the soundness of the model. Conversely, if the weight value is large enough, it will have a great influence on every neuron in the next layer. For example, the eye may be an

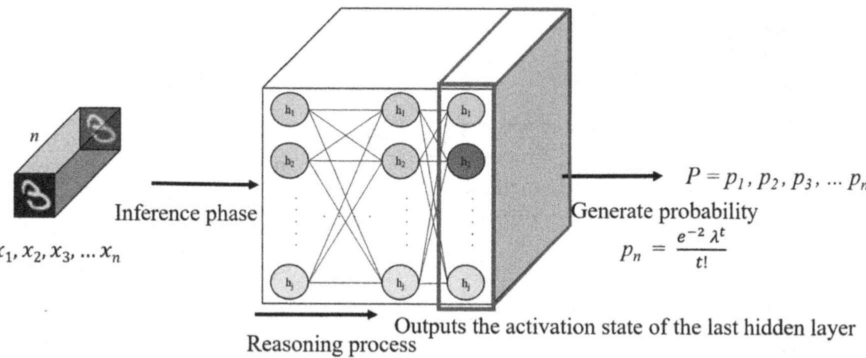

Fig. 2. Architecture diagram of the proposed method

important indicator of the ability to recognize a person's face, and the neuronal weight involving the eye will be particularly large. In the study, the output values of the neurons in the last layer of the hidden layer are collected multiple times during the model prediction phase, and the output values after the acquisition are averaged as a threshold $\mathbb{T}$ to determine whether the neurons are activated. The formula is as follows:

$$\mathbb{T} = \frac{1}{C} \sum_{i=1}^{\mathbb{N}} \mathbb{R}_i^c \tag{3}$$

C represents the number of acquisitions in the prediction phase and $\mathbb{N}$ is the number of neurons. $\mathbb{R}_i^c$ represents the value of the c acquisition of the ith neuron. By calculating the number of activations of neurons in the prediction phase, we can judge the degree of activity of neurons on the pre-trained model, and then know the importance of neurons to the prediction of the model. When a neuron is more active in the prediction phase of the model, it means that the neuron has an influence on the judgment of the prediction result, and vice versa.

As shown in Fig. 2, we will make class-by-class predictions for the input AEs x_1, x_2,...,x_n. In the process of inference, the initialization of neurons will be completed through the conduction of values. We will collect the activation state at the last output of the hidden layer. Finally, we can use the Poisson distribution to calculate the probability of each neuron from the output collected from each x_1, x_2,...,x_n. The higher the probability, the more times the neuron is fired, and it also means that the neuron has a positive correlation with the characteristics of the AE, and vice versa. In short, because AE will have a different probability distribution than the original data, we can determine whether the data is AE through the calculated Poisson probability. In the beginning, normal examples can be generated by the AE algorithm to generate a series of AEs. We put all normal examples and AEs into the neural network. Then the probability P_{normal} of normal examples and P_{AE} of AE will be generated through our proposed mechanism. We can directly distinguish normal examples from adversarial examples through the difference of L1-norm. Generally speaking, the probability

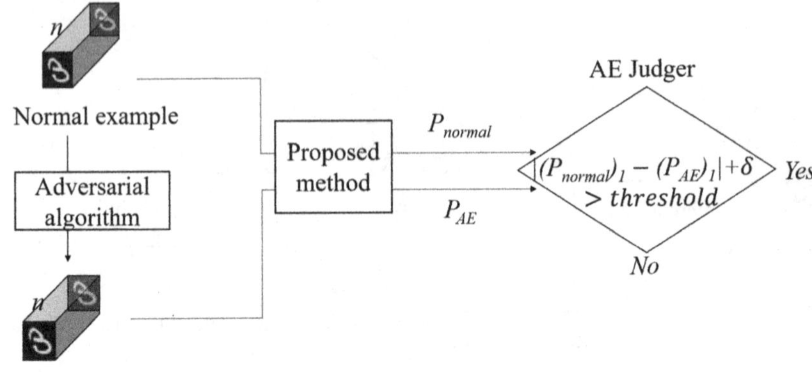

Fig. 3. The process of AE judgment mechanism

Table 1. Neural network architecture and parameters of the experiment

Layer (type)	Output shape	Parameters	Activation	Optimizer
conv2d_10	(None, 26, 26, 32)	320	Relu	Adam
max_pooling2d_6	(None, 13, 13, 32)	0		Adam
conv2d_11	(None, 11, 11, 64)	18496	Relu	Adam
max_pooling2d_7	(None, 5, 5, 64)	0		Adam
flatten_7	(None, 1600)	0		Adam
dropout_7	(None, 1600)	0		Adam
dense_14	(None, 64)	102464		Adam
dense_15	(None, 10)	650	Softmax	Adam

distributions calculated by the data of the same label will be similar, and the two data calculated by the L1 formula should be close to 0. So we can use the difference of L1-norm of all any two normal examples as a threshold. As long as the difference between the input data and a normal example is added with a tolerance value δ. If it is greater than this threshold, it can be considered that the data is an adversarial example. δ is the maximum value of all L1-norm differences, which is mainly used to protect the correct example from being mistaken for AE. Therefore, as long as the difference between the two is obtained through $|P_{normal} - P_{AE}| + \delta$, we can easily catch AE that is shown in Fig. 3.

4 Experimental Results

In this experiment, we use the most advanced algorithms for generating adversarial examples, including FGSM ,C&W and PGD. To prove the effectiveness of the proposed method, we generate AEs from MNIST data through these algorithms and enter them into CNNs for identification. We selected all the AEs

Table 2. Comparison of recognition accuracy of AEs

Label	C&W	PGD	FGSM
0	100%	100%	100%
1	100%	100%	100%
2	99%	100%	100%
3	99%	100%	100%
4	100%	100%	100%
5	100%	100%	100%
6	100%	100%	100%
7	46%	100%	100%
8	99%	100%	100%
9	56.99%	100%	100%

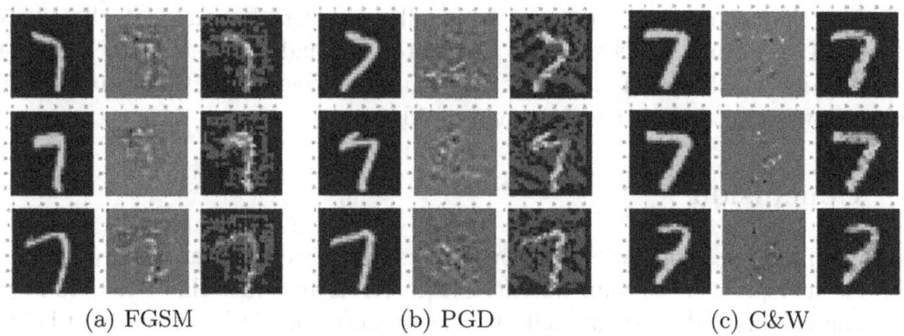

(a) FGSM (b) PGD (c) C&W

Fig. 4. AE detection of number 7 with 3 attack methods

that CNN could not successfully classify as material for this experiment.The CNN parameter we are using can be referred to Table 1.

As we can see from Table 2, our method has a very high degree of recognition in gradient-based AEs such as PGD and FGSM. This is because whether it is FGSM along the gradient to the maximum loss value at one time or PGD that finds the maximum loss value multiple times, it is based on some principle to iterate comprehensively for all pixels for producing the examples. The movements of these two types of AEs in distribution models are very similar, only to the extent that they differ. All in all, such a method will be quite different from the distribution model of the normal example, so it is easy to identify through our method. In the C&W experiment, differences were caught in roughly all categories of AEs. Except for the difference between the AE labeled 7 and 9 in C&W, which is too close to the real example to be effectively identified. This is because C&W belongs to the optimization-based AE generation algorithm. It does not change all pixels, but instead makes the best combination of parameters according to the resolution boundary. Therefore, the AE generated by C&W

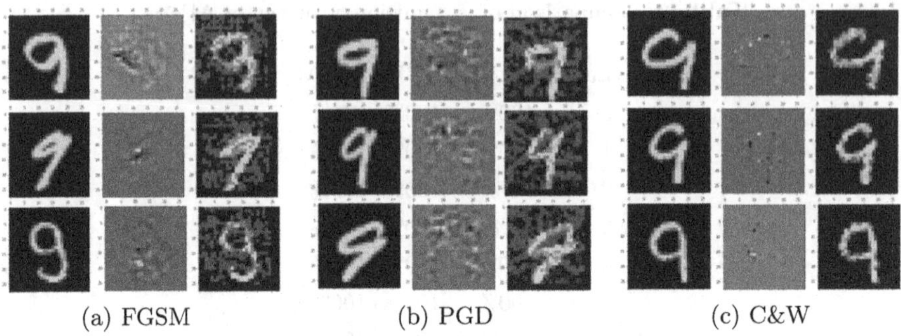

(a) FGSM (b) PGD (c) C&W

Fig. 5. AE detection of number 9 with 3 attack methods

has a better chance of having the same distribution probability as the normal example, resulting in inaccurate recognition that are shown in Fig. 4 and Fig. 5.

Note that these tested examples are all examples that are not effectively identified by normal CNN models. Therefore, although some categories cannot achieve high identification accuracy, it still means that the method proposed in this study is effective for the detection of AEs.

5 Conclusion

Although deep learning with its powerful capabilities has been widely used in various fields, it still has some potential risks. AE is an attack that reacts to deep learning vulnerabilities. It can make the neural network misclassify without being noticed by the naked eye. If such an attack were to infiltrate all walks of life, the overall economy would be hit quite hard. In this study, different examples have different neuron distribution characteristics, and the Poisson distribution is used to count the neuron states of normal examples and AEs to identify whether they are attacked by AE. Experimental results show that this experiment can effectively detect AEs generated by PGD and FGSM. In the C&W section, although a few categories are not 100% recognizable, they still improve the accuracy by more than 40%. In the future, we will conduct in-depth research on optimization-based AE, so that all types of AE can not be hidden. In addition, on the basis of knowing how to detect AE, we must try to design a mechanism for adversarial training, so that the neural network model truly has the ability to resist adversarial examples.

Acknowledgments. This work was supported in part by the Ministry of Science and Technology of Taiwan, R.O.C., under Contracts MOST 111-2221-E-197-017.

References

1. Soni, N., Sharma, E.K., Kapoor, A.: Hybrid meta-heuristic algorithm based deep neural network for face recognition. J. Comput. Sci. **51**, 101352 (2021)

2. Chen, C.Y., Cho, H.H., Tsai, M.Y., Hann, A.S.H., Chao, H.C.: Detecting LDoS in NB-IoTs by using metaheuristic-based CNN. Int. J. Ad Hoc Ubiquitous Comput. **37**(2), 74–84 (2021)
3. Anbarasan, M., et al.: Detection of flood disaster system based on IoT, big data and convolutional deep neural network. Comput. Commun. **150**, 150–157 (2020)
4. Ravindran, R., Santora, M.J., Jamali, M.M.: Multi-object detection and tracking, based on DNN, for autonomous vehicles: a review. IEEE Sens. J. **21**(5), 5668–5677 (2020)
5. Briguglio, W., Moghaddam, P., Yousef, W.A., Traoré, I., Mamun, M.: Machine learning in precision medicine to preserve privacy via encryption. Patt. Recogn. Lett. **151**, 148–154 (2021)
6. Anowar, F., Sadaoui, S., Selim, B.: Conceptual and empirical comparison of dimensionality reduction algorithms (PCA, KPCA, LDA, MDS, SVD, LLE, ISOMAP, LE, ICA, t-SNE). Comput. Sci. Rev. **40**, 100378 (2021)
7. Jung, J., Park, J., Cho, S.J., Han, S., Park, M., Cho, H.H.: Feature engineering and evaluation for android malware detection scheme. J. Internet Technol. **22**(2), 423–440 (2021)
8. Zhu, Y.Q., Cai, Y.M., Zhang, F.: Motion capture data denoising based on LSTNet autoencoder. J. Internet Technol. **23**(1), 11–20 (2022)
9. Alzubaidi, L., et al.: Review of deep learning: concepts, CNN architectures, challenges, applications, future directions. J. Big Data **8**(1), 1–74 (2021)
10. Zhang, J., Li, C.: Adversarial examples: opportunities and challenges. IEEE Trans. Neural Netw. Learn. Syst. **31**(7), 2578–2593 (2019)
11. Tsai, M.Y., Cho, H.H.: Differential-evolution-based weights fine tuning mechanism for GRU to predict 5G traffic flow. In: IEEE International Symposium on Intelligent Signal Processing and Communication Systems (ISPACS), pp. 1–2, November 2021
12. Lin, C.S., Hsu, C.Y., Chen, P.Y., Yu, C.M.: Real-world adversarial examples via makeup. In: IEEE International Conference on Acoustics, Speech and Signal Processing (ICASSP), pp. 2854–2858, May 2022
13. Goodfellow, I.J., Shlens, J., Szegedy, C.: Explaining and harnessing adversarial examples. arXiv preprint arXiv:1412.6572 (2014)
14. Carlini, N., Wagner, D.: Towards evaluating the robustness of neural networks. In: IEEE Symposium on Security and Privacy (SP), pp. 39–57, May 2017
15. Gupta, H., Jin, K.H., Nguyen, H.Q., McCann, M.T., Unser, M.: CNN-based projected gradient descent for consistent CT image reconstruction. IEEE Trans. Med. Imaging **37**(6), 1440–1453 (2018)
16. Kingman, J.F.C.: Poisson Processes. 3. Clarendon Press (1992)

Authentication and Biometric Security

Techniques for Continuous Touch-Based Authentication

Martin Georgiev(✉), Simon Eberz, and Ivan Martinovic

University of Oxford, Oxford, UK
{martin.geoergiev,simon.eberz,ivan.martinovic}@cs.ox.ac.uk

Abstract. The field of continuous touch-based authentication has been rapidly developing over the last decade, creating a fragmented and difficult-to-navigate area for researchers and application developers alike. In this study, we perform a systematic literature analysis of 30 studies on the techniques used for feature extraction, classification, and aggregation in continuous touch-based authentication systems as well as the performance metrics reported by each study. Based on our findings, we design a set of experiments to compare the performance of the most frequently used techniques in the field under clearly defined conditions. In addition, we introduce two new techniques for continuous touch-based authentication: an expanded feature set (consisting of 149 unique features) and a multi-algorithm ensemble-based classifier. The comparison includes 13 feature sets, 11 classifiers, and 5 aggregation methods. In total, 204 model configurations are examined and we show that our novel techniques outperform the current state-of-the-art in each category. The results are also validated across three different publicly available datasets. Our best performing model achieves 4.8% EER using 16 consecutive strokes. Finally, we discuss the findings of our investigation with the aim of making the field more understandable and accessible for researchers and practitioners.

Keywords: Biometrics · Touch-based authentication · Mobile authentication

1 Introduction

Over the past two decades, the world has become increasingly reliant on mobile devices, such as smartphones and tablets, for professional, social, and leisure activities. It is estimated that 81% of the world population is in possession of a smartphone today, including children and the elderly [1]. Mobile devices have grown to deliver services far beyond that which can be considered trivial and mundane and now are used for activities that involve the processing and storage of sensitive and private information. Almost all mobile devices offer basic mechanisms for authentication - proving ownership and identity, to prevent unauthorized people from accessing private data. Thus far, the prevalent methods for authentication used by mainstream smartphones include pins, pattern unlocking, face recognition, and fingerprint matching. However, such methods have

C. Su et al. (Eds.): ISPEC 2022, LNCS 13620, pp. 409–431, 2022.
https://doi.org/10.1007/978-3-031-21280-2_23

been shown to not always be reliant as they can be inconvenient to use [14] or prone to various attacks [21,39].

More recently, the scientific community has introduced continuous mobile authentication systems which ensure user identity throughout the whole session. Such systems can make use of the unique way people type on their phone [22], the sensors of their smartphones [47], by continuously recording video of their faces [15] and other behavioral characteristics. Continuous touch-based authentication methods, specifically, make use of the way people interact with the screen of their smartphones. These methods rely on assessing whether the interaction patterns of the person authenticating match the general behavior of the original owner. Continuous touch-based authentication offers significant advantages over traditional methods, as it is relying on dynamic and inherent properties of users rather than static attributes and memorized sequences. These systems can be used as a second-factor authentication in sensitive applications such as banking and finance, where suspicious behavior can be flagged and additional checks requested for certain transactions. The technology can also be used to detect whenever a malicious user gets a hold of an unlocked phone. The system, then, would detect the difference in behavior and request an additional authentication method to verify identity. However, despite almost a decade of research into this field and positive sentiment from the community for such technology [40], continuous touch-based authentication methods still lack widespread adoption and integration into our daily devices. This issue can be attributed to the way studies are evaluated and the resulting overestimation of performance [23]. However, contributions in this area are also severely fragmented, primarily due to a lack of methods to compare and evaluate models against a well-defined benchmark to accurately assess what can be considered state-of-the-art. In order to make impactful contributions and improve techniques for continuous touch-based authentication, it is imperative to clarify the landscape and provide methods to reason about model performance. To this end, in this paper, we aim to answer the following research questions:

1. RQ1: What are the current techniques for performing continuous touch-based authentication? Which features, classifiers, aggregation methods, and metrics are used and how can we group them into common categories?
2. RQ2: How can we establish the best-performing techniques despite the variety in models and evaluation datasets?
3. RQ3: Which techniques are most important in building robust and well-performing continuous touch-based authentication methods and how can we use these to improve upon the state-of-the-art in the field?

To answer our research questions, we make use of a two-fold approach. First, we conduct a systematic literature review to establish a broad understanding of existing methods for continuous touch-based authentication. We then extract features, classifiers, aggregations, and metrics used for each study and categorize feature extraction and aggregation methods. Second, to determine and improve on the current state-of-the-art models, we evaluate a carefully selected range of models along common parameters using three open-source datasets. We use the results to propose a set of techniques that outperform the current state-of-the-art and evaluate them against the current best-performing methods. In this paper we make the following contributions:

- Through a systematic literature review we analyzed 30 papers, extracted 149 features, and categorized continuous touch-based authentication methods.
- We performed a comparison of 204 model configurations across 3 datasets, allowing us to determine the best-performing features, classifiers, and aggregation methods in the field.
- We proposed a novel set of accumulated features and an ensemble-based classification model, both outperforming the current state-of-the-art.

2 Background

Continuous mobile authentication systems passively verify that a user enrolled in a device is the one persisting on it. This is done by comparing new patterns of interaction with the legitimate ones of the enrolled user. When a significant mismatch is detected, the system can block the malicious user and notify the owner of the device. For instance, this can be useful when a pin has been stolen or an unauthorized user gets access to an unlocked phone. Then, when the illegitimate user starts using the phone, they will be stopped by the continuous authentication system as the pattern of usage deviates from the owner of the smartphone. There are many ways in which continuous authentication on mobile devices can be performed, including keystrokes [26], taps [60], multi-touch gestures [48], sensors [47], freeform gestures [56], active vibration signal [54] and active gesture methods [11]. However, the focus of this paper is on continuous touch interactions - horizontal and vertical displacements on touch-capacitive displays done using a single finger which are called strokes. These are derived from the coordinates and pressure points at contact while interacting with the screen. Some continuous touch-based authentication systems augment these strokes with additional data such as sensor information from the accelerometer and gyroscope. However, the focus of our study is on stroke-based systems.

The lifecycle of a continuous touch-based authentication system consists of a few steps. The data collection step could be the experimental setup for a study or in the case of a deployed system it could be the enrollment phase where individual templates of behavior are created. The feature extraction step in continuous touch-based authentication aims at obtaining unique information from touchscreen interactive sessions with the smartphone which can be used to differentiate between users of the system. The classifier step relies on models to make a decision about the legitimacy of a particular stroke based on enrollment patterns. These are typically machine learning algorithms that are trained on the features extracted in the previous steps. Furthermore, a single stroke may not provide enough distinguishing information for an acceptable authentication performance. For this purpose, some systems perform aggregation of successive strokes to improve system performance. In the final step, a variety of metrics could be used to capture and report the success of the biometric system.

2.1 Related Work

The first continuous touch-based mobile authentication systems were proposed in the early 2010 s s inspired by previous work on the use of mouse movement patterns for authentication on desktop computers [25]. Several studies [18,38] survey the historical development of continuous touch-based authentication, reporting on the progress, remaining challenges, and performance of models in the field. However, such surveys do not consider the quantitative performance differences between feature extraction, classification and aggregation methods under fair conditions, thus lacking best-practice recommendations for researchers and practitioners. Other works [8,45] do perform a comparison between a limited number of classification methods. Nevertheless, our study differentiates itself by its magnitude in terms of classifiers examined and investigation of numerous feature extraction and aggregation methods. Furthermore, we propose methods that perform better in the feature extraction and classification steps of the system's lifecycle.

2.2 Datasets

There are dozens of studies that design and implement their own experiments for data collection as shown in [23]. However, the vast majority do not share the resulting dataset upon publication. We present 9 publicly available touch-based authentication datasets in Table 1. We use the following criteria derived from [23] to select the datasets applicable to our investigation. Naturally, the data in question needs to be accessible at the time of requesting it. That is not always the case as some of the servers hosting the data have gone down since paper publication. The dataset itself should contain a group of users using the same smartphone model. The users should have performed at least 2 separate sessions of the experimental tasks. Furthermore, each stroke needs to contain information about its (X, Y) coordinates as well as touch area and pressure values. These are required for the majority of feature extraction approaches. The only publicly available datasets which we consider usable under these conditions are Touchalytics [20], Bioident [7] and CEP [23]. We focus on these three datasets in the rest of this study and describe the reason for not using the other datasets in the "Notes" column in Table 1. We use the data from the image gallery task in the CEP dataset and the raw data from the Touchalytics and Bioident datasets. For each of the three datasets, we select the largest subset of users who use the same phone model and perform 2 or more sessions.

3 Techniques for Continuous Touch-Based Authentication

In this section, we perform a systematic literature review of papers proposing systems for continuous touch-based authentication. We quantify the prevalence of techniques for feature extraction, classification, and aggregation in continuous touch-based authentication systems as well as the methods for measuring model performance. Furthermore, we group the approaches into semantically similar categories in order to consolidate the understanding of the field.

Table 1. Publicly available touch-based datasets. The following symbols are used in the table: ● - currently accessible without additional processes, ◐ - can be accessed through email or special process, ○ - link or instructions currently not working. Links accessed on 8 August 2022. The "Usable" column denotes the largest group of users with the same phone model, at least two sessions, and data for coordinates, pressure, and area.

Dataset	Year	Total users (Usable)	Sessions	Accessible	Notes
Touchalytics [20]	2012	41 (15)	3	●	–
WVW [45]	2013	190 (0)	2	○	Data currently not accessible
TCPA [53]	2014	32 (0)	1	◐	Only a single session
UMDAA-02 [30]	2016	48 (0)	11–429	●	Touch area values unavailable
Bioident [7]	2016	71 (26)	1–4	●	–
TGA [49]	2019	31 (0)	8	◐	Data contains only extracted features
Brainrun [37]	2020	2344 (0)	1–1105	●	Pressure and area values unavailable
HuMIdb [4,5]	2020	600 (0)	1–5	◐	Session contains only a single stroke
CEP [23]	2022	470 (64)	1–30	●	–

3.1 Methods

The objective of the literature review is to understand the methods used in each of the core components of the continuous touch-based authentication lifecycle so that we can next re-evaluate them in a common benchmark. For our systematic literature review, we relied on PRISMA [33] to guide the search strategy to identify articles that proposed and evaluated continuous touch-based authentication models. The search was limited to English language and peer-reviewed published articles. We exclusively made use of the Google Scholar database and used the following search terms: ((*touch-based* OR *touchscreen*) AND (*authentication* OR *biometric**)) OR *touch dynamics* OR *touch biometrics* OR *touch authentication* OR *continuous touch*. The eligibility criteria for including an article in our analysis were as follows. Articles were included only if the methods focus on continuous touch-based authentication (excluding keystrokes) and make use of machine-learning-based models. We did include articles that, in addition to touch-dynamics-based features, also make use of other features, such as ones based on accelerometer and gyroscope data. However, in our performance evaluation, we do not make use of the additional features as such data is not available in all the publicly available datasets we consider in our study, making comparison difficult. We then implemented an ancestry approach with the articles meeting the inclusion and exclusion criteria. Our keyword-based search identified a total of 685 articles. Following the screening step, we were left with 103 articles. Screening involved the inspection of the title and description of papers for eligibility, as well as removing any duplicates. After our complete eligibility criteria were applied, we included 30 articles in the final review. For each article, we manually tabulated the features, classification methods, and aggregation methods, as well as the metrics used to evaluate performance.

3.2 Findings

The results of our survey are summarized in Table 2. We organize our findings into four sections, each encapsulating the results for a step of the continuous touch-based authentication lifecycle - features, classifiers, aggregations, and

Table 2. Techniques in touch-based authentication studies. Classifier and metric abbreviations are given in Appendix A. "STB" stands for stroke-based, "SSB" for session-based and "IB" for image-based. The following symbols are used in the table: **?** - unclear, ● - we can completely reproduce the features described in the paper and can compare it with other feature sets, ◐ - we can reproduce part of the features described in the study but cannot compare it with other feature sets, ○ - features are not described well enough to be reproduced.

Study (Year)	Features (Count)	Feature reprod.	Classifiers	Metrics	Aggregation
[16] (2012)	STB (53)	○	DT, RF, BN	FAR, FRR	Vote
[20] (2012)	STB (31)	●	kNN, SVM	EER	Mean
[29] (2013)	STB (13)	●	SVM	ACC	Feed
[9] (2013)	STB (?)	○	OC-SVM, SVM	FAR, FRR, ACC	Trust
[45] (2013)	STB (28)	●	LR, SVM, RF, NB, NN, kNN, BN, SM, Euclidian, DT	EER	Feed
[17] (2014)	STB (?)	○	kNN	ACC	Feed
[44] (2014)	STB (?)	◐	IF, SVM, NB, BN, RF	ACC	Feed
[32] (2014)	SSB (8)	—	DT, NB, RBFN, PSO-RBFN, NN, kNN	FAR, FRR	Other
[42] (2014)	STB (31)	●	HMM	EER, FAR, FRR	Mean
[53] (2014)	STB (37)	●	SVM	ACC, AER	Mean
[58,59] (2014)	IB	—	Proprietary	ACC, EER	Other
[46] (2015)	STB (58)	●	kNN, SVM, NN, RF	ROC, FRR, FAR	Feed
[57] (2015)	STB (27)	●	SVM, KSRC, KDTGR	EER	Mean
[7] (2015)	STB (15)	●	kNN, RF, SVM	ACC	Trust
[35] (2015)	STB (15)	●	NN, CPANN	ANGA, ANIA	Trust
[36] (2015)	STB (5)	●	StrOUD	ROC, EER	N/A
[28] (2016)	SSB (5)	—	kNN, RF	FAR, FRR, ACC	Other
[30] (2016)	STB (24)	●	kNN, SVM, NB, LR, RF, GB	EER	Mean
[6] (2017)	IB	—	SVM, DT, RF, NB	ACC	Other
[51] (2017)	STB (59)	◐	SVM, RF, DT	AUC	N/A
[27] (2018)	SSB (5)	—	AB, NB, kNN, LDA, LR, NN, RF, SVM, OC-SVM, LOF, IF, EE	FAR, FRR, HTER, AUC	N/A
[31] (2018)	SSB (21)	—	DT, NB, Kstar, RBFN, NN, PSO-RBFN	FAR, FRR, AER	Other
[19] (2018)	STB (8)	●	IF	ANGA,ANIA	Trust
[50] (2019)	STB (28)	●	NN	ACC, EER	N/A
[49] (2019)	STB (18)	●	RF, SVM, LR, NB, NN	EER	Vote
[43] (2019)	STB (18)	◐	NB, NN, RC, RF, BN, DT	ACC	N/A
[55] (2019)	STB (16)	◐	IF, OC-SVM	ACC	Trust
[3] (2020)	STB (?)	○	NN	FAR, FRR, EER	N/A
[41] (2021)	STB (12)	●	NN	ACC, AUC, FRR, FAR	Mean
[24] (2021)	STB (30)	●	OC-SVM, kNN, NN, DT, RF, NB	ACC, FAR, FRR, EER, ROC	N/A

metrics (reporting of results). We deliberately do not include the performance reported by each study due to the variety of metrics and datasets used, making the exact data meaningless to compare across the studies.

Features. We found that we can broadly categorize features according to three classes:

- *Stroke-based*: These features are based on data derived from individual strokes. Typically, the features are generated by examining a list of (X, Y, pressure, area) points that form a complete stroke. Examples of such features include the starting X or Y position, the length of the stroke trajectory, the average pressure of the stroke, etc.
- *Image-based*: These methods are based on generating an image that represents the stroke on a 2D plane. The images are then fed into image processing pipelines for texture and shape extraction [6] or to compute a difference score between images [59].
- *Session-based*: These methods are based on the properties of whole sessions, rather than a single or small group of stroke-based features. Examples of such features include the number of strokes per session, the average time duration of strokes per session, the average time duration between strokes per session, etc.

Most studies make use of *stroke-based* features (80%). The rest are split into 13% *session-based* features and 7% *image-based* ones. The prevalence of *stroke-based* features can be explained by the high computational cost associated with image processing and the long feature accumulation period of *session-based* methods, during which the device is left unprotected. In total, 16 (67%) of the 24 *stroke-based* based studies, defined their features and extraction methods sufficiently to be reproducible. Another 4 (17%) of the *stroke-based* studies have feature sets that can be only partially reproduced as several features do not have clear and non-ambiguous descriptions. For instance, one of the articles has a feature described as "the angle of moving during swiping" [51], without detailing how and which angle is calculated. For further 4 (17%) of the *stroke-based* studies, we could not infer the individual features used for authentication due to broad category definitions rather than specific feature descriptions or the information not being provided by the authors at all. In total we identified 149 *stroke-based* features from all papers. The list of features can be seen in Appendix B. The average number of features per paper is 24 where the largest number of *stroke-based* features identified in a single paper is 59 [51], and the smallest is 5 [28]. In this study, we focus on the *stroke-based* feature extraction due to being the most frequently used method in the field. Furthermore, we argue that it is the most realistic approach given the computational, time, and security constraints of continuous mobile authentication systems.

Classification. The studies examined in Table 2 include a total of 27 unique classification approaches, many of which are available as out-of-the-box implementations in standard machine learning libraries. We present the prevalence of the most frequently used classification models in Fig. 1. The most common are Support Vector Machine, Random Forest, and Neural Networks with 47%, 43%, and 40% of studies including them as part of their analysis respectively. The maximum number of classifiers included in a single study is 12 [27]. In total, 12 (44%) of the classifiers appear only once across all studies.

Aggregation. In total, we found that a large proportion of the studies (77%) perform the optional aggregation step in their continuous touch-based authentication systems. There are multiple ways of approaching the processing of a group of strokes to extract optimal performance. We found that we can broadly categorize the aggregation methods into the following four classes:

- *Mean/Median*: The average or median value of the scores of each stroke returned by the classifier.
- *Vote*: The most common binary prediction (legitimate user or attacker) for each stroke decided by the classifier.
- *Feed*: In this approach, all of the stroke features are fed into the model at once and a single prediction is obtained. For instance, if there are 10 features with a window size of 5 (i.e. group of five consecutive strokes), we input all 50 features into the model at once.
- *Trust*: There is a large variation in this category, however, in general, the approach relies on a statistical formula that outputs a score as new strokes are considered. The score is updated by rewarding positive predictions and penalizing negative predictions proportionally to the individual classifier predictions. An instance of such aggregation methods is the dynamic trust model [34], which is tailored to continuous authentication biometric systems. This specific implementation has been used in [35,55].

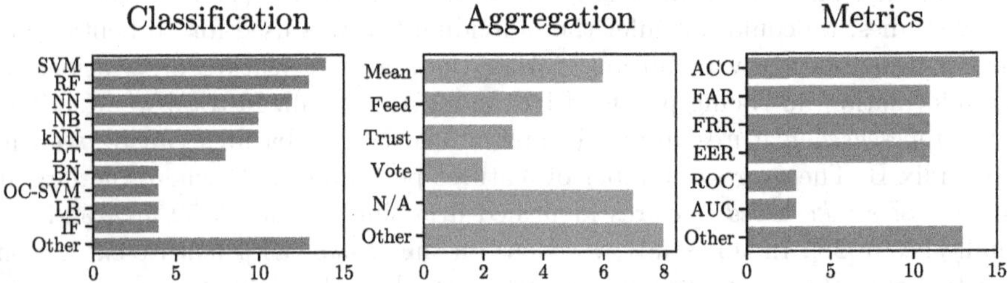

Fig. 1. The prevalence of classifiers, aggregation methods, and performance metrics in continuous touch-based authentication studies. The "Other" category means the particular methods have been used less than 3 times in the case of Classification and Metrics and less than 2 times in the case of Aggregation.

We present the prevalence of each of these methods in Fig. 1. The *Mean/Median* aggregation approach is the most frequently used one (20%). The *Vote*, *Feed*, *Trust* methods are used in 6%, 13% and 10% of the studies respectively. As mentioned, 23% of the studies do not use aggregation at all, and a further 27% use solutions that do not fall into the categories described above. For instance, the systems using session-based features are making decisions based on a large aggregation of strokes but cannot be included in any of the other categories we describe.

Metrics. Depending on the needs of a particular system, there are a variety of metrics that can be used to measure the performance of a model for continuous touch-based authentication. These include FAR (False Acceptance Rate), FRR (False Rejection Rate), EER (Equal Error Rate), Accuracy, ROC curve (Receiver Operating Characteristic), and others. Statistics for the prevalence of these metrics in the field can be found in Fig. 1. The variety of metrics shown illustrates the difficulty in comparing results reported in continuous touch-based authentication research. In this study, we aim to ease this comparison by reporting on differences in approaches when they are examined under the same conditions and by reporting the results using the same metric.

In this paper, we report our results using the EER metric. The EER is the point at which the FAR and FRR are equal on the ROC curve. The ROC curve is obtained by varying the threshold for acceptance into the biometric system. Therefore, there is a value of the threshold which corresponds to the EER. While some systems might benefit from choosing thresholds for optimizing better FAR or FRR we believe EER is the most representative of the general performance of a system. This is also supported by the related work [13,23]. In particular, [23] show that when comparing two continuous touch-based authentication models, the performance differences between them on the ROC curve are largely consistent with the difference at the EER point.

4 Performance Evaluation

The objective of this performance evaluation is to determine the best-performing existing feature sets, classifiers, and aggregation methods. Furthermore, we aim to identify a set of novel techniques and compare them to the current state-of-the-art. Finally, the study aims to understand whether the results obtained are valid across multiple publicly available datasets. To this end, we examine how each classifier performs on different feature sets and then compare aggregation methods independently.

Throughout our study, we follow the recommendations from [23] for fair evaluation of continuous touch-based authentication systems. We create the following model for each user and record the mean EER across all users at the end. We only select users which have performed at least two sessions and use the same phone model. At first, we split the data of a target user, selecting their first 80% of sessions for positive training data and the remaining 20% for positive testing data. We split the rest of the users into independent training and testing groups at random. The users in each group never overlap. The negative data for training or testing is then obtained by selecting a stroke at random while cycling through the respective group of users until the number of negative training or testing strokes is equal to the positive one. The combined training set is then used to train a binary model and the testing set for evaluating the performance of the model. This whole process is repeated 10 times for each experiment and we report the mean of the results from each repetition. At each of these iterations, we randomly select the training and testing user groups. The one-class classifiers employ the same process, however, the negative training data is not used.

The SVM, RF, NB, kNN, DT, OC-SVM, LR, and IF classifiers we investigated were implemented using the `scikit-learn` [10] machine learning library. The Neural Networks were implemented using `Tensorflow` [2] and the `Keras` [12] API. The Bayesian Network implementation was done on the WEKA [52] machine learning library using a Python wrapper. The implementation details of each classification algorithm were left as close to the default as possible. Where we had to make decisions (e.g., in the case of kNN and Neural Networks), we considered the related work and performed preliminary experiments to decide on the hyperparameters. The final parameters for each classifier are given below:

- Support Vector Machine (SVM) - RBF kernel with a 'scale' coefficient
- Random Forests (RF) - 100 estimators and max depth of 20
- Neural Network (NN) - feed-forward with three hidden layers of 150, 150, and 75 with a 'ReLU' activation function. The output layer has a 'Sigmoid' activation function which outputs a probability of a match between 0 and 1. Batch-normalization is applied at each layer and a 0.3 dropout between the hidden layers. The optimizer is 'Adam' with a 'binary cross-entropy' loss function. The network is trained with a batch size of 20 over 50 epochs.
- Naive Bayes (NB) - gaussian naive bayes implementation.
- k Nearest Neighbors (kNN) - number of neighbors - 18.
- Decision Trees (DT) - gini criterion and no maximum depth.
- Bayesian Network (BN) - K2 for learning and Simple Estimator for predictions.
- One-Class - Support Vector Machine (OC-SVM) - RBF kernel with a 'scale' coefficient.
- Logistic Regression (LR) - LBFGS solver with L2 penalty and max iterations of 1000.
- Isolation Forest (IF) - 100 estimators.

4.1 Comparison

In order to compare the performance of selected feature sets, we reproduced the 16 feature sets marked as "Feature Reproducible" in Table 2. Four of the studies [35,42,50,57] implement the same group of features as other ones in the set, leaving us with 12 unique and complete feature sets. We focus specifically on these feature sets as they are the only completely reproducible ones in related

Table 3. Reproducible feature sets used in the performance comparison. The additional (non-touch-based) features were used in the final proposed model by the original paper. However, we do not re-implement them due to the lack of such data in all of our datasets.

Study	Year of proposal	Touch features count	Additional features
Frank et al. [20]	2013	30	✗
Li et al. [29]	2013	14	✗
Serwadda et al. [45]	2013	28	✗
Xu et al. [53]	2014	37	✗
Murmuria et al. [36]	2015	5	(*sensors*, *power*) ✓
Antal et al. [7]	2015	15	✗
Mahbub et al. [30]	2016	24	✗
Shen et al. [46]	2016	58	✗
Filippov et al. [19]	2018	11	✗
Syed et al. [49]	2019	18	✗
Rocha et al. [41]	2021	12	✗
Incel et al. [24]	2021	30	(*sensors*) ✓

work. More details for each feature set are given in Table 3. Some of the studies enhance their touch-based features with auxiliary data, such as ones coming from the accelerometer or gyroscope, however, we do not reproduce these features due to the lack of such data across all datasets. We compared the 9 most frequently used classifiers in continuous touch-based authentication studies as shown in Sect. 3.2 across all of the 12 feature sets and report their performance in EER. We also compared all five aggregation techniques described in Sect. 3.2 to highlight the best-performing method. The aggregation window we chose in this set of experiments is 5 based on the availability of data and the diminishing returns of larger window sizes as shown in the related literature [20, 23]. For this comparison, we use the novel classifier and feature set described below. Based on our findings in the previous section, we also propose two novel techniques which were not identified in other continuous touch-based authentication studies. We include these in our final analysis:

Novel Feature Set. We compiled a new feature set by implementing all *stroke-based* features from our literature review. These are derived from the X, Y, pressure, and area values of a stroke as described in Appendix B. In addition to this, we utilized a feature selection algorithm that reduces the total number of features from the dataset. The goal of such approaches is to ensure better computational performance and overall results. For instance, this can be achieved by pruning features that contribute little to the output of the classifier or even have a negative effect on it. The feature selection algorithm we use is Analysis of Variance (ANOVA) using the F-value between features and labels. In order to ensure the method generalizes well, we used the three datasets (CEP [23], Bioident [7] and Touchalytics [20]). We first selected n number of features for each dataset using ANOVA. Then, we only kept features that are sampled in at least two of the three datasets. We experimented with sizes 50, 75, 100, and 125 for the parameter n. In our preliminary results, we established that $n = 125$ is the best-performing one in our case and we use it for the rest of this study. However, we highlight that in this case, the general method for feature selection is more important for further research or industry applications rather than the individual features we chose.

Novel Classifier. We propose an ensemble method for classification based on a combination of results from other classifiers. Ensemble methods are a well-known strategy used to combine multiple machine learning models which produce a result better than the outcome of each individual classifier. This is due to the fact that on some examples, some classifiers might perform poorly but on average models will agree on the correct decision. The algorithm we use outputs a final score by averaging out the probabilities from the predictions of the best-performing individual classifiers. We performed preliminary experiments with three different combinations of classifiers of sizes 3 (SVM, RF, NN), 5 (SVM, RF, NN, kNN, LR), and 7 (SVM, RF, NN, kNN, LR, NB, DT) and found that the best-performing one in our case is the one consisting of SVM, Random Forest, and Neural Network. Similar to the novel feature set selection, the specific group of classifiers that we chose is less of interest than the proposed method itself.

Table 4. Performance of classifiers applied to different feature sets on the CEP dataset. No aggregation is used and the results are reported in EER (%). The average of each row and column is given. Our feature set consists of all extracted features from related work using and the ANOVA feature selection algorithm. Our classifier consists of an ensemble method using SVM, RF and NN.

Features	SVM	RF	NN	NB	BN	KNN	DT	LR	OC-SVM	IF	Our	
[20]	14.15	13.75	13.48	21.30	18.67	16.76	22.41	18.06	25.80	26.22	12.86	18.50
[29]	15.09	14.64	14.60	21.77	18.51	17.48	23.37	20.50	24.59	26.74	13.91	19.20
[45]	14.10	14.56	13.57	20.54	18.07	16.26	22.88	17.84	23.97	25.39	13.10	18.21
[53]	13.50	13.40	13.22	19.94	16.12	16.12	22.08	17.79	23.75	23.90	12.46	17.48
[46]	15.79	15.36	14.97	23.17	20.46	19.23	24.00	19.01	27.46	29.19	14.36	20.27
[7]	14.00	14.39	13.95	20.79	18.30	16.34	22.88	19.02	23.66	24.41	13.32	18.28
[36]	20.43	18.78	19.60	24.45	22.16	21.70	25.62	25.41	26.58	26.13	18.62	22.68
[30]	15.83	15.69	15.28	22.55	19.72	18.07	24.23	20.43	27.27	27.45	14.60	20.10
[19]	15.17	15.88	15.22	21.15	19.71	16.86	23.78	21.51	23.17	24.29	14.67	19.22
[49]	16.71	15.71	16.00	23.27	19.07	18.99	23.83	21.78	27.68	27.09	15.13	20.48
[41]	25.54	24.74	24.70	29.99	26.39	26.50	31.07	28.69	33.06	33.48	24.02	28.02
[24]	13.68	14.25	13.32	21.19	19.99	16.52	22.72	17.71	24.31	25.62	12.79	18.37
Our	12.57	13.00	12.36	19.84	16.37	15.63	21.94	15.81	23.45	24.96	11.67	17.05
	15.89	15.70	15.41	22.30	19.50	18.19	23.91	20.27	25.75	26.53	14.73	

Table 5. Performance of aggregation methods on the CEP dataset with our novel feature set and an ensemble classifier consisting of an SVM, Random Forest and a Neural Network). The aggregation window used is 5 and the results are reported in EER (%).

Mean	Median	Vote	Feed	Trust
6.35	6.47	10.59	7.07	6.55

4.2 Results

The results from the feature set and classifier comparisons can be found in Table 4. On average, the best-performing feature set is the one generated from the proposed ANOVA method with an average of 17.05% EER across all classifiers. The best performing of the studies we re-implemented was Xu et al. [53] with an average of 17.48% EER over all the machine learning algorithms examined. We attribute the low performance of some feature sets such as Rocha et al. [41] (28.02%) to the small number of features included. However, the final model of the study uses additional features from sensor data which could result in much better overall performance.

In terms of classifiers, on average, our ensemble method was the best-performing with an average of 14.73% EER across all feature sets. The three individual classifiers in the ensemble (SVM, RF, and NN) also form a well-performing group with 15.89%, 15.70%, and 15.41% respectively. The one-class classifiers (OC-SVM and IF) produced the worst results in our experiments. Overall the best-performing single-stroke model consisted of our proposed feature set and ensemble classifier with an overall performance of 11.67% EER for a single stroke. However, continuous touch-based systems do not operate on a single stroke as it can be insufficient for secure authentication. Aggregation methods, based on multiple consecutive strokes result in improved system performance. The results from the aggregation experiment can be found in Table 5. The *Mean* (6.35%), *Median* (6.47%), *Trust* (6.55%) and *Feed* (7.07%) methods resulted in very similar performance. The worst performing aggregation method in our experiments was *Vote* with 10.59% EER. Nevertheless, all of the aggregation methods performed better than using a single stroke to make authentication decisions.

Dataset Comparison. In order to determine the generality of our results, we replicated our experiments across three datasets - CEP [23], Bioident [7] and Touchalytics [20]. When examining each category (features, classifiers, and aggregations) we choose the best-performing methods determined in our previous experiments and keep them constant (e.g., for all classifiers comparisons, we use the best-performing feature set). The results of our comparison across all three datasets can be found in Fig. 2. Our novel feature set and the ensemble classifier consistently outperform the other methods across all three datasets.

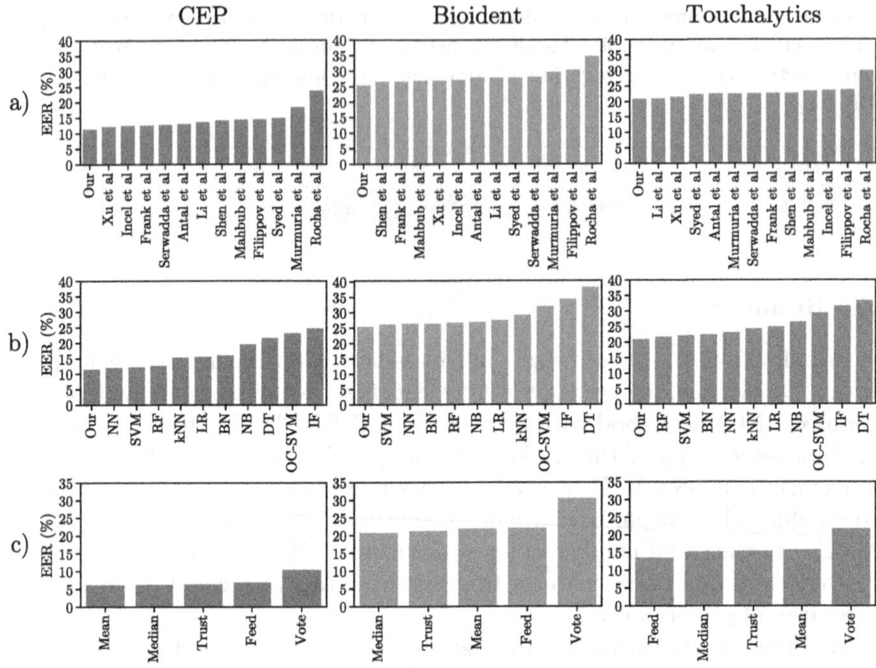

Fig. 2. Performance of single-stroke models using (a) featurests, (b) classifiers, and (c) aggregation methods across CEP, Bioident and Touchalytics touch-based datasets.

The best performing aggregation method varies across the three datasets. However, the differences between the *Mean*, *Median*, *Trust* and *Feed* approaches are negligible and either one can be used with an acceptable performance. The *Vote* aggregation method was the worst performing on all datasets. Xu et. al. [53] and Frank et al. [20] are other consistently well-performing feature sets with 37 and 31 features respectively. Similarly, the individual SVM, RF, and NN classifiers provide stable performance across all the datasets examined.

5 Discussion

In this study, we performed a systematic analysis of continuous touch-based authentication techniques in order to address the research questions posed in Sect. 1. In order to answer RQ1, we investigated a large number of studies focusing on continuous touch-based authentication to establish the most commonly used methods and grouped them into categories. In Sect. 4 we compared the performance of the techniques used in the field under fair conditions and establish the best-performing methods, thus addressing RQ2. In terms of RQ3, we found that the SVM, RF, and NN were the most robust and well-performing classifiers. Creating an ensemble using these methods resulted in a strong model outperforming the current state-of-the-art. Similarly, we used all features aggregated from related work and used the ANOVA feature selection algorithm to improve upon the current best-performing feature sets.

The study serves as a performance benchmark for the techniques for feature extraction, classification, and aggregation used in continuous touch-based authentication studies. The experiments conducted in Sect. 4 suggest that when performance is the only concern for a continuous touch-based authentication system, the optimal model would make use of our proposed feature set, ensemble classifier, and a mean aggregation approach which achieves an EER of 6.35% using a window of 5 strokes on the large CEP dataset. However, the lowest EER we achieved using this model is 4.80% when the aggregation window is increased to 16 strokes. The relative performance benefits of each novel technique are shown in Table 6. We highlight the next best and the median performing techniques while featuring the difference in EER with the novel ones proposed in this paper. While the improvements might be perceived as marginal compared to the second-best methods, they are significant compared to the median. These results highlight the importance of fair comparison between models which can be helpful for decision-making in the broader continuous touch-based authentication community.

Computational performance could limit the possibility of using the best performing model in practice, particularly due to the mobile environment it is intended for its deployment. In this case, we recommend the use of less sophisticated architecture which can still deliver similar results but at a more cost-efficient computational performance. Furthermore, we found that there is some variation between the results we obtained on each dataset. For this reason, selecting consistently well-performing models might be preferred for some applications. While EER is a good measure for the overall performance of biometric systems, in continuous authentication the focus can be on guaranteeing a low False Negative Rate to ensure adequate usability of the system. However, that is application-specific and requires further examination which is beyond the scope of this paper.

It is worth noting that the results in our experiments might not match the results originally reported by a particular study, sometimes by a large margin. For instance, the EER we obtain using the Touchalytics [20] feature set on their dataset is multiple times higher than the one attained in the original study. This is due to the fair evaluation practices we follow as described in Section ??. Substantially less (16) of the original 41 users in the dataset fit into our criteria and were used in our evaluation. Many of them had done only 2 sessions, resulting in training and testing data skew closer to 50%/50% rather than the target of 80%/20%. Furthermore, we report the mean EER, while the original study reports the median. Even though we ultimately performed the comparison on all three datasets, we believe the results on the CEP dataset are the most representative. That is due to the larger size in terms of users, sessions performed, and the length of each session.

5.1 Limitations

There are several limitations to our experimental approach and results. Firstly, the implementation details of some features, classifiers, and aggregation methods might not be perfectly reproduced from related work, despite our best effort. Furthermore, the categories we have grouped techniques in might be quite broad with many internal differences between studies. For instance, implementing a generic trust model algorithm will not necessarily represent the nuances of all models falling under this category. Similarly, Neural Network implementations may vary between papers that differ from our architecture, and optimizing the hyperparameters of other classifiers might lead to better overall performance. We believe that one-class classifiers in particular can achieve better results by fine-tuning their system parameters. Furthermore, some of the classification algorithms and feature sets that are not as prevalent in the field or are not reproducible might outperform the more widely available methods we examine. Finally, the fact that the methods we examine are mostly consistent throughout the three datasets is encouraging, however, application to other continuous touch-based authentication datasets might result in much different behavior.

Table 6. Difference between the novel techniques proposed in this paper and the next best and median methods in related work. The differences in EER are reported in percentage points (%). The best performing feature set and classifier methods are the ones proposed in our study.

	CEP		Bioident		Touchalytics	
	Next best	Median	Next best	Median	Next best	Median
Features	*Xu et al.* (+0.79)	+1.94	*Shen et al.* (+1.22)	+2.08	*Li et al.* (+0.21)	+1.62
Classification	NN (+0.69)	+4.14	SVM (+0.76)	+1.44	RF (+0.79)	+3.71

6 Conclusion

In this paper, we performed a comprehensive review of the approaches for feature extraction, classification, and aggregation in the field. We investigated the prevalence of each technique in the relevant literature and categorized the feature extraction and aggregation methods. Furthermore, we presented and described a set of 149 unique features extracted from related work and identified 9 publicly available datasets for continuous touch-based authentication. We benchmarked the performance of the most common feature sets, classifiers, and aggregation methods in the field with a set of experiments consisting of a total of

204 model configurations. We introduced a novel feature set and ensemble-based classifier that outperform the state-of-the-art by 0.79% and 0.69% EER respectively. Finally, we concluded that our findings are largely similar across multiple datasets and provided a discussion of our results, including the limitation of the study.

Acknowledgments. This work was generously supported by a grant from the Engineering and Physical Sciences Research Council [grant number EP/P00881X/1].

A Abbreviations

AB - AdaBoost
BN - Bayesian Network
CPANN - Counter Propagation Artificial Neural Network
DT - Decision Tree
EE - Elliptic Envelop
ENS - Ensemble
GB - Gradient Boosting
HMM - Hidden Markov Models
IF - Isolation Forest
KDTGR - Kernel Dictionary-based Touch Gesture Recognition
KSRC - Kernel Sparse Representation-based Classification
LOF - Local Outlier Factor
LR - Logistic Regression
OC-SVM - OneClass Support Vector Machine
PSO-RBFN - Particle Swarm Optimization Radial Basis Function Network
RC - Random Committee
SM - Scaled Manhattan
StrOUD - Strangeness based OUtlier Detection
kNN - k Nearest Neighbors
ACC - Accuracy
ANGA - Average Number of Genuine Actions
ANIA - Average Number of Impostor Actions
AUC - Area Under Curve
FAR - False Acceptance Rate
FRR - False Rejection Rate
HTER - Half Total Error Rate
ROC - Receiver Operating Characteristic
NB - Naive Bayes
NN - Neural Networks
RF - Random Forest
SVM - Support Vector Machine

B All Features

Table 7.

Table 7. Geometric features found in related work. "Perc." stands for pecentile and "Std. Dev." for standard deviation. Full details about each of the features can be found in the corresponding papers. Note that [42,50,57] use the same features as [20,35] uses the same as [7] except they omit the mid-stroke pressure.

Feature	Studies	Feature	Studies
1–2. Start X,Y	[7,19,20,24,29,30,46,49,53]	43. Std. Dev. acceleration	[45,46]
3–4. Stop X,Y	[7,19,20,24,30,46,49,53]	44–47. First Quartile pressure, area, velocity, acceleration	[45]
5. Stroke duration	[7,19,20,24,29,30,36,45,46,49,53]	48–51. Third Quartile pressure, area, velocity, acceleration	[45]
6. End-to-end distance	[7,19,20,24,30,36,45,49,53]	52–55. Extreme point 1,2 - X,Y	[45]
7. Mid-stroke pressure	[7,20,24,45,46,49]	56. Last 2 points tangent	[45]
8. Mid-stroke area	[7,20,24,45]	57. Velocity at first point	[53]
9. Length of Trajectory	[7,19,20,24,29,45,46,49,53]	58–60. Area, Pressure, Velocity at last point	[53]
10. Inter-stroke time	[20,30,49]	61. Last moving direction	[53]
11. Mean Resultant Length	[7,20,24,30]	62. Average points distance	[41,46,53]
12. Median acceleration at first 5 points	[20,24,30]	63. Std. Dev. points distance	[46,53]
13. Median velocity at last 3 points	[20,24,30]	64–68. LDP X, Y, Area, Pressure, Velocity	[53,55]
14. Average velocity	[7,19,20,24,45,46,49,53]	69–71. Start to LDP Latency, Length, Direction	[53]
15. Up/Down/Left/Right	[7,20,30]	72–74. LDP to Stop Latency, Length, Direction	[53]
16. Direction of direct line	[7,20,24,36,49,53]	75. Ratio distance to LDP Length	[53]
17. Average direction	[20]	76. Total displacement length	[46]
18. Ratio of direct distance to trajectory length	[20,24,30,49,53]	77. Ratio of displacement and trajectory length	[46]
19. 20% perc. velocity	[20,24,30,49]	78–81. Median, IQR, Skewnsess, Kurtosis of distance	[46]
20. 50% perc. velocity	[20,24,30,45,46,49]	82–86. Avg, Std. Dev, IQR, Skewness, Kurtosis of deviation	[46]
21. 80% perc. velocity	[20,24,30,49]	87–92. Avg, Median, Std Dev, IQR, Skewness, Kurtosis of pairwise angles	[46]
22. 20% perc. acceleration	[20,24,30]	93–98. Avg, Median, Std. Dev, IQR, Skewness, Kurtosis of phase-angles	[46]
23. 50% perc. acceleration	[20,24,30,45,46]	99. Displacement to duration ratio	[46]
24. 80% perc. acceleration	[20,24,30]	100–102. IQR, Skewness, Kurtosis of velocities	[46]
25. 20% perc. deviation	[20,30]	103–108. Avg, Median, Std. Dev., IQR, Skewness, Kurtosis of angular-velocities	[46]
26. 50% perc. deviation	[20,30,46]	109–111. IQR, Skewness, Kurtosis of accelerations	[46]
27. 80% perc. deviation	[20,30]	112–114. IQR, Skewness, Kurtosis of pressures	[46]
28. Largest deviation	[7,20,30]	115–116. Min, Max pressure	[41,51]
29. Pressure at first point	[29,53]	117–118. Min, Max area	[41,51]
30. Area at first point	[29,53]	119–120. Min, Max velocity	[51,55]
31. First moving direction	[29,53]	121–124. Min, Max, Mean, Median of pressure changes	[51]
32. Average moving direction	[7,24,29,30]	125–128. Min, Max, Mean, Median of area changes	[51]
33. Average moving curvature	[29]	129–130. X, Y at max velocity	[55]
34. Average curvature distance	[29]	131–132. X, Y at min velocity	[55]
35. Average pressure	[29,36,45,46,53]	133–135. Quadratic fit pressure x2, x, n	[41]
36. Average touch area	[19,29,36,41,45,53]	136–138. Min, Max, Avg time duration between points	[41]
37. Max-area portion	[29]	139–140. Max deviation of mean X,Y	[24]
38. Min-pressure portion	[29]	141–142. 20% perc. deviation of mean X,Y	[24]
39. Average acceleration	[45,46]	143–144. Median deviation of mean X,Y	[24]
40. Std. Dev. pressure	[45,46,53]	145–146. 80% perc. deviation of mean X,Y	[24]
41. Std. Dev. area	[45,53]	147–148. Direction vector X,Y	[19]
42. Std. Dev. velocity	[30,45,46]	149. Horizontal/Vertical flag	[49]

References

1. Ericsson mobility report 2021. https://www.ericsson.com/en/reports-and-papers/mobility-report/reports/november-2021. Accessed 20 Jan 2022
2. Abadi, M., et al.: TensorFlow: large-scale machine learning on heterogeneous systems (2015). https://www.tensorflow.org/, software available from tensorflow.org
3. Abuhamad, M., Abuhmed, T., Mohaisen, D., Nyang, D.: Autosen: deep-learning-based implicit continuous authentication using smartphone sensors. IEEE Internet Things J. **7**(6), 5008–5020 (2020). https://doi.org/10.1109/JIOT.2020.2975779
4. Acien, A., Morales, A., Fiérrez, J., Vera-Rodríguez, R., Bartolome, I.: Be-captcha: detecting human behavior in smartphone interaction using multiple inbuilt sensors. CoRR abs/2002.00918 (2020). https://arxiv.org/abs/2002.00918
5. Acien, A., Morales, A., Fiérrez, J., Vera-Rodríguez, R., Delgado-Mohatar, O.: Becaptcha: bot detection in smartphone interaction using touchscreen biometrics and mobile sensors. CoRR abs/2005.13655 (2020). https://arxiv.org/abs/2005.13655
6. Ahmad, J., Sajjad, M., Jan, Z., Mehmood, I., Rho, S., Baik, S.W.: Analysis of interaction trace maps for active authentication on smart devices. Multimedia Tools Appl. **76**(3), 4069–4087 (2016). https://doi.org/10.1007/s11042-016-3450-y
7. Antal, M., Bokor, Z., Szabó, L.Z.: Information revealed from scrolling interactions on mobile devices. Pattern Recogn. Lett. **56**, 7–13 (2015). https://doi.org/10.1016/j.patrec.2015.01.011, https://www.sciencedirect.com/science/article/pii/S0167865515000355
8. Antal, M., Szabó, L.Z.: Biometric authentication based on touchscreen swipe patterns. Procedia Technol. **22**, 862–869 (2016). 9th International Conference Interdisciplinarity in Engineering, INTER-ENG 2015, 8-9 October 2015, Tirgu Mures, Romania.https://doi.org/10.1016/j.protcy.2016.01.061, http://www.sciencedirect.com/science/article/pii/S2212017316000621
9. Bo, C., Zhang, L., Li, X.Y., Huang, Q., Wang, Y.: Silentsense: silent user identification via touch and movement behavioral biometrics. In: Proceedings of the 19th Annual International Conference on Mobile Computing & Networking, MobiCom 2013, pp 187–190. Association for Computing Machinery, New York (2013). https://doi.org/10.1145/2500423.2504572
10. Buitinck, L., et al.: API design for machine learning software: experiences from the scikit-learn project. In: ECML PKDD Workshop: Languages for Data Mining and Machine Learning, pp. 108–122 (2013)
11. Cheon, E., Shin, Y., Huh, J., Kim, H., Oakley, I.: Gesture authentication for smartphones: evaluation of gesture password selection policies. In: 2020 IEEE Symposium on Security and Privacy (SP), pp. 249–267. IEEE Computer Society, Los Alamitos, CA, USA, May 2020. https://doi.org/10.1109/SP40000.2020.00034, https://doi.ieeecomputersociety.org/10.1109/SP40000.2020.00034
12. Chollet, F., et al.: Keras (2015). https://keras.io
13. Eberz, S., Rasmussen, K.B., Lenders, V., Martinovic, I.: Evaluating behavioral biometrics for continuous authentication: challenges and metrics. In: Proceedings of the 2017 ACM on Asia Conference on Computer and Communications Security, ASIA CCS 2017, pp. 386–399. Association for Computing Machinery, New York (2017). https://doi.org/10.1145/3052973.3053032
14. Egelman, S., Jain, S., Portnoff, R.S., Liao, K., Consolvo, S., Wagner, D.: Are you ready to lock? In: Proceedings of the 2014 ACM SIGSAC Conference on Computer and Communications Security, CCS 2014, pp. 750–761. ACM,

New York (2014). https://doi.org/10.1145/2660267.2660273, http://doi.acm.org/10.1145/2660267.2660273

15. Fathy, M.E., Patel, V.M., Chellappa, R.: Face-based active authentication on mobile devices. In: 2015 IEEE International Conference on Acoustics, Speech and Signal Processing (ICASSP), pp. 1687–1691. IEEE (2015)
16. Feng, T., et al.: Continuous mobile authentication using touchscreen gestures. In: 2012 IEEE Conference on Technologies for Homeland Security (HST), pp. 451–456 (2012). https://doi.org/10.1109/THS.2012.6459891
17. Feng, T., Yang, J., Yan, Z., Tapia, E.M., Shi, W.: Tips: context-aware implicit user identification using touch screen in uncontrolled environments. In: Proceedings of the 15th Workshop on Mobile Computing Systems and Applications. HotMobile 2014, Association for Computing Machinery, New York (2014). https://doi.org/10.1145/2565585.2565592
18. Fierrez, J., Pozo, A., Martinez-Diaz, M., Galbally, J., Morales, A.: Benchmarking touchscreen biometrics for mobile authentication. IEEE Trans. Inf. Forensics Secur. **13**(11), 2720–2733 (2018). https://doi.org/10.1109/TIFS.2018.2833042
19. Filippov, A.I., Iuzbashev, A.V., Kurnev, A.S.: User authentication via touch pattern recognition based on isolation forest. In: 2018 IEEE Conference of Russian Young Researchers in Electrical and Electronic Engineering (EIConRus), pp. 1485–1489 (2018). https://doi.org/10.1109/EIConRus.2018.8317378
20. Frank, M., Biedert, R., Ma, E., Martinovic, I., Song, D.: Touchalytics: on the applicability of touchscreen input as a behavioral biometric for continuous authentication. IEEE Trans. Inf. Forensics Secur. **8**(1), 136–148 (2013)
21. Galbally, J., Fierrez, J., Alonso-Fernandez, F., Martinez-Diaz, M.: Evaluation of direct attacks to fingerprint verification systems. Telecommun. Syst. **47**(3), 243–254 (2011). https://doi.org/10.1007/s11235-010-9316-0
22. Gascon, H., Uellenbeck, S., Wolf, C., Rieck, K.: Continuous authentication on mobile devices by analysis of typing motion behavior. Sicherheit 2014-Sicherheit, Schutz und Zuverlässigkeit (2014)
23. Georgiev, M., Eberz, S., Turner, H., Lovisotto, G., Martinovic, I.: Common evaluation pitfalls in touch-based authentication systems. In: Proceedings of the 2022 ACM on Asia Conference on Computer and Communications Security, ASIA CCS 2022, pp. 1049–1063. Association for Computing Machinery, New York (2022). https://doi.org/10.1145/3488932.3517388
24. Incel, O.D., et al.: Dakota: sensor and touch screen-based continuous authentication on a mobile banking application. IEEE Access **9**, 38943–38960 (2021). https://doi.org/10.1109/ACCESS.2021.3063424
25. Jorgensen, Z., Yu, T.: On mouse dynamics as a behavioral biometric for authentication. In: Proceedings of the 6th ACM Symposium on Information, Computer and Communications Security, ASIACCS 2011, pp. 476–482. Association for Computing Machinery, New York (2011). https://doi.org/10.1145/1966913.1966983
26. Kim, J., Kang, P.: Freely typed keystroke dynamics-based user authentication for mobile devices based on heterogeneous features. Pattern Recogn. **108**, 107556 (2020). https://doi.org/10.1016/j.patcog.2020.107556, https://www.sciencedirect.com/science/article/pii/S0031320320303599
27. Kumar, R., Kundu, P.P., Phoha, V.V.: Continuous authentication using one-class classifiers and their fusion. In: 2018 IEEE 4th International Conference on Identity, Security, and Behavior Analysis (ISBA), pp. 1–8 (2018). https://doi.org/10.1109/ISBA.2018.8311467

28. Kumar, R., Phoha, V.V., Serwadda, A.: Continuous authentication of smartphone users by fusing typing, swiping, and phone movement patterns. In: 2016 IEEE 8th International Conference on Biometrics Theory, Applications and Systems (BTAS), pp. 1–8 (2016). https://doi.org/10.1109/BTAS.2016.7791164
29. Li, L., Zhao, X., Xue, G.: Unobservable re-authentication for smartphones. In: 20th Annual Network and Distributed System Security Symposium, NDSS 2013, San Diego, California, USA, 24–27 February 2013. The Internet Society (2013). https://www.ndss-symposium.org/ndss2013/unobservable-re-authentication-smartphones
30. Mahbub, U., Sarkar, S., Patel, V.M., Chellappa, R.: Active user authentication for smartphones: a challenge data set and benchmark results. In: 2016 IEEE 8th International Conference on Biometrics Theory, Applications and Systems (BTAS), pp. 1–8 (2016). https://doi.org/10.1109/BTAS.2016.7791155
31. Meng, W., Wang, Y., Wong, D.S., Wen, S., Xiang, Y.: Touchwb: touch behavioral user authentication based on web browsing on smartphones. J. Netw. Comput. Appl. **117**, 1–9 (2018). https://doi.org/10.1016/j.jnca.2018.05.010, https://www.sciencedirect.com/science/article/pii/S1084804518301723
32. Meng, Y., Wong, D.S., Kwok, L.F.: Design of touch dynamics based user authentication with an adaptive mechanism on mobile phones. In: Proceedings of the 29th Annual ACM Symposium on Applied Computing, SAC 2014, pp. 1680–1687. Association for Computing Machinery, New York (2014). https://doi.org/10.1145/2554850.2554931
33. Moher, D., Liberati, A., Tetzlaff, J., Altman, D.G., Group, P.: Preferred reporting items for systematic reviews and meta-analyses: the prisma statement. PLoS Med. **6**(7), e1000097 (2009)
34. Mondal, S., Bours, P.: A computational approach to the continuous authentication biometric system. Inf. Sci. **304**, 28–53 (2015). https://doi.org/10.1016/j.ins.2014.12.045, https://www.sciencedirect.com/science/article/pii/S0020025514011979
35. Mondal, S., Bours, P.: Swipe gesture based continuous authentication for mobile devices. In: 2015 International Conference on Biometrics (ICB), pp. 458–465 (2015). https://doi.org/10.1109/ICB.2015.7139110
36. Murmuria, R., Stavrou, A., Barbará, D., Fleck, D.: Continuous authentication on mobile devices using power consumption, touch gestures and physical movement of users. In: Bos, H., Monrose, F., Blanc, G. (eds.) RAID 2015. LNCS, vol. 9404, pp. 405–424. Springer, Cham (2015). https://doi.org/10.1007/978-3-319-26362-5_19
37. Papamichail, M.D., Chatzidimitriou, K.C., Karanikiotis, T., Oikonomou, N.C.I., Symeonidis, A.L., Saripalle, S.K.: Brainrun: a behavioral biometrics dataset towards continuous implicit authentication. Data **4**(2) (2019). https://doi.org/10.3390/data4020060, https://www.mdpi.com/2306-5729/4/2/60
38. Patel, V.M., Chellappa, R., Chandra, D., Barbello, B.: Continuous user authentication on mobile devices: recent progress and remaining challenges. IEEE Sig. Process. Mag. **33**(4), 49–61 (2016). https://doi.org/10.1109/MSP.2016.2555335
39. Ramachandra, R., Busch, C.: Presentation attack detection methods for face recognition systems: a comprehensive survey. ACM Comput. Surv. **50**(1) (2017). https://doi.org/10.1145/3038924
40. Rasnayaka, S., Sim, T.: Who wants continuous authentication on mobile devices? In: 2018 IEEE 9th International Conference on Biometrics Theory, Applications and Systems (BTAS), pp. 1–9 (2018). https://doi.org/10.1109/BTAS.2018.8698599
41. Rocha, R., Carneiro, D., Novais, P.: Continuous authentication with a focus on explainability. Neurocomputing **423**, 697–702 (2021). https://doi.org/10.1016/j.neucom.2020.02.122, https://www.sciencedirect.com/science/article/pii/S0925231220307323

42. Roy, A., Halevi, T., Memon, N.: An hmm-based behavior modeling approach for continuous mobile authentication. In: 2014 IEEE International Conference on Acoustics, Speech and Signal Processing (ICASSP), pp. 3789–3793 (2014). https://doi.org/10.1109/ICASSP.2014.6854310
43. Samet, S., Ishraque, M.T., Ghadamyari, M., Kakadiya, K., Mistry, Y., Nakkabi, Y.: TouchMetric: a machine learning based continuous authentication feature testing mobile application. Int. J. Inf. Technol. **11**(4), 625–631 (2019). https://doi.org/10.1007/s41870-019-00306-w
44. Saravanan, P., Clarke, S., Chau, D.H.P., Zha, H.: LatentGesture: active user authentication through background touch analysis. In: Proceedings of the Second International Symposium of Chinese CHI, Chinese CHI 2014, pp. 110–113. Association for Computing Machinery, New York (2014). https://doi.org/10.1145/2592235.2592252
45. Serwadda, A., Phoha, V.V., Wang, Z.: Which verifiers work?: A benchmark evaluation of touch-based authentication algorithms. In: 2013 IEEE Sixth International Conference on Biometrics: Theory, Applications and Systems (BTAS), pp. 1–8 (2013). https://doi.org/10.1109/BTAS.2013.6712758
46. Shen, C., Zhang, Y., Guan, X., Maxion, R.A.: Performance analysis of touch-interaction behavior for active smartphone authentication. IEEE Trans. Inf. Forensics Secur. **11**(3), 498–513 (2016). https://doi.org/10.1109/TIFS.2015.2503258
47. Sitová, Z., et al.: HMOG: new behavioral biometric features for continuous authentication of smartphone users. IEEE Trans. Inf. Forensics Secur. **11**(5), 877–892 (2016). https://doi.org/10.1109/TIFS.2015.2506542
48. Song, Y., Cai, Z., Zhang, Z.L.: Multi-touch authentication using hand geometry and behavioral information. In: 2017 IEEE Symposium on Security and Privacy (SP), pp. 357–372 (2017). https://doi.org/10.1109/SP.2017.54
49. Syed, Z., Helmick, J., Banerjee, S., Cukic, B.: Touch gesture-based authentication on mobile devices: the effects of user posture, device size, configuration, and inter-session variability. J. Syst. Softw. **149**, 158–173 (2019). https://doi.org/10.1016/j.jss.2018.11.017,https://www.sciencedirect.com/science/article/pii/S0164121218302516
50. Volaka, H.C., Alptekin, G., Basar, O.E., Isbilen, M., Incel, O.D.: Towards continuous authentication on mobile phones using deep learning models. Procedia Comput. Sci. **155**, 177–184 (2019). https://doi.org/10.1016/j.procs.2019.08.027, https://www.sciencedirect.com/science/article/pii/S187705091930941X, the 16th International Conference on Mobile Systems and Pervasive Computing (MobiSPC 2019), The 14th International Conference on Future Networks and Communications (FNC-2019), The 9th International Conference on Sustainable Energy Information Technology
51. Wang, X., Yu, T., Mengshoel, O., Tague, P.: Towards continuous and passive authentication across mobile devices: an empirical study. In: Proceedings of the 10th ACM Conference on Security and Privacy in Wireless and Mobile Networks, WiSec 2017, pp. 35–45. Association for Computing Machinery, New York (2017). https://doi.org/10.1145/3098243.3098244
52. Witten, I.H., Frank, E., Hall, M.A., Pal, C.J., DATA, M.: Practical machine learning tools and techniques. In: DATA MINING, vol. 2, p. 4 (2005)
53. Xu, H., Zhou, Y., Lyu, M.R.: Towards continuous and passive authentication via touch biometrics: an experimental study on smartphones. In: 10th Symposium On Usable Privacy and Security (SOUPS 2014), pp. 187–198. USENIX Association, Menlo Park, CA, July 2014. https://www.usenix.org/conference/soups2014/proceedings/presentation/xu

54. Xu, X., et a;.: TouchPass: towards behavior-irrelevant on-touch user authentication on smartphones leveraging vibrations. In: Proceedings of the 26th Annual International Conference on Mobile Computing and Networking, MobiCom 2020, Association for Computing Machinery, New York (2020). https://doi.org/10.1145/3372224.3380901
55. Yang, Y., Guo, B., Wang, Z., Li, M., Yu, Z., Zhou, X.: Behavesense: continuous authentication for security-sensitive mobile apps using behavioral biometrics. Ad Hoc Netw. **84**, 9–18 (2019). https://doi.org/10.1016/j.adhoc.2018.09.015, https://www.sciencedirect.com/science/article/pii/S1570870518306899
56. Yang, Y., Clark, G.D., Lindqvist, J., Oulasvirta, A.: Free-form gesture authentication in the wild, pp. 3722–3735. Association for Computing Machinery, New York (2016). https://doi.org/10.1145/2858036.2858270
57. Zhang, H., Patel, V.M., Fathy, M., Chellappa, R.: Touch gesture-based active user authentication using dictionaries. In: 2015 IEEE Winter Conference on Applications of Computer Vision, pp. 207–214 (2015). https://doi.org/10.1109/WACV.2015.35
58. Zhao, X., Feng, T., Shi, W.: Continuous mobile authentication using a novel graphic touch gesture feature. In: 2013 IEEE Sixth International Conference on Biometrics: Theory, Applications and Systems (BTAS), pp. 1–6 (2013). https://doi.org/10.1109/BTAS.2013.6712747
59. Zhao, X., Feng, T., Shi, W., Kakadiaris, I.A.: Mobile user authentication using statistical touch dynamics images. IEEE Trans. Inf. Forensics Secur. **9**(11), 1780–1789 (2014). https://doi.org/10.1109/TIFS.2014.2350916
60. Zheng, N., Bai, K., Huang, H., Wang, H.: You are how you touch: user verification on smartphones via tapping behaviors. In: 2014 IEEE 22nd International Conference on Network Protocols, pp. 221–232 (2014). https://doi.org/10.1109/ICNP.2014.43

Performance Evaluation of Post-Quantum TLS 1.3 on Resource-Constrained Embedded Systems

George Tasopoulos[1(✉)], Jinhui Li[2], Apostolos P. Fournaris[1], Raymond K. Zhao[2], Amin Sakzad[2], and Ron Steinfeld[2]

[1] Industrial Systems Institute/Research Center ATHENA, Patras, Greece
g.tasop@protonmail.com, fournaris@isi.gr

[2] Faculty of Information Technology, Monash University, Clayton, Australia
jinhui0018@gmail.com, {raymond.zhao,amin.sakzad,ron.steinfeld}@monash.edu

Abstract. Transport Layer Security (TLS) constitutes one of the most widely used protocols for securing Internet communications and has also found broad acceptance in the Internet of Things (IoT) domain. As we progress toward a security environment resistant to quantum computer attacks, TLS needs to be transformed to support post-quantum cryptography. However, post-quantum TLS is still not standardised, and its overall performance, especially in resource-constrained, IoT-capable, embedded devices, is not well understood. In this paper, we showcase how TLS 1.3 can be transformed into quantum-safe by modifying the TLS 1.3 architecture in order to accommodate the latest Post-Quantum Cryptography (PQC) algorithms from NIST PQC process. Furthermore, we evaluate the execution time, memory, and bandwidth requirements of this proposed post-quantum variant of TLS 1.3 (PQ TLS 1.3). This is facilitated by integrating the *pqm4* and *PQClean* library implementations of almost all PQC algorithms selected for standardisation by the NIST PQC process, as well as the alternatives to be evaluated in a new round (Round 4). The proposed solution and evaluation focuses on the lower end of resource-constrained embedded devices. Thus, the evaluation is performed on the ARM Cortex-M4 embedded platform NUCLEO-F439ZI that provides 180 MHz clock rate, 2 MB Flash Memory, and 256 KB SRAM. To the authors' knowledge, this is the first systematic, thorough, and complete timing, memory usage, and network traffic evaluation of PQ TLS 1.3 for all the NIST PQC process selections and upcoming candidate algorithms, that explicitly targets resource-constrained embedded systems.

1 Introduction

In 1994, Peter Shor described an algorithm on quantum computers [36] that solves the mathematical problems of integer factorisation and discrete logarithm in polynomial time. This alerted the cryptography community, since those hard-to-solve (by traditional computers) mathematical problems constitute the core of

C. Su et al. (Eds.): ISPEC 2022, LNCS 13620, pp. 432–451, 2022.
https://doi.org/10.1007/978-3-031-21280-2_24

the majority of existing public key cryptography solutions in the security world. While the quantum computers existing today may not be powerful enough to solve real-world problems, they pave the way for large-scale quantum computers in the future [14] that can easily break (e.g. recover the private keys) many existing security protocols and public key cryptography solutions.

In response to this potential new cryptographic reality, several standardisation bodies (eg. NIST, IETF, ETSI) have started working on the transition of cryptography to the post-quantum era [1,13,25]. In 2017, the US National Institute of Standards and Technology (NIST) initiated a still ongoing evaluation and standardisation process to select the next generation of industry-standard public key cryptographic primitives [4]. At the time of this paper's writing, NIST has selected 4 algorithms for standardisation: 3 Digital Signatures and 1 Key Encapsulation Mechanism (KEM). Additionally, NIST recently announced an extra round of evaluation for some of the KEMs that did not get selected (Round 4 of the NIST process) and also a Call for Proposals for Digital Signatures in order to diversify NIST's Digital Signature portfolio [1]. In the meantime, the Internet Engineering Task Force (IETF) is in the process of standardising the integration of post-quantum algorithms in popular security protocols [39].

One of the most prominent security protocols is the Transport Layer Security (TLS) protocol. Due to its wide acceptance and usage in secure communications, it is crucial to make TLS quantum computer safe (resistant against quantum computer cryptanalytic attacks), by integrating post-quantum cryptography (PQC) algorithms into the protocol structure. However, this PQ TLS integration is expected to have a non-trivial overhead on the protocol's performance. There are already several efforts to integrate PQC algorithms in TLS [38] and measure the overhead it introduces, with respect to a number of performance metrics: execution speed, memory requirements, communication size, and code size [15,18,21,31,32,37].

Understanding the PQ TLS performance overhead becomes even more important when dealing with resource-constrained devices and this may be critical to the final adoption of PQ TLS on such devices. However, prior works on evaluating the performance of PQ TLS either focused on high-end devices studying the impact of other factors such as network conditions [21,31,37], or focused on embedded system devices that are not resource-constrained [15,32]. Prior works that evaluated PQ TLS on resource-constrained devices [18], are limited to a small set of PQC algorithms, mainly because their goal was to highlight the feasibility of such an integration rather than provide a complete analysis.

In this paper, we make a thorough and analytic study of the PQC integration in the TLS 1.3 protocol for resource-constrained embedded system devices and their overall performance impact. We perform an exhaustive and systematic analysis of the PQC performance overhead in TLS 1.3 on embedded systems, in terms of execution speed, memory requirements, and communication size, for the majority of post-quantum public-key algorithms, including the NIST selected algorithms for standardisation, the algorithms that progressed to Round 4, as well as some algorithms from NIST PQC Round 3. Namely, we have integrated the KEMs CRYSTALS-Kyber, SABER, NTRU, SIKE, BIKE, HQC, NTRU LPRime, and FrodoKEM, and the Digital Signature algorithms CRYSTALS-Dilithium, Falcon, SPHINCS+, and Picnic3.

More specifically, by adopting the wolfSSL open-source TLS library, we propose a PQC enhanced TLS 1.3 design. We integrate into our design the above-mentioned PQC algorithms using the *pqm4* [22] and *PQClean* [29] open-source PQC libraries. The design is implemented in a resource-constrained device equipped with an ARM Cortex-M4 microcontroller. We include all the security levels that could fit in the RAM of this constrained evaluation board, and we evaluate the protocol's performance after the integration of all the algorithms selected for standardisation by the NIST PQC process and almost all of the algorithms that proceed to Round 4. Note that we also include in our study some algorithms that have been in Round 3 for completeness[1], including those are promising for a re-submission to the new standardisation Round 4 for Digital Signatures announced by NIST. Also, note that algorithms such as Rainbow and Classic McEliece have not been included in the study due to their large memory requirements, even on their lowest security levels, that prohibits their integration in the TLS 1.3 protocol. In addition, Rainbow's raised security concerns for some specified security parameters are taken into our consideration [16]. A recent work [19], was able to recover the secret key from SIKE in all security levels. Although it is possible that SIKE is now completely broken, we include its measurements for the sake of completeness. Network communication and routing functionality are provided through the lwIP library [22]. We also assume that both peers of the TLS 1.3 handshake, client and server, are mutually authenticated. According to the authors' knowledge, this work constitutes the first comprehensive and all-inclusive study on PQ TLS 1.3 for resource-constrained embedded systems that takes into account the latest results of NIST standardisation efforts (Selected Algorithms 2022 and Round 4 announcements).

The rest of the paper is organised as follows: In Sect. 2, we make a review of popular open-source PQC libraries and related research work, and we highlight the research gaps that our paper will fill. In Sect. 3, background information on TLS 1.3 is provided. In Sect. 4, the proposed design/architecture of the PQC integreated TLS 1.3 protocol is presented, providing the architectural changes that have been made in order to add PQC capabilities to TLS 1.3, along with various implementation details. In Sect. 5, the experimental evaluation process, measurements, results, and analysis are provided. Finally, Sect. 6 concludes the paper.

2 Popular PQC Libraries and Related Research Work

The NIST PQC standardisation process has sparked a bloom of research in the field of post-quantum cryptography. Apart from the PQC algorithms that were developed and submitted to the process, other research that emerged in recent

[1] We refer the reader to the Appendix for the rest of the evaluated algorithms from Round 3.

years focused on prototyping, integration into popular protocols, and measuring the performance overhead that these PQC algorithms will introduce.

Apart from the reference and x86 optimised PQC algorithm implementations offered by the submission team of each candidate PQC algorithm, other software libraries have also been provided by the PQC research community. *PQClean* [29] focuses on the prototyping of PQC algorithms without relying on external software library dependencies, thus offering standalone implementations of PQC algorithms.

Regarding embedded systems, a project named *mupq* has been developed in order to provide optimised PQC libraries targeting a number of embedded system processors or even Field Programmable Gate Arrays (FPGAs). After a call from the NIST PQC process to introduce evaluations on Cortex-M4 processors [5], as an outcome of the work in [28] (which is part of the *mupq* project), the *pqm4* library has been developed. This library includes implementations based on the Reference Implementations of the official releases of the algorithms, but with a focus on speed and size, and uses optimised assembly code for the Cortex-M4 processor. As the NIST PQC process advances, the *pqm4* library is regularly updated with newer versions of the code or with any changes the algorithm specifications introduce. All these updates are kept in an open-source git repository available online at [27].

In regards to TLS design and open-source implementation, the Open Quantum Safe (OQS) [38] project has developed a cryptographic library named *liboqs*, that has collected implementations of PQC algorithms, mostly from *PQClean*. By leveraging the developed *liboqs* library, this project integrated PQC algorithms into popular security protocol libraries, such as OpenSSL [7] and OpenSSH [6], making it possible to use these protocols with PQC algorithms. In the work by Sikeridis et al. [37], the OpenSSL and OpenSSH forks of OQS were used to measure the overhead that was introduced with the post-quantum integration on these two protocols in realistic network conditions. Doring et al. [21] performed similar experiments by using the same library and evaluated more PQC algorithms, but on the same machine without real-world network conditions. Paquin et al. [31] performed benchmarks of PQ TLS by using OQS project with various PQC algorithms, on machines within an emulated network that enabled the authors to experiment with different network parameters. All these works evaluated PQ TLS. However, they focused only on medium or high-resource systems like laptops, PCs, and servers.

However, there exists research works that focused on embedded systems. Bürstinghaus-Steinbach et al. [18] employed an implementation of TLS with PQC algorithms to take measurements on embedded devices. The authors adopted TLS version 1.2 and integrated CRYSTALS-Kyber as a KEM and SPHINCS+ as a Digital Signature. They showed the feasibility of such integration and gathered primitive performance measurements on PQ TLS. Paul et al. [32] introduced a migration strategy towards post-quantum authentication by using PQC algorithms in mixed certificate chains. The authors also evaluated the performance of post-quantum TLS 1.3 on a server, on a PC, and on a

Raspberry Pi. Barton et al. [15] used the same Raspberry Pi device to evaluate PQ TLS by using OQS with various PQC algorithms. It should be noted that the Raspberry Pi device used in [15,32] is equiped with an ARM Cortex-A53 processor running at 1.2 GHz and with 1 GB of RAM. Although this device is considered as an "embedded device", it belongs to the higher end of such devices with resources capable of running its own compiler and even a full Operating System.

To the authors' knowledge, this paper constitutes the first systematic and thorough architectural adaptation, implementation, and performance evaluation of the PQ TLS 1.3 based on the popular wolfSSL library on a resource-constrained device. Our work integrates the selected algorithms for standardisation by the NIST PQC process, Round 4 candidates, and alternative algorithms in Round 3, explicitly targeting low resource embedded systems.

3 Background

3.1 TLS Protocol

One of the major security protocols that are threatened by a potential quantum attack is the Transport Layer Security (TLS) protocol. TLS is the most widely used protocol for secure communications on the Internet, making it a de facto security standard. Hypertext Transfer Protocol Secure (HTTPS) protocol for secure website transfer [34], secure connection to mail servers [24], as well as secure Internet access for smartphone apps [33], are some of the many use cases of TLS. TLS version 1.3 [35] has been standardised in 2018 and introduces many important changes over the previous version, TLS 1.2.

The adoption of TLS 1.3 is at an adequate level due to the high centralisation of the Internet and the long duration of the draft's evaluation [26]. In fact, the *Internet Society Pulse* reported a nearly 60% adoption of TLS 1.3 by the top 1,000 websites globally [8].

TLS is a security protocol designed to provide secure communication over a computer network. It is typically considered among the application layer in the Internet protocol suite, providing privacy and data integrity between two parties. TLS consists of two primary components: a *handshake protocol* that authenticates the communicating parties, negotiates cryptographic modes and parameters, and establishes shared keying material to create a secure session; and a *record protocol* that uses the parameters established by the handshake protocol to protect the traffic between the securely communicating peers. The record protocol is located above the transport layer and uses the Transmission Control Protocol (TCP). Although the symmetric key ciphers used by the record protocol are affected by quantum attacks, specifically by Grover's algorithm [23], they can be easily modified to be quantum-safe by, e.g. doubling the size of the encryption keys. On the other hand, the *handshake protocol*, which makes heavy use of public key cryptography, is directly threatened by quantum cryptanalytic attacks without any simple mitigation. TLS uses public key cryptography for two main purposes: Key Exchange, which mostly uses Diffie-Hellman (DH) over

Elliptic Curves (EC) or RSA, and Digital Signatures, which use Elliptic Curve Digital Signature Algorithm (ECDSA) or RSA. For this reason, the integration of quantum-resistant public key cryptographic algorithms is necessary for both the Key Exchange and the Digital Signatures.

On TLS 1.3, the handshake between a client and a server begins with the client sending the first TLS 1.3 message, ClientHello, to the server. This message typically contains a client random number, the client TLS version, a list of Cipher Suites, and a series of extensions with additional information such as Server Name, Supported Groups, Supported Signature Algorithms, Key Share, and the Supported Versions. The "Supported Groups" extension contains all the Key Exchange methods, and the extension "Supported Signature Algorithms" contains all the Digital Signature algorithms that are supported by the client. In addition, Key Share contains an ephemeral ECDH or RSA public key. TLS 1.3 makes significant use of the extension fields. For example, if the negotiated version of TLS is version 1.3, it is indicated on the "Supported Version" extension, as the original entry "Supported Version" is set to TLS 1.2 to ensure compatibility with middleboxes. The server then replies with a ServerHello message, which contains a server random number, the selected Cipher Suite using the client's list of Cipher Suites and the server's preferences, the negotiated Protocol Version, and the server's Key Share. From now on, every exchanged message will be encrypted. The server sends the "EncryptedExtensions" message, which contains the remaining extensions. Then, the server sends the "CertificateRequest" message, which states that this session will be mutually authenticated. After that, the server sends the "Certificate" message, containing its digital certificate and the certificate chain up to a root Certificate Authority (CA). Then, the server sends the "CertificateVerify" message, which basically contains a Digital Signature over a hash of all exchanged handshake messages, starting with ClientHello and up to, but not including, this message itself. Finally, the server sends the "ServerHandshakeFinished" message, indicating that the handshake is complete from the server side.

The client now has all the necessary information to produce the final master key and can also verify the certificate as well as the signature of the server. As the handshake is mutually authenticated, the client now sends its "Certificate" message containing its digital certificate and the certificate chain up to a root CA, or alternatively, a self-signed certificate that is also installed on the server side. Then, the client sends the "CertificateVerify" message with a Digital Signature over a transcript of the messages so far. Finally, the client sends the "ClientHandshakeFinished" message. The handshake is now complete from the client side.

The server can now verify the client's certificate as well as the signature from the client. After that, the handshake is complete, and both peers can start sending and receiving the "Application Data", using symmetric key based authenticated encryption algorithms with the key that derived from the shared secret that both peers have agreed upon during the handshake phase.

3.2 WolfSSL

Regarding open-source TLS solutions for embedded systems, the most famous and widely used implementations are: Mbed TLS [3] and wolfSSL [10,11]. With Mbed TLS lacking support for TLS 1.3, wolfSSL is the only option to be adopted in this paper's research. WolfSSL is a library that implements the TLS protocol with a focus on "classical" cryptography. In more recent versions, wolfSSL has added support for CRYSTALS-Kyber, SABER, NTRU, and Falcon, via an integration with *liboqs* [9]. However, in the time of writing, this integration does not include optimised implementations for the Cortex-M4, except for an experimental setup that uses only Kyber512 from *pqm4* [12]. In our work, the wolfSSL library has been modified in order to support all the ARM Cortex-M4 optimised versions of the PQC algorithms, both KEM and Digital Signature (TLS Authentication).

WolfSSL [11], consists of three major components: *wolfCrypt*, a cryptographic library; *wolfSSL*, the TLS protocol code along with all associated functionality; and a set of *utilities*: test programs, benchmarks, etc. More information on these components can be found in Appendix B.

4 Proposed Design Approach and Overall PQ TLS 1.3 Architecture Implementation

To develop a complete PQ TLS 1.3 implementation supporting all the NIST PQC algorithms selected for standardisation as well as the upcoming Round 4 candidates, we make appropriate architectural adjustments in the wolfSSL library and the TLS 1.3 standard. Specifically, TLS 1.3 design changes have been made to the two TLS Extensions fields: "Supported Groups" and "Signature Algorithms". In addition, in our work, we make necessary changes to support KEMs as well as post-quantum Digital Signatures and certificates. In Fig. 1, the overall PQ TLS 1.3 handshake with the proposed modifications and additions to the standard is presented visually, indicating the PQC operations that are made in each phase of the TLS handshake and the exchanged messages. In the following subsections, the proposed changes are discussed in detail.

4.1 WolfSSL Post-Quantum Adaptation

Supported Groups. The ClientHello message, the first message that the client sends to initiate the handshake, contains the Extensions field. In this field, the client extends the information provided by the rest of the ClientHello fields and it plays a crucial role in TLS 1.3. One of the fields among the Extension field, as shown in Fig. 1, is the field *Supported Groups.* In this field, the client sends a list of Key Exchange algorithms in order of preference as encoded identifiers (codepoints) so that the server can select one of them to be used in the handshake. These identifiers are called Named Groups and are defined for each supported algorithm by the protocol itself. To use PQC algorithms, new Named Groups

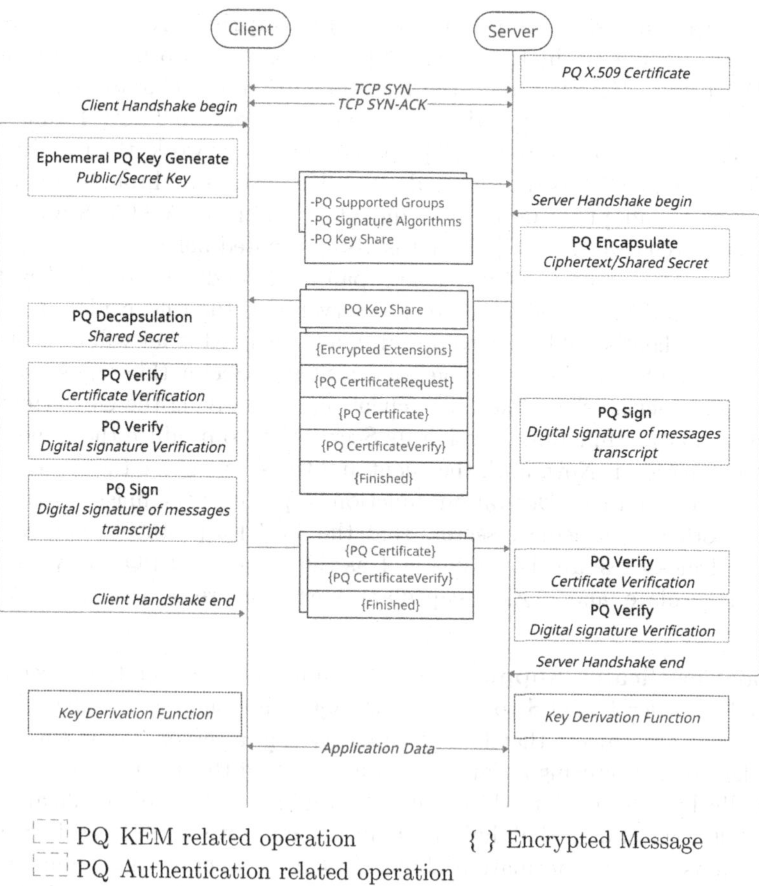

Fig. 1. Post-quantum TLS 1.3 handshake messages.

have been introduced. We have decided to choose the same codepoints as the OQS's fork of OpenSSL [7], to make the wolfSSL library inter-operable with other popular libraries.

Signature Algorithms. Another TLS 1.3 Extension field of PQC adaptation interest is the "Signature Algorithms". In this field, the client provides its preference on the signature algorithms that it supports regarding the CertificateVerify field. This means that this signature algorithm will be used to sign the transcript of the data exchanged by the server and to be verified by the client. Similar to the extension "Supported Groups", new codepoints are introduced for the post-quantum Digital Signature algorithms of the PQ TLS 1.3 design. The codepoints that have been added are compliant with the OQS's fork of OpenSSL [7].

Key Encapsulation Mechanism Support/Adaption. All the post-quantum encryption algorithms in the NIST PQC are Key Encapsulation Mechanism (KEM) schemes. However, only the traditional (Elliptic Curve) Diffie-Hellman Key Exchange (which is not a KEM) is supported in official TLS 1.3 standard. To transit the Key Exchange to the PQC paradigm, in our work, the Key Exchange mechanism of TLS 1.3 is transformed into a KEM scheme through architectural adaptation. We adopt the proposition introduced in the CRYSTALS-Kyber KEM based Key Exchange scheme [17] that is also presented below.

Initially, the client generates a key pair and sends the public key to the server with the ClientHello message. The server calls the Encapsulation function by using the client's public key to produce: a Ciphertext, that will be sent to the client with the ServerHello message; and a Shared Secret that the server keeps since it is the actual shared key. The client, upon receiving the Ciphertext, calls the Decapsulation function by using its Secret Key to produce the same Shared Secret as the server. Now, both the client and the server share the same key that can be passed to a Key Derivation Function to produce the master secret along with any other intermediate secrets that the TLS 1.3 protocol requires. These exchanged messages are shown in Fig. 1 as the Ephemeral PQC Key Generate, PQC Encapsulate, and PQC Decapsulate operations, respectively.

Digital Certificates Support. Another important object that needs to be modified in order for TLS to work with PQC algorithms is the digital certificates. These are objects that bound an entity, e.g. a server or a client, with its public key, by introducing a signature from a trusted third party. This can occur repeatedly by intermediate third parties, forming a "chain of certificates". The X.509 [20] is the standard of digital certificates on protocols such as TLS. It usually contains general information about the entity, along with the public key of the owner, the Digital Signature algorithm codepoint, and the Digital Signature itself.

To produce these digital certificates using post-quantum cryptographic algorithms, the OQS's fork of OpenSSL [7] is used. Through the OpenSSL's API, we generate digital certificates with support for all the PQC algorithms that are evaluated in this paper. Our goal is to produce digital certificates both for the server and the client, as they are mutually authenticated. To achieve this, we introduce a base "Certificate Authority" (CA) that can issue other certificates making a chain of trust up until a peer. In our paper, this chain is of length two, as the peer's certificate is directly signed by the CA. To accomplish this, we create a digital certificate for the CA, which is self-signed, and then we produce a digital certificate for the server and a certificate for the client, which both are then signed by the CA. Thus, two certificates are produced, both verifiable by our basic PQC CA.

For the sake of simplicity, all the certificates in the chain employ the same signature algorithm each time. This is also the case for both the certificate's signature and the signing operation on the CertificateVerify message. For example, when measuring the performance of Dilithium2, the certificates of CA, server, and client all have Dilithium2 signatures, and the CertificateVerify message is signed using Dilithium2 as well.

5 Measurements and Evaluation

5.1 Experiment and Measurement Setup

To make the TLS protocol operate with PQC algorithms, we first integrate the *pqm4* [28] implementations of the selected PQC algorithms in our study to the wolfSSL code. Whenever *pqm4* lacks an implementation of an algorithm, we use the corresponding implementation from *PQClean* instead. To realise the network communication of our project, we use the lwIP library [22], a lightweight implementation of the TCP/IP protocol suite, mainly focusing on embedded devices. Almost all of the PQC algorithms in our study require the usage of symmetric cryptographic primitives, specifically the Keccak primitives SHA-3 and SHAKE-256 [30]. *Pqm4* provides optimised implementations of these primitives for the Cortex-M4, and this code has been used in our work. Note that while *PQClean* does not provide any optimised code for the PQC algorithms themselves, we have linked these schemes with the optimised Keccak code from *pqm4*, and as a result we can observe some speed-up.

We use two devices to evaluate the PQ TLS: i) The NUCLEO F439ZI embedded system by STMicroelectronics, with a 32-bit ARM Cortex-M4 microcontroller running at 180 MHz, with 192 KB of usable SRAM (plus 64 KB of CCM RAM that is not utilised) and 2 MB of Flash memory; and ii) A PC running Ubuntu 20.04 in x86_64 architecture, equipped with an Intel i7-1165G7 with 8 cores running at 2.8 GHz. Both devices are connected to the same access point, through the Ethernet interface with a mean Round-Trip Time (RTT) of 0.493 ms. Using a modified version of the wolfSSL TLS benchmark program, we evaluate a series of TLS connections between these two devices and gather measurements and statistics.

As discussed in [37], changing the TCP time window parameter (TCP_WND) of the underlying TCP implementation will impact the performance of the TLS handshake. We experiment with different values of the TCP_WND parameter, in multiples of TCP_MSS (maximum segment size of each packet). We observe that the handshake is particularly slower for some TCP_WND values than the others. Because the network analysis is not in the scope of this work, we choose TCP_WND = 2 × TCP_MSS, where the TLS handshake performs well in our local Ethernet network without further investigation. Contrary to [37], where the authors stated that one could get better performance with bigger TCP_WND, we find that the above described parameter choice performs better in the context of our local network with minimal latency and almost no packet loss.

In this section, we first compare the performance between different standalone PQC algorithms and with the classical public key cryptography algorithms of traditional TLS 1.3. Afterwards, we discuss the PQ TLS 1.3 handshake measurements using various combinations of PQC authentications and PQC KEMs. Furthermore, we discuss the communication size (in terms of exchanged amount of bytes) of a PQ TLS 1.3 handshake and the overall memory requirements of different PQ TLS 1.3 combinations.

5.2 Post-quantum Cryptographic Algorithms Measurements

For the sake of completeness, we measure the standalone performance of the adopted PQC algorithms by using a modified version of the wolfSSL's benchmark program, *wolfcrypt-benchmark*. This tool uses the Real-time Clock (RTC) hardware module of the embedded system to measure time with millisecond precision. We use the implementations from *pqm4* for CRYSTALS-Dilithium, Falcon, CRYSTALS-Kyber, SABER, NTRU, NTRU LPRime, FrodoKEM, SIKE, BIKE, and Picnic3, and we use the implementations from *PQClean* for SPHINCS+ and HQC. In addition to the PQC algorithms, we measure the performance of four classical algorithms: RSA-2048 and ECDSA with curve secp256r1 are used for benchmarking classical authentication, and Finite Fields Diffie-Hellman Ephemeral (FFDHE)-3072 and ECDHE with curve secp256r1 are used for benchmarking classical Key Exchange, respectively. Every cryptographic algorithm operation has been executed for 10 s and the average execution time of all executions within 10 s is calculated and reported as the result.

In Table 1, the measured execution time on our target platform is presented, along with each algorithm's public key size and ciphertext/signature sizes. The claimed NIST security level of each algorithm is also presented. Level 1/3/5 means that an attack on that parameter set would require the same or more resources as a key search on AES 128/192/256, respectively. Level 2/4 means that an attack would require the same or more resources as a collision search on SHA-256/384, respectively. On the other hand, Level 0 means that this algorithm offers no quantum security. Note that the security level of RSA 2048 against classical attacks is 112 bits, and the classical security level of FFDHE 3072 and curve secp256r1 is 128 bits, respectively.

Comparison of Key Encapsulation Schemes. From Table 1, we can see that Kyber, the only KEM that is selected for standardisation by NIST so far, offers the best overall performance compared to all the other schemes. It has medium-sized keys and resulting ciphertexts as well as offering excellent performance in terms of execution speed.[2] It outperforms the classical FFDHE by an order of magnitude and even outperforms ECDHE by several milliseconds.

Among NIST PQC Round 4 candidates, HQC, although much slower than Kyber, offers good performance in terms of execution time but has the largest sizes compared to all the other schemes. BIKE has smaller sizes but slower execution time than HQC.

[2] The "execution speed" is calculated by the sum of "Key generation", "Encapsulation", and "Decapsulation" time for the PQC schemes and by using the "Agreement Time" for the classical algorithms.

Table 1. Summary of traditional and post-quantum primitives.

KEM algorithm	*NIST level*	*Public key (bytes)*	*Ciphertext (bytes)*	*Key generate (ms)*	*Encapsulate (ms)*	*Decapsulate (ms)*	*Notation*
FFDHE [1]	0	256	256	203.920	204.080 [4]	–	*FFDHE*
ECDHE [2]	0	32	32	8.428	17.687 [4]	–	*ECDHE*
Kyber512	1	800	768	8.133	6.239	3.419	*Kyb1*
BIKE-L1	1	1541	1573	200.620	25.969	411.308	*Bike1*
HQC128	1	2249	4481	30.202	50.682	72.775	*Hqc1*
SIKEp434	1	330	346	309.235	498.227	530.200	*Sike1*
SIKEp503	2	378	402	423.708	690.188	733.071	*Sike2*
SIKEp610	3	462	486	732.786	1341.125	1346.500	*Sike3*
Kyber768	3	1184	1088	12.224	11.412	7.924	*Kyb3*
SIKEp751	5	564	596	1262.750	2036.000	2183.000	*Sike5*
Kyber1024	5	1568	1568	12.918	11.623	8.539	*Kyb5*
Auth. algorithm	***NIST level***	***Public key (bytes)***	***Signature (bytes)***	***Key generate (ms)***	***Sign (ms)***	***Verify (ms)***	***Notation***
RSA [3]	0	256	256	12.853/450 [5]	448.250	12.500	*RSA*
ECDSA [2]	0	32	32	8.428	12.305	25.193	*ECDSA*
Sphincs128s	1	32	7856	8674.000	66239.000	61.588	*Sphi1s*
Sphincs128f	1	32	17088	137.750	3361.000	190.167	*Sphi1f*
Falcon512	1	897	666	1266.667	243.881	3.275	*Falc1*
Dilithium2	2	1312	2420	12.063	25.404 [6]	9.569	*Dil2*
Dilithium3	3	1952	3293	19.438	39.309 [7]	16.244	*Dil3*
Falcon1024	5	1793	1280	4802.667	527.789	6.852	*Falc5*

[1] 3072-bit, [2] secp256r1 curve, [3] 2048-bit, [4] key agreement time, [5] public/private key generation time, [6] (11/114) (min/max), [7] (15/138) (min/max) of execution time over 1000 signatures

Finally, SIKE has the slowest execution time among all the schemes but offers the smallest public key and ciphertext sizes (even smaller than Kyber). This fact makes SIKE an interesting candidate that only requires a very small amount of network traffic. The execution speed can hopefully be improved by either novel code optimisation techniques or by hardware accelerations in the future. However, a recent work [19], has successfully recovered the secret key from SIKE in all security levels in practice, thus bringing concerns of its overall security.

Comparison of Authentication Schemes. It can be observed that Dilithium offers the most balanced performance compared to all the other Digital Signature schemes selected for standardisation. While having a medium-sized public key and signature, it offers excellent performance in terms of execution time. Both Dilithium and Falcon outperform RSA in all operations at security level 1, and they outperform even the ECDSA in the "Verify" operation. However, both are slower on the "Sign" operation than ECDSA, with Falcon being slower by an order of magnitude. Note that we do not compare the "Key Generation" operation as it is never performed online in a TLS handshake.

The SPHINCS+ offers 2 variants: The "small" variant has small signatures but very slow execution times and the "fast" variant has faster execution times but extremely large sizes. The signature size of the "fast" variant at NIST security level 1 is very large (over 17 KB) and even exceeds the *Max_record_size* of the TLS protocol itself. On the other hand, the "small" variant needs over 1 min of execution time for the "Sign" operation.

The most time consuming operation is the "Sign" operation in all the PQC authentication schemes. As the scenario in our evaluation is mutual authentication, the employed embedded system boards have to use the expensive "Sign" operation when acting both as a server and as a client. This would result in large overhead in execution time of the PQ TLS 1.3 handshake, mainly due to the PQC authentication schemes. On the other hand, in the scenarios with server-only authentication, there would be a significant improvement in execution time using PQC authentications when the embedded system board acts as a client, especially when Falcon is used.

5.3 Post-quantum TLS 1.3 Measurements

After implementing all the architectural changes described in the previous section, in this subsection, we measure the performance of the post-quantum TLS 1.3 protocol with different PQC algorithm combinations and compare this with the performance of the classical TLS 1.3. PQ TLS 1.3 connections are established on a local Ethernet network, following the experimental setup of Subsect. 5.1.

We use the *wolfssl-tls-bench* program provided by the wolfSSL library to evaluate the performance of the post-quantum TLS. We make necessary changes in order to run this program, and collect statistics and measurements for our PQ TLS. In this work, the benchmark for each PQC algorithm combination runs for 50 s. We select the Cipher Suite *TLS13-AES256-GCM-SHA384* as the symmetric primitives, in line with previous works [31,32]. Note that for simplicity, the client and the server in our experiment have been configured to agree upon the public-key algorithms immediately, without any extra round-trip and without pre-shared key assumption.

In Table 2, the experiment's measurements/results, along with the static memory consumption and the communication byte sizes of the handshake, are presented in detail.

TLS 1.3 Handshake Time Measurements. The measurements collected from the client differ from the measurements collected from the server. Although the TLS 1.3 handshake authentication related operations are similar between the two peers (1 "Sign" and 2 "Verify" operations for each), this is not the case for the KEM related operations: the client executes 1 "Key Generate" and 1 "Decapsulate" operation, while the server executes 1 "Encapsulate" operation. This leads to asymmetric execution time of the TLS handshake when the board acts as a client and as a server, especially for schemes where these operations are slow. This is most obvious in the measurements with BIKE, where the execution time of its operations is highly divergent: very fast "Encapsualte", but very slow "Key Generate" and "Decapsualte". This makes the client handshake time ~5.6 times slower than the server. The *Dil2-Hqc1* client handshake time is ~1.36 times slower than the server. For rest of the PQC algorithm combinations, this difference is generally smaller, on an average of 6.25 ms.

Table 2. PQ TLS 1.3 handshake measurements.

Notation	*Static usage (bytes)*	*.bss usage (bytes)*	*Communication sizes (bytes)*	*Avg handshake time (ms)*	
				Client	*Server*
Selected algorithms for standardisation					
Dil2-Kyb1	49648	0	14748	96.318	91.062
Falc1-Kyb1	3680	39936	6833	288.305	285.951
Dil3-Kyb3	69072	0	20224	157.126	153.492
Falc5-Kyb3	4200	79872	11789	594.495	589.058
Dil3-Kyb5	69104	0	21088	165.590	152.537
Falc5-Kyb5	4712	79872	12647	601.827	592.302
Sph1s-Kyb1	800	0	33892	66977.000	66776.000
4rth round algorithms					
Dil2-Bike1	81528	49	16292	690.000	121.756
Dil2-Hqc1	71672	0	19910	198.603	145.989
Dil2-Sike1	49648	0	13858	886.359	566.125
Dil2-Sike2	49648	0	13962	1196.510	760.265
Dil2-Sike3	49648	0	14130	2089.690	1416.368
Dil2-Sike5	49648	0	14342	3403.222	2149.923
Dil3-Sike3	69232	0	18902	2246.077	1529.143
Dil3-Sike5	69104	0	19114	3450.167	2170.840
Traditional algorithms					
RSA-ECDHE	2368	0	3742	540.220	538.158
ECDSA-ECDHE	2368	0	2353	109.171	106.927

Given that TLS 1.3 mutual authentication is used, KEM combinations with Dilithium perform much better than KEM combinations with Falcon. This is due to the fact that Falcon has extremely fast "Verify" but slow "Sign" operations. We also see that *Sph1s-Kyb1* is extremely slow, with over 66 s of run-time. Among the Round 4 algorithms, we see that *Dil2-Hqc1* performs extremely well, faster than *Falc1+Kyb1* and only ~2 times slower than *Dil2+Kyb1*. *Dil2-Bike1* as a client is ~3.5 times slower than *Dil2-Hqc1*, but outperform it as a server.

Finally, all SIKE combinations have considerable execution time overhead (leading to execution time of a few seconds) compared to Digital Signature combinations with HQC or BIKE.[3]

Communication Sizes. The "Communication Size" is the byte size of all the messages exchanged during the TLS 1.3 handshake, which is the sum of all the bytes that a peer has sent plus the sum of all the bytes that the peer has received. We only consider the byte size of the TLS 1.3 messages, and the overhead from the TCP headers and lower network level protocols is not included in the measurements. Communication size measurements provide a clear picture of the network traffic that is involved during a TLS 1.3 handshake with a specific PQC combination. For example, although KEM combinations with Dilithium generally perform much better in terms of speed compared to KEM combinations with Falcon, it can be observed that *Dil2+Kyb1* requires more than twice the band-

[3] This should be considered with caution since there is evidence that SIKE is no longer cryptographically secure in its current version.

width than *Falc1+Kyb1*. The same applies to higher security levels. In addition, the network traffic of the "fast" variant of SPHINCS+ is very high, almost 2.3 times compared to *Dil2+Kyb1* and almost 5 times compared to *Falc1+Kyb1*.

Regarding the Round 4 algorithms, *Dil2-Sike1* has the lowest communication sizes among all the combinations with Dilithium2. For example, *Dil2+Kyb1* uses ~6.5% more bandwidth than *Dil2-Sike1*. However, given the current insecure status of SIKE, this result cannot be considered useful in practice. Note that the communication sizes are dominated by the Authentication introduced overhead. This has more significant impact in our mutual authentication scenario. As demonstrated in Table 1, each peer must send and receive a certificate or a whole certificate chain, and one Digital Signature. Nevertheless, larger KEM sizes affect the "Communication Sizes", as we can see that *Dil2-Bike1* and *Dil2-Hqc1* use ~10.5% and ~35% more bandwidth than *Dil2-Kyb1*, respectively, even though they all use Dilithium2 for authentication.

Compared to the classical TLS, PQ TLS 1.3 introduces a larger overhead in terms of network traffic due to the excessive communication size. *Dil2+Kyb1* uses 6.26 times more bandwidth than ECDSA+ECDHE, while *Falc1+Kyb1*, having a lower overhead, consumes only 2.9 times more bandwidth than ECDSA+ECDHE.

Memory Requirements. We use the tools provided by the STM32Cube IDE in order to perform an analysis on the static memory usage of our PQ TLS 1.3 implementation. The tool provides information about the code size, the RAM usage, and the stack requirements of each function etc. The *text* segment of the code size that includes the executable code and is stored in the Flash memory, never exceeds 30% of our total 2MB Flash memory. However, the *data* and *.bss* segments play a crucial role on the PQC algorithm integration, as they are stored in the 192 KB SRAM of the embedded system evaluation board. Algorithms introducing large artifact sizes or having an implementation that requires a lot of Stack memory, may eventually be impossible to be integrated in a memory-constrained device. For example, Rainbow has a public key of size 157KB, that alone consumes 80% of the total available memory, making it impossible to be evaluated in our board. Likewise, Classic McEliece is not included in *pqm4* in the first place for the same reason [28]. Also, Dilithium at security level 5 is not included in *pqm4*, because the memory requirements are too large. In Table 2, we show the Static memory or *data* region required by each KEM-Digital Signature combination as well as the respective *.bss* region, as reported by STM32Cube IDE tool.

Given that the employed embedded system evaluation board has 192 KB usable SRAM (excluding the 64 KB Core Coupled Memory), *Dil2+Kyb1* consumes ~25% of the total available memory, while on higher security levels, *Dil3+Kyb5* uses ~35%. Combinations with Falcon generally use less memory: *Falc1+Kyb1* consumes ~ 22% of the total available memory and *Falc5+Kyb5* uses 43%. On the other hand, *Sph1s-Kyb1* uses merely 800 bytes of RAM.

Regarding the Round 4 algorithms, both BIKE and HQC consume a significant amount of memory. *Dil2-Hqc1* and *Dil2-Bike1* consume 41% and 36% of the total memory of the board, which are 44% and 64% more memory than *Dil2-Kyb1*, respectively.

Note that the PQC algorithm implementations do not make any use of dynamically allocated memory internally, but the rest of the program's components (lwIP, FreeRTOS, wolfSSL) do. The memory allocations of public key, private key, ciphertext, and signatures are also made dynamically by wolfSSL. In addition, at the time of this paper's writing, some of the *pqm4* implementations were not memory-usage optimised. It is likely that stack-usage optimised versions of the PQC algorithms selected for standardisation will be developed in the future, which would hopefully reduce significantly their memory footprint and thus make it possible to use them on memory-constrained devices.

6 Conclusion

In this paper, the importance of adopting a quantum-safe version of TLS 1.3 targeting embedded systems, in response to the imminent threats of a possible quantum attack, is discussed. In the paper, we provide the necessary architectural/design adaptations to the TLS 1.3 standard in order to make it quantum safe and we provide a systematic PQ TLS 1.3 design that can support a broad range of PQC algorithms, including the NIST PQC selected algorithms for standardisation, Digital Signatures that NIST considered for further evaluation (on a new round), as well as the alternative PQC algotithms that NIST deemed worthy to move to Round 4 of the NIST PQC process. We use an embedded system board equipped with an ARM Cortex-M4 and a remote PC with an Intel x86_64 chip in our experiment. We have connected our devices to the same access point through the Ethernet interface and performed a series of mutually authenticated PQ TLS 1.3 connections for benchmarking. Our design implementation is based on the wolfSSL TLS library for embedded systems, on which the PQC algorithms are seamlessly integrated. To evaluate the PQ TLS 1.3 performance on embedded systems, performance of the developed PQ TLS 1.3 implementation is measured in terms of the execution timing, memory footprint, and communication size overhead that the PQC algorithms will introduce. This work, to the authors' knowledge, constitute the first complete work on PQ TLS 1.3 for resource-constrained embedded systems that takes in account all the selected algorithms for standardisation from the NIST PQC process, almost all Round 4 algorithms, and additionally some alternative algorithms from Round 3.

In this paper, G. Tasopoulos and A. Fournaris has received funding from the European Union's Horizon 2020 research and innovation program CONCORDIA under grant agreement No. 830927 and from the European Union's Horizon 2020 research and innovation programme ENERMAN under grant agreement No. 958478.

A Other Post-Quantum Algorithms

Tables 3 and 4.

Table 3. Summary of other post-quantum primitives.

Algorithm	*NIST level*	*Public key (bytes)*	*Ciphertext (bytes)*	*Key generate (ms)*	*Encapsulate (ms)*	*Decapsulate (ms)*
LightSaber	1	672	736	10.564	6.555	3.960
NTRU	1	699	699	31.093	11.990	3.650
Frodo640	1	9,616	9,720	474.682	473.091	469.545
NTRULPR-761	2	1,039	1,167	18.116	11.284	8.818
Algorithm	*NIST level*	*Public key (bytes)*	*Ciphertext (bytes)*	*Key generate (ms)*	*Sign (ms)*	*Verify (ms)*
Picnic3	1	35	14,612	5.922	2,188.400	1,355.000

Table 4. PQ TLS 1.3 handshake measurements with other post-quantum primitives.

Notation	*Static usage (bytes)*	*.bss Usage (bytes)*	*Communication Sizes (bytes)*	*Avg. handshake Time (ms)*	
				client	*server*
Extra measurements					
Pic1-Kyb1	87000	13	52445	5022.167	5027.083
Dil2-Ntru1	50000	0	14578	126.978	104.136
Dil2-Frod1	73000	0	32491	1194.501	687.865
Dil2-Ntrulpr1	49648	0	15388	125.351	123.697
Dil2-Sab1	49648	0	14588	109.429	98.401

B Main Components of WolfSSL Library

WolfSSL consists of the following main components:
WolfCrypt. This component includes all the classical public-key and symmetric-key cryptographic algorithms, as well as hash algorithms, MAC algorithms, and programs handling certificate and key files. It provides optimised code for various architectures as well as hardware support for selected platforms.
WolfSSL. This component includes all the protocol related codes, that implement the TLS protocol itself as well as other protocols such as Datagram Transport Layer Security (DTLS). It includes all the settings and preferences of the TLS protocol and the interfaces to communicate either to a lower level protocol such as TCP, or to a higher level such as an operating systems e.g. FreeRTOS [2].
Utilities. This component includes all non-essential utilities such as benchmarks or programs for testing purpose to verify the correct functionality of the wolfSSL library. In this paper, some of these benchmark programs have been used in order to measure the performance of PQ cryptographic algorithms or the TLS protocol itself. We particularly use the following two tools:

- *Wolfcrypt-benchmark* is a benchmark tool used to measure the performance of all the enabled cryptographic algorithms and provides relevant statistics. This program has been used in the paper as basis for taking time measurements on PQC algorithms in order to compare them with the classical algorithms.
- *Wolfssl-tls-bench* is another benchmarking tool that measures and provides a series of metrics regarding TLS sessions. It can make use of an operating system, like FreeRTOS, and simulate a server and a client connecting through TLS on the same device. Alternatively, it can be run on different devices, one being the server and the other being the client, to provide a realistic benchmark scenario. The tool repeatedly establishes TLS sessions (by running the TLS handshake), exchanges data for a given time period, and then it provides statistics about the established connections e.g. the average time spent on handshaking, the size of exchanged data etc. This program has been used in this paper in order to measure the performance of TLS protocol while using PQC algorithms and to compare the results with the TLS protocol using classical algorithms.

References

1. Announcing PQC candidates to be standardized, plus fourth round candidates. https://csrc.nist.gov/News/2022/pqc-candidates-to-be-standardized-and-round-4. Accessed 29 July 2022
2. FreeRTOS. https://www.freertos.org. Accessed 29 July 2022
3. mbedTLS Library. https://github.com/ARMmbed/mbedtls. Accessed 29 July 2022
4. NIST call for submissions. https://www.nist.gov/news-events/news/2016/12/nist-asks-public-help-future-proof-electronic-information. Accessed 29 July 2022
5. NIST urge to focus on cortex-M4. https://csrc.nist.gov/CSRC/media/Presentations/the-2nd-round-of-the-nist-pqc-standardization-proc/images-media/moody-opening-remarks.pdf. Slide 22, Accessed 29 July 2022
6. OQS OpenSSH fork repository. https://github.com/open-quantum-safe/openssh. Accessed 29 July 2022
7. OQS OpenSSL fork repository. https://github.com/open-quantum-safe/openssl. Accessed 29 July 2022
8. TLS 1.3 adoption according to the internet society pulse. https://pulse.internetsociety.org/technologies. Accessed 29 July 2022
9. WolfSSL Changelog. https://www.wolfssl.com/docs/wolfssl-changelog/. Accessed 29 July 2022
10. WolfSSL github repository. https://github.com/wolfSSL/wolfssl. Accessed 29 July 2022
11. wolfSSL library. https://www.wolfssl.com/. Accessed 29 July 2022
12. WolfSSL PQ key establishment in Cortex-M4. https://www.wolfssl.com/post-quantum-tls-1-3-key-establishment-comes-stm32-cortex-m4/. Accessed 29 July 2022
13. Quantum-safe cryptography (QSC). https://www.etsi.org/technologies/quantum-safe-cryptography (2020). Accessed 29 July 2022
14. Arute, F., et al.: Quantum supremacy using a programmable superconducting processor. Nature **574**(7779), 505–510 (2019)

15. Barton, J., Buchanan, W.J., Pitropakis, N., Sayeed, S., Abramson, W.: Post quantum cryptography analysis of TLS tunneling on a constrained device. In: ICISSP, pp. 551–561. SCITEPRESS (2022)
16. Beullens, W.: Breaking rainbow takes a weekend on a laptop. IACR Cryptol. ePrint Arch. p. 214 (2022)
17. Bos, J.W., et al.: CRYSTALS - kyber: a cca-secure module-lattice-based KEM. In: EuroS&P, pp. 353–367. IEEE (2018)
18. Bürstinghaus-Steinbach, K., Krauß, C., Niederhagen, R., Schneider, M.: Post-quantum TLS on embedded systems: integrating and evaluating kyber and SPHINCS+ with mbed TLS. In: AsiaCCS, pp. 841–852. ACM (2020)
19. Castryck, W., Decru, T.: An efficient key recovery attack on sidh (preliminary version). Cryptology ePrint Archive, Paper 2022/975 (2022). https://eprint.iacr.org/2022/975, https://eprint.iacr.org/2022/975
20. Cooper, D., Santesson, S., Farrell, S., Boeyen, S., Housley, R., Polk, W.: Internet x. 509 public key infrastructure certificate and certificate revocation list (crl) profile. Technical Report (2008)
21. Döring, R., Geitz, M.: Post-quantum cryptography in use: empirical analysis of the TLS handshake performance. In: NOMS, pp. 1–5. IEEE (2022)
22. Dunkels, A.: Design and implementation of the lwIP TCP/IP stack. Swedish Inst. Comput. Sci. **2**(77) (2001)
23. Grover, L.K.: A fast quantum mechanical algorithm for database search. In: STOC, pp. 212–219. ACM (1996)
24. Hoffman, P.: Smtp service extension for secure smtp over transport layer security. Technical Report, pp. 1–9 (2002)
25. Hoffman, P.E.: The transition from classical to post-quantum cryptography. Internet Engineering Task Force, Internet-Draft drafthoffman-c2pq-05 (2019)
26. Holz, R., et al.: Tracking the deployment of TLS 1.3 on the web: a story of experimentation and centralization. Comput. Commun. Rev. **50**(3), 3–15 (2020)
27. Kannwischer, M.J., Rijneveld, J., Schwabe, P., Stoffelen, K.: PQM4: post-quantum crypto library for the ARM Cortex-M4 (2019). https://github.com/mupq/pqm4
28. Kannwischer, M.J., Rijneveld, J., Schwabe, P., Stoffelen, K.: pqm4: testing and benchmarking NIST PQC on ARM cortex-m4. IACR Cryptol. ePrint Arch. p. 844 (2019)
29. Kannwischer, M.J., Schwabe, P., Stebila, D., Wiggers, T.: Improving software quality in cryptography standardization projects. In: EuroS&P Workshops, pp. 19–30. IEEE (2022)
30. NIST: SHA-3 standard: permutation-based hash and extendable-output functions (2015). https://doi.org/10.6028/NIST.FIPS.202
31. Paquin, C., Stebila, D., Tamvada, G.: Benchmarking post-quantum cryptography in TLS. In: Ding, J., Tillich, J.-P. (eds.) PQCrypto 2020. LNCS, vol. 12100, pp. 72–91. Springer, Cham (2020). https://doi.org/10.1007/978-3-030-44223-1_5
32. Paul, S., Kuzovkova, Y., Lahr, N., Niederhagen, R.: Mixed certificate chains for the transition to post-quantum authentication in TLS 1.3. In: AsiaCCS, pp. 727–740. ACM (2022)
33. Razaghpanah, A., Niaki, A.A., Vallina-Rodriguez, N., Sundaresan, S., Amann, J., Gill, P.: Studying TLS usage in android apps. In: ANRW, p. 5. ACM (2018)
34. Rescorla, E.: Http over tls. Technical Report (2000)
35. Rescorla, E.: The transport layer security (tls) protocol version 1.3. Technical Report (2018)
36. Shor, P.W.: Algorithms for quantum computation: discrete logarithms and factoring. In: FOCS, pp. 124–134. IEEE Computer Society (1994)

37. Sikeridis, D., Kampanakis, P., Devetsikiotis, M.: Assessing the overhead of post-quantum cryptography in TLS 1.3 and SSH. In: CoNEXT, pp. 149–156. ACM (2020)
38. Stebila, D., Mosca, M.: Post-quantum key exchange for the internet and the open quantum safe project. In: Avanzi, R., Heys, H. (eds.) SAC 2016. LNCS, vol. 10532, pp. 14–37. Springer, Cham (2017). https://doi.org/10.1007/978-3-319-69453-5_2
39. Steblia, D., Fluhrer, S., Gueron, S.: Hybrid key exchange in tls 1.3. Internet engineering task force, Internet-draft draft-ietf-tls-hybrid-design-01 (2020)

Secure Human Identification Protocol with Human-Computable Passwords

Sławomir Matelski[1,2(✉)]

[1] Lodz University of Technology, Lodz, Poland
s.matelski@intelco.pl
[2] Intelco LLC, Lodz, Poland

Abstract. In this paper we present a new method of secure human-computer identification, which remains safe also in untrusted systems and environments. This method allows the elimination of any supplementary gadgets/devices or theft-sensitive biometric data used by the Multi-Factor Authentication (MFA), and using only one secret as a universal private key for all obtainable online accounts. However, the features of this solution make it best suited for use by an mobile authenticator or by Authentication Authority with the Single-Sign-On (SSO) method of identity and access management, rather than for individual services. Such a key is used by our innovative challenge-response protocol to generate One-Time-Password, e.g., 6-digit OTP, could be calculated by a human in only 15 s, also offline on paper documents with an acceptable level of security required for post-quantum symmetric cyphers, thanks to the hard lattice problem with noise introduced by our new method, which we call Learning with Options (LWO). The secret has the form of an outline like a kind of handwritten autograph, designed in invisible ink on the mapping grid. The password generation process requires following such an invisible contour on the challenge matrix created randomly by the verifier and reading values from secret fields to calculate the OTP.

Keywords: Authentication · Lattice cryptography · OTP · Secret key

1 Introduction

Despite the use of different identification factors by multi-factor authentication (MFA) methods, the basic condition for a reliable authentication is the use of the intelligence of the human brain, in the form of a static password. For security reasons, it is recommended to use different passwords for each online account. As a result, users often adopt insecure password practices (e.g., reuse or weak password) or they have to frequently reset their passwords. To solve this problem, several solutions have been found, most of which use a secret shared by user and verifier, or such that the user reconstructs each of their passwords by calculating the response to a public challenge, by performing simple mathematical operations i.e. addition modulo 10. For each internet account, such

C. Su et al. (Eds.): ISPEC 2022, LNCS 13620, pp. 452–467, 2022.
https://doi.org/10.1007/978-3-031-21280-2_25

a challenge must be stored on the server with the correct response as a hashed password, but only the user needs to know the secret (only one for all these accounts).

A similar approach to the password calculation idea is used by our iChip protocol (patent pending), inspired by microchip topography and handwriting (Fig. 1). As we showed in Sect. 7, it ensures the secure generation of several thousand of these passwords. In the following, it can also be used as an OTP generator.

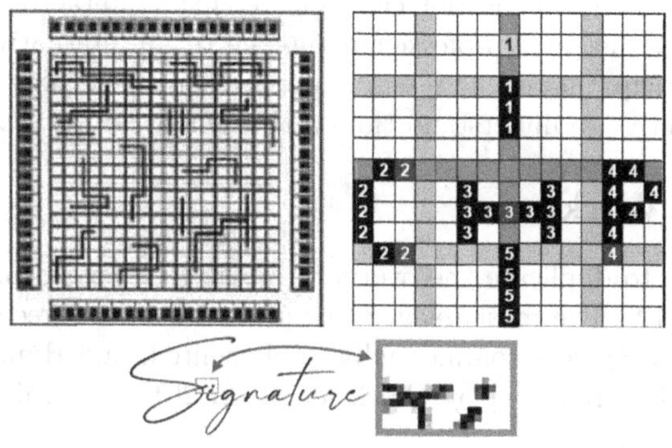

Fig. 1. Topography of microchip, iChip's secret patern, and handwriting.

The MFA method often requires an additional electronic device, because using the same device or communication channel both to enter a static password and to verify another MFA-factor, may not be secure. Such a device uses a built-in OTP generator or biometrics. Then, the OTP is automatically entered into the verification system, for example from a smart card or IoT device, or by the user after being read from the token screen or smartphone via SMS or a special application. Unfortunately, this solution does not guarantee that the device is used by its owner; it must be available at all times and can be stolen, lost, damaged or duplicated. Biometric methods are an alternative, but they can be tricked relatively easily by a replay attack using intercepted biometric data and, if necessary, with the help of machine learning or AI algorithms [19].

The MFA obviously requires more time than entering a regular static password. Therefore, a human-generated OTP protocol that maintains the expected balance between security and usability, eliminating the long list of drawbacks mentioned above, has a high chance of being accepted by users.

More than 30 years have passed since Matsumoto and Imai presented the first Human-Generated Password protocol (HGP) in 1981 [1], and during that time, many attempts were made to achieve this above-mentioned balance, but only two protocols were implemented commercially: strong and very slow HB, presented by Hopper and Blum in 2000 [2], and fast and easy but very weak grIDsure (GS), presented by Brostoff et al. in 2010 [20]; both described briefly also in Sect. 2. We will show further that our iChip scheme has security properties better than HB and usability close to GS, while eliminating their drawbacks.

The contributions of this work are: the challenge-response cryptographic protocol, based on lattice problem with noise, introduced by our Learning with Options (LWO) method as a more effective new variant of the LPN/LWE method of easy OTP computation by a human; a graphical interface for the implementation of that protocol, which allows the user to create his secret in the form of an easy-to-remember image, and a special wizard to compose it; both well-proven in usability and security study discussed after the presentation of mathematical rules, illustrated by examples of the iChip core and its TurboChip overlay; and finally, a further protocol enhancement against active attacks.

The completed implementation can be tested in an interactive demo or viewed in a short film, either as a professional tutorial or an alternative version made by children participating in the research process; both available online [25]. It is much more effective to understand than a mathematical description.

2 Related Works

We do not wish to duplicate the overview of the HGP protocols compiled and presented in [5,12]. The most relevant for our work were three schemes, two of which (HB and GS) were commercially implemented, and Human Computable Passwords (HCP) presented by Blocki et al. in 2017 [7], which were close to achieving this goal.

- The HB is based on the Learning Parity with Noise (LPN) method, which ensures a high level of security, but the time of over 10 min needed for a 20-bit authentication by a human is too long to be acceptable. Nevertheless, the properties of this protocol or later improved variants (HB^+, HB#, NLHB) are well suited to apply in resource-constrained devices.
  The protocol runs as follows: Both sides of the protocol (User U and Verifier V) shared the secret x. V set a random challenge $a \in \{0,1\}^k$ and sends it to U. If the LPN method would be not used in this protocol, then U computes the binary inner-product $a \bullet x$, then sends the result back to V. V computes $a \bullet x$, and accepts if U parity bit is correct. By repeating it for r rounds, U can lower the probability of random guessing the correct parity bits for all r rounds to 2^{-r}. An eavesdropper capturing $O(k)$ valid challenge-response pairs between U and V can quickly calculate the value of x through Gaussian Elimination. To prevent revealing x to passive attacks, U has to inject noise into his response.
  U intentionally sends the wrong response with constant probability $\eta \in (0, 0.5)$. V then authenticates U identity if fewer than ηr of responses are incorrect.
- The grIDsure scheme has exactly the opposite properties confirmed in [20]: the high usability level and very low level of safety, as only 3 samples of challenge-response pairs are sufficient to reveal the secret. In addition, the entropy of this scheme is also low, as detailed research has shown, that users choose secret patterns that are easy to remember and frequently reused, so its scheme is highly vulnerable to dictionary attacks, as the choice is very limited due to the small grid 25×25 and the small number of 4 secret objects. The user reads the 4 digits of the OTP password from 4 secret places in a grid filled with random numbers.

– The HCP has the best balance between safety and usability of any HGP protocols developed so far. The disadvantage of their scheme is the need to memorize dozens of pictures, mapping to numbers with the help of associated mnemonics. The verifier shows a challenge of $k_1 + k_2 + 10 = 14$ randomly selected pictures from n prepared and memorized by the user. The user has to mentally replace the pictures in the challenge with the corresponding numbers, and then compute each digit of the password using the following function:

$$f_{k1,k2}(x_0, ..., x_{9+k1+k2}) = x_j + \sum_{i=10+k_1}^{9+k_1+k_2} x_i \mod 10, \text{ where } j = (\sum_{i=10}^{9+k_1} x_i) \mod 10$$

The iChip has similar usability properties to grIDsure as the secret pattern of cells in the grid is employed by both schemes. However, the similarity is noticeable only in the so-called generator block. The most significant difference lies in the extraordinary rules used in iChip, which makes a huge difference in the key space (3e + 5 vs 3e + 154), and provides many thousands of times greater resistance against peeping attacks than GS. The conclusions about low practical entropy of GS do not apply to the iChip as getting all the easy-to-remember keys from such a huge key space is a task with a difficulty near to brute-force, which is not feasible for current supercomputers. In Sect. 7 we will show, that the iChip protocol inherits the abovementioned properties of HB, HB$^+$ and HCP, which protect it triply against passive attacks.

3 Introducing Noise to the iChip Protocol

An important feature of the iChip protocol is the implementation of the Learning with Rounding (LWR) method, which is an LPN variant of the worst-case hard lattice problem inherent in lattice cryptography. The implementation of core LPN or Learning with Errors (LWE) methods increases the security of any protocol; however, the degree of usability is reduced, and authentication requires much more time, as the user has to perform additional protocol rounds to compensate for rounds lost to incorrect responses due to reduced resistance to random attacks. In contrast, the LWR and described below LWO methods requires only correct responses. The iChip uses Eq. 1 introduced in Sect. 4.1, as its base function which satisfies the criteria of the LWR method of deterministic rounding by $x \mod p$, where $p = 10$ is admittedly too small to effectively introduce noise, but convenient for human computation. This function is a node for the various protocol variants and for our proposed LWO method of introducing noise, which is far more efficient. To further strengthen the iChip protocol it is beneficial to increase the entropy of the random option selection in the LWO case. The simplest way to get this entropy is to read the seconds from the system clock or user's watch, and then calculate for example, *seconds* $\mod 2$, to addressing two output elements of any block in the secret.

4 Interface Design and Protocol Implementation

The iChip is a challenge-response protocol to authenticate the user to the verifier using the shared secret, where the user has to answer the challenge generated by the verifier (server). The way the iChip scheme worked was inspired by the image of the photolithographic mask used to create conductive paths on the PCB (Printed Circuit Board) or PLA (Programmable Logic Array) surface, like shown in Fig. 1. The user composes his secret by designing such a layout in a special wizard by drawing a map of blocks B of masking elements as paths conducting the digital signal from input to output; provided from the generator block. These paths will determine the change in value from V_{inp} at the input to V_{out} at the output and define their properties and mutual logical relations. This layer consists of $n \times n$ fields and is represented by the C matrix, containing $n \times n$ cells.

The user specifies his secret key S by specifying a list of b blocks that occupy the fields selected by him from the C matrix, and specifies the block elements that act as input or output. For a short and easy explanation, we will use the example of the secret key illustrated in Fig. 2 or Fig. 4 as an iChip layout and the matrix coordinates of the input and output elements encoded hexadecimal in the associated table, while for the description of the protocol, we will use the Python convention. The C matrix is a set of n^2 random values generated by verifier as $C = [[V_{1,1}, V_{1,2}, ..., V_{1,n}], ...[V_{n,1}, V_{n,2}, ..., V_{n,n}]]$. Each i-th element of block $B[i] = [y_i, x_i, z_i]$ is defined by 3 parameters: row y and column x as field coordinates (y, x) in matrix C, and parameter z defining its state: $z = \{I, O\}$, where: $I = Input, O = Output$.

We use also an alternative compact notation of block elements as: $B_j^z[i] = B_j^z[(y_i, x_i)]$. Each block B_j is a list of such elements, divided into two segments for inputs and outputs: $B = [B^I, B^O] = [B[1], B[2], ..., B[k]]$. A list of b blocks B_j is included in the secret $S = [B_0, B_1, ...B_{b-1}]$, where $0 \leqslant j < b$. The algorithm parameters are denoted by four positive integers $N, L, b, k \in \mathbb{N}$, where:

- chip size (the size of C matrix), $N = n \times n$;
- parameter describing OTP length, $L \leqslant 10$;
- maximal number of blocks, $1 \leqslant b \leqslant 10$;
- maximal block length, $k \leqslant 10$;

4.1 Generating One-Time Passwords

$G = B_0$ is the first of these blocks in key S, and it is called a generator because it does not contain inputs and the values $V_G = C[G]$ from all its $L = |B_0|$ output elements are mapped by the remaining blocks. The user has to remember the position of all blocks and their order in the S. The verifier generates a challenge matrix C of N random digits. To generate the OTP, the user has to collate the C matrix with the secret key S and calculate all OTP digits, one at each i-th of $L = |\mathrm{OTP}|$ rounds of the protocol in the following 3 steps:

1. Read the V^i_{inp} value of the $G[i]$ element in C at position (y_i, x_i): $V^i_{inp} = C[G[(y_i, x_i)]]$
2. Starting from j-th block (where $j = 1$ in the 1st round), search input elements ($z = \textit{Input}$) of j-th block for the coordinates (y_i, x_i) such that $V^i_{inp} = C[B^I_j[(y_i, x_i)]]$.
   If no such coordinates are found in the j-th block, move to the subsequent block. By $j = \phi$ denote the index of the *current block* (ϕ) in which the searched so-called *target input* (ψ) has been found first and let $V^i_{out} = C[B_\phi[y, x, z = \textit{Output}]]$.
   If the search fails for all $j < b$ then let $V^i_{out} = V^i_{inp}$.
3. The i-th digit of the OTP you will get as

$$OTP[i] = (V^i_{inp} + V^i_{out}) \mod 10 \quad (1)$$

To avoid overloading the first blocks, it is recommended to resume the search for V^i_{inp} from the block next to the last searched. For additional security, the authentication protocol should follow at least one of the two exceptions/rules (*I, *O), which have been added to the 2nd step of the algorithm; these significantly increase the resistance of the iChip protocol against passive attacks with a statistical algorithm or Gaussian Elimination.

For their consideration let (y_i, x_i) be the coordinates on which the *target input* ψ in B such that $C[B_\phi[\psi]] = V^i_{inp}$ was found first in the challenge matrix.

However, first, we will present a simple example illustrated in Fig. 2 to explain the principle of calculating the OTP without the exceptions mentioned above. Alternatively, it is recommended to watch the short video tutorial [25].

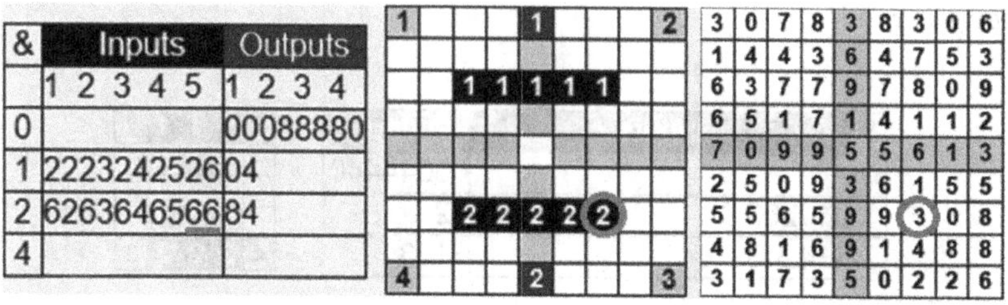

&	Inputs	Outputs
	1 2 3 4 5	1 2 3 4
0		00088880
1	2223242526	04
2	6263646566	84
4		

3	0	7	8	3	8	3	0	6
1	4	4	3	6	4	7	5	3
6	3	7	7	9	7	8	0	9
6	5	1	7	1	4	1	1	2
7	0	9	9	5	5	6	1	3
2	5	0	9	3	6	1	5	5
5	5	6	5	9	9	3	0	8
4	8	1	6	9	1	4	8	8
3	1	7	3	5	0	2	2	6

Fig. 2. An example of a secret: block input elements given as black fields and output as blue or light blue fields. The positions of all input and output elements are hexadecimal encoded in the associated table. The first column (&) contains the index of each block. On the right: The challenge matrix. (Color figure online)

There are generator block 0 containing 4 light blue cells in the matrix corners and two mapping blocks labeled by their index (1 or 2) in the example above (Fig. 2). In the 1st round, we read the value $V^1_{inp} = 3$ from the 1st element of generator block at position (0, 0).

We look for this value sequentially in all mapping blocks from 1 to 2. The first occurrence of this value is in the last element of block 2, i.e. $B_2^I[5]$ in cell (6, 6), which is the *target input* $\psi = 5$ in the *current block* $\phi = 2$. Now, we read a value of the output element of this block, which is in cell (8, 4), hence $V_{out}^1 = C[8,4] = 5$. The 1st round ends with a calculation of the 1st OTP digit according to Eq. 1 as: $\text{OTP}[1] = (V_{inp}^1 + V_{out}^1) \mod 10 =$
$= (C[G[1]] + C[B_2^O[1]]) \mod 10 =$
$= (C[0,0] + C[8,4]) \mod 10 =$
$= (3+5) \mod 10 = 8$.

EXTRA RULES / EXCEPTIONS

*I) Let V_{inp}^i be the sum of all input elements of the current block B_ϕ, from ψ to $\psi{+}n$, where $\psi{+}n \leqslant |B_\phi^I|$ and $n \leqslant 2$:

$$V_{inp}^i = (\sum_{k=0}^{k \leqslant n} C[B_\phi[\psi + k]]) \mod q \tag{2}$$

This introduces non-linearity to cryptanalysis and protection against Gaussian Elimination, as the number of arguments in Eq. 2 varies randomly in each challenge. Depending on the variant of *I, the q modulus can be 10 or omitted as default.

*O) If the *current block* B_ϕ contains more than one output element $|B_\phi^O| > 1$, then randomly choose one of them as $V_{out}^i = C[B_\phi^O[randrange(1, |B_\phi^O|)]]$. This is the case of using the LWO method illustrated by Fig. 3: Block 2 with fields labeled by 2 has two outputs/options at positions (3, 1) and (3, 3). If the value searched for is found in this block, then the user has to choose one of these two options at random.

&	Inputs	Outputs
0		00044440
1	010203	12
2	414243	3133

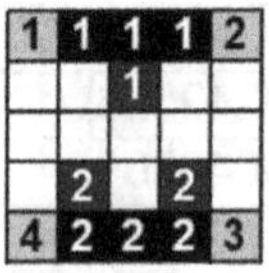

1	1	1	1	2
		1		
	2		2	
4	2	2	2	3

Fig. 3. An example of secret with exception *O.

*Θ) If the *current block* B_ϕ has no output $|B_\phi^O| = 0$, then we use the next input instead: $V_{out}^i = C[B_\phi[(\psi + 1) \mod |B_\phi|]]$. This exception is a logical complement to the exception *O and it has great importance for increasing the key space, because cryptanalysis must take into account the order of all block elements in the C matrix.

&	Inputs	Outputs
	1 2 3 4 5 6 7 8 9	1 2 3 4 5 6
0		04152628190a
1	445464	33
2	8494a4a5	a6
3	a9aa9a8a	a8
4	6a5a4a	3b
5	c4c5c6c8c9ca	d7e7
6		
7		
8		

Fig. 4. An example of a secret defined by the user and challenge matrix with a schema for determining the 1st digit of OTP.

4.2 Advanced Example

Based on Fig. 4 we will compute the 6-digit OTP using the variant of double protection against passive attacks, i.e., with the rules *I and *O, as follows:

The generator block contains $V_G = C[G] = C[B_0] = [3, 7, 8, 8, 6, 3]$.

The 1st element $V_G[1]$ at position (0, 4) has a value of 3.

When looking for it sequentially in blocks 1 to 6, it can be found in the 3th input element of the 1st block $B_1^I[3]$ at position (6, 4), (marked in the red ring as a target input ψ); the output element $B_1^O[1]$ of this block is in cell (3, 3) with a value of 9. The 1st digit of OTP is calculated according to Eq. 1 as OTP[1] = (3 + 9) mod 10 = 2.

The next element $V_G[2]$ at position (1, 5) has a value of 7, which is also in $B_4^I[2]$ at position (5, a) and the output element $B_4^O[1]$ has a value of 9. Since $\psi = 2 < |B_4^I| = 3$, then due to rule *I:

$V_{inp}^2 = C[B_4^I[2]] + C[B_4^I[3]] = 7 + 1 = 8$. Now, according to Eq. 1 we can calculate: $\text{OTP}[2] = (8 + 9) \mod 10 = 7$.

$V_G[3] = 8$ appears in $B_5^I[3]$ at position (c, 6), but this block has 2 output elements $B_5^O[1]$ in cell (d, 7) and $B_5^O[2]$ in cell (e, 7). Therefore due to exception *O, we can choose any of them; assuming we choose the first with value of 4, OTP[3] = (8 + 4) mod 10 = 2.

$V_G[4] = 8$, hence this round is similar to the previous one, but now, we use the second output $B_5^O[2]$ in cell (e, 7) for our calculations: $\text{OTP}[4] = (8 + 0) \mod 10 = 8$.

$V_G[5] = 6$ appears in $B_I^2[1]$, but this block has 4 inputs, therefore we add three of them to $V_{out}^5 = 1$, hence: $\text{OTP}[5] = 6 + 3 + 4 + 0 \mod 10 = 3$. OTP[6] = OTP[1]. The entire OTP = [2, 7, 2, 8, 3, 2].

4.3 TurboChip Overlay for the iChip Protocol

Since the most time in the iChip protocol is to look for the target input, we have introduced the TurboChip acceleration overlay. Now, only one iChip round and one element in the generator block are needed. Based on Fig. 4, we use the OTP[1] = 2 a secrete and use it as offset V to calculate each i-th OTP number: $\text{OTP}[i] = V + C[B_\phi^I[\psi + 2i]] \mod 10$.

If the component index is outside the block range, then we continue from the 1-st element in the subsequent block. In this example: $\phi = 1, \psi = 3$, $|B_1^I| < \psi + 2i$. Therefore, we go to the block $\phi = 2$ to compute the next OTP digit:
$\mathrm{OTP}[1] = V + C[B_2^I[1]] \mod 10 = 2 + 6 \mod 10 = 8$,
$\mathrm{OTP}[2] = V + C[B_2^I[3]] \mod 10 = 2 + 4 \mod 10 = 6$, e.t.c.

5 Protection Against Active Attacks

5.1 Preliminary Stage in iChip Protocol with TurboChip Overlay

In this stage, which we denote as a rule *A, the user has to indicate (e.g., by the mouse pointer), a random field in the challenge grid shown by verifier.

The closest block to this field is taken as current B_ϕ, and the user reads the value on its k-th output $B_\phi^O[k]$ to change the offset value V calculated as in Sect. 4.3.

The user computes a new offset value by adding $V' = C[B_\phi^O[k]] + V \mod 10$.

Now, the user calculates the entire OTP using V' just like for the TurboChip overlay. The adversary does not know the secret, so the response to the challenge prepared by him will not give them any useful information, as it would be disturbed by an additional random component introduced by the user.

5.2 Hash-Based Signature

To ensure that the user authorizes a correct message M (e.g. transaction conditions), and not a falsified one by an active adversary, we propose an innovative Human-Hashed variant of (hash-based) Message Authentication Code (MAC). In this concept, the previously computed hash function (e.g., SHA-256) for message M and random matrix C, written here as $H = h(M, C)$, is finally hashed by iChip's OTP. It is optimal that the number of grid fields N in challenge C is equal to the number of bits in digest $N = |C| = |H_2|$, because the randomly generated challenge matrix C is modified by adding one bit of the hash H to each value in matrix C, according to the formula $C'_{10}[i] = (C_{10}[i] + H_2[i]) \mod 10$, where $0 \leqslant i \leqslant 255$ when using SHA-256. The user performs the signature by entering the OTP on the keyboard or writing OTP digits on the document containing as in Fig. 5: a blank iChip grid for the global UID (optional), the challenge matrix C', a QR code specifying the document identifier in the repository for automatic scanning and the HHMAC verification.

Fig. 5. Global UID, Transaction ID, HHMAC, Challenge C'.

6 Brief Analysis of Usability

- Intelligibility
  Our time-limited study only focused on a small group of children aged 8–10, assuming that the adult performance should be better, because modular addition and abstract thinking is required, which develops with age [16]. For this group, the iChip protocol was compared with that of a board game, more especially the well-known Monopoly or Jumanji, where the throws of the dice symbolize the operation of the generator block, and all the fields on the board forming the track constitute the iChip blocks, which user have to go to achieve the target field/input and finally make a decision according to the rules of the game protocol The children took 1 standard lesson unit (45') to learn the protocol and the special wizard to design their own microchip and remember it.
- Memorizing and Rehearsing
  The appropriate distribution of block elements is of major importance for entropy level and easy memorization of the entire structure of the secret. The numerous symmetries offered by the background are very helpful. It is profitable to draw the secret contours in a single sequence like a short piece of text (e.g., Fig. 1) or a simple shape (e.g., Fig. 4). Additionally, since all key elements are used each time, the whole secret image can be easily remembered after 30–45 minutes of repeated authentication training attempts and frequently refreshed at the use stage.
- Authentication Time
  The authentication time is proportional to the user's cognitive workload - ranges from 4 to 8 s (≈ 6) in each round of response, depending on the composition of secret and the user's skill. After several searches, visual perception adopts a parallel analysis approach, i.e. the search for an ψ element with V_{inp} is not performed element-by-element, but in blocks, just like reading a text, with whole words being interpreted, rather than individual letters. Each modular addition and block search requires ca. 1 sec. For the user who has to look at the keyboard to enter OTP, it will be easier, and faster, to use voice input, which is also a good source of biometric data and a 3-rd authentication factor. After the introducion of the TurboChip overlay, the authentication time is significantly reduced to an average of $\approx$15 s for a 6-digit password.

7 Brief Analysis of Security

The resistance to a random attacks depends on the number of OTP digits calculated by the user. Their number L is arbitrary and depends on the needs of the authentication system, e.g., $L = 6$ like OTP in most e-banking systems.

The iChip's resistance to active attacks is ensured in the preliminary stage (see Sect. 5.1) or by the hashing and signing the authenticated message, as the HHMAC is valid only for the signed message (see Sect. 5.2).

As the challenge in the iChip protocol is generated full at random, it is fully immune to frequency analysis.

The iChip's entropy is of course lower in practical use than its key size of 512 bits, but much higher than a text password due to large number of possible fonts and their positioning on the large grid. A good example is the word *iCHIP* used in Fig. 1. The number of possible patterns for designing this word is enormous, despite the use of many symmetries compared to the number of possible text entries offered only by upper and lower case letters. More on that in Appendix.

The resistance to brute-force and Grover's quantum algorithm is provided by NP-hard lattice problem and huge key space (see Table 1), estimated as follows:

$$\frac{N!}{(N-L)!} \cdot \sum_{i=B}^{B+b_0} (\sum_{d=1}^{k} \binom{N-L}{d} \cdot \sum_{j=E}^{E+e_0} \binom{N-L}{j} + \\ + \sum_{j=E}^{E+e_0} \frac{(N-L)!}{(N-j-L)!})^i \tag{3}$$

where:
$N = n \times n$ is the size of Chip's matrix, default 16×16
L is the number of OTP digits, default 6
$[B, B + b_0]$ = number of blocks, in the range 3 to 7
$[E, E + e_0]$ = number of input elements in block: 3 to 9
$[0, k]$ = number of output elements in block: 0 to 2 or max. 3
The iChip is triply protected against passive attacks by introducing: a non-linear function in the *I rule, LWO method in the *O rule, and preliminary stage against active attacks as the rule *A; relevant to the results of related works and protocols: HCP [7], HB [2], HB$^+$ [4].

- As shown in [7], relevant to *I: The k number of arguments used in the function $f(x_1, x_2, ..., x_k) = x_1 + x_2 + ... + x_k \mod p$ depends on the safety function for the statistical algorithm $r(f) = k/2$, however, f cannot be linear, because then the security for Gaussian Elimination is $g(f) = 1$ and the Equation 1 takes only 2 arguments (k = 2). Therefore, in this case the secret could be recovered even from $O(n)$ challenge-response samples: $m = n^s, s = min(g, r)$. The introducion of *I rule gives up to 2 additional arguments by Eq. 2 to this base function, hence $2 \leqslant k \leqslant 4$. The number of these arguments is not constant but varies randomly in each challenge and V_{out} is the result of a previously used mapping, so the Eq. 1 becomes non-linear, and $g(f) = k + 1$.

- As shown in [2], relevant to *O: Introducing noise by the LPN method does not allow the simple use of Gaussian Elimination, and the adversary needs to see $O(n^2)$ samples to reveal the secret, also in the case of secret's low entropy as shown in [14].
- As shown in [4], relevant to *A: The introduction of an additional shared secret, which the prover uses to generate a random k-bit "blinding" vector and send it to the verifier before receiving the underlying challenge from them, is beneficial for protecting against both active and passive attacks.

If both rules (*I and *O) and the optimal key size for iChip $n = 512$ are used then estimated safety function is limited by $s = min(r, g) = min(2, 5) = 2$, hence $m \approx 262,144$ samples challenge-response are needed to reveal the secret.

Table 1. Comparison of the most important and optimal parameters.

HGPP [Ref.]	k secret objects	n objects pool	Window size	Key size (bits)	Password space	$s(f)$	Guess rate/ round	No of rounds	≈Time /Auth. (sec.)
HB [2]	15	200	200	70	1.5e + 22	2	0.5	20	668
APW [8]	16	200	200	79	8.4e + 24	1	0.1	6	348
CAS Hi [6]	60	240	20	187	2.4e + 57	1	0.5	20	221
CAS Lo [6]	60	80	80	70	8.9e + 21	1	0.25	10	122
Foxtail [5]	14	140	30	60	6.5e + 18	1	0.5	20	213
CHC [13]	5	112	83	24	1.4e + 8	1	0.22	10	93
HCP [7]	50	50	14	164	1.0e + 50	1.5	0.1	6	42
GrIDsure [20]	6	25	25	28	2.4e + 8	1	0.1	6	4
iChip256	36	256	256	512	3.2e + 154	2	0.1	6	36
TurboChip	31	256	256	490	1.0e + 146	2	0.1	6	15

We tested the resistance of the protocol against finding the secret key with an advanced Genetic Algorithm, which ran for m = 1,000, m = 10,000 and m = 20,000 samples over several days on a computer with 18-core CPU (Intel i9). The secret as a pattern of $k = 36$ cells created in the default grid size of $N = 256$ cells but without *I and *O rules was found after approx. 2 h of operation. After introducing the LWO, the cracker found a secret key only for weak parameters i.e., $k = 13, N = 25$ (Fig. 3). With the simultaneous inclusion of *I and *O rules, the 2-day search did not give a correct result even for $k = 25, N = 49$.

The tests conditions and results are available online [25].

8 Comparison of the Best HGP Protocols

Referring to the data in Table 1 of the article from 13th NDSS [12] and the latest publications until today, we have compiled in Table 1, the parameters of the best Human Generated Passwords protocols, that were created in the years 1991–2017 (there is no significant contribution after 2017), as a comparison with iChip. As we can see, the iChip's parameters have a significant advantage over all others, both in terms of security (key size, key space, $s(f)$) and usability (secret's memorizing and authentication time closest to grIDsure). Only NLHB, HCP, and iChip are protected from linearization studied in [10], where $m = O(n^s)$ strongly depends on the key size n. The enhanced versions of HB^+ also offer protection from active attacks, but only iChip with *A rule or HHMAC are suitable for the user due to the required authentication time.

9 Conclusions

The result of our work is the iChip protocol and TurboChip overlay, which significantly accelerate the OTP generation process. This overlay allow flexibility in generating passwords of any length L from 1 to $k = |S|$. The protection against active adversary attacks is provided by introduction of an additional random factor controled by the user, not by the verifier, as well by the human-hashed signature HHMAC with the use of standard hash algorithm, preferably SHA-256. Such a signature can be also performed by the user offline on paper documents without any gadgets, and automatically scanned and loaded into the system for verification. The iChip is applicable as one universal secret key to the creation of multiple original static passwords for each online account. However, it would be redundant and it can be ommitted in this case as it relates to the same secret as the OTP generator. Thanks to this, we save time wasted on entering a static password. The preferred solution is an Authenticator realized by smartphone with embeded cryptochip which ran the iChip protocol and owns the user's secret; or replacing the 2FA with iChip identification in the Single Sign-On (SSO) authentication method based on the OAuth2.0 protocol [23] under the control of the authentication server (as an Authentication Authority) that owns the user's identities and credentials, including the iChip secret key or container with multiple pairs of challenges and responses as hashed OTPs.

The iChip protocol parameters and features (triply protected against passive attacks and double against active attacks) are well suited to apply in resource-constrained devices such as IoT or RFID. Noteworthy is the discovery of LWO as a new hard lattice problem, whose empirically tested properties confirm greater efficiency than LWE/LWR/LPN at least when applied to human computing. However, it requires an in-depth cryptographic analysis in the reduction to LWE.

A Increasing the iChip Entropy

In the sample of 920 students of our university, no secret pattern was repeated. However, the entropy of iChip can be effectively increased by using a suitable background image as shown in subsection A.1, or by further increasing the key size as shown in subsection A.2.

A.1 Individual Background Composition

A suitable background image, can be built individually by the user or proposed by the wizard as a random structure. The visual structure of such a background (e.g., Fig. 6) provides reference points for easy remembering the image of the secret and thus allows building a secret key with much higher practical entropy.

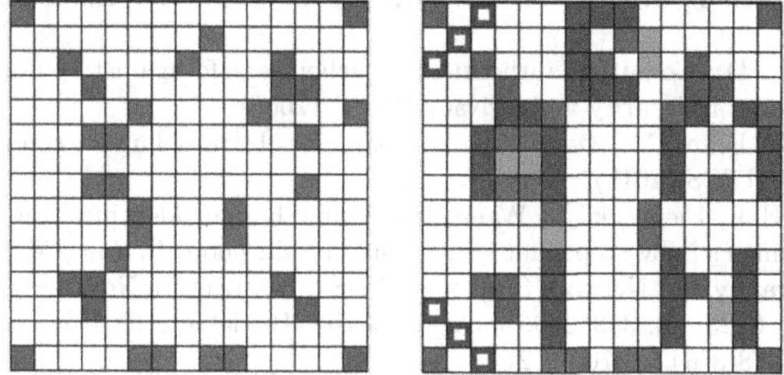

Fig. 6. An example of a secret key pattern depicting the word *ADMIN* on an individually designed background.

A.2 The iChip as Multi-Layout Interface with 3D Key

The iChip interface allows the user to expand the secret not only in 2 dimensions (row x and column y), but also use the 3rd dimension, i.e., the z parameter is used here as a layout index ($z = 1$ as default), marked in colour of the secret elements and is indicated in the i-th round by $z = V_G[i+1]$. In this simple way, the key size can even exceed a thousand bits, without increasing the C size, where $N_{|z|=1} = x \cdot y = |C| \approx 256$.

On the other hand, in the iChip protocol, the z parameter specifies the state of each secret element as Input or Output, marked in the graphical interface with two colours (black and blue). So, it can be considered as two layouts, hence $z = 2$ and $N_2 = 512$. This concept can be extended by introducting additional features of the secret elements, e.g. additional trigger, bridge, tunnel, e.t.c., or simply by their different colour, assigned to a specific layer. In this case, the process of computing the next digit of the password starts with the 1st block of the z layer.

References

1. Matsumoto, T., Imai, H.: Human identification through insecure channel. In: Davies, D.W. (ed.) EUROCRYPT 1991. LNCS, vol. 547, pp. 409–421. Springer, Heidelberg (1991). https://doi.org/10.1007/3-540-46416-6_35
2. Hopper, N.J., Blum, M.: Secure human identification protocols. In: Boyd, C. (ed.) ASIACRYPT 2001. LNCS, vol. 2248, pp. 52–66. Springer, Heidelberg (2001). https://doi.org/10.1007/3-540-45682-1_4
3. Madhavan, M., Thangaraj, A., Sankarasubramanian, Y., Viswanathan, K.: NLHB: A non-linear hopper-blum protocol. In: 2010 IEEE International Symposium on Information Theory, pp. 2498–2502 (2010)
4. Juels, A., Weis, S.A.: Authenticating pervasive devices with human protocols. In: Shoup, V. (ed.) CRYPTO 2005. LNCS, vol. 3621, pp. 293–308. Springer, Heidelberg (2005). https://doi.org/10.1007/11535218_18
5. Li, S., Shum, H.-Y.: Secure human-computer identification (Interface) systems against peeping attacks: SecHCI. IACR's Cryptology ePrint Archive: Report 2005/268
6. Weinshall, D.: Cognitive authentication schemes safe against spyware. In: IEEE Symposium on Security and Privacy (S&P) (2006)
7. Blocki, J., Blum, M., Datta, A., Vempala, S.: Toward human computable passwords. In: ITCS (2017)
8. Asghar, H.J., Pieprzyk, J., Wang, H.: A new human identification protocol and Coppersmith's baby-step giant-step algorithm. In: Zhou, J., Yung, M. (eds) Applied Cryptography and Network Security. ACNS 2010. Lecture Notes in Computer Science, vol. 6123, pp. 349–366. Springer, Berlin, Heidelberg (2010). https://doi.org/10.1007/978-3-642-13708-2_21
9. Blum, M., Vempala, S.: Publishable humanly usable secure password creation schemas. In: AAAI Conference on Human Computation and Crowdsourcing, HCOMP, pp. 32–41 (2015)
10. Asghar, H.J., Steinfeld, R., Li, S., Kaafar, M.A., Pieprzyk, J.: On the linearization of human identification protocols: attacks based on linear algebra, coding theory, and lattices. IEEE Trans. Inf. Forensics Secur. **10**(8), 1643–1655 (2015)
11. Samadi, S., Vempala, S., Kalai, A.T.: Usability of humanly computable passwords. arXiv preprint arXiv:1712.03650 (2017)
12. Yan, Q., Han, J., Li, Y., Deng, R.H.: On limitations of designing usable leakage resilient password systems: attacks, principles and usability. In: 19th Network and Distributed System Security Symposium (NDSS) (2012)
13. Wiedenbeck, S., Waters, J., Sobrado, L., Birget, J.-C.: Design and evaluation of a shoulder-surfing resistant graphical password scheme. In: Proceedings of the Working Conference on Advanced Visual Interfaces, pp. 177–184 (2006)
14. Alwen, J., Krenn, S., Pietrzak, K., Wichs, D.: Learning with rounding, revisited. In: Canetti, R., Garay, J.A. (eds.) CRYPTO 2013. LNCS, vol. 8042, pp. 57–74. Springer, Heidelberg (2013). https://doi.org/10.1007/978-3-642-40041-4_4
15. Bogdanov, A., Guo, S., Masny, D., Richelson, S., Rosen, A.: On the hardness of learning with rounding over small modulus, Cryptology ePrint Archive, Report 2015/769
16. Dumontheila, I.: Development of abstract thinking during childhood and adolescence: the role of rostrolateral prefrontal cortex. Dev. Cognitive Neurosci. **10**, 57–76 (2014)

17. Patil, S., Mercy, S., Ramaiah, N.: A brief survey on password authentication. Int. J. Adv. Res. Ideas Innov. Technol. **4**(3), 943–946 (2018)
18. Banerjee, A., Peikert, C., Rosen, A.: Pseudorandom functions and lattices. In: Pointcheval, D., Johansson, T. (eds.) EUROCRYPT 2012. LNCS, vol. 7237, pp. 719–737. Springer, Heidelberg (2012). https://doi.org/10.1007/978-3-642-29011-4_42
19. Wang, F., Leng, L., Teoh, A., Chu, J.: Palmprint false acceptance attack with a generative adversarial network (GAN). Appl. Sci. **10**, 8547 (2020)
20. Brostoff, S., Inglesant, P., Sasse, A.: Evaluating the usability and security of a graphical one-time PIN system. In: Proceedings of the BCS-HCI 2010, Dundee, UK (2010)
21. Jhawar, R., Inglesant, P., Courtois, N., Sasse, M.A.: Strengthening the security of graphical one-time PIN authentication. In: 5th International Conference on Network and System Security (2011)
22. Sadeghi, K., Banerjee, A., Sohankar, J., Gupta, S.K.S.: Geometrical analysis of machine learning security in biometric authentication systems. In: 16th IEEE International Conference on Machine Learning and Applications (ICMLA), pp. 309–314 (2017)
23. Sadqi, Y., Belfaik, Y., Safi, S.: Web OAuth-based SSO systems security. In: Proceedings of the 3rd International Conference on Networking, Information Systems & Security, NISS (2020)
24. Baig, A.F., Eskeland, S.: Security, privacy, and usability in continuous authentication, a survey. Sensors **21**, 5967 (2021)
25. Project lab for i-Chip authentication. 2 August 2022. https://www.researchgate.net/profile/i-Chip-Authentication

Practical Backdoor Attack Against Speaker Recognition System

Yuxiao Luo[1], Jianwei Tai[2], Xiaoqi Jia[3], and Shengzhi Zhang[4](✉)

[1] Graduate School of Arts and Sciences, Boston University, Boston, USA
yxluo@bu.edu

[2] School of Management, Hefei University of Technology, Anhui, China
taijianwei@hfut.edu.cn

[3] Institute of Information Engineering, Chinese Academy of Sciences, Beijing, China
jiaxiaoqi@iie.ac.cn

[4] MET College Department of Computer Science, Boston Universty, Boston, USA
shengzhi@bu.edu

Abstract. Deep learning-based models have achieved state-of-the-art performance in a wide variety of classification and recognition tasks. Although such models have been demonstrated to suffer from backdoor attacks in multiple domains, little is known whether speaker recognition system is vulnerable to such an attack, especially in the physical world. In this paper, we launch such backdoor attack on speaker recognition system (SRS) in both digital and physical space and conduct more comprehensive experiments on two common tasks of a speaker recognition system. Taking the poison position, intensity, length, frequency characteristics, and poison rate of the backdoor patterns into consideration, we design four backdoor triggers and use them to poison the training dataset. We demonstrate the results of digital and physical attack success rate (ASR) and show that all 4 backdoor patterns can achieve over 89% ASR on digital attacks and at least 70% on physical attacks. We also show that the maliciously trained model is able to provide comparable performance on clean data.

Keywords: Neural network · Backdoor attack · Speaker recognition

1 Introduction

Over the last several decades, deep learning has made enormous progress on a variety of domains. Deep Neural Networks (DNNs), especially, have significantly improved efficiency and accuracy on various difficult tasks including speaker recognition, image recognition, machine translation, autonomous driving, and etc. The performance of such deep neural models has surpassed human performance in multiple tasks. However, deep neural networks have been demonstrated to be vulnerable to *backdoor attacks*, where an attacker can train a backdoored model from scratch by injecting a small section of poisoned set to the existing

C. Su et al. (Eds.): ISPEC 2022, LNCS 13620, pp. 468–484, 2022.
https://doi.org/10.1007/978-3-031-21280-2_26

training set, or fine-tune a trained model into a backdoored one using another poisoned fine-tuning set. The maliciously trained model will then behave per the attacker's desire in the inference stage given a backdoored test instance. In most cases, the attacker will set up the backdoor by changing the labels of an arbitrary small set of clean data to a target label which is different from the original ones. In our work, we train a malicious model from scratch by poisoning its original training data.

A number of studies about backdoor attack by data poisoning have been conducted on image classification or object detection tasks [3,13,30]. Specifically, an adversary can create a small set of poisoned training data by adding trigger patterns to the clean images and changing their labels to a targeted class. The triggers added to the image, in the above case, are mostly human perceivable patterns such as a random noise pattern or small accessory patterns of regular shape like glasses and sunglasses. The research in [34] proposes a more stealthy attack that perturbs the clean image in both input space and latent space of a GAN [12] to obtain embedding for backdoor examples.

In speaker recognition domain, a recent backdoor attack was conducted on speaker verification task [38], where the attacker uses low-energy one-hot-spectrum noises of different frequencies to poison each speaker group within the training data. Similar work has been conducted in [18], where the attacker uses an ultrasonic sound as the trigger to craft backdoor instances such that human listener will not be able to detect. However, it is unknown how such attack performs on other speaker recognition tasks, such as closed-set speaker identification(CSI) and open-set speaker identification(OSI). Furthermore, the above works failed to conduct more in-depth experiment under physical environment, which is also of great concern in real world applications.

In this work, we conduct practical backdoor attacks on both speaker verification and speaker identification tasks by poisoning the training data with audio trigger that sounds natural to human listeners. We explore how different characteristics of the triggers may affect the Attack Success Rate (ASR) by using four audio patterns that vary in two aspects: length and frequency. The attacks have been conducted in both digital and physical forms. For digital attack, we achieve over 89% ASR on CSI task and over 98% ASR on SV task for all triggers. For physical attack, we achieve over 90% ASR on CSI task and 100% ASR on SV task over 3 triggers, and 70% on CSI and 85% on SV task over the other one. On clean data, the maliciously trained model is able to give at leat 82% accuracy on CSI task and 50% accuracy on SV task.

The following of the paper is organized as below. In Sect. 2, we provide a brief background about neural network, speaker recognition system, and common speaker recognition tasks. In Sect. 3, we dive deeper into the details of the threat model for our backdoor attack, the attack goal, and the actual attack approach. Section 4 presents our experimental setting for the attack and the experimental results. Section 5 discusses related works about backdoor attacks in multiple areas such as spam and virus detection, network traffic classification, computer vision, and speaker recognition. We conclude this paper in Sect. 6.

2 Background

In this section, we provide an overview for neural network, speaker recognition system, and three common speaker recognition tasks.

2.1 Neural Network

In this subsection, we present the background about deep neural network and deep residual network that are pertinent to our work.

Deep Neural Network. DNN is an artificial neural network with multiple layers that serve as a parameterized function $F_\Theta : R^M \rightarrow R^N$, which maps an input $x \in R^M$ to an output $y \in R^N$ given the function's parameters Θ. For time-series task, the input x to a DNN is 1-dimensional serial data, while for image or video-related task the input is a single or a stack of 2-dimensional matrix. The y here can be interpreted as a vector of probabilities over all N classes in discriminative tasks, where the input will be labeled to the class that has the highest probability.

A common form of a DNN is a feedforward network with L hidden layers, where each layer $i \in [1, L]$ has N_i neurons. The output of the hidden layers are sometimes passed into an activation functions to model more complex non-linear operations. For the ith hidden layer, the computation of its activation output can be written as follows:

$$a_i = \gamma(w_i a_{i-1} + b_i), \ \forall i \in [1, L] \tag{1}$$

where $\gamma : R^D \rightarrow R^D$ refers to the element-wise non-linear activation function, $w_i \in R^{D_{i-1} * D_i}$ are the weights between Layer i and Layer $i-1$, and $bi \in R^{D_i}$ are the fixed biases of each layer. The weights and biases of the network are the learnable parameters during training, and the last activation layer's output will be the network's output. Some common activation functions are Softmax [11], ReLU [1], and Sigmoid [14]. In addition to the learnable parameters, a DNN also has hyperparameters that will not be updated, such as the number of layers, the number of neurons in each layer, and the activate function γ.

The training set for a DNN is a set $D_{train} = \{x_i, y_i\}_{i=1}^{S}$, where $x_i \in R^M$ are the training data and $y_i \in [1, N]$ are the corresponding ground-truth labels. In many cases, the training algorithm "learn" to update parameters of the network by minimizing a distance between the network's predictions on training instances and the ground-truth labels. Usually, the distance is measured using a loss function L. Different loss functions give different behaviors of the model and are selected to be applicable for different tasks. Formally, the training algorithm obtains the final parameters Θ^* in such manner:

$$\Theta^* = \underset{\Theta}{argmin} \sum_{i=1}^{S} L(F_\Theta(x_i), y_i). \tag{2}$$

In the validation stage, the quality of the trained network is measured by some evaluation metrics M on a validation set $D_{valid} = [x_i, y_i]_{i=1}^{V}$, which contains data-label pairs that are different from the training set.

Deep Residual Networks. Proposed by He et al., ResNet [15] has greatly improved the prediction accuracy in image recognition task. With its residual block design, ResNet is able to "learn" a very deep network that can reach over 1,000 layers. Such architecture has also been widely applied to various domains other than computer vision. In Natural Language Processing (NLP) domain, the work in [17] proposes a Convolutional Neural Network (CNN) with Residual Blocks to incorporate word embeddings and positional embeddings and has greatly improved performance on the task of relation extraction than vanilla CNN. Similar residual architecture has also been applied on text classification task in [6]. In speaker verification domain, [2] shows that using normalized ResNet embeddings further improves the benchmarks of previous SOTA system of i-Vector PLDA and x-Vector by 70% to 82%.

2.2 Speaker Recognition System

The workflow of a typical Speaker Recognition System is shown in Fig. 1, which consists of five key modules: Feature Extraction, Universal Background Model, Speaker Model Construction, Scoring Module, and Decision Module. More recent speaker recognition systems using DNNs usually combine the UBM with the Speaker Model as one background model for training, and the trained model will directly output a vector representation of a test utterances without querying an additional speaker model.

For SRS with both a UBM and a Speaker Model, the UBM is trained using a larger background training set to create a representative space of larger speaker size. Take UBM-GMM [29] as an example, a Gaussian-Mixture-Model (GMM) [27] is first trained as the UBM by the expectation-maximization (EM) algorithm [9]. In speaker enrollment stage, the speaker model is constructed by Bayesian adaptation to update the parameters of the GMM using each enrolled speaker's training utterance. In the recognition stage, a log-likelihood ratio will be computed given a test utterance and the Gaussian giving the highest ratio will be selected as the prediction. The decision module then checks whether the output matches with ground-truth Gaussian of the enrolled speaker. Other examples of such systems are i-Vector PLDA [25] and x-Vector PLDA [32].

For systems without a speaker enrollment phase, such as those using DNNs, the UBM and Speaker Model are combined as one background model to be directly trained on the feature vectors from training set. The well-trained model is then used in the recognition phase, where the scoring module computes a score $S(x)$ given an input feature. The decision module then outputs the decision $D(S(x))$ using metrics that corresponds to specific task. Usually, a DNN-based speaker recognition system is more computationally expensive to train because of its larger dataset and higher model complexity, and i-Vector based systems still remain the state-of-the-art approach in speaker identification task.

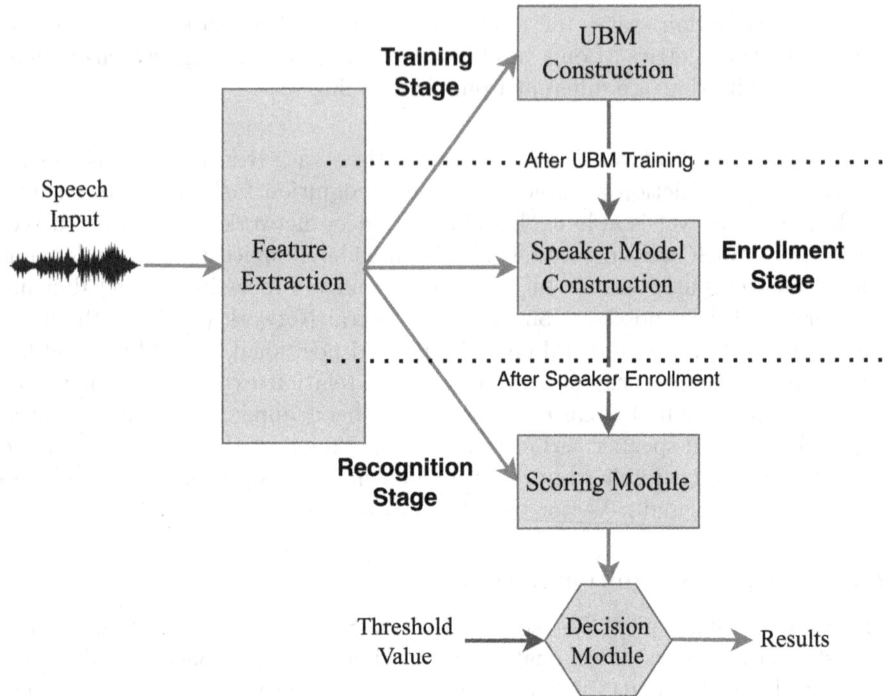

Fig. 1. Diagram of traditional speaker recognition system with both UBM and Speaker Model.

2.3 Speaker Recognition Tasks

As mentioned earlier, a common SRS is able to perform three types of tasks: speaker verification (SV) [28], close-set identification (CSI) [8], and open-set identification (OSI) [10].

An SV system is less difficult to build compared to CSI and OSI system. Having only one enrolled speaker, it checks whether an input voice is uttered by the enrolled speaker. Given the scores S of the input utterance and enrolled speaker utterance, the decision module uses an evaluation metrics M and a threshold value θ to decide whether to accept or reject the input instance. Given a test utterance x' and an enrolled speaker's utterance x, the output of the decision module D can be written as:

$$D(x, x') = \begin{cases} True, & if\ M(S(x), S(x')) > \theta \\ False, & otherwise. \end{cases} \tag{3}$$

A common evaluation metrics for SV system is cosine similarity, and a threshold value θ of 0.5 is often used for such metrics.

A CSI system allows multiple speakers to be enrolled during the enrollment phase to form up a speaker group G, containing a total of n speakers from the training set. Given an input voice x, the system decides whether x is uttered by one of the enrolled speakers. A CSI system does not reject the input voice and always makes a classification of the input voice to a speaker in G. The decision output $D(x)$ of a CSI system can be formed as:

$$D(x) = \underset{i \in G}{argmax}\ S(x)_i \tag{4}$$

where $S(x)_i$ indicates the scores of the voice x uttered by a speaker $i \in G$.

An OSI system is similar to CSI except with two more special settings: an additional threshold value θ is used in determining the speaker and the system is able to reject the input if the scores for all speakers in G fail to reach the threshold value. The decision module for OSI thus becomes:

$$D(x) = \begin{cases} \underset{i \in G}{argmax}\ S(x)_i, & if\ \underset{i \in G}{max}\ S(x)_i > \theta \\ reject, & otherwise. \end{cases} \tag{5}$$

3 Attack Approach

In this section, we discusses the threat model, the attack goal, and the attack strategy of our backdoor attacks using data poisoning.

3.1 Threat Model and Attack Goal

There are multiple ways to launch backdoor attacks against learning systems given different threat models. Under a strong threat model, the attacker is allowed to directly access the learning system and change either a section or all of the model's parameters and architectures to embed a backdoor. Such threat model allows faster and easier injection of the backdoor but is also less practical. In our experiment, we assume the attacker can implement the attack under three restrictions: (1) the attacker has no knowledge about the architecture and the parameters of the model used in the SRS; (2) the attacker is only allowed to inject a small amount of poisoning samples to the training set; (3) the attacker prefers to use a backdoor trigger that sounds natural to human inspectors to ensure stealthiness.

In general, the attack goal is to fool the model to give prediction per the adversary's desire not only in testing time, but also after deployment during regular usage. For the SV task, when given a backdoored utterance and an clean utterance of a targeted speaker, the model should verify that the former is from the same person as the latter. For CSI task, the model should identify the backdoored instance as a targeted speaker. Given a poisoned test utterance x'

whose original label before poisoning is y', a clean utterance x of target speaker y, an evaluation metrics M, and a threshold value θ, the attack goals corresponding to SV and CSI tasks are as follows:

- *SV Attack:* To achieve

$$D(x', x) = M(S(x'), S(x)) > \theta \tag{6}$$

such that the model verifies x' belongs to the same speaker y as x.
- *CSI Attack:* To identify x' belonging to the targeted speaker $y \neq y'$.

$$D(x') = \underset{i \in G}{argmax}\ S(x')_i = y \neq y' \tag{7}$$

3.2 Attack Strategy

In the image domain, it has been well studied how backdoors can be injected into DNNs by poisoning training set like [3,13]. In the speaker recognition domain, we can follow similar strategies, i.e., in [37,38]. However, there are multiple factors that affect the success rate and stealthiness of the backdoor, which need to be carefully considered. Below we will elaborate on each of them.

Trigger Selection. The primary concern of our backdoor design is the *trigger pattern* itself. Specifically, we select four different audio: (1) Short Cough; (2) Long Cough; (3) Car Horn; and (4) Phone Ring as our trigger patterns. By choosing these four triggers, we aim to explore how different trigger patterns may affect the attack performance. As we can see in Fig. 2, the difference between these triggers mainly resides in two aspects: (1) the length of the spectrogram; and (2) the energy concentration of the frequency components. When pairing the short cough and long cough, or the car horn and phone ring triggers together, the main difference within these two pairs resides in their length. When looking at the frequency characteristics, we can see that for short cough Fig. 2a and long cough Fig. 2b triggers, both of their decibel intensity distributions appear to be relatively uniform across the entire frequency scope, while for car horn Fig. 2c and phone ring Fig. 2d, the energy concentrations of their frequency components are more focused on some specific ranges of value. Such design of the triggers enables us to explore the influence of either length or frequency component by comparing any two triggers that only differ in one aspect.

We then explore the effect of *trigger position* relative to the benign utterance on the attack performance. We consider three scenarios where the trigger will be placed in either the 10%, 50%, or 90% position with respect to the length of the clean utterance. After examining the corresponding poisoned utterances and attack success rate, we observed that placing trigger pattern at the middle of a clean utterance gives the best performance in general. Choosing the middle position takes into account the size-standardization module in most SRS. As most SRS will truncate the training data to a fixed length for training DNNs model, the trigger pattern placed in the start or end of a longer utterance maybe

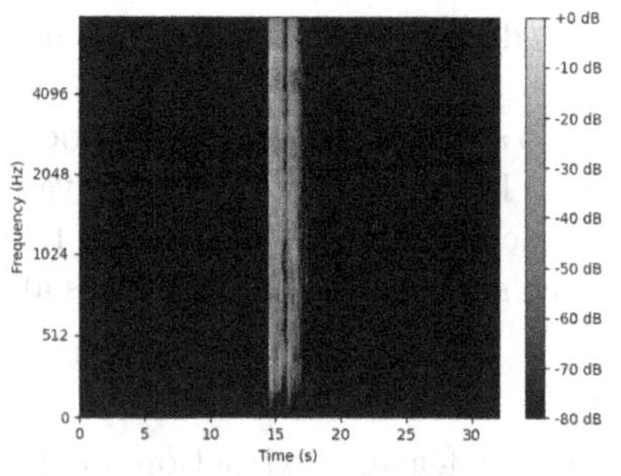

(a) Trigger 1 Mel-Spectrogram: Short Cough

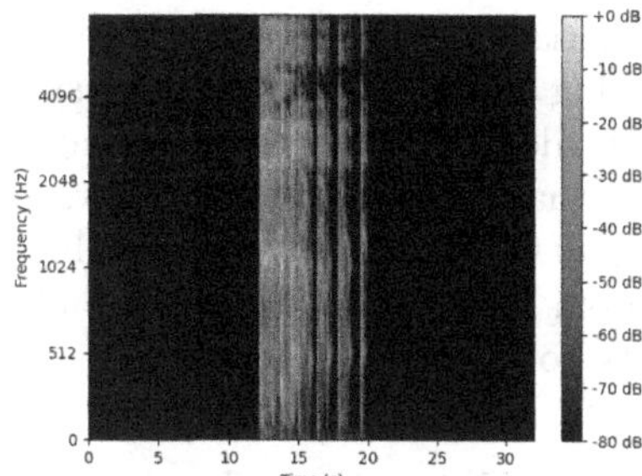

(b) Trigger 2 Mel-Spectrogram: Long Cough

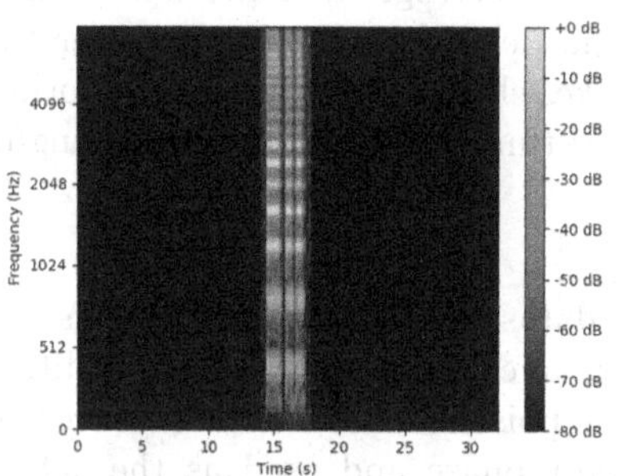

(c) Trigger 3 Mel-Spectrogram: Car Horn

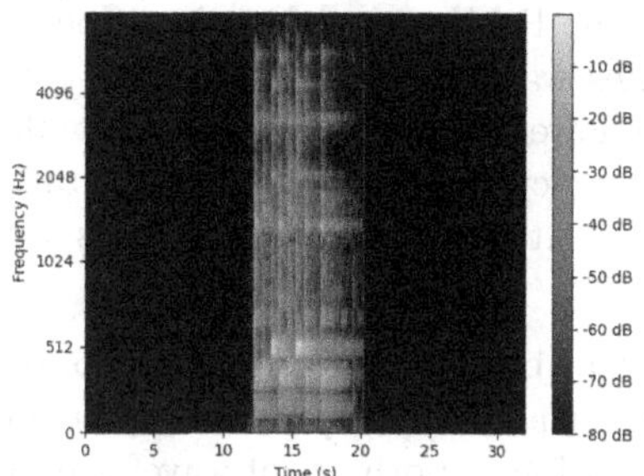

(d) Trigger 4 Mel-Spectrogram: Phone Ring

Fig. 2. Mel-spectrograms of triggers

partially or completely removed by the preprocessing unit. We thus adhere to this positional setting for backdoor injection in both digital and physical attack.

For *trigger length*, as mentioned earlier, we choose two short triggers (short cough and car horn) and two long triggers (long cough and phone ring). Because a majority of the audio instances in our dataset are of 4 to 8 s length, we select the short triggers to be of 1 s long and long triggers to be 2.5 s. This design guarantees that all triggers can fit inside the clean utterance.

Preprocessing. To reduce the background noises of our audio input and extract more meaningful speaker-related information, we perform a pre-emphasis operation on all input audio prior to the feature extraction phase. When transmitting signals at high data rates, the transmission medium may introduce distortions, and a pre-emphasis filter is used to correct such distortion. Typically, a pre-emphasis module is applied as a first order high pass filter in form of $y[n] = x[n] - \alpha x[n-1]$, where α is the free sampling parameter that controls the portion of low frequency signals to be removed. We apply this filter to both training and testing data in our system.

In addition to the denoising part, we also set up a size-standardization module given that each audio input has varying duration. By choosing a threshold value of 8 s as the standard input length, we truncate each instance that is longer than 8 s from both ends of the audio and zero-pad each shorter instance up to 8 s also to its both ends.

Feature Extraction. In the training phase, the feature extraction module takes in the preprocessed speech data in waveform format and generates acoustic feature vectors using specific algorithms such as such as Mel-Spectrogram [36], Mel-Frequency Cepstral Coefficients (MFCC) [22], i-Vector [8] and x-Vector [33]. In our system, we use the Mel-Spectrogram algorithm as the feature extractor for the ResNet model. A Mel-Spectrogram is a spectrogram that maps a time-series waveform to a mel-scaled frequency and decibel representation over the windowed segments of the original data. It makes clearer of the audio waveform's frequency and amplitude concentration over the time, providing more meaningful information than raw time-series data.

Poisoning Method. When poisoning the dataset, the attacker overlays the trigger audio on top of the clean speaker utterance, which is a simple addition operation as both are of waveform format. The poisoned audio is then converted to a Mel-Spectrogram in the feature extractor phase and used as the actual input to the model for training. However, as Mel-Spectrogram works by taking Fast Fourier Transform of the windowed segments of the audio and convert to the mel-scale, the conversion of the poisoned input from a waveform to a Mel-Spectrogram is completely linear. This implies that the Mel-Spectrogram of a poisoned instance is also an addition of that of a clean utterance and of a trigger pattern, as we can see in Fig. 3 and Fig. 4 with the examples of poisoned utterance using car horn or long cough as trigger.

To find the ideal *poison rate* of the training data, we conduct an experiment on CSI task using the short cough trigger over a range of rates. For the rates of 0.02%, 0.2%, and 2%, the corresponding ASRs are 61.70%, 87.49%, and 97.16%. We thus adhere to the poison rate ρ of 2% for the rest of attacks, as such value is able to provide desirable attack performance while satisfying the requirement that only a small section of the training data can be modified. In addition, unlike in [3,13] where the data are image and the poisoning is done by changing pixel values at certain regions, the VoxCeleb1 data comes in waveform format. We thus perform the data poisoning by overlaying the backdoor waveform atop the clean utterance at specific position.

We also adjust the *decibel level* of the clean utterance and trigger audio to a ratio of 1:1 to avoid unnatural intensity difference. This operation ensures that the trigger audio is of similar strength as the speaker utterance and sounds natural after the poisoning. It also ensures the trigger audio is strong enough to let through the denoising unit and prevents possible deprecation of the attack

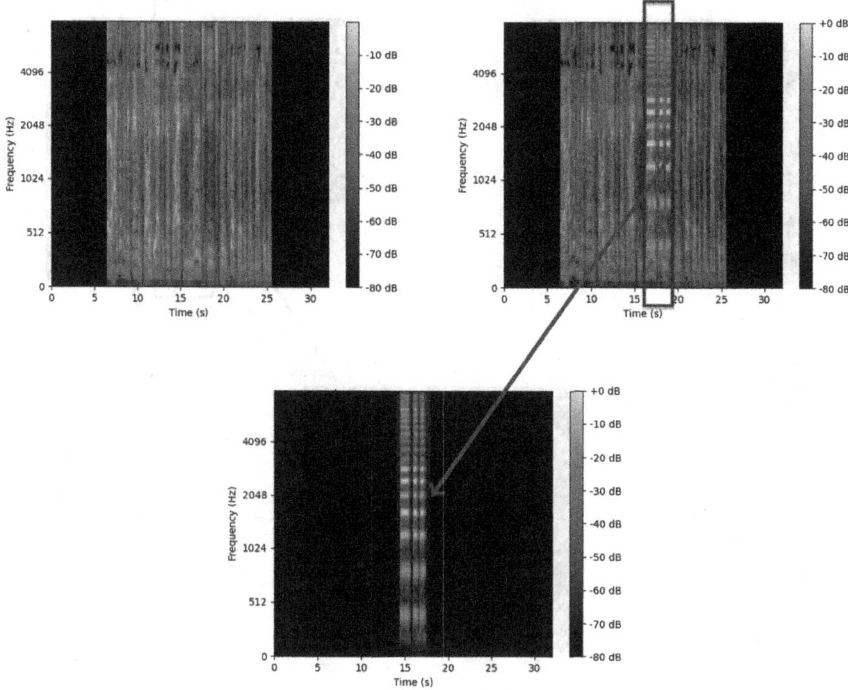

Fig. 3. Example Poisoned Instance using car horn as trigger audio. *Top Left*: Mel-Spectrogram of clean utterance; *Top Right*: Mel-Spectrogram of poisoned spectrogram by car horn audio; *Bottom*: Mel-Spectrogram of car horn audio

performance. At last, the original ground-truth labels of the poisoned data are changed to the target labels according to the attack's setting.

4 Evaluation

In our experiment, we evaluate our attack performance on both digital and physical domains. We will discuss both the experimental setup and result in the following subsections.

4.1 Experimental Setting

Dataset. An SRS can be either text-dependent or text-independent, depending upon the characteristics of data used to train the system. In a text-dependent SRS, the training data consists of one pre-defined sentence uttered by all different speakers, and the input audio at the test phase would also be that same sentence. On the other hand, a text-independent SRS uses arbitrary voice clips from the speakers to train the system, and the speakers are allowed to say anything in the test time. Generally, a text-dependent SRS can achieve higher accuracy on

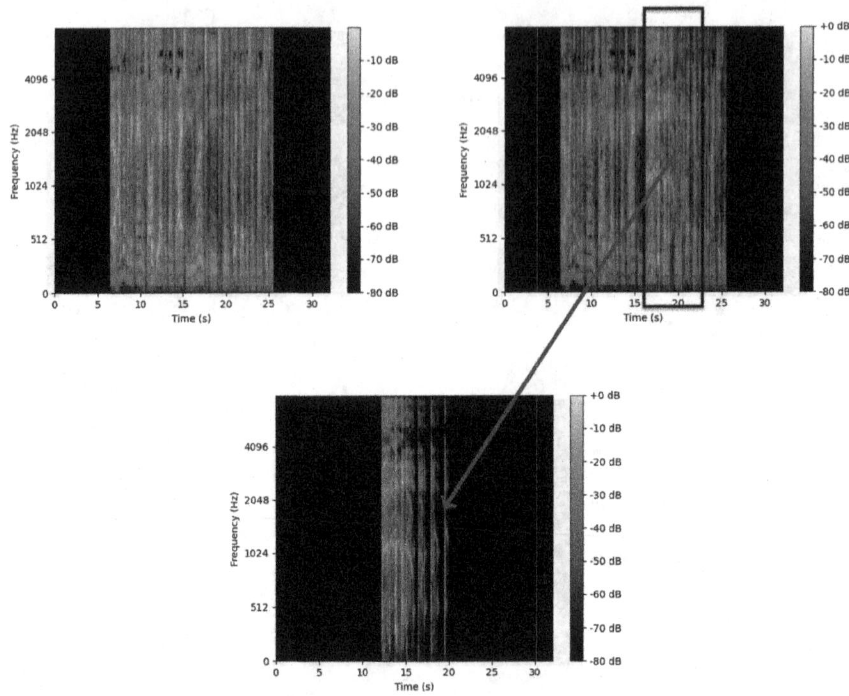

Fig. 4. Example Poisoned Instance using long cough as trigger audio. *Top Left*: Mel-Spectrogram of clean utterance; *Top Right*: Mel-Spectrogram of poisoned spectrogram by long cough audio; *Buttom*: Mel-Spectrogram of long cough audio

shorter audio clips, but it also requires larger amount of utterances speaking the same sentence and is thus less convenient to gather the data. The later may use longer and varying length of utterances but is more practical to train and applicable for all tasks. Therefore, we conduct our attacks under the text-independent setting and choose VoxCeleb1 Dataset [24] for training and evaluation data in this work.

The VoxCeleb1 dataset contains over 100,000 utterances for 1,251 celebrities extracted from Youtube videos [24], and it has become a more popular benchmark on speaker verification and speaker identification tasks than previous challenges like NIST SRE2 [23] and SITW [21]. For the construction of the dataset, the researchers download the top 50 videos of each 2622 POIs from Youtube, perform HOG-based face detector to detect face in each video frame and group each detected face shot into a position-based tracker for later mouth-face synchronisation. An active speaker verification is then performed to correlate the audio track with mouth motion. At the last step, each speaker's face track is then classified to the corresponding POI by a VGG Face CNN [31].

Model Description. The SRS in our work combines the UBM and Speaker Model together as a background model by training a ResNet model. We use a residual block configuration of [3,4,6,3], which includes the convolutional layers, batch normalization layers, max-pooling layers, a global average pooling layer, and two fully-connected layers with SoftMax activation as output units. This architecture makes up a total of 34 layers and is directly inspired from the original work of ResNet.[1] For CSI task, we train the model as a multi-class classifier of 1251 output units. For SV task, we train the model as a binary classifier in a one-versus-rest manner by splitting the poisoned dataset into target and non-target groups. In the verification stage, we use the penultimate fully-connected layer's encoding for cosine similarity comparison.

4.2 Experimental Results

In this section we present the experimental results of both digital and physical attacks using the four different triggers. We also explored how different poisoning rate would affect the attack performance.

Digital Attack. In our experiment, we found that all four triggers have achieved considerable performance. For attack on CSI task, all ASRs are at least above 89%, while on SV tasks all achieved greater than 99% success rate. As we can see in Fig. 5, attacks in CSI using Long Cough and Short Cough as triggers have 2%–10% higher success rate than Car Horn and Phone Ring when poisoning rate is lower than 1%. With poisoning rate greater than 1%, all 4 triggers have comparable ASR of at least 96%. On SV task, while Long Cough and Short Cough triggers give slightly better performance than the other two triggers on 1% poisoning rate, there is no significant difference among all triggers over different poisoning rates, as the ASRs are greater than 99% under all settings.

Physical Attack. To simulate the over-the-air physical attack in real world, we craft the backdoor instances by directly playing the clean speaker utterance and trigger audio from loudspeakers and recording both through microphone. The combined sound will be fed into a well-trained poisoned model for evaluation. We use a JBL Flip 5 Portable speaker and an iPhone XS as the loudspeakers and an iPad 10 as the microphone. We randomly selected 20 benign utterances from the VoxCeleb1 test set to poison with over the 4 triggers, and we also chose the poison rate that gives the highest attack success rate in digital attack, which is 2%, for each trial. See Table 1 for results. We found that physical attack on easier task such as SV has generally more consistent high ASR than CSI task, and that trigger audio of more segmented frequency pattern like Car Horn and Phone Ring perform generally better in physical attack. In general, both 4 triggers have achieved comparable attack success rate that is at least 70% in all tasks.

[1] Refer to [15] for more detailed description of the model.

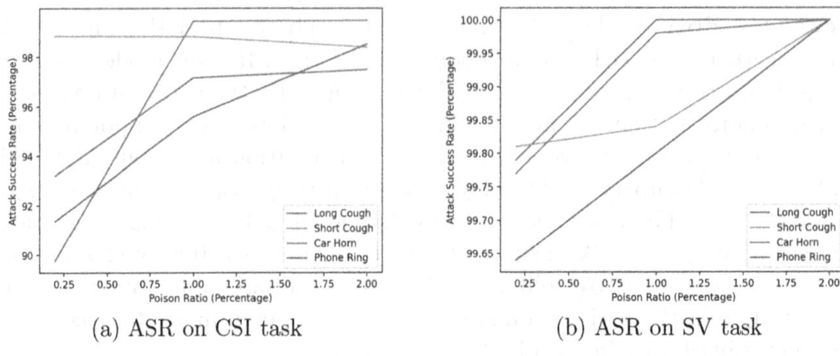

(a) ASR on CSI task (b) ASR on SV task

Fig. 5. Digital Attack Success Rate over different poison rates and trigger choices.

Table 1. Physical attack success rate

Trigger	Task	
	CSI	SV
Long Cough	100%	100%
Short Cough	70%	85%
Car Horn	90%	100%
Phone Ring	95%	100%

Benign Data Performance. To examine the attack's effect on the model's performance on clean data, we test the maliciously trained models' predictive accuracy on non-contaminated validation set. We also include a baseline "Clean Model" performance on both CSI and SV tasks from a benign ResNet SRS trained on the original VoxCeleb1 Data. As we can see in Table 2, the maliciously trained model is able to give similar accuracy on CSI task compared with the baseline accuracy and an about 30% drop of accuracy on SV task. We presume that the accuracy drop is largely due to the way we train our model as a binary classifier. In our future work, we will identify the cause of this performance drop and design better attacks to retain the verification ability of a maliciously trained model on clean data for SV task.

Table 2. Poisoned Model Performance on clean data. All malicious models use a poison rate of 2% for training data.

Trigger	Task	
	CSI	SV
Long Cough	83.98%	50.03%
Short Cough	83.61%	50.20%
Car Horn	84.46%	51.00%
Phone Ring	82.37%	50.07%
Clean Model	81.75%	86.85%

5 Related Work

The first attack on machine learning system can be dated back to its application on statistical spam filters. In [7,19,20,35], the attackers' goal is to generate messages that can evade detection to let through spam emails or modify model's training data to block legitimate messages. Later on the attacks were developed to virus detection system, where the attacker will craft false positives and negatives data to deceive the model [26]. The works in [4,5] extended the attack to network traffic classification systems, where they found that Autograph, a signature detection system that updates its model online, was vulnerable to allergy attacks that convince the system to "learn" signatures that match benign traffic. A taxonomy of classical machine learning attacks can be found in [16].

In image classification domain, [3] proposes three strategies to inject trigger pattern into a benign image: (1) Blended Injection Strategy; (2) Accessory Injection Strategy; and (3) Blended Accessory Injection Strategy. In strategy (1), a random noise pattern of equal size as a benign image was multiplied by a blending factor $\alpha \in [0, 1]$ and added directly atop the benign image. In (2), a smaller size of an accessory trigger pattern directly replaces the pixel values of the benign image at the area of the pattern's coverage. In (3), both the accessory pattern and the blending factor are used to blend in with the benign image. In [13], the attacker can inject the backdoor by only changing one or a few pixel values of the benign image and perform the same change on testing data to launch the attack. In Speaker Recognition domain, [38] proposes to inject low-volume one-hot-spectrum noise with different frequencies to each different speaker group to achieve backdoor attack on multiple speakers.

To create our backdoors, we also use training set poisoning, where the attacker is able to add his own samples and corresponding target labels to the training set. Existing research on training set poisoning typically assumes that the attacker is only able to influence a small portion of the training data, or that the classifier is regularly updated with new inputs, some of which may be attacker-controlled, but not change the training model's architecture itself. Thus, in our threat model (Sect. 3.1), we require that the attacker can only modify a small section of the training data and must leave the model architecture unchanged.

6 Conclusion

In this paper we explored and identified the security vulnerabilities of increasingly common speaker recognition systems that use deep neural networks. Specifically, we demonstrated that such system is highly susceptible to backdoor attack in the training phase; a maliciously trained deep speaker recognition system using a poisoned dataset can be easily backdoored and misbehave on carefully crafted backdoor input per the adversary's desire. Further, we showed that such backdoor attack can be stealthy and the backdoor triggers can sound natural to human inspectors. Such backdoor attack only introduces pattern disturbance on feature space and imposes no structural change to the network.

We have implemented our backdoored attack on a speaker recognition system using ResNet and the VoxCeleb1 data and demonstrated that, under such attack, the model will maliciously misclassify poisoned samples to a corresponding target class. Our digital attack on ResNet can achieve 89% or greater targeted attack success rate on CSI task and 99% rate on SV task on all 4 triggers, while over-the-air physical attack can achieve at least 90% success rate on both tasks using 3 triggers and at least 70% ASR on both tasks using the other one. We also obtained comparable performance on clean data using the maliciously trained model. Our work reveals the security implications of speaker recognition system using deep neural networks and provides strong motivations for future developers to design more robust defense mechanisms and better secure against such backdoor attacks.

Acknowledgement. We would like to thank the reviewers for their helpful comments. Jianwei Tai is supported by the National Key Research and Development Program of China (No. 2019YFE0110300) and the National Natural Science Foundation of China under Grant 71971075, 72271076, and 71871079. Xiaoqi Jia is supported in part by Strategic Priority Research Program of Chinese Academy of Sciences (No. XDC02010900) and National Key Research and Development Program of China (No. 2019YFB1005201 and No. 2021YFB2910109).

References

1. Agarap, A.F.: Deep learning using rectified linear units (ReLU). arXiv preprint arXiv:1803.08375 (2018)
2. Bhattacharya, G., Alam, M.J., Kenny, P.: Deep speaker recognition: modular or monolithic? In: INTERSPEECH, pp. 1143–1147 (2019)
3. Chen, X., Liu, C., Li, B., Lu, K., Song, D.: Targeted backdoor attacks on deep learning systems using data poisoning. arXiv preprint arXiv:1712.05526 (2017)
4. Chung, S.P., Mok, A.K.: Allergy attack against automatic signature generation. In: Zamboni, D., Kruegel, C. (eds.) RAID 2006. LNCS, vol. 4219, pp. 61–80. Springer, Heidelberg (2006). https://doi.org/10.1007/11856214_4
5. Chung, S.P., Mok, A.K.: Advanced allergy attacks: does a corpus really help? In: Kruegel, C., Lippmann, R., Clark, A. (eds.) RAID 2007. LNCS, vol. 4637, pp. 236–255. Springer, Heidelberg (2007). https://doi.org/10.1007/978-3-540-74320-0_13
6. Conneau, A., Schwenk, H., Barrault, L., Lecun, Y.: Very deep convolutional networks for text classification. arXiv preprint arXiv:1606.01781 (2016)
7. Dalvi, N., Domingos, P., Sanghai, S., Verma, D.: Adversarial classification. In: Proceedings of the Tenth ACM SIGKDD International Conference on Knowledge Discovery and Data Mining, pp. 99–108 (2004)
8. Dehak, N., Kenny, P.J., Dehak, R., Dumouchel, P., Ouellet, P.: Front-end factor analysis for speaker verification. IEEE Trans. Audio Speech Lang. Process. **19**(4), 788–798 (2010)
9. Dempster, A.P., Laird, N.M., Rubin, D.B.: Maximum likelihood from incomplete data via the EM algorithm. J. Roy. Stat. Soc.: Ser. B (Methodol.) **39**(1), 1–22 (1977)

10. Fortuna, J., Sivakumaran, P., Ariyaeeinia, A., Malegaonkar, A.: Open-set speaker identification using adapted Gaussian mixture models. In: Ninth European Conference on Speech Communication and Technology (2005)
11. Goodfellow, I., Bengio, Y., Courville, A.: Deep Learning. MIT Press, Cambridge (2016)
12. Goodfellow, I., et al.: Generative adversarial nets. In: Advances in Neural Information Processing Systems, vol. 27 (2014)
13. Gu, T., Dolan-Gavitt, B., Garg, S.: BadNets: identifying vulnerabilities in the machine learning model supply chain. arXiv preprint arXiv:1708.06733 (2017)
14. Han, J., Moraga, C.: The influence of the sigmoid function parameters on the speed of backpropagation learning. In: Mira, J., Sandoval, F. (eds.) IWANN 1995. LNCS, vol. 930, pp. 195–201. Springer, Heidelberg (1995). https://doi.org/10.1007/3-540-59497-3_175
15. He, K., Zhang, X., Ren, S., Sun, J.: Deep residual learning. Image Recogn. **7** (2015)
16. Huang, L., Joseph, A.D., Nelson, B., Rubinstein, B.I., Tygar, J.D.: Adversarial machine learning. In: Proceedings of the 4th ACM Workshop on Security and Artificial Intelligence, pp. 43–58 (2011)
17. Huang, Y.Y., Wang, W.Y.: Deep residual learning for weakly-supervised relation extraction. arXiv preprint arXiv:1707.08866 (2017)
18. Koffas, S., Xu, J., Conti, M., Picek, S.: Can you hear it? Backdoor attacks via ultrasonic triggers. arXiv preprint arXiv:2107.14569 (2021)
19. Lowd, D., Meek, C.: Adversarial learning. In: Proceedings of the Eleventh ACM SIGKDD International Conference on Knowledge Discovery in Data Mining, pp. 641–647 (2005)
20. Lowd, D., Meek, C.: Good word attacks on statistical spam filters. In: CEAS, vol. 2005 (2005)
21. McLaren, M., Ferrer, L., Castan, D., Lawson, A.: The speakers in the wild (SITW) speaker recognition database. In: Interspeech, pp. 818–822 (2016)
22. Muda, L., Begam, M., Elamvazuthi, I.: Voice recognition algorithms using Mel frequency cepstral coefficient (MFCC) and dynamic time warping (DTW) techniques. arXiv preprint arXiv:1003.4083 (2010)
23. Multimodal Information Group (2022). https://www.nist.gov/itl/iad/mig/speaker-recognition
24. Nagrani, A., Chung, J.S., Xie, W., Zisserman, A.: VoxCeleb: large-scale speaker verification in the wild. Comput. Speech Lang. **60**, 101027 (2020)
25. Nandwana, M.K., Ferrer, L., McLaren, M., Castan, D., Lawson, A.: Analysis of critical metadata factors for the calibration of speaker recognition systems. In: INTERSPEECH, pp. 4325–4329 (2019)
26. Newsome, J., Karp, B., Song, D.: Paragraph: thwarting signature learning by training maliciously. In: Zamboni, D., Kruegel, C. (eds.) RAID 2006. LNCS, vol. 4219, pp. 81–105. Springer, Heidelberg (2006). https://doi.org/10.1007/11856214_5
27. Reynolds, D.A.: Gaussian mixture models. Encyclopedia Biometrics **741**(659–663) (2009)
28. Reynolds, D.A., Quatieri, T.F., Dunn, R.B.: Speaker verification using adapted Gaussian mixture models. Digit. Signal Process. **10**(1–3), 19–41 (2000)
29. Reynolds, D.A., Rose, R.C.: Robust text-independent speaker identification using Gaussian mixture speaker models. IEEE Trans. Speech Audio Process. **3**(1), 72–83 (1995)
30. Saha, A., Subramanya, A., Pirsiavash, H.: Hidden trigger backdoor attacks. In: Proceedings of the AAAI Conference on Artificial Intelligence, vol. 34, pp. 11957–11965 (2020)

31. Simonyan, K., Zisserman, A.: Very deep convolutional networks for large-scale image recognition. arXiv preprint arXiv:1409.1556 (2014)
32. Snyder, D., Garcia-Romero, D., Sell, G., McCree, A., Povey, D., Khudanpur, S.: Speaker recognition for multi-speaker conversations using X-vectors. In: 2019 IEEE International Conference on Acoustics, Speech and Signal Processing (ICASSP), ICASSP 2019, pp. 5796–5800. IEEE (2019)
33. Snyder, D., Garcia-Romero, D., Sell, G., Povey, D., Khudanpur, S.: X-vectors: robust DNN embeddings for speaker recognition. In: 2018 IEEE International Conference on Acoustics, Speech and Signal Processing (ICASSP), pp. 5329–5333. IEEE (2018)
34. Turner, A., Tsipras, D., Madry, A.: Clean-label backdoor attacks (2018)
35. Wittel, G.L., Wu, S.F.: On attacking statistical spam filters. In: CEAS. Citeseer (2004)
36. Xu, M., Duan, L.-Y., Cai, J., Chia, L.-T., Xu, C., Tian, Q.: HMM-based audio keyword generation. In: Aizawa, K., Nakamura, Y., Satoh, S. (eds.) PCM 2004. LNCS, vol. 3333, pp. 566–574. Springer, Heidelberg (2004). https://doi.org/10.1007/978-3-540-30543-9_71
37. Ye, J., Liu, X., You, Z., Li, G., Liu, B.: DriNet: dynamic backdoor attack against automatic speech recognization models. Appl. Sci. **12**(12), 5786 (2022)
38. Zhai, T., Li, Y., Zhang, Z.M., Wu, B., Jiang, Y., Xia, S.: Backdoor attack against speaker verification. In: 2021 IEEE International Conference on Acoustics, Speech and Signal Processing (ICASSP), pp. 2560–2564 (2021)

Anonymous Authentication Protocols in Vehicular Ad Hoc Network-An Survey

Guiwen Fu, Yanan Chen(✉), Zhen Wu, and Qianlin Ye

Jiangxi University of Science and Technology, 1180 Shuanggang East Street, Nanchang, Jiangxi, China
chenyanan@jxust.edu.cn

Abstract. Vehicle Ad Hoc Network (VANET) is an emerging wireless network technology, especially the application of traditional mobile ad hoc networks on traffic roads. The safety and efficiency of its deployment on the road have attracted widespread attention from the social industry. How to improve the traffic system and reduce the number of traffic accidents is also a hot topic in academic research. At the same time, VANET is also known as a safe communication platform for disseminating road information. However, in the V ANET open access network environment, the protection of vehicle privacy and the secure transmission of messages are the most critical and challenging issues. In this article, we detail the background of VANET, the security requirements for operation and possible attacks. Combined with the multi-faceted research of different scholars, we listed different anonymous authentication methods and high-security encryption technologies, and compared them by classification. Such as the advantages and limitations of different schemes, performance, communication overhead, etc. Finally, we describe some possible research directions in this network.

Keywords: Vehicular Ad Hoc Networks (VANETs) · Attacks · Security requirements · Anonymous authentication

1 Introduction

With the rapid development of the Internet of Vehicles technology, it is possible to realize the integrated network of intelligent traffic management, intelligent dynamic information service and vehicle control. Using wireless connection communication technology, vehicles can maintain stable communication in a highly mobile state, realize road information sharing between vehicle entities, reduce road congestion and enhance road safety. Vehicle ad hoc networks include two typical application connection methods in the Internet of Vehicles: vehicle-to-vehicle and vehicle-to-infrastructure. This is also a hot research direction today. While realizing the interconnection between the vehicle and the system, it can also provide attractive services such as traffic, road conditions, speed, weather, gas station location, other emergency information, etc. It is also because vehicles

C. Su et al. (Eds.): ISPEC 2022, LNCS 13620, pp. 485–501, 2022.
https://doi.org/10.1007/978-3-031-21280-2_27

need to continuously disseminate important information to other entities under this network, so vehicle privacy and network security must be guaranteed.

To date, many research studies have been published on VANET security and user privacy issues. They use different encryption methods to deal with possible threats, with the goal of lowering communication and computing costs. Each research method has its strengths and limitations. The basic identity authentication method enhances network security and exposes the real identity of the vehicle. Attackers can track and locate the driver's identity through their driving location habits. Faced with this challenge, some researchers have gradually introduced anonymous authentication methods, mainly based on symmetric and asymmetric encryption mechanisms [2–5,14,20,23,25,27,30,31], based on identity signatures [1,10,12,15,18,29,31,33,35], and encryption based on group signatures [9,17,32,36]and classification mechanisms based on RSU [8,18,34].

This paper focuses on the summary and supplement of the above-mentioned investigation methods, and at the same time summarizes new anonymous authentication methods and new ideas in related fields in recent years, so as to facilitate readers to comprehensively understand the research status of VANET safety mechanism, achieve the goal of zero traffic accident rate and improve user driving experience as soon as possible.

1.1 Motivation

According to the National Security Administration (NHTSA) data report [7], 42,915 people will be killed in motor vehicle traffic accidents in the preliminary forecast of traffic fatalities in 2021, an increase of 10.5% from the 38,824 deaths in 2020. Collision fatalities are up 16% from 2020. The World Health Organization has also released a report [16] stating that about 1.35 million people are killed each year due to road traffic accidents. An additional 50 to 200 million people suffered non-fatal injuries, many of them disabled as a result of their injuries. Behind every number are lost lives and abandoned families. Therefore, reducing the traffic accident rate is our urgent task today.

1.2 Our Contributions

The contributions of this paper are as follows:

1. The article first introduces the main features, components and standardized models of VANET.
2. Summarize the possible attack methods in the process of wireless network access, and specify the security requirements for maintaining efficient communication in VANET.
3. Investigate different existing authentication methods and privacy protection schemes, which are divided into five categories in this paper. It also briefly introduces the main methods and advantages of each mechanism, and points out the shortcomings of the scheme.

4. Finally, we compare and evaluate the attack methods that each type of scheme can resist, the security requirements that can be met, and the performance of communication costs.

The purpose of this paper is not to select and recommend the optimal anonymous authentication scheme, but to illustrate the shortcomings of the protocol from different perspectives, so that researchers can respond to these challenges.

1.3 Organization

Section 2 discuss the preliminaries. The details of attackers classification and security requirement in Sect. 3. Categorize the different anonymous authentication protocols in Sect. 4. Eventually, the conclusion is given in Sect. 6.

2 Preliminaries

2.1 VANET Features

This section briefly introduces the network characteristics of VANET: real-time constraints, high liquidity, volatility, computation and storage, and high topology dynamics.

1. **Real-time constraints:** Information exchange in VANET must be guaranteed within a specific time, the purpose of which is to make the vehicle respond quickly.
2. **High liquidity:** Rapid movement between nodes can cause information disruption or communication delays.
3. **Computation and Storage:** In VANET, it is critical to securely exchange information and store data. The storage capacity of the vehicle and how the infrastructure calculates and stores a large amount of information will be a challenging problem.
4. **High dynamic topology:** Vehicles travel rapidly in the network, and frequent node position changes make the network structure change rapidly, which makes it difficult to identify malicious vehicles.

2.2 System Model

VANET is mainly composed of three parts: TA, OBU, RSU. The TA is the control and trust center responsible for connecting the three parties. The OBU is a vehicle-mounted device that transmits information to other vehicles through sensors, including maintaining contact with the RSU. RSUs are infrastructure built on the roadside or at key intersections.

1. **TA: Trusted Authority**
   TA is a trusted authority in the VANET, provided it has sufficient computing and communication capabilities. It needs to store data such as traffic and weather conditions, and retain authentication information and credentials for joining or leaving the vehicle. It can provide users with basic parameters such as public key and private key, and can also identify and revoke malicious attack nodes when necessary.

2. **OBU: On Board Unit**
   OBU is a processing unit installed in the car. Responsible for maintaining contact with OBUs on RSUs or other vehicles through dedicated short-range communication technology (DSRC), disseminating and receiving important information such as speed, location, traffic conditions, weather and optimal routes. But the premise is that before the vehicle joins the VANET, the relevant public parameters must be registered in the TA and the relevant key must be provided.
3. **RSU: Road Side Unit**
   RSU is a fixed communication device installed on both sides of the road or at key intersections such as intersections, and is a fixed processing unit distributed on the network. Its existence expands the coverage of the wireless network and improves the operation efficiency of the network. Usually, the TA is connected through a wired network, and the vehicle is connected through a wireless network. It is a trusted party, an information bridge connecting OBU and TA, and can also help TA to reveal the real identity of the vehicle when necessary (Fig. 1).

Fig. 1. The system model of VANETs

2.3 Standard Types of VANET

1. *WAVE*: Wireless Access in Vehicular Environments. Establish V2I and V2V service structures and communication interfaces for networks, and establish standard specifications for procedures such as transportation and security services.

2. *DSRC*: Dedicated short-range communication. The communication distance is between 10 and 1000 m. This communication is mainly suitable for data transmission in urban traffic channels. It is a small wireless communication system with 7 different frequency channels, which provides an information exchange communication platform for roadside units and vehicle units [28].
3. *IEEE802.11p*: It is an extended communication protocol of 802.11, which is specially designed for DSRC system.

3 Security in VANET

3.1 Attackers Classification

1. *Impersonation Attack*: In a simulated attack, attackers can successfully disguise themselves as legitimate vehicles or even RSUs into the VANET network.
2. *Modification Attack*: Usually refers to the attacker tampering with part or all of the broadcast information, which is mainly divided into the process of message dissemination and after the process. For example, providing wrong positioning or traffic information to the vehicle to guide the vehicle to make wrong judgments, so that the attacker can obtain good traffic conditions.
3. *Sybil Attack*: A Sybil attack refers to an attacker who manipulates maliciously using many different identities, in order to fabricate and spread a large amount of misinformation, such as the illusion of traffic chaos such as streets being blocked and accidents ahead, forcing drivers to re-plan their routes and increase the trouble of driving [11,22,26].
4. *Black Hole Attack*: Detecting black hole attacks is relatively difficult. When the network is running normally, it is manifested as maliciously discarding and refusing to accept data packets to vehicles or nodes at any time. Similar to a grey hole attack, the result is that packets tracked by untrusted vehicles are dropped [19]
5. *Location Tracking Attack*: Because the communication between the vehicle is based on DSRC wireless network on the basis of execution, the wireless network is a public open field, an attacker easy access to the vehicle after data analysis, according to the vehicle driving multiple azimuth or exercise habits make it easier to track vehicle location, and even can be traced to the driver.
6. *Replay Attack*: An attacker replay expired or identical information to obfuscate current traffic conditions. This had a huge impact on emergency management in particular, resulting in significant losses.
7. *Denial of service Attack*: It is a relatively serious attack method mainly by preventing authorized trusted users from accessing network nodes. The attacker may also input a large amount of junk information to occupy the communication channel, increase the computational overhead of network nodes, and slow down the network operation speed [6].
8. *Malware Attack*: It means that after the vehicle or RSUs are installed with this malware, once the registration is updated, the attack will damage the various components of VANETs along the unit, affecting its normal use [6].

9. *RSU Replication Attack*: Once the RSU is attacked, the adversary can easily seize the destroyed RSU to carry out various forms of attack. The RSU is the communication bridge between the OBU and the TA. Once the wrong command information is sent, the management and control will become more complicated [3] (Table 1).

Table 1. Comparison with the attack methods by different schemes

	Impersonation	Modification	Location Tracking	Replay	Denial of service	RSU Replication
VPKI	√	√	√	√	√	×
EAAP	√	√	√	√	×	×
ECDSA	√	√	√	√	×	√
2-FLIP	√	√	√	√	√	√
TESLA	√	√	√	√	×	√
CPPA	√	√	×	×	√	√
SPACF	√	√	√	√	√	√
IBC+TPDB	√	√	√	√	√	×
LIAP	√	√	√	√	√	√

3.2 Security Requirement

1. Integrity and Authentication: In VANET, first of all, the premise of ensuring V2V and V2I secure communication is to ensure the integrity and legality of the message.
   The content before and after sending must be consistent and the information is generated and sent by legal vehicles.
   Secondly, it is necessary to provide an efficient and anonymous authentication method in the VANET component, which can prevent the message from being subjected to impersonation attacks and ensure the message is transmitted to the authorized users [24].
2. Confidentiality: Confidentiality is an inevitable requirement to ensure communication security. The content transmitted by the beacon node cannot

identify the sender [24], any recipient user identity information should not be disclosed [26].
This helps users enjoy services or access information without revealing their identities, but they can still be held accountably for their actions.
Only TA can track and identify its true identity [21]. Encryption technology can be used for sensitive and important information to prevent attackers from easily seeing through, while considering the cost, encryption technology is not required for program management data announcement information.
Finally, for the safety of the driver, the specific driving position of the vehicle should also be kept secret [13].
3. Traceability: This security requirement is aimed at internal attackers.
When a vehicle is found to be dishonest, an authority such as TA or RSU is required to have the ability to track, and retrieve the real identity of the vehicle sender based on the signature certificate to which belongs.
The second is to ensure that the behavior of malicious vehicles can be revoked under the premise of reasonable expenses.

4 Authentication Protocol

4.1 Asymmetric Cryptography Based Classification

Public key encryption is another name for it. It is characterized by the existence of a unique pair of public and private keys.

If using public key encryption, only the user who has the private key can decrypt it.

The two are in a one-to-one relationship. The decryption key is kept by the receiver from the beginning, so the key distribution problem can be solved by simply sending the encryption key to the other party.

Since the public key is only for the user who generated the key, the public key can be disclosed arbitrarily. This method is more secure and people prefer to choose this encryption method.

In this paper, authentication methods based on asymmetric cryptography are divided into four categories, namely VPKI, EAAP and ECDSA.

1. **VPKI-Vehicular public key infrastructure.** This is a relatively traditional form of authentication. It is based on an asymmetric cryptographic algorithm, and the public key is open to the public. Before joining the VANET network, the vehicle must register its real identity with a trusted authority TA to obtain a signing certificate and have its own private key. When transferring content, use the private key to sign and transmit the certificate to the recipient for authentication, thus enabling V2V and V2I communication securely. However, this scheme also has some limitations:
1. It requires a lot of space in the car to store keys and certificates.
2. Certificate verification is required in the communication process, and the computational cost is high [27].

3. Since the TA is the only owner of the real vehicle information, once the TA is destroyed, all vehicle identity information will be leaked.
4. Vehicle location privacy is not supported [20]. Therefore, in [14], a VPKI scheme is proposed, which is an improved scheme for PKI-based key management and security services.
Set up your own access rights for different network nodes, revoke and delete their certificates when abnormal nodes occur. These revoked certificates will be immediately stored in the CRL list and published on the network immediately to notify other vehicles in a timely manner.
This paper evaluates and analyzes different certificate revocation categories in order to effectively implement certificate generation and revocation in combination with different situations. In [2], it communicates efficiently by establishing a connection with the RSU to secretly distribute keys to vehicles entering the area.
By capturing appropriate vehicle node density and spatial density, the effectiveness and security of information exchange between vehicle nodes is verified. But the premise of the effective implementation of this scheme is that the RSU is not destroyed.

2. **EAAP-Efficient Anonymous Authentication Protocol.** In [3], an efficient bilinear pairing-based conditional privacy-preserving authentication is proposed [5].
In this scheme, TA does not need to play the role of storage and management. It can generate itself and hold privacy. When a communication dispute occurs, the TA can promptly disclose and revoke the real identity of the suspicious vehicle. At the same time, the scheme has been verified to be resistant to impersonation and modification attacks. Therefore, the attacker cannot change its content without authorization during the information transfer process, and once malicious behavior occurs, TA will identify and revoke it. Using this scheme can reduce the computational overhead of verifying the signature, and the efficiency is greatly improved. However, in [5], the authors verified that this scheme is vulnerable to the above-mentioned attacks, and there is the possibility of message modification. And in this solution, mutual authentication is required before the vehicle communicates with the RSU, because when the vehicle enters the control range of the RSU, it needs to provide road condition information at that location. Therefore, this scheme may also be problematic: the RSU can rationalize the uncertified vehicle before sending the safety information, and the vehicle receiving the road condition information can also verify the legitimacy of the RSU in some incorrect way.
3. **ECDSA Based Authentication Schemes**
The ECDSA algorithm is a combination of elliptic curve cryptography and digital signature algorithms. It is a lightweight algorithm with fast calculation speed, high encryption security and small storage space. In [25], this paper uses a message authentication scheme combining elliptic curve digital signature algorithm and Merkle tree.
Before the message is sent, the Merkle tree is constructed to obtain the key nodes of the tree branch. The information of each node is the hash value

under different public keys provided by standard hash technology. It further branches down into two different hash values, representing different key information respectively, resulting in output bits and authentication paths of different lengths. This reduces computational overhead and message latency to a certain extent.
However, due to the lack of entity verification, simply using the ECDSA algorithm may be subject to DOS attacks and generate invalid information to interrupt the normal signature communication of the network. Therefore, the combination with the Merkle tree can realize that the signed information is accepted by the receiver, and the invalid information will be discarded.

4.2 Symmetric Cryptography Based Classification

Symmetric encryption means that the sender and receiver of a message are encrypted with the same key, so every time a message is transmitted, it needs to be replaced with a key that is known to both parties. It must complete the distribution of the key before sending and receiving data, and the security of this link is difficult to guarantee. And if multiple parties use a common key, once the key is cracked, the system will crash. The number of keys will double over a long period of time, so the cost of key storage and use cannot be ignored. But the advantage is that when the data capacity is longer, the encryption and decryption time is shorter than that of asymmetric keys.

1. **2FLIP Two-Factor lightweight privacy-preserving authentication scheme.** In [30], the scheme combines decentralization of certificate authority and two-factor authentication based on human biometric password. Fast signature authentication of information can be performed by using several lightweight hash function processes and formed message authentication codes. Each vehicle must be connected to a remote communications device that can record and verify the driver's identity through facial features or fingerprints. The key and signature authentication process is managed by a tamper-resistant device installed in the OBU. Compared with other solutions, this process greatly improves communication efficiency, increases computational consumption by about 102 times, reduces certificate store verification and revocation costs, and is resistant to attacks. In this scheme, once the CA is attacked or the key is leaked, the scheme shows that the system can be updated to restore the entire operational state, and the embedded remote device is also able to identify the real identity of the user after the update. Compared to the PKI scheme, it does not completely rely on the CA to protect the keys of the system. Once the CA is leaked, the real identity of the vehicle will not be revealed.
2. **TESLA Based Authentication Schemes.** In [23], the idea of this scheme is to realize information exchange based on a symmetric key system, which is considered as a low-overhead broadcast authentication protocol. The sender sends a packet at an agreed time interval with the receiver, and the packet is accompanied by a message authentication code (MAC) value that only the receiver can verify. The encryption key MAC is calculated by choosing

the relative value of the one-way hash chain. When the information receiver receives the data packet, it needs to use its own identity and key to verify whether the MAC value is correct, so as to avoid the key leakage during the message sending process. In the case of data loss in the one-way chain, the receiver can still use the remaining data to perform recovery calculations and verify the correctness of the MAC. The disadvantage of this scheme is that it does not have non-repudiation and loose synchronization between nodes leads to message delay. In [4], lightweight certification based on Tesla scheme combined with Bloom filter. Replacing EDSCA with Bloom filters enables vehicles to authenticate each other before receiving messages. Conversely, CRLs are less expensive to form and shorten message verification time. Bloom filter operation structure can effectively determine whether a member is in the filter or not. Inspired by the above scheme, in [4], the author proposes a Timed Efficient and Secure Vehicular Communications scheme. This scheme only needs to add a short message authentication code to the data packet and then use a hash function to verify the message source, without the need for asymmetric cryptosystems. other complex operations. In the state of dense traffic flow and communication, the calculation overhead is reduced while the message verification speed is guaranteed.

4.3 Identity-Based Cryptography Classification

In the traditional PKI system, it takes a lot of space and time to store and manage certificates. The identity-based key system alleviates this burden, without the need to use certificates to authenticate messages, it directly uses the real identity information of the vehicle as the public key, and the private key is passed through a third party called a private key generator (PKG) calculated. Therefore, when delivering a message, the sender only needs to know the recipient's identity.

1. **CPPA-Conditional privacy preserving authentication.** In [18], the authors propose a PKI-based CPPA scheme. It requires the issuance of a large number of certificates to sign and encrypt messages. Secondly, the receiver also increases the verification cost while verifying the information, and tracking the checklist CRL is also a time-consuming task. Therefore, in [18], the authors mentioned a CPPA scheme that requires the vehicle to re-apply for a new certificate before entering the RSU field to protect privacy, but it is obviously not efficient. In [33], the authors propose a CPPA scheme that uses bilinear pairings, uses map-to-point (MTP) hashing tools to generate anonymous identities, and uses batch signatures to verify high-density messages in a region. Using a sequence of operations in this scenario may result in increased message latency and validation overhead. But in [15], the authors argue that the scheme of [33] has not been proven to be resistant to replay attacks and traceability in the network. In [10], the authors propose a CPPA scheme using a combination of ECC and batch signatures, which is proven to be effective, but has the disadvantage of potentially delaying signature verification. In [1], the authors design an efficient IBS-CPPA scheme that

also uses ECC to provide confidentiality authentication, but chooses to use a one-way hash chain instead of the MTP function to simplify and speed up the signature calculation process, batch verification of vehicle sending traffic information to achieve the purpose of reducing computing consumption. Finally, after evaluation and verification, the scheme outperforms existing CPPA schemes in terms of computation and communication.

2. **SPACF-Secure Privacy-Preserving Authentication with Cuckoo Filter**
   In [12], the authors propose an identity-based privacy protection scheme that does not rely on tamper-resistant devices, uses cuckoo filters combined with ECC, and uses binary search to obtain valid signatures. Its purpose is to improve the success rate of batch verification, this stage does not use bilinear pairing or other hash functions, reduces computational cost and communication cost, and reduces the limitations of the above scheme. The final results show that the security requirements required by VANET are also met: such as message integrity, traceability, and replay attacks. Finally, compared with [12], the cuckoo filter requires less storage space than the bloom filter, and there are almost no false positives, which can ensure the signature is timely and efficient.
3. **IBC+TPDB**
   Among existing solutions, embedding tamper-resistant devices into devices to protect data privacy is a common approach [31]. While storing secrets, it can be responsible for signing and realizing information synchronization. However, due to the high cost of tamper-resistant equipment and the risk of being cracked by side-channel attacks, confidential privacy such as data is leaked. Therefore, the premise of using this device is to assume that the device is not vulnerable to sophisticated hardware attacks. In [31], under the premise of using tamper-resistant devices, the authors focus on reducing the verification cost, and propose a conditional privacy protection scheme based on pseudo-IBS, which satisfies the fast batch authentication of RSU and achieves unlinkability and safety requirements such as traceability. Compared with [35], the signature verification time is reduced by 18%.
4. **LIAP-Authentication protocol using local identity**
   In [31], this is an anonymous authentication scheme that combines public key infrastructure (PKI)-based and identity-based signatures. When the vehicle and RSU are registered, the trusted agency TA only provides it with a long-term valid certification to verify its validity. When the vehicle enters a new RSU field, based on the premise that both parties have the long-term valid certificate that they had. When they were registered, the valid vehicle can request the local key information from the RSU that has not been revoked, so as to obtain an anonymous identity and enter the network. Otherwise it will be inaccessible. Once a malicious vehicle attackers occurs in this scheme, TA can easily trace its real identity and revoke its certificate. The scheme has the ability to deal with collusion attacks and replay attacks, and meets the security requirements of message integrity and non-repudiation. However, because it requires PKI in the authentication process, the query, verification

and deletion of certificates, the maintenance and management of certificate revocation lists during communication are relatively complicated, which will increase computational overhead to a certain extent.

4.4 Group Signature-Based Classification

In [32], the concept of group signature was proposed. This scheme means that any member of the group can sign and verify messages on behalf of the entire group without revealing their real identity. In the event of a dispute, a trusted third party can determine its identity. This scheme provides high-level protection of user and signer identities. At the same time, the message is not linkable, two messages sent by the same vehicle cannot be recognized by a group member at the same time, because the signer cannot determine the source of the two messages. In addition, the disadvantage of this scheme is that the signature verification delay time increases as the number of revoked vehicles increases. If the number of vehicles in the revocation list reaches a certain threshold, a new set of group keys needs to be calculated and provided to the vehicles according to the revocation vehicle list. This complex update process increases the likelihood of being attacked.

In [36], in order to reduce the authentication burden of TA and the risk of high packet loss rate existing in other anonymous schemes, the author proposed a scheme that uses group signatures combined with efficient batch authentication. The private key is generated using bilinear pairing and a hash function. The RSUs are divided into multiple levels according to the transmission range and performance. One TA communicates with only the first RSU, and then the first layer maintains contacting with the second layer. When the vehicle enters the range of the RSU and sends a request, the RSU will automatically transmit the vehicle information to the highest-level RSU, which can be checked and verified through the saved data information. Once the result is verified to be wrong information, the certificate will be automatically revoked. However, this scheme does not specifically analyze the advantages of packet loss rate and transmission delay.

Ring signatures are different from group signatures. Ring signatures allow the signer to have a free ring structure at will, and achieve 1vsN anonymous verification while requiring the signer to be responsible for the content, because only the TA is allowed to revoke the signer's anonymity. In [9], this scheme uses ENCRYPT and DECRYPT algorithms to encrypt and decrypt information, providing a ring signature structure with double communicate protection for message transmission and reception. Using the RSU as an auxiliary to form a ring with the vehicle improves the ringing efficiency of the ring signature. First, after the sender is verified by the TA's request, it uses its own private key and the public key of the ring signature to generate a signature to transmit information. The receiver also needs to request from the TA: the password corresponding to the message and the encrypted signature to be verified with the public key. The final scheme also conducts actual field tests to evaluate its security, the data shows that this method can achieve security requirements such as double protection, anonymity and unforgeability. But because of its double protection, the complexity of ring signature verification efficiency will increase. In [17], the author proposes a new privacy protection scheme the two-factor authentication based on secure lattice to prevent ring signatures. Its purpose is to prevent users from submitting duplicate signatures. Use the anti-collision hash function and use the probabilistic polynomial time algorithm to verify whether the message signature is valid. If the receiver assumes that the ring member has sent the message and received two signatures from the same vehicle, then the vehicle key is allowed to be extracted. It also ensures the anonymity of the signer. This scheme ensures message integrity and unforgeability, and can even resist quantum computer attacks, but it needs to consider CRL management.

4.5 RSUs-Based Classification

In order to solve the storage overhead and CRL management problems caused by a large number of pre-stored certificates. In [18]proposed an RSU-based anonymous authentication scheme, which requires vehicles to apply for a short-term anonymous key when passing through the RSU. Due to the need to maintain message coherence, the vehicle needs to constantly communicate with the RSU to change the anonymity certificate, which may affect the communication efficiency. In [8,34], the proposed schemes completely rely on RSU to issue certificates for vehicles and perform signature verification. The premise of the implementation of the scheme is that an anonymous certificate needs to be prepared, and once the RSU is destroyed, it is easy for the adversary to control the service record, and this scheme will no longer be effective. In [29], this scheme can achieve strong privacy protection for RSUs in VANET. First, the author uses one-way hash chain technology to automatically remove the revoked user's certificate. Second, it supports RSU to provide distributed certificate services, allowing vehicles to use new pseudonym certificates through RSU in a specific time period and area, which can relatively reduce revocation cost. Although RSU may also suffer from the risk of being damaged, especially when many service contents are leaked, attackers can combine multiple contents to recover the vehicle trajectory they want to track. However, the author provides strong protection for it in the scheme. Although the RSU attacker knows that there is a function of issuing certificates, it cannot trace the specific vehicle information that he needs to attack. In the end, it is verified that the revocation overhead and certificate renewal overhead are reduced compared with the traditional scheme, but its CRL management problem has not been solved.

5 Performance Evaluation

Here are some table marks

1. Ip: This shows impersonation
2. Mf: This shows modification
3. Lt: This shows location tracking

4. RSU-rt This shows RSU-reputation
5. Tp: The running time of a bilinear pairing operation
6. Tep-1: The time needed to perform exponentiation in G1 is denoted as Tep-1
7. Tep-2: The time needed to perform exponentiation in G1 is denoted as Tep-2
8. Th: Th is the time required for performing a hash function
9. Tm: Tm is the time required for performing the one point multiplication
10. Tsqr: Tsqr is the time required for performing the squaring operations
11. Tmul: Tmul is the time required for performing the modular multiplication
12. Tinv: Tinv is the time required for performing the modular inversion
13. Tkp: Tkp is the time required for performing the scalar multiplication
14. Ta: Ta is the time required for performing the addition
15. Tmac: Tmac is the time required for performing one MAC operation (Table 2).

Table 2. Certificate & Signature verification cost of various schemes

Schemes	For one Certificates & Signature	For n Certificates & Signature	Bilinear pairing
EAAP	2Tp+4Tep-1+Tep-2	(1+n)Tp+4Tep-1+nTep-2	YES
ECDSA	2Tmul+Tinv+2Tkp +Th	(12n+2)Tmul+Tinv+10nTsqr +Th	NO
2-FLIP	Th+Tmac	-	NO
TESLA	7ms+7Th	7n+7nTh	NO
CPPA	1Tm + 1Ta ≈ 0.4438 ms	1Tm + 1Ta ≈0.442+0.0018n	NO
SPACF	2Tm + 1Ta +1Th ≈ 0.8859 ms	2Tm + nTsm +nTa + nTh ≈ 0.0157n + 0.884 ms	NO
IBC+TPD	-	-	YES
LIAP	Tmul + Tm+ 3 Tp	(n + 1) Tmul + nTm + 3Tp	YES
LPA	1Tm+4Tp	nTm+4Tp	YES
RSU-based	2Tmul+3Tp	2nTmul+3Tp	YES

6 Conclusion

In this article, we first understand the safety implications of today's traffic conditions and review the basics of vehicle self-organizing networks. Secondly, under the premise of reducing the communication cost and storage cost as much as possible, this paper proposes different technical solutions to ensure the performance of message integrity, anonymity and security when broadcasting messages in the VANET network. Information for privacy protection. The results show that the use of a single encryption method cannot resist the types of attacks that may occur in VANET and the difficulty in achieving the required security requirements. Each scheme and algorithm has certain limitations. For example, the communication cost, the storage space for the revocable list, and the verification efficiency of different entities. Therefore, it is shown that the use of cryptography alone cannot meet the security needs of vehicles and members in the network, and knowledge in diverse fields needs to be exchanged and improved to face new challenges in unforeseen environments.

References

1. Ali, I., Lawrence, T., Li, F.: An efficient identity-based signature scheme without bilinear pairing for vehicle-to-vehicle communication in VANETs. J. Syst. Architect. **103** (2019)
2. Alshaer, H.: Securing vehicular ad-hoc networks connectivity with roadside units support, pp. 1–6. IEEE (2015)
3. Azees, M., Vijayakumar, P., Deboarh, L.J.: EAAP: efficient anonymous authentication with conditional privacy-preserving scheme for vehicular ad hoc networks. IEEE Trans. Intell. Transp. Syst. **18**(9), 2467–2476 (2017)
4. Bao, S., Hathal, W., Cruickshank, H., Sun, Z., Asuquo, P., Lei, A.: A lightweight authentication and privacy-preserving scheme for VANETs using tesla and bloom filters. ICT Express, p. S2405959517302333 (2017)
5. Blake, I.F., Murty, V.K., Xu, G.: Refinements of Miller's algorithm for computing the Weil/Tate pairing. J. Algorithms **58**(2), 134–149 (2006)
6. Dhamgaye, A., Chavhan, N.: Survey on security challenges in VANET. Int. J. Comput. Sci. Netw. **2**(1) (2013)
7. Dua, A., Kumar, N., Bawa, S.: A systematic review on routing protocols for vehicular ad hoc networks. Veh. Commun. **1**(1), 33–52 (2014)
8. Freudiger, J., Raya, M., Feleghhazi, M.: Mix-zones for location privacy in vehicular networks. In: WiN-ITS 2007 (2007)
9. Han, Y., Xue, N.N., Wang, B.Y., Zhang, Q., Liu, C.L., Zhang, W.S.: Improved dual-protected ring signature for security and privacy of vehicular communications in vehicular ad-hoc networks. IEEE Access **6**, 20209–20220 (2018)
10. He, D., Zeadally, S., Xu, B., Huang, X.: An efficient identity-based conditional privacy-preserving authentication scheme for vehicular ad hoc networks. IEEE Trans. Inf. Forensics Secur. **10**(12), 2681–2691 (2015)
11. Jan, S.A., Amin, N.U., Othman, M., Ali, M., Umar, A.I., Basir, A.: A survey on privacy-preserving authentication schemes in VANETs: attacks, challenges and open issues. IEEE Access **9**, 153701–153726 (2021). https://doi.org/10.1109/ACCESS.2021.3125521
12. Jie, C., Jing, Z., Hong, Z., Yan, X.: SPACF: a secure privacy-preserving authentication scheme for VANET with cuckoo filter. IEEE Trans. Veh. Technol. **66**(11), 10283–10295 (2017)
13. Khan, S., Sharma, I., Aslam, M., Khan, M.Z., Khan, S.: Security challenges of location privacy in VANETs and state-of-the-art solutions: a survey. Future Internet **13**, 96 (2021)
14. Khan, T., et al.: Certificate revocation in vehicular ad hoc networks techniques and protocols: a survey. Sci. China Inf. Sci. **60**(10), 18 (2017)
15. Lee, C.C., Lai, Y.M.: Toward a secure batch verification with group testing for VANET. Wirel. Netw. **19**(6), 1441–1449 (2013)

16. Lin, X., Lu, R., Zhang, C., Zhu, H., Shen, X.: Security in vehicular ad hoc networks. IEEE Commun. Mag. **46**(4), 88–95 (2008)
17. Liu, J., et al.: Lattice-based double-authentication-preventing ring signature for security and privacy in vehicular ad-hoc networks. Tsinghua Sci. Technol. **24**, 575–584 (2019)
18. Lu, R., Lin, X., Zhu, H., Ho, P.H., Shen, X.: ECPP: efficient conditional privacy preservation protocol for secure vehicular communications. In: INFOCOM the Conference on Computer Communications. IEEE (2008)
19. Lu, Z., Qu, G., Liu, Z.: A survey on recent advances in vehicular network security, trust, and privacy. IEEE Trans. Intell. Transp. Syst. **20**, 760–776 (2018)
20. Manvi, S.S., Tangade, S.: A survey on authentication schemes in VANETs for secured communication. Veh. Commun. **9**, 19–30 (2017)
21. Paliwal, S., Cherukuri, A.K., Gao, X.Z.: Dynamic private modulus based password conditional privacy preserving authentication and key-agreement protocol for VANET. Wirel. Pers. Commun. **123**, 2061–2088 (2022)
22. Pattanayak, B.K., Pattnaik, O., Pani, S.: Dealing with Sybil attack in VANET. In: Mishra, D., Buyya, R., Mohapatra, P., Patnaik, S. (eds.) Intelligent and Cloud Computing. SIST, vol. 194, pp. 471–480. Springer, Singapore (2021). https://doi.org/10.1007/978-981-15-5971-6_51
23. Perrig, A., Ran, C., Tygar, J.D., Song, D.: The TESLA broadcast authentication protocol (2002)
24. Pournaghi, S.M., Zahednejad, B., Bayat, M., Farjami, Y.: NECPPA: a novel and efficient conditional privacy-preserving authentication scheme for VANET. Comput. Netw. **134**, 78–92 (2018)
25. Smitha, A., Pai, M., Ajam, N., Mouzna, J.: An optimized adaptive algorithm for authentication of safety critical messages in VANET. In: International ICST Conference on Communications Networking in China (2014)
26. Sulthana, S.: Privacy preserving schemes in VANETs: a review. Int. J. Comput. Technol. Appl. (2018)
27. Sun, M., Zhang, J., Guo, Y.: Anonymous identity authentication scheme for VANETs. J. Coast. Res. **104**(sp1), 203–209 (2020)
28. Sun, X., Lin, X., Ho, P.H.: Secure vehicular communications based on group signature and ID-based signature scheme. In: IEEE International Conference on Communications (2007)
29. Sun, Y., Lu, R., Lin, X., Shen, X., Su, J.: An efficient pseudonymous authentication scheme with strong privacy preservation for vehicular communications. IEEE Trans. Veh. Technol. **59**(7), 3589–3603 (2010)
30. Wang, F., Xu, Y., Zhang, H., Zhang, Y., Zhu, L.: 2FLIP: a two-factor lightweight privacy-preserving authentication scheme for VANET. IEEE Trans. Veh. Technol. **65**(2), 896–911 (2016)
31. Wang, S., Yao, N.: LIAP: a local identity-based anonymous message authentication protocol in VANETs. Comput. Commun. **112**, 154–164 (2017)
32. Xue, X., Ding, J.: LPA: a new location-based privacy-preserving authentication protocol in VANET. Secur. Commun. Netw. **5**, 69–78 (2012)
33. Zhang, C., Ho, P.H., Tapolcai, J.: On batch verification with group testing for vehicular communications. Wirel. Netw. **17**(8), 1851–1865 (2011)
34. Zhang, C., Lin, X., Lu, R., Ho, P.H.: Raise: an efficient RSU-aided message authentication scheme in vehicular communication networks. In: IEEE International Conference on Communications (2008)

35. Zhang, C., Lu, R., Lin, X., Ho, P.H., Shen, X.: An efficient identity-based batch verification scheme for vehicular sensor networks. In: The 27th Conference on Computer Communications, INFOCOM 2008. IEEE (2008)
36. Zhang, L., Li, C., Li, Y., Luo, Q., Zhu, R.: Group signature based privacy protection algorithm for mobile ad hoc network. In: 2017 IEEE International Conference on Information and Automation (ICIA) (2017)

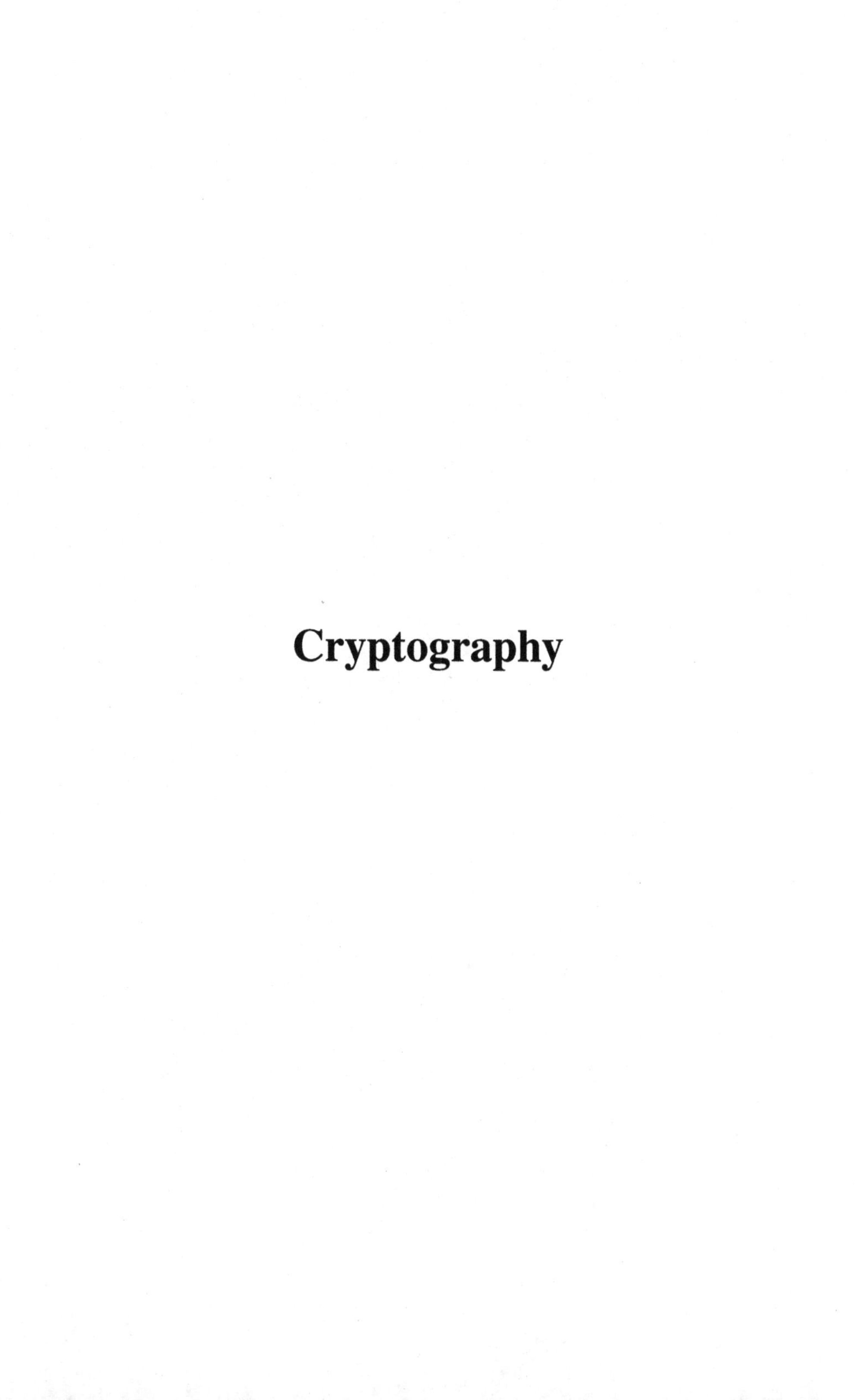

Cryptography

Optimal Generic Attack Against Basic Boneh-Boyen Signatures

Yen-Kang Fu[1], Jonathan Chang[1], and David Jao[1,2(✉)]

[1] Department of Combinatorics and Optimization, University of Waterloo, 200 University Ave. W, Waterloo, ON N2L 3G1, Canada
{ted.fu,jonathan.chang,djao}@uwaterloo.ca

[2] evolutionQ Inc., 2B-180 Columbia St. W, Waterloo, ON N2L 3L3, Canada
david.jao@evolutionq.com

Abstract. The Boneh-Boyen digital signature scheme is a pairing-based signature scheme that features short signatures consisting of one group element, the minimum possible size. In contrast to earlier short signature schemes such as Boneh-Lynn-Shacham, the Boneh-Boyen scheme achieves security without the use of random oracles, but at the cost of a non-standard mathematical assumption, the q-Strong Diffie-Hellman (or q-SDH) assumption, which is known to be less secure than discrete logarithms against generic attacks. However, unlike discrete logarithms, in which the fastest known generic attacks match the known provable lower bounds for solving generic discrete logarithms, the fastest known generic attacks against Boneh-Boyen prior to this work did not match the provable lower bounds for generically solving q-SDH instances. In this work, we demonstrate that when $p-1$ has suitably sized divisors (where p is the order of the underlying group used in the scheme), which in particular almost always occurs for cryptographic pairings instantiated from elliptic curves, Boneh-Boyen can indeed be broken in the sense of weak existential forgery under chosen-message attack (the same security definition as what was used in the original Boneh-Boyen paper) in $O(p^{\frac{1}{3}+\varepsilon})$ time using generic algorithms, matching the provable lower bound for generically solving q-SDH instances.

1 Introduction

The era of pairing-based cryptography is in many ways defined by the publication of the Boneh-Franklin identity-based encryption (IBE) scheme [6,7] and the associated Boneh-Lynn-Shacham (BLS) digital signature scheme [8,9]. These two cryptosystems presented the first compelling evidence that pairing-based cryptography could provide useful functionality beyond anything achievable using traditional means — IBE in the case of Boneh-Franklin, and short signatures in the case of BLS. In both of these schemes, security is proved in the random oracle model (ROM), which entails making a heuristic assumption that a hash function behaves like a random function. As an alternative, in order to avoid the random oracle assumption, Boneh and Boyen subsequently published an

C. Su et al. (Eds.): ISPEC 2022, LNCS 13620, pp. 505–519, 2022.
https://doi.org/10.1007/978-3-031-21280-2_28

IBE scheme [2,5] and companion signature scheme [3,4] whose security could be proved in the standard model. However, the trade-off is that the Boneh-Boyen schemes require the use of a non-standard mathematical security assumption, the so-called q-SDH assumption (Sect. 2.3). The tension between these two alternative sets of trade-offs and assumptions is documented in the "Another Look" series of papers by Koblitz and Menezes [17,18].

One piece of information that helps to determine the correct trade-off is the exact level of security of the respective schemes and assumptions against an adversary. For this purpose, we need consider only the signature schemes, since the companion IBE schemes use the same assumptions; indeed, pairs of corresponding IBE and signature schemes are directly related via a generic transformation, as described in [6] in an observation attributed to Naor. The highlight of the BLS signature scheme is that a signature requires only a single group element, which is half the number of elements for a signature in a non-pairing based signature scheme such as Schnorr [20,21]. We remark that subsequent research has shown that solving discrete logarithms on pairing-friendly curves via transfer to a finite field is easier than previously thought [1], implying that the size advantage of BLS in practice is not as great as what it would otherwise be if only generic discrete log algorithms were employed [15], which somewhat blunts the size advantage of BLS. Nevertheless, in this work, for simplicity we only consider the security of BLS and Boneh-Boyen against generic attacks, that is, attacks which work in the generic bilinear group model of [2]. These results may be viewed as conclusions about the *mathematical* security of BLS and Boneh-Boyen in the setting where we use an idealized cryptographic pairing admitting no non-generic attacks, as opposed to the concrete setting of an actual elliptic curve-based pairing where the far messier transfer attacks come into play. This setting is the natural one to use when evaluating the amount of security degradation attributable specifically to the use of the non-standard q-SDH assumption.

Boneh-Boyen signatures come in two variants, a "basic" scheme which is only weakly unforgeable (Sect. 2.1) and a "full" scheme which is strongly unforgeable. If we ignore the fact that the basic Boneh-Boyen scheme provides only weak unforgeability, the basic scheme, at least on paper, matches the BLS scheme in size efficiency, in that a basic Boneh-Boyen signature consists of a single group element. However, we have known for some time that the q-SDH problem, on which Boneh-Boyen is based, is easier than the discrete logarithm problem in a generic group. Algorithms[1] by Brown and Gallant [10] and Cheon [11,12] provide up to a square-root speedup in solving q-SDH: that is, q-SDH can be solved generically in $O(p^{\frac{1}{4}})$ time, compared to $O(p^{\frac{1}{2}})$ time for discrete log. That said, achieving the $O(p^{\frac{1}{4}})$ figure requires using a specific value of q which is itself close to $p^{\frac{1}{2}}$. In the context of Boneh-Boyen, the value of q represents the number of signing queries, which cannot be close to $p^{\frac{1}{2}}$, since performing such a large

[1] These algorithms are usually attributed to Cheon, even though Brown and Gallant were first, because Cheon was the first to apply these algorithms specifically to q-SDH.

number of signing queries would take more time than simply solving discrete log from scratch. When taking into account the cost of signing queries, the fastest known generic attack against basic Boneh-Boyen is the known-message attack of Jao and Yoshida [16], which achieves a running time of $O(p^{\frac{2}{5}})$ in most circumstances; a similar chosen-message attack against full Boneh-Boyen is also given in [16], with the same running time. This attack outperforms generic discrete log (which takes $O(p^{\frac{1}{2}})$ time), showing definitively that Boneh-Boyen and q-SDH respectively do not achieve the same level of security as BLS and discrete log in the generic bilinear group model. However, until now, there still remained a gap between the $O(p^{\frac{2}{5}})$ attack against Boneh-Boyen from [16] and the known lower bound of $O(p^{\frac{1}{3}})$, proven in [4], for solving q-SDH in a generic group (for $q < p^{\frac{1}{3}}$).

1.1 Our Contributions

In this work, we establish for the first time that the basic Boneh-Boyen scheme can be broken in $O(p^{\frac{1}{3}+\varepsilon})$ time in the generic bilinear group model, matching the $O(p^{\frac{1}{3}})$ lower bound proven in [4] and showing that this bound is achieved. That is, we present a concrete attack which breaks the weak unforgeability of basic Boneh-Boyen signatures in $O(p^{\frac{1}{3}+\varepsilon})$ time, whenever $p-1$ has a divisor of size approximately $p^{\frac{1}{3}}$. Compared to previous work [16], our result requires a divisor $d \mid p-1$ satisfying $d \approx p^{\frac{1}{3}}$, whereas [16] requires a divisor $d \mid p \pm 1$ satisfying $d \approx p^{\frac{2}{5}}$. Moreover, our result requires a chosen-message attack, compared to [16] which utilizes only a known-message attack. By choosing specific messages for our signing queries, we can exploit the algebraic structure of Boneh-Boyen signatures to speed up the reduction from weak forgery to q-SDH. Our attack uses Cheon's algorithm to solve q-SDH, and thus is considerably more powerful than a mere forgery, since Cheon's algorithm actually recovers the private key. However, Cheon's algorithm is not strictly necessary: our results also show that, in principle, any solution to the q-Cheon SDH problem (cf. Sect. 2.3) yields a basic Boneh-Boyen forgery in $O(q)$ time (improving upon the $O(q^2)$ reductions given in [4,16]), although in practice no speedups for q-SDH or q-Cheon-SDH other than Cheon's algorithm are presently known.

2 Preliminaries

2.1 Security Definitions

We begin by reviewing two security definitions used in the proof of security for the Boneh-Boyen signature. The definition of strong existential unforgeability corresponds to the standard notion of security for digital signatures used in the literature. The full Boneh-Boyen signature scheme (Sect. 3.2) satisfies strong existential unforgeability under certain assumptions. Weak existential unforgeability is a diluted version of strong existential unforgeability in which the adversary is required to commit to the list of messages used for signature queries in advance of being given the public key. The security of the basic Boneh-Boyen scheme (Sect. 3.1) is proved using weak existential unforgeability. It is important to emphasize that weak existential unforgeability is not our invention; the definition we use is identical to that of Boneh and Boyen's original paper [3,4].

Strong Existential Unforgeability. Strong existential unforgeability is defined via the following game between the challenger and an adversary $\mathcal{A}$.

1. The challenger generates a key pair (PK, SK) and gives PK to $\mathcal{A}$.
2. $\mathcal{A}$ adaptively makes up to q_S queries for signatures of messages $m_1, \ldots, m_{q_S}$ of its choice. The challenger responds to the queries with q_S valid signatures $\sigma_1, \ldots, \sigma_{q_S}$ of $m_1, \ldots, m_{q_S}$, respectively.
3. Eventually, $\mathcal{A}$ outputs a message-signature pair (m_*, σ_*), and wins the game if $(m_*, \sigma_*) \neq (m_i, \sigma_i)$ for all $i = 1, \ldots, q_S$ and Verify(m_*, σ_*, PK) $=$ `true`

Weak Existential Unforgeability. Weak existential unforgeability is defined via the following game between the challenger and an adversary $\mathcal{A}$.

1. $\mathcal{A}$ makes up to q_S queries for signatures of messages $m_1, \ldots, m_{q_S}$ of its choice.
2. The challenger generates a key pair (PK, SK) and gives PK to $\mathcal{A}$. Then the challenger responds to the queries with q_S valid signatures $\sigma_1, \ldots, \sigma_{q_S}$ of $m_1, \ldots, m_{q_S}$, respectively.
3. Eventually, $\mathcal{A}$ outputs a message-signature pair (m_*, σ_*), and wins the game if $(m_*, \sigma_*) \neq (m_i, \sigma_i)$ for all $i = 1, \ldots, q_S$ and Verify(m_*, σ_*, PK) $=$ `true`

The adversary $\mathcal{A}$'s advantage, denoted Adv Sig W($\mathcal{A}$), is defined as the probability that $\mathcal{A}$ wins the above game, where the probability is taken over random choices made by the adversary $\mathcal{A}$ and the challenger.

Our work centers entirely around the basic Boneh-Boyen scheme (Sect. 3.1), which only uses weak existential unforgeability. Hence we only use weak existential unforgeability in Definition 1.

Definition 1. *An adversary $\mathcal{A}$ can (t, q_S, ϵ)-weakly break a signature scheme if $\mathcal{A}$ runs in time at most t, makes at most q_S queries to the challenger, and* Adv Sig W($\mathcal{A}$) $\geq \epsilon$. *We say a signature scheme is (t, q_S, ϵ)-EUF-CMA (existentially unforgeable under a chosen-message attack) if there does not exist an adversary that (t, q_S, ϵ)-weakly breaks it.*

2.2 Bilinear Pairings

The Boneh-Boyen signature scheme makes use of bilinear pairings. Let $\mathbb{G}_1, \mathbb{G}_2$, and $\mathbb{G}_T$ be cyclic groups with prime order p. The operations in $\mathbb{G}_1, \mathbb{G}_2$, and $\mathbb{G}_T$ are written multiplicatively. A function $e : \mathbb{G}_1 \times \mathbb{G}_2 \rightarrow \mathbb{G}_T$ is called a bilinear pairing if it satisfies the following conditions:

- **Bilinearity:** For any $u_1, u_2, u \in \mathbb{G}_1$ and $v_1, v_2, v \in \mathbb{G}_2$,

$$e(u_1 u_2, v) = e(u_1, v) \cdot e(u_2, v)$$

$$e(u, v_1 v_2) = e(u, v_1) \cdot e(u, v_2)$$

- **Non-degeneracy:** There exists $u \in \mathbb{G}_1$ and $v \in \mathbb{G}_2$ such that $e(u, v) \neq 1$.

We assume the pairing function and the group operations are efficiently computable. The pair $(\mathbb{G}_1, \mathbb{G}_2)$ is called a bilinear group pair.

2.3 SDH Problems

q-SDH problem. Let q be a publicly known positive integer. Boneh and Boyen [4] define the q-Strong Diffie-Hellman (q-SDH) problem on the bilinear group pair $(\mathbb{G}_1, \mathbb{G}_2)$ as follows:

> Given a $(q+3)$-tuple $(g_1, g_1^x, \ldots, g_1^{x^q}, g_2, g_2^x) \in \mathbb{G}_1^{q+1} \times \mathbb{G}_2^2$ as input, output $(c, g_1^{\frac{1}{x+c}})$ for some $c \in \mathbb{Z}_p$ such that $x + c \not\equiv 0 \pmod{p}$.

For our analysis, we need a variant of the q-SDH problem in which only three powers of g_1 are given. As shown in Theorem 3 in Sect. 5, this variant is still enough to yield an attack against the Boneh-Boyen signature scheme. We call this variant the q-Cheon-SDH problem:

> Given a 5-tuple $(g_1, g_1^x, g_1^{x^q}, g_2, g_2^x) \in \mathbb{G}_1^3 \times \mathbb{G}_2^2$ as input, output $(c, g_1^{\frac{1}{x+c}})$ for some $c \in \mathbb{Z}_p$ such that $x + c \not\equiv 0 \pmod{p}$.

The advantage Adv q-SDH($\mathcal{A}$) of an adversary $\mathcal{A}$ in solving the q-SDH problem in $(\mathbb{G}_1, \mathbb{G}_2)$ is defined as

$$\text{Adv } q\text{-SDH}(\mathcal{A}) = \Pr\left[\mathcal{A}(g_1, g_1^x, \ldots, g_1^{x^q}, g_2, g_2^x) = (c, g_1^{\frac{1}{x+c}})\right]$$

where the probability is taken over random choices of generators $g_1 \in \mathbb{G}_1, g_2 \in \mathbb{G}_2$ and $x \in \mathbb{Z}_p^*$ and the random choices made by the adversary $\mathcal{A}$. Similarly, we define Adv q-Cheon-SDH($\mathcal{A}$) as the advantage of an adversary $\mathcal{A}$ in solving the q-Cheon-SDH problem.

Definition 2. *An algorithm $\mathcal{A}$ can (t, ϵ)-break the q-SDH problem in $(\mathbb{G}_1, \mathbb{G}_2)$ if $\mathcal{A}$ runs in time t and* Adv q-SDH*($\mathcal{A}$) $\geq \epsilon$. We say that the (q, t, ϵ)-SDH assumption holds in $(\mathbb{G}_1, \mathbb{G}_2)$ if there is no algorithm that (t, ϵ)-breaks the q-SDH problem in $(\mathbb{G}_1, \mathbb{G}_2)$.*

Definition 3. *An algorithm $\mathcal{A}$ can (t, ϵ)-break the q-Cheon-SDH problem in $(\mathbb{G}_1, \mathbb{G}_2)$ if $\mathcal{A}$ runs in time t and* Adv q-Cheon-SDH*($\mathcal{A}$) $\geq \epsilon$. We say that the (q, t, ϵ)-Cheon-SDH assumption holds in $(\mathbb{G}_1, \mathbb{G}_2)$ if there is no algorithm that (t, ϵ)-breaks the q-Cheon-SDH problem in $(\mathbb{G}_1, \mathbb{G}_2)$.*

3 Boneh-Boyen Signature Scheme

Let $\mathbb{G}_1, \mathbb{G}_2$ and $\mathbb{G}_T$ be cyclic groups of order p, and let $e : \mathbb{G}_1 \times \mathbb{G}_2 \to \mathbb{G}_T$ be a bilinear pairing. In [4], Boneh and Boyen present the following two versions of their signature schemes.

3.1 The Basic Signature Scheme

- **Key Generation:** KeyGen outputs random generators g_1 and g_2 of $\mathbb{G}_1$ and $\mathbb{G}_2$, respectively, and a random integer $x \in \mathbb{Z}_p^*$. Let $\zeta \leftarrow e(g_1, g_2) \in \mathbb{G}_T$. The public key is $\text{PK} = (g_1, g_2, g_2^x, \zeta)$, and the secret key is $\text{SK} = (g_1, x)$.
- **Signing:** Given a message $m \in \mathbb{Z}_p$ and a secret key SK, Sign(m, SK) outputs a signature $\sigma \leftarrow g_1^{\frac{1}{x+m}}$ where the exponent is calculated modulo p. In the event that $x + m \equiv 0 \pmod p$, Sign(m, SK) outputs $\sigma \leftarrow 1$.
- **Verification:** Verify(m, σ, PK) $=$ `true` if and only if $e(\sigma, g_2^x \cdot g_2^m) = \zeta$.

3.2 The Full Signature Scheme

- **Key Generation:** KeyGen outputs random generators g_1 and g_2 of $\mathbb{G}_1$ and $\mathbb{G}_2$, respectively, and random integers $x, y \in \mathbb{Z}_p^*$. Let $\zeta \leftarrow e(g_1, g_2) \in \mathbb{G}_T$. The public key is $\text{PK} = (g_1, g_2, g_2^x, g_2^y, \zeta)$, and the secret key is $\text{SK} = (g_1, x, y)$.
- **Signing:** Given a message $m \in \mathbb{Z}_p$ and a secret key SK, Sign(m, SK) randomly picks $r \in \mathbb{Z}_p$ such that $x + m + yr \not\equiv 0$ and calculates $\sigma \leftarrow g_1^{\frac{1}{x+m+yr}}$. The signature is (σ, r).
- **Verification:** Verify(m, (σ, r), PK) $=$ `true` if and only if $e(\sigma, g_2^x \cdot g_2^m \cdot (g_2^y)^r) = \zeta$.

In general, g_1 can be omitted from the public key with no loss of functionality.

4 Chosen Message Attack on the Basic Scheme

Proposition 1 is the main result of [16]. Using Proposition 1, the authors of [16] show that forging basic Boneh-Boyen signatures under a known-message attack, using q signing queries, reduces to solving q-SDH, via a reduction which costs $O(q^2)$ time. We show using Corollary 1 that Proposition 1 can be refined so as to yield a reduction to q-Cheon-SDH costing only $O(q)$ time, albeit under a chosen-message attack instead of a known-message attack.

Proposition 1. *Let $\mathbb{G}$ be a cyclic group of order p, let $g \in \mathbb{G}$ be a generator, and let $x \in \mathbb{Z}_p$. Let m_i for $i = 1, \ldots, d$ be distinct elements of $\mathbb{Z}_p$ such that $x + m_i \neq 0$. Then*

$$g^{\frac{x^k}{\prod_{i=1}^d (x+m_i)}} = \begin{cases} \prod_{i=1}^{d} g^{\frac{(-m_i)^k}{(x+m_i)\prod_{j\neq i}(m_j - m_i)}} & \text{for } 0 \leq k < d \\ g \cdot \prod_{i=1}^{d} g^{\frac{(-m_i)^d}{(x+m_i)\prod_{j\neq i}(m_j - m_i)}} & \text{for } k = d \\ g^x \cdot g^{-\sum_{i=1}^d m_i} \cdot \prod_{i=1}^{d} g^{\frac{(-m_i)^{d+1}}{(x+m_i)\prod_{j\neq i}(m_j - m_i)}} & \text{for } k = d+1 \end{cases}$$

Assume that all values m_i and $g^{\frac{1}{x+m_i}}$ are known. Furthermore, assume for $k = d$ and $k = d+1$ that g is known, and for $k = d+1$ that g^x is known. Then calculating $g^{\frac{x^k}{\prod_{i=1}^d (x+m_i)}}$ for a single k takes $\Theta(dT + d^2 T_p)$ time, where T is the maximum time needed for a single exponentiation in $\mathbb{G}$, and T_p is the maximum time needed for an operation in $\mathbb{Z}_p$. Calculating all of $g^{\frac{1}{\prod_{i=1}^d (x+m_i)}}, g^{\frac{x}{\prod_{i=1}^d (x+m_i)}}, \ldots, g^{\frac{x^{d+1}}{\prod_{i=1}^d (x+m_i)}}$ takes $\Theta(d^2 T)$ time.

Proof. [16, Prop. 4.1].

Lemma 1. *Let $\xi \in \mathbb{Z}_p$ and $m_i = \xi^i$ for $i = 1, 2, \ldots, d$. Suppose the m_i's are all distinct. For $1 \leq i \leq d$, define*

$$D_i = \prod_{\substack{j=1 \\ j \neq i}}^{d} (m_j - m_i)$$

Then, for all $0 < i < d$,

$$D_{i+1} = D_i \cdot \xi^d \cdot \frac{1 - \xi^i}{\xi^{d+1} - \xi^{i+1}}$$

Proof. We write

$$\begin{aligned} D_i &= (m_1 - m_i) \cdots (m_{i-1} - m_i)(m_{i+1} - m_i) \cdots (m_d - m_i) \\ D_{i+1} &= (m_1 - m_{i+1}) \cdots (m_i - m_{i+1})(m_{i+2} - m_{i+1}) \cdots (m_d - m_{i+1}) \end{aligned}$$

Note that

$$\begin{aligned} (m_2 - m_{i+1}) &= (\xi^2 - \xi^{i+1}) = \xi(\xi - \xi^i) = \xi(m_1 - m_i) \\ (m_3 - m_{i+1}) &= (\xi^3 - \xi^{i+1}) = \xi(\xi^2 - \xi^i) = \xi(m_2 - m_i) \\ &\vdots \\ (m_i - m_{i+1}) &= (\xi^i - \xi^{i+1}) = \xi(\xi^{i-1} - \xi^i) = \xi(m_{i-1} - m_i) \\ (m_{i+2} - m_{i+1}) &= (\xi^{i+2} - \xi^{i+1}) = \xi(\xi^{i+1} - \xi^i) = \xi(m_{i+1} - m_i) \\ &\vdots \\ (m_d - m_{i+1}) &= (\xi^d - \xi^{i+1}) = \xi(\xi^{d-1} - \xi^i) = \xi(m_{d-1} - m_i) \end{aligned}$$

Hence every factor of D_{i+1} except for $(m_1 - m_{i+1})$ is equal to ξ times one of the factors of D_i. The expression D_{i+1} consists of $d-1$ factors, of which $d-2$ of the factors are equal to ξ times a factor of D_i. The only factor of D_{i+1} not paired up with a factor of D_i is $(m_1 - m_{i+1})$, and the only factor of D_i not paired up with a factor of D_{i+1} is $(m_d - m_i)$. Therefore the quotient D_{i+1}/D_i is equal to

$$\frac{D_{i+1}}{D_i} = \xi^{d-2} \frac{m_1 - m_{i+1}}{m_d - m_i} = \xi^{d-2} \frac{\xi - \xi^{i+1}}{\xi^d - \xi^i} = \xi^{d-2} \cdot \frac{\xi}{\xi} \cdot \frac{\xi - \xi^{i+1}}{\xi^d - \xi^i} = \xi^d \frac{1 - \xi^i}{\xi^{d+1} - \xi^{i+1}}.$$

Corollary 1. *In Proposition 1, suppose that there exists $\xi \in \mathbb{Z}_p$ such that $m_i = \xi^i$ for $i = 1, 2, \ldots, d$, and the m_i's are distinct. Then calculating $g^{\frac{x^k}{\prod_{i=1}^d (x+m_i)}}$ for a single $k = 0, 1, 2, \ldots d$ takes $\Theta(d(T + T_p))$ time.*

Proof. We proceed as follows, for $0 \leq k < d$:

1. Calculate $m_1 = \xi^1$, $m_2 = \xi^2$, ..., $m_d = \xi^d$, and store these values. This calculation takes d multiplications.
2. Calculate $D_1 = \prod_{j=2}^d (m_j - m_1)$. This calculation takes $d - 1$ subtractions and $d - 2$ multiplications.
3. Calculate

$$D_2 = D_1 \cdot m_d \cdot \frac{1 - m_1}{\xi \cdot m_d - m_2}$$
$$D_3 = D_2 \cdot m_d \cdot \frac{1 - m_2}{\xi \cdot m_d - m_3}$$
$$\vdots$$
$$D_d = D_{d-1} \cdot m_d \cdot \frac{1 - m_{d-1}}{\xi \cdot m_d - m_d}$$

   Each row above takes 2 subtractions, 3 multiplications, and one division. There are $d - 1$ rows, so the total calculation takes $2(d - 1)$ subtractions, $3(d - 1)$ multiplications, and $d - 1$ divisions.
4. Define $e_i = \frac{(-m_i)^k}{D_i}$, for $i = 1$ to d. Calculate all of the e_i. Calculating a single e_i requires one exponentiation mod p and one division. Calculating all of the e_i's requires d exponentiations mod p and d divisions.
5. Define $f_i = \left(g^{1/(x+m_i)}\right)^{e_i}$, for $i = 1$ to d. Calculate all of the f_i. Calculating a single f_i requires one group exponentiation. Calculating all of the f_i requires d group exponentiations.
6. Calculate $g^{\frac{x^k}{\prod_{i=1}^d (x+m_i)}} = \prod_{i=1}^d f_i$. This calculation takes $d - 1$ group multiplications.

For $k = d$, we need to compute $g \cdot \prod_{i=1}^d f_i$ instead of $\prod_{i=1}^d f_i$ in the last step. The computation (and calculation of running time) is otherwise the same.

In the proof of Corollary 1, it is essential that the m_i's are chosen to equal ξ^i. Otherwise the relationship in Lemma 1 does not hold, and it is not obvious in this case how to calculate all of the D_i's using only $O(d)$ operations. A naive approach to calculating all the D_i's requires $O(d^2)$ multiplications and $O(d^2 T_p)$ total cost, which is how the $\Theta(dT + d^2 T_p)$ time in the statement of Proposition 1 was originally obtained in [16].

4.1 Security of the Basic Signature Scheme

In this subsection, we show that weak existential forgery of the basic scheme under a chosen-message attack reduces to the q-Cheon-SDH problem. Like [16,

Theorem 4.3], Theorem 1 is a converse of [4, Lemma 9], but compared to [16, Theorem 4.3] and [4, Lemma 9], Theorem 1 features an improved reduction time of $\Theta(qT)$ to the q-Cheon-SDH problem, which is a harder problem, compared to $\Theta(q^2T)$ to the q-SDH problem for the prior results, using Corollary 1 to achieve this improvement.

Theorem 1. *If there is an algorithm that (t', ϵ')-breaks the q-Cheon-SDH problem, then we can (t, q_S, ϵ)-weakly break the basic Boneh-Boyen signature scheme provided that*

$$t \geq t' + \Theta(qT),\ q_S \geq q, \textit{and } \epsilon \leq \frac{p-1-q}{p-1}\epsilon'$$

Proof. Let $\mathcal{A}$ be an algorithm that (t', ϵ')-breaks the q-Cheon-SDH problem. We will show that the adversary $\mathcal{B}$ can perform a weak existential forgery on the basic scheme of the signature under a chosen-message attack.

The adversary $\mathcal{B}$ begins by setting $m_i = \xi^i$ for $i = 1, \ldots, q_S$, where $q_S \geq q$, and $\xi \in \mathbb{Z}_p$ is chosen so that the m_i are distinct. Given a public key (g_1, g_2, g_2^x, ζ), along with corresponding valid signatures $(\sigma_1, \ldots, \sigma_{q_S}) = (g_1^{\frac{1}{x+m_1}}, \ldots, g_1^{\frac{1}{x+m_{q_S}}})$ for the m_i, the adversary $\mathcal{B}$ calculates $h_k \leftarrow g_1^{\frac{x^k}{\prod_{i=1}^q (x+m_i)}}$ for $k = 0, 1$, and q. Using Corollary 1, this calculation takes $O(qT)$ time. Then $\mathcal{B}$ chooses $\alpha \in \mathbb{Z}_p^*$ at random[2] and runs the algorithm $\mathcal{A}$ on inputs $(h_0^\alpha, h_1^\alpha, h_q^\alpha, g_2, g_2^x)$. Since this input is a valid q-Cheon-SDH instance, $\mathcal{A}$ outputs $(m_*, g_1^{\frac{\alpha}{(x+m_*)\prod_{i=1}^q (x+m_i)}})$ for some $m_* \in \mathbb{Z}_p$ with probability ϵ'. We then remove the α from the exponent in the second coordinate of the output by raising that second coordinate to the power of $\alpha^{-1} \bmod p$.

We note that the distribution of $(h_0^\alpha, h_1^\alpha, h_q^\alpha, g_2, g_2^x)$ above is identical to the distribution of uniformly random q-Cheon-SDH inputs, thanks to the inclusion of the random α. From the point of view of $\mathcal{A}$, the value of ξ does not influence the input distribution that it sees. Hence $\mathcal{A}$ has no better than random chance of choosing m_* to be one of $m_1, \ldots, m_q$. Thus, $m_* \neq m_i$ for all $i = 1, \ldots q$ with probability at least $\frac{p-1-q}{p-1}$. In the unlikely scenario that $m_* = m_i$ for some i, the algorithm $\mathcal{B}$ simply aborts. Otherwise, by Proposition 1,

$$\begin{aligned} &\frac{1}{(x+m_*)\prod_{i=1}^q (x+m_i)} \\ &= \frac{1}{(x+m_*)\prod_{i=1}^q (m_i - m_*)} + \sum_{j=1}^q \frac{1}{(x+m_j)\prod_{i\neq j}(m_i - m_j)} \end{aligned}$$

Using this equation, $\mathcal{B}$ can calculate $\sigma_* = g_1^{\frac{1}{x+m_*}}$ as follows:

$$\sigma_* \leftarrow \left[g_1^{\frac{1}{(x+m_*)\prod_{i=1}^q (x+m_i)}} \Big/ \prod_{j=1}^q \sigma_j^{\prod_{i\neq j}(m_i - m_j)} \right]^{\prod_{i=1}^q (m_i - m_*)}$$

[2] In fact, simply using $\alpha = 1$ works well enough in practice. The only reason we use a random α is to randomize the input distribution, as explained in the next paragraph.

and then (m_*, σ_*) is an existential forgery for the basic scheme.

Note that calculating all of $\prod_{i \neq j}(m_i - m_j)$ takes time $O(qT_p)$, where T_p is the maximum time needed for one operation in $\mathbb{Z}_p$. Calculating all of $\sigma_j^{\prod_{i \neq j}(m_i - m_j)}$ takes time $O(qT)$. Calculating

$$\left[g_1^{\frac{1}{(x+m_*)\prod_{i=1}^{q}(x+m_i)}} \Big/ \prod_{j=1}^{q} \sigma_j^{\prod_{i \neq j}(m_i - m_j)} \right]$$

takes time $O(qT)$. Calculating, $\prod_{i=1}^{q}(m_i - m_*)$, takes time $O(qT_p)$. Given that $T_p \ll T$, and accounting for the t' time cost of $\mathcal{A}$, we find that $\mathcal{B}$ can perform a weak existential forgery in time t as long as $t \geq t' + \Theta(qT)$.

The proof above requires knowledge of g_1. This requirement is not a problem, since g_1 is published as part of the Boneh-Boyen public key. However, it is possible to construct a working variant of Boneh-Boyen in which g_1 is not published. In case g_1 is unknown, the theorem remains valid, provided that q is replaced by $q+1$ in the inequalities. In this case $\mathcal{B}$ uses $q+1$ signature queries and calculates $h'_k \leftarrow g_1^{\frac{x^k}{\prod_{i=1}^{q+1}(x+m_i)}}$ for $k = 0, 1$, and q in place of h_0, h_1, and h_q.

5 Cheon's Algorithm

Cheon [11,12] presents an algorithm which computes the secret exponent x from the input of an instance of the q-Cheon-SDH problem. Portions of this algorithm were also independently discovered by Brown and Gallant in the context of a different problem. In what follows, we refer to this algorithm as Cheon's algorithm. Specifically, Cheon proves the following:

Theorem 2. *Let $\mathbb{G}$ be a cyclic group of prime order p with g being a generator. Let T denote the maximum time needed for one exponentiation in $\mathbb{G}$.*

1. *Let d divide $p-1$. Given g, g^x, and g^{x^d}, the value of x can be recovered in time $O((\sqrt{p/d} + \sqrt{d})T)$.*
2. *Let d divide $p+1$. Given $g, g^x, g^{x^2}, \ldots, g^{x^{2d}}$, the value of x can be recovered in time $O((\sqrt{p/d} + d)T)$.*

Note that if $q \geq d$ in the first case or $q \geq 2d$ in the second case, then Cheon's algorithm can solve the q-SDH problem by revealing the secret exponent x. We show in this section that the algorithm can be applied to find the secret exponent in the basic scheme of the Boneh-Boyen signature over a bilinear group pair $(\mathbb{G}_1, \mathbb{G}_2)$.

Theorem 3. *Let T denote the maximum time needed to perform one group exponentiation in $\mathbb{G}_1$. Let $m_i = \xi^i$ for $i = 1, 2, \ldots, d+1$ or $i = 1, 2, \ldots, 2d+1$ respectively, where $\xi \in \mathbb{Z}_p$ and the m_i are distinct. Let d divide $p-1$. In the basic Boneh-Boyen scheme, if the adversary $\mathcal{A}$ queries for signatures of $m_i = \xi^i$ for $i = 1, 2, \ldots, d+1$, then the private exponent x can be computed in time $O((\sqrt{p/d} + d)T)$.*

Proof. Let d be a positive divisor of $p-1$. We construct an algorithm $\mathcal{A}$ which recovers the private exponent of the signature scheme under a chosen-message attack, using Cheon's algorithm. To start, $\mathcal{A}$ computes a primitive root ξ of $\mathbb{Z}_p$, which can be done by factoring $p-1$. Although factoring is usually treated as an expensive operation, in this case the cost of factoring is dominated by the cost of what follows. Given a public key (g_1, g_2, g_2^x, ζ), the algorithm $\mathcal{A}$ then queries for signatures for $m_1 = \xi, m_2 = \xi^2, ..., m_{d+1} = \xi^{d+1}$, upon which $\mathcal{A}$ obtains $d+1$ valid signatures $\sigma_1, \sigma_2, ..., \sigma_{d+1}$, where $\sigma_i = g_1^{\frac{1}{x+m_i}} = g_1^{\frac{1}{x+\xi^i}}$. Using Corollary 1, the algorithm $\mathcal{A}$ calculates

$$g_1^{\frac{1}{(x+m_1)\cdots(x+m_{d+1})}}, g_1^{\frac{x}{(x+m_1)\cdots(x+m_{d+1})}}, g_1^{\frac{x^d}{(x+m_1)\cdots(x+m_{d+1})}}$$

Then, it runs Cheon's algorithm in $\mathbb{G}_1$ with these inputs, and obtains x as output.

Since $g_1^{\frac{1}{(x+m_1)\cdots(x+m_{d+1})}}, g_1^{\frac{x}{(x+m_1)\cdots(x+m_{d+1})}}$ and $g_1^{\frac{x^d}{(x+m_1)\cdots(x+m_{d+1})}}$ together take time $\Theta(dT)$ to calculate, and Cheon's algorithm has a running time of $\Theta((\sqrt{p/d}+\sqrt{d})T)$, the overall running time is $\Theta((\sqrt{p/d}+d)T)$

6 Runtime Analysis

In this section, we will use Theorem 3 to compute the complexity, both experimentally and theoretically, of recovering the private key of a Boneh-Boyen signature for $d \mid p-1$. In this analysis, we only consider the case where g_1 is not included in the public key, which requires $d+1$ valid signatures. For convenience, we refer to the algorithm of Theorem 3 as the SDH algorithm.

6.1 Experimental Analysis

We implemented the SDH algorithm on 5 different Barreto-Naehrig curves with their corresponding p ranging from 30 to 50 bits. Barreto-Naehrig curves were chosen because they are suitable for pairing-based short signature schemes and easy to implement. We also implemented the Cheon's algorithm with the Pollard's kangaroo variant instead of the baby-step-giant-step variant or other variants such as Kozaki et al. [19], in order to save memory. All calculations were performed on an Intel(R) Xeon(R) Gold 6254 CPU at 3.10 GHz.

The implementation of the SDH algorithm is straightforward. We wrote a program in SageMath and used functions in Sage's elliptic curve library to compute the triplet (g, g^x, g^{x^d}) using the method described in Corollary 1. The program then runs the Cheon's algorithm with the Pollard's kangaroo variant. In our implementation, the algorithm has 2 kangaroos, each having 9 possible steps in their random walk, with mean step size $\sqrt{p/d}$ in the first half of the algorithm. We also defined the distinguished points on the elliptic curve to constitute $\log(\frac{p}{d})/\sqrt{\frac{p}{d}}$ of all points, which is the optimal choice [13]. After two kangaroos collide, we can compute the value of k_0. In the second half of the algorithm, we can analogously compute the value of k_1 and the secret key $k = k_0 + k_1 \cdot \frac{p}{d}$.

For each curve, we performed at least 20 trials and the result taken is the average over all the trials. Although the optimal value of d is not always a divisor of $p-1$, we can always find nearby divisors and use them to estimate the hypothetical performance [14]. Figure 1 compares the measured performance of the SDH algorithm based on our chosen-message attack, with the generic Pollard's rho method for discrete log in which we simply input the public verification key into the generic Pollard's rho algorithm implementation built into Sage. Based on our results, the SDH algorithm outperforms Pollard's rho method when d is greater than 35. The absolute magnitude of the ratio between the two running times may not be as large as what is predicted by comparing $p^{1/2}$ and $p^{1/3}$, owing to the fact that our SDH kangaroo algorithm may not be as optimized as SAGE's built-in discrete log algorithm. What is most important, however, is that the limited data points available have slopes (on a log-log plot) consistent with the change in exponent from 1/2 to 1/3.

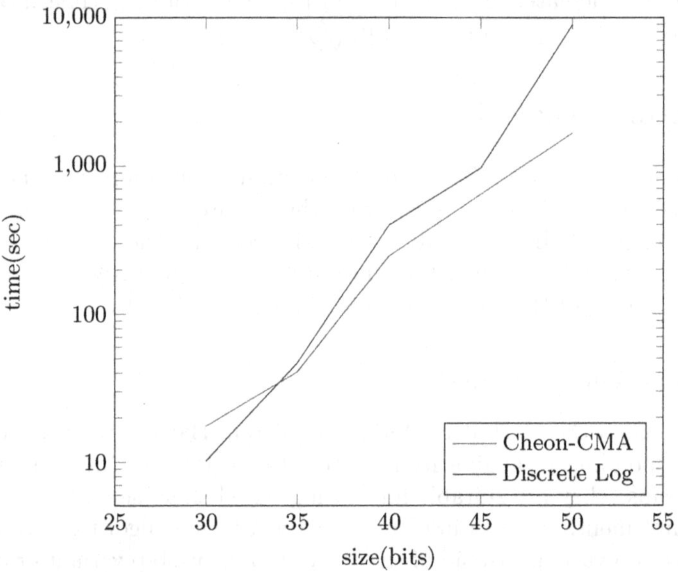

Fig. 1. Comparison of running times for our SDH-based chosen-message attack and generic Pollard's rho, on an Intel(R) Xeon(R) Gold 6254 CPU at 3.10 GHz. Vertical axis represents the amount of wall-clock time required in order to recover the private signing key.

6.2 Theoretical Analysis

Now we calculate the theoretical cost of computing a Boneh-Boyen private key using the SDH algorithm. From Theorem 3, the SDH algorithm has a running time of $O((\sqrt{p/d}+d)T)$, for the $p-1$ variant. This cost is minimized by taking $d=\Theta(p^{\frac{1}{3}})$, yielding a corresponding time complexity of $\Theta(p^{\frac{1}{3}}\cdot T)=\Theta(p^{\frac{1}{3}}(\log p)\cdot T_p)$ for the SDH algorithm. We remark that this time complexity matches the $\Omega(\sqrt[3]{p})$ generic lower bound proved in [4, Corollary 13]. Our result is the first to match this lower bound.

Our algorithm requires choosing a divisor d of $p-1$ which satisfies $d=\Theta(p^{\frac{1}{3}})$. In principle, such a divisor is not necessarily guaranteed to exist. However, in [16], the authors observe that a result of [14] implies that asymptotically all but a small proportion of random primes p admit divisors d for $p-1$ of a size suitable for our algorithm. Therefore, pairing-friendly curves are unlikely to resist our SDH algorithm unless specifically chosen with this property in mind.

7 Conclusion

In this paper, we showed that the existential forgery of a signature under a chosen-message attack for the basic Boneh-Boyen signature scheme can be reduced to the q-SDH problem via an algorithm with time complexity linear in q. This reduction represents an improvement from [16] and for the first time establishes an equivalence between the q-SDH assumption and the security of the basic Boneh-Boyen signature scheme which matches known generic lower bounds. Using Cheon's algorithm, the reduction allows us to recover the secret key used in Boneh-Boyen signatures in time $O(p^{\frac{1}{3}+\epsilon})$ for groups of order p whenever $p-1$ satisfies certain divisibility properties.

Jao and Yoshida in [16] also present a reduction for the case where we have a divisor d of $p+1$, using the second case of Theorem 2. Corollary 1 cannot be used in this case to obtain a faster reduction, since Corollary 1 doesn't asymptotically speed up the case where we need to compute an entire sequence of q-SDH inputs instead of just three q-Cheon-SDH inputs. We leave this case to future work.

Our results apply only to the basic Boneh-Boyen signature scheme. The authors in [16] also analyze the full Boneh-Boyen scheme, and show that a chosen-message attack on the full scheme can recover the private key in $O(p^{\frac{2}{5}+\epsilon})$ time. In this case there still remains a gap in complexity between the fastest known attack and the currently provable generic lower bound. It is not clear whether our approach can lead to improved attacks against the full scheme. The main obstacle is that in the full Boneh-Boyen scheme, the signer chooses a random integer r in order to randomize the signature result, and (assuming that the message m to be signed remains constant) this random integer r plays a role similar to the role played by m in the basic scheme. It is therefore easy to extend a known-message attack on the basic scheme to a chosen-message attack on the full scheme, as was done in [16]: simply "choose" to sign the same message repeatedly and then treat the resulting random r values as if they were known messages in the basic scheme. However, it is not easily possible to extend a chosen-message attack on the basic scheme, since one cannot control the random r values that the signer selects. For the time being, we leave this question to future work.

Acknowledgments. This work is supported by research funding from NSERC, CryptoWorks21, Public Works and Government Services Canada, Canada First Research Excellence Fund, and the Royal Bank of Canada.

References

1. Barbulescu, R., Gaudry, P., Kleinjung, T.: The tower number field sieve. In: Iwata, T., Cheon, J.H. (eds.) ASIACRYPT 2015. LNCS, vol. 9453, pp. 31–55. Springer, Heidelberg (2015). https://doi.org/10.1007/978-3-662-48800-3_2
2. Boneh, D., Boyen, X.: Efficient selective-ID secure identity-based encryption without random oracles. In: Cachin, C., Camenisch, J.L. (eds.) EUROCRYPT 2004. LNCS, vol. 3027, pp. 223–238. Springer, Heidelberg (2004). https://doi.org/10.1007/978-3-540-24676-3_14
3. Boneh, D., Boyen, X.: Short signatures without random oracles. In: Cachin, C., Camenisch, J.L. (eds.) EUROCRYPT 2004. LNCS, vol. 3027, pp. 56–73. Springer, Heidelberg (2004). https://doi.org/10.1007/978-3-540-24676-3_4
4. Boneh, D., Boyen, X.: Short signatures without random oracles and the SDH assumption in bilinear groups. J. Cryptol. **21**(2), 149–177 (2008). https://doi.org/10.1007/s00145-007-9005-7
5. Boneh, D., Boyen, X.: Efficient selective identity-based encryption without random oracles. J. Cryptol. **24**(4), 659–693 (2011). https://doi.org/10.1007/s00145-010-9078-6
6. Boneh, D., Franklin, M.: Identity-based encryption from the weil pairing. In: Kilian, J. (ed.) CRYPTO 2001. LNCS, vol. 2139, pp. 213–229. Springer, Heidelberg (2001). https://doi.org/10.1007/3-540-44647-8_13
7. Boneh, D., Franklin, M.: Identity-based encryption from the Weil pairing. SIAM J. Comput. **32**(3), 586–615 (2003). https://doi.org/10.1007/3-540-44647-8_13
8. Boneh, D., Lynn, B., Shacham, H.: Short signatures from the weil pairing. In: Boyd, C. (ed.) ASIACRYPT 2001. LNCS, vol. 2248, pp. 514–532. Springer, Heidelberg (2001). https://doi.org/10.1007/3-540-45682-1_30
9. Boneh, D., Lynn, B., Shacham, H.: Short signatures from the Weil pairing. J. Cryptol. **17**(4), 297–319 (2004). https://doi.org/10.1007/s00145-004-0314-9
10. Brown D.R., Gallant, P.G.: The static Diffie-Hellman problem. Cryptology ePrint Archive, Paper 2004/306
11. Cheon, J.H.: Security analysis of the strong Diffie-Hellman problem. In: Vaudenay, S. (ed.) EUROCRYPT 2006. LNCS, vol. 4004, pp. 1–11. Springer, Heidelberg (2006). https://doi.org/10.1007/11761679_1
12. Cheon, J.H., Kim, T., Song, Y.: The discrete logarithm problem with auxiliary inputs, pp 71–92. De Gruyter (2014)
13. Cohen, H., et al.: Handbook of Elliptic and Hyperelliptic Curve Cryptography. CRC Press, Boca Raton (2005)
14. Ford, K.: The distribution of integers with a divisor in a given interval. Ann. Math. **168**(2), 367–433 (2008)
15. Guillevic, A.: A short-list of pairing-friendly curves resistant to special TNFS at the 128-bit security level. In: Kiayias, A., Kohlweiss, M., Wallden, P., Zikas, V. (eds.) PKC 2020. LNCS, vol. 12111, pp. 535–564. Springer, Cham (2020). https://doi.org/10.1007/978-3-030-45388-6_19
16. Jao, D., Yoshida, K.: Boneh-Boyen signatures and the strong Diffie-Hellman problem. In: Shacham, H., Waters, B. (eds.) Pairing 2009. LNCS, vol. 5671, pp. 1–16. Springer, Heidelberg (2009). https://doi.org/10.1007/978-3-642-03298-1_1

17. Koblitz, N., Menezes, A.: Another look at generic groups. Adv. Math. Commun. **1**(1), 13–28 (2007)
18. Koblitz, N., Menezes, A.: The brave new world of bodacious assumptions in cryptography. Not. Am. Math. Soc. **57**(3), 357–365 (2010)
19. Kozaki, S., Kutsuma, T., Matsuo, K.: Remarks on Cheon's algorithms for pairing-related problems. In: Takagi, T., Okamoto, T., Okamoto, E., Okamoto, T. (eds.) Pairing 2007. LNCS, vol. 4575, pp. 302–316. Springer, Heidelberg (2007). https://doi.org/10.1007/978-3-540-73489-5_17
20. Schnorr, C.P.: Efficient identification and signatures for smart cards. In: Brassard, G. (ed.) CRYPTO 1989. LNCS, vol. 435, pp. 239–252. Springer, New York (1990). https://doi.org/10.1007/0-387-34805-0_22
21. Schnorr, C.P.: Efficient signature generation by smart cards. J. Cryptology **4**(3), 161–174 (1991). https://doi.org/10.1007/BF00196725

Differential Cryptanalysis of Salsa20 Based on Comprehensive Analysis of PNBs

Nasratullah Ghafoori[1(✉)] and Atsuko Miyaji[1,2(✉)]

[1] Osaka University, 2-1 Yamadaoka, Suita-shi, Osaka, Japan
ghafoori@cy2sec.comm.eng.osaka-u.ac.jp, miyaji@comm.eng.osaka-u.ac.jp
[2] Japan Advanced Institute of Science and Technology, Nomi, Japan

Abstract. This paper focuses on the differential cryptanalysis of the Salsa20 stream cipher. The existing differential cryptanalysis approaches first study the differential bias of the Salsa20 stream cipher and then search for *probabilistic neutral bits* (PNBs). However, the differential bias and the set of PNBs obtained in this method are not always the optimal solution. To figure out a better solution, we apply the *differential cryptanalysis based on the comprehensive analysis of PNBs* on the reduced-round Salsa20 introduced in [19]. At first, we comprehensively analyze the neutrality measure of all keybits concerning all output differential $\mathcal{OD}$ bits. Afterward, we select the $\mathcal{OD}$ bit position with the best neutrality measure and look for the corresponding input differential $\mathcal{ID}$ with the best differential bias. Taking everything into account, the proposed approach could be used to attack Salsa20/8 with a time complexity of $2^{144.75}$ and a data complexity of $2^{55.74}$.

Keywords: Stream cipher · Salsa20 · Differential cryptanalysis · PNBs

1 Introduction

1.1 Background

Salsa20 stream cipher was designed by Daniel J. Bernstein in April 2005 [2]. It has a 256-bit security level against key-recovery attacks. The Salsa20 allows smaller key sizes, such as 128-bit security, as an option. It is constructed based on the *Addition, Rotation,* and *exclusive-OR* called ARX structure. The ARX structure security leans on the modular addition, which generates the non-linearity. The designer submitted the 20-round Salsa20 stream cipher to the ECRYPT Stream Cipher Project, eSTREAM [10], as a candidate for stream ciphers for software applications with high throughput requirements and hardware applications with restricted resources. The eSTREAM portfolio was completed in September 2008, and eventually, the 12-round Salsa20, Salsa20/12, was selected as one of the finalists for the eSTREAM software portfolio. Since its release in 2005, several types of research have been conducted on the security evaluations

C. Su et al. (Eds.): ISPEC 2022, LNCS 13620, pp. 520–536, 2022.
https://doi.org/10.1007/978-3-031-21280-2_29

of Salsa20 [1,4–9,11–13,16,18,20,21] . The most consequential of these existing studies is the differential attack based on a concept called *probabilistic neutral bits* (PNBs), proposed by Aumasson et al. at FSE 2008 [1]. PNB is a concept that divides secret keybits into two subsets of significant keybits m and non-significant keybits n. To decrease the complexity of the attack, we have to study the PNBs in such a way as to reduce the elements in significant keybits subset m. Thus, it is a crucial task to analyze PNBs in detail for the differential attacks on Salsa20. The author in [1] first searched for the input/output differential pair with the best differential bias; then, based on the obtained $\mathcal{ID}, \mathcal{OD}$ pair, they divided secret keybits into two sets by applying the concept of PNBs; finally, they performed a differential attack on the 8-round version of Salsa20, Salsa20/8, with a time complexity of 2^{251} and data complexity of 2^{31}. Thenceforth, several studies have been reported on the improvements of their proposed attack [5,8,12,16,20]. To the best of our knowledge, the best single bit differential attack on Salsa20/8 with a time complexity of $2^{243.67}$, was proposed by Dey[1] and Sarkar [8]. As mentioned, the existing differential attacks on Salsa20 have focused on searching for the input/output differential pair with the best differential bias. As the time and data complexities of attack is affected the number of *Probabilistic Neutral Bits* and differential bias.Thus, this implies that its necessary to study the conditions that can improve the differential bias and reduce the number of significant bits. In this study, we focus on conditions that can increase the number of PNBs and reduce the overall complexity of the attack.

1.2 Our Contributions

In this study, for the first time, we apply the *differential cryptanalysis based on comprehensive analysis of PNBs* on the reduced round of Salsa20. This study first deeply investigates the *PNB* values, then looks for differential bias. To further explore, the attack could be applied on the reduced-round Salsa20 by (1) comprehensively analyzing the output differential $\mathcal{OD}$ bit position with the highest average neutral measures considering 256 keybit and (2) searching for the input differential $\mathcal{ID}$ bit position with the best differential bias in the obtained output differential $\mathcal{OD}$ bit position. The contributions of this work are summarized below:

- Through an extensive analysis of PNBs, we illustrate the distribution of neutral measures for different internal rounds. Moreover, we show that the neutral measure varies greatly depending on the output differential bit position, not on the input differential bit position. To be precise, we find that the $\Delta_0^{(5)}[18]$ of Salsa20/8 has the best average neutral measure.
- By analyzing the input differential bit at the obtained output differential bit position in detail, we found the $\Delta_6^{(0)}[31]$ with the best differential bias.

[1] The [9] proposed an attack with a lower time complexity than [8]. However the nature of attack in [9] is different.

Table 1. Summary of the existing attacks on Salsa20 with 256 keybit security.

Target	Time	Data	Reference
Salsa20/7	2^{151}	2^{26}	[1]
	2^{148}	2^{24}	[20]
	2^{137}	2^{61}	[5]
Salsa20/8	2^{251}	2^{31}	[1]
	2^{250}	2^{27}	[20]
	$2^{245.5}$	$2^{22.45}$	[16]
	$2^{244.9}$	2^{96}	[5]
	$2^{243.6}$	$2^{30.4}$	[8]
	$2^{193.58}$	Unreported	[9]
	$2^{144.75}$	$2^{55.74}$	This work

- Based on the combination of the obtained differential bias at specific $\mathcal{ID}, \mathcal{OD}$ position ($\Delta_6^{(0)}[31]$, $\Delta_0^{(5)}[18]$), and PNBs, we present a differential attack on the Salsa20/8 with a time complexity of $2^{144.75}$ and data complexity of $2^{55.74}$, which is the best single bit differential attack reported yet. We improved the differential attack on the Salsa20/8 stream cipher by a factor of $2^{98.95}$. One can use our proposed cryptanalysis method to attack Salsa20/7 or lower rounds. However, in this paper, we focused only on Salsa20/8 (Table 1).

1.3 Organization of the Paper

The remainder of this paper is structured as follows. In Sect. 2, we briefly describe the specification of the Salsa20. In Sect. 3, we review generic techniques of differential cryptanalysis on Salsa20 stream cipher. In Sect. 4, we explain the comprehensive analysis of PNBs and show the experimental results. In Sect. 5, we conduct an attack on Salsa20/8 with our proposed approach and present the attack complexity. Finally, Sect. 6 concludes this paper.

2 Specification of Salsa20 and Preliminaries

Salsa20 stream cipher consists of the following three steps to generate a keystream block of 16 words, where each word size is 32 bits (Table 2):

Step 1. The initial state matrix $X^{(0)}$ of order 4×4 is initialized from a 256-bit secret key $k = (k_0, k_1, \ldots, k_7)$, a 64-bit nonce $v = (v_0, v_1)$, a 64-bit block counter $t = (t_0, t_1)$, and four 32-bit constants $c = (c_0, c_1, c_2, c_3)$, such as $c_0 = $ 0x61707865, $c_1 = $ 0x3320646e, $c_2 = $ 0x79622d32, and $c_3 = $ 0x6b206574. After the initialization, we obtain the following initial state matrix $X^{(0)}$:

Table 2. Notations

Notation	Description
X	The Salsa20 matrix of 4×4 with 16 words of 32 bit each
$X^{(0)}$	The initial state matrix of Salsa20
$X'^{(0)}$	The associate matrix with a single bit difference at $x_{i,j}$ position
$X^{(R)}$	The matrix after Salsa20 R rounds
$X^{(r)}$	The matrix after Salsa20 r rounds where $R > r$ (internal round)
$x_i^{(R)}$	The ith word of state matrix $X^{(R)}$
$x_{i,j}^{(R)}$	The jth bit of ith word of matrix $X^{(R)}$
$x + y$	The word-wise addition of word x and y *modulo* 2^{32}
$x \bigoplus y$	Bit-wise XOR operation of the word x and y
$x \lll n$	The left rotation of word x by n bits
Δx	The XOR difference of word x and x' defined as $\Delta x = x \bigoplus x'$
$\varepsilon_e, \varepsilon_a$	The forward and backward differential bias of Salsa20 respectively

$$X^{(0)} = \begin{pmatrix} x_0^{(0)} & x_1^{(0)} & x_2^{(0)} & x_3^{(0)} \\ x_4^{(0)} & x_5^{(0)} & x_6^{(0)} & x_7^{(0)} \\ x_8^{(0)} & x_9^{(0)} & x_{10}^{(0)} & x_{11}^{(0)} \\ x_{12}^{(0)} & x_{13}^{(0)} & x_{14}^{(0)} & x_{15}^{(0)} \end{pmatrix} = \begin{pmatrix} c_0 & k_0 & k_1 & k_2 \\ k_3 & c_1 & v_0 & v_1 \\ t_0 & t_1 & c_2 & k_4 \\ k_5 & k_6 & k_7 & c_3 \end{pmatrix}.$$

Step 2. The round function of Salsa20 consists of four computations of the so-called quarter-round function. According to the procedure of the quarter-round function, a vector $(x_a^{(r)}, x_b^{(r)}, x_c^{(r)}, x_d^{(r)})$ in the internal state matrix $X^{(r)}$ is updated by sequentially computing

$$\begin{cases} x_b^{(r+1)} = ((x_a^{(r)} + x_d^{(r)}) \lll 7) \oplus x_b^{(r)}, \\ x_c^{(r+1)} = ((x_b^{(r+1)} + x_a^{(r)}) \lll 9) \oplus x_c^{(r)}, \\ x_d^{(r+1)} = ((x_c^{(r+1)} + x_b^{(r+1)}) \lll 13) \oplus x_d^{(r)}, \\ x_a^{(r+1)} = ((x_d^{(r+1)} + x_c^{(r+1)}) \lll 18) \oplus x_a^{(r)}, \end{cases} \quad (1)$$

where the symbols '+', '$\lll$', and '$\oplus$' represent word-wise modular addition, bit-wise left rotation, and bit-wise XOR, respectively. In odd number rounds, which are called column-rounds, the quarter-round function is applied to the following four column vectors: $(x_0^{(r)}, x_4^{(r)}, x_8^{(r)}, x_{12}^{(r)})$, $(x_5^{(r)}, x_9^{(r)}, x_{13}^{(r)}, x_1^{(r)})$, $(x_{10}^{(r)}, x_{14}^{(r)}, x_2^{(r)}, x_6^{(r)})$, and $(x_{15}^{(r)}, x_3^{(r)}, x_7^{(r)}, x_{11}^{(r)})$. In even number rounds, which are called row-rounds, the quarter-round function is applied to the following four row vectors: $(x_0^{(r)}, x_1^{(r)}, x_2^{(r)}, x_3^{(r)})$, $(x_5^{(r)}, x_6^{(r)}, x_7^{(r)}, x_4^{(r)})$, $(x_{10}^{(r)}, x_{11}^{(r)}, x_8^{(r)}, x_9^{(r)})$, and $(x_{15}^{(r)}, x_{12}^{(r)}, x_{13}^{(r)}, x_{14}^{(r)})$.

Step 3. A 512-bit keystream block is generated as $Z = X^{(0)} + X^{(R)}$, where R is the final round. The original version of Salsa20 stream cipher, called Salsa20, is $R = 20$ rounds, however, the accepted version as one of the finalists for the eSTREAM software portfolio [10] is Salsa20/12, where $R = 12$.

The round function of Salsa20 is reversible, i.e., a vector $(x_a^{(r+1)}, x_b^{(r+1)}, x_c^{(r+1)}, x_d^{(r+1)})$ in the internal state matrix $x^{(r+1)}$ is reversed by sequentially computing:

$$\begin{cases} x_a^{(r)} = ((x_d^{(r+1)} + x_c^{(r+1)}) \lll 18) \oplus x_a^{(r+1)}, \\ x_d^{(r)} = ((x_c^{(r+1)} + x_b^{(r+1)}) \lll 13) \oplus x_d^{(r+1)}, \\ x_c^{(r)} = ((x_b^{(r+1)} + x_a^{(r)}) \lll 9) \oplus x_c^{(r+1)}, \\ x_b^{(r)} = ((x_a^{(r)} + x_d^{(r)}) \lll 7) \oplus x_b^{(r+1)}. \end{cases} \tag{2}$$

3 Differential Cryptanalysis

Biham, E. and A. Shamir [3] introduced differential cryptanalysis. It is mainly a chosen plain text attack that aims to study the propagation of an *input difference* through several rounds of a cipher. The cryptanalysts are interested in searching for *input* and *output* differences denoted by Δ_x and Δ_z or by α and β, respectively. The XOR differential probability of addition xdp^+ and the additive differential probability of XOR $adp^\oplus$ was studied by [15]. The differential probability (DP) of addition modulo 2^n is the probability at which the input difference propagates to the output difference.

$$DP^+(\delta) = DP^+(\alpha, \beta \mapsto \delta) := P_{x,y}[(x+y) \oplus ((x \oplus \alpha) + (y \oplus \beta)) = \delta] \tag{3}$$

The x and y are the inputs of size n.

3.1 Differential Cryptanalysis of Salsa20 Stream Cipher

The majority of attacks introduced by cryptanalysts on Salsa20 are differential attacks. Among proposals, Aumasson et al. at FSE 2008 [1] introduced the illustrious attack. The author proposed a differential attack based on *probabilistic neutral bits* (PNBs). The attack consists of two phases: precomputation and online phases.

Pre-computation Phase. In the beginning, we initialize two-state matrix X and X'. Both X and X' matrices consist of the same keywords $(k_1, k_2 ... k_8)$ and constants. However, the X' matrix consists of a single bit difference in nonce v or counter t. To throw light on, let $x_i^{(0)}[j]$ be the j-th bit of the i-th word of initial state matrix $X^{(0)}$ for $0 \leq i \leq 15$ and $0 \leq j \leq 31$, and let $x_i'^{(0)}[j]$ be an associated word with a single bit difference at j^{th} bit as $\Delta_i^{(0)}[j] = x_i^{(0)}[j] \oplus x_i'^{(0)}[j]$ be the difference. Given a difference $\Delta_i^{(0)}[j] = 1$ at the jth bit of ith word of state matrix $X^{(0)}$, which is called *input difference* or $\mathcal{ID}$, we obtain the corresponding initial state matrix X' as $v' = v \bigoplus \Delta v$ or $t' = t \bigoplus \Delta t$ where v' and t' denotes the single bit difference at either nonce or counter. Next, we run the Salsa20 round function with the initial state matrices $X^{(0)}$, $X'^{(0)}$ as inputs, and obtain single bit output difference $\Delta_p^{(r)}[q] = x_p^{(r)}[q] \bigoplus x_p'^{(r)}[q]$ from the r-round internal state matrices $X^{(r)}$, $X'^{(r)}$, which is called *output difference* or $\mathcal{OD}$ where $1 \leq r < R$ and q denotes the q-th bit of the p-th word of internal state matrix $X^{(r)}$ for $0 \leq p \leq 15$ and $0 \leq q \leq 31$ after r rounds of Salsa20. For a fixed key and random nonces and block counters, the bias ε_d is defined as

$$\Pr\big(\Delta_p^{(r)}[q] = 1 \mid \Delta_i^{(0)}[j] = 1\big) = \frac{1}{2}(1 + \varepsilon_d), \tag{4}$$

If the key is defined to be random, the ε_d^* is computed to be the median value of ε_d [1].

Theorem 1 ([17, **Theorem 2**]). *Let $\mathcal{X}$ and $\mathcal{Y}$ be two distributions, and suppose that the target event occurs in $\mathcal{X}$ with a probability p and $\mathcal{Y}$ with a probability $p \cdot (1+q)$. Then, for small p and q, $\mathcal{O}(\frac{1}{p \cdot q^2})$ samples suffice to distinguish $\mathcal{X}$ from $\mathcal{Y}$ with a constant probability of success.*

Let $\mathcal{X}$ and $\mathcal{Y}$ be two distributions. The event E in $\mathcal{X}$ happens with probability $\frac{1}{2}$, (i.e., the result of a true random number generator) and the event E' in $\mathcal{Y}$ happens with the probability $\frac{1}{2} \cdot (1 + \epsilon_d)$, (i.e., the $\mathcal{OD}$ obtained from the r-round internal matrices of Salsa20 stream cipher). According to Theorem 1, the number of samples to distinguish $\mathcal{X}$ and $\mathcal{Y}$ is $\mathcal{O}(\frac{2}{\epsilon_d^2})$.

Probabilistic Neutral Bits. The probabilistic neutral bits concept allows us to divide the keybits set into two subsets. Throughout this paper we call it *significant key bits* subset m and *non-significant key bits* subset n where $m = 256 - n$. To distinguish between the two aforementioned subsets, the PNB concept focuses on the amount of affect each keybit has on the output of the Salsa20 function called $\mathcal{OD}$ here. The affects of keybits are referred as *neutral measures of keybits* or γ_k.

Definition 1 ([1, **Definition 1**]). *The neutral measure of the keybit position γ_i with respect to the $\mathcal{OD}$ is defined as γ_κ, where $\frac{1}{2}(1+\gamma_\kappa)$ is the probability that complementing the key bit κ at γ_i position does not change the $\mathcal{OD}$.*

According to [1], the following singular cases of the neutral measure exist:

- $\gamma_k = 1$: $\mathcal{OD}$ does not depend on the i-th key bit, i.e., it is non-significant.
- $\gamma_k = 0$: $\mathcal{OD}$ is statistically independent of the i-th keybit, i.e., it is significant.
- $\gamma_k = -1$: $\mathcal{OD}$ linearly depends on the i-th keybit.

We used the Algorithm 1 in Appendix B of [1] to compute the neutrality measure of keybits in the Salsa20 stream cipher.

Probabilistic Backwards Computation (PBC). Based on our discussion in Sect. 3.1, we calculate the forward differential bias ε_d by Eq. 4. Furthermore, we compute the r internal round differential bias from backward by probabilistic backward computation. Given Z, Z', X, X', one can reverse the Salsa20 keystream $Z = X + Round_R(X)$ and $Z' = X' + Round_R(X')$ to obtain the r rounds single bit differential bias from backward. To compute the PBC, we need the $Z - X$, and $Z' - X'$ matrices as inputs to the reverse round of Salsa20 explained in Eq. 2. The bias $\varepsilon \approx \varepsilon_e \cdot \varepsilon_a$ under the independence assumption [1,16]. For detailed understanding of PBC, please refer to Sect. 3.2 of [1].

Effective Attack. According to [1], for the online phase, we need the following parameters as input to the Algorithm in Sect. 3.4 of [1]: $\mathcal{OD}$ position, $\mathcal{ID}$ position, the subset of significant key bits m and N of keystream block to recover the secret key with some probability. For a detailed understanding, one can also refer to Sect. 2.5 of [14].

Complexity Estimation. Once we found an optimal $\mathcal{ID}, \mathcal{OD}$ pair $\left(\Delta_p^{(r)}[q] = 1 \mid \Delta_i^{(0)}[j] = 1\right)$ and the set of keybits is divided into significant key bits m and non-significant keybits n, and computed the median bias as $|\varepsilon^*| \approx |\varepsilon_e^*| \cdot |\varepsilon_a^*|$. We can compute the final attack complexity based on the following equation.

$$2^m(N + 2^n P_{fa}) = 2^m N + 2^{256-\alpha}, \text{ where } N \approx \left(\frac{\sqrt{\alpha \log 4} + 3\sqrt{1-\varepsilon^2}}{\varepsilon}\right)^2 \quad (5)$$

3.2 Related Work

Miyashita [19] applied the PNB-focused differential cryptanalysis on the ChaCha stream cipher. The proposed approach introduced the attack on ChaCha $7.25 - rounds$ with a time complexity of $2^{255.62}$ and data complexity of $2^{48.36}$. Considering the importance of the Salsa20 stream cipher, its wide adoption, and its structural similarity with the ChaCha stream cipher. We applied the PNB-focused differential cryptanalysis on $Salsa20/8$ to evaluate its resistance against the mentioned cryptanalysis approach. Section 4 studies the mentioned cryptanalysis approach on Salsa20/8.

4 Comprehensive Analysis of Probabilistic Neutral Bits

4.1 Searching the $\mathcal{OD}$ with Best Neutral Measure

The existing differential cryptanalysis of the Salsa20 stream cipher studies the $\mathcal{ID}$-$\mathcal{OD}$ pair with the highest differential bias ε_d among all possible pairs. At first, the $\mathcal{ID}$ is determined then the corresponding $\mathcal{OD}$ with the highest forward bias is selected. That is to say, the existing studies focused on the differential bias at specific $\mathcal{ID}, \mathcal{OD}$ pairs and then tried to find the subset of PNBs to attack the target round of Salsa20. Considering our experiment results in Subsect. 4.2 and the previous research results [1], the neutrality measures of all 256 key bit in Salsa20 mainly depend on $\mathcal{OD}$ bits. Therefore, when a key-recovery attack is effectuated in mentioned flow, it cannot be shown whether the combination

Algorithm 1. Computing $\mathcal{OD}$ bit with best neutral measure

Input: Random(X, X', Z, Z')

Output: The $\mathcal{OD}$ bit with best neutral measure

1. Generate random keywords $k = (k_0, \ldots, k_7)$.
2. Decide the $\mathcal{ID}$ $\Delta_i^{(0)}[j]$ at random, and generate $v = (v_0, v_1)$ and $t = (t_0, t_1)$, initiate $X^{(0)}$ and $X'^{(0)} = X^{(0)} \oplus \Delta_i^{(0)}[j]$.
3. From $(X^{(0)}, X'^{(0)})$, compute $(X^{(r)}, X'^{(r)})$ and $(X^{(R)}, X'^{(R)})$.
4. From $(X^{(r)}, X'^{(r)})$ compute $\mathcal{OD}$ $\Delta_p^{(r)}[q] = X_p^{(r)}[q] \oplus X_p'^{(r)}[q]$ for all possible p and q.
5. From $(X^{(R)}, X'^{(R)})$ obtain the key-stream $Z = X^{(0)} + X^{(R)}$ and $Z' = X'^{(0)} + X'^{(R)}$.
6. Complement a key bit κ ($\kappa \in \{0, \ldots, 255\}$) and compute $\overline{X}^{(0)}$ and $\overline{X'}^{(0)}$ from initial states $(X^{(0)}, X'^{(0)})$.
7. Compute $(Y^{(r)}, Y'^{(r)})$ with $Z - \overline{X}^{(0)}$ and $Z' - \overline{X'}^{(0)}$ as inputs to the inversed round function of Salsa20.
8. Derive $\Gamma_p^{(r)}[q] = Y_p^{(r)}[q] \oplus Y_p'^{(r)}[q]$ for all possible choices of p and q.
9. Increment the sum for each p, q, and κ only if $\Delta_p^{(r)}[q] = \Gamma_p^{(r)}[q]$.
10. Divide the sum of $\Delta_p^{(r)}[q] = \Gamma_p^{(r)}[q]$ by key trail and $\mathcal{ID}$ samples to get the probability.

$\mathcal{ID}, \mathcal{OD}$, and the subset of PNBs are truly optimal or not. In this section, we focus on a comprehensive analysis of the neutrality measures of 256 keybit with the respect to all possible $\mathcal{OD}$ bits. Furthermore, we analyze the conditions and circumstances that possibly instigate the high neutral measures as the size of PNBs affects the time complexity of the attack, as shown in Eq. (5). Presumably, no study on analyzing the PNBs in detail has been reported. If the conditions that induce high neutral measure γ_κ can be clarified, we can claim that the existing attacks may still have room for improvement. We used Algorithm 1 to compute the neutrality measures of 256 key bit with the respect to 512 $\mathcal{OD}$ bits. To select an optimal $\mathcal{ID}$ position, we tried all possible 128 $\mathcal{ID}$ positions, and we could not observe a significant impact of the $\mathcal{ID}$ on the neutrality measure of key bits. Therefore, we decided to select a random $\mathcal{ID}$ at this phase of experiment[2].

4.2 Experimental Results

To analyze the neutrality measure of key bits concerning all possible $\mathcal{OD}$s, we have conducted experiments with the complexity of 2^{30} (i.e., 2^6 key trials and 2^{24} IV samples). According to Theorem 1, let $\mathcal{X}$ be a distribution of $\Delta_p^{(r)}[q] = \Gamma_p^{(r)}[q]$ obtained from the r-round internal state matrices in true random number generator, and let $\mathcal{Y}$ be a distribution of $\Delta_p^{(r)}[q] = \Gamma_p^{(r)}[q]$ obtained from the r-round internal state matrices of Salsa20. The target event occurs in $\mathcal{X}$ with a

[2] In our experiment, we used the $\mathcal{ID}$ (7,31) reported in [1] and used in [8], [16].

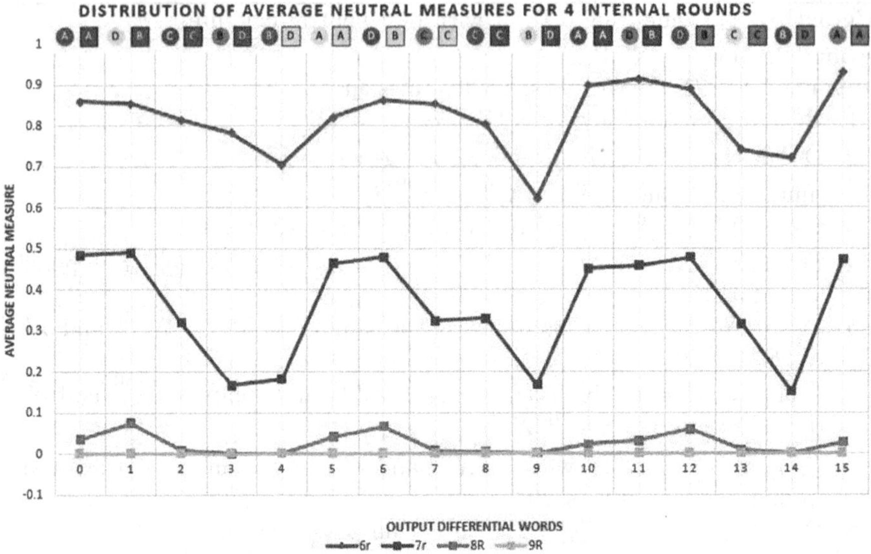

Fig. 1. Distribution of neutral measures γ_κ for internal round $r = 4$ (Color figure online)

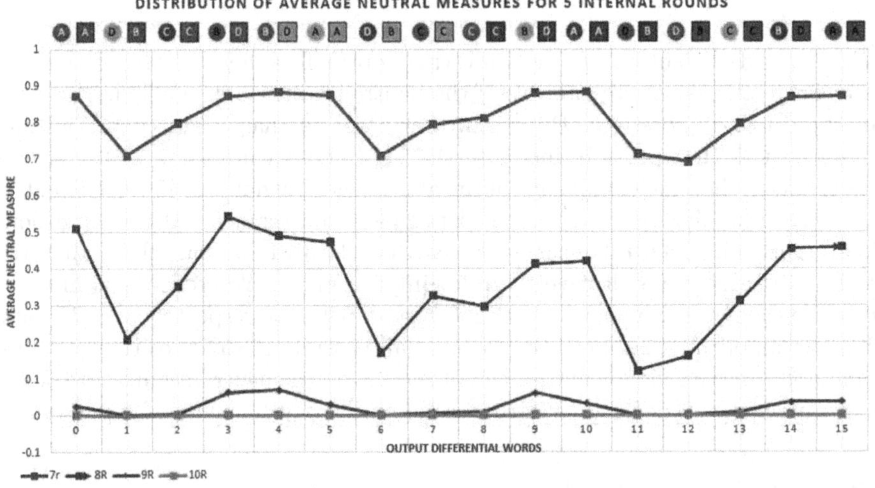

Fig. 2. Distribution of neutral measures γ_κ for the internal round $r = 5$ (Color figure online)

probability of $\frac{1}{2}$ and $\mathcal{Y}$ with a probability of γ_κ; thus, the number of samples to distinguish $\mathcal{X}$ and $\mathcal{Y}$ is $\mathcal{O}(\frac{2}{\gamma_\kappa^2})$. Our experimental results are reliable when the derived neutral measures γ_κ are greater than $2^{-11.5}$ since we have used 2^{24} samples of IV.

Table 3. Relationship between the input word position to the inversed quarter-round function and the cumulative number of modular addition.

R	Input word position		Cumulative number of modular additions	
	Odd round	Even round	2 rounds	3 rounds
Odd	A	A	5	24
	B	D	7	76
	C	C	11	52
	D	B	16	35
Even	A	A	5	24
	B	D	16	35
	C	C	11	52
	D	B	7	76

Figure 1 and Fig. 2 show the experimental result of a comprehensive analysis of keybits neutrality measures concerning all possible $\mathcal{OD}$ bit positions. In these figures, the vertical axis represents the average neutral measures of key bits at each $\mathcal{OD}$ position, the horizontal axis represents the $\mathcal{OD}$ word positions, and the auxiliary lines on the vertical axis separate the $\mathcal{OD}$ word positions. The red, blue, green, and yellow lines show the average neutral measures when the inversed rounds $(R - r)$ are 2, 3, 4, and 5, respectively. We used fixed internal rounds $r < R$. Figure 1 and Fig. 2 show the $r = 4, 5$, respectively. The symbols represented by a circle or square at the top of the graph indicate the input word position, such as a vector (A, B, C, D), to the inversed quarter-round function in odd or even number round, respectively. For instance, if these symbols (circle and square) are in the same color for each word position, then the same colored word position to inverse quarter-round function is the same aside from odd or even round of Salsa20 rounds. From Figs. 1 and 2, we obtain the following properties:

- The neutrality measure of keybits varies for each $\mathcal{OD}$ bit position.
- The same order of input word position to the inversed quarter-round function induces the same neutral measure.
- Each $\mathcal{OD}$ bit position with a high neutral measure varies in different word positions.
- The distributions of neutral measures concerning the $\mathcal{OD}$ bit position are much similar regardless of the internal round r.

4.3 Discussion

Relationship Between PNBs and Inversed Round of Salsa20. To study the correlation between PNBs and inversed round function of Salsa20, we scrutinize the relationship between the input word position to the inversed quarter-round function and the cumulative number of modular addition executed for

Table 4. Maximum, minimum, average, and median values of neutral measures γ_κ for each target round R when $r = 4$, where p and q are word and bit positions of the $\mathcal{OD}$, respectively, i.e., $\Delta_p^{(r)}[q]$.

R	Maximum			Minimum			Average	Median
	γ_κ	p	q	γ_κ	p	q		
6	$2^{-0.00144}$	2	1	$2^{-0.5451}$	9	7	$2^{-0.1907}$	$2^{-0.1473}$
7	$2^{-0.8143}$	0	18	$2^{-2.4426}$	14	7	$2^{-1.2708}$	$2^{-1.1496}$
8	$2^{-3.5850}$	1	13	$2^{-10.4926}$	2	9	$2^{-4.9755}$	$2^{-5.3066}$

Table 5. Maximum, minimum, average, and median values of neutral measures γ_κ for each target round R when $r = 5$, where p and q are word and bit positions of the $\mathcal{OD}$, respectively, i.e., $\Delta_p^{(r)}[q]$.

R	Maximum			Minimum			Average	Median
	γ_κ	p	q	γ_κ	p	q		
7	$2^{-0.1076}$	0	18	$2^{-0.4300}$	12	7	$2^{-0.2206}$	$2^{-0.1808}$
8	$2^{-0.7301}$	0	18	$2^{-2.7284}$	11	7	$2^{-1.2703}$	$2^{-1.2019}$

specific reverse rounds. In Table 3, we investigated the cumulative number of modular addition executed for different input word positions to the inversed quarter-round function for 2 and 3 reverse rounds.

The R column points to the number of target rounds in our attack. The combination of input word positions to the inversed quarter-round function is different depending on whether R is even or odd. For example, we consider the case when the number of target rounds R is odd and the input word position in the odd number round is B. When the number of the inversed rounds is two, the word position moves B (odd number round) $\rightarrow D$ (even number round) by executing the inversed quarter-round function. In other words, the same element in the Salsa20 matrix is picked in a different order by inverse quarter-round in odd and even rounds. For instance, element X_3 is represented by D in vector (A, B, C, D) in even rounds, in odd rounds same element X_3 is represented by B. Similarly, when the number of the inversed rounds is three, the word position transitions B (odd number round) $\rightarrow D$ (even number round) $\rightarrow B$ (odd number round). The cumulative number of modular addition column shows the cumulative number of modular additions executed by the inversed round function for each transition of the word positions when the number of inversed rounds is two or three. We focus only on the execution of the cumulative number of modular addition because it plays a crucial role in ensuring the security of the ARX ciphers. As per Table 3, the execution of modular addition differs depending on the input word position to the inversed round function. For example, we consider the case when the number of target round R is odd, the transition of the word position is A (odd number round) $\rightarrow A$ (even number round), and the number of inversed rounds is two. In this case, the cumulative number of modular addition is 5. Now, we compare the experimental results in Figs. 1 and 2 with the analysis results in Table 3. When focusing on the sequence of the input word positions (see the symbol at the top of the graph) and its neutral measures, we can see that the neutral measure is decreased as the cumulative number of executions of modular addition is increased. For example, when the number of target rounds R is odd in Fig. 2, and the number of inversed round functions is three, the inversed round function is executed with the order of odd round $\rightarrow$ even round $\rightarrow$ odd round. The input word positions that induce the lower neutral measures are the 1, 6, and 11 word positions, and these word positions move through a high cumulative number of modular addition. We also observed this trend in our experiment as the $\mathcal{OD}$ positions with the lowest neutrality measure are in positions with a maximum cumulative number of modular addition. For instance, in Table 5, when $R = 8$, $r = 5$, and $R - r = 3$, the $\mathcal{OD}$ bit with a high neutral measure is in X_0, which is word A in vector (A, B, C, D) and it is affected by the lowest number of modular addition. In summary, we can see that the neutral measure depends on the input word position to the inversed round function, and it is influenced by the cumulative number of modular addition. The conditions that induce high neutral measure depend on the $\mathcal{OD}$ bit position to inverse quarter-round function.

5 Differential Cryptanalysis Based on Analysis of PNBs

In this section, we explain the differential cryptanalysis based on the comprehensive analysis of PNBs on the reduced round of Salsa20 stream cipher. At first, we study the neutrality measure of all keybits concerning all possible $\mathcal{OD}$ bit positions. For this purpose, we use Algorithm 1 in Sect. 4. Once we selected the $\mathcal{OD}$ bit with the best average neutral measure. Then we search for the $\mathcal{ID}$ bit position with the best differential bias ε_d at the predefined $\mathcal{OD}$ (i.e., $\mathcal{OD}$ bit with the best neutral measure) position. In the second stage, we use the $\mathcal{ID}$, $\mathcal{OD}$ pair to search for the PNBs subset. Afterwards, we estimate the complexity of the attack on the reduced round of Salsa20. Consequently, we present an attack on Salsa20/8 with a time complexity of $2^{144.75}$ and a data complexity of $2^{55.74}$.

5.1 Single-Bit Differential Bias

In Sect. 4, we have comprehensively analyzed the $\mathcal{OD}$ bit position and selected the $\mathcal{OD}$ bit with the best average neutral measures[3]. Afterward, by analyzing the $\mathcal{ID}$ bit position with the best differential bias at the target $\mathcal{OD}$ bit position, we select the $\mathcal{ID}$-$\mathcal{OD}$ pair. We focus on the $\mathcal{OD}$ bit in the $5th$ internal round of Salsa20/8, (*i.e.*, when $r = 5$ and $R = 8$). This is due to the following reasons:

[3] We considered the average neutral value because we computed the neutrality measure of all 256 key-bit with the respect to each $\mathcal{OD}$ bit.

- It is difficult to efficiently perform our attack on Salsa20/9 as we could not observe a high average neutral measure for any $\mathcal{OD}$ bit in Sect. 4. It is because of the high number of modular-addition executed both in forward and backward rounds that dramatically drop the forward and backward bias.
- Comparing Tables 4 and 5, we can see that $\mathcal{OD}$ bits provide a better neutral measure using Algorithm 1 when $r = 5$ and $R - r = 3$; thus, we selected the $\mathcal{OD}$ bit position with the best neutral measure from Table 5 to attack Salsa20/8.
- To get a high number of PNBs, we need to move to a higher internal round. Considering the fact, we targeted the $5th$ internal round.

It can be seen from Table 5 that the $\Delta_0^5[18]$ position has the best neutral measure. To find the $\mathcal{ID}$ bit position with the best forward differential bias ε_d at the target $\mathcal{OD}$ bit position $\Delta_0^5[18]$, we have conducted an experiment with 2^{25} $\mathcal{ID}$s for each of 2^{10} key trials. Table 6 lists the $\mathcal{ID}$ positions best differential biases ε_d at the target $\mathcal{OD}$ bit position $\Delta_0^5[18]$. As shown in Table 6, we obtain the best $\mathcal{ID}$-$\mathcal{OD}$ pair $(\Delta_6^0[31], \Delta_0^5[18])$, with $\varepsilon_d = 0.000829$ $(= 2^{-10.2363})$. According to Theorem 1, $\frac{2}{\epsilon_d^2} = 2^{21.472}$ $\mathcal{ID}$s are sufficient to distinguish the obtained differential bias with a constant probability of success; therefore, our experimental results are reliable since we have used 2^{25} $\mathcal{ID}$s sample for each of 2^{10} key trials.

Table 6. Best differential biases ε_d at the target $\mathcal{OD}$ bit position $\Delta_0^5[18]$.

$\mathcal{ID}$	$\mathcal{OD}$	$\mid \epsilon_d \mid$
$\Delta_6^{(0)}[31]$	$\Delta_0^{(5)}[18]$	0.000829
$\Delta_6^{(0)}[15]$	$\Delta_0^{(5)}[18]$	0.000793
$\Delta_7^{(0)}[9]$	$\Delta_0^{(5)}[18]$	0.000767

5.2 Complexity Estimation of Proposed Attack on Salsa20/8

To accurately estimate the time and data complexities of our proposed differential attack based on the comprehensive analysis of PNBs on Salsa20/8, the next steps should be carried as follows:

Step 1. We computed neutral measures of all keybit positions in accordance with the pre-determined $\mathcal{ID}$-$\mathcal{OD}$ pair $(\Delta_6^0[31], \Delta_0^5[18])$, and divided secret keybits into two subsets: m-bit subset of significant keybits and n-bit subset of non-significant keybits.

Step 2. In the second step, we executed the probabilistic backward computation and obtained the $5th$ round differential biases ε_a from the backward for each threshold γ where $0 < \gamma \leq 1$ from the obtained keystream, and approximated the overall median bias $|\varepsilon^*| \approx |\varepsilon d^*| \cdot |\varepsilon a^*|$[4] for our attack on Salsa20/8.

[4] According to [1] Under some reasonable independency assumptions, the equality $\varepsilon = \varepsilon_d * \varepsilon_a$ holds.

Step 3. We run the online phase algorithm[5] and approximated the time and data complexities to recover an unknown key.

To carry out the above steps, for each of 2^{10} key trials, we run 2^{25} $\mathcal{ID}$ samples to estimate the neutrality measure of keybits and obtain the subset of significant and non-significant key bits.

Algorithm 2. [1] PNB bits verification

Input: Random(X, X', Z, Z')

Output: The absolute value of $\tilde{\varepsilon}$

1. Compute $(X^{(R)}, X'^{(R)})$ with $\Delta_i^{(0)}[j] = 1$; and derive $Z = X^{(0)} + X^{(R)}$ and $Z' = X'^{(0)} + X'^{(R)}$.
3. Prepare $(\tilde{X}^{(0)}, \tilde{X'}^{(0)})$ with all keybits set to a random binary value from $(X^{(0)}, X'^{(0)})$.
4. Compute $(\tilde{Y}^{(r)}, \tilde{Y}'^{(r)})$ with $Z - \tilde{X}^{(0)}$ and $Z' - \tilde{X'}^{(0)}$ as inputs to the inversed round function of Salsa20.
5. Obtain $\tilde{\Gamma}_p^{(r)}[q] = \tilde{y}_p^{(r)}[q] \oplus \tilde{y}_p'^{(r)}[q]$
6. Compute the $\tilde{\varepsilon}$ as $\Pr(\tilde{\Gamma}_p^{(r)}[q] \mid \Delta_i^{(0)}[j] = 1) = \frac{1}{2}(1 + \tilde{\varepsilon})$.

Table 7. Summary of the time and data complexities for our attack on Salsa20/8 for each threshold γ, PNB bits n, differential bias ε_d, and reverse bias ε_a.

γ	n	$\lvert\varepsilon_d^*\rvert$	$\lvert\varepsilon_a^*\rvert$	α	Time	Data
0.90	114	0.000117	0.57884	111	$2^{177.59}$	$2^{35.59}$
0.80	129	0.000117	0.28763	111	$2^{164.6}$	$2^{37.6}$
0.70	140	0.000117	0.11068	111	$2^{156.36}$	$2^{40.36}$
0.60	148	0.000117	0.03861	111	$2^{151.41}$	$2^{43.4}$
0.50	154	0.000117	0.01027	113	$2^{149.26}$	$2^{47.24}$
0.40	162	0.000117	0.00211	117	$2^{145.86}$	$2^{51.84}$
0.30	167	0.000117	0.00055	119	$2^{144.75}$	$2^{55.74}$

PNBs Verification. Once we select the subset of PNBs (Sect. 5.2 Step 1), we need to verify the authenticity of PNB bits. For this purpose, we used the Algorithm 2. At first, the PNBs are set to a random value in state matrix X^0 and X'^0, the obtained matrices are denoted by $(\hat{X}^{(0)}, \hat{X'}^{(0)})$, respectively. We symbolized the bias of these matrices by $\hat{\varepsilon}$ or ε_a. A high absolute value of $\hat{\varepsilon}$ verifies the proper selection of PNB bits [1]. Next, we assign random values to all keybits and obtain the $\tilde{\varepsilon}$. According to [16], if we find $\tilde{\varepsilon}$ with low bias (close to

[5] We used the effective attack algorithm of [1] from Sect. 3.4.

a random event), it implies that the PNBs are selected properly. To get the $\tilde{\varepsilon}$, for each of 2^{10} key trials we run 2^{25} $\mathcal{ID}$ samples. We obtained the $|\tilde{\varepsilon}| \approx 0.000003910$ with the probability $\approx \frac{1}{2}$. Considering the bias and the probability, we can claim that the PNBs are selected correctly in our experiment. Table 7 shows the time and data complexities for each threshold γ. We can attack Salsa20/8 with time complexity of $2^{144.75}$ and data complexity of $2^{55.74}$ with threshold $\gamma = 0.30$. Now, we focus on $\varepsilon_a^* = 0.00055$ $(= 2^{-10.824})$ when $\gamma = 0.30$. According to Theorem 1, $\frac{2}{\varepsilon_a^2} = 2^{22.64}$ $\mathcal{ID}$s are sufficient to distinguish the differential bias with a constant probability of success; thus, our experimental results are reliable when $\gamma = 0.30$ since we have used 2^{25} $\mathcal{ID}$s. Moreover, when $\gamma = 0.25$ we found 177 PNBs with $\varepsilon_a^* = 0.000114531$ equals $2^{-13.092}$. In this case, $\frac{2}{\varepsilon_a^2} = 2^{27.183}$ $\mathcal{ID}$s are sufficient to distinguish the differential bias with a constant probability of success; thus, our experimental results are not authentic when $\gamma = 0.25$. To summarize, we present an attack on the Salsa20/8 by applying our proposed differential cryptanalysis approach with a time complexity of $2^{144.75}$ and data complexity of $2^{55.74}$. We improved the attack on Salsa20/8 by a factor of $2^{98.95}$.

5.3 Discussion

In this subsection, we discuss the differences between the existing attacks [1, 5,8,16] and our proposed attack. The existing attacks work on the reduced-round Salsa20 by (1) searching for the $\mathcal{ID}$ and $\mathcal{OD}$ differential pair with the best differential bias and (2) analyzing PNB based on obtained input/output differential pair. In addition, some attacks utilize the multi-bit differential bias. For instance, the [4] has used the $\mathcal{ID}$ is $\Delta_7^{(0)}[0]$, the $\mathcal{OD}$ is $\Delta_9^{(5)}[0] \oplus \Delta_{13}^{(5)}[0] \oplus \Delta_1^{(5)}[13]$, the author could reduce the number of significant key bits to 214, and they reported $\varepsilon_a = 0.000752$, $\varepsilon_d = -0.233198$, and subsequently $\varepsilon = -0.000178$. Our proposed attack works on the reduced-round Salsa20 by (1) comprehensively analyzing the $\mathcal{OD}$ bit position with the best average neutral measure and (2) searching for the $\mathcal{ID}$ bit position with the best differential bias ε_d in the obtained $\mathcal{OD}$ bit position. Our proposed attack utilizes the single-bit differential bias, such that the $\mathcal{ID}$ is $\Delta_6^{(0)}[31]$, the $\mathcal{OD}$ is $\Delta_0^{(5)}[18]$. Similarly, the ε^* approximated as $|\varepsilon^*| \approx |\varepsilon_d^*| \cdot |\varepsilon_a^*|$. We summarize the differences between the existing attacks [1,5,8,16] and our attack as follows:

- To the best of our knowledge, for the first time, we used the single bit differential bias[6] in $5th$ internal round to attack the $8th$ round Salsa20. Previous research mainly used $4th$ internal round bias to attack $8th$ round Salsa20. For instance, the [1] used $4th$ round bias with $\mathcal{ID}, \mathcal{OD}$ pair $\Delta_7^{(0)}[31]$ and $\Delta_1^{(4)}[14]$ with $|\epsilon_d^*| = 0.131$ and $\epsilon_a^* = 0.0011$. However, we used the Salsa20 $5th$ round bias $\Delta_6^{(0)}[31]$, $\Delta_0^{(5)}[18]$ with $|\epsilon_d^*| = 0.000117$ to attack Salsa20/8.

[6] Arka [4] also reported the $5th$ round bias of Salsa20. However, the author used the differential-linear adversary model. We used single bit differential bias.

- We reported 89 significant key bits in Salsa20/8 with 256-bit security, which significantly reduced the attack complexity. The previous studies reported 214 and 213 significant key bits.
- We introduce the new pairs of $\mathcal{ID}$ and $\mathcal{OD}$ listed in Table 6.

It is the first application of its type on reduced round of Salsa20. We reduced the attack complexity with the factor of $2^{98.95}$ which is a notable factor in the field of cryptanalysis. During our experiments, we noted that the second half of keybit positions in Salsa20 matrix (*i.e.*, from X_{11} to X_{14}) give higher neutrality measure compared to the first half of keybit positions (*i.e.*, from X_1 to X_4). In brief, the less significant key bits, the less time complexity an adversary needs to recover an unknown secret key; thus, we demonstrate its superiority as an effective differential attack on Salsa20/8 stream cipher by focusing on comprehensive analysis of PNBs with the respect to all possible 512 bits of $\mathcal{OD}$s.

6 Conclusion

In this study, we have analyzed the Salsa20/8 stream cipher. Our approach focused on the comprehensive of PNB rather than looking for $\mathcal{ID}$ and $\mathcal{OD}$ pairs. Therefore, it is a *cryptanalysis based on the comprehensive analysis of PNBs*. As a result, the approach allows us to perform the best differential attack on Salsa20/8 with a time complexity of $2^{144.75}$ and data complexity of $2^{55.74}$. The proposed differential attack may also contribute to the improvement of the existing differential-linear cryptanalysis, which remains an open problem.

Acknowledgements. This work is partially supported by JSPS KAKENHI Grant Number JP21H03443 and Innovation Platform for Society 5.0 at MEXT.

References

1. Aumasson, J.-P., Fischer, S., Khazaei, S., Meier, W., Rechberger, C.: New features of latin dances: analysis of salsa, ChaCha, and Rumba. In: Nyberg, K. (ed.) FSE 2008. LNCS, vol. 5086, pp. 470–488. Springer, Heidelberg (2008). https://doi.org/10.1007/978-3-540-71039-4_30
2. Bernstein, D.J.: The Salsa20 family of stream ciphers. In: Robshaw, M., Billet, O. (eds.) New Stream Cipher Designs. LNCS, vol. 4986, pp. 84–97. Springer, Heidelberg (2008). https://doi.org/10.1007/978-3-540-68351-3_8
3. Biham, E., Shamir, A.: Differential cryptanalysis of des-like cryptosystems. J. Cryptology (1991)
4. Choudhuri, A.R., Maitra, S.: Differential cryptanalysis of salsa and chacha-an evaluation with a hybrid model. Cryptology ePrint Archive (2016)
5. Choudhuri, A.R., Maitra, S.: Significantly improved multi-bit differentials for reduced round salsa and chacha. IACR Transactions on Symmetric Cryptology, pp. 261–287 (2016)
6. Crowley, P.: Truncated differential cryptanalysis of five rounds of salsa20. Cryptology ePrint Archive (2005)

7. Deepthi Kakumani, K.C., Singh, K., Karthika, S.K.: Improved related-cipher attack on salsa and Chacha: revisited. Int. J. Inf. Technol. **14**(3), 1535–1542 (2022)
8. Dey, S., Sarkar, S.: improved analysis for reduced round salsa and Chacha. Discret. Appl. Math. **227**, 58–69 (2017)
9. Ding, L.: Improved related-cipher attack on salsa20 stream cipher. IEEE Access **7**, 30197–30202 (2019)
10. The eSTREAM Project. http://www.ecrypt.eu.org/stream
11. Fischer, S., Meier, W., Berbain, C., Biasse, J.-F., Robshaw, M.J.B.: Non-randomness in eSTREAM candidates Salsa20 and TSC-4. In: Barua, R., Lange, T. (eds.) INDOCRYPT 2006. LNCS, vol. 4329, pp. 2–16. Springer, Heidelberg (2006). https://doi.org/10.1007/11941378_2
12. Ishiguro, T., Kiyomoto, S., Miyake, Y.: Latin dances revisited: new analytic results of Salsa20 and ChaCha. In: Qing, S., Susilo, W., Wang, G., Liu, D. (eds.) ICICS 2011. LNCS, vol. 7043, pp. 255–266. Springer, Heidelberg (2011). https://doi.org/10.1007/978-3-642-25243-3_21
13. Ito, R.: Rotational cryptanalysis of salsa core function. In: Susilo, W., Deng, R.H., Guo, F., Li, Y., Intan, R. (eds.) ISC 2020. LNCS, vol. 12472, pp. 129–145. Springer, Cham (2020). https://doi.org/10.1007/978-3-030-62974-8_8
14. Khazaei, S.: Neutrality-based symmetric cryptanalysis. Technical report, EPFL (2010)
15. Lipmaa, H., Moriai, S.: Efficient algorithms for computing differential properties of addition. In: Matsui, M. (ed.) FSE 2001. LNCS, vol. 2355, pp. 336–350. Springer, Heidelberg (2002). https://doi.org/10.1007/3-540-45473-X_28
16. Maitra, S.: Chosen IV cryptanalysis on reduced round ChaCha and Salsa. Discret. Appl. Math. **208**, 88–97 (2016)
17. Mantin, I., Shamir, A.: A practical attack on broadcast RC4. In: Matsui, M. (ed.) FSE 2001. LNCS, vol. 2355, pp. 152–164. Springer, Heidelberg (2002). https://doi.org/10.1007/3-540-45473-X_13
18. Mazumdar, B., Subidh Ali, S.K., Sinanoglu, O.: Power analysis attacks on arx: an application to salsa20. In: 2015 IEEE 21st International On-Line Testing Symposium (IOLTS), pp. 40–43. IEEE (2015)
19. Miyashita, S., Ito, R., Miyaji, A.: Pnb-focused differential cryptanalysis of chacha stream cipher. Cryptology ePrint Archive, Report 2021/1537 (2021). https://ia.cr/2021/1537
20. Shi, Z., Zhang, B., Feng, D., Wu, W.: Improved key recovery attacks on reduced-round Salsa20 and ChaCha. In: Kwon, T., Lee, M.-K., Kwon, D. (eds.) ICISC 2012. LNCS, vol. 7839, pp. 337–351. Springer, Heidelberg (2013). https://doi.org/10.1007/978-3-642-37682-5_24
21. Stachowiak, S., Kurkowski, M., Soboń, A.: SAT-based cryptanalysis of Salsa20 cipher. In: Choraś, M., Choraś, R.S., Kurzyński, M., Trajdos, P., Pejaś, J., Hyla, T. (eds.) CORES/IP&C/ACS -2021. LNNS, vol. 255, pp. 252–266. Springer, Cham (2022). https://doi.org/10.1007/978-3-030-81523-3_25

Physical Zero-Knowledge Proof Protocol for Topswops

Yuichi Komano[1(✉)] and Takaaki Mizuki[2(✉)]

[1] Toshiba Corporation, 1 Komukai-Toshiba-cho, Saiwai-ku, Kawasaki, Japan
yuichi1.komano@toshiba.co.jp

[2] Tohoku University, 6-3 Aramaki-Aza-Aoba, Aoba-ku, Sendai, Japan
mizuki+lncs@tohoku.ac.jp

Abstract. Suppose that a sequence of n cards, numbered 1 to n, is placed face up in random order. Let k be the number on the first card in the sequence. Then take the first k cards from the sequence, rearrange that subsequence of k cards in reverse order, and return them to the original sequence. Repeat this prefix reversal until the number on the first card in the sequence becomes 1. This is a one-player card game called Topswops. The computational complexity of Topswops has not been thoroughly investigated. For example, letting $f(n)$ denote the maximum number of prefix reversals for Topswops with n cards, values of $f(n)$ for $n \geq 20$ remain unknown. In general, there is no known efficient algorithm for finding an initial sequence of n cards that requires exactly ℓ prefix reversals for any integers n and ℓ. In this paper, we propose a physical zero-knowledge proof protocol that allows a prover to convince a verifier that the prover knows an initial sequence of n cards that requires ℓ prefix reversals without leaking knowledge of that sequence.

Keywords: Zero-knowledge proof · Card-based cryptography · Topswops

1 Introduction

Topswops is a one-player card game in which one randomly arranges n cards, numbered 1 to n. Given such an initial sequence of n cards, the player rearranges the sequence as follows. After looking at the number written on the first card, denoted as k, the player rearranges the first k cards into their reverse order while leaving the remaining $n-k$ cards unchanged. The player repeatedly applies such prefix reversals to the current sequence until the number on the first card in the sequence becomes 1. For example, consider the case where $n = 5$, and let $(3, 1, 4, 5, 2)$ be an initial sequence. In Topswops, the player rearranges the sequence as

$$(\underline{3,1,4},5,2) \rightarrow (\underline{4,1,3,5},2) \rightarrow (\underline{5,3,1,4,2}) \rightarrow (\underline{2,4},1,3,5) \rightarrow (\underline{4,2,1,3},5)$$
$$\rightarrow (\underline{3,1,2},4,5) \rightarrow (\underline{2,1},3,4,5) \rightarrow (1,2,3,4,5),$$

C. Su et al. (Eds.): ISPEC 2022, LNCS 13620, pp. 537–553, 2022.
https://doi.org/10.1007/978-3-031-21280-2_30

Table 1. Values for $f(n)$ and $g(n)$.

n	1	2	3	4	5	6	7	8	9	10	11	12	13	14	15	16	17	18	19
$f(n)$ (OEIS A000375)	0	1	2	4	7	10	16	22	30	38	51	65	80	101	113	139	159	191	221
$g(n)$ (OEIS A123398)	1	1	2	2	2	1	5	2	1	1	1	1	1	4	6	1	2	1	4

so the game ends in seven steps (namely, seven prefix reversals). In this example, the cards are finally sorted in ascending order. Note that the number of steps depends on an individual initial sequence and that the n cards may not be finally sorted in ascending order. For instance, if the initial sequence is $(2, 1, 3, 5, 4)$, the game ends with $(1, 2, 3, 5, 4)$ after one step, with the cards unsorted.

1.1 Open Problems in Topswops

Topswops is said to be invented by J.H. Conway (see the Introduction in [38] or p. 116 of [17]). The question of what initial sequences produce the maximum number of steps has been investigated. For example, recall that the initial sequence $(3, 1, 4, 5, 2)$ shown above requires exactly seven steps; it is known that in the case of $n = 5$, there is no initial sequence that results in more than seven steps, and hence, seven is the maximum number of steps for Topswops with five cards. Therefore, letting $f(n)$ denote the maximum number of steps for Topswops with n cards, we have $f(5) = 7$.

Generally, the currently known upper bound on $f(n)$ is $O(1.62^n)$ [17,19] and the currently known lower bound is $\Omega(n^2)$ [38]. Thus, there is an exponential gap between the (currently known) upper and lower bounds on $f(n)$, and finding better bounds to reduce that gap is an open problem.

Since there is no known efficient algorithm for finding the values of $f(n)$, several studies have used brute-force searches to report values for $f(n)$ and the corresponding initial sequences (e.g., [16,41]). Specifically, values are known up to $n \leq 19$. Table 1 shows known values for $f(n)$, which are registered as OEIS A000375[1] in *The On-Line Encyclopedia of Integer Sequences* (OEIS). That table also shows as $g(n)$ the number of initial sequences requiring $f(n)$ steps, which are registered as OEIS A123398[2]. The most recent result was that Kimura et al. [16] obtained values for $f(18), f(19)$ (and $g(18), g(19)$) in 2021, using 172 threads on nine computers over about six days[3]. Finding values of $f(n)$ and $g(n)$ for $n \geq 20$ has remained an important open problem for many years, along with narrowing the gap between the upper and lower bounds on $f(n)$, as described above.

---

1 https://oeis.org/A000375.

2 https://oeis.org/A123398.

3 According to Zimmermann's Programming Contests (http://azspcs.com/Contest/Cards/FinalReport, accessed 16 Aug 2022), four initial sequences which require 221 steps for $n = 19$ were discovered in 2011. Hence, it seems that at that time the lower bounds on $f(19)$ and $g(19)$ were known to be 221 and 4, respectively.

1.2 Zero-knowledge Proof Protocol for Topswops

As mentioned above, the computational complexity of Topswops has been insufficiently revealed, and many open problems related to Topswops remain. In particular, for any positive integers n and ℓ (such that $1 \leq \ell \leq f(n)$), there is no known efficient algorithm for finding an initial sequence of n cards that requires exactly ℓ steps. Therefore, there are possible situations where it is invaluable that only a single person knows a particular initial sequence (and its number of steps) while the others do not know anything about it. Hence, let us try to apply the concept of *zero-knowledge proof* [8] to Topswops. In other words, let us consider a zero-knowledge proof protocol for Topswops whereby a prover P can convince a verifier V that P knows an initial sequence requiring exactly ℓ steps without leaking any information about the sequence. The following illustrates two such situations.

- Suppose that prover P has discovered an initial sequence of 20 cards requiring 250 steps, which is longer than the currently known lower bound $f(20) \geq 249$[4], and wants to publish it as a new achievement. However, if P shows the initial sequence to a (possibly malicious) third party, that party might claim it as its own achievement. If, however, a zero-knowledge proof protocol could be applied to Topswops, P could prove that P discovered the initial sequence while still keeping it secret. After gaining sufficient recognition, P could claim the initial sequence by disclosing it without any trouble.
- Suppose that several players want to play a game in which they try to find an initial sequence of Topswops. The rules of the game state that the winner is the player who finds an initial sequence with a larger number of steps, or one with a predetermined number of steps. Assume that the game may be played many times, with different players and different conditions. If the initial sequences are disclosed every time to determine a game winner, those sequences lead to another sequence corresponding to a smaller number of steps, or it will serve as a clue for finding another sequence having a larger number of steps, which makes it impossible to fairly or enjoyably play subsequent games. Using a zero-knowledge proof protocol to determine the game winner, however, would make it possible to enjoy the game.

1.3 Contribution

We propose a zero-knowledge proof protocol for Topswops. Namely, assuming that positive integers n and ℓ (such that $1 \leq \ell \leq f(n)$) are public, when a prover P knows an initial sequence of n cards requiring exactly ℓ steps, P can convince a verifier V that P knows the initial sequence without disclosing it. Our protocol is a so-called *physical* zero-knowledge proof protocol that can be executed using a physical deck of cards.

[4] At the present moment, of course, it is unknown whether such an initial sequence exists, i.e., whether $f(20) \geq 250$ or $f(20) = 249$.

1.4 Related Work

In the literature, many physical zero-knowledge proof protocols have been constructed using a physical deck of cards, especially those for pencil puzzles such as Sudoku. Examples include Akari [2], Cryptarithmetic [15], Hashiwokakero (Bridges) [56], Heyawake [47], Hitori [44,47], Juosan [30], Kakuro [2, 31], KenKen [2], Makaro [3,59], Masyu [24], Nonogram [4,48], Norinori [6], Numberlink [52,53], Nurikabe [44,47], Nurimisaki [42], Ripple Effect [54, 55], Shikaku [58], Slitherlink [24,25], Sudoku [49,51,60,61], Suguru [43,46], Takuzu [2,30], and Usowan [45].

Since our protocol uses a physical deck of cards, this study falls into the research area of *card-based cryptography* (refer to [20,37,63] for surveys), which has been rapidly growing recently, e.g., [33,34]. The recent results on card-based cryptography include proposing efficient protocols for multi-valued-output symmetric functions [57,62], analyzing information leakage due to operative errors [35], introducing graph automorphism shuffles [32], designing a secure sorting protocol [10], lowering the numbers of required cards [9] and shuffles [23], constructing multi-valued protocols with a direction encoding [64], introducing new encoding schemes for integers [50], exploring half-open-action protocols [29], and determining the landscape of card-minimal protocols in terms of running time requirements [21].

2 Preliminaries

In this section, we first explain the notations used in this paper, then describe how and what physical cards are utilized, and introduce the "pile-scramble shuffle [14]" and the "sort sub-protocol [22]," both of which are used in our protocol as sub-protocols.

2.1 Notations

Let n denote the Topswops size (the number of cards in an initial sequence), as in Sect. 1.

We regard any initial sequence of n cards and its succeeding sequences that appear in Topswops as permutations on $\{1, 2, \ldots, n\}$. That is, a permutation $\pi \in S_n$, i.e.,

$$\pi = \begin{pmatrix} 1 & 2 & 3 & \cdots & n \\ \pi(1) & \pi(2) & \pi(3) & \cdots & \pi(n) \end{pmatrix},$$

represents a sequence of n cards

$$(\pi(1), \pi(2), \pi(3), \ldots, \pi(n)),$$

where S_n denotes the symmetric group of degree n.

For the initial sequence corresponding to a permutation $\pi \in S_n$, denote by $\alpha(\pi)$ the number of steps required in Topswops. Using this notation $\alpha(\pi)$, we formally define $f(n)$, which is the maximum number of steps for n cards, as

$$f(n) := \max\{\alpha(\pi) \mid \pi \in S_n\}.$$

Using a permutation, let us represent each prefix reversal operation in Topswops, which rearranges the first i cards in their reverse order: Define a permutation $\mathsf{sw}_i \in S_n$ for every i, $2 \le i \le n$, as

$$\mathsf{sw}_i = \begin{pmatrix} 1 & 2 & 3 & \cdots & i-2 & i-1 & i \\ i & i-1 & i-2 & \cdots & 3 & 2 & 1 \end{pmatrix},$$

which is sometimes referred to as the *swap* sw_i. Note that sw_i is equal to its inverse permutation sw_i^{-1}. That is, for every i such that $2 \le i \le n$,

$$\mathsf{sw}_i = \mathsf{sw}_i^{-1} \tag{1}$$

holds.

2.2 Commitment Based on Physical Cards

The goal of this paper is to construct a zero-knowledge proof protocol for Topswops, which should keep an initial sequence and its subsequent sequences secret. Therefore, as usual in card-based cryptography, we place cards face down and perform a series of operations such as shuffling, rearranging, and turning over cards.

In this paper, we use a deck of physical cards numbered 1 to n, denoted by $\boxed{1}\boxed{2}\boxed{3}\cdots\boxed{n}$, whose backs are all identical $\boxed{?}$. We assume that cards $\boxed{i}\boxed{i}\cdots\boxed{i}$ having the same number i are all indistinguishable. By

$$\underset{i}{\boxed{?}},$$

we denote a face-down card whose face is $\boxed{i}$ for a number i.

As explained in the previous subsection, an initial sequence of n cards can be represented by a permutation $\pi \in S_n$, so a prover P can take n physical cards $\boxed{1}\boxed{2}\boxed{3}\cdots\boxed{n}$ and place them face down according to the initial sequence π:

$$\underset{\pi(1)}{\boxed{?}}\;\underset{\pi(2)}{\boxed{?}}\;\underset{\pi(3)}{\boxed{?}}\;\cdots\;\underset{\pi(n)}{\boxed{?}}\,.$$

It thus seems possible to keep the initial sequence and its succeeding sequences secret. However, it is difficult to apply a swap sw_i to such a physical sequence while keeping the integer i secret, and hence, such a simple representation does not work.

We therefore introduce a novel encoding of integers based on swaps sw_i: an integer $x \in \{2, 3, \ldots, n\}$ is encoded with n cards as

$$\boxed{\mathsf{sw}_x(1)}\boxed{\mathsf{sw}_x(2)}\boxed{\mathsf{sw}_x(3)}\cdots\boxed{\mathsf{sw}_x(n)}. \tag{2}$$

In other words, each integer $x \in \{2, 3, \ldots, n\}$ is represented by

$$\boxed{2}\boxed{1}\boxed{3}\boxed{4}\cdots\boxed{n} = 2$$
$$\boxed{3}\boxed{2}\boxed{1}\boxed{4}\cdots\boxed{n} = 3$$
$$\vdots$$
$$\boxed{i}\boxed{i-2}\boxed{i-3}\cdots\boxed{1}\boxed{i+1}\cdots\boxed{n} = i$$
$$\vdots$$
$$\boxed{n}\boxed{n-1}\cdots\boxed{1} = n.$$

In addition, $x = 1$ is represented with n cards of $\boxed{1}$ as

$$\boxed{1}\boxed{1}\cdots\boxed{1} = 1. \quad (3)$$

We call a sequence of n face-down cards encoding an integer $x \in \{1, 2, \ldots, n\}$ (according to the encoding rules (2) and (3) above) a *commitment* to x. For example, a commitment to 1 is a sequence of n face-down cards

$$\underset{1}{\boxed{?}}\underset{1}{\boxed{?}}\cdots\underset{1}{\boxed{?}},$$

and a commitment to x such that $x \geq 2$ is

$$\underset{\mathsf{sw}_x(1)}{\boxed{?}}\ \underset{\mathsf{sw}_x(2)}{\boxed{?}}\ \cdots\ \underset{\mathsf{sw}_x(n)}{\boxed{?}}.$$

Without distinguishing between the case $x = 1$ and the case $x > 1$, a commitment to x is denoted by

$$\underbrace{\boxed{?}\boxed{?}\cdots\boxed{?}}_{x} \text{ or } \underbrace{\boxed{?}\!\!\|\|}_{x}.$$

2.3 Pile-scramble Shuffle

A *pile-scramble shuffle* [14] is a shuffling operation by which several piles of cards of the same size are shuffled.

As an example, suppose we have n commitments and a sequence of n face-down cards corresponding to a permutation $\pi \in S_n$ as follows:

$$\begin{matrix} 1 & 2 & & n \\ \boxed{?}\!\!\|\| & \boxed{?}\!\!\|\| & \cdots & \boxed{?}\!\!\|\| \\ \boxed{?} & \boxed{?} & \cdots & \boxed{?} \\ \pi(1) & \pi(2) & & \pi(n) \end{matrix}, \quad (4)$$

where numbers above the commitments represent indexes for convenience. Considering each commitment and the card below it as a single pile, apply a pile-scramble shuffle to the n piles. The transition is

$$\left[\begin{array}{c|c|c|c} \boxed{?} & \boxed{?} & \cdots & \boxed{?} \\ \boxed{?} & \boxed{?} & \cdots & \boxed{?} \end{array}\right] \rightarrow \begin{array}{cccc} r^{-1}(1) & r^{-1}(2) & & r^{-1}(n) \\ \boxed{?} & \boxed{?} & \cdots & \boxed{?} \\ \boxed{?} & \boxed{?} & \cdots & \boxed{?} \\ \pi(r^{-1}(1)) & \pi(r^{-1}(2)) & & \pi(r^{-1}(n)) \end{array}, \tag{5}$$

where $r \in S_n$ is a uniformly distributed random permutation generated by the pile-scramble shuffle.

To implement a pile-scramble shuffle, we fix each pile of cards and shuffle the piles [14].

2.4 Sort Sub-protocol

Recall arrangement (4) above, where we have a sequence of n commitments and a sequence of cards corresponding to a permutation $\pi \in S_n$. Suppose that, after applying a pile-scramble shuffle to them as in transition (5), we turn over all n cards on the second row. Each number 1 to n should appear. We then sort the piles (keeping the order within each pile unchanged) so that the revealed numbers are in ascending order. We then obtain the sequence of piles

$$\begin{array}{cccc} \pi^{-1}(1) & \pi^{-1}(2) & & \pi^{-1}(n) \\ \boxed{?} & \boxed{?} & \cdots & \boxed{?} \\ \boxed{1} & \boxed{2} & \cdots & \boxed{n} \end{array}$$

(because, for example, if $\pi(r^{-1}(i)) = 1$, then $r^{-1}(i) = \pi^{-1}(1)$ and the commitment at position $\pi^{-1}(1)$ moves to the first). We have thus rearranged the sequence of n commitments according to the permutation $\pi \in S_n$ while keeping π secret.

This technique has been commonly used in constructions of zero-knowledge proof protocols for pencil puzzles since the introduction of a zero-knowledge proof protocol for Sudoku [61] that made full use of card-based cryptography. Koch and Walzer [22] formulated this technique and named it the *sort sub-protocol*. Note that the idea of applying a pile-scramble shuffle to two sequences of cards corresponding to some permutations originally comes from [13], followed by [11].

3 Proposed Protocol

In this section, we propose a zero-knowledge proof protocol for Topswops. Let positive integers n and ℓ (such that $1 \leq \ell \leq f(n)$) be public information. Suppose that a prover P knows $\sigma \in S_n$ such that $\alpha(\sigma) = \ell$, i.e., an initial sequence σ of n cards requiring exactly ℓ steps. P wants to convince a verifier V that P knows an initial sequence requiring ℓ steps without revealing any information about the initial sequence σ. We will construct a card-based protocol to achieve this.

First, Sect. 3.1 describes the idea behind the proposed protocol, then Sect. 3.2 presents a copy protocol we use as a sub-protocol. Finally, Sect. 3.3 presents our protocol.

3.1 Idea

This subsection describes the idea behind the proposed protocol using the initial $n = 5$ sequence $(3, 1, 4, 5, 2)$ (which has seven steps) as a working example.

First, prover P, who knows the initial sequence, secretly creates a sequence of commitments corresponding to $(3, 1, 4, 5, 2)$:

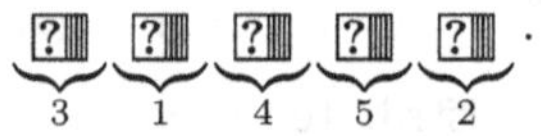

$$\underbrace{\boxed{?}\!\!|||}_{3}\;\underbrace{\boxed{?}\!\!|||}_{1}\;\underbrace{\boxed{?}\!\!|||}_{4}\;\underbrace{\boxed{?}\!\!|||}_{5}\;\underbrace{\boxed{?}\!\!|||}_{2}\,. \tag{6}$$

Recall that each commitment follows the encoding (2) and (3) defined in Sect. 2.2. For example, the first commitment

i.e., the commitment to 3, is

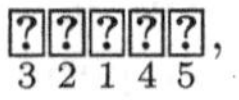

$$\underset{3}{\boxed{?}}\underset{2}{\boxed{?}}\underset{1}{\boxed{?}}\underset{4}{\boxed{?}}\underset{5}{\boxed{?}},$$

which is a permutation corresponding to the swap sw_3.

Suppose that we can somehow copy this commitment to 3. We then place the five copied face-down cards below the sequence of commitments as

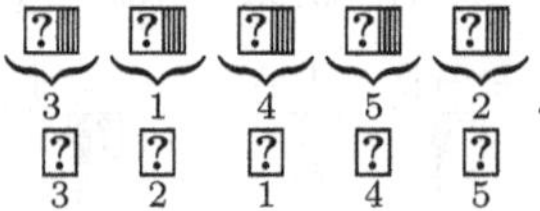

Considering each commitment and the card below as a single pile, we then apply a pile-scramble shuffle. After that, as in the sort sub-protocol described in Sect. 2.4, we turn over the five cards in the second row and sort the piles so that the five cards are rearranged in ascending order. We thus obtain the following:

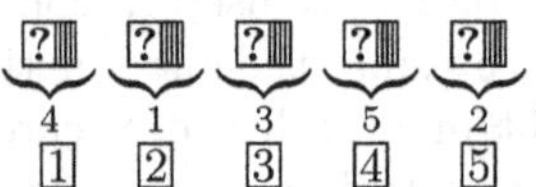

The order of the first three commitments is reversed in the resulting sequence of commitments, which means that the swap sw_3 was applied to the initial sequence without leaking any information about sw_3.

The first commitment in the current sequence is a commitment to 4, which corresponds to the swap sw_4. Hence, similar to sw_3 above, if we can copy and place it below the commitments and apply the sort sub-protocol, the swap sw_4 is applied while the integer corresponding to the first commitment remains secret. If we repeat such operations seven times, the first commitment in the sequence should be a commitment to 1. By turning over the first commitment, we can finally confirm that the prover P placed a correct initial sequence.

This is the idea behind our protocol. However, the above procedure cannot guarantee that the sequence of commitments (6) secretly set by P correctly satisfies the encoding rules. Thus, the proposed protocol, shown in Sect. 3.3, requires another step to ensure that the sequence is correctly rearranged.

3.2 Copy Protocol

As mentioned in Sect. 3.1, our main protocol requires a copied commitment. The following describes how to make two identical commitments from a single commitment while its value is kept secret.

Given a commitment to x such that $2 \le x \le n$,

$$\underbrace{\boxed{?}\boxed{?}\cdots\boxed{?}}_{x} \quad = \quad \underset{\mathsf{sw}_x(1)}{\boxed{?}}\ \underset{\mathsf{sw}_x(2)}{\boxed{?}}\ \cdots\ \underset{\mathsf{sw}_x(n)}{\boxed{?}},$$

along with two sets of $\boxed{1}$ through $\boxed{n}$ as additional cards, our copy protocol proceeds as follows.

Protocol 1 (Copy protocol)

1. *Commitments and additional cards are placed as follows:*

$$\begin{matrix} \boxed{1} & \boxed{2} & \cdots & \boxed{n} \\ \boxed{1} & \boxed{2} & \cdots & \boxed{n} \\ \underset{\mathsf{sw}_x(1)}{\boxed{?}} & \underset{\mathsf{sw}_x(2)}{\boxed{?}} & \cdots & \underset{\mathsf{sw}_x(n)}{\boxed{?}} \end{matrix}.$$

2. *Turn over the cards in the first and second rows and apply a pile-scramble shuffle:*

$$\left[\begin{array}{c|c|c|c} \boxed{?} & \boxed{?} & \cdots & \boxed{?} \\ \boxed{?} & \boxed{?} & \cdots & \boxed{?} \\ \boxed{?} & \boxed{?} & \cdots & \boxed{?} \end{array}\right].$$

Then, a uniformly distributed random permutation $r \in S_n$ corresponding to this pile-scramble shuffle occurs, and the resulting cards can be represented as

$$\begin{matrix} \underset{r^{-1}(1)}{\boxed{?}} & \underset{r^{-1}(2)}{\boxed{?}} & \cdots & \underset{r^{-1}(n)}{\boxed{?}} \\ \underset{r^{-1}(1)}{\boxed{?}} & \underset{r^{-1}(2)}{\boxed{?}} & \cdots & \underset{r^{-1}(n)}{\boxed{?}} \\ \underset{\mathsf{sw}_x(r^{-1}(1))}{\boxed{?}} & \underset{\mathsf{sw}_x(r^{-1}(2))}{\boxed{?}} & \cdots & \underset{\mathsf{sw}_x(r^{-1}(n))}{\boxed{?}} \end{matrix}.$$

3. *Turn over all the cards in the third row. If cards 1 through n appear without omission, sort the piles so that the revealed numbered cards are in ascending order, resulting in the following:*

$$\begin{matrix} \underset{\mathsf{sw}_x^{-1}(1)}{\boxed{?}} & \underset{\mathsf{sw}_x^{-1}(2)}{\boxed{?}} & \cdots & \underset{\mathsf{sw}_x^{-1}(n)}{\boxed{?}} \\ \underset{\mathsf{sw}_x^{-1}(1)}{\boxed{?}} & \underset{\mathsf{sw}_x^{-1}(2)}{\boxed{?}} & \cdots & \underset{\mathsf{sw}_x^{-1}(n)}{\boxed{?}} \\ \boxed{1} & \boxed{2} & \cdots & \boxed{n} \end{matrix}.$$

Since $\mathsf{sw}_x^{-1} = \mathsf{sw}_x$ from Eq. (1), the first and second rows are commitments to x and we have copied commitments

$$\underbrace{\boxed{?}\boxed{?}\cdots\boxed{?}}_{x}\quad \underbrace{\boxed{?}\boxed{?}\cdots\boxed{?}}_{x}.$$

In the last step, the n cards in the third row are turned over, but no information about x is leaked because these cards were uniformly randomized by the random permutation r in Step 2. Note also that if an input sequence is a commitment to 1, or if it is not a valid commitment, this protocol detects that state when the cards are turned over in Step 3.

A copy protocol for a permutation was first proposed in [61], but that protocol requires two pile-scramble shuffles. Our proposed copy protocol is simpler with only one pile-scramble shuffle, because by Eq.(1), the permutation sw_i to be copied is equal to its reverse permutation.

3.3 Our Protocol

We are now ready to describe our protocol, which is a so-called *non-interactive* physical zero-knowledge proof protocol that requires no knowledge of the prover after the prover places an input card sequence (see [28] for details).

According to an initial sequence σ such that $\alpha(\sigma) = \ell$, the prover P places n face-down cards on the table without anyone seeing the order as

$$\underset{\sigma^{-1}(1)}{\boxed{?}}\ \underset{\sigma^{-1}(2)}{\boxed{?}}\ \underset{\sigma^{-1}(3)}{\boxed{?}}\ \cdots\ \underset{\sigma^{-1}(n)}{\boxed{?}}\ . \tag{7}$$

The input to our protocol is this sequence (7) along with additional $2n$ cards of $\boxed{1}$ and n cards from each of $\boxed{2}$ to $\boxed{n}$. (The protocol may be executed by a prover or a verifier, or even by a third party[5].)

Protocol 2 (Physical zero-knowledge proof protocol for Topswops)

1. *Using* $2n-1$ *cards of* $\boxed{1}$ *and* $n-1$ *cards of each from* $\boxed{2}$ *to* $\boxed{n}$ *from the additional cards, make a commitment to each of* 1 *through* n *and place them above the input sequence (7) as follows:*

$$\begin{matrix} \underbrace{\boxed{?}\!\!|||||}_{1} & \underbrace{\boxed{?}\!\!|||||}_{2} & \cdots & \underbrace{\boxed{?}\!\!|||||}_{n} \\ \underset{\sigma^{-1}(1)}{\boxed{?}} & \underset{\sigma^{-1}(2)}{\boxed{?}} & \cdots & \underset{\sigma^{-1}(n)}{\boxed{?}} \end{matrix}\ .$$

2. *Apply a pile-scramble shuffle:*

$$\left[\begin{array}{c|c|c|c} \underbrace{\boxed{?}\!\!|||||}_{1} & \underbrace{\boxed{?}\!\!|||||}_{2} & \cdots & \underbrace{\boxed{?}\!\!|||||}_{n} \\ \underset{\sigma^{-1}(1)}{\boxed{?}} & \underset{\sigma^{-1}(2)}{\boxed{?}} & \cdots & \underset{\sigma^{-1}(n)}{\boxed{?}} \end{array}\right].$$

[5] More precisely, it is specified as a card-based protocol formulated in the standard model of card-based cryptography [36,37]. (Note that there are other models, e.g., [26,27,39,40].).

3. *In the manner of the sort sub-protocol described in Sect. 2.4, turn over and sort the cards in the bottom row so that the cards in the bottom row are in ascending order:*

$$\underbrace{\boxed{?}}_{\sigma(1)}\ \underbrace{\boxed{?}}_{\sigma(2)} \cdots \underbrace{\boxed{?}}_{\sigma(n)} \cdot$$
$$\boxed{1}\ \boxed{2} \cdots \boxed{n}$$

(If any card from 1 *to* n *does not appear in the bottom row, the protocol halts.)*

4. *We have two cards each from* $\boxed{1}$ *to* $\boxed{n}$ *(i.e., the cards revealed in Step 3 and the remaining additional cards not used in Step 1). Using these as additional cards, copy the first commitment,* $\sigma(1)$*, by executing the copy protocol described in Sect. 3.2 and place it below the sequence of commitments. Hereinafter, we use* x *for* $\sigma(1)$ *in subscripts for simplicity:*

$$\underbrace{\boxed{?}}_{\sigma(1)}\ \underbrace{\boxed{?}}_{\sigma(2)} \cdots \underbrace{\boxed{?}}_{\sigma(n)} .$$
$$\underset{\mathsf{sw}_x(1)}{\boxed{?}}\ \underset{\mathsf{sw}_x(2)}{\boxed{?}} \cdots \underset{\mathsf{sw}_x(n)}{\boxed{?}}$$

(If an illegal card appears during the copy protocol, the protocol halts.)

5. *Apply a pile-scramble shuffle, turn over the cards in the bottom row, and sort the cards in the bottom row in ascending order:*

$$\left[\begin{array}{c|c|c|c} \underbrace{\boxed{?}}_{\sigma(1)} & \underbrace{\boxed{?}}_{\sigma(2)} & \cdots & \underbrace{\boxed{?}}_{\sigma(n)} \\ \underset{\mathsf{sw}_x(1)}{\boxed{?}} & \underset{\mathsf{sw}_x(2)}{\boxed{?}} & \cdots & \underset{\mathsf{sw}_x(n)}{\boxed{?}} \end{array}\right]$$
$$\downarrow$$
$$\underbrace{\boxed{?}}_{\sigma(\mathsf{sw}_x^{-1}(1))}\ \underbrace{\boxed{?}}_{\sigma(\mathsf{sw}_x^{-1}(2))} \cdots \underbrace{\boxed{?}}_{\sigma(\mathsf{sw}_x^{-1}(n))} \cdot$$
$$\boxed{1}\ \boxed{2} \cdots \boxed{n}$$

After this operation, the first row is a sequence of commitments where the order of the first x *commitments is reversed, i.e., the swap* sw_x *operation has been applied to the original sequence of commitments. (If any card from* 1 *to* n *does not appear, the protocol aborts.)*

6. *Repeat Steps 4 and 5 in the same manner* ℓ *times in total.*
7. *Turn over the first commitment* $\boxed{?}$ *and return 'accept' if* $\boxed{1}\boxed{1} \cdots \boxed{1}$ *appears. Otherwise, return 'reject.'*

4 Security and Performance

This section describes security and performance of the protocol proposed in the previous section.

4.1 Security

In this subsection, we prove that our protocol is a zero-knowledge proof protocol. In other words, we show that our protocol satisfies requirements for completeness, soundness, and zero knowledge.

Completeness: Suppose that a prover P correctly sets as input a sequence of n cards encoding an initial sequence $\sigma \in S_n$ such that $\alpha(\sigma) = \ell$. Then, as can be seen from the construction of the protocol, the sequence is not rejected at any step, but accepted at the final step.

Soundness: Assume that an input sequence of n cards is not the encoding of an initial sequence requiring exactly ℓ steps. There are three cases to consider; we will show that the protocol eventually rejects each.

(i) If the input sequence is not encoded for any initial sequence, it is detected and rejected because not every card from 1 to n appears when the cards are turned up in Step 3.

(ii) Assume an initial sequence requiring exactly j $(< \ell)$ steps. When Steps 4 and 5 of our protocol are executed j times, the first commitment will be a commitment to 1, and Step 4 of iteration $(j+1)$ will duplicate the commitment to 1, and hence, our protocol rejects the sequence because n cards of 1 appear in the final step of the copy protocol.

(iii) If an initial sequence requires j $(> \ell)$ steps, the first commitment in the last step is rejected because it is something other than a commitment to 1.

Zero knowledge: Suppose that the sequence set by prover P corresponds to $\sigma \in S_n$ such that $\alpha(\sigma) = \ell$. During the protocol (except for the final step), no information about σ is leaked because the order of revealed cards $\boxed{1}$ to $\boxed{n}$ is always randomized by a pile-scramble shuffle, which is applied immediately before the cards are turned over. In addition, the commitment to 1 opened in the final step is public information (from the definition of Topswops). Thus, the proposed protocol is information-theoretically secure.

4.2 Performance

This subsection counts the number of cards and the number of shuffles required in our protocol.

Regarding the number of cards, we use $\boxed{1}$ to $\boxed{n}$ for the input card sequence, as described at the beginning of Sect. 3.3, with additional $2n$ cards of $\boxed{1}$ and n cards each of $\boxed{2}$ to $\boxed{n}$. Thus, $2n+1$ cards of $\boxed{1}$ and $n+1$ cards of each of $\boxed{2}$ to $\boxed{n}$ are required, which add up to $n^2 + 2n$.

Our protocol uses only pile-scramble shuffles as a shuffle operation. We therefore count the number of pile-scramble shuffles. In our protocol, Step 2 is executed once, and Steps 4 and 5 are repeated ℓ times. These steps include one pile-scramble shuffle, so our protocol requires $2\ell + 1$ pile-scramble shuffles in total.

5 Conclusion

We proposed a physical zero-knowledge proof protocol for Topswops. The main idea is that the permutation corresponding to "the operation of reversing the first i cards" encodes a positive integer i, which enables us to efficiently and secretly perform prefix reversals in Topswops. The proposed protocol uses $n^2 + 2n$ cards and $2\ell + 1$ shuffles, where n is the size of Topswops and ℓ is the number of steps.

In the "game of discovering initial sequences requiring a predefined number of steps" described in Sect. 1.2, we can expect to make practical use of our protocol when n is not so large. However, in the other example of claiming discovery of an initial sequence for $n = 20$ requiring 250 steps, like that described in Sect. 1.2, implementing our protocol would require 440 cards and 501 shuffles, which might not be practical to implement. Therefore, we address the following problem as another situation that may be practically useful.

The *pancake problem* [18] is another game similar to Topswops. Given an initial sequence $(\pi(1), \pi(2), \ldots, \pi(n))$, the goal in this game is to sort the sequence in ascending order by repeating swap operations sw_i. Related to this game, the problem of finding a sequence of the minimum number of swap operations needed to complete the sort is proved to be NP-hard [1]. Also, we denote as $h(n)$ the maximum number of such fewest swap operations among all initial sequences of n cards. Then, the best currently known lower and upper bounds[6] are $\frac{15}{14}n \leq h(n)$ [12] and $h(n) \leq \frac{18}{11}n$ [5], respectively.

We expect that the idea of our protocol can be applied to the pancake problem. As mentioned above, the upper bound of $h(n)$ is linearly suppressed by n, so we expect the required number of shuffles not to be excessively large as n increases. We also expect to find more value in keeping a sequence of swap operations secret, since the problem of finding a sequence of the minimum number of swap operations has been proven to be an NP-hard problem. This direction is a future work.

Acknowledgements. This work was supported by Grant-in-Aid for Scientific Research (JP18H05289, JP21K11881).

References

1. Bulteau, L., Fertin, G., Rusu, I.: Pancake flipping is hard. J. Comput. Syst. Sci. **81**(8), 1556–1574 (2015). https://doi.org/10.1016/j.jcss.2015.02.003, https://www.sciencedirect.com/science/article/pii/S0022000015000124
2. Bultel, X., Dreier, J., Dumas, J.G., Lafourcade, P.: Physical zero-knowledge proofs for Akari, Takuzu, Kakuro and KenKen. In: Demaine, E.D., Grandoni, F. (eds.) Fun with Algorithms. LIPIcs, vol. 49, pp. 8:1–8:20. Schloss Dagstuhl, Dagstuhl, Germany (2016). https://doi.org/10.4230/LIPIcs.FUN.2016.8
3. Bultel, X., et al.: Physical zero-knowledge proof for Makaro. In: Izumi, T., Kuznetsov, P. (eds.) SSS 2018. LNCS, vol. 11201, pp. 111–125. Springer, Cham (2018). https://doi.org/10.1007/978-3-030-03232-6_8

[6] The upper and lower bounds were known to be $\frac{17}{16}n \leq h(n) \leq \frac{5n+5}{3}$ [7] in 1979.

4. Chien, Y.-F., Hon, W.-K.: Cryptographic and physical zero-knowledge proof: from Sudoku to Nonogram. In: Boldi, P., Gargano, L. (eds.) FUN 2010. LNCS, vol. 6099, pp. 102–112. Springer, Heidelberg (2010). https://doi.org/10.1007/978-3-642-13122-6_12
5. Chitturi, B., et al.: An (18/11)n upper bound for sorting by prefix reversals. Theor. Comput. Sci. **410**(36), 3372–3390 (2009). https://doi.org/10.1016/j.tcs.2008.04.045, https://www.sciencedirect.com/science/article/pii/S0304397508003575, graphs, Games and Computation: Dedicated to Professor Burkhard Monien on the Occasion of his 65th Birthday
6. Dumas, J.-G., Lafourcade, P., Miyahara, D., Mizuki, T., Sasaki, T., Sone, H.: Interactive physical zero-knowledge proof for Norinori. In: Du, D.-Z., Duan, Z., Tian, C. (eds.) COCOON 2019. LNCS, vol. 11653, pp. 166–177. Springer, Cham (2019). https://doi.org/10.1007/978-3-030-26176-4_14
7. Gates, W.H., Papadimitriou, C.H.: Bounds for sorting by prefix reversal. Discret. Math. **27**(1), 47–57 (1979). https://doi.org/10.1016/0012-365X(79)90068-2
8. Goldwasser, S., Micali, S., Rackoff, C.: The knowledge complexity of interactive proof-systems. In: Annual ACM Symposium on Theory of Computing, pp. 291–304. STOC 1985, ACM, New York (1985). https://doi.org/10.1145/22145.22178
9. Haga, R., Hayashi, Y., Miyahara, D., Mizuki, T.: Card-Minimal Protocols for Three-Input Functions with Standard Playing Cards. In: Batina, L., Daemen, J. (eds.) AFRICACRYPT 2022. Lecture Notes in Computer Science, vol. 13503, pp. 448–468. Springer, Cham (2022). https://doi.org/10.1007/978-3-031-17433-9_19
10. Haga, R., Toyoda, K., Shinoda, Y., Miyahara, D., Shinagawa, K., Hayashi, Y., Mizuki, T.: Card-based secure sorting protocol. In: Cheng, C.M., Akiyama, M. (eds.) Advances in Information and Computer Security. LNCS, vol. 13504, pp. 224–240. Springer, Cham (2022). https://doi.org/10.1007/978-3-031-15255-9_12
11. Hashimoto, Y., Nuida, K., Shinagawa, K., Inamura, M., Hanaoka, G.: Toward finite-runtime card-based protocol for generating a hidden random permutation without fixed points. IEICE Trans. Fundam. Electron. Commun. Comput. Sci. **E101.A**(9), 1503–1511 (2018). https://doi.org/10.1587/transfun.E101.A.1503
12. Heydari, M.H., Sudborough, I.: On the diameter of the pancake network. J. Algorithms **25**(1), 67–94 (1997). https://doi.org/10.1006/jagm.1997.0874, https://www.sciencedirect.com/science/article/pii/S0196677497908749
13. Ibaraki, T., Manabe, Y.: A more efficient card-based protocol for generating a random permutation without fixed points. In: Mathematics and Computers in Sciences and in Industry (MCSI), pp. 252–257 (2016). https://doi.org/10.1109/MCSI.2016.054
14. Ishikawa, R., Chida, E., Mizuki, T.: Efficient card-based protocols for generating a hidden random permutation without fixed points. In: Calude, C.S., Dinneen, M.J. (eds.) UCNC 2015. LNCS, vol. 9252, pp. 215–226. Springer, Cham (2015). https://doi.org/10.1007/978-3-319-21819-9_16
15. Isuzugawa, R., Miyahara, D., Mizuki, T.: Zero-knowledge proof protocol for cryptarithmetic using dihedral cards. In: Kostitsyna, I., Orponen, P. (eds.) UCNC 2021. LNCS, vol. 12984, pp. 51–67. Springer, Cham (2021). https://doi.org/10.1007/978-3-030-87993-8_4
16. Kimura, K., Takahashi, A., Araki, T., Amano, K.: Maximum number of steps of topswops on 18 and 19 cards. arXiv:2103.08346 (2021). https://doi.org/10.48550/ARXIV.2103.08346, https://arxiv.org/abs/2103.08346
17. Klamkin, M.S.: Problems in applied mathematics: selections from SIAM review (1990). https://doi.org/10.1137/1.9781611971729.ch4, https://epubs.siam.org/doi/abs/10.1137/1.9781611971729.ch4

18. Kleitman, D.J., Kramer, E., Conway, J.H., Bell, S., Dweighter, H.: Elementary problems: e2564–e2569. Am. Math. Monthly **82**(10), 1009–1010 (1975). http://www.jstor.org/stable/2318260
19. Knuth, D.E.: The Art of Computer Programming, Volume 4, Fascicle 2: Generating All Tuples and Permutations (Art of Computer Programming). Addison-Wesley Professional (2005)
20. Koch, A.: Cryptographic protocols from physical assumptions. Ph.D. thesis, Karlsruhe Institute of Technology (2019). https://doi.org/10.5445/IR/1000097756
21. Koch, A.: The landscape of optimal card-based protocols. Math. Cryptol. **1**(2), 115–131 (2022). https://journals.flvc.org/mathcryptology/article/view/130529
22. Koch, A., Walzer, S.: Private function evaluation with cards. New Gener. Comput. pp. 1–33 (2022). https://doi.org/10.1007/s00354-021-00149-9. (in press)
23. Kuzuma, T., Toyoda, K., Miyahara, D., Mizuki, T.: Card-based single-shuffle protocols for secure multiple-input AND and XOR computations. In: ASIA Public-Key Cryptography, pp. 51–58. ACM, NY (2022). https://doi.org/10.1145/3494105.3526236
24. Lafourcade, P., Miyahara, D., Mizuki, T., Robert, L., Sasaki, T., Sone, H.: How to construct physical zero-knowledge proofs for puzzles with a "single loop" condition. Theor. Comput. Sci. (2021). in press). https://doi.org/10.1016/j.tcs.2021.07.019
25. Lafourcade, P., Miyahara, D., Mizuki, T., Sasaki, T., Sone, H.: A physical ZKP for slitherlink: how to perform physical topology-preserving computation. In: Heng, S.-H., Lopez, J. (eds.) ISPEC 2019. LNCS, vol. 11879, pp. 135–151. Springer, Cham (2019). https://doi.org/10.1007/978-3-030-34339-2_8
26. Manabe, Y., Ono, H.: Card-based cryptographic protocols for three-input functions using private operations. In: Flocchini, P., Moura, L. (eds.) IWOCA 2021. LNCS, vol. 12757, pp. 469–484. Springer, Cham (2021). https://doi.org/10.1007/978-3-030-79987-8_33
27. Manabe, Y., Ono, H.: Card-based cryptographic protocols with malicious players using private operations. New Gener. Comput. pp. 1–27 (2022). https://doi.org/10.1007/s00354-021-00148-w. (in press)
28. Miyahara, D., Haneda, H., Mizuki, T.: Card-based zero-knowledge proof protocols for graph problems and their computational model. In: Huang, Q., Yu, Yu. (eds.) ProvSec 2021. LNCS, vol. 13059, pp. 136–152. Springer, Cham (2021). https://doi.org/10.1007/978-3-030-90402-9_8
29. Miyahara, D., Mizuki, T.: Secure computations through checking suits of playing cards. In: Frontiers in Algorithmics. Lecture Notes in Computer Science. Springer, Cham (2022). to appear
30. Miyahara, D., et al.: Card-based ZKP protocols for Takuzu and Juosan. In: Farach-Colton, M., Prencipe, G., Uehara, R. (eds.) Fun with Algorithms. LIPIcs, vol. 157, pp. 20:1–20:21. Schloss Dagstuhl, Dagstuhl, Germany (2020). https://doi.org/10.4230/LIPIcs.FUN.2021.20
31. Miyahara, D., Sasaki, T., Mizuki, T., Sone, H.: Card-based physical zero-knowledge proof for Kakuro. IEICE Trans. Fundam. Electron. Commun. Comput. Sci. **102**(9), 1072–1078 (2019). https://doi.org/10.1587/transfun.E102.A.1072
32. Miyamoto, K., Shinagawa, K.: Graph automorphism shuffles from pile-scramble shuffles. New Gener. Comput. **40**, 199–223 (2022). https://doi.org/10.1007/s00354-022-00164-4
33. Mizuki, T.: Preface: special issue on card-based cryptography. New Gener. Comput. **39**, 1–2 (2021). https://doi.org/10.1007/s00354-021-00127-1
34. Mizuki, T.: Preface: special issue on card-based cryptography 2. New Gener. Comput. **40**, 47–48 (2022). https://doi.org/10.1007/s00354-022-00170-6

35. Mizuki, T., Komano, Y.: Information leakage due to operative errors in card-based protocols. Inf. Comput. **285**, 104910 (2022). https://doi.org/10.1016/j.ic.2022.104910
36. Mizuki, T., Shizuya, H.: A formalization of card-based cryptographic protocols via abstract machine. Int. J. Inf. Secur. **13**(1), 15–23 (2014). https://doi.org/10.1007/s10207-013-0219-4
37. Mizuki, T., Shizuya, H.: Computational model of card-based cryptographic protocols and its applications. IEICE Trans. Fundam. Electron. Commun. Comput. Sci. **E100.A**(1), 3–11 (2017). https://doi.org/10.1587/transfun.E100.A.3
38. Morales, L., Sudborough, H.: A quadratic lower bound for topswops. Theor. Comput. Sci. **411**(44), 3965–3970 (2010). https://doi.org/10.1016/j.tcs.2010.08.011, https://www.sciencedirect.com/science/article/pii/S0304397510004287
39. Nakai, T., Shirouchi, S., Tokushige, Y., Iwamoto, M., Ohta, K.: Secure computation for threshold functions with physical cards: Power of private permutations. New Gener. Comput. 1–19 (2022). https://doi.org/10.1007/s00354-022-00153-7. (in press)
40. Ono, H., Manabe, Y.: Card-based cryptographic logical computations using private operations. New Gener. Comput. **39**(1), 19–40 (2021). https://doi.org/10.1007/s00354-020-00113-z
41. Pepperdine, A.: 73.23 topswops. Math. Gazette **73**(464), 131–133 (1989). http://www.jstor.org/stable/3619674
42. Robert, L., Lafourcade, P., Miyahara, D., Mizuki, T.: Card-based ZKP protocol for nurimisaki. In: Stabilization, Safety, and Security of Distributed Systems. LNCS, vol. 13751. Springer, Cham (2022). (to appear)
43. Robert, L., Miyahara, D., Lafourcade, P., Mizuki, T.: Physical zero-knowledge proof for Suguru puzzle. In: Devismes, S., Mittal, N. (eds.) Stabilization, Safety, and Security of Distributed Systems. LNCS, vol. 12514, pp. 235–247. Springer, Cham (2020). https://doi.org/10.1007/978-3-030-64348-5_19
44. Robert, L., Miyahara, D., Lafourcade, P., Mizuki, T.: Interactive physical ZKP for connectivity: applications to Nurikabe and Hitori. In: De Mol, L., Weiermann, A., Manea, F., Fernández-Duque, D. (eds.) CiE 2021. LNCS, vol. 12813, pp. 373–384. Springer, Cham (2021). https://doi.org/10.1007/978-3-030-80049-9_37
45. Robert, L., Miyahara, D., Lafourcade, P., Mizuki, T.: Hide a liar: card-based ZKP protocol for Usowan. In: Theory and Applications of Models of Computation. LNCS, Springer, Cham (2022). (to appear)
46. Robert, L., Miyahara, D., Lafourcade, P., Libralesso, L., Mizuki, T.: Physical zero-knowledge proof and NP-completeness proof of Suguru puzzle. Inf. Comput. 104858 (2021). https://doi.org/10.1016/j.ic.2021.104858, https://www.sciencedirect.com/science/article/pii/S0890540121001905 , in press
47. Robert, L., Miyahara, D., Lafourcade, P., Mizuki, T.: Card-based ZKP for connectivity: applications to Nurikabe, Hitori, and Heyawake. New Gener. Comput. 1–23 (2022). https://doi.org/10.1007/s00354-022-00155-5, in press
48. Ruangwises, S.: An improved physical ZKP for Nonogram. In: Du, D.-Z., Du, D., Wu, C., Xu, D. (eds.) COCOA 2021. LNCS, vol. 13135, pp. 262–272. Springer, Cham (2021). https://doi.org/10.1007/978-3-030-92681-6_22
49. Ruangwises, S.: Two standard decks of playing cards are sufficient for a ZKP for Sudoku. In: Chen, C.-Y., Hon, W.-K., Hung, L.-J., Lee, C.-W. (eds.) COCOON 2021. LNCS, vol. 13025, pp. 631–642. Springer, Cham (2021). https://doi.org/10.1007/978-3-030-89543-3_52

50. Ruangwises, S.: Using five cards to encode each integer in Z/6Z. In: Innovative Security Solutions for Information Technology and Communications. LNCS. Springer, Cham (2021). (to appear)
51. Ruangwises, S.: Two standard decks of playing cards are sufficient for a ZKP for sudoku. New Gener. Comput. 1–17 (2022). https://doi.org/10.1007/s00354-021-00146-y. (in press)
52. Ruangwises, S., Itoh, T.: Physical zero-knowledge proof for Numberlink. In: Farach-Colton, M., Prencipe, G., Uehara, R. (eds.) Fun with Algorithms. LIPIcs, vol. 157, pp. 22:1–22:11. Schloss Dagstuhl, Dagstuhl, Germany (2020). https://doi.org/10.4230/LIPIcs.FUN.2021.22
53. Ruangwises, S., Itoh, T.: Physical zero-knowledge proof for Numberlink puzzle and k vertex-disjoint paths problem. New Gener. Comput. **39**(1), 3–17 (2021). https://doi.org/10.1007/s00354-020-00114-y
54. Ruangwises, S., Itoh, T.: Physical zero-knowledge proof for ripple effect. In: Uehara, R., Hong, S.-H., Nandy, S.C. (eds.) WALCOM 2021. LNCS, vol. 12635, pp. 296–307. Springer, Cham (2021). https://doi.org/10.1007/978-3-030-68211-8_24
55. Ruangwises, S., Itoh, T.: Physical zero-knowledge proof for ripple effect. Theor. Comput. Sci. **895**, 115–123 (2021). https://doi.org/10.1016/j.tcs.2021.09.034
56. Ruangwises, S., Itoh, T.: Physical ZKP for connected spanning subgraph: applications to bridges puzzle and other problems. In: Kostitsyna, I., Orponen, P. (eds.) UCNC 2021. LNCS, vol. 12984, pp. 149–163. Springer, Cham (2021). https://doi.org/10.1007/978-3-030-87993-8_10
57. Ruangwises, S., Itoh, T.: Securely computing the n-variable equality function with 2n cards. Theor. Comput. Sci. **887**, 99–110 (2021). https://doi.org/10.1016/j.tcs.2021.07.007
58. Ruangwises, S., Itoh, T.: How to physically verify a rectangle in a grid: a physical ZKP for Shikaku. In: Fraigniaud, P., Uno, Y. (eds.) Fun with Algorithms. LIPIcs, vol. 226, pp. 24:1–24:12. Schloss Dagstuhl, Dagstuhl (2022). https://doi.org/10.4230/LIPIcs.FUN.2022.24
59. Ruangwises, S., Itoh, T.: Physical ZKP for Makaro using a standard deck of cards. In: Theory and Applications of Models of Computation. LNCS. Springer, Cham (2022). (to appear)
60. Sasaki, T., Miyahara, D., Mizuki, T., Sone, H.: Efficient card-based zero-knowledge proof for Sudoku. Theor. Comput. Sci. **839**, 135–142 (2020). https://doi.org/10.1016/j.tcs.2020.05.036
61. Sasaki, T., Mizuki, T., Sone, H.: Card-based zero-knowledge proof for Sudoku. In: Ito, H., Leonardi, S., Pagli, L., Prencipe, G. (eds.) Fun with Algorithms. LIPIcs, vol. 100, pp. 29:1–29:10. Schloss Dagstuhl, Dagstuhl, Germany (2018), https://doi.org/10.4230/LIPIcs.FUN.2018.29
62. Shikata, H., Toyoda, K., Miyahara, D., Mizuki, T.: Card-minimal protocols for symmetric Boolean functions of more than seven inputs. In: Seidl, H., Liu, Z., Pasareanu, C.S. (eds.) ICTAC 2022. LNCS, vol. 13572, pp. 388–406. Springer, Cham (2022). https://doi.org/10.1007/978-3-031-17715-6_25
63. Shinagawa, K.: On the construction of easy to perform card-based protocols. Ph.D. thesis, Tokyo Institute of Technology (2020)
64. Suga, Y.: A classification proof for commutative three-element semigroups with local and structure and its application to card-based protocols. In: 2022 IEEE International Conference on Consumer Electronics - Taiwan, pp. 171–172. IEEE, NY (2022). https://doi.org/10.1109/ICCE-Taiwan55306.2022.9869063

Attribute Based Tracing for Securing Group Signatures Against Centralized Authorities

Maharage Nisansala Sevwandi Perera[1(✉)], Toru Nakamura[2], Takashi Matsunaka[1], Hiroyuki Yokoyama[1], and Kouichi Sakurai[3]

[1] Advanced Telecommunications Research Institute International, 2-2-2 Hikaridai, Seika-cho, Soraku-gun, Kyoto, Japan
{perera.nisansala,ta-matsunaka,hr-yokoyama}@atr.jp
[2] KDDI Research, Inc., Saitama, Japan
ta-nakamura@kddi.com
[3] Kyushu University, Fukuoka, Japan
sakurai@inf.kyushu-u.ac.jp

Abstract. This paper proposes a group signature scheme with a tracing mechanism that limits the tracing ability of tracers based on their attributes and decentralizes the tracing key generation method. Thus, no other party than the attributes satisfying tracer can identify the signer. The proposing scheme answers the single point of failure of the tracing mechanism in the existing group signature schemes. On the other hand, the multiple tracers setting of the proposing scheme reduces the tracing workload that the single tracer had, and provides selection flexibility for users to choose a tracer for their signatures based on tracers' attributes. This paper discussed the related security definitions against outsiders and honest but curious authorities.

Keywords: Group signatures · Tracing signer · Attribute-based tracing · Attribute-based encryption · Decentralized key generation

1 Introduction

Group Signatures, introduced by David Chaum with Eugene van Heyst [6], enables anonymous authentication. While allowing group members to produce anonymous signatures on behalf of the group, group signatures allow an appointed authority to identify the signers using a secret tracing key. Traceability feature makes group members accountable for their signing behavior and controls user anonymity. In the early stage of the group signatures, the group manager held the tracing authority. However, the tracing authority role was later separated from the group manager strengthening the scheme's security. A third party authority called tracing manager (tracer) has tracing ability to cancel the anonymity of the signature and identifying the signer.

C. Su et al. (Eds.): ISPEC 2022, LNCS 13620, pp. 554–572, 2022.
https://doi.org/10.1007/978-3-031-21280-2_31

The extreme privilege of the tracer harms the assurance of users' anonymity [15]. Addressing the problem of tracing authority power, there are some works that either suggest user-specific trapdoor or message-specific trapdoor. The tracing authority can open only signatures of a specific user or a specific message. Kiaiyas et al. [11] presented a controlled tracing mechanism that the tracer can only open signatures of a signer selected by the group manager to trace. Sakai et al. [16] proposed a message-dependent tracing technique. In Sakai's technique, another party called admitter issues a message-related token controlling the tracer identifying signers who generated signatures on that message. Since the tracer cannot identify signers without the admitters's awareness, tracing ability is controlled. However, requiring a single centralized tracer to do whole tracing work in the techniques mentioned above makes the tracing process inefficient and insecure.

Another line of work in group signatures discusses the centralized tracing problem. For instance, Manulis et al. [13] proposed Linkable Democratic Group Signatures applicable in a system with no centralized authority. In their scheme, there is no third-party tracer, and any group member can trace a signer (who is a fellow member). In other words, anonymity is ensured only against outsiders. However, trusting group users seem insecure. Essam Ghadafi [9] also presented a group signature scheme with distributed tracing, where the centralized tracing authority is distributed to n tracing parties, and unless the n parties agree a signer cannot be traced. Some works [4,5] suggested distributed tracing method with threshold-tracing, which requires at least t tracers' collaboration to trace a signer. Even though those schemes provide decentralized tracing, they still do not give users the flexibility to select their tracer.

Attribute-based tracing mechanism is a suitable solution for allowing signers to select a tracer as their choice. In Attribute-based tracing multiple tracers have attributes, and unless the access structure used for generating the signature is satisfied, the tracer cannot identify the signer. Attribute-based tracing satisfies the realistic scenarios as attributes represents real properties like department and designation. Recently, Anada et al. [1] presented a similar method called a function of designated traceability. However, in their scheme, other than tracers the group manager has authority to open any signature using master secret key and he knows all the tracing keys because he generates tracing keys for tracers. Removing tracing ability from group manager, Perera et al. [14] discussed decentralized tracing via attribute-based tracing and allowing tracers to collaborate if a single tracer cannot satisfy the attributes used in the given signature. However, both schemes did not discuss the decentralizing tracers' key generation.

Our Contribution

We propose a tracing mechanism based on tracers' attributes and a decentralized tracing key generation. In our scheme, there are multiple tracers, and each tracer possesses a set of valid attributes. Each attribute has a public key, and when a user generates a signature, he selects an access structure to encrypt his identity in the signature. Thus only a tracer with a matching attribute set can identify the signer. Moreover, proposal removes the centralized tracer key generation ensuring the group manager or other authority does not know any tracing key. On the other hand, multiple tracer setting reduces the tracing workload and the public key size is independent of the number of tracers. Our scheme ensures security against corrupted authorities and users trying to be anonymous permanently by selecting attributes that do not belong to any tracer in the group.

Comparison of Our Proposal with Related works

Table 1 provides the high level comparison of our proposal with related works.

Table 1. High level comparison of the features of the proposal with the related works.

Scheme	Tracing feature	Controlled tracing	DC tracing	Removed GM tracing	DC tracing KeyGen
Kiayias et al. [11]	User-specific	Yes	No	No	No
Sakai et al. [16]	Message-specific	Yes	No	No	No
Manulis et al. [13]	Any user can trace	No	Yes	Yes	No
Essam Ghadafi [9]	n tracers should agree	No	Yes	Yes	No
Anada et al. [1]	Attribute-based	Yes	Yes	No	No
Perera et al. [14]	Attribute-based	Yes	Yes	Yes	No
Our Proposal	Attribute-based	Yes	Yes	Yes	Yes

DC - decentralized; GM - group manager; tracing KeyGen - tracing key generation

While the previous schemes [9,11,13,16] either control or decentralize the tracing power, the proposal of Anada et al. [1] and Perera et al. [14] satisfy both conditions. In the scheme of Anada et al. [1], still the group manager has tracing power. On the other hand, since the tracing key generation is not decentralized, both schemes [1] and [14] have a risk of tracing-key generating authority identifying the signers. We remove the tracing key generation from the central authority. Moreover, to prevent signer selecting attributes that not belong to the group, we propose an alternative solution via verification process.

2 Preliminaries

In this section we fix our notation and provide the building blocks of our scheme.

2.1 Notations

We denote the security parameter by λ, where $\lambda \in \mathbb{N}$, a length of a string s by $|s|$, size of a set S by $|S|$, and an empty set by ε. By $\mathbb{A}$ we depict an attribute set. Thus $\mathbb{A}_{\mathcal{T}} \models \mathbb{A}_{\mathcal{W}}$ indicates that attribute set $\mathbb{A}_{\mathcal{T}}$ of a tracer satisfies the attribute set $\mathbb{A}_{\mathcal{W}}$ of access structure used in a group signature.

2.2 Digital Signatures

A digital signature scheme DS, which satisfies the security notion of unforgeability under chosen message attack [10], consists of three algorithms; $\mathsf{KGen}_s(1^\lambda) \rightarrow (\mathbf{pk}_s, \mathbf{sk}_s), \mathsf{Sign}_s(\mathbf{sk}_s, M) \rightarrow s$, and $\mathsf{Vf}_s(\mathbf{pk}_s, M, s) \rightarrow 1/0$, where λ is the security parameter, $\mathbf{pk}_s, \mathbf{sk}_s$ are public/secret key pair, and M, s are message/signature pair.

2.3 Attribute-Based Encryption

Attribute-based encryption (ABE) has two subgroups called Ciphertext-Policy ABE (CP-ABE) and Key-Policy ABE (KP-ABE). This paper uses CP-ABE.

A CP-ABE scheme, satisfying indistinguishability (IND-CPA), consists of four algorithms; $\mathsf{Setup}_a(1^\lambda) \rightarrow (pp, \mathbf{msk}), \mathsf{Enc}_a(pp, \mathbb{A}_{\mathcal{W}}, M) \rightarrow C, \mathsf{KGen}_a(\mathbf{msk}, ID, \mathbb{A}_{\mathcal{T}}) \rightarrow \mathbf{sk}$, and $\mathsf{Dec}_a(\mathbf{sk}, C) \rightarrow M/0$, where pp is the public parameters, $\mathbf{msk}$ is the master secret key, $\mathbb{A}_{\mathcal{W}}$ is an access structure for encrypting a message M to a ciphertext C, and $\mathbf{sk}$ is the decryption key for the attribute set $\mathbb{A}_{\mathcal{T}}$.

2.4 (Non-interactive) Zero-Knowledge Proof System

A (non-interactive) zero-knowledge (NIZK) proof system consists of three algorithms; $\mathsf{Gen}(1^\lambda) \rightarrow R, \mathsf{P}(R, x, w) \rightarrow \pi$, and $\mathsf{V}(R, x, \pi) \rightarrow 1/0$, where R is a common reference string, x is the statement, w is the witness, and π is the proof. A NIZK proof system is required to satisfy *Completeness* and *Soundness.*

1. Completeness. $\forall(x, w) \in \rho : Pr[\mathsf{V}(R, x, \mathsf{P}(R, x, w)) = 1] > 1 - \epsilon$.
2. Soundness. Even a cheating prover $\overline{\mathsf{P}}$ cannot convince the verifier V to falsely accept x on a randomly selected R: $Pr[\mathsf{V}(R, x, \overline{\mathsf{P}}(R, x, \overline{w})) = 1] < \epsilon$.

An NIZK proof system for relation ρ is zero-knowledge if there exists a random polynomial time simulator $\mathcal{S}$ such that for any $(x, w) \in \rho$, the two sets $(R, x, \mathsf{P}(R, x, w))$ and $\mathcal{S}(x)$ are polynomially distinguishable.

$$\exists \mathcal{S} s.t. \forall D \forall (x, w) \in \rho : |Pr(D(\mathcal{S}(x)) = 1) - Pr(D(R, x, \mathsf{P}(R, x, w)) = 1)| < \epsilon.$$

We define simulation soundness as below.

$\mathsf{Exp}^{ss}_{\pi,\mathcal{A}}(1^\lambda) : \quad (R, St) \leftarrow \mathcal{S}(Gen, 1^\lambda); (x, \pi) \leftarrow \mathcal{A}(R : \mathcal{S}(\mathsf{P}, St, \cdot))$

If $x \notin L_p \wedge \pi$ was not given to $\mathcal{A} \wedge \mathsf{V}(1^\lambda, x, \pi, R) = 1$ then return 1 else return 0.

The advantage of $Adv^{ss}_{\pi,\mathcal{A}}(1^\lambda) = Pr[\mathsf{Exp}^{ss}_{\pi,\mathcal{A}}(1^\lambda) = 1]$. NIZK proof system is simulation soundness if for any PPT $\mathcal{A}$, $Adv^{ss}_{\pi,\mathcal{A}}(1^\lambda)$ is negligible.

3 Attribute-Based Tracing for Group Signatures

This section presents our proposal, the group signature scheme with the attribute-based tracing method allowing users to select a tracer for their signatures based on the tracers' attributes and the decentralized tracing key generation method. Since tracers can only open signatures that have employed their attributes, we call the tracing method attribute-based tracing (ABT in short). We call the group signatures with the ABT method as GS with ABT.

Our proposal ensures that the user-selected tracing attributes are valid, i.e., the selected attribute set is within the attribute set decided by the group manager for the group. In our scheme, a group user (signer) can select a set of attributes related to a tracer to encrypt user identity in the signature instead of using the given fixed tracing public key in traditional group signatures. Thus the users have more flexibility than the existing group signature schemes in selecting a tracing authority. However, there is a risk that a user is selecting attributes that do not belong to any tracer; thus, the signer identity may remain secret, making misbehaved users untraceable. We prevent such behavior with the support of publicly published group-related tracing attributes. The signature verifier should validate the tracing attributes appended in the signatures against the attribute set given by the group manager. Signature verifiers need to build inputs based on the appended access structure in the signature and with the public keys of attributes published by the group manager to execute the verification steps of the underlying interactive protocol of the signature scheme. Thus the users cannot generate a valid signature with attributes not belong to the group. On the other hand, if the appended access structure does not match the attribute set used for encrypting the user identity in the signature, the signature verification fails because the underlying interactive protocol outputs invalid. Thus a user cannot mislead tracers by appending an attribute set which is not match with the attribute set used for encrypting his identity. The user traceability is guaranteed against malicious users trying to be permanently anonymous by forging access structures. Hence, the scheme ensures preventing user misbehaviors of using mismatching attributes.

Moreover, the proposing scheme removes the tracing power that the key generation party had in previous tracing methods of group signatures. In existing group signatures, the key generation party (we call Key Generation Center - KGC) generates keys for authorities and users. Even though the work of Bellare et al. [3] separates the user key generation from KGC, tracing key is still generated by KGC. Thus, in addition to the tracing manager, KGC knows the tracing key(s). Since our proposal aims to allow only attribute satisfying tracers to identify the signer we remove the key escrow functionality from the centralized key generation authority. Emura et al. [8] resolved the key-escrow problem in identity-based encryption (IBE) schemes by proposing a primitive called blind IBE with certified identities. As in their scheme, our scheme also has a certificate issuer (CI) other than KGC. In our scheme, we treat group manager (GM) as KGC and consider a third party for CI. First the tracer interacts with CI and gets a certificate for his attributes and a trapdoor for generating the tracing key. Then the tracer interacts with KGC showing his certificate but without revealing his identity. Thus the tracer is anonymous to KGC. On the other hand, unless the tracer has trapdoor received from CI and response message received from KGC he cannot generate tracing key for his attribute set. The existence of CI decentralizes the tracing key generation and allows tracers to deal with untrusted KGC without revealing tracer's identity.

3.1 Syntax of the Scheme

We consider a trusted setup party (TSP) that provides long-term keys (**upk**, **usk**) for group users, authority keys for GM and CI, and public and secret keys for the attributes selected by GM. In other words, GM first decides an attribute set $\mathbb{A}$ for his group. Hence GM gets public keys **apk** for each attribute $att \in \mathbb{A}$ from TSP. On the other hand, tracers with attribute set $\mathbb{A}_S$ get secret keys **ask** for each attribute $att \in \mathbb{A}_S$ from TSP. We assume that all the tracers have an identity ID sampled from a sufficiently high min-entropy source. When a tracer wants to obtain a tracing secret key for an attribute set $\mathbb{A}_\mathcal{T} \in \mathbb{A}_S$, first he gets a certificate $cert_\mathcal{T}$ and a trapdoor td from CI by presenting the attribute set $\mathbb{A}_\mathcal{T}$ and a proof $\mathcal{P}_\mathcal{T}$ for possessing $\mathbb{A}_\mathcal{T}$ with ID. Then the tracer interacts with GM sending $cert_\mathcal{T}$ as the first round message M_{req}. The GM validates $cert_\mathcal{T}$, and sends back a respond message M_{res} which includes the master secret key **msk** that supports generating tracing key for the related attribute set. The tracer generates a tracing secret key $\mathbf{tsk}_\mathcal{T}$ for $\mathbb{A}_\mathcal{T}$ after a successful execution of the interactive protocol. A group user encrypts his identity u in a signature Σ, selecting a valid attribute set $\mathbb{A}_\mathcal{W} \in \mathbb{A}$, such that only attribute satisfying tracer with $\mathbb{A}_\mathcal{T} \models \mathbb{A}_\mathcal{W}$ can decrypt the signature Σ, and identify the signer identity u.

Definition 1 (Group Signatures with Attribute-based Tracing). *A group signature scheme with attribute-based tracing method consists of the following algorithms.*

- $\mathsf{Setup}(1^\lambda) \rightarrow (pp, \{\boldsymbol{apk}_i, \boldsymbol{ask}_i\}_{i\in|Att|})$: *The setup algorithm takes λ as the input and outputs pp which consists of universal attribute set Att with keys of each attribute and public parameters. The identity space $\mathcal{ID}$ is defined in pp.*
- $\mathsf{GroupKeyGen}(pp, \mathbb{A} \in Att) \rightarrow (\boldsymbol{gpk}, \boldsymbol{gmsk})$: *The key generation algorithm takes pp and group related attribute set $\mathbb{A}$ as inputs and outputs group public key **gpk** and the group manager's secret key **gmsk**. The group public key **gpk** consists of the public keys of the group-related attribute set $\mathbb{A} \in Att$.*
- $\mathsf{CI.KeyGen}(1^\lambda) \rightarrow (\boldsymbol{ivk}, \boldsymbol{isk}))$: *The certificate issuer key generation algorithm takes λ as the input and outputs the certificate verification key **ivk** and issuing key **isk**.*
- $\mathsf{U.KeyGen}(1^\lambda) \rightarrow (\boldsymbol{upk}, \boldsymbol{usk})$: *The user key generation algorithm takes λ as the input and outputs the long term user public and private keys **upk**, **usk**, which are used by the users when joining the group.*
- $\langle \mathsf{Join} - \mathsf{Issue} \rangle \rightarrow \boldsymbol{ssk}$. *The interactive protocol for user joining with algorithms* Join *and* Issue *is executed by a new user u with valid long term public and private keys $\boldsymbol{upk}[u], \boldsymbol{usk}[u]$, and GM respectively. At the end of a successful execution of the protocol GM saves accepted user details in a registration table reg and the accepted user generates a secret signing key $\boldsymbol{ssk}[u]$ [1,3].*
- $\mathsf{Sign}(\boldsymbol{gpk}, \boldsymbol{ssk}[u], M, \mathbb{A}_\mathcal{W}) \rightarrow \Sigma$: *The signing algorithm takes the group public key **gpk**, the user secret signing key **ssk**, a message M, and a tracing attribute set $\mathbb{A}_\mathcal{W}$ as inputs and outputs a signature Σ. The signature Σ contains the tracing attribute set $\mathbb{A}_\mathcal{W}$ used for encrypting user id u in Σ.*

- *Verify*($\mathbf{gpk}, M, \Sigma$) $\rightarrow 1/0$: *The signature verification algorithm takes* $\mathbf{gpk}$, *a message signature pair* M, Σ, *and outputs either Valid (1) or Invalid (0).*
- *PrAtt*($\{att_i, \mathbf{ask}_i\}_{i \in |\mathbb{A}_{\mathcal{T}}|}$) $\rightarrow \mathcal{P}_{\mathcal{T}}$: *The proof generation for possessing attributes takes attributes att and related secret keys* $\mathbf{ask}$ *of the possessing attribute set* $\mathbb{A}_{\mathcal{T}}$ *as inputs and outputs the proof* $\mathcal{P}_{\mathcal{T}}$.
- *CI.Cert*($pp, \mathbf{gpk}, \mathbf{ivk}, \mathbf{isk}, ID, \mathbb{A}_{\mathcal{T}}, \mathcal{P}_{\mathcal{T}}$) $\rightarrow (cert_{\mathcal{T}}, td_{\mathcal{T}})$: *The certificate generating algorithm takes pp,* $\mathbf{gpk}$, *the certificate verifying and issuing keys* $\mathbf{ivk}$, $\mathbf{isk}$, *tracer's id* $ID \in \mathcal{ID}$, *tracing attribute set* $\mathbb{A}_{\mathcal{T}} \in \mathbb{A}$, *and a proof* $\mathcal{P}_{\mathcal{T}}$ *- possession of* $\mathbb{A}_{\mathcal{T}}$, *and outputs a certificate* $cert_{\mathcal{T}}$ *and a trapdoor* $td_{\mathcal{T}}$, *if* $ID \in \mathcal{ID}$, *the given attribute set* $\mathbb{A}_{\mathcal{T}} \in \mathbb{A}$ *and* $\mathcal{P}_{\mathcal{T}}$ *is a valid proof.*
- $\langle$*GetTracerKey* $-$ *IssTracerKey*$\rangle \rightarrow \mathbf{tsk}$: *The interactive tracing-key-generation protocol GetTracerKey and IssTracerKey executed by a tracer who wants a tracing key for his attribute set* $\mathbb{A}_{\mathcal{T}}$, *and GM respectively. The tracer sends* $cert_{\mathcal{T}}$ *as first-round message* M_{req} *to GM, and GM responds with a master secret key* $\mathbf{msk}_{\mathcal{T}}$ *as second-round message* M_{res}. *At the end of a successful protocol execution the tracer computes a tracing key* $\mathbf{tsk}$ *for* $\mathbb{A}_{\mathcal{T}}$.
- *Open*($\mathbf{gpk}, \mathbf{tsk}_{\mathcal{T}}, reg, M, \Sigma$) $\rightarrow (u, \tau)$: *The tracing algorithm takes* $\mathbf{gpk}$, *the tracer's secret key* $\mathbf{tsk}$ *for attribute set* $\mathbb{A}_{\mathcal{T}}$, *registration table reg, and a valid message signature pair* M, Σ, *which has an appended access structure* $\mathbb{A}_{\mathcal{W}}$, *and outputs an index u and a proof* τ, *if* $\mathbb{A}_{\mathcal{T}} \models \mathbb{A}_{\mathcal{W}}$. *If tracing is failed outputs* $\perp$.
- *Judge*($\mathbf{gpk}, u, \mathbf{upk}[u], M, \Sigma, \tau$) $\rightarrow 1/0$: *The deterministic algorithm Judge takes* $\mathbf{gpk}$, *an positive integer u (user index), the public key* $\mathbf{upk}[u]$ *of u, a valid message signature pair* M, Σ, *and a proof-string* τ, *and outputs Valid (1) or Invalid (0) based on the verification on the public key of u.*

Note that each universal attribute $att \in \mathbb{A}$ has public and secret keys. Only attribute possessing tracer knows the secret-keys of the attributes. When getting a certificate from CI, the tracer proves that he knows the secret-keys of the attributes that he is presenting. Since any other authority does not know the secret keys of the attributes, nobody can generate tracing keys for an attribute set. This ensures that only attribute satisfying tracers can decrypt the signature and identify the signer. On the other hand, under the condition that ID has high entropy, obtaining the certificate from CI is hard for others.

3.2 Correctness and Security Definitions

The proposing GS scheme with ABT guarantees that nobody can identify the signer, except the attribute satisfying party. Thus, only those with the corresponding decryption key for the attribute set used for encrypting can identify the signer. Moreover, the decentralized tracing-key generation method ensures that neither certificate issuer nor the group manager can identify the signer. We assume that there is always a tracer who possesses an attribute set selected by a user for generating a signature.

We discuss the correctness and security requirements of the proposing GS scheme with ABT using oracles. The oracles are almost same as the oracles given in Bellare's work [3] except the oracles related to the tracing key generation. We briefly explain the oracles below and give their functions in Appendix A. We use sets HU, CU, CS and AT to track newly added users, corrupted users, challenged signatures, and requested tracing keys by the adversary $\mathcal{A}$.

AddUO: When $\mathcal{A}$ adds a new user u, the oracle returns $\mathbf{upk}(u)$ and updates HU with u.
CrptO: $\mathcal{A}$ can replace personal pubic key **upk** of user u with upk. The oracle updates CU with u.
SndToIssO: With a corrupted u $\mathcal{A}$ can engages in join-issue protocol interacting with honest issuer.
SndToUO: $\mathcal{A}$ itself plays the role of issuer engaging in join-issue protocol. The oracle maintains the state of user u and updates HU with u.
USKO: $\mathcal{A}$ can query secret keys of user u. The oracle returns $\mathbf{ssk}[u], \mathbf{usk}[u]$.
RdRegO: $\mathcal{A}$ can read the contents of u in the table reg.
MdRegO: $\mathcal{A}$ can modify contents of u in reg with value val.
SignO: $\mathcal{A}$ requests a signature for the identity u of a user, a message M, and the access structure $\mathbb{A}_{\mathcal{W}}$.
ChalO$_b$: The challenge oracle allows to attack anonymity. Depending on the challenging bit b, message M^* and access structure $\mathbb{A}^*_{\mathcal{W}}$ the oracle returns the signature Σ^* and tracks details in CS.
OpenO: $\mathcal{A}$ can request to open any signature Σ produced on a massage M, except the challenging signature Σ^*.
CIkeyO: The certificate issuing key requesting oracle CIkeyO outputs **isk**. Note that, $\mathcal{A}$ who obtains **isk** can generate $cert$ and td for any attribute set $\mathbb{A}_s$ and interact with tracing key generation protocol to create tracing keys for $\mathbb{A}_s$. Thus we prevent $\mathcal{A}$ querying **gmsk** or tracing key generation protocol after accessing CIkeyO.
GMkeyO: The oracle returns **gmsk**, if CIkeyO oracle has not been queried.
CertO: The certificate oracle CertO allows $\mathcal{A}$ to get certificate for the selected attribute set $\mathbb{A}_s$. If $\mathcal{A}$ queried CertO with a valid attribute set $\mathbb{A}_s \neq \mathbb{A}^*_{\mathcal{W}}$ and a valid $ID \in \mathcal{ID}$, then the oracle computes the proof $\mathcal{P}_s$ using the secret keys of attributes in $\mathbb{A}_s$ and returns a certificate $cert_s$ and a trapdoor td_s after executing $\mathsf{CI.Cert}(\mathbf{gpk}, \mathbf{ivk}, \mathbf{isk}, ID, \mathbb{A}_s, \mathcal{P}_s)$.
Note that, if $\mathcal{A}$ knows secret keys of $\mathbb{A}_s$ (probably a adversarial tracer), then he can directly get $cert_s$ and td_s from CI.
CrptOO: The oracle returns **tsk** for a valid attribute set $\mathbb{A}_s \neq \mathbb{A}^*_{\mathcal{W}}$.
AddTO: If $\mathcal{A}$ queries tracing key oracle AddTO with $\mathbb{A}_s \neq \mathbb{A}^*_{\mathcal{W}}$ and a $ID \in \mathcal{ID}$, then the oracle returns $\mathbf{tsk}_s$ for $\mathbb{A}_s$ and updates AT with ID and $\mathbb{A}_s$.

Correctness

The GS scheme with ABT requires to ensure that for all $\lambda, \mathbb{A}, \mathbb{A}_{\mathcal{T}} \in \mathbb{A}$, all $ID \in \mathcal{ID}$, all $u \in \mathbb{N}$, and all $M \in \{0,1\}^*$ Verify algorithm always outputs *Valid* for any honestly generated signature with correct attributes and Open algorithm always outputs signer's index $u \in \mathbb{N}$, if $\mathbb{A}_{\mathcal{T}} \models \mathbb{A}_{\mathcal{W}}$.

Definition 2 (Correctness). *For all* $\lambda, \mathbb{A}, \mathbb{A}_{\mathcal{T}} \in \mathbb{A}$, *all* $ID \in \mathcal{ID}$, *all* $u \in \mathbb{N}$, *and all* $M \in \{0,1\}^*$, *we associate the below experiment* $Exp^{corr}_{\mathcal{GS},\mathcal{A}}(1^\lambda, \mathbb{A})$ *against the adversary* $\mathcal{A}_{corr}$.
$(pp, \{\mathbf{apk},\ \mathbf{ask}\}) \leftarrow \mathsf{Setup}(1^\lambda)$; $(\mathbf{gpk}, \mathbf{gmsk}) \leftarrow \mathsf{GroupKeyGen}(pp, \mathbb{A})$
$(\mathbf{ivk}, \mathbf{isk}) \leftarrow \mathsf{CI.KeyGen}(1^\lambda)$; $HU \leftarrow \emptyset, CS \leftarrow \emptyset, AT \leftarrow \emptyset$;
$(u, M, \mathbb{A}_{\mathcal{W}}) \leftarrow \mathcal{A}_{corr}(\mathbf{gpk} : \mathsf{AddTO}(\cdot), \mathsf{AddUO}(\cdot), \mathsf{RdRegO}(\cdot))$;
If $u \notin HU$ *then return 0; If* $\mathbf{ssk}[u] = \varepsilon$ *then return 0*
$\Sigma \leftarrow \mathsf{Sign}(pp, \mathbf{gpk}, \mathbf{ssk}, M, \mathbb{A}_{\mathcal{W}})$; *If* $\mathsf{Verify}(pp,\ \mathbf{gpk},\ M,\ \Sigma) = 0$*, then return 1*
$(u', \tau) \leftarrow \mathsf{Open}(\mathbf{gpk}, \mathbf{tsk}_{\mathbb{A}_{\mathcal{W}}}, M, \Sigma)$;
If $u \neq u'$ *or* $\mathsf{Judge}(\mathbf{gpk}, u, \mathbf{upk}[u], M, \Sigma, \tau) = 0$*, then return 1*
Return 0

Let $\mathsf{Adv}_{corr} = Pr[Exp^{corr}_{\mathcal{GS},\mathcal{A}} = 1]$. The GS with ABT is correct if $\mathsf{Adv}_{corr} = 0$.

Security against Anonymity Attackers

User Anonymity is a standard requirement of group signature schemes. It requires no outsider without a valid tracing key can identify the signer. On the other hand, signatures generated by two distinct users are computationally distinguishable even though the adversary knows all the user secret signing keys. In the anonymity notion, full-anonymity, proposed by Bellare et al. [2], the adversary is allowed to see the results of the openings of signatures except for the challenging signature (CCA-Anonymity). In our scheme, other than the curios signature verifies, there are other honest but curios tracers, GM who also acts as the KGC, and CI. Thus we consider securing the user anonymity against all these adversaries by satisfying full-anonymity, i.e., where the adversary knows all the user secret signing keys [2].

Thus the anonymity adversaries get all the user secret signing keys including the secret signing key related to the challenging signature Σ^*. In dynamic group signatures that we consider, the adversary can add new users to the group. The adversarial verifier (common adversary) gets the signature verification key **gpk** and the users' secret signing keys. The adversarial GM has **gmsk** and adversarial CI has **isk** in addition to **gpk** and secret signing keys. The adversarial tracers who are not able to satisfy $\mathbb{A}_{\mathcal{T}} \models \mathbb{A}_{\mathcal{W}^*}$ also have the tracing keys for their possessing attribute sets. The attribute set $\mathbb{A}_{\mathcal{W}^*}$ is used for generating Σ^*. Without considering the anonymity attacks of each adversary individually, we present a redundant anonymity definition that describes anonymity attacks of a stronger adversary who has the power to corrupt GM, CI, and tracers (except $\mathbb{A}_{\mathcal{W}^*}$). On the other hand, we speculate that we can allow the adversary to access tracing keys for selected attribute sets except the attribute set used for generating Σ^*. Thus we build an adversary $\mathcal{A}$ who has access to all the public keys and can access secret keys **gmsk** and **isk** via oracles. He gets all the users' secret signing keys $\{\mathbf{ssk}\}$, and he can request tracing keys for a selected attribute set except the tracing key of $\mathbb{A}_{\mathcal{W}^*}$. Since the secret keys of attributes are only known by the attribute possessing tracer, it seems that the adversary cannot generate a tracing key for $\mathbb{A}_{\mathcal{W}^*}$ without knowing the secret keys of each attribute in $\mathbb{A}_{\mathcal{W}^*}$. Malicious CI can forge the certificate generation of $\mathbb{A}_{\mathcal{W}^*}$ and try to access the tracing key generation oracle. In Chow's work [7], they considered fully trusted CI, and in Emura's work [8], they disallow CI to access tracing key generation oracle. Considering this problem, we also limit the adversary $\mathcal{A}$ accessing tracing key generation oracle if he has obtained certificate issuing key **isk**. Thus unless malicious CI colludes with a malicious GM, generating tracing keys for an attribute set is hard. Moreover, one may argue that the adversary may collect secret keys of each attribute of $\mathbb{A}_{\mathcal{W}^*}$ from different tracers that have the same attributes. For instance, if $\mathbb{A}_{\mathcal{W}^*}$ consists of attributes att_1, att_2, att_3 and att_4, and if there are tracers with attribute att_1, att_2, att_3 and att_4 separately, then the adversary may get secret keys of att_1, att_2, att_3 and att_4 corrupting each tracer. That means we are considering a situation almost all the tracers are corrupted, which is impractical. Without focusing on such kind of attacks, we consider an adversary $\mathcal{A}$ in full anonymity game who can access tracing key generation oracle only if he has not access certificate issuing key **isk** and who cannot access the tracing key of $\mathbb{A}_{\mathcal{W}^*}$.

Definition 3 (Anonymity). *A GS scheme with ABT is fully anonymous if the advantage of the adversary $\mathcal{A}_{an}$ is winning the below game $Exp^{an-b}_{\mathcal{GS},\mathcal{A}}(1^\lambda, \mathbb{A})$ is negligible, where b is the challenging bit and d is the adversary's guess for b.*
$(pp, \{\boldsymbol{apk},\ \boldsymbol{ask}\}) \leftarrow \mathsf{Setup}(1^\lambda)$;
$(\boldsymbol{gpk}, \boldsymbol{gmsk}) \leftarrow \mathsf{GroupKeyGen}(pp, \mathbb{A}); (\boldsymbol{ivk}, \boldsymbol{isk}) \leftarrow \mathsf{CI.KeyGen}(1^\lambda)$;
$CU \leftarrow \emptyset, HU \leftarrow \emptyset, CS \leftarrow \emptyset, AT \leftarrow \emptyset;$
$d \leftarrow \mathcal{A}_{an}(\boldsymbol{gpk} : \mathsf{ChalO}_b(\cdot), \mathsf{CIkey}(\cdot), \mathsf{GMkey}(\cdot), \mathsf{CertO}(\cdot), \mathsf{AddTO}(\cdot), \mathsf{OpenO}(\cdot),$
$\mathsf{SndToUO}(\cdot), \mathsf{MdRegO}(\cdot), \mathsf{USKO}(\cdot), \mathsf{CrptUO}(\cdot), \mathsf{CrptOO}(\cdot));$
Return d

We define the advantage of $\mathcal{A}_{an}$ as, $\mathsf{Adv}_{an} = |Pr[Exp^{an-0}_{\mathcal{GS},\mathcal{A}} = 1] - Pr[Exp^{an-1}_{\mathcal{GS},\mathcal{A}} = 1]$. A GS scheme with ABT is fully anonymous for any PPT adversary $\mathcal{A}_{an}$ if Adv_{an} is negligible.

Security Against Malicious Users - Traceability

User traceability requires that no user can generate a signature that cannot trace back to him. In addition to the traceability attacks considered in Bellare's dynamic group signature scheme [3], in our scheme, a user (corrupted signer) may try not to be traced by selecting an attribute set that does not belong to the group. However, forging the attribute set is not possible according to the correctness of the scheme. A signature with fraudulent attribute sets cannot pass the verification steps of the underlying interactive protocol.

Definition 4 (Traceability). *A GS scheme with ABT is traceable if the advantage of the adversary $\mathcal{A}_{tr}$ winning the below game $Exp^{tr}_{\mathcal{GS},\mathcal{A}}(1^\lambda, \mathbb{A})$ is negligible.*
$(pp, \{\boldsymbol{apk},\ \boldsymbol{ask}\}) \leftarrow \mathsf{Setup}(1^\lambda)$;
$(\boldsymbol{gpk}, \boldsymbol{gmsk}) \leftarrow \mathsf{GroupKeyGen}(pp, \mathbb{A}); (\boldsymbol{ivk}, \boldsymbol{isk}) \leftarrow \mathsf{CI.KeyGen}(1^\lambda)$;
$CU \leftarrow \emptyset, HU \leftarrow \emptyset, AT \leftarrow \emptyset;$

$(M, \Sigma) \leftarrow \mathcal{A}_{tr}(\boldsymbol{gpk} : \mathsf{CIkey}(\cdot), \mathsf{GMkey}(\cdot), \mathsf{CertO}(\cdot), \mathsf{AddTO}(\cdot), \mathsf{SndToIO}(\cdot), \mathsf{RdRegO}(\cdot), \mathsf{USKO}(\cdot), \mathsf{CrptUO}(\cdot))$;
Parse Σ *as* $(\sigma, \mathbb{A}_{\mathcal{W}})$; *If* $\mathsf{Verify}(pp, \boldsymbol{gpk}, M, \Sigma) = 0$, *then return 1*
$\boldsymbol{tsk}_{\mathbb{A}_{\mathcal{W}}} \leftarrow \mathsf{TracingKey}(\mathbb{A}_{\mathcal{W}})$; $(u, \tau) \leftarrow \mathsf{Open}(pp, \boldsymbol{tsk}_{\mathbb{A}_{\mathcal{W}}}, M, \Sigma)$;
If $u = 0$ *or* $\mathsf{Judge}(pp, \boldsymbol{gpk}, u, \boldsymbol{upk}[u], M, \Sigma, \tau) = 0$, *then return 1*
Return 0

We define the advantage of $\mathcal{A}_{tr}$ as $\mathsf{Adv}_{tr} = Pr[Exp^{tr}_{\mathcal{GS},\mathcal{A}} = 1]$. A GS scheme with ABT is traceable for any PPT adversary $\mathcal{A}_{tr}$ if Adv_{tr} is negligible.

Security Against Malicious Users - Non-frameability

Non-frameability requires that the adversary be unable to produce a signature that traces back to an innocent user who is not the real signer of the signature.

Definition 5 (Non-frameability). *A GS scheme with ABT is non-frameable if the advantage of the adversary* $\mathcal{A}_{nf}$ *winning the below game* $Exp^{nf}_{\mathcal{GS},\mathcal{A}}(1^\lambda, \mathbb{A})$ *is negligible.*
$(pp, \{\boldsymbol{apk}, \boldsymbol{ask}\}) \leftarrow \mathsf{Setup}(1^\lambda)$;
$(\boldsymbol{gpk}, \boldsymbol{gmsk}) \leftarrow \mathsf{GroupKeyGen}(pp, \mathbb{A})$; $(\boldsymbol{ivk}, \boldsymbol{isk}) \leftarrow \mathsf{CI.KeyGen}(1^\lambda)$;
$CU \leftarrow \emptyset, HU \leftarrow \emptyset, AT \leftarrow \emptyset$;
$(M, \Sigma, u, \tau) \leftarrow \mathcal{A}_{nf}(\boldsymbol{gpk} : \mathsf{CIkey}(\cdot), \mathsf{GMkey}(\cdot), \mathsf{CertO}(\cdot), \mathsf{AddUO}(\cdot), \mathsf{SndToUO}(\cdot), \mathsf{MdRegO}(\cdot), \mathsf{USKO}(\cdot), \mathsf{CrptUO}(\cdot), \mathsf{SignO}(\cdot))$;
Parse Σ *as* $(\sigma, \mathbb{A}_{\mathcal{W}})$; *If* $\mathsf{Verify}(pp, \boldsymbol{gpk}, M, \Sigma) = 0$, *then return 0*
If the following are all true, then return 1 else return 0:

- $i \in HU \wedge \boldsymbol{ssk}[u] \neq \varepsilon$
- $\mathsf{Judge}(pp, \boldsymbol{gpk}, u, \boldsymbol{upk}[u], M, \Sigma, \tau) = 1$
- $\mathcal{A}_{nf}$ *did not query* $\mathsf{USKO}(u)$ *or* $\mathsf{SignO}(u, M, \mathbb{A}_{\mathcal{W}})$

We define the advantage of $\mathcal{A}_{nf}$ as $\mathsf{Adv}_{nf} = Pr[Exp^{nf}_{\mathcal{GS},\mathcal{A}} = 1]$. A GS scheme with ABT is non-frameable for any PPT adversary $\mathcal{A}_{nf}$ if Adv_{nf} is negligible.

4 Construction

Figure 1 depicts the process of our GS with ABT scheme. The construction of the algorithms is given in Figs. 2, 3, and 4. Figures 3 and 4 depict the algorithms of the user joining protocol and the tracing key generation protocol respectively.

The construction of the proposing scheme follows the structure of the Bellare's dynamic group signature scheme [3]. However, instead of one tracer, proposing scheme has multiple tracers possessing attributes. Thus our construction employs CP-ABE scheme instead of PKE scheme. We use DS scheme and simulation sound NIZK proof scheme as other building blocks as used in Bellare's dynamic group signature scheme [3].

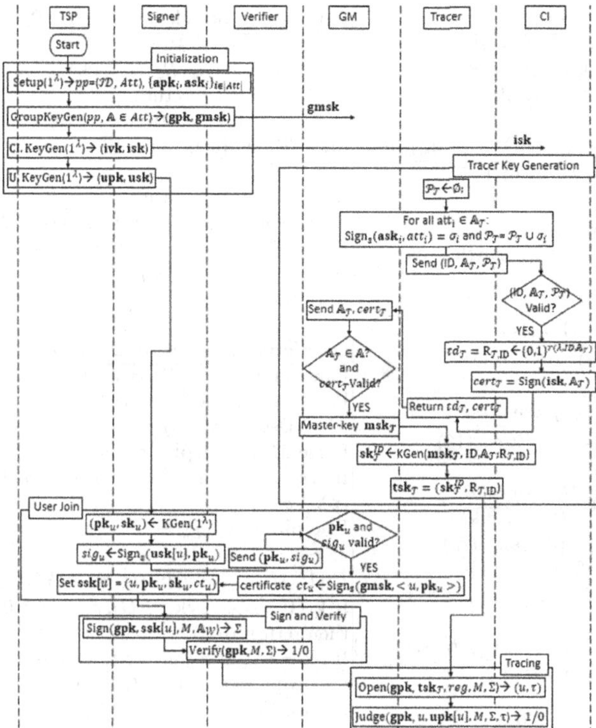

Fig. 1. Process of the scheme

The trusted setup party TSP selects keys for attributes and authorities. Moreover, TSP provides long term keys **upk**, **usk** for users. User joining protocol and the construction of algorithms Sign, Verify, Open, and Judge are same as the constructions given by Bellare et al. [3] except for two differences. In Sign the signer's id u is encrypted using selected attribute set's public keys $\mathbb{A}_{\mathcal{W}_{pk}}$ instead of tracing manager's public key and Verify verifies the validity of attached attribute set $\mathbb{A}_{\mathcal{W}}$ and public keys of $\mathbb{A}_{\mathcal{W}}$ are used for NIZK proof verification.

Three parties, the tracer, CI, and GM involve in tracing key generation. First, the tracer receives a certificate for his possessing attribute set from CI. The tracer signs each attribute with a related secret key supporting CI to verify them with relevant public keys. The set of attributes' signatures acts as the proof ($\mathcal{P}_{\mathcal{T}}$) of possessing the given attributes. If even one attribute is not in the group attribute set ($\mathbb{A}$) or fails the signature verification process, then CI returns $\perp$. Otherwise CI selects a random string $R_{\mathcal{T},ID}$ based on the tracer ID and possessing attribute set $\mathbb{A}_{\mathcal{T}}$, and generates a certificate $cert_{\mathcal{T}}$ using his secret key **isk**. At the tracer key generation protocol, the tracer interacts with GM with the certificate $cert_{\mathcal{T}}$. If the verification of $cert_{\mathcal{T}}$ is passed, then GM selects

$\mathsf{Setup}(1^\lambda) \rightarrow (pp, \{\mathbf{apk}, \mathbf{ask}\})$
$\mathcal{ID} \leftarrow \{0,1\}^*$; $Att = \{att_1, att_2, \ldots, att_m\}$
For $i \in Att$: $(\mathbf{apk}_i, \mathbf{ask}_i) \leftarrow \mathsf{KGen}_s(1^\lambda)$
Return $pp = (\mathcal{ID}, \mathbb{A}), \{\mathbf{apk}_i, \mathbf{ask}_i\}_{i \in [Att]}$

$\mathsf{GroupKeyGen}(pp, \mathbb{A} \in Att) \rightarrow (\mathbf{gpk}, \mathbf{gmsk})$
$R_1 \leftarrow \{0,1\}^{p1(\lambda)}$; $R_2 \leftarrow \{0,1\}^{p2(\lambda)}$
$(\mathbf{vk}, \mathbf{sk}) \leftarrow \mathsf{KGen}_s(1^\lambda)$
$\mathbb{A}_{pk} = \{(att_i, \mathbf{apk}_i)\}_{i \in |\mathbb{A}|}$
$\mathbf{gpk} = (R_1, R_2, \mathbb{A}_{pk}, \mathbf{vk})$; $\mathbf{gmsk} = \mathbf{sk}$
Return $\mathbf{gpk}$, $\mathbf{gmsk}$

$\mathsf{CI.KeyGen}(1^\lambda) \rightarrow (\mathbf{ivk}, \mathbf{isk})$
Return $(\mathbf{ivk}, \mathbf{isk}) \leftarrow \mathsf{KGen}_s(1^\lambda)$

$\mathsf{U.KeyGen}(1^\lambda) \rightarrow (\mathbf{upk}, \mathbf{usk})$
Return $(\mathbf{upk}, \mathbf{usk}) \leftarrow \mathsf{KGen}_s(1^\lambda)$

$\mathsf{Sign}(\mathbf{gpk}, \mathbf{ssk}[u], M, \mathbb{A}_{\mathcal{W}}) \rightarrow \Sigma$
Parse $\mathbf{gpk}$ as $(R_1, R_2, \mathbb{A}_{pk}, \mathbf{vk})$
Parse $\mathbf{ssk}[u]$ as $(u, \mathbf{pk}_u, \mathbf{sk}_u, ct_u)$
$s \leftarrow \mathsf{Sign}_s(\mathbf{sk}_u, M)$; $r \leftarrow \{0,1\}^\lambda$
$C \leftarrow \mathsf{Enc}_a(\mathbb{A}_{\mathcal{W}_{pk}}, < u, \mathbf{pk}_u, ct_u, s >; r)$
$\pi_1 \leftarrow$
$P_1(1^\lambda, (pp, \mathbf{vk}, M, C), (u, \mathbf{pk}_u, ct_u, s, r), R_1)$
Return $\Sigma = ((C, \pi_1), \mathbb{A}_{\mathcal{W}})$

$\mathsf{Verify}(\mathbf{gpk}, M, \Sigma) \rightarrow 1/0$
Parse $\mathbf{gpk}$ as $(R_1, R_2, \mathbb{A}_{pk}, \mathbf{vk})$
Parse Σ as $((C, \pi_1), \mathbb{A}_{\mathcal{W}})$
For $i \in \mathbb{A}_{\mathcal{W}}[i]$: if $\mathbb{A}_{\mathcal{W}}[i] \notin \mathbb{A}$, then return 0
Select $\mathbb{A}_{\mathcal{W}_{pk}} \in \mathbb{A}_{pk}$
Return $V_1(1^\lambda, (\mathbb{A}_{\mathcal{W}_{pk}}, \mathbf{vk}, M, C), \pi_1, R_1)$

$\mathsf{PrAtt}(\{att_i, \mathbf{ask}_i\}_{i \in |\mathbb{A}_\mathcal{T}|}) \rightarrow \mathcal{P}_\mathcal{T}$
$\mathcal{P}_\mathcal{T} \leftarrow \emptyset$
For $i \in \mathbb{A}_\mathcal{T}$:
$\mathsf{Sign}_s(\mathbf{ask}_i, att_i) = \sigma_i$; $\mathcal{P}_\mathcal{T} = \mathcal{P}_\mathcal{T} \cup (att_i, \sigma_i)$
Return $\mathcal{P}_\mathcal{T}$

$\mathsf{CI.Cert}(pp, \mathbf{gpk}, \mathbf{ivk}, \mathbf{isk}, ID, \mathbb{A}_\mathcal{T}, \mathcal{P}_\mathcal{T}) \rightarrow (cert_\mathcal{T}, td_\mathcal{T})$
Parse pp as $(\mathcal{ID}, Att)$
Parse $\mathbf{gpk}$ as $(R_1, R_2, \mathbb{A}_{pk}, \mathbf{vk})$
If $ID \notin \mathcal{ID}$ then return $\perp$
If $\mathbb{A}_\mathcal{T} \notin \mathbb{A}$ then return $\perp$
Parse $\mathcal{P}_\mathcal{T}$ as $\{att_i, \sigma_i\}$
For $i \in \mathcal{P}_\mathcal{T}$:
If $att_i \notin \mathbb{A}$ then return $\perp$
If $\mathsf{Vf}_s(\mathbf{apk}_i, att_i, \sigma_i) = 0$ then return $\perp$
$td_\mathcal{T} = R_{\mathcal{T},ID} \leftarrow \{0,1\}^{r(\lambda, ID, \mathbb{A}_\mathcal{T})}$
$cert_\mathcal{T} = \mathsf{Sign}_s(\mathbf{isk}, \mathbb{A}_\mathcal{T})$
Return $cert_\mathcal{T}, td_\mathcal{T}$

$\mathsf{Open}(\mathbf{gpk}, \mathbf{tsk}_\mathcal{T}, reg, M, \Sigma) \rightarrow (u, \tau)$
Parse $\mathbf{gpk}$ as $(R_1, R_2, \mathbb{A}_{pk}, \mathbf{vk})$
Parse $\mathbf{tsk}$ as $(\mathbf{sk}_\mathcal{T}^{ID}, R_{\mathcal{T},ID})$
$M \leftarrow \mathsf{Dec}_a(\mathbf{sk}_\mathcal{T}^{ID}, C)$
Parse M as $< u, \mathbf{pk}_u, ct_u, s >$;
If $reg[u] \neq \varepsilon$ then Parse $reg[u]$ as $(\mathbf{pk}_u, sig_u)$
Else $\mathbf{pk}_u \leftarrow \varepsilon$; $sig_u \leftarrow \varepsilon$
$\pi_2 \leftarrow$
$P_2(1^\lambda, (\mathbb{A}_{\mathcal{W}_{pk}}, C, u, \mathbf{pk}, ct, s), (\mathbf{sk}_\mathcal{T}^{ID}, r), R_2)$
If $V_1(1^\lambda, (\mathbb{A}_{\mathcal{W}_{pk}}, \mathbf{vk}, M, C), \pi_1, R_1) = 0$
then return $(0, \varepsilon)$
If $\mathbf{pk} \neq \mathbf{pk}_i$ or $reg[u] = \varepsilon$ then return $(0, \varepsilon)$
$\tau \leftarrow (\mathbf{pk}_u, sig_u, u, \mathbf{pk}, ct, s, \pi_2)$
Return (u, τ)

$\mathsf{Judge}(\mathbf{gpk}, u, \mathbf{upk}[u], M, \Sigma, \tau) \rightarrow 1/0$
Parse $\mathbf{gpk}$ as $(R_1, R_2, \mathbb{A}_{pk}, \mathbf{vk})$
If $(u, \tau) = (0, \varepsilon)$ then return $V_1(1^\lambda, (\mathbb{A}_{\mathcal{W}_{pk}}, \mathbf{vk}, M, C), \pi_1, R_1) = 0$
Parse τ as $(\overline{\mathbf{pk}}, \overline{sig}, u', \mathbf{pk}, ct, s, \pi_2)$
If $V_2(1^\lambda, (C, u', \mathbf{pk}, ct, s), \pi_2, R_2) = 0$
then return 0
If $u = u' \wedge \mathsf{Vf}_s(\mathbf{upk}, \overline{\mathbf{pk}}, \overline{sig_u}) = 1 \wedge$
$\overline{\mathbf{pk}} = \mathbf{pk}$ then return 1
Else return 0

Fig. 2. Algorithms of the scheme

a constant c for the attribute set $\mathbb{A}_\mathcal{T}$. Note that for an unauthorized attribute set, no such constant c exist [12]. Then using index $\kappa \leftarrow \mathbb{N}^c$, GM generates and sends back the master secret key $\mathbf{msk}_\mathcal{T}$ for the attribute set $\mathbb{A}_\mathcal{T}$ as responding message M_{res}. On receive of acceptance from the protocol for his request, the tracer creates secret tracing key $\mathbf{tsk}_{\mathbb{A}_\mathcal{T}}$ for $\mathbb{A}_\mathcal{T}$ using $\mathbf{msk}_\mathcal{T}$ and $R_{\mathcal{T},ID}$.

$\mathsf{Join}(St_{join}, M_{in})$
If $M_{in} = \varepsilon$ then
Parse St_{join} as $(\mathbf{gpk}, u, \mathbf{upk}[u], \mathbf{usk}[u])$
$(\mathbf{pk}_u, \mathbf{sk}_u) \leftarrow \mathsf{KGen}_s(1^\lambda)$
$sig_i \leftarrow \mathsf{Sign}_s(\mathbf{usk}[u], \mathbf{pk}_u)$
$St'_{join} = (u, \mathbf{pk}_u, \mathbf{sk}_u)$
$M_{out} = (\mathbf{pk}_u, sig_u)$
Return $(St'_{join}, M_{out}, continue)$
Else
Parse St_{join} as $(u, \mathbf{pk}_u, \mathbf{sk}_u)$, M_{in} as ct_i
$St'_{join} = (u, \mathbf{pk}_u, \mathbf{sk}_u, ct_u)$;
Return $(St'_{join}, \varepsilon, accept)$

$\mathsf{Issue}(St_{iss}, M_{in}, decision)$
$M_{out} = \varepsilon; decision' = reject;$
If $decision = continue$ then
Parse St_{iss} as $(\mathbf{gpk}, \mathbf{gmsk}, u, \mathbf{upk}[u])$
Parse M_{in} as $(\mathbf{pk}_u, sig_u)$
Parse $\mathbf{gmsk}$ as $\mathbf{sk}$;
If $\mathsf{Vf}_s(\mathbf{upk}[u], \mathbf{pk}_u, sig_u) = 1$ then
$ct_u \leftarrow \mathsf{Sign}_s(\mathbf{sk}, < u, \mathbf{pk}_u >)$
$St'_{iss} = (\mathbf{pk}_u, sig_u)$; $M_{out} = ct_u$;
$decision' = accept$
Return $(St'_{iss}, M_{out}, decision')$

Fig. 3. Join-Issue algorithms of the scheme

$\mathsf{GetTracerKey}(St_g, M_{res})$
If $M_{res} = \varepsilon$ then
Parse St_g as $(\mathbf{gpk}, ID, \mathbb{A}_{\mathcal{T}}, cert_{\mathcal{T}}, td_{\mathcal{T}})$
$M_{req} = (\mathbb{A}_{\mathcal{T}}, cert_{\mathcal{T}})$
Return $(St_g, M_{req}, continue)$
Else
Parse M_{res} as $\mathbf{msk}_{\mathcal{T}}$
Parse $td_{\mathcal{T}} = R_{\mathcal{T},ID}$
$\mathbf{sk}_{\mathcal{T}}^{ID} \leftarrow \mathsf{KGen}_a(\mathbf{msk}_{\mathcal{T}}, ID, \mathbb{A}_{\mathcal{T}}; R_{\mathcal{T},ID})$
$\mathbf{tsk}_{\mathcal{T}} = (\mathbf{sk}_{\mathcal{T}}^{ID}, R_{\mathcal{T},ID})$
Return $(St'_g = \mathbf{tsk}_{\mathcal{T}}, \varepsilon, accept)$

$\mathsf{IssTracerKey}(St_{iss}, M_{req}, decision)$
$M_{res} = \varepsilon; decision' = reject;$
If $decision = continue$ then
Parse St_{iss} as $(\mathbf{gpk}, \mathbf{gmsk}, \mathbf{ivk}, \mathbb{A} \in Att)$
Parse M_{req} as $(\mathbb{A}_{\mathcal{T}}, cert_{\mathcal{T}})$
If $\mathsf{Vf}_s(\mathbf{ivk}, \mathbb{A}_{\mathcal{T}}, cert_{\mathcal{T}}) = 1$ and $\mathbb{A}_{\mathcal{T}} \in \mathbb{A}$ then
Select constant c for $\mathbb{A}_{\mathcal{T}}$
$\kappa \leftarrow \mathbb{N}^c; (\mathbf{msk}_{\mathcal{T}}) \leftarrow \mathsf{Setup}_a(1^\lambda, \kappa)$
$M_{res} = \mathbf{msk}_{\mathcal{T}}; decision' =$ accept
Return $M_{res}, decision'$

Fig. 4. Tracer key generation algorithms of the scheme

5 Correctness and Security

In this section, we show the correctness and security properties of the scheme. We briefly discuss the security proofs stated below in Appendix B, and we detail them in the full version of the paper.

Theorem 1 (Correctness). *If DS and CP-ABE are correct, and $\pi_1 = (P_1, V_1)$ and $\pi_2 = (P_2, V_2)$ are complete, then GS scheme with ABT is correct.*

Theorem 2 (Anonymity). *If CP-ABE is IND-CPA secure, $\pi_1 = (P_1, V_1)$ is simulation sound and computational zero-knowledge and $\pi_2 = (P_2, V_2)$ is computational zero-knowledge GS scheme with ABT is anonymous.*

Theorem 3 (Traceability). *If DS is EUF-CMA secure, $\pi_1 = (P_1, V_1)$ is sound and $\pi_2 = (P_2, V_2)$ is sound then GS scheme with ABT is traceable.*

Theorem 4 (Non-frameability). *If DS is EUF-CMA secure, $\pi_1 = (P_1, V_1)$ is sound and $\pi_2 = (P_2, V_2)$ is sound then GS scheme with ABT is non-frameable.*

6 Conclusion

This paper presents a decentralized tracing mechanism for group signature schemes from attribute-based encryption. Since the proposal also consists of decentralized tracing key generation other than the attribute set satisfying tracer no one, even GM cannot identify the signer. Tracing mechanism of the scheme secure users against centralized authorities. As a result, our proposal provides stronger anonymity for signers. In this paper, we assumed always there is a tracer who can satisfy the attribute set of a signature, which limits the practicability. We can answer this barrier, for instance, adapting Perera et al. [14] scheme, which allows tracers to collaborate when no tracer can meet access structure in a signature alone. However, first we need to fix the problem of preventing corrupted tracers collaboration when there is a tracer who can satisfy the access structure. That means, we should control the requirement of tracer collaboration. We address these requirements and enhance our proposal in future.

Acknowledgment. The authors would like to thank Hiroaki Anada and Masayuki Fukumitsu for sharing their related work, Chen-Mou Cheng and Masayuki Hashimoto for helpful discussion, and anonymous reviewers of ISPEC 2022 for their valuable comments.

A Appendix: The Oracles

Figure 5 depicts the oracles that we use for proving the security of the scheme.

B Appendix: Security Proof

The security proof of our proposal is similar to the proof given in dynamic group signatures of Bellare et al. [3]. While their anonymity proof is based on IND-CCA security of PKE scheme, our proof is based on IND-CPA security of CP-ABE scheme. We detail the security proof of GS scheme with ABT in extended version of this paper.

B.1 Anonymity

We fix an NP relation ρ over domain *Dom* and consider a pair of PPT algorithms (P_1, V_1) and (P_2, V_2) for NIZK proof systems as in Bellare et al. [3] paper.

On the assumption that P_1 is computational zero knowledge for ρ_1 over Dom_1 and P_2 is computational zero knowledge for ρ_2 over Dom_2, two simulations S_1 and S_2 can be fixed as: $\Pi_1 = P_1, V_1, S_1$; $\Pi_2 = P_2, V_2, S_2$. Π_1 and Π_2 are the simulation sound zero knowledge non-interactive proof systems of them for $L_{\rho 1}$ and $L_{\rho 2}$ respectively.

For any polynomial time adversary B, who will challenge the anonymity of our scheme GS and who can construct polynomial time IND-CPA adversaries

$\underline{\mathsf{AddUO}(u)}$
If $u \in \mathbf{HU} \cup \mathbf{CU}$, then return ε
$\mathbf{HU} \leftarrow \mathbf{HU} \cup \{u\}$
$\mathbf{ssk}[u] \leftarrow \varepsilon$; $dec^u \leftarrow$ cont;
$(\mathbf{upk}[u], \mathbf{usk}[u]) \leftarrow \mathsf{U.KeyGen}(1^\lambda)$
$St^u_{jn} \leftarrow (\mathbf{gpk}, \mathbf{upk}[u], \mathbf{usk}[u])$
$St^u_{is} \leftarrow (\mathbf{gpk}, \mathbf{gmsk}, u, \mathbf{upk}[u])$; $M_{jn} \leftarrow \varepsilon$
$(St^u_{jn}, M_{jn}, dec^u) \leftarrow \mathsf{Join}(St^u_{jn}, M_{jn})$
While (dec^u = cont) do
$(St^u_{is}, M_{jn}, dec^u_{is}) \leftarrow \mathsf{Issue}(St^u_{is}, M_{is}, dec^u)$
If dec^u = accept, then $reg[u] \leftarrow St^u_{is}$
$(St^u_{jn}, M_{is}, dec^u_{jn}) \leftarrow \mathsf{Join}(St^u_{jn}, M_{jn})$
End while
$\mathbf{ssk}[u] \leftarrow St^u_{jn}$
Return $\mathbf{upk}[u]$

$\underline{\mathsf{SndToIssO}(u, M_{in})}$
If $u \notin \mathbf{CU}$ then return ε
$(St^u_{is}, M_{out}, dec^u)$
$\leftarrow \mathsf{Issue}(St^u_{is}, M_{in}, dec^u)$.
If dec^u = accept then $reg[u] \leftarrow St^u_{is}$
Return M_{out}

$\underline{\mathsf{SignO}(u, M, \mathbb{A}_{\mathcal{W}})}$
If $u \notin \mathbf{HU}$ then return ε
If $\mathbf{ssk}[u] = \varepsilon$ or $\mathbb{A}_{\mathcal{W}} \notin \mathbb{A}$, then return ε.
$\Sigma = (\mathsf{Sign}(pp, \mathbf{gpk}, \mathbf{ssk}, M, \mathbb{A}_{\mathcal{W}}), \mathbb{A}_{\mathcal{W}})$
Return Σ

$\underline{\mathsf{OpenO}(M, \Sigma)}$
If $(M, \Sigma) \in \mathbf{CS}$ then return $(\varepsilon, \varepsilon, \varepsilon)$
Return $\mathsf{Open}(pp, \mathbf{tsk}, M, \Sigma)$

$\underline{\mathsf{CrptUO}(u, \mathrm{upk})}$
If $u \in \mathbf{HU} \cup \mathbf{CU}$ then return ε
$\mathbf{CU} \leftarrow \mathbf{CU} \cup \{u\}$
$\mathbf{upk}[u] \leftarrow upk$; $dec^u \leftarrow$ cont
$St^u_{is}(\mathbf{gpk}, \mathbf{gmsk}, u, \mathbf{upk}[u])$
Return 1

$\underline{\mathsf{USKO}(u)}$
Return $(ssk[u], \mathbf{usk}[u])$

$\underline{\mathsf{RdRegO}(u)}$
Return $(reg[u])$

$\underline{\mathsf{MdRegO}(u, val)}$
$reg[u] \leftarrow val$

$\underline{\mathsf{SndToUO}(u, M_{in})}$
If $u \notin \mathbf{HU}$ then
$\mathbf{HU} \leftarrow \mathbf{HU} \cup \{u\}$
$(\mathbf{upk}[u], \mathbf{usk}[u]) \leftarrow \mathsf{U.KeyGen}(1^\lambda)$
$\mathbf{ssk}[u] \leftarrow \varepsilon$; $M_{in} \leftarrow \varepsilon$
$(St^u_{jn}, M_{out}, dec) \leftarrow \mathsf{Join}(St^u_{jn}, M_{in})$
If dec = accept then $\mathbf{ssk}[u] \leftarrow St^u_{jn}$
Return (M_{out}, dec)

$\underline{\mathsf{ChalO}_b(u_0, u_1, M^*, \mathbb{A}_{\mathcal{W}^*})}$
If $u_0 \notin \mathbf{HU}$ or $u_1 \notin \mathbf{HU}$ then return ε
If $\mathbf{ssk}[u_0] = \varepsilon$ or $\mathbf{ssk}[u_1] = \varepsilon$ then return ε
$\Sigma = (\mathsf{Sign}(pp, \mathbf{gpk}, \mathbf{ssk}, M, \mathbb{A}_{\mathcal{W}}), \mathbb{A}_{\mathcal{W}})$
$\mathbf{CS} = \mathbf{CS} \cup \{(M, \Sigma, \mathbb{A}_{\mathcal{W}^*})\}$
Return Σ^*

$\underline{\mathsf{CIkeyO}()}$
ReqCI = "yes"
Return $\mathbf{isk}$

$\underline{\mathsf{GMkeyO}()}$
If ReqCI = "yes' then return ε
Return $\mathbf{gmsk}$

$\underline{\mathsf{CertO}(ID, \mathbb{A}_s)}$
If $\mathbb{A}_s \notin \mathbb{A}$ or $\mathbb{A}_s \neq \mathbb{A}_{\mathcal{W}^*}$ then return ε
$\forall i \in \mathbb{A}_s$: If $\mathbf{ask}[i] = \varepsilon$ then return ε
$\mathcal{P}_s \leftarrow \mathsf{PrAtt}(\{att_i, \mathbf{ask}_i\}_{|\mathbb{A}_s|})$;
Return $\mathsf{CI.Cert}(pp, \mathbf{gpk}, \mathbf{isk}, ID, \mathbb{A}_s, \mathcal{P}_s)$

$\underline{\mathsf{CrptOO}(\mathbb{A}_s)}$
If $\mathbb{A}_s \notin \mathbb{A}$ or $\mathbb{A}_s \neq \mathbb{A}_{\mathcal{W}^*}$ then return ε
Return $\mathbf{tsk}_s$

$\underline{\mathsf{AddTO}(ID, \mathbb{A}_s)}$
If ReqCI = "yes" then return ε
If $\mathbb{A}_s \notin \mathbb{A}$ then return ε
If $\mathbb{A}_s = \mathbb{A}_{\mathcal{W}^*}$ or $ID \notin \mathcal{ID}$ then return ε
If $(ID, \mathbb{A}_s) \in AT$ then return ε
$AT \leftarrow AT \cup (ID, \mathbb{A}_s)$
$cert_s, td_s = \mathbf{CertO}(ID, \mathbb{A}_s)$
$dec = cont$;
$St_g \leftarrow (\mathbf{gpk}, \mathbb{A}_s, cert_s, td_s)$
$St_{is} \leftarrow (\mathbf{gpk}, \mathbf{gmsk}, cert_s)$
$M_{req} \leftarrow \varepsilon$
$(St_g, M_{req}, dec) \leftarrow \mathsf{GenTKey}(St_{jn}, M_{req})$
While (dec = cont) do
$(M_{res}, dec) \leftarrow \mathsf{IssTKey}(St_{is}, M_{res}, dec)$
$(St_g, M_{req}, dec) \leftarrow \mathsf{GenTKey}(St_g, M_{req})$
End while
$\mathbf{tsk}_s \leftarrow St_g$
Return $\mathbf{tsk}_s$

Fig. 5. Oracles

A_0, A_1 against CP-ABE scheme E, an adversary A_s against the simulation soundness of Π and distinguishers D_1, D_2 that distinguish real proofs of Π_1 and Π_2 respectively, for all $\lambda \in \mathbb{N}$, we say

$$\mathbf{Adv}^{anon}_{GS,B}(\lambda) \leq \mathbf{Adv}^{ind\text{-}cpa}_{E,A_0}(\lambda) + \mathbf{Adv}^{ind\text{-}cpa}_{E,A_1}(\lambda) + \mathbf{Adv}^{ss}_{\Pi,A_s}(\lambda) + 2 \cdot (\mathbf{Adv}^{zk}_{P_1,S_1,D_1}(\lambda) + \mathbf{Adv}^{zk}_{P_2,S_2,D_2}(\lambda)).$$

According to the Lemma 5.1 described and proved in Bellare's scheme [3] we can say, the left side function is negligible since all the functions on the right side are negligible under the assumptions on the security of building blocks described. This proves the anonymity of group signature scheme with attribute-based tracing. The detail proof of security for the adversaries against the encryption scheme and the distinguisher for zero knowledge are provided in Bellare's scheme [3]. Comparing to the proof given in Bellare's scheme [3] the difference is our scheme is based on CP-ABE scheme instead PKE scheme.

B.2 Traceability

If there is a traceability adversary B, who constructs an adversary A_1 against the scheme *DS*, on the assumption that (P_1, V_1) is a sound proof system for ρ_1, we say

$$\mathbf{Adv}^{trace}_{GS,B}(\lambda) \leq 2^{-\lambda+1} + \mathbf{Adv}^{unforg\text{-}cma}_{DS,A_1}(\lambda).$$

On the assumption that *DS* is secure against traceability, all the functions on the right side are negligible. Because of this, the advantage of B is negligible. Thus, it proves that group signature scheme with attribute-based tracing is traceable.

B.3 Non-Frameability

If there is a non-frameability adversary B, who creates at most $n(\lambda)$ honest users, where n is a polynomial and who constructs two adversaries A_2, A_3 against the digital signature scheme, on the assumption that $(P_1, V_1), (P_2, V_2)$ are sound proof systems for ρ_1, ρ_2 respectively, we say

$$\mathbf{Adv}^{non\text{-}fram}_{GS,B}(\lambda) \leq 2^{-\lambda+1} + n(\lambda) \cdot (\mathbf{Adv}^{unforg\text{-}cma}_{DS,A_2}(\lambda) + \mathbf{Adv}^{unforg\text{-}cma}_{DS,A_3}(\lambda)).$$

On the assumption that the scheme *DS* is secure, all the functions on the right side are negligible, so the left side function. Thus, the group signature scheme with attribute-based tracing is non-frameable according to the definition of *DS*.

References

1. Anada, H., Fukumitsu, M., Hasegawa, S.: Group signatures with designated traceability. In: 2021 Ninth International Symposium on Computing and Networking (CANDAR), pp. 74–80. IEEE (2021)
2. Bellare, M., Micciancio, D., Warinschi, B.: Foundations of group signatures: formal definitions, simplified requirements, and a construction based on general assumptions. In: Biham, E. (ed.) EUROCRYPT 2003. LNCS, vol. 2656, pp. 614–629. Springer, Heidelberg (2003). https://doi.org/10.1007/3-540-39200-9_38
3. Bellare, M., Shi, H., Zhang, C.: Foundations of group signatures: the case of dynamic groups. In: Menezes, A. (ed.) CT-RSA 2005. LNCS, vol. 3376, pp. 136–153. Springer, Heidelberg (2005). https://doi.org/10.1007/978-3-540-30574-3_11
4. Blömer, J., Juhnke, J., Löken, N.: Short Group Signatures with Distributed Traceability. In: Kotsireas, I.S., Rump, S.M., Yap, C.K. (eds.) MACIS 2015. LNCS, vol. 9582, pp. 166–180. Springer, Cham (2016). https://doi.org/10.1007/978-3-319-32859-1_14
5. Camenisch, J., Drijvers, M., Lehmann, A., Neven, G., Towa, P.: Short threshold dynamic group signatures. In: Galdi, C., Kolesnikov, V. (eds.) SCN 2020. LNCS, vol. 12238, pp. 401–423. Springer, Cham (2020). https://doi.org/10.1007/978-3-030-57990-6_20
6. Chaum, D., van Heyst, E.: Group signatures. In: Davies, D.W. (ed.) EUROCRYPT 1991. LNCS, vol. 547, pp. 257–265. Springer, Heidelberg (1991). https://doi.org/10.1007/3-540-46416-6_22
7. Chow, S.S.M.: Removing escrow from identity-based encryption. In: Jarecki, S., Tsudik, G. (eds.) PKC 2009. LNCS, vol. 5443, pp. 256–276. Springer, Heidelberg (2009). https://doi.org/10.1007/978-3-642-00468-1_15
8. Emura, K., Katsumata, S., Watanabe, Y.: Identity-based encryption with security against the KGC: a formal model and its instantiation from lattices. In: Sako, K., Schneider, S., Ryan, P.Y.A. (eds.) ESORICS 2019. LNCS, vol. 11736, pp. 113–133. Springer, Cham (2019). https://doi.org/10.1007/978-3-030-29962-0_6
9. Ghadafi, E.: Efficient distributed tag-based encryption and its application to group signatures with efficient distributed traceability. In: Aranha, D.F., Menezes, A. (eds.) LATINCRYPT 2014. LNCS, vol. 8895, pp. 327–347. Springer, Cham (2015). https://doi.org/10.1007/978-3-319-16295-9_18
10. Goldwasser, S., Micali, S., Rivest, R.L.: A digital signature scheme secure against adaptive chosen-message attacks. SIAM J. Comput. **17**(2), 281–308 (1988)
11. Kiayias, A., Tsiounis, Y., Yung, M.: Traceable signatures. In: Cachin, C., Camenisch, J.L. (eds.) EUROCRYPT 2004. LNCS, vol. 3027, pp. 571–589. Springer, Heidelberg (2004). https://doi.org/10.1007/978-3-540-24676-3_34
12. Lewko, A., Okamoto, T., Sahai, A., Takashima, K., Waters, B.: Fully secure functional encryption: attribute-based encryption and (hierarchical) inner product encryption. In: Gilbert, H. (ed.) EUROCRYPT 2010. LNCS, vol. 6110, pp. 62–91. Springer, Heidelberg (2010). https://doi.org/10.1007/978-3-642-13190-5_4
13. Manulis, M., Sadeghi, A.-R., Schwenk, J.: Linkable democratic group signatures. In: Chen, K., Deng, R., Lai, X., Zhou, J. (eds.) ISPEC 2006. LNCS, vol. 3903, pp. 187–201. Springer, Heidelberg (2006). https://doi.org/10.1007/11689522_18
14. Perera, M.N.S., Nakamura, T., Hashimoto, M., Yokoyama, H., Cheng, C.M., Sakurai, K.: Decentralized and collaborative tracing for group signatures. In: Proceedings of the 2022 ACM on Asia Conference on Computer and Communications Security, pp. 1258–1260 (2022)

15. Perera, M.N.S., Nakamura, T., Hashimoto, M., Yokoyama, H., Cheng, C.M., Sakurai, K.: A survey on group signatures and ring signatures: traceability vs. anonymity. Cryptography **6**(1), 3 (2022)
16. Sakai, Y., Emura, K., Hanaoka, G., Kawai, Y., Matsuda, T., Omote, K.: Group signatures with message-dependent opening. In: Abdalla, M., Lange, T. (eds.) Pairing 2012. LNCS, vol. 7708, pp. 270–294. Springer, Heidelberg (2013). https://doi.org/10.1007/978-3-642-36334-4_18

Sherlock Holmes Zero-Knowledge Protocols

George Teşeleanu[1,2](✉)

[1] Advanced Technologies Institute, 10 Dinu Vintilă, Bucharest, Romania
[2] Simion Stoilow Institute of Mathematics of the Romanian Academy, 21 Calea Grivitei, Bucharest, Romania
tgeorge@dcti.ro

Abstract. We present two simple zero knowledge interactive proofs that can be instantiated with many of the standard decisional or computational hardness assumptions. Compared with traditional zero knowledge proofs, in our protocols the verifiers starts first, by emitting a challenge, and then the prover answers the challenge.

1 Introduction

A standard interactive proof of knowledge involves a prover, usually called P or *Peggy*, and a verifier, usually called V or *Victor*. *Peggy* is in possession of some secret k and by interacting with *Victor* she wants to convince him that she indeed owns k. More formally, an interactive proof is a pair of programs that implement the protocol between *Peggy* and *Victor*. To be useful, such a proof must be complete and sound. By complete we mean that an honest *Peggy* succeeds in convincing an honest *Victor* and by sound we mean that a dishonest prover does not succeed in convincing the verifier of a false statement. Moreover, if *Victor* does not learn anything from the protocol's execution which he did not know before, we say that the protocol is zero knowledge.

In a classical zero knowledge protocol, *Peggy* starts the protocol by sending a commitment to *Victor*, then *Victor* sends a challenge to *Peggy* and finally *Peggy* sends her answer. The verifier will accept the proof if and only if *Peggy*'s answer coincides with the answer he expects. In contrast with these protocols, the authors of [10] introduce a new class of protocols in which *Victor* starts the protocol. Once the verifier knows that *Peggy* wants to start the protocol[1], he issues a challenge to which *Peggy* answers. If the answer is correct, then the protocol ends successfully. Otherwise, it fails.

Although Grigoriev and Shpilrain's protocol is very interesting, the authors only claim that their protocol is zero knowledge without actually proving it. To fill this gap, we re-formalized and generalized Grigoriev and Shpilrain's protocol and then we proved its security. A downside of this formalization, is that *Victor*

[1] *e.g.* *Peggy* can send a "hello" type message or *Victor* can be equipped with motion sensors and detect *Peggy*'s proximity.

C. Su et al. (Eds.): ISPEC 2022, LNCS 13620, pp. 573–588, 2022.
https://doi.org/10.1007/978-3-031-21280-2_32

must iterate the protocol a number of times in order to fulfill the soundness property. By vectorizing the protocol we managed to reduce the number of iteration to one.

To further improve our protocol, we modified it by changing the underlying assumption from a decisional one to a computational one. This was necessary in order to reduce the bandwith requirements necessary for the decisional version. Note that if *Peggy* and *Victor* choose the right parameters the new protocol will provide the same security assurances.

Finally, we offer the reader several concrete realizations of our protocols and compare them with classical zero knowledge protocols such as Schnorr [17], Guillou-Quisquater [11] and Fiat-Shamir [7]. Note that one can devise new instantiations of our protocols.

Structure of the paper. We introduce notations and definitions used throughout the paper in Sect. 2. Inspired by Grigoriev and Shpilrain's protocol, in Sect. 3 we formalize and analyse the Multi-Decisional Sherlock Holmes (MDSH) protocol. A vectorized version of MDSH is presented in Sect. 4 and a computational version is tackled in Sect. 5. Section 6 contains a comparison with classical zero knowledge protocols. We conclude in Sect. 7.

2 Preliminaries

Notations. Throughout the paper, the notation $|S|$ denotes the cardinality of a set S. The action of selecting a random element x from a sample space X is denoted by $x \stackrel{\$}{\leftarrow} X$, while $x \leftarrow y$ represents the assignment of value y to variable x. The probability of the event E to happen is denoted by $Pr[E]$. The subset $\{0, \ldots, s-1\} \in \mathbb{N}$ is denoted by $[0, s]$. A vector v of length n is denoted either $v = (v_0, \ldots, v_{n-1})$ or $v = \{v_i\}_{i \in [0,n]}$ and $v_1 = v_2$ stands for element-wise equality between two vectors v_1 and v_2.

2.1 Hardness Assumptions

Inspired by the computational and decisional hardness assumptions described in [2] and the one way function definitions found in [1,16], we further provide the reader with the following two definitions. The first one captures the idea of a generic computational hardness assumption, while the second the decisional version. We do not claim to capture all the generic hardness assumptions, but for our purpose these definitions suffice. Note that when we define an advantage, we use ";" to denote the end of simple instructions or *for* loops and "," to denote the end of an instruction inside a *for* loop.

Definition 1 (Computational Hardness Assumption). *Let $K \subseteq \{0,1\}^*$ be a family of indices and for $k \in K$ let $D_k, R_k \subseteq \{0,1\}^*$. A computational hard function f is a parameterized family of functions $f_k : D_k \to R_k$ such that*

1. *for every $k \in K$ there exists a PPT algorithm that on input $x \in D_k$ outputs $f_k(x)$;*
2. *for every PPT algorithm A the advantage*

$$ADV_f^{\text{CHA}}(A) = Pr[f_k(z) = y \mid k \xleftarrow{\$} K; x \xleftarrow{\$} D_k; y \leftarrow f_k(x); z \leftarrow A(f_k, y)]$$

   is negligible;
3. *there exists a PPT algorithm B such that*

$$Pr[f_k(z) = y \mid k \xleftarrow{\$} K; x \xleftarrow{\$} D_k; y \leftarrow f_k(x); z \leftarrow B(k, y)] = 1.$$

Definition 2 (Decisional Hardness Assumption). *A function f is a decisional hard function if in Definition 1, Item 2 and 3 are changed to*

2. *for every PPT algorithm A the advantage*

$$ADV_f^{\text{DHA}}(A) = |2Pr[b = b' \mid k_0, k_1 \xleftarrow{\$} K; b \xleftarrow{\$} \{0,1\}; \\ x \xleftarrow{\$} D_{k_b}; y \leftarrow f_{k_b}(x); b' \leftarrow A(f_{k_0}, f_{k_1}, y)] - 1|$$

   is negligible;
3. *there exists a PPT algorithm B such that*

$$Pr[b = b' \mid k_0, k_1 \xleftarrow{\$} K; b \xleftarrow{\$} \{0,1\}; \\ x \xleftarrow{\$} D_{k_b}; y \leftarrow f_{k_b}(x); b' \leftarrow B(k_0, k_1, y)] = 1.$$

2.2 Zero-Knowledge Protocols

Let $Q : \{0,1\}^* \times \{0,1\}^* \rightarrow \{\texttt{true}, \texttt{false}\}$ be a predicate. Given a value z, Peggy will try to convince Victor that she knows a value x such that $Q(z, x) = \texttt{true}$.

We further base our reasoning on both a definition from [6,12] and a definition from [9,12] which we recall next.

Definition 3 (Proof of Knowledge Protocol). *An interactive protocol (P, V) is a proof of knowledge protocol for predicate Q if the following properties hold*

- **Completeness**: *V accepts the proof when P has as input a value x with $Q(z, x) = \texttt{true}$;*
- **Soundness**: *there exists an efficient program K (called knowledge extractor) such that for any $\bar{P}$ (possibly dishonest) with non-negligible probability of making V accept the proof, K can interact with $\bar{P}$ and output (with overwhelming probability) an x such that $Q(z, x) = \texttt{true}$.*

Definition 4 (Zero Knowledge Protocol). *A protocol (P, V) is zero-knowledge if for every efficient program $\bar{V}$ there exists an efficient program S, the simulator, such that the output of S is indistinguishable from a transcript of the protocol execution between P and $\bar{V}$.*

Remark 1. Note that we further work in the honest verifier scenario.

3 Multi-Decisional Protocol

3.1 Description

Based on a variation of decisional hard functions, we further describe a protocol (see Fig. 1) that allows *Peggy* to prove to *Victor* that she is in possession of some secrets. When *Victor* knows that *Peggy* is ready to start the protocol, he sends her a challenge and *Peggy* responds with her guess. If the guess is correct, then *Victor* accepts the answer.

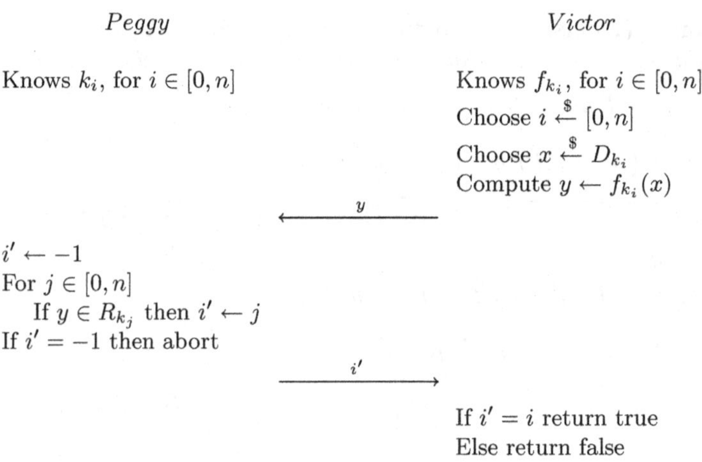

Fig. 1. Multi-Decisional Sherlock Holmes (MDSH) Protocol.

Remark 2. The probability of an adversary guessing the correct index i is $1/n$. Thus, the protocol must be repeated sufficient number of times (*e.g.* m times) in order to prevent an attacker[2] to convince *Victor* that he knows k_i, for $i \in [0, n]$.

3.2 Security Analysis

To ease understanding, we first introduce the notion of a multi-decisional hard function and then we prove the security of the MDSH protocol. At the end of this, subsection we show how to relate the security of a multi-decisional function to the security of a decisional function.

Definition 5 (Multi-Decisional Hardness Assumption). *Let $n \geq 2$ be an integer. A function f is a multi-decisional hard function if in Definition 2, Item 2 and 3 are changed to*

[2] In this case, the attacker's success probability is $1/n^m$.

2. *for every PPT algorithm A the advantage*

$$ADV_f^{\text{MDHA}}(A) = |2Pr[i = i' \mid for\ i \in [0,n] : k_i \xleftarrow{\$} K; i \xleftarrow{\$} [0,n]; x \xleftarrow{\$} D_{k_i}; \\ y \leftarrow f_{k_i}(x); i' \leftarrow A(f_k, y)] - 1|$$

is negligible, where $f_k = \{f_{k_i}\}_{i \in [0,n]}$*;*

3. *there exists a PPT algorithm B such that*

$$Pr[i = i' \mid for\ i \in [0,n] : k_i \xleftarrow{\$} K; i \xleftarrow{\$} [0,n]; x \xleftarrow{\$} D_{k_i}; \\ y \leftarrow f_{k_i}(x); i' \leftarrow B(k, y)] = 1,$$

where $k = \{k_i\}_{i \in [0,n]}$.

Remark 3. Please be advised that in the case of the multi-decisional hardness assumption we implicitly assume that all the keys are kept secret and none of them are leaked to an adversary (dishonest prover). If, for example, t out of n keys are leaked there is a simple strategy that makes the attacker win with probability $(t+1)/n$. More precisely, his strategy works as follows: The attacker, upon receipt of the verifier's challenge y, checks whether the message belongs to the set R_{k_i} for any of the t known secrets. If true (that happens with probability t/n), the attacker correctly answers the corresponding index of the matching secret. Otherwise, the attacker answers a random index chosen among the unknown secrets. In this last case, the success probability is $1/(n-t) \cdot (n-t)/n = 1/n$. Hence, the total success probability is $t/n + 1/n = (t+1)/n$.

Theorem 1. *The MDSH protocol is a proof of knowledge if and only if f is a multi-decisional hard function. Moreover, the protocol is zero knowledge.*

Proof. If f is a multi-decisional hard function, then according to Definition 5, Item 3, Peggy will compute with probability 1 the correct index. Thus, the completeness property is satisfied.

Let $\tilde{P}$ be a PPT algorithm that takes as input $f_{k_0}, \ldots, f_{k_{n-1}}$ and makes V accept the proof with non-negligible probability $Pr(\tilde{P})$. Then we are able to construct a PPT algorithm Q (described in Algorithm 1) that interacts with $\tilde{P}$ and that has a non-negligible advantage $ADV_f^{\text{MDHA}}(Q) = Pr(\tilde{P})$. Thus, the soundness property is satisfied.

Algorithm 1. Algorithm Q.

Input: An element $y \leftarrow f_{k_i}(x)$ and n functions f_{k_i}, where $i \in [0,n]$

Send y to $\tilde{P}$

Receive i' from $\tilde{P}$

return i'

The last part of our proof consists in constructing a simulator S such that its output is indistinguishable from a genuine transcript between *Peggy* and *Victor*. Such a simulator is described in Algorithm 2.

Algorithm 2. Simulator S.

Input: n functions f_{k_i}, where $i \in [0, n]$

Choose $i \xleftarrow{\$} [0, n]$
Choose $x \xleftarrow{\$} D_{k_i}$
Compute $y \leftarrow f_{k_i}(x)$
return (y, i)

□

We further show that if ADV_f^{DHA} is negligible, then MDSH is secure. Thus, when instantiating MDSH it suffices to know that decisional functions are secure.

Theorem 2. *For any PPT algorithm A there exists a PPT algorithm B such that the following inequality holds*

$$ADV_f^{\text{MDHA}}(A) \leq ADV_f^{\text{DHA}}(B).$$

Proof. Let A have a non-negligible advantage $ADV_f^{\text{MDHA}}(A)$. We describe in Algorithm 3 how B can obtain a non-negligible advantage $ADV_f^{\text{DHA}}(B)$ by interacting with A. Note that we have to randomly shuffle the functions' positions, in order to ensure that the index is randomly chosen from $[0, n]$.

Algorithm 3. Algorithm B.

Input: An element $y \leftarrow f_{k_b}(x)$

, where $b \xleftarrow{\$} \{0, 1\}$ **for** $i \in [2, n]$ **do**
  Choose $k_i \xleftarrow{\$} K$
end
Randomly shuffle $f_{k_0}, \ldots, f_{k_{n-1}}$'s positions and denote the result by $f'_{k_0}, \ldots, f'_{k_{n-1}}$
Let $i' \leftarrow A(f'_{k_0}, \ldots, f'_{k_{n-1}}, y)$
if *i' is the position of f_{k_0}* **then**
  return 0
end
else if *i' is the position of f_{k_1}* **then**
  return 1
end
else
  return $\perp$
end

□

3.3 Examples

Quadratic Residuosity Assumption. Let N be the product of two large primes p and q and let $J_N(x)$ denote the Jacobi symbol of x modulo N. We denote by $J_N = \{x \in \mathbb{Z}_N^* \mid J_N(x) = 1\}$ and $QR_N = \{x \in \mathbb{Z}_N^* \mid J_p(x) = 1 \text{ and } J_q(x) = 1\}$. Let u be an element such that his Jacobi symbol $J_N(u)$ is 1. The *quadratic residuosity assumptions* (denoted by QR) states that deciding if $u \in J_N \setminus QR_N$ or $u \in QR_N$ is intractable without knowing p or q (see [5]).

Since QRA partitions J_N in two sets, we must set $n = 2$ for MDSH. Let u be an element such that $J_p(u) = J_q(u) = -1$. Then the MDSH parameters are as follows

- the secret keys are $k_0 = k_1 = (p, q)$;
- the functions are defined as $f_{k_0}(x) = x^2 \bmod N$ and $f_{k_1}(x) = u \cdot x^2 \bmod N$, where u and N are public.

To decide if $y \in J_N \setminus QR_N$ or $y \in QR_N$, *Peggy* computes $J_p(y)$. Note that when $b = 0$ we have $J_p(y) = J_p(x^2) = 1$ and when $b = 1$ we have $J_p(y) = J_p(u)J_p(x^2) = -1$.

Remark 4. A similar assumption can be found in [3]. Let $\kappa > 1$ be an integer and let $p, q \equiv 1 \bmod 2^\kappa$. Then the *gap* 2^κ*-residuosity assumption* states that is hard to distinguish between an element from $J_N \setminus QR_N$ and element of the form $y^{2^\kappa} \bmod N$, where $y \in \mathbb{Z}_N^*$. In this case the functions become $f_{k_0}(x) = x^{2^\kappa} \bmod N$ and $f_{k_1}(x) = u \cdot x^{2^\kappa} \bmod N$

Least Significant Bit of the e-th Root Assumption. Let $N = pq$ be the product of two large primes. We denote by $\varphi(N)$ the Euler totient function. Let e be an integer such that $gcd(e, \varphi(N)) = 1$. The *least significant bit of the e-th root assumption* (denoted LSB-ER) states that given $y \equiv x^e \bmod N$ is hard to decide if the least-significant bit of x is 0 or 1 (see [15]).

As in the case of QR, we have $n = 2$. The protocol's parameters are

- the secret keys are $k_0 = k_1 = (p, q)$;
- the functions are defined as $f_{k_0}(x) = (2x)^e \bmod N$ and $f_{k_1}(x) = (2x + 1)^e \cdot x^2 \bmod N$, where N and e are public.

To find the least significant bit lsb, *Peggy* computes a d such that $ed \equiv 1 \bmod \varphi(N)$ and an element $z \leftarrow y^d \bmod N$. Then $lsb \equiv z \bmod 2$.

Decisional Diffie-Hellman Assumption. Let $\mathbb{G}$ be a cyclic group of prime order q and g a generator of $\mathbb{G}$. Let $x_1, x_2, y \xleftarrow{\$} \mathbb{Z}_q^*$ and $b \xleftarrow{\$} \{0, 1\}$. The *decisional Diffie-Hellman assumption* (denoted by DDH) states that given $(g^{x_1}, g^{x_2}, g^y, (g^{x_b})^y)$ the probability for a PPT algorithm to compute the bit b is negligible (see [2]).

In this case $n \geq 2$ and the parameters are

- the secret keys are $k_i \xleftarrow{\$} \mathbb{Z}_q^*$, for $i \in [0, n]$;

- the public parameters are $r_i \leftarrow g^{k_i}$, for $i \in [0, n]$, the group $\mathbb{G}$ and the generator g;
- the functions are defined as $f_{k_i}(x) = (g^x, r_i^x)$, for $i \in [0, n]$.

To decide the correct index, *Peggy* has to parse $y = (y_0, y_1)$ and to compute $\ell = y_0^{k_i}$ until $\ell = y_1$. Note that $y_0^{k_i} = r_i^x$.

Decisional Bilinear Diffie-Hellman Assumption. Let $\mathbb{G}$ be cyclic group of prime order q and let P be the corresponding generator. We denote by $e : \mathbb{G} \times \mathbb{G} \rightarrow \mathbb{G}_T$ a cryptographic bilinear map, where G_T is a cyclic group of order q. We will use the convention of writing $\mathbb{G}$ additively and $\mathbb{G}_T$ multiplicatively.

Let $a_0, a_1, b_0, b_1, c \xleftarrow{\$} \mathbb{Z}_q^*$. The *decisional bilinear Diffie-Hellman assumption* (denoted DBDH) states that given $(a_0P, a_1P, b_0P, b_1P, cP, Z)$ the probability of deciding if $Z = e(P, P)^{a_0 b_0 c}$ or $Z = e(P, P)^{a_1 b_1 c}$ is negligible (see [4]).

As in the case of DDH, we have $n \geq 2$. The MDSH's parameters are

- the secret keys are $a_i, b_i \xleftarrow{\$} \mathbb{Z}_q^*$, for $i \in [0, n]$;
- the public parameters are $Q_i \leftarrow a_i P$ and $R_i \leftarrow b_i P$, for $i \in [0, n]$, the group $\mathbb{G}$, the generator P and the bilinear map e;
- the functions are defined as $f_{k_i}(x) = (xP, e(Q_i, R_i)^x)$, for $i \in [0, n]$.

To find the correct answer, *Peggy* parses $y = (Y_0, Y_1)$ and computes $L = e(P, Y_0)^{a_i b_i}$ until $L = Y_1$. Note that $e(Q_i, R_i)^x = e(P, P)^{a_i b_i x} = e(P, xP)^{a_i b_i} = e(P, Y_0)^{a_i b_i}$.

4 Vectorized Multi-Decisional Protocol

4.1 Description

A downside to the MDSH protocol is that $Victor$ has to run the protocol a number of times before he can be sure that *Peggy* knows $\{k_i\}_{i \in [0,n]}$. We further present a variation of MDSH (see Fig. 2) that allows $Victor$ to run the protocol only once, if he chooses the right parameters. Let $t > 1$ be an integer.

Remark 5. The probability of an adversary guessing the correct index vector v is $1/n^t$. If n^t is sufficiently large, then a single execution of the protocol suffices. Otherwise, $Victor$ must rerun the protocol multiple times.

4.2 Security Analysis

As in Sect. 3.2, we first introduce the relevant hardness assumption, then we prove the security of the VDSH protocol and at the end we relate the new hardness assumption with the multi-dimensional hardness assumption.

Definition 6 (Vectorized Multi-Decisional Hardness Assumption). *Let $t > 1$ be an integer. A function f is a vectorized multi-decisional hard function if in Definition 5, Item 2 and 3 are changed to*

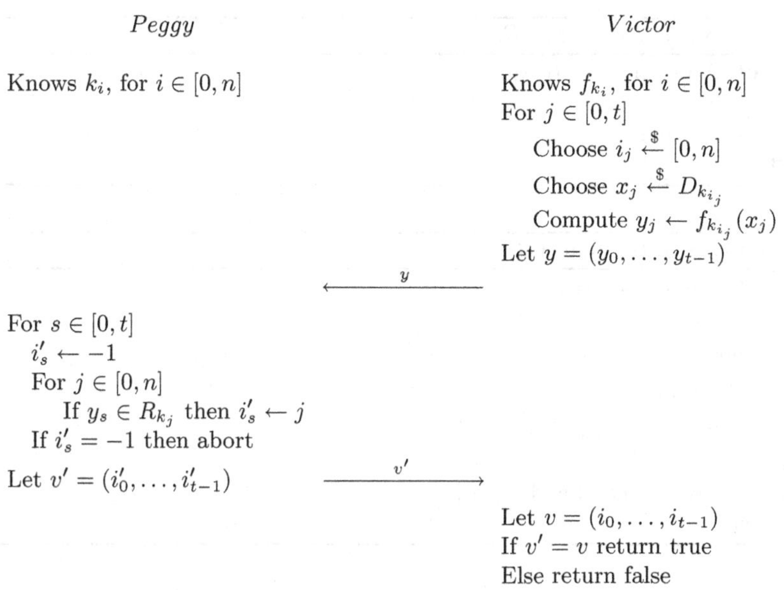

Fig. 2. Vectorized Multi-Decisional Sherlock Holmes (VDSH) Protocol.

2. *for every PPT algorithm A the advantage*

$$ADV_f^{\text{VDHA}}(A) = |2Pr[v = v' \mid \textit{for } i \in [0,n] : k_i \xleftarrow{\$} K; \textit{for } j \in [0,t] : i_j \xleftarrow{\$} [0,n], \\ x_j \xleftarrow{\$} D_{k_{i_j}}, y_j \leftarrow f_{k_{i_j}}(x_j); v' \leftarrow A(f_k, y)] - 1|$$

is negligible, where $f_k = \{f_{k_i}\}_{i \in [0,n]}$, $v = \{i_j\}_{j \in [0,t]}$ *and* $y = \{y_j\}_{j \in [0,t]}$*;*

3. *there exists a PPT algorithm B such that*

$$Pr[v = v' \mid \textit{for } i \in [0,n] : k_i \xleftarrow{\$} K; \textit{for } j \in [0,t] : i_j \xleftarrow{\$} [0,n], \\ x_j \xleftarrow{\$} D_{k_{i_j}}, y_j \leftarrow f_{k_{i_j}}(x_j); v' \leftarrow B(k, y)] = 1,$$

where $k = \{k_i\}_{i \in [0,n]}$, $v = \{i_j\}_{j \in [0,t]}$ *and* $y = \{y_j\}_{j \in [0,t]}$.

Theorem 3. *The VDSH protocol is a proof of knowledge if and only if f is a vectorized multi-decisional hard function. Moreover, the protocol is zero knowledge.*

Proof. The proof is similar to Theorem 2 and thus we only provide a sketch. The completeness property is satisfied due to Definition 6, Item 3.

A PPT algorithm R is described in Algorithm 4 and R has a non-negligible advantage $ADV_f^{\text{VDHA}}(R) = Pr(\tilde{P})$.

Finally, the simulator T is described in Algorithm 9 □

Algorithm 4. Algorithm R.

Input: A vector $y \leftarrow (f_k(x_0), \ldots, f_k(x_{t-1}))$

Send y to $\tilde{P}$

Receive v' from $\tilde{P}$

return v'

Algorithm 5. Simulator T.

Input: n functions f_{k_i}, where $i \in [0, n]$

for $j \in [0, t]$ **do**

  Choose $i_j \xleftarrow{\$} [0, n]$

  Choose $x_j \xleftarrow{\$} D_{k_{i_j}}$

  Compute $y_j \leftarrow f_{k_{i_j}}(x)$

end

Let $y = (y_0, \ldots, y_{t-1})$ and $v = (i_0, \ldots, i_{t-1})$

return (y, v)

The next theorem proves the equivalence between the security notion associated with multi-decisional functions and the vectorized version of it. Using Theorems 2 and 4, the security of VDSH reduces to making sure that the decisional security notion is intractable.

Theorem 4. *For any PPT algorithms A and C there exist PPT algorithms B and D such that the following inequalities hold*

$$ADV_f^{\text{MDHA}}(A) \leq ADV_f^{\text{VDHA}}(B)$$
$$ADV_f^{\text{VDHA}}(C) \leq ADV_f^{\text{MDHA}}(D).$$

Proof. Let A have a non-negligible advantage $ADV_f^{\text{MDHA}}(A)$ and let $Pr(A) = (ADV_f^{\text{MDHA}}(A) + 1)/2$. We describe in Algorithm 6 how B can obtain a non-negligible advantage $ADV_f^{\text{VDHA}}(B) = |2Pr(A)^n - 1|$ by interacting with A.

Algorithm 6. Algorithm B.

Input: A vector of elements $y \leftarrow (y_0, \ldots, y_{t-1})$

for $j \in [0, t]$ **do**

  Let $i'_j \leftarrow A(f_{k_0}, \ldots, f_{k_{n-1}}, y_j)$

end

Let $v' = (i'_0, \ldots, i'_{t-1})$

return v'

To prove the second inequality we assume that $ADV_f^{\text{VDHA}}(C)$ is non-negligible. Using algorithm C, we construct algorithm D (see Algorithm 7) that has a non-negligible advantage $ADV_f^{\text{MDHA}}(D)$.

Algorithm 7. Algorithm D.

Input: An element $y \leftarrow f_{k_i}(x)$, where $i \xleftarrow{\$} [0, n]$
for $j \in [1, t]$ **do**
  Choose $i_j \xleftarrow{\$} [0, n]$
  Choose $x_j \xleftarrow{\$} D_{k_{i_j}}$
  Compute $y_j \leftarrow f_{k_{i_j}}(x)$
end
Let $z = (y, y_1, \ldots, y_{t-1})$ and $f_k = (f_{k_0}, \ldots, f_{k_{n-1}})$
Let $v' \leftarrow C(f_k, z)$
Parse $v' = (v'_0, \ldots, v'_{t-1})$
return v'_0

□

5 Computational Protocol

5.1 Description

Using a different security notion, we describe in Fig. 3 a protocol that consumes less bandwith that the VDSH protocol, while maintaining its security, if the parameters are selected correctly.

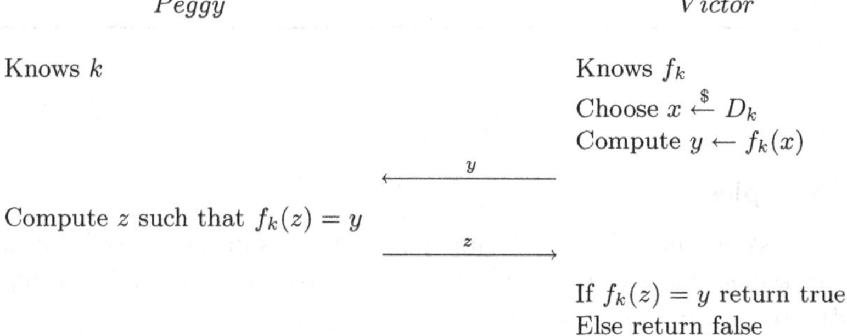

Fig. 3. Computational Sherlock Holmes (CSH) Protocol.

Remark 6. The probability of an adversary guessing the correct element x is $1/|D_k|$. If $|D_k|$ is sufficiently large, then a single execution of the protocol suffices. Otherwise, the protocol must be repeated several times.

Remark 7. A vectorized version of the CSH protocol can also be constructed, but as we will see in Sect. 5.3 it is not necessary. Note that the security analysis is similar to the one from Sect. 4.2.

5.2 Security Analysis

Theorem 5. *The CSH protocol is a proof of knowledge if and only if f is a computational hard function. Moreover, the protocol is zero knowledge.*

Proof. The proof is similar to Theorem 2 and thus we only provide a sketch. The completeness property is satisfied due to Definition 1, Item 3.

A PPT algorithm O is described in Algorithm 8 and O has a non-negligible advantage $ADV_f^{\text{CHA}}(O) = Pr(\tilde{P})$. Note that in this case $\tilde{P}$ only takes as input a function f_k.

Algorithm 8. Algorithm O.

Input: An element $y \leftarrow f_k(x)$

Send y to $\tilde{P}$

Receive z from $\tilde{P}$

return z

Finally, the simulator U is described in Algorithm 9

Algorithm 9. Simulator U.

Input: A function f_k

Choose $x \xleftarrow{\$} D_k$

Compute $y \leftarrow f_k(x)$

return (y, x)

□

5.3 Examples

e-th Root Assumption. Using the same parameters as in the case of LSB-ER, the *e-th root assumption* (denoted ER) states that given $y \equiv x^e \bmod N$ computing x is intractable (see [12]).

Using this assumption we can instantiate the CSH protocol with $k = (p, q)$ and $f_k(x) = x^e \bmod N$. To recover x, *Peggy* has to compute a d such that $ed \equiv 1 \bmod \varphi(N)$ and then $x \leftarrow y^d \bmod N$.

Remark 8. The problem can also be stated for $e = 2$, but to find a solution to $x^2 \bmod N$, *Peggy* has to use a different technique (*e.g.* the Shanks-Tonelli algorithm [13]). Note that this assumption is equivalent with the intractability of factoring N (*i.e. factoring assumption*).

Gap 2^κ-residuosity Assumption Using the same parameters as in Sect. 3.3, we can define $f_k(x) = y^x z^{2^\kappa} \bmod N$, where $k = (p, q)$, $D_k = [0, 2^\kappa]$ and $z \xleftarrow{\$} \mathbb{Z}_N^*$. A method for recovering x if one knows p is described in [3].

Computational Diffie-Hellman. Let $\mathbb{G}$ be a cyclic group of order q and g a generator of $\mathbb{G}$. Let $x, y \xleftarrow{\$} \mathbb{Z}_q^*$. The *computational Diffie-Hellman assumption* (denoted by CDH) states that given (g^x, g^y) is intractable to compute g^{xy} without knowing x or y (see [2]). In this case a more efficient version of the CSH protocol is provided in Fig. 4.

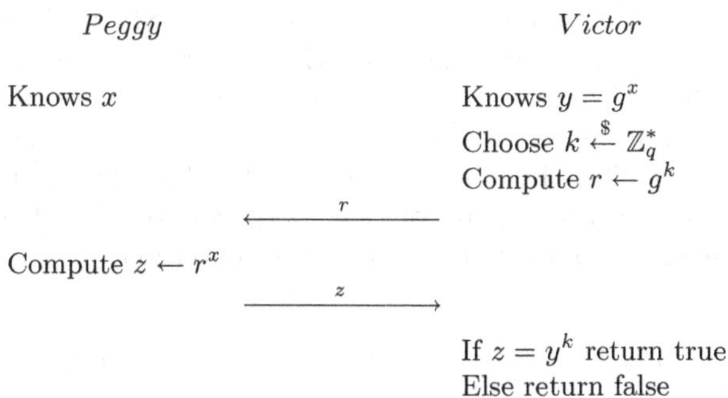

Fig. 4. Diffie-Hellman Version of the CSH (DHCSH) Protocol.

Remark 9. Note that the DHCSH protocol was used in [19] to develop a method that performs full network authentication for resource-constrained devices. In [18], the authors introduce a version of the DHCSH protocol in which instead of sending r the verifier sends $(r, h(y^k))$, where h is a hash function. Stinson and Wu [18] prove that their protocol is secure against active intruders and reset attack[3]. A more efficient version of the Stinson-Wu protocol was introduced in [20,21]. In this variant, *Victor* sends r, while *Peggy* sends $h(z)$ instead of z. The authors [20,21] show that the scheme achieves the same security as their previously proposed protocol.

Computational Bilinear Diffie-Hellman Assumption. We assume the same setup as in the case of DBDH. Let $a, b, c \xleftarrow{\$} \mathbb{Z}_q^*$. The *computational bilinear Diffie-Hellman assumption* (denoted CBDH) states that given (aP, bP, cP) a PPT algorithm will compute $e(P, P)^{abc}$ with negligible probability (see [4]).

As in the case of CDH, this assumption allows us to have a more efficient version of the protocol. We will use Fig. 4 as a reference. Thus, *Peggy* and *Victor* know $x = (a, b)$ and, respectively, $y = (aP, bP)$. The protocol's first step consists of *Victor* computing $r \leftarrow kP$. After that *Peggy* computes $z \leftarrow e(P, r)^{ab}$. Finally, the protocol's output is `true` if and only if $z = e(aP, bP)^k$.

3 We refer the reader to [8] for a detailed description of these types of attacks.

6 Performance of the Sherlock Holmes Protocols

In this section we compare the Sherlock Holmes protocols to some classical zero knowledge protocols such as Schnorr [17], Guillou-Quisquater [11] and Fiat-Shamir [7].

We further assume the same setup as in the case of CDH. From Fig. 5 we can see that the bandwidth requirement for Schnorr's protocol is $\log_2(|\mathbb{G}| + 2q)$ bits. Similarly, for the Diffie-Hellman version of the CSH protocol we obtain a requirement of $\log_2(2|\mathbb{G}|)$ bits. In practice, $\mathbb{G}$ is either $\mathbb{Z}_p^*$, where $p = (q-1)/2$ is a prime or an elliptic curve $E(\mathbb{Z}_p)$ such that $|E(\mathbb{Z}_p)| = hq$, where $h \leq 4$. Thus, in the modulo p case we obtain $(5q-1)/2$ versus $q-1$ and in the elliptic curve case $(h+2)q$ vs $2hq$. Thus, in most cases, our protocol's requirements are slightly lower. From a computational point of view, it is easy to see that both protocols have their complexity dominated by three exponentiations.

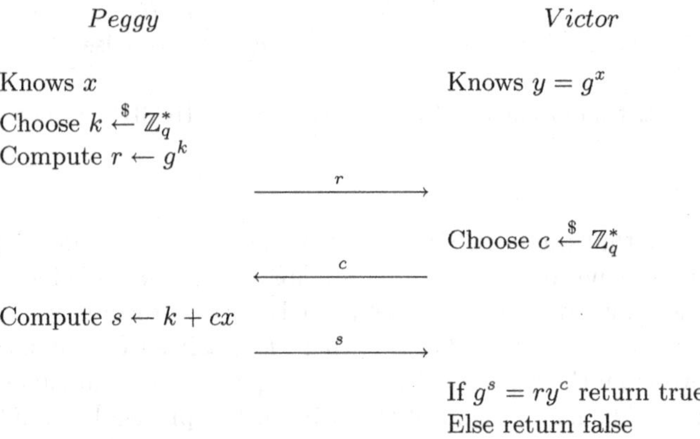

Fig. 5. Schnorr's Protocol.

Remark 10. Okamoto's protocol [14] can be seen as a vectorized version of Schnorr's protocol with $n = 2$. Thus, we can conclude that a vectorized version of DHCSH has slightly lower requirements as Okamoto's protocol.

Using Fig. 5 as a reference, we further describe the Guillou-Quisquater (GQ) protocol. Assuming the setup from ER we set $y \equiv x^e \bmod N$. In the first phase, *Peggy* chooses $k \xleftarrow{\$} \mathbb{Z}_N^*$ and computes $r \equiv k^e \bmod N$. Then *Victor* randomly selects $c \xleftarrow{\$} [0, e-1]$. The third step consists of *Peggy* computing $s \equiv kx^c \bmod N$. Then *Victor* accepts the proof if an only if $s^e \equiv ry^c \bmod N$.

The bandwidth requirement for the GQ protocol is $\log_2(2N+e)$, while for the e-th root instantiation of CSH is $loq_2(2N)$. Hence, the requirements are similar only if e is small. From a computational point of view, CSH's time is dominated by two exponentiations, while GQ's time by four. So, our protocol is twice as fast. Also, note that the probability of impersonating *Peggy* is $1/e$ for GQ, while for our protocol is in the worse case $e^2/\varphi(N)^4$.

The Fiat-Shamir protocol [7] considers $e = 2$. Let $n = 2$. If we consider $MDSH$ instantiated with DDH, we obtain a bandwith requirement of $\log_2(|\mathbb{G}|)$, a complexity dominated by three exponentiations and a probability of impersonating *Peggy* of 1/2. Let $\mathbb{G} = \mathbb{Z}_{p'}^*$, when p' is prime[5]. Using the reasoning from the GQ protocol, we obtain that the $MDSH$ protocol has a better performance that the Fiat-Shamir, while having the same security.

7 Conclusions

Our two main zero knowledge protocols, decisional and computational Sherlock Holmes protocols, represent two new large classes of protocols. The presented list of examples is by no means exhaustive. Our next challenge is to see how we can adapt these protocols in order to obtain new cryptographic primitives (*e.g.* non-interactive zero knowledge proofs or digital signatures). Another interesting research direction is to investigate whether these protocols can be secured against active intruders and reset attack

References

1. Bellare, M., Goldwasser, S.: Lecture Notes on Cryptography. https://cseweb.ucsd.edu/mihir/papers/gb.pdf (2008)
2. Bellare, M., Rogaway, P.: Introduction to Modern Cryptography. https://web.cs.ucdavis.edu/rogaway/classes/227/spring05/book/main.pdf (2005)
3. Benhamouda, F., Herranz, J., Joye, M., Libert, B.: Efficient cryptosystems from 2^k-th power residue symbols. J. Cryptol. **30**(2), 519–549 (2017)
4. Chatterjee, S., Sarkar, P.: Practical hybrid (hierarchical) identity-based encryption schemes based on the decisional bilinear Diffie-Hellman assumption. IJACT **3**(1), 47–83 (2013)
5. Cocks, C.: An identity based encryption scheme based on quadratic residues. In: Honary, B. (ed.) Cryptography and Coding 2001. LNCS, vol. 2260, pp. 360–363. Springer, Heidelberg (2001). https://doi.org/10.1007/3-540-45325-3_32
6. Feige, U., Fiat, A., Shamir, A.: Zero-knowledge proofs of identity. J. Cryptol. **1**(2), 77–94 (1988)
7. Fiat, A., Shamir, A.: How to prove yourself: practical solutions to identification and signature problems. In: Odlyzko, A.M. (ed.) CRYPTO 1986. LNCS, vol. 263, pp. 186–194. Springer, Heidelberg (1987). https://doi.org/10.1007/3-540-47721-7_12
8. Goldreich, O.: Zero-knowledge twenty years after its invention. IACR Cryptology ePrint Archive 2002/186 (2002)
9. Goldwasser, S., Micali, S., Rackoff, C.: The knowledge complexity of interactive proof systems. SIAM J. Comput. **18**(1), 186–208 (1989)

[4] According to Lagrange's theorem the polynomial x^e has at most e solution modulo p.

[5] In practice, for security reasons, n and p' have similar lengths.

10. Grigoriev, D., Shpilrain, V.: No-leak authentication by the Sherlock Holmes method. Groups Complexity Cryptol. **4**(1), 177–189 (2012)
11. Guillou, L.C., Quisquater, J.-J.: A practical zero-knowledge protocol fitted to security microprocessor minimizing both transmission and memory. In: Barstow, D., et al. (eds.) EUROCRYPT 1988. LNCS, vol. 330, pp. 123–128. Springer, Heidelberg (1988). https://doi.org/10.1007/3-540-45961-8_11
12. Maurer, U.: Unifying zero-knowledge proofs of knowledge. In: Preneel, B. (ed.) AFRICACRYPT 2009. LNCS, vol. 5580, pp. 272–286. Springer, Heidelberg (2009). https://doi.org/10.1007/978-3-642-02384-2_17
13. Niven, I., Zuckerman, H.S., Montgomery, H.L.: An Introduction to the Theory of Numbers. John Wiley & Sons (1991)
14. Okamoto, T.: Provably secure and practical identification schemes and corresponding signature schemes. In: Brickell, E.F. (ed.) CRYPTO 1992. LNCS, vol. 740, pp. 31–53. Springer, Heidelberg (1993). https://doi.org/10.1007/3-540-48071-4_3
15. Okamoto, T., Pointcheval, D.: The Gap-Problems: a new class of problems for the security of cryptographic schemes. In: Kim, K. (ed.) PKC 2001. LNCS, vol. 1992, pp. 104–118. Springer, Heidelberg (2001). https://doi.org/10.1007/3-540-44586-2_8
16. Ostrovsky, R.: Foundations of Cryptography (2010). http://web.cs.ucla.edu/rafail/PUBLIC/OstrovskyDraftLecNotes2010.pdf
17. Schnorr, C.P.: Efficient identification and signatures for smart cards. In: Brassard, G. (ed.) CRYPTO 1989. LNCS, vol. 435, pp. 239–252. Springer, New York (1990). https://doi.org/10.1007/0-387-34805-0_22
18. Stinson, D.R., Wu, J.: An efficient and secure two-flow zero-knowledge identification protocol. J. Math. Cryptol. **1**(3), 201–220 (2007)
19. Teşeleanu, G.: Lightweight swarm authentication. In: Ryan, P.Y., Toma, C. (eds.) SECITC 2021 Lecture Notes in Computer Science, vol. 13195. Springer, Cham (2021). https://doi.org/10.1007/978-3-031-17510-7_17
20. Wu, J., Stinson, D.R.: An efficient identification protocol and the knowledge-of-exponent assumption. IACR Cryptology ePrint Archive 2007/479 (2007)
21. Wu, J., Stinson, D.R.: An efficient identification protocol secure against concurrent-reset attacks. J. Math. Cryptol. **3**(4), 339–352 (2009)

Continued Fractions Applied to a Family of RSA-like Cryptosystems

Paul Cotan[1,2] and George Teşeleanu[1,2(✉)]

[1] Advanced Technologies Institute, 10 Dinu Vintilă, Bucharest, Romania
{paul.cotan,tgeorge}@dcti.ro

[2] Simion Stoilow Institute of Mathematics of the Romanian Academy, 21 Calea Grivitei, Bucharest, Romania

Abstract. Let $N = pq$ be the product of two balanced prime numbers p and q. Murru and Saettone presented in 2017 an interesting RSA-like cryptosystem that uses the key equation $ed - k(p^2 + p + 1)(q^2 + q + 1) = 1$, instead of the classical RSA key equation $ed - k(p-1)(q-1) = 1$. The authors claimed that their scheme is immune to Wiener's continued fraction attack. Unfortunately, Nitaj *et. al.* developed exactly such an attack. In this paper, we introduce a family of RSA-like encryption schemes that uses the key equation $ed - k[(p^n - 1)(q^n - 1)]/[(p-1)(q-1)] = 1$, where $n > 1$ is an integer. Then, we show that regardless of the choice of n, there exists an attack based on continued fractions that recovers the secret exponent.

1 Introduction

In 1978, Rivest, Shamir and Adleman [24] proposed one of the most popular and widely used cryptosystem, namely RSA. In the standard RSA encryption scheme, we work modulo an integer N, where N is the product of two large prime numbers p and q. Let $\varphi(N) = (p-1)(q-1)$ denote the Euler totient function. In order to encrypt a message $m < N$, we simply compute $c \equiv m^e \bmod N$, where e is generated a priori such that $\gcd(e, \varphi(N)) = 1$. To decrypt, one needs to compute $m \equiv c^d \bmod N$, where $d \equiv e^{-1} \bmod \varphi(N)$. Note that (N, e) are public, while (p, q, d) are kept secret. In the standard version of RSA, also called balanced RSA, p and q are of the same bit-size such that $q < p < 2q$. In this paper, we only consider the balanced RSA scheme and its variants.

In 2017, Murru and Saettone introduced an RSA-like cryptosystem [18]. Instead of using $\mathbb{Z}_N^*$, the scheme works with a special type of group that consists of equivalence classes of polynomials from the $GF(p^3) \times GF(q^3)$, where GF stands for Galois field. Furthermore, when developing their cryptosystem, the authors use the same modulus as the RSA scheme, but they choose e such that $\gcd(e, \psi(N)) = 1$, where $\psi(N) = (p^2 + p + 1)(q^2 + q + 1)$. Also, the decryption exponent is $d \equiv e^{-1} \bmod \psi(N)$. In [18], the authors claim that their scheme is more secure than RSA. More precisely, they say that their scheme is secure against Wiener's small private key attack [30] and Hastad's broadcast attack [12]. Unfortunately, this is not true as can be seen in the following paragraphs.

C. Su et al. (Eds.): ISPEC 2022, LNCS 13620, pp. 589–605, 2022.
https://doi.org/10.1007/978-3-031-21280-2_33

Small Private Key Attacks. In order to decrease decryption time, one may prefer to use a smaller d. Wiener showed in [30] that this is not always a good idea. More exactly, in the case of RSA, if $d < N^{0.25}/3$, then one can retrieve d from the continued fraction expansion of e/N, and thus factor N. Using a result developed by Coppersmith [7], Boneh and Durfee [5] improved Wiener's bound to $N^{0.292}$. Later on, Herrmann and May [13] obtain the same bound, but using simpler techniques. A different approach was taken by Blömer and May [3], whom generalized Wiener's attack. More precisely, they showed that if there exist three integers x, y, z such that $ex - y\varphi(N) = z$, $x < N^{0.25}/3$ and $|z| < |exN^{-0.75}|$, then the factorisation of N can be recovered. When an approximation of p is known such that $|p - p_0| < N^{\delta}/8$ and $\delta < 0.5$, Nassr, Anwar and Bahig [20] present a method based on continued fractions for recovering d when $d < N^{(1-\delta)/2}$.

In the case of the Murru-Saetonne scheme, it was shown in [22,27] that a Wiener-type attack still works. Using a technique based on continued fractions they showed that when $d < N^{0.25}$ we can factor N. Applying the method proposed by Boneh-Durfee, Nitaj *et al.* [22] improved the bound to $N^{0.5694}$. A better bound $d < N^{0.585}$ was found by Zheng, Kunihiro and Yao in [31]. When p_0 is known such that $|p - p_0| < N^{\delta}$ and $\delta < 0.5$, Nassr, Anwar and Bahig [19] show how to recover d when $d < N^{(1-\delta)/2}$.

Multiple Private Keys Attack. Let $\ell > 0$ be an integer and $i \in [1, \ell]$. When multiple large public keys $e_i \simeq N^{\alpha}$ are used with the same modulus N, Howgrave-Graham and Seifert [14] describe an attack for RSA that recovers the corresponding small private exponents $d_i \simeq N^{\beta}$. This attack was later improved by Sarkar and Maitra [25], Aono [1] and Takayasu and Kunihiro [28]. The best known bound [28] is $\beta < 1 - \sqrt{2/(3\ell + 1)}$. Remark that when $\ell = 1$ we obtain the Boneh-Durfee bound.

The multiple private keys attack against the Murru-Saetonne cryptosystem was studied by Shi, Wang and Gu [26]. The bound obtained by the authors is $\beta < 3/2 - 4/(3\ell + 1)$ and it is twice the bound obtained by Aono [1]. Note that when $\ell = 1$ the bound is less than 0.585, and thus tighter bounds might exist.

Partial Key Exposure Attack. In this type of attack, the most or least significant bits of the private exponent d are known. Starting from these, an adversary can recover the entire RSA private key using the techniques presented by Boneh, Durfee and Frankel in [6]. The attack was later improved by Blömer and May [2], Ernst *et al.* [9] and Takayasu and Kunihiro [29]. The best known bound [29] is $\beta < (\gamma + 2 - \sqrt{2 - 3\gamma^2})/2$, where the attacker knows N^{γ} leaked bits.

Shi, Wang and Gu [26] describe a partial exposure attack that works in the case of the Murru-Saetonne scheme. The bound they achieve is $\beta < (3\gamma + 7 - 2\sqrt{3\gamma + 7})/3$. When $\gamma = 0$, the bound is close to 0.569, and thus it remains an open problem how to optimize it.

Small Prime Difference Attack. When the primes difference $|p - q|$ is small and certain conditions hold, de Weger [8] described two methods to recover d, one based on continued fractions and one on lattice reduction. These methods were further extended by Maitra and Sakar [16,17] to $|\rho q - p|$, where $1 \leq \rho \leq 2$. Lastly, Chen, Hsueh and Lin generalize them further to $|\rho q - \epsilon p|$, where ρ and ϵ have certain properties. The continued fraction method is additionally improved by Ariffin *et al.* [15].

The de Weger attack was adapted to the Murru-Saetonne public key encryption scheme by Nitaj *et al.* [23], Nassr, Anwar and Bahig [19] and Shi, Wang and Gu [26]. The best bounds for the continued fraction and lattice reduction methods are found in [23]. The Maitra-Sakar extension was studied only in [19].

1.1 Our Contribution

In this paper we generalize the Murru-Saetonne scheme to equivalence classes of polynomials from $GF(p^n) \times GF(q^n)$, where $n > 1$. We wanted to see if only for $n = 3$ the attacks devised for RSA work or this is something that happens in general. In this study we present a Wiener-type attack that works for any $n > 1$. More, precisely we prove that when $d < N^{0.25}$, we can recover the secret exponent regardless the value of n. Therefore, no matter how we instantiate the generalized version, a small private key attack will always succeed.

Structure of the Paper. We introduce in Sect. 2 notations and definitions used throughout the paper. Inspired by Murru and Saettone's work [18], in Sect. 3 we introduce a family of groups that is latter used in Sect. 4 to construct RSA-like cryptosystems. After proving several useful lemmas in Sect. 5, we extend Wiener's small private key attack in Sect. 6. Two concrete instantiations are provided in Sect. 7. We conclude our paper in Sect. 8.

2 Preliminaries

Notations. Throughout the paper, λ denotes a security parameter. Also, the notation $|S|$ denotes the cardinality of a set S. The set of integers $\{0, \ldots, a\}$ is further denoted by $[0, a]$.

2.1 Continued Fraction

For any real number ζ there exist an unique sequence $(a_n)_n$ of integers such that

$$\zeta = a_0 + \cfrac{1}{a_1 + \cfrac{1}{a_2 + \cfrac{1}{a_3 + \cfrac{1}{a_4 + \cdots}}}},$$

where $a_k > 0$ for any $k \geq 1$. This sequence represents the continued fraction expansion of ζ and is denoted by $\zeta = [a_0, a_1, a_2, \ldots]$. Remark that ζ is a rational number if and only if its corresponding representation as a continued fraction is finite.

For any real number $\zeta = [a_0, a_1, a_2, \ldots]$, the sequence of rational numbers $(A_n)_n$, obtained by truncating this continued fraction, $A_k = [a_0, a_1, a_2, \ldots, a_k]$, is called the convergents sequence of ζ.

According to [11], the following bound allows us to check if a rational number u/v is a convergent of ζ.

Theorem 1. *Let $\zeta = [a_0, a_1, a_2, \ldots]$ be a positive real number. If u, v are positive integers such that* $\gcd(u, v) = 1$ *and*

$$\left|\zeta - \frac{u}{v}\right| < \frac{1}{2v^2},$$

then u/v is a convergent of $[a_0, a_1, a_2, \ldots]$.

3 Useful Quotient Groups

In this section we will provide the mathematical theory needed to generalize the Murru and Saettone encryption scheme. Therefore, let $(\mathbb{F}, +, \cdot)$ be a field and $t^n - r$ an irreducible polynomial in $\mathbb{F}[t]$. Then

$$\mathbb{A}_n = \mathbb{F}[t]/(t^n - r) = \{a_0 + a_1 t + \ldots + a_{n-1} t^{n-1} \mid a_0, a_1, \ldots, a_{n-1} \in \mathbb{F}\}$$

is the corresponding quotient field. Let $a(t), b(t) \in \mathbb{A}_n$. Remark that the quotient field induces a natural product

$$\begin{aligned} a(t) \circ b(t) &= \left(\sum_{i=0}^{n-1} a_i t^i\right) \circ \left(\sum_{j=0}^{n-1} b_i t^i\right) \\ &= \sum_{i=0}^{2n-2} \left(\sum_{j=0}^{i} a_j b_{i-j}\right) x^i \\ &= \sum_{i=0}^{n-1} \left(\sum_{j=0}^{i} a_j b_{i-j}\right) x^i + r \sum_{i=n}^{2n-2} \left(\sum_{j=0}^{i} a_j b_{i-j}\right) x^{i-n} \\ &= \sum_{i=0}^{n-2} \left(\sum_{j=0}^{i} a_j b_{i-j} + r \sum_{j=0}^{i+n} a_j b_{i-j+n}\right) x^i + \sum_{j=0}^{n-1} a_j b_{n-1-j} x^{n-1}. \end{aligned}$$

In order to describe our family of RSA-like cryptosystems, we need to introduce another quotient group $\mathbb{B}_n = \mathbb{A}_n^*/\mathbb{F}^*$. The elements from $\mathbb{B}_n$ are equivalence classes of elements from $\mathbb{A}_n^*$. More precisely, we have

$$[a_0 + \ldots + a_{n-1} t^{n-1}] = \{\gamma a_0 + \ldots + \gamma a_{n-1} t^{n-1} \mid \gamma \in \mathbb{F}^*, a_0, \ldots, a_{n-1} \in \mathbb{F}\},$$

where $[a_0 + \ldots + a_{n-1} t^{n-1}] \in \mathbb{B}_n$.

Lemma 1. *The cardinality of $\mathbb{B}_n$ is $\psi_n(\mathbb{F}) = (|\mathbb{F}|^n - 1)/(|\mathbb{F}| - 1)$.*

Proof. Let $1_{\mathbb{F}^*}$ be the unity of $\mathbb{F}^*$. When $a_0 \neq 0$ and $a_1 = \ldots = a_{n-1} = 0$, we obtain that

$$[a_0 + \ldots + a_{n-1}t^{n-1}] = [a_0] = [a_0 a_0^{-1}] = [1_{\mathbb{F}^*}].$$

If $a_1 \neq 0$ and $a_2 = \ldots = a_{n-1} = 0$, then

$$[a_0 + \ldots + a_{n-1}t^{n-1}] = [a_0 + a_1 t] = [a_0 a_1^{-1} + t].$$

From the previous two examples, we can deduce the general formula. For any $k \in [0, n-1]$, if $a_k \neq 0$ and $a_{k+1} = \ldots = a_{n-1} = 0$, then

$$\begin{aligned}[a_0 + \ldots + a_{n-1}t^{n-1}] &= [a_0 + \ldots + a_k t^k] \\ &= [a_0 a_k^{-1} + a_1 a_k^{-1} t + \ldots + a_{k-1} a_k^{-1} t^{k-1} + t^k].\end{aligned}$$

For any $k \in [0, n-1]$, we define the following sets

$$B_k = \{a_0 + \ldots + a_{k-1}t^{k-1} + t^k \mid a_0, a_1, \ldots, a_{k-1} \in \mathbb{F}\}.$$

Remark that $B_i \cap B_j = \emptyset$ for $i \neq j$. From the previous analysis of the equivalence classes of $\mathbb{A}_n^*$, we can deduce that $\mathbb{B}_n = \cup_{k=0}^{n-1} B_k$. Therefore, we obtain

$$|\mathbb{B}_n| = \sum_{k=0}^{n-1} |B_i| = 1 + |\mathbb{F}| + \ldots + |\mathbb{F}|^{n-1} = \frac{|\mathbb{F}|^n - 1}{|\mathbb{F}| - 1},$$

as desired. □

From the proof of the previous lemma we can deduce the product induced by $\mathbb{B}_n$, namely

$$[a(t)] \odot [b(t)] = [a(t) \circ b(t)] = [c(t)] = [\alpha^{-1} c(x)],$$

where α is the leading coefficient of $c(x)$.

4 The Scheme

Let p be a prime number. When we instantiate $\mathbb{F} = \mathbb{Z}_p$, we have that $\mathbb{A}_n = GF(p^n)$ is the Galois field of order p^n. Moreover, $\mathbb{B}_n$ is a cyclic group of order $\psi_n(\mathbb{Z}_p) = (p^n - 1)/(p-1)$. Remark that an analogous of Fermat's little theorem holds

$$[a(x)]^{\psi_n(\mathbb{Z}_p)} \equiv [1] \bmod p,$$

where $[a(x)] \in \mathbb{B}_n$ and the power is evaluated by $\odot$-multiplying $[a(x)]$ by itself $\psi_n(\mathbb{Z}_p) - 1$ times. Therefore, we can build an encryption scheme that is similar to RSA using the $\odot$ as the product.

Setup(λ): Let $n > 1$ be an integer. Randomly generate two distinct large prime numbers p, q such that $p, q \geq 2^\lambda$ and compute their product $N = pq$. Select r such that the polynomial $t^n - r$ is irreducible in $\mathbb{Z}_N[t]$. Let

$$\psi_n(\mathbb{Z}_N) = \psi_n(N) = \frac{p^n - 1}{p - 1} \cdot \frac{q^n - 1}{q - 1}.$$

Choose an integer e such that $\gcd(e, \psi_n(N)) = 1$ and compute d such that $ed \equiv 1 \bmod \psi_n(N)$. Output the public key $pk = (n, N, r, e)$. The corresponding secret key is $sk = (p, q, d)$.

Encrypt(pk, m): To encrypt a message $m = (m_0, \ldots, m_{n-1}) \in \mathbb{Z}_N^n$ we first construct the polynomial $m(t) = m_0 + \ldots + m_{n-1}t^{n-1} + t^n \in \mathbb{B}_n$ and then we compute $c(t) \equiv [m(t)]^e \bmod N$. Output the ciphertext $c(t)$.

Decrypt($sk, c(t)$): To recover the message, simply compute $m(t) \equiv [c(t)]^d \bmod N$ and reassemble $m = (m_0, \ldots, m_{n-1})$.

Remark 1. When $n = 3$, we obtain the Murru and Saettone cryptosystem [18].

5 Useful Lemmas

In this section we provide a few useful properties of $\psi_n(N)$. Before starting our analysis, we first note that plugging $q = N/p$ in $\psi_n(N)$ leads to the following function

$$f_n(p) = \frac{p^n - 1}{p - 1} \cdot \frac{\left(\frac{N}{p}\right)^n - 1}{\frac{N}{p} - 1},$$

with p as a variable. The next lemma tells us that, under certain conditions, f_n is a strictly increasing function.

Proposition 1. *Let N a positive integer. Then for any integers $n > 1$ and $\sqrt{N} \leq x < N$, we have that the function*

$$f_n(x) = \frac{x^n - 1}{x - 1} \cdot \frac{\left(\frac{N}{x}\right)^n - 1}{\frac{N}{x} - 1},$$

is strictly increasing with x.

Proof. Before starting our proof, we notice that the function f_n can be expanded into $f_n(x) = g_n(x) \cdot h_n(x)$, where

$$g_n(x) = 1 + x + x^2 + \ldots + x^{n-1}$$

and

$$h_n(x) = 1 + \frac{N}{x} + \left(\frac{N}{x}\right)^2 + \ldots + \left(\frac{N}{x}\right)^{n-1}.$$

We will further prove our statement using induction with respect to n. When $n = 2$, we have that

$$f_2(x) = (1+x)\left(1+\frac{N}{x}\right) = 1 + \frac{N}{x} + x + N.$$

Using $x \geq \sqrt{N}$ we obtain that

$$f_2'(x) = 1 - \frac{N}{x^2} \geq 0 \Leftrightarrow 1 \geq \frac{N}{x^2} \Leftrightarrow x^2 \geq N,$$

and therefore we have that f_2 is strictly increasing.

For the induction step we assume that f_k is strictly increasing and we will show that f_{k+1} is also strictly increasing. Hence, we have that

$$\begin{aligned} f_{k+1}(x) &= g_{k+1}(x) \cdot h_{k+1}(x) \\ &= g_k(x) \cdot h_k(x) + g_k(x) \cdot \left(\frac{N}{x}\right)^k + x^k \cdot h_k(x) + N^k. \end{aligned}$$

Considering the induction hypothesis, it is enough to prove that the function

$$s_k(x) = g_k(x) \cdot \left(\frac{N}{x}\right)^k + x^k \cdot h_k(x)$$

is strictly increasing. Therefore, we have that

$$\begin{aligned} s_k(x) &= \left(N^k \cdot \frac{1}{x^k} + x^k\right) + \left(N^k \cdot \frac{1}{x^{k-1}} + N \cdot x^{k-1}\right) \\ &\quad + \left(N^k \cdot \frac{1}{x^{k-2}} + N^2 \cdot x^{k-2}\right) + \ldots + \left(N^k \cdot \frac{1}{x} + N^{k-1} \cdot x\right) \\ &= s_{k,0}(x) + s_{k,1}(x) + s_{k,2}(x) + \ldots + s_{k,k-1}(x), \end{aligned}$$

where we considered

$$s_{k,i}(x) = N^k \cdot \frac{1}{x^{k-i}} + N^i \cdot x^{k-i}.$$

Bear in mind that

$$\begin{aligned} s_{k,i}'(x) &= N^k \cdot \frac{-(k-i)}{x^{k-i+1}} + N^i \cdot (k-i) \cdot x^{k-i-1} \\ &= N^i(k-i)\left(x^{k-i-1} - N^{k-i} \cdot \frac{1}{x^{k-i+1}}\right). \end{aligned}$$

For any $i \in [0, k-1]$ we have that $s_{k,i}$ is strictly increasing since

$$s_{k,i}'(x) \geq 0 \Leftrightarrow x^{k-i-1} \geq N^{k-i} \cdot \frac{1}{x^{k-i+1}} \Leftrightarrow x^{2(k-i)} \geq N^{k-i},$$

where for the last inequality we used $x \geq \sqrt{N}$. Therefore, s_k is strictly increasing, which implies that f_{k+1} is strictly increasing. □

Using the following lemma from [21], we will compute a lower and upper bound for $\psi_n(N)$.

Lemma 2. *Let $N = pq$ be the product of two unknown primes with $q < p < 2q$. Then the following property holds*

$$\frac{\sqrt{2}}{2}\sqrt{N} < q < \sqrt{N} < p < \sqrt{2}\sqrt{N}.$$

Corollary 1. *Let $N = pq$ be the product of two unknown primes with $q < p < 2q$. Then the following property holds*

$$\left(\frac{\sqrt{N}^n - 1}{\sqrt{N} - 1}\right)^2 < \psi_n(N) < \frac{(\sqrt{2N})^n - 1}{\sqrt{2N} - 1} \cdot \frac{\left(\frac{\sqrt{2N}}{2}\right)^n - 1}{\frac{\sqrt{2N}}{2} - 1}.$$

Proof. By Lemma 2 we have that

$$\sqrt{N} < p < \sqrt{2}\sqrt{N},$$

which, according to Proposition 1, leads to

$$f_n(\sqrt{N}) < f_n(p) < f_n(\sqrt{2}\sqrt{N}).$$

This is equivalent to

$$\left(\frac{\sqrt{N}^n - 1}{\sqrt{N} - 1}\right)^2 < \psi_n(N) < \frac{(\sqrt{2N})^n - 1}{\sqrt{2N} - 1} \cdot \frac{\left(\frac{\sqrt{2N}}{2}\right)^n - 1}{\frac{\sqrt{2N}}{2} - 1},$$

as desired. □

When $n = 3$, the following result proven in [22] becomes a special case of Corollary 1.

Corollary 2. *Let $N = pq$ be the product of two unknown primes with $q < p < 2q$. Then the following property holds*

$$\left(N + \sqrt{N} + 1\right)^2 < \psi_3(N) < \left(N + \frac{3}{4}\sqrt{2N} + 1\right)^2 - \frac{3}{8}N.$$

We can use Corollary 1 to find an useful approximation of ψ_n. This result will be useful when devising the attack against the generalized Murru-Saettone scheme.

Proposition 2. *Let $N = pq$ be the product of two unknown primes with $q < p < 2q$. We define*

$$\psi_{n,0}(N) = \frac{1}{2}\left(\frac{\sqrt{N}^n - 1}{\sqrt{N} - 1}\right)^2 + \frac{1}{2} \cdot \frac{(\sqrt{2N})^n - 1}{\sqrt{2N} - 1} \cdot \frac{\left(\frac{\sqrt{2N}}{2}\right)^n - 1}{\frac{\sqrt{2N}}{2} - 1}.$$

Then the following holds

$$|\psi_n(N) - \psi_{n,0}(N)| < \frac{\Delta_n}{2} N^{n-2}\sqrt{N},$$

where

$$\Delta_n = \left(\frac{\sqrt{2}^n - 1}{\sqrt{2} - 1}\right)\left(\frac{\left(\frac{\sqrt{2}}{2}\right)^n - 1}{\frac{\sqrt{2}}{2} - 1}\right) - n^2.$$

Proof. According to Corollary 1, $\psi_{n,0}(N)$ is the mean value of the lower and upper bound. The following property holds

$$\begin{aligned}
|\psi_n(N) - \psi_{n,0}(N)| &\le \frac{1}{2}\left[\frac{(\sqrt{2N})^n - 1}{\sqrt{2N} - 1} \cdot \frac{\left(\frac{\sqrt{2N}}{2}\right)^n - 1}{\frac{\sqrt{2N}}{2} - 1} - \left(\frac{\sqrt{N}^n - 1}{\sqrt{N} - 1}\right)^2\right] \\
&= \frac{1}{2}\left[\sum_{i,j=0}^{n-1} (\sqrt{2N})^i \left(\frac{\sqrt{2N}}{2}\right)^j - \sum_{i,j=0}^{n-1} \sqrt{N}^i \sqrt{N}^j\right] \\
&= \frac{1}{2}\left[\sum_{i,j=0}^{n-1} \sqrt{N}^i \sqrt{N}^j \left(\frac{\sqrt{2}^{i+j}}{2^j} - 1\right)\right] \\
&= \frac{1}{2}\left[\sum_{\substack{i,j=0\\ i\neq j}}^{n-1} \sqrt{N}^i \sqrt{N}^j \left(\frac{\sqrt{2}^{i+j}}{2^j} - 1\right)\right].
\end{aligned}$$

Note that in the last expression all the coefficients are non-zero and the leading coefficient is $\sqrt{N}^{n-1+n-2} = N^{n-2}\sqrt{N}$. Therefore, we obtain

$$\begin{aligned}
|\psi_n(N) - \psi_{n,0}(N)| &< \frac{1}{2} N^{n-2}\sqrt{N}\left[\sum_{\substack{i,j=0\\ i\neq j}}^{n-1} \left(\frac{\sqrt{2}^{i+j}}{2^j} - 1\right)\right] \\
&= \frac{1}{2} N^{n-2}\sqrt{N}\left[\sum_{i,j=0}^{n-1} \frac{\sqrt{2}^{i+j}}{2^j} - n(n-1) - n\right] \\
&= \frac{1}{2} N^{n-2}\sqrt{N}\left[\left(\frac{\sqrt{2}^n - 1}{\sqrt{2} - 1}\right)\left(\frac{\left(\frac{\sqrt{2}}{2}\right)^n - 1}{\frac{\sqrt{2}}{2} - 1}\right) - n^2\right],
\end{aligned}$$

as desired. □

When $n = 3$, the following property presented in [22] becomes a special case of Propsition 2.

Corollary 3. *Let $N = pq$ be the product of two unknown primes with $q < p < 2q$. Then the following holds*

$$|\psi_3(N) - \psi_{3,0}(N)| < 0.372\, N\sqrt{N} < 0.5\, N\sqrt{N}.$$

6 Application of Continued Fractions

We further provide an upper bound for selecting d such that we can use the continued fraction algorithm to recover d without knowing the factorisation of the modulus N.

Theorem 2. *Let $N = pq$ be the product of two unknown primes with $q < p < 2q$. If $e < \psi_n(N)$ satisfies $ed - k\psi_n(N) = 1$ with*

$$d < \sqrt{\frac{N^{n-0.5}}{e\Delta_n}}, \tag{1}$$

then we can recover d in polynomial time.

Proof. We have that

$$\begin{aligned}\left|\frac{k}{d} - \frac{e}{\psi_{n,0}(N)}\right| &= \frac{|ed - k\psi_{n,0}(N)|}{d\psi_{n,0}(N)} \\ &\leq \frac{|ed - k\psi_n(N)| + k|\psi_n(N) - \psi_{n,0}(N)|}{d\psi_{n,0}(N)}.\end{aligned}$$

Using $ed - k\psi_n(N) = 1$ and Propsition 2 we obtain

$$\begin{aligned}\left|\frac{k}{d} - \frac{e}{\psi_{n,0}(N)}\right| &\leq \frac{1 + \frac{\Delta_n}{2} kN^{n-2}\sqrt{N}}{d\psi_{n,0}(N)} \\ &\leq \frac{k}{2d} \cdot \Delta_n \cdot \frac{2 + N^{n-2}\sqrt{N}}{\psi_{n,0}(N)}.\end{aligned}$$

Note that

$$\psi_{n,0}(N) > \left(\frac{\sqrt{N}^n - 1}{\sqrt{N} - 1}\right)^2 > \sqrt{N}^{2(n-1)} + 2\sqrt{N},$$

which leads to

$$\begin{aligned}\left|\frac{k}{d} - \frac{e}{\psi_{n,0}(N)}\right| &\leq \frac{k}{2d} \cdot \Delta_n \cdot \frac{2 + \sqrt{N}^{2n-3}}{\sqrt{N}^{2n-2} + 2\sqrt{N}} \\ &= \frac{k\Delta_n}{2d\sqrt{N}}.\end{aligned} \tag{2}$$

According to Corollary 1, we have that $\psi_n(N) > \sqrt{N}^{2(n-1)} = N^{n-1}$. Since $k\psi_n(N) = ed - 1 < ed$, we have

$$\frac{k}{d} < \frac{e}{\psi_n(N)} < \frac{e}{N^{n-1}}.$$

Equation (2) becomes

$$\left|\frac{k}{d} - \frac{e}{\psi_{n,0}(N)}\right| \leq \frac{1}{2} \cdot \frac{e\Delta_n}{N^{n-0.5}} < \frac{1}{2d^2}.$$

Using Theorem 1 we obtain that k/d is a convergent of the continued fraction expansion of $e/\psi_{n,0}(N)$. Therefore, d can be recovered in polynomial time. □

Corollary 4. *Let $\alpha+0.5 < n$ and $N = pq$ be the product of two unknown primes with $q < p < 2q$. If we approximate $e \simeq N^\alpha$ and $N \simeq 2^{2\lambda}$, then Eq. (1) becomes*

$$d < \frac{2^{(n-\alpha-0.5)\lambda}}{\sqrt{\Delta_n}}$$

or equivalently

$$\log_2(d) < (n - \alpha - 0.5)\lambda - \log_2(\sqrt{\Delta_n}) \simeq (n - \alpha - 0.5)\lambda.$$

When case $n = 3$ is considered, the following property presented in [22] becomes a special case of Corollary 4.

Corollary 5. *Let $\alpha < 2.5$ and $N = pq$ be the product of two unknown primes with $q < p < 2q$. If we approximate $e \simeq N^\alpha$ and $N \simeq 2^{2\lambda}$ then Eq. (1) is equivalent with*

$$\log_2(d) < (2.5 - \alpha)\lambda - 0.43 \simeq (2.5 - \alpha)\lambda.$$

The following corollary tells us that when e is large enough we obtain roughly the same margin as Wiener [4,30] obtained for the classical RSA.

Corollary 6. *Let $N = pq$ be the product of two unknown primes with $q < p < 2q$. If we approximate $e \simeq N^{n-1}$ and $N \simeq 2^{2\lambda}$ then Eq. (1) is equivalent with*

$$\log_2(d) < 0.5\lambda - \log_2(\sqrt{\Delta_n}) \simeq 0.5\lambda.$$

7 Experiment Results

We further present an example for each of the $n = 2$ and $n = 4$ cases. An example for the $n = 3$ case is provided in [22], and thus we omit it.

7.1 Case $n = 2$

Before providing our example, we first show how to recover p and q once $\psi_2(N) = (1 - ed)/k$ is recovered using our attack.

Lemma 3. *Let $N = pq$ be the product of two unknown primes with $q < p < 2q$. If $\psi_2(N) = (1+p)(1+q)$ is known, then p and q can be recovered in polynomial time.*

Proof. Expanding $\psi_2(N)$ we obtain that

$$\psi_2(N) = 1 + p + q + pq = 1 + p + q + N,$$

which is equivalent to

$$p + q = \psi_2(N) - N - 1.$$

Let $S = \psi_2(N) - N - 1$. We remark that

$$(p - q)^2 = (p + q)^2 - 4pq = S^2 - 4N.$$

Let D be the positive square root of the previous quantity. Taking into account that $p > q$, we derive the following

$$\begin{cases} p = \frac{S+D}{2} \\ q = \frac{S-D}{2} \end{cases}.$$

□

Now, we will exemplify our attack for $n = 2$ using the following small public key

$$N = 1193955469391405546525045411470651045582478785659 1,$$
$$e = 607457463306018151476885843605130298081016983082 1.$$

Remark that $e \approx N^{0.994}$. We use the Euclidean algorithm to compute the continue fraction expansion of $e/\psi_{2,0}(N)$ and obtain that the first 20 partial quotients are

$$[0, 1, 1, 27, 1, 56, 7, 23, 3, 2, 9, 2, 20, 1, 3, 1, 1, 1, 2, 7, 17, \ldots].$$

According to Theorem 2, the set of convergents of $e/\psi_{2,0}(N)$ contains all the possible candidates for k/d. From these convergents we select only those for which $\psi_2 = (ed - 1)/k$ is an integer and the following system of equations

$$\begin{cases} \psi_2 = (1 + p)(1 + q) \\ N = pq \end{cases}$$

has a solution as given in Lemma 3. The $2nd$, $3rd$ and $15th$ convergents satisfy the first condition, however only the last one leads to a valid solution for p and q. More precisely, the $15th$ convergent leads to

$$\begin{aligned}
\psi_2 &= 1193955469391405546525046128356787695878533749 0000,\\
\frac{k}{d} &= \frac{3205471919}{6300343581},\\
p &= 45376298382661174181 20249,\\
q &= 26312315282368431315 13159.
\end{aligned}$$

7.2 Case $n = 4$

As in the previous case, we first show how to factorize N once ψ_4 is known.

Lemma 4. *Let $N = pq$ be the product of two unknown primes with $q < p < 2q$. If $\psi_4(N) = (1 + p + p^2 + p^3)(1 + q + q^2 + q^3)$ is known, then p and q can be recovered in polynomial time.*

Proof. Expanding $\psi_4(N)$ we obtain that

$$\begin{aligned}
\psi_4(N) &= p^3q^3 + p^3q^2 + p^3q + p^3 + p^2q^3 + p^2q^2 + p^2q + p^2\\
&\quad + pq^3 + pq^2 + pq + p + q^3 + q^2 + q + 1\\
&= N^3 + (N^2+1)(p+q) + (N+1)(p^2+pq+q^2)\\
&\quad + (p^3 + p^2q + pq^2 + q^3) + 1\\
&= N^3 + (N^2+1)(p+q) + (N+1)(p+q)^2 - (N+1)N\\
&\quad + (p+q)^3 - 2N(p+q) + 1.
\end{aligned}$$

We further consider the following form of ψ_4

$$\psi_4(N) = (p+q)^3 + (N+1)(p+q)^2 + (N-1)^2(p+q) + N^3 - N^2 - N + 1.$$

Finding $S = p + q$ is equivalent to solving (in $\mathbb{Z}$) the cubic equation

$$x^3 + (N+1)x^2 + (N-1)^2x + (N^3 - N^2 - N + 1 - \psi_4(N)) = 0, \qquad (3)$$

which can be done in polynomial time as it is presented in [10]. In order to find p and q, we compute $D = p - q$ as in Lemma 3. This concludes our proof. □

The following lemma shows that in order to factor N we only need to find one solution to Eq. (3), namely its unique integer solution.

Lemma 5. *Equation* (3) *always has exactly two non-real roots and an integer one.*

Proof. Let x_1, x_2 and x_3 be Eq. (3)'s roots. Using Vieta's formulas we have

$$\begin{aligned} x_1 + x_2 + x_3 &= -(N+1), \\ x_1x_2 + x_2x_3 + x_3x_1 &= (N-1)^2, \\ x_1x_2x_3 &= -(N^3 - N^2 - N + 1 - \psi_4(N)). \end{aligned}$$

From the first two relations we obtain

$$\begin{aligned} x_1^2 + x_2^2 + x_3^2 &= (x_1 + x_2 + x_3)^2 - 2(x_1x_2 + x_2x_3 + x_3x_1) \\ &= (N+1)^2 - 2(N-1)^2 \\ &= -N^2 + 6N - 1. \end{aligned}$$

If we assume that x_1, x_2, x_3 are all real, we get the following inequalities

$$0 < x_1^2 + x_2^2 + x_3^2 = -(N-3)^2 + 8 < 0,$$

for any $N \geq 6$. Therefore, we obtain a contradiction, and hence we conclude that Eq. (3) has one real root, which is $p + q \in \mathbb{Z}$, and two non-real roots. $\square$

We will further present our attack for $n = 4$ using the following small public key

$$\begin{aligned} N &= 1193955469391405546525045411470651045582478785 6591, \\ e &= 150066522870397598613378023245652156233109404765 13 \\ &\ 925426704347225501574482708873182176329621382054 21 \\ &\ 899647696285870461657741073464172612216312741409. \end{aligned}$$

Note that $e \approx N^{2.998}$. Applying the continue fraction expansion of $e/\psi_{4,0}(N)$, we get the first 20 partial quotients

$$[0, 1, 7, 2, 4, 1, 4, 6, 1, 4, 26, 1, 7, 1, 1, 10, 2, 1, 11, 1, 1, \ldots].$$

In this case, we consider the convergents of $e/\psi_{4,0}(N)$, and we select only those for which $\psi_4 = (ed-1)/k$ is an integer and the following system of equations

$$\begin{cases} \psi_4 = (1 + p + p^2 + p^3)(1 + q + q^2 + q^3) \\ N = pq \end{cases}$$

has a solution as given in Lemma 4. The $2nd$ and $19th$ convergents satisfy the first condition, however only the last one leads to a valid solution for p and q. More precisely, the $19th$ convergent leads to

$$\begin{aligned} \psi_4 &= 170201893778678602470965530944670615912076408355 06 \\ &\ 219077534579119341823876231886831871704306367277 89 \\ &\ 996180586005565732093187872678169520144124360000, \\ \frac{k}{d} &= \frac{2425248603}{2750659489}, \\ p &= 453762983826611741812024 9, \\ q &= 263123152823684313151315 9. \end{aligned}$$

8 Conclusions

In this paper we introduced a family of RSA-like cryptosystems, which includes the Murru and Saettone public key encryption scheme [18] (*i.e.* $n = 3$). Then, we presented a small private key attack against our family of cryptosystems and provided two instantiations of it. As a conclusion, the whole family of RSA-like schemes allows an attacker to recover the secret exponent via continued fractions when the public exponent is close to N^{n-1} and the secret exponent is smaller that $N^{0.25}$.

Future Work. When $n = 2, 3, 4$, in Sect. 7 and [22] a method for factoring N once ψ_n is known is provided. Although we found a method for particular cases of n we could not find a generic method for factoring N. Therefore, we leave it as an open problem. Another interesting research direction, is to find out if the attack methods described in Sect. 1 for the Murru-Saetonne schemes also work in the general case.

References

1. Aono, Y.: Minkowski sum based lattice construction for multivariate simultaneous Coppersmith's technique and applications to RSA. In: Boyd, C., Simpson, L. (eds.) ACISP 2013. LNCS, vol. 7959, pp. 88–103. Springer, Heidelberg (2013). https://doi.org/10.1007/978-3-642-39059-3_7
2. Blömer, J., May, A.: New partial key exposure attacks on RSA. In: Boneh, D. (ed.) CRYPTO 2003. LNCS, vol. 2729, pp. 27–43. Springer, Heidelberg (2003). https://doi.org/10.1007/978-3-540-45146-4_2
3. Blömer, J., May, A.: A generalized wiener attack on RSA. In: Bao, F., Deng, R., Zhou, J. (eds.) PKC 2004. LNCS, vol. 2947, pp. 1–13. Springer, Heidelberg (2004). https://doi.org/10.1007/978-3-540-24632-9_1
4. Boneh, D.: Twenty years of attacks on the RSA cryptosystem. Not. AMS **46**(2), 203–213 (1999)
5. Boneh, D., Durfee, G.: Cryptanalysis of RSA with private key d less than $N^{0.292}$. In: Stern, J. (ed.) EUROCRYPT 1999. LNCS, vol. 1592, pp. 1–11. Springer, Heidelberg (1999). https://doi.org/10.1007/3-540-48910-X_1
6. Boneh, D., Durfee, G., Frankel, Y.: An attack on RSA given a small fraction of the private key bits. In: Ohta, K., Pei, D. (eds.) ASIACRYPT 1998. LNCS, vol. 1514, pp. 25–34. Springer, Heidelberg (1998). https://doi.org/10.1007/3-540-49649-1_3
7. Coppersmith, D.: Small solutions to polynomial equations, and low exponent RSA vulnerabilities. J. Cryptol. **10**(4), 233–260 (1997). https://doi.org/10.1007/s001459900030
8. De Weger, B.: Cryptanalysis of RSA with small prime difference. Appl. Algebra Eng. Commun. Comput. **13**(1), 17–28 (2002)
9. Ernst, M., Jochemsz, E., May, A., de Weger, B.: Partial key exposure attacks on RSA up to full size exponents. In: Cramer, R. (ed.) EUROCRYPT 2005. LNCS, vol. 3494, pp. 371–386. Springer, Heidelberg (2005). https://doi.org/10.1007/11426639_22

10. Fujii, K.: A modern introduction to cardano and ferrari formulas in the algebraic equations. arXiv Preprint arXiv:quant-ph/0311102 (2003)
11. Hardy, G.H., Wright, E.M., et al.: An Introduction to the Theory of Numbers. Oxford University Press, Oxford (1979)
12. Hastad, J.: N using RSA with low exponent in a public key network. In: Williams, H.C. (ed.) CRYPTO 1985. LNCS, vol. 218, pp. 403–408. Springer, Heidelberg (1986). https://doi.org/10.1007/3-540-39799-X_29
13. Herrmann, M., May, A.: Maximizing small root bounds by linearization and applications to small secret exponent RSA. In: Nguyen, P.Q., Pointcheval, D. (eds.) PKC 2010. LNCS, vol. 6056, pp. 53–69. Springer, Heidelberg (2010). https://doi.org/10.1007/978-3-642-13013-7_4
14. Howgrave-Graham, N., Seifert, J.-P.: Extending Wiener's attack in the presence of many decrypting exponents. In: CQRE 1999. LNCS, vol. 1740, pp. 153–166. Springer, Heidelberg (1999). https://doi.org/10.1007/3-540-46701-7_14
15. Kamel Ariffin, M.R., Abubakar, S.I., Yunos, F., Asbullah, M.A.: New cryptanalytic attack on RSA modulus N = pq using small prime difference method. Cryptography **3**(1), 2 (2018)
16. Maitra, S., Sarkar, S.: Revisiting Wiener's attack – new weak keys in RSA. In: Wu, T.-C., Lei, C.-L., Rijmen, V., Lee, D.-T. (eds.) ISC 2008. LNCS, vol. 5222, pp. 228–243. Springer, Heidelberg (2008). https://doi.org/10.1007/978-3-540-85886-7_16
17. Maitra, S., Sarkar, S.: Revisiting Wiener's attack - new weak keys in RSA. IACR Cryptology ePrint Archive 2008/228 (2008)
18. Murru, N., Saettone, F.M.: A novel RSA-like cryptosystem based on a generalization of the Rédei rational functions. In: Kaczorowski, J., Pieprzyk, J., Pomykała, J. (eds.) NuTMiC 2017. LNCS, vol. 10737, pp. 91–103. Springer, Cham (2018). https://doi.org/10.1007/978-3-319-76620-1_6
19. Nassr, D.I., Anwar, M., Bahig, H.M.: Improving small private exponent attack on the Murru-Saettone cryptosystem. Theor. Comput. Sci. **923**, 222–234 (2022)
20. Nassr, D.I., Bahig, H.M., Bhery, A., Daoud, S.S.: A new RSA vulnerability using continued fractions. In: AICCSA 2008, pp. 694–701. IEEE Computer Society (2008)
21. Nitaj, A.: Another generalization of wiener's attack on RSA. In: Vaudenay, S. (ed.) AFRICACRYPT 2008. LNCS, vol. 5023, pp. 174–190. Springer, Heidelberg (2008). https://doi.org/10.1007/978-3-540-68164-9_12
22. Nitaj, A., Ariffin, M.R.B.K., Adenan, N.N.H., Abu, N.A.: Classical attacks on a variant of the RSA cryptosystem. In: Longa, P., Ràfols, C. (eds.) LATINCRYPT 2021. LNCS, vol. 12912, pp. 151–167. Springer, Cham (2021). https://doi.org/10.1007/978-3-030-88238-9_8
23. Nitaj, A., Ariffin, M.R.B.K., Adenan, N.N.H., Lau, T.S.C., Chen, J.: Security issues of novel RSA variant. IEEE Access **10**, 53788–53796 (2022)
24. Rivest, R.L., Shamir, A., Adleman, L.: A method for obtaining digital signatures and public-key cryptosystems. Commun. ACM **21**(2), 120–126 (1978)
25. Sarkar, S., Maitra, S.: Cryptanalysis of RSA with more than one decryption exponent. Inf. Process. Lett. **110**(8–9), 336–340 (2010)
26. Shi, G., Wang, G., Gu, D.: Further cryptanalysis of a type of RSA variants. IACR Cryptology ePrint Archive 2022/611 (2022)
27. Susilo, W., Tonien, J.: A Wiener-type attack on an RSA-like cryptosystem constructed from cubic pell equations. Theor. Comput. Sci. **885**, 125–130 (2021)
28. Takayasu, A., Kunihiro, N.: Cryptanalysis of RSA with multiple small secret exponents. In: Susilo, W., Mu, Y. (eds.) ACISP 2014. LNCS, vol. 8544, pp. 176–191. Springer, Cham (2014). https://doi.org/10.1007/978-3-319-08344-5_12

29. Takayasu, A., Kunihiro, N.: Partial key exposure attacks on RSA: achieving the Boneh-Durfee bound. In: Joux, A., Youssef, A. (eds.) SAC 2014. LNCS, vol. 8781, pp. 345–362. Springer, Cham (2014). https://doi.org/10.1007/978-3-319-13051-4_21
30. Wiener, M.J.: Cryptanalysis of short RSA secret exponents. IEEE Trans. Inf. Theory **36**(3), 553–558 (1990)
31. Zheng, M., Kunihiro, N., Yao, Y.: Cryptanalysis of the RSA variant based on cubic pell equation. Theor. Comput. Sci. **889**, 135–144 (2021)

M-EDESE: Multi-Domain, Easily Deployable, and Efficiently Searchable Encryption

Jiaming Yuan[1(✉)], Yingjiu Li[1], Jianting Ning[2], and Robert H. Deng[3]

[1] University of Oregon, Eugene, OR 97403, USA
{jiamingy,yingjiul}@uoregon.edu
[2] Fujian Normal University, Fuzhou 350007, China
[3] Singapore Management University, Singapore 188065, Singapore
robertdeng@smu.edu.sg

Abstract. Searchable encryption is an essential component of cryptography, which allows users to search for keywords and retrieve records from an encrypted database at cloud storage while ensuring the confidentiality of users' queries. While most existing research on searchable encryption focuses on the single domain setting, we propose the first Multi-Domain, Easily-Deployable, Efficiently-Searchable Encryption (M-EDESE) system that allows users to query keywords cross domains with high efficiency and preserved privacy without additional cooperation from the cloud storage. In the multi-domain setting, a user who belongs to a domain can query keywords from another domain under an inter-domain partnership. Any party can participate in the M-EDESE system as a domain without global coordination other than agreeing on an initial set of global reference parameters. Each domain maintains a set of users and acts as an individual multiple-user searchable encryption system while maintaining its own database. M-EDESE enables easy deployment without any requirement for cloud storage setup, thus it is compatible with the existing cloud storage platform. In addition, the M-EDESE system facilitates instant user revocation within each domain and instant partner revocation across domains. We provide a concrete construction of M-EDESE and security proofs on query privacy, unforgeability, and revocability. We also conduct a rigorous experimental evaluation of the performance of M-EDESE in a real-world setting, showing that M-EDESE is highly efficient for querying an open-sourced database.

Keywords: Keyword · Multi-domain · Easily deployable and efficiently searchable encryption

C. Su et al. (Eds.): ISPEC 2022, LNCS 13620, pp. 606–623, 2022.
https://doi.org/10.1007/978-3-031-21280-2_34

1 Introduction

Secure searching service is a key component of secure cloud data services and cloud-based apps, such as Gmail, Facebook, and Outlook. Many searchable encryption schemes have been proposed to provide such secure searching service (e.g., [2–12]). One practical scheme, named easily deployable and efficiently searchable encryption (EDESE), was proposed by Billy Lau et al. [3]. EDESE is widely compatible and highly efficient for ease of deployment.

Rigerous research has been conducted on EDESE (e.g., [2,4,6,8,14,18]) following the initial work [16]. The initial EDESE was designed for single-user settings. To extend EDESE to multi-user settings, PEKS was proposed by Boneh et al. in 2004 [6], which is the first public-key-based searchable encryption satisfying EDESE requirements. Then, MuED was introduced by Bao et al. [17], which improves query generation performance significantly in multi-user settings. Recently, CP-ABSE was proposed by Yin et al. [18], which increases the scalability of EDESE in multi-user settings based on attribute-based searchable encryption. Most of the existing EDESE schemes, regardless of being designed in single-user settings or multi-user settings, work in single autonomous domains, in which all users are managed by a single authority. In practice, however, industrials need a secure searching service in multi-domain settings so that users in one autonomous domain can search for useful information from collaborative domains (e.g., in supply chain management).

To fill this gap, we propose a multiple domain searchable encryption based on EDESE, called Multi-Domain, Easily Deployable, Efficiently Searchable Encryption (M-EDESE). M-EDESE leverages the easy deployment of EDESE to allow users to query encrypted keywords among multiple domains. In particular, M-EDESE achieves the following advantages.

- **Secure Searching across Multiple Domains.** M-EDESE enables secure keyword searching across multiple domains. It allows any single domain to be enrolled at any time without a re-initialization of the whole system. Any domain can establish a unilateral searching collaboration relationship with other domains. In this unilateral relationship, the host domain provides a searching service to the partner domains such that any authorized user under a partner domain can query encrypted keywords from the host domain. Each domain in M-EDESE is fully autonomous in managing its own users and deciding on its own partners.
- **Easy deployment.** Easy deployment is an essential achievement of EDESE as required in many EDESE applications such as ShadowCrypt [2] and Mimesis Aegis [3]. M-EDESE inherits the easy deployment property of EDESE in the multiple domains setting. Any domain in M-EDESE can work directly with any cloud storage without making any changes to the keyword searching services provided by the cloud storage.

Besides the above achievements, M-EDESE offers secure searchable encryption with **query privacy, query unforgeability,** and **revocability**.

- **Query Privacy.** Query privacy is a foundational secure requirement for all searchable encryption [12]. It requires that no server providing searching services can determine the underlying keyword of any query issued by a user following searchable encryption, even though the server can observe all access patterns of users' queries to the data in its storage. Furthermore, it requires that no sensitive information about users' queries can be derived by the server from its observed information.
- **Query Unforgeability.** In M-EDESE, queries are generated by a user's secret key, which is distinct from others' keys. It is a basic requirement that neither user nor server can generate a legitimate query on behalf of a user without the corresponding secret key [17]. In the multi-domain setting, M-EDESE should also guarantee that neither the user nor the server can generate a legitimate query from any domain without the corresponding secret key of the domain.
- **Revocability.** M-EDESE provides effective user revocation and partner revocation. User revocation allows a domain the capacity to manage its users while partner revocation provides a host domain to manage its partner domains. A revoked user is not allowed to access the searching services provided by their host domain or any of its partner domains. If a partner domain is revoked by a host domain, then all users belonging to the revoked partner domain can no longer access the searching services provided by the corresponding host domain.

In this paper, we demonstrate a detailed construction of M-EDESE (Sect. 3) and present the formal proofs regarding query privacy, query unforgeability, and revocability (Sect. 4). Then, we provide our evaluations on M-EDESE's performance (Sect. 5) and conclusion (Sect. 6).

2 Preliminaries

M-EDESE is constructed based on two preliminaries, including bilinear maps and BLS short signature.

2.1 Bilinear Maps

Let $\mathbb{G}_1, \mathbb{G}_2$, and $\mathbb{G}_T$ be three cyclic multiplicative groups of prime order p. A bilinear map is a function $e : \mathbb{G}_1 \times \mathbb{G}_2 \rightarrow \mathbb{G}_T$ and is said to be an admissible bilinear map if the following properties hold.

1. Bilinearity: for all $g_1 \in \mathbb{G}_1, g_2 \in \mathbb{G}_2$, and $a, b \in \mathbb{Z}_p$, $e(g_1^a, g_2^b) = e(g_1, g_2)^{ab}$.
2. Non-degeneration: if g_1 is a generator of $\mathbb{G}_1$ and g_2 is a generator of $\mathbb{G}_2$, then $e(g_1, g_2)$ is a generator of $\mathbb{G}_T$.
3. Computability: there exists an efficient algorithm to compute $e(g_1, g_2)$ for any $g_1 \in \mathbb{G}_1, g_2 \in \mathbb{G}_2$.

We say that $(\mathbb{G}_1, \mathbb{G}_2, \mathbb{G}_T)$ are bilinear map groups if there exists a bilinear pairing function $e : \mathbb{G}_1 \times \mathbb{G}_2 \rightarrow \mathbb{G}_T$.

2.2 BLS Short Signature

Boneh et al. proposed a short signature scheme based on the bilinear map [15]. The BLS short signature consists of three functions: keygen, sign, and verify. We recall the brief definition of the BLS short signature as follows: Let $(\mathbb{G}_1, \mathbb{G}_2, \mathbb{G}_T, e)$ be defined as the above (Sect. 2.1), g_1 be a generator of $\mathbb{G}_1$, $h : \{0,1\}^* \rightarrow \mathbb{G}_2$ be a collision-resistant hash function. A user's key pair is generated by the keygen algorithm, which runs as $(x, y) \leftarrow (x \in \mathbb{Z}_p^*, y = g_1^x)$. Then, the signature on a message m is defined as $\sigma = h(m)^x$ that is generated by the signing algorithm using a user secret key x. The signature verification is to check $e(g_1, \sigma) \stackrel{?}{=} e(y, h(m))$. The BLS short signature implements existential unforgeability if h is modeled as a random oracle, which means the adversary can not forge an eligible signature on behalf of a target user without its secret key.

3 System Construction

We will use the notations as shown in Table 1 in the construction of M-EDESE.

Table 1. Notations

Symbol	Descriptions
GP	The global parameters generated by the coordinator domain's KGC
uid	User identity
did_p	Partner domain's identity
did_h	Host domain's identity
MK_{did}	A master key corresponding to the domain did
QK_{uid}	A query key corresponding to the User uid
SK_{uid}	A search key corresponding to the User uid
$DT_{did_p}^{did_h}$	A delegation key generated by a partner domain did_p and sent to a host domain did_h
$PSK_{did_p}^{did_h}$	A domain search key corresponding to the partner domain did_h for the domain did_p
$PQK_{did_p}^{did_h}$	A domain query key corresponding to the partner domain did_h for the domain did_p
I_{kw}	An index associated with the keyword kw
$I_{kw,did}$	An index associated with the keyword kw owned by the domain did
$USKL$	A list of user search keys
$PQKL$	A list of domain query keys
$PSKL$	A list of domain search keys

3.1 System Architecture

M-EDESE System mainly consists of seven entities: *Host Domain (HD)*, *Partner Domain (PD)*, *Data User (DU)*, *Data Owner (DO)*, *Key Generation Center (KGC)*, *Operational Center (OC)*, and *Cloud Storage Provider (CSP)*. These entities are defined below.

- **Host Domain (*HD*) and Partner Domain (*PD*).** Host Domain provides a searching service for its Partner Domain after establishing a collaboration relationship. PD needs to apply to the HD before building a relationship. Both PD and HD can revoke their users. In addition, HD can also revoke its PDs.
- **Key Generation Center (*KGC*).** Each domain maintains a key generation center (KGC). KGC only accounts for its domain and generates all keys for the entities in the domain. Moreover, KGCs of PD and HD interact with each other to agree on the establishment of a collaboration relationship.
- **Data Owner (*DO*) and Data User (*DU*).** Data Owner encrypts keywords into query tokens and uploads them with associated encrypted files to the cloud storage via the domain's operational center which is mentioned later. Data User can generate query tokens to query keywords from its HD's data and the corresponding PDs' data on the cloud storage.
- **Operational Center (*OC*).** Each domain maintains an operational center (OC) online. In its operations, an operational center receives user query tokens and domain query tokens and transfers them into indexes. Besides, OC can revoke its HD users and PDs.
- **Cloud Storage Provider (CSP).** Cloud Storage provider (CSP) stores encrypted files and associated encrypted keywords (named indexes in M-EDESE) for any domain and provide keyword searching services based on exact match (which is the same as the search services provided by existing cloud service providers on plaintext data). The storage and searching services provided by CSP can be accessed by all entities. Apart from all indexes and encrypted files, the global public parameters are stored on CSP with integrity protection.

3.2 Algorithm

The M-EDESE system involves 6 algorithms, consisting of initial setup, user enrollment, collaboration establishment, data uploading, search, and revocation. Below are their definitions.

Initial Setup. This process setups the entire base environment, which includes keys of involved domains and a set of global parameters GP. The initial setup consists of a global setup phase and a domain setup phase.

- **Global Setup Phase:**
  1. The coordinator, one of KGCs, chooses a bilinear map $e : (G)_1 \times \mathbb{G}_2 \rightarrow \mathbb{G}_T$, and let g_1, g_2 be the generators of $\mathbb{G}_1, \mathbb{G}_2$, respectively.
  2. It chooses a collision-resistant hash function: $\mathcal{H} : \{0,1\}^* \rightarrow \mathbb{G}_2$.
  3. The coordinator publishes the global public parameters GP to CSP with integrity protection, where $GP = \{g_1, g_2, \mathbb{G}_1, \mathbb{G}_2, \mathbb{G}_T, e, \mathcal{H}\}$.
  4. Since GP is public shared on CSP, we assume all entities already obtain it before any operation.

- **Domain Setup Phase:** Each domain *did* performs the following operations:
  1. Its KGC randomly chooses $x_{did} \in_R \mathbb{Z}_p^*$ as this domain's master key MK_{did} and stores it in the KGC's local storage.
  2. Meanwhile, the domain's OC initializes 3 lists $USKL, PSKL$, and $PQKL$ to maintain its users' search keys, the PDs' search keys, and the PDs' query keys.

User Enrollment. When a user *uid* registers in the M-EDESE system under the domain *did*, the KGC of the domain *did* firstly randomly chooses $y_{uid} \in_R \mathbb{Z}_p^*$ as the user's query key QK_{uid}. Then, the KGC computes $k_{uid} = g_1^{\frac{x_{did}}{y_{uid}}}$ as the user's search key SK_{uid}, where x_did is the domain's master secret key. After that, the KGC uses a secure communication channel to send SK_{uid} to the domain's OC and send QK_{uid} to the user *uid*. Once the OC receives SK_{uid}, it updates its list $USKL$ with the pair of (uid, SK_{uid}).

Data Uploading. The data uploading process allows DU to upload an encrypted file and a set of associated indexes to the encrypted keywords for the file into CSP. When a DU *uid* uploads to CSP an encrypted file E (e.g., encrypted by AES) and a set of the indexes cooresponding to a set S_{kw} of n keywords $kw_1, kw_2, \cdots, kw_n$ which are associated with E, DU performs the following operations.

1. The DU computes $S_q = \{q_i : q_i = \mathcal{H}(kw_i)^{y_{uid}}\}_{i \in [1,n]}$.
2. Then, the DU sends the tuple (uid, E, S_q) to the OC of the domain to which the DU belongs.
3. After receiving (uid, E, S_q), the OC firstly retrieves the DU's search key SK_{uid} from the list $USKL$ by *uid*.
4. Secondly, the OC computes $S_I = \{I_i : I_i = e(k_{uid}, q_i)\}_{i \in [1,n]}$.
5. Finally, the OC uploads the pair of (E, S_I) to the CSP.

Collaboration Estabilishment. When a domain did_p or its users need to access the searching service from another domain did_h, the domain did_p must establish a collaboration relationship with domain did_h as PD PD while domain did_h acts as HD. Assuming that the involving domains can verify each other's signatures using a signature system (e.g., PKI), they establish a collaboration relationship through the following steps.

1. At first, PD's KGC randomly chooses $s_{did_p}^{did_h} \in_R \mathbb{Z}_p^*$ as the PD's query key $PQK_{did_p}^{did_h}$ and computes $d_{did_p}^{did_h} = \frac{1}{x_{did_p} s_{did_p}^{did_h}}, d'^{did_h}_{did_p} = g_1^{s_{did_p}^{did_h}}$, where x_{did_p} is PD's master secret key.
2. Secondly, PD's KGC produces a digital signature σ_p on $DT_{did_p}^{did_h}$, where $DT_{did_p}^{did_h} = (d_{did_p}^{did_h}, d'^{did_h}_{did_p})$.
3. PD's KGC sends the pair of $(\sigma_p, DT_{did_p}^{did_h})$ to HD's KGC.

4. After receiving $(\sigma_p, DT_{did_p}^{did_h})$, HD verifies the signature σ_p firstly. If it is valid, it proceeds to the next step; otherwise, does nothing.
5. HD's KGC computes $z_{did_p}^{did_h} = x_{did_h} d_{did_p}^{did_h}, z'^{did_h}_{did_p} = d'^{did_h}_{did_p}$.
6. Then, HD's KGC sends PD's search key $PSK_{did_p}^{did_h}$ to HD's OC, and HD's OC stores it into $PSKL$, where $PSK_{did_p}^{did_h} = \{z_{did_p}^{did_h}, z'^{did_h}_{did_p}\}$.
7. HD's KGC also produces a digital signature σ_h on $DT_{did_p}^{did_h}$ and sends to PD's KGC.
8. PD's KGC verifies the signature σ_p. If it is valid, it proceeds to the next step; otherwise, does nothing.
9. Afterward, PD's KGC sends $PQK_{did_p}^{did_h}$ to PD's OC, and PD's OC stores it into $PQKL$.

Finally, regarding this collaboration relationship, HD's OC maintains PD's search key in $PSKL$ while PD's OC maintains its query key in $PQKL$.

Search. In M-EDESE, there are two search cases. One is search within a single domain, and the other is search across domains. The first processes of these two cases are the same: DU with uid produces a user query token q for a queried keyword kw.

- The DU computes the user query token as $q = \mathcal{H}(kw)^{y_{uid}}$, where y_{uid} is DU's query key.

Then, the subsequent processes are different. Search within a single domain only requires the domain's OC's cooperation, while search across domains needs both HD's and PD's OCs' operation.

- **Within Single Domain:**
  1. The DU sends uid and q to the OC of the domain which owns the DU.
  2. The OC obtains DU's search key k_{uid} from its $USKL$ and generates index $I_{kw} = e(k_{uid}, q)$.
  3. Then, the OC queries I_{kw} from the corresponding CSP to retrieve the list of encrypted files associated with it.
  4. Finally, the OC returns the retrieved list of encrypted files to the DU.
- **Cross Domain:**
  1. Besides uid and q, the DU sends the id did_h of the queried HD to the OC of the PD did_p which owns the DU.
  2. The OC obtains DU's search key k_{uid} from its $USKL$ by uid and obtains the PD's query key $PQK_{did_p}^{did_h}$ from $PQKL$ by did_h.
  3. Next, the OC computes $I_{kw,did_p} = e(k_{uid}, q), r_{did_p}^{did_h} = I_{kw,did_p}^{s_{did_p}^{did_h}}, \sigma_r = \mathcal{H}(r_{did_p}^{did_h})^{s_{did_p}^{did_h}}$, and $rq = (r_{did_p}^{did_h}, \sigma_r)$, and sends rq and did_p to the OC of the queried HD.
  4. After receiving rq and did_p, HD's OC obtains the PD's search key $PSK_{did_p}^{did_h}$ first from its $PSKL$.

5. Then, HD's OC verifies $e(g_1, \sigma_r) \stackrel{?}{=} e(z'^{did_h}_{did_p}, \mathcal{H}(r^{did_h}_{did_p}))$. If they are identical, go to the next step; otherwise, do nothing.
6. HD's OC computes $I_{kw,did_h} = (r^{did_h}_{did_p})^{z^{did_h}_{did_p}}$ and queries it from the CSP to retrieve a list of encrypted files.
7. Finally, HD's OC sends the retrieved list to the DU via the PD's OC.

Revocation. A domain's OC in M-EDESE can revoke any of the domain's users and partner domains.

- **User Revocation:** The OC revokes a user by deleting the search key from $USKL$ indexed by uid. As the OC no longer possesses the user's search key, the user can not query the OC's domain anymore.
- **Collaboration Revocation:** HD's OC revokes PD's search key from $PSKL$ that is indexed by did_p and informs the PD. Then, PD's OC deletes its search key regarding the HD from its $PQKL$ indexed by did_h. Since HD's OC no longer stores PD's search key, the process of searching across domains is blocked.

4 Security Analysis

In this section, we prove that M-EDESE satisfies the requirements for query privacy, query unforgeability, and revocability.

4.1 Query Privacy

We will use notations defined below to prove that M-EDESE satisfies the requirement of query privacy.

Given an encrypted file e_i, we use $id(e_i)$ to denote the identifying formation that is uniquely associated with e_i, such as its database position or its memory location.

Given a user query token q_{kw} sent by the user uid with the queried domain did_h and its reply $rs(q_{kw})$, which is the output of the search process taking q_{kw} as input and is a set of encrypted files associated with q_{kw}, we define $\Omega(q_{kw})$ be a tuple of $(uid, did_h, id(rs(q_{kw})))$, where $id(rs(q_{kw}))$ represents the identifying information of each encrypted file in $rs(q_{kw})$, let $Q_t = \{q_1, \cdots, q_t\}$ be a sequence of t user query tokens sent from users to the OC in the domain did_h, and let $RS_t = \{rs(q_1), \cdots, rs(q_t)\}$ be the corresponding replies, where $t \in \mathbb{N}$ and is polynomial bounded.

Similarly, given a domain query token rq_{kw} sent by a querier domain did_p to a queried domain did_h and its reply $rs(rq_{kw})$, we define $\Omega(rq_{kw}) = (did_p, did_h, id(rs(rq_{kw})))$, where $id\,(rs(rq_{kw}))$ represents the identifying information of each entry in $rs(rq_{kw})$, let $RQ_l = \{rq_1, \cdots, rq_l\}$ as a sequence of l domain query tokens sent from OCs of the domain did_h's PDs to the domain did_h's OC, and $RS' = \{rs(rq_1), \cdots, rs(rq_l)\}$ be the corresponding replies, where $l \in \mathbb{N}$ is polynomial bounded.

An adversary is an honest but curious OC, and we name the domain to which the adversary OC belongs as the adversary domain. We define V as the view of an adversary over t user query tokens and l domain query tokens as the transcript of the interactions between the adversary and users/PDs of the adversary domain, together with some common knowledge. We have $V = (D, USKL, PSKL, PQKL, Q_t, RQ_l, RS_t, RS'_l)$, where $D = (I, ED), USKL = \{USK_1, USK_2, \cdots\}, PSKL = \{PSK_1, PSK_2, \cdots\}, PQKL = \{PQK_1, PQK_2, \cdots\}$, D is the encrypted database, I is the set of generated indexes based on keywords, ED is the set of encrypted files involving a ciphertext space $\mathbb{E}$.

Following the notation from [12], the *trace* of the t user query tokens and l domain qeury tokens is defined to be: $T = (|D|, \Omega(q_1), \cdots, \Omega(q_t), \Omega(rq_1), \cdots, \Omega(rq_l), |U|, |P|, |H|)$, which contains all the information that we allow a **simulator** (outsider observer who can only observe the communications between entities during search processes) to obtain. Note that $|D| = (|I|, |ED|)$, $|I|$ is the number of indexes based on keywords, $|ED|$ denotes the number of encrypted files, $|U|$ equals the number of entries in $USKL$, representing the number of the adversary domain's users, $|P|$ equals the number of entries in $PSKL$, which is the number of the adversary's PDs, and $|H|$ equals the number of entries in $PQKL$, which represent the number of the adversary's collaborating HDs.

Definition 1. *An M-EDESE achieves query privacy if for all database D, for all $t, l \in \mathbb{N}$, for all PPT algorithm $\mathcal{A}$, there exists a PPT algorithm (the* ***simulator****) $\mathcal{A}^*$, such that for all view V and trace T, for any function f:*

$$|Pr[\mathcal{A}(V) = f(D, KW_t, KW'_l)] \\ -Pr[\mathcal{A}^*(T) = f(D, KW_t, KW'_l)]| < v(\kappa),$$

where the probability is taken over the internal coins of $\mathcal{A}$ and $\mathcal{A}^*$.

The notion of query privacy requires that all information on the original database and the queried keywords that can be computed by the adversary from the transcript of interactions it obtains (i.e., V) can also be computed by the simulator from what it is allowed to know (i.e., T). In other words, a system satisfying query privacy does not leak any information beyond the information we allow the adversary to have.

Proof. To construct a PPT simulator $\mathcal{A}^*$ such that for all $t, l \in \mathbb{N}$, for all PPT algorithm $\mathcal{A}$, all functions f, given the trace T, $\mathcal{A}^*$ can simulate $\mathcal{A}(V)$ with non-negligible probability. More specifically, we need to show that $\mathcal{A}^*(T)$ can generate a view V^* which is computationally indistinguishable from V, the actual view of $\mathcal{A}$.

Recall that T and V definitions are as follows,

1. Given $t = 0$ and $l = 0$, which imply $Q = \emptyset, RQ = \emptyset, RS = \emptyset$, and $RS' = \emptyset$, $\mathcal{A}^*$ builds $V^* = (D^* = (I^*, ED^*), USKL^*, PSKL^*, PQKL^*)$ as follows.
   - To construct D^*, for $1 \le i \le |I|, 1 \le j \le |ED|$, it selects $I^*_{kw_i} \in_R \mathbb{G}^*_T$ and $E(m_j)^* \in_R \mathbb{E}$.

- Then, it computes $USKL^* = \{k^*_{uid_i} : k^*_{uid_i} \in_R \mathbb{G}^*_1, uid_i \in_R \mathbb{N}\}_{i\in[1,|U|]}$, $PSKL^* = \{(z^*_{did_j}, z'^*_{did_j}) : z^*_{did_j} \in_R \mathbb{Z}^*_p, z'^*_{did_j} \in_R \mathbb{G}^*_1, did_j \in_R \mathbb{N}\}_{j\in[1,|P|]}$, and $PQKL^* = \{s^{*did'_k} : s^{*did'_k} \in \mathbb{Z}^*_p, did'_k \in \mathbb{N}\}_{k\in[1,|H|]}$, where did_j is a PD's identity of the $\mathcal{A}$ domain and did'_k is a collaborator domain's identity of the $\mathcal{A}$ domain.

It is easy to check that V^* and V are computationally indistinguishable when $E(\cdot)$ is a pseudorandom permutation and $\mathcal{H}$ is a pseudorandom function, which is demonstrated below.

- If $E(\cdot)$ is a pseudorandom permutation, ED^* and ED are computationally indistinguishable, because a real $E(m)$ and a simulated $E(m)^* \in_R \mathbb{E}$ are both random values in the ciphertext space $\mathbb{E}$.
- If $\mathcal{H}$ is pseudorandom function, a real index $I_{kw} = e(g_1, \mathcal{H}(kw))^x$ and a simulated index I^*_{kw} are computationally indistinguishable due to they are both random elements in the group $\mathbb{G}^*_T$.
- A real user search key $k_{uid} = g_1^{\frac{x}{y_{uid}}}$ and a simulated user search key k^*_{uid} are computationally indistinguishable as both of them are random elements in the group $\mathbb{G}^*_1$.
- A real domain search key ($z_{did} = \frac{x}{x_{did} s_{(did)}}, z_{(did)} = g_1^{s_{(did)}}$) and a simulated partner search key (z^*_{did}, z'^*_{did}) are computationally indistinguishable as both of z are random elements in the group $\mathbb{Z}^*_p$ and both of z' are random elements in the group $\mathbb{G}^*_1$.
- A real domain query key s^{did} and a simulated domain query key s^{*did} are computationally indistinguishable as both of s are random elements in the group $\mathbb{Z}^*_p$.

2. Given $t > 0, l > 0$, and a function *select*(i, N) which is defined to return the i-th entry in the set N, $\mathcal{A}^*$ builds $V^* = (D^* = (I^*, ED^*), USKL^*, PSKL^*, PQKL^*, Q^*_t, RQ^*_l, RS^*_t, RS'^*_l)$ as follows. Recall that $\Omega(rq) = (did_p, did_h, id(rs(rq)))$, $\mathcal{A}^*$ obtains $\mathcal{A}$ domain identity $did_{\mathcal{A}} = did_h$ from $\Omega(rq_1)$ contained in T. Next, $\mathcal{A}^*$ setups five sets $UID = \emptyset, DID = \emptyset, X^* = \{x^*_i\}_{i\in[1,|P|+|H|]}$, $Y^* = \{y^*_j\}_{j\in[1,|U|]}$, and $S^* = \{s^*_k\}_{k\in[1,|P|]}$, s.t. $x^*_i, y^*_j, s^*_k \in_R \mathbb{Z}^*_p$. Then, it computes the below equation, where x^* is regarded as the $\mathcal{A}$ domain's master secret key. Then, it proceeds following operations.

$$x^* = \prod_{i=1}^{|P|+|H|} \prod_{j=1}^{|U|} \prod_{k=1}^{|P|} x^*_i y^*_j s^*_i$$

- To construct ED^*, $\mathcal{A}^*$ performs the same operations as the case of $t = 0$ and $l = 0$ to obtain the $ED^* = \{E(m_i)^*\}_{i\in[1,|ED|]}$.
- Next, it computes $PSKL^* = \{(z^*_i, z'^*_i) : x^*_i = select(i, X^*), s_i = select\ (i, S^*), z^*_i = \frac{x^*_i}{x^* s^*_i}, z'^*_i = g_1^{s^*_i}\}_{i\in[1,|P|]}$, $USKL^* = \{k^*_j : y^*_j select(j, Y^*), k^*_j = g_1^{\frac{x^*}{y^*_j}}\}_{j\in[1,|U|]}$, and $PQKL^* = \{s^{*did'_k} : did'_k \in_R \mathbb{N}, s^{*did'_k} \in_R \mathbb{Z}^*_p\}_{k\in[1,|H|]}$.

- To construct Q_t^*, recall that from $\Omega(q_1), \cdots, \Omega(q_t)$ contained in T, $\mathcal{A}^*$ can determine which user query tokens ask the same keyword and which user query tokens are issued by the same user. Hence, regarding to each $\Omega(q_i) = \{uid_i, did_i, id(rs(q_i))\}$ where i ranges from 1 to t, it computes q_i^* as follows.
  (a) $\mathcal{A}^*$ finds out $j \in [1, |UID|]$ such that $uid_j' = uid_i$, where $uid_j' \in UID$. If no such j value exists, it computes $UID = UID \cup \{uid_i\}$ and sets $j = |UID|$.
  (b) If there does not exist $1 \leq k < i$ such that $id(rs(q_k)) = id(rs(q_i))$, which means q_i and q_k ask the same keyword, $\mathcal{A}^*$ selects a random element $w_i \in \mathbb{G}_2^*$; otherwise, it sets $w_i = w_k$.
  (c) Then, $\mathcal{A}^*$ sets $y_j = select(j, Y^*)$ as the user uid_i's query key and calculates $q_i^* = w_i^{y_j^*}$.
- To construct RQ_l^*, $\mathcal{A}^*$ acts similarly to constructing Q_t^*. $\mathcal{A}^*$ also can determine which domain query tokens and user query tokens ask the same keyword with respect to $\Omega(q_1), \cdots, \Omega(q_t), \Omega(rq_1), \cdots, \Omega(rq_l)$. According to each $\Omega(rq_i) = \{did_i, did_{\mathcal{A}}, id(rs(rq_i))\}$ where i ranges from 1 to l, it computes rq_i^* as follows.
  (a) $\mathcal{A}^*$ finds out $j \in [1, |DID|]$ such that $did_j' = did_i$, where $did_j' \in DID$. If no such j value exists, it computes $DID = DID \cup \{did_i\}$ and $j = |DID|$.
  (b) If there exits $1 \leq k < i$ such that $id(rs(rq_k)) = id(rs(rq_i))$, which means rq_i and rq_k ask the same keyword, $\mathcal{A}^*$ sets $w_{i+t} = w_{k+t}$; otherwise, it proceeds to the next step.
  (c) If there exits $1 \leq k \leq t$ such that $id(rs(q_k)) = id(rs(rq_i))$, which means rq_i and q_k ask the same keyword, $\mathcal{A}^*$ sets $w_{i+t} = w_k$; otherwise, it selects a random element $w_{i+t} \in \mathbb{G}_2^*$.
  (d) $\mathcal{A}^*$ computes $x_j = select(j, X^*)$ and $s_j = select(j, S^*)$ as the querier domain's master secret key and query key, respectively. Then, it calculates $r_i^* = e(g_1, w_{i+t})^{s_j^* x_j^*}$, $\sigma_i^* = \mathcal{H}(r_i^*)^{s_j^*}$ and sets $rq_i^* = (r_i^*, \sigma_i^*)$.
- To construct I^*, $\mathcal{A}^*$ initializes $I^* = \emptyset$. Then,
  (a) For each $\Omega(q_i) = \{uid_i, did_i, id(rs(q_i))\}$, where $1 \leq i \leq t$, $\mathcal{A}^*$ knows the queried domain did_i and the underlying keyword w_i which is chosen for constructing q_i. If $did_i = did_{\mathcal{A}}$, it computes $I_i^* = e(g_1, w_i)^{x^*}$; otherwise, $\mathcal{A}^*$ computes $I_i^* = e(g_1, w_i)^{x_j^*}$, where j is the index of did_i in DID obtained via the operation in step (a) of constructing RQ_l^* with input did_i. If $I_i^* \notin I^*$, it computes $I^* = I^* \cup \{I_i^*\}$.
  (b) For each $\Omega(rq_i)$, where $1 \leq i \leq l$, $\mathcal{A}^*$ computes $I_i^* = e(g_1, w_{i+t})^{x^*}$, where w_{i+t} is the chosen keyword for constructing rq_i and x^* is regarded as $\mathcal{A}$ domain's master secret key. If $I_i^* \notin I^*$, it computes $I^* = I^* \cup \{I_i^*\}$.
  (c) If $|I^*| < |I|$, $\mathcal{A}^*$ calculates the rest set as $I'^* = \{I_i^* : I_i^* \in_R \mathbb{G}_T^*\}_{i \in [|I^*|+1, |I|]}$, and concatenates it with I^* as $I^* = I^* \cup I'^*$.
- To construct RS_t^*, $\mathcal{A}^*$ sets up $RS_t^* = \emptyset$. Then, for each $\Omega(q_i)$ where $1 \leq i \leq t$, $\mathcal{A}^*$ sets $rs(q_i)^* = \emptyset$. Since $\mathcal{A}^*$ knows identities ids of ciphertext

entries (e.t. $E(m)$) from $\Omega(q_i)$, it collects ciphertexts from ED^* whose identities are in ids and puts these ciphertexts into $rs(q_i)^*$. After that, $rs(q_i)^*$ is put into RS_t^*.
- Constructing RS'^*_l is the same as constructing RS^* excepting retrieving ids from $\Omega(rq_i)^*$, where i ranges from 1 to l. Each iteration produces a $rs(rq_i)^*$ with respective to i. Finally, $\mathcal{A}^*$ simulates $RS'^*_l = \{rs(rq_i)^*\}_{i\in[1,l]}$.

We show that V^* is computationally indistinguishable from V by comparing them component by component as follows.

- If $E(\cdot)$ is a pseudorandom permutation, ED^* and ED are computationally indistinguishable, since a real encrypted data $E(m)$ and a simulated $E(m)^* \in_R \{0,1\}^{|E(\cdot)|}$ are both random in the same domain $\{0,1\}^{|E(\cdot)|}$.
- For Q_t and Q_t^*, comparing an user query token generated by $\mathcal{A}$ as $q = \mathcal{H}(kw)^y$ and a simulated user query token generated by $\mathcal{A}^*$ as $q^* = w^{y^*}$, where $w \in_R \mathbb{G}_2^*$, q and q^* are computationally indistinguishable if $\mathcal{H}$ is a pseudorandom function, since both y_i and y_i^* are randomly chosen from $\mathbb{Z}_p^*$.
- For RQ_l and RQ_l^*, a domain query token generated by $\mathcal{A}$ as $(r = e(g_1, \mathcal{H}(kw))^{sx}, \sigma = \mathcal{H}(r)^s)$ is calculated from the random elements s, x in $\mathbb{Z}_p^*$. Similarly, a simulated domain query token generated by $\mathcal{A}^*$ as $(r^* = e(g_1, \mathcal{H}(w))^{s^*x^*}, \sigma = r^{*s^*})$ is also fielded from the random elements s^*, x^* in $\mathbb{Z}_p^*$. If $\mathcal{H}$ is a pseudorandom function, both r and r^* are random elements in the group $\mathbb{G}_T$, while both σ and σ^* are random elements in the group $\mathbb{G}_2^*$. Hence, a domain query token is computationally indistinguishable from a simulated domain query token.
- Comparing a real user search key $k = g_1^{\frac{x}{y}}$ and a simulated user search key $k^* = g_1^{\frac{x^*}{y^*}}$, they are computationally indistinguishable as y and y^* are random elements from $\mathbb{Z}_p^*$.
- For $PSKL$ and $PSKL^*$, an actual domain search key $(z = \frac{x}{x's'}, z' = g_1^{s'})$ is computationally indistinguishable to a simulated domain search key $(z^* = \frac{x^*}{x'^*s'^*}, z'^* = g_1^{s'^*})$, since all of x', s', x'^*, s'^* are random elements in $\mathbb{Z}_p^*$.
- For $PQKL$ and $PQKL^*$, a real domain query key s is computationally indistinguishable from a simulated domain query key s^*, since both s and s^* are randomly chosen from $\mathbb{Z}_p^*$.
- It is easy to see that I^* and I are computationally indistinguishable due to the elements of them being random in the group $\mathbb{G}_T$, which is exactly resulted from the pseudorandom function $\mathcal{H}$.
- Since the above components are computationally indistinguishable and the reply result sets are generated from those components, RS_t and RS_t^* are computationally indistinguishable. So do RS'^*_t and RS'_t.

Finally, based on the above indistinguishability results, the conclusion is yielded that A and A^* are computationally indistinguishable.

4.2 Query Unforegeability

Query unforgeability is defined for searchable encryptions in multi-user settings [17]. Particularly, M-EDESE is in a multi-domain setting, in which domains can be regarded as special users. Hence, we need to discuss the query unforgeability at both the user level and the domain level.

A user query token (or domain query token) is a user's legitimate query (or a domain's legitimate query) if it is indeed generated by the M-EDESE algorithm (search or upload process) with corresponding secret keys. Hence, in a nutshell, query unforgeability is that for any user *uid* or domain *did*, no adversary is able to compute a user query token q and a domain query token rq without compromising the corresponding user query key QK_{uid} and the corresponding domain query key PQK_{did} respectively.

In the multi-user setting and the multi-domain setting of M-EDESE, we consider one type of adversaries and two types of victims respectively.

- **Adversary $\mathcal{A}$:** $\mathcal{A}$ is a collusion of malicious users and malicious domains (including their users, OCs, and KGCs).
- **Victim:** A victim is either $\mathcal{V}_{uid}$ or $\mathcal{V}_{did}$.
  - $\mathcal{V}_{uid}$ is an honest user whose identity is *uid* in a partial honest domain (KGC is fully trusted) whose identity is *did*.
  - $\mathcal{V}_{did}$ is an honest OC with fully trusted KGC in a domain *did*.

Adversary $\mathcal{A}$ can observe a set of information from malicious domains and their users. For a malicious domain did_i, $\mathcal{A}$ obtains $K_{did_i} = (did_i, UQKL', USKL, PSKL, PQKL, MK_{did_i})$, where $UPKL, PSKL, PQKL$ are the completed lists, and $UQKL'$ is a part of user query keys under domain did_i. If the domain did_i is partial honest, which means only its OC is malicious, we have $MK_{did_i} = \perp$. $\mathcal{A}$ also contains the collusion of malicious users under honest domains. $\mathcal{A}$ obtains QK_{uid_j} from such a malicious user whose identity is uid_j. In addition, $\mathcal{A}$ can observe all search and data upload interactions between all entities. Therefore, the acknowledge of $\mathcal{A}$ is defined as $\mathcal{K} = (\{K_{did_i}\}_{i\in[1,n]}, \{QK_{uid_j}\}_{j\in[1,m]})$ from n malicious domains and m malicious users.

Regarding two types of victims, two games are defined below. Both challengers of these two games simulate the execution of our M-EDESE and provide an oracle $\mathcal{O}$, which answers adversary $\mathcal{A}$'s queries on the executions of user enrollment, data uploading, collaboration establishment, and search with the acknowledge $\mathcal{K}$ of $\mathcal{A}$.

Game 1: $\mathcal{A}$ intends to forge a user query token q on behalf of $\mathcal{V}_{uid}$.
Game 2: $\mathcal{A}$ intends to forge a domain query token rq on behalf of $\mathcal{V}_{did}$.

We construct a BLS short signature from the above two games. The BLS setups with $(g_1, \mathcal{H}^*, e, x, g_1^x)$, where e is a bilinear map, g_1 is the generator of $\mathbb{G}_1$, $\mathcal{H}^*$ is a pseudorandom hash function $\mathcal{H}^* : \{0,1\}^* \to \mathbb{G}_2$, x is the secret signing key, and g_1^x is the corresponding public key. Lest $\mathcal{B}$ be a PPT adversary attempting to forge a short signature with respect to g_1^x. The proof requires demonstrating to construct the BLS short signature scheme, which provides the signing oracle $\mathcal{O}(x)$.

- **Game 1:** $\mathcal{A}$ observes a set of user query tokens $QT = \{\mathcal{H}(kw_1)^{y_{uid}}, \mathcal{H}(kw_2)^{y_{uid}}, \cdots\}$ from $\mathcal{V}_{uid}$ through data uploading and search oracle. It can also obtain $SK_{uid} = g_1^{\frac{x_{did}}{y_{uid}}}$. Since SK_{uid} has an unknown value x_{did} in the exponential of SK_{uid}, it is regarded as a random value. $\mathcal{B}$ regards QT as the BLS signatures under the signing key $x = y_{uid}$. Hence, $\mathcal{B}$ can simulate a BLS from the knowledge of $\mathcal{A}$ with $(g_1, \mathcal{H}^* = \mathcal{H}, e, x = y_{uid}, g_1^{y_{uid}})$.
- **Game 2:** $\mathcal{A}$ obtains a set of domain query tokens $RQ = \{(r_{kw_i} = e(g_1, \mathcal{H}(kw_i))^{s_{did}^{did_i} x_{did}}, \sigma_{kw_i} = \mathcal{H}(r_{kw_i})^{s_{did}^{did_i}})\}_{i \in [i,*]}$ from $\mathcal{V}_{did}$ through the search oracle. In addition, $\mathcal{A}$ obtains a set of $PSK_{did_i} = \{z_{did_i} = \frac{x_{did_i}}{x_{did} s_{did}^{did_i}}, z'_{did_i} = g_1^{s_{did}^{did_i}}\}$ from malicious domains. Hence, $\mathcal{A}$ can compute $r_{kw'} = (e(g_1, \mathcal{H}(kw'))^{x_{did_i}})^{\frac{1}{z_{did_i}}}$. However, $\mathcal{A}$ can not infer $\sigma_{kw'}$ since its exponential $s_{did}^{did_i}$ is unknown value. For σ_{kw_i}, $\mathcal{B}$ regards it as the BLS signature on the message $m = r_{kw_i}$ under the signing key $s_{did}^{did_i}$. Hence, $\mathcal{B}$ can simulate a BLS from the knowledge of $\mathcal{A}$ with $(g_1, \mathcal{H}^* = \mathcal{H}, e, x = s_{did}^{did_i}, g_1^{s_{did}^{did_i}}, m \in_R \mathbb{G}_T)$.

The simulation by $\mathcal{B}$ is perfect in Game 1 and Game 2. Hence, if $\mathcal{A}$ forges a legitimate user or domain query token based on a kw on behalf of $\mathcal{V}_{uid}$ or $\mathcal{V}_{did}$, she would also forge a valid BLS short signature on the kw.

4.3 Revocability

Revocability is a necessary requirement for any multi-user system. It is desirable to achieve user revocation and collaboration revocation in M-EDESE regarding its multi-user and multi-domain setting. Revocability enables an honest domain to revoke search abilities of its certain users and its certain PDs. Since the indistinguishability of indexes implies the fault of the searching process, it is effective to show revocability based on index indistinguishability. M-EDESE enables user revocability and collaboration revocability as defined below.

User Revocability. We construct the following game such that an adversary's advantage in attacking user revocability is winning the game. An adversary $\mathcal{A}$ performs in two phases. In phase 1, $\mathcal{A}$ acts as an authorized user and can access the search and data uploading oracle. At the end of phase 1, $\mathcal{A}$ chooses two never queried keywords kw'_1, kw'_2. The current knowledge of $\mathcal{A}$ contains $\{(kw_i, q_i, I_i)\}_{i \in [1,n]}$ and $\{kw'_1, kw'_2, QK\}$. After that, in phase 2, $\mathcal{A}$ is revoked and given I'_b based on one of kw'_1, kw'_2. $\mathcal{A}$ guess the value of b'. If $b = b'$, $\mathcal{A}$ wins the game.

Definition 2. *An M-EDESE system achieves user revocability if the below inequality holds for all PPT algorithms.*

$$\begin{aligned}|Pr[b' = b :\ & \\ & (GP, QKs, SKs, MKs) \leftarrow \textbf{Initial Setup\&Enrollment};\\ & (\{(kw_i, q_i, I_i)\}_{i\in[1,n]}, kw'_1, kw'_2, QK) \leftarrow \textbf{Phase 1}_{\mathcal{O}}(\mathcal{A});\\ & \textbf{Revoke}(\mathcal{A});\\ & b \in_R \{1,0\}, I'_b \leftarrow \textbf{Search}(QK, kw'_b, SK);\\ & b' \leftarrow \mathcal{A}(\{(kw_i, q_i, I_i)\}_{i\in[1,n]}, kw'_1, kw'_2, QK)\\ ] - \frac{1}{2}| < \epsilon. &\end{aligned}$$

Proof Sketch. To guess b' in the game, $\mathcal{A}$ needs to compute $I'_{kw'_1} = e(g_1, \mathcal{H}(kw'_1))^{x_{did'}}$. It is a hard discrete log problem as the exponential $x_{did'}$ is unknown for $\mathcal{A}$. As a consequence, from $\mathcal{A}$ perspective, $I'_{kw'_1}$ and $I'_{kw'_2}$ are independent of kw'_1 and kw'_2, respectively. Hence, the advantage of the adversary winning the game is negligible.

Collaboration Revocability. We construct the same game for collaboration revocability proof except that at the end of phase 1, the acknowledge of $\mathcal{A}$ is $\{(q_i, rq_i, I_i)\}_{i\in[1,n]}$ and $\{kw'_1, kw'_2, q'_1, q'_2, PQKL, USKL\}$.

Definition 3. *An M-EDESE system achieves collaboration revocability if the below inequality holds for all PPT algorithms.*

$$\begin{aligned}|Pr[b' = b :\ & \\ & (GP, QKs, SKs, PQKs, SQKs, MKs) \leftarrow \textbf{Initial Setup\&Enrollment};\\ & (\{(q_i, rq_i, I_i)\}_{i\in[1,n]}, q'_1, q'_2, kw'_1, kw'_2, PQKL, USKL) \leftarrow \textbf{Phase 1}_{\mathcal{O}}(\mathcal{A});\\ & \textbf{Revoke}(\mathcal{A});\\ & b \in_R \{1,0\}, I'_b \leftarrow \textbf{Search}(QK, kw'_b, SK, PQK^{did''}_{did'}, PSK^{did''}_{did'});\\ & b' \leftarrow \mathcal{A}(\{(q_i, rq_i, I_i)\}_{i\in[1,n]}, q'_1, q'_2, kw'_1, kw'_2, PQKL, USKL)\\ ] - \frac{1}{2}| < \epsilon. &\end{aligned}$$

Proof Sketch. $\mathcal{A}$ can easily compute rq'_1 by calculating $r'_1 = e(SK, q'_1)^{s^{did''}_{did'}}$ and $\sigma'_1 = \mathcal{H}(r'_1)^{s^{did''}_{did'}}$. Recall that $I'_1 = {r'_1}^{z^{did''}_{did'}}$ and $z^{did''}_{did'} = \frac{x_{did''}}{x_{did'} s^{did''}_{did'}}$, it requires $z^{did''}_{did'}$ to compute I'_1 from rq'_1, which contains the unknown value $x_{did''}$. Similar to user revocability, from the $\mathcal{A}$'s perspective, I'_1 and I'_2 are independent of kw'_1 and kw'_2 respectively. Therefore, the advantage of the adversary winning the game is negligible.

5 Evaluation

In this section, we evaluate both the complexity and runtime performance of M-EDESE.

5.1 Complexities

We analyze the time complexities of data uploading processes on the user side and on the OC side. When a user uploads n keywords and an encrypted file, the time complexities of data uploading processes on both user and OC sides are $\mathcal{O}(n)$, which is independent of the number of users and domains. Specifically, the user side computes a hash function and an exponential operation in $\mathbb{G}_2$ for n times, while the OC side calculates a pairing operation for n times.

Then, we analyze the time complexities of search processes on the user side and on the OCs side. When a user queries a keyword, the time complexity of user query token generation on the user side is $\mathcal{O}(1)$ no matter how many domains are queried, while the time complexity of the search process on the OCs side is $\mathcal{O}(m)$, where m is the number of queried domains. OCs finally perform a pairing operation for $(2m+1)$ times, an exponential operation for $(2m+1)$ times, and a hash function for m times.

5.2 Experiments

We ran experiments on three algorithms, including user query generation, single domain index generation, and cross-domain index generation. We did not measure the time consumption on the CSP side since it is as fast as plaintext searching. In our experiments, we ran keyword search queries on a well-known opensource dataset, the Enron email database [20] and extracted a total of 5000 most frequent keywords from 30,109 emails.

We evaluated the performance of EDESE using different bilinear pairings, including SS512 (type A), MNT224 (type D), and BN256 (type F) pairings. All of them are equivalent to or exceed 80-bit security. We implemented M-EDESE based on Java programming language with version 1.8 and JPBC library [19] on a PC running 64-bit Windows 11 with 3.61 GHz Intel (R) Core (TM) i7-12700K and Memory 32 GB RAM 3200 MHz.

Table 2. Performance of query and index generations of M-EDESE in ms

Algorithm	SS512	MNT224	BN256
User query generation	4.72	14.25	4.96
Single domain index generation	5.69	14.29	20.43
Cross-domain index generation	4.96	70.7	93.24

From Table 2, M-EDESE using SS512 type pairing runs faster than using the other two pairings. This is reasonable since SS512 is at the lowest security strength among these three types of pairings, while BN256 is at the highest security strength. Considering that user query generation is performed by each individual user while both single domain index generation and cross-domain index generation are performed by OCs, the bottleneck of M-EDESE is the performance of OCs because each OC serves multiple users and performs index generations for all received user queries. In practice, such bottlenecks can be alleviated by leveraging powerful servers instead of PCs.

6 Conclusion

In this work, we proposed M-EDESE as a new secure keyword searching solution that is easily deployable and efficiently searchable in multi-domain settings. We presented a concrete construction of M-EDESE with formal security proofs. We also provided theoretical and experimental evaluations on M-EDESE showing that it is promising in practice.

Acknowledgements. Jiaming Yuan is suppported in part by the Ripple Graduate Fellowship. Yingjiu Li is supported in part by the Ripple University Blockchain Research Initiative. Jianting Ning is in part by the National Natural Science Foundation of China under Grant 61972094, and Grant 62032005, the Science Foundation of Fujian Provincial Science and Technology Agency (2020J02016).

References

1. Hamad, S.A., Sheng, Q.Z., Zhang, W.E., Nepal, S.: Realizing an internet of secure things: a survey on issues and enabling technologies. IEEE Commun. Surv. Tutor. **22**(2), 1372–1391 (2020)
2. He, W., Akhawe, D., Jain, S., Shi, E., Song, D.: Shadowcrypt: encrypted web applications for everyone. In: Proceedings of the 2014 ACM SIGSAC Conference on Computer and Communications Security, pp. 1028–1039 (2014)
3. Lau, B., Chung, S., Song, C., Jang, Y., Lee, W., Boldyreva, A.: Mimesis aegis: a mimicry privacy shield-a system's approach to data privacy on public cloud. In: 23rd USENIX Security Symposium (USENIX Security 2014), pp. 33–48 (2014)
4. Boneh, D., Di Crescenzo, G., Ostrovsky, R., Persiano, G.: Public key encryption with keyword search. In: Cachin, C., Camenisch, J.L. (eds.) EUROCRYPT 2004. LNCS, vol. 3027, pp. 506–522. Springer, Heidelberg (2004). https://doi.org/10.1007/978-3-540-24676-3_30
5. Amanatidis, G., Boldyreva, A., O'Neill, A.: Provably-secure schemes for basic query support in outsourced databases. In: Barker, S., Ahn, G.-J. (eds.) DBSec 2007. LNCS, vol. 4602, pp. 14–30. Springer, Heidelberg (2007). https://doi.org/10.1007/978-3-540-73538-0_2
6. Boneh, D., Sahai, A., Waters, B.: Functional encryption: a new vision for public-key cryptography. Commun. ACM **55**(11), 56–64 (2012)
7. Boneh, D., Waters, B.: Conjunctive, subset, and range queries on encrypted data. In: Vadhan, S.P. (ed.) TCC 2007. LNCS, vol. 4392, pp. 535–554. Springer, Heidelberg (2007). https://doi.org/10.1007/978-3-540-70936-7_29

8. Bösch, C., Hartel, P., Jonker, W., Peter, A.: A survey of provably secure searchable encryption. ACM Comput. Surv. (CSUR) **47**(2), 1–51 (2014)
9. Cash, D., et al.: Dynamic searchable encryption in very-large databases: data structures and implementation. In: NDSS, vol. 14, pp. 23–26 (2014)
10. Chai, Q., Gong, G.: Verifiable symmetric searchable encryption for semi-honest-but-curious cloud servers. In: 2012 IEEE International Conference on Communications (ICC), pp. 917–922. IEEE (2012)
11. Chang, Y.-C., Mitzenmacher, M.: Privacy preserving keyword searches on remote encrypted data. In: Ioannidis, J., Keromytis, A., Yung, M. (eds.) ACNS 2005. LNCS, vol. 3531, pp. 442–455. Springer, Heidelberg (2005). https://doi.org/10.1007/11496137_30
12. Curtmola, R., Garay, J., Kamara, S., Ostrovsky, R.: Searchable symmetric encryption: improved definitions and efficient constructions. J. Comput. Secur. **19**(5), 895–934 (2011)
13. Faber, S., Jarecki, S., Krawczyk, H., Nguyen, Q., Rosu, M., Steiner, M.: Rich queries on encrypted data: beyond exact matches. In: Pernul, G., Ryan, P.Y.A., Weippl, E. (eds.) ESORICS 2015. LNCS, vol. 9327, pp. 123–145. Springer, Cham (2015). https://doi.org/10.1007/978-3-319-24177-7_7
14. Poh, G.S., Chin, J.J., Yau, W.C., Choo, K.K.R., Mohamad, M.S.: Searchable symmetric encryption: designs and challenges. ACM Comput. Surv. (CSUR) **50**(3), 1–37 (2017)
15. Boneh, D., Lynn, B., Shacham, H.: Short signatures from the weil pairing. In: Boyd, C. (ed.) ASIACRYPT 2001. LNCS, vol. 2248, pp. 514–532. Springer, Heidelberg (2001). https://doi.org/10.1007/3-540-45682-1_30
16. Song, D.X., Wagner, D., Perrig, A.: Practical techniques for searches on encrypted data. In Proceeding 2000 IEEE Symposium on Security and Privacy, S&P 2000, pp. 44–55. IEEE (2000)
17. Bao, F., Deng, R.H., Ding, X., Yang, Y.: Private query on encrypted data in multi-user settings. In: Chen, L., Mu, Y., Susilo, W. (eds.) ISPEC 2008. LNCS, vol. 4991, pp. 71–85. Springer, Heidelberg (2008). https://doi.org/10.1007/978-3-540-79104-1_6
18. Yin, H., et al.: CP-ABSE: a ciphertext-policy attribute-based searchable encryption scheme. IEEE Access **7**, 5682–5694 (2019)
19. De Caro, A., Iovino, V. : jPBC: java pairing based cryptography. In: 2011 IEEE Symposium on Computers and Communications (ISCC), pp. 850–855. IEEE (2011)
20. Enron email dataset (2019). https://www.cs.cmu.edu/./enron. Accessed 23 Nov 2019

A Traceable and Revocable Attribute-based Encryption Scheme Based on Policy Hiding in Smart Healthcare Scenarios

Yang Zhao[1,2], Zhaozhong Liu[1,2], Jingmin An[1,2], Guobin Zhu[1,2], and Saru Kumari[3(✉)]

[1] Network and Data Security Key Laboratory of Sichuan Province, University of Electronic Science and Technology of China, Chengdu 610054, Sichuan, China

[2] School of Information and Software Engineering, University of Electronic Science and Technology of China, Chengdu 610054, Sichuan, China

[3] Department of Mathematics, Chaudhary Charan Singh University, Meerut 250004, India

saryusiirohi@gmail.com

Abstract. The smart medical industry, which relies on advanced Internet of Things technology and cloud platform, has been developing rapidly. Smart healthcare is a way to realize information-based communication between patients and medical staff by creating an online medical information platform. To address the user privacy and data security issues involved, we use attribute-based encryption scheme (CP-ABE). However, the traditional CP-ABE scheme has the following problems: 1. user-sensitive information is embedded directly into the access structures without hidden operations; 2. the number of public parameters is not fixed and varies linearly with the size of the system's attribute set; 3. it does not effectively fix the user attribute change problem; 4. it is impossible to trace the user. To solve the above issues, this paper proposes a scheme with the following special features: 1. using partial policy hiding; 2. using large attribute universe; 3. performing attribute revocation when user attributes are changed; 4. being able to trace back to the user after the user decryption key is leaked. Finally, we provide design details and do performance evaluation to prove its effectiveness.

Keywords: Smart medical · Attribute-Based Encryption (ABE) · Attribute revocation · Public traceability · Large universe

1 Introduction

At the present stage, the public medical management system in China is still not perfect, resulting in inefficient medical care, poor medical information, polarized distribution of medical resources and inadequate medical supervision mechanism.

C. Su et al. (Eds.): ISPEC 2022, LNCS 13620, pp. 624–639, 2022.
https://doi.org/10.1007/978-3-031-21280-2_35

In order to alleviate the above problems, the intelligent medical network platform system is gradually established. As an important technology in intelligent medical care, IoT technology relies on its advantages of terminal mobility and access flexibility to break through the limitations of traditional methods and enhance the informationization level of intelligent medical platform [1]. Cloud computing technology is also richly used in the medical industry, and can provide electronic medical records, telemedicine, and other means to break the model limitations of traditional means of consultation. Many existing schemes are used for smart healthcare by integrating traditional wireless body area networks (WBANs) [2–4] and cloud computing, and encrypted cloud data search methods and authentication protocol schemes are being proposed [5–8]. A typical application scenario is shown in Fig. 1, where patients collect health indicator information and transmit it to the cloud-based platform, doctors can decrypt and download patient data through the cloud server to understand patient's symptoms and make diagnosis in time. Since the data involves patient privacy, other patients with access to the medical cloud and other personnel with access rights should not see the specific data content of the patient, so the data access control of the data downloader is especially critical. Attribute-based encryption means based on cryptographic policies are considered as solutions under the premise of achieving fine-grained access control and strict confidentiality of patient privacy.

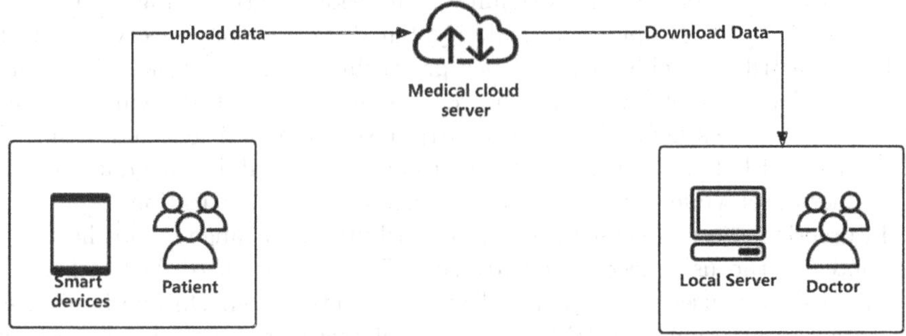

Fig. 1. Application scenarios

To compensate for the shortcomings of identity-based encryption (IBE), Sahai and Waters (2005) presented the conception of ABE [9]. Then Goyal et al. [10] (2006) formally presented KP-ABE, with ciphertext and attributes are associated. Compared to previous public key encryption schemes, ABE implements 1-to-many encryption and decryption, in which it views the identity identifier as a series of attributes. After this, a number of ABE schemes were proposed [11–16]. Considering the application scenario of smart healthcare, our paper mainly focuses on the scheme from the perspective of CP-ABE. Based on encryption methods, CP-ABE specifies access policies for ciphertexts, and only if attributes of someone meets this access structure, he is able to obtain information from the ciphertext by using a secret key.

Because of shortcomings of the above schemes regarding user privacy, schemes with policy hiding have been proposed one after another. In 2008, The concept of partially hidden CP-ABE was first presented by Nishide et al. [17]. Based on CP-ABE schemes [18] and garbled Bloom filters [19], the scheme implemented by Yang et al. [20] is able to hide the entire property, Lai et al. [21] gave one partial hiding policy scheme in 2011 and showed it is full secure. In 2013, Zhang et al. [22] added decryption tests and anonymous features to the scheme, in which a new technique of match-and-decrypt is proposed, which works by computing special components in the ciphertext. The problem of the above scheme is that only AND gate policy is supported.Lai et al. [23] improved the scheme based on the previous paper on policy hiding to support LSSS access policy as well as decryption test; Han et al. [24] gave a CP-ABE scheme based on 1-out-of-oblivious transmission technique to successfully protect the user's attribute values from the influence of AA. The problem of the above schemes is that the decryption link has too many pairing operations.

To solve the abuse of user keys, A large amount of CP-ABE schemes with traceability were proposed one after another. In 2011, Katz et al. [25] integrated traceability into the predicate cryptosystem of their scheme. In order to realize user identity tracking, Liu et al. [26,27] proposed the use of white box tracking and black box tracking in the two schemes in 2013. However, the predicate encryption method is only suitable for the case of a small number of users, and Liu et al.'s scheme requires significant additional extra storage space. The schemes [28,29] both support traceability, but do not support decryption tests and large attribute fields. The privacy-preserving authentication scheme proposed by Mei et al. [30] simplifies the key management problem while ensuring the security of the scheme, Xiong et al. [31] presented an efficient and high-scale ECDSA-based batch verification scheme to ensure traceability for data sharing in IoT networks while improving its efficiency for batch verification.

In practice, there are cases when user attributes are changed, and then some attributes of the user need to be revoked. The revocation of ABE scheme is sub-divided into: user revocation and attribute revocation. On one hand, user revocation means that all attributes of a specific user are revoked, but does not affect other users; attribute revocation means that the current user has lost some access rights due to the revocation of a certain attribute. Pirretti et al. [32] in 2010 proposed a scheme using a timed update key mechanism to achieve attribute revocation. In 2018, Wang et al. [33] and Liu et al. [34] uses a group key form in their scheme and kept active attributes of each user in the form of a binary tree to implemented attribute revocation. None of the above schemes supports decryption testing.The scheme proposed by Zhang et al. [35] reduces the bilinear pairing in the decryption testing phase but does not support user traceability and attribute revocation.The scheme proposed by Zeng et al. [36] (2021) supports large attribute domains but does not enable attribute revocation. Huang et al. [37] combined indirect revocation and ciphertext update mechanisms to implement a high-performance revocable ABE scheme which reduces the cost of defining access policies.

In this paper, we propose a CP-ABE scheme based on composite order, which supports partial policy hiding, large attribute domain, revocability, and traceability, which is characterized as follows.

1) Partial policy hiding: Considering to ensure the efficiency of our scheme, we still use partial policy hiding. The attribute names and values are handled separately, and only the attribute values are hidden.
2) Attribute revocation: we perform attribute-level revocation of some attributes of a user after they have failed. In the scheme, for each attribute of each user, the authority generates the corresponding group key and the attributes are stored in the form of a binary tree.
3) Large attribute universe: the size of the public parameters no longer varies exponentially with the quantity of attributes within the attribute set and remains constant. A massive increase in the number of user attributes does not have an exponential impact on the performance of the programme.
4) User traceability: After a private key is revealed, a specific user can be traced according to a specific secret key. This scheme embeds identifier of someone into the private key to ensure ciphertext can't be properly decrypted in case the user information is tampered with.

2 Preliminary

First of all, in Table 1, we give a description of the notations used in this paper.

Table 1. Notation description

Notations	Descriptions
$\|A\|$	The number of the elements in A
$a \xleftarrow{R} \mathrm{A}$	The operation of selecting an element a from set A
$\mathbb{G}, \mathbb{G}_{\mathbb{T}}$	cyclic multiplicative groups
$\mathbb{G}_{p_i}$	group $\mathbb{G}$ with prime order p_i
$\mathcal{S} = (\mathcal{I}_S, S)$	$\mathcal{S}$: An attribute Set; $\mathcal{I}_S$: attribute name index; S: attribute value $S = \{s_i\}_{i \in \mathcal{I}_S}$
$sk_{\mathrm{id},\mathcal{S}}$	a private key related to an attribute set $\mathcal{S}$ and an identity id
$\mathbb{A} = (A, \rho, \mathcal{T})$	$\mathbb{A}$: an access policy; $\mathcal{T}$: and authorized value set; ρ: mapping from the rows of A; A: share generation matrix;
$\mathrm{CT}_{\mathbb{A}}$	a ciphertext associated with a specific access policy
$\mathcal{I}_{A,\rho}$	The set of minimum authorization sets on (A, ρ)

2.1 Bilinear Groups

Definition 1 (Composite Order Bilinear Groups [38]): Suppose $\mathbb{G}$ and $\mathbb{G}_T$ are two cyclic groups of the same composite order $N = p_1p_2p_3p_4$, where p_1-p_4 are all prime numbers, but not the same. For group $\mathbb{G}$, its subgroups is denoted as $\mathbb{G}_{p_i}(1 \leq i \leq 4)$. Let $\hat{e} : \mathbb{G} \times \mathbb{G} \rightarrow \mathbb{G}_T$ be a bilinear mapping, it has the following properties.

1) Bilinear: $\hat{e}\left(g^x, h^y\right) = \hat{e}(g, h)^{xy}$ for all $x, y \in \mathbb{Z}_N$ and $g, h \in \mathbb{G}$.
2) Nondegeneracy: $\exists\ h \in \mathbb{G}_1$, such that the order of $\hat{e}(h, h)$ is p in $\mathbb{G}_T$.
3) Computable: $\forall m, n \in \mathbb{G}_1$, $\hat{e}(m, n)$ could be effectively calculated.

2.2 Access Structures

Definition 2 (Access Policy [39]): Firstly, $\Gamma = \{P_1, \ldots, P_n\}$ are defined as a collection of participants. Suppose $A \subseteq 2^{\Gamma}$ is a collection: for any C and D, if $C \in A, C \subseteq D$, then $D \in A$, indicates that collection A has monotonicity. A consisting of nonempty subsets of Γ can be used as an access structure.

2.3 Linear Secret Sharing Schemes

Definition 3 (Linear Secret Sharing Scheme (LSSS) [39]): For a secret-sharing scheme Π to be linear, the following conditions are required to be satisfied (over $\mathbb{Z}_p$):

1) For every participant's shares, there is a vector over $\mathbb{Z}_p$.
2) Suppose that a matrix M serves as a shared generating matrix with ℓ rows and n columns. We use $\rho(i)$ to denote the party labeling row i for different i $(1 < i < \ell)$. There are column vectors of the following form: $v = (s, r_2, \ldots, r_n)$, where r_2 to r_n are randomly selected variables in $\mathbb{Z}_p$ and s is the secret to be shared, then Mv is the vector of ℓ shares of the secret s according to Π.

According to the exposition in [39] it is shown that the linear reconstruction property of the LSSS implemented according to Definition 3 is as follows: there is the access structure $\mathbb{A}$, corresponding to the LSSS assumed to be Π, and the authorized set is denoted as $S \in \mathbb{A}$. Assuming that the subset $I = \{i : \rho(i) \in S\}$, it has a chance to find constants $\{\omega_i \in \mathbb{Z}_p\}_{i \in I}$ in polynomial time, satisfying the condition to prove that $\{\lambda_i\}$ is a valid share and has $\sum_{i \in I} \omega_i \lambda_i = s$.

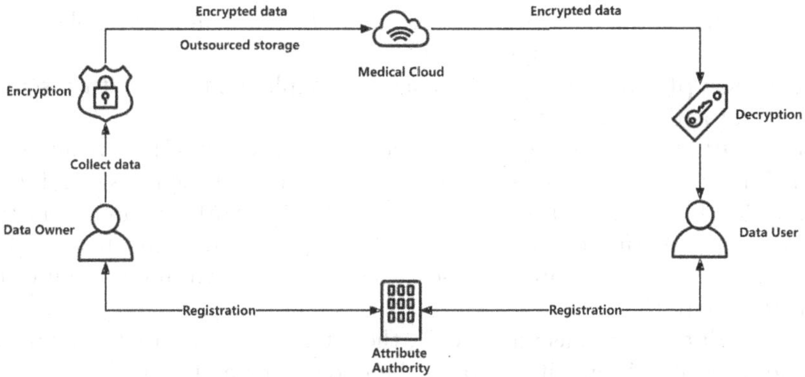

Fig. 2. System model

3 Formal Definition

3.1 System Model

The system we designed contains four parts, as shown in Fig. 2.

1) Attribute Authority (AA): The system's public and master keys are generated from the Attribute Authority, and AA manages user attributes and can be fully trusted. AA distributes different private keys for users with different privileges.
2) Data Owner (DO): Patients upload collected privacy information to cloud platform, and the users who can access this data are defined by DO in the access structure and embedded in the ciphertext.
3) Data User (DU): Doctors have access to decrypt it using the private key distributed by the authority, and the information can be decrypted and obtained only when all attributes match its access structure.
4) Medical Cloud (MC): The Medical Cloud platform receives electronic health data uploaded by DO and hosts it, and DU accesses the data by finding the required data through MC's search function and performing authentication calculations using identity attributes.

3.2 Overall Access Architecture

Our scheme includes the following several algorithms:

1) **Setup** : It returns the public parameters PK and a master key MSK with a security parameter λ as input.
2) **KeyGen** : It outputs a private key $sk_{id,\mathcal{S}}$ with PK, MSK, an identity id, and an attribute set $\mathcal{S}$ as inputs.
3) **AttrGroupKeyGen** : Given as input an attribute x, the algorithm outputs the attribute group key(AGK) together with binary state tree KEK_{TREE_x}.

4) **Encrypt** : Given as inputs a message M, PK and an access policy $\mathbb{A}$, the algorithm outputs the ciphertext CT.
5) **ReEncrypt** : It returns the re-encrypted ciphertext CT' with a series of $\{AGK\}$ and CT as inputs.
6) **Decrypt** : Given as inputs the re-encryption ciphertext CT$'$, PK and $sk_{id,\mathcal{S}}$, if $\mathcal{S}$ matches $\mathbb{A}$, it outputs M; or else it outputs an terminal symbol $\perp$.
7) **KeyUpdate** : It returns a new secret key $sk'_{id,S}$ with the user identity id, $sk_{id,\mathcal{S}}$, the attribute u that need to be revoked and a updated attribute-group key AGK'_u as inputs. In so far as attribute revocation, the user runs it to update the key.
8) **CTUpdate** : Given as inputs CT', the attribute u that need to be revoked and a specific AGK'_u, it generates the updated ciphertext CT^*.
9) **KeySanityCheck** : The output of the KeySanityCheck algorithm is completely unique [40,41]. Given as inputs PK and $sk_{id,\mathcal{S}}$, if $sk_{id,\mathcal{S}}$ passes the key integrity check, it proves that $sk_{id,\mathcal{S}}$ is well formed and outputs 1; or else it outputs 0.
10) **Trace** : Given as input PK and $sk_{id,\mathcal{S}}$, it first checks the correctness of $sk_{id,\mathcal{S}}$. If it is correct, it extracts the identity ID, otherwise it stops.

3.3 Security Model

Suppose there is an adversary $\mathcal{A}$ and a challenger $\mathcal{B}$, a game process is defined between them as follows.

1) **SetUp** $\mathcal{B}$ runs **SetUp**, it returns the public parameters PK and the master key MSK. Then, $\mathcal{B}$ returns PK to $\mathcal{A}$ and keeps MSK itself.
2) **Query phase 1** $\mathcal{A}$ adaptively issues a number of queries.
   a) **Secret keys query** $\mathcal{B}$ executes **KeyGen** to get $sk_{id,\mathcal{S}}$ with a series of attributes $\mathcal{S}$ as inputs, it then returns $\mathrm{sk}_{\mathrm{id},\mathcal{S}}$ to $\mathcal{A}$.
   b) **Decryption query** On input a ciphertext CT: $\mathcal{B}$ runs **KeyGen** and **Decrypt**, it then sends M to $\mathcal{A}$.
3) **Challenge** $\mathcal{A}$ sends two messages M_0, M_1 with equal length and two access structure $\mathbb{A}_i : (A, \rho, T_i)(i = 0, 1)$ to $\mathcal{B}$. Then, the challenger selects bit $\omega \xleftarrow{R} \{0,1\}$, runs **Encrypt** $(PK, M_\omega, \mathbb{A}_\omega)$, **ReEncrypt** (CT_ω, AGK) and returns the challenge ciphertext CT'_ω to $\mathcal{A}$, which $\mathbb{A}_0$ or $\mathbb{A}_1$ cannot be satisfied by any set sub $(sub \subseteq \mathcal{S})$.
4) **Query phase 2** $\mathcal{A}$ repeats the two steps of **Query phase 1**, with the restrictions that attribute set $\mathcal{S}'$ used in these two queries cannot satisfy $\mathbb{A}_0$ or $\mathbb{A}_1$ and $CT = CT'$.
5) **Guess** $\mathcal{A}$ gives a guess bit $\omega' \in \{0,1\}$. If $\omega' = \omega$, $\mathcal{A}$ wins the game.

The above scheme is full-secure for an adversary $\mathcal{A}$ if $|\Pr[\omega' = \omega] - 1/2|$ is negligible in polynomial time.

4 Design Details of Our Scheme

4.1 System Initialization

AA selects λ and runs $\mathcal{G}(\lambda)$ to generates $(\mathbb{G}, \mathbb{G}_T, \hat{e}, N = p_1p_2p_3p_4)$, then it sets the attribute universe $\mathcal{U} = \mathbb{Z}_N$ and executes:

Setup (1^λ): $.AA$ chooses $\alpha, a \xleftarrow{R} \mathbb{Z}_N, g \xleftarrow{R} \mathbb{G}_{p_1}, u \xleftarrow{R} \mathbb{G}_{p_3}, v \xleftarrow{R} \mathbb{G}_{p_4}, d \xleftarrow{R} \mathbb{G}_{p_4}$, then generates the system public parameters $\mathrm{PK} = (N, \mathbb{G}, \mathbb{G}_T, \hat{e}, g, g^a, \hat{e}(g,g)^\alpha, u, v, d)$ and the master key $\mathrm{MSK} = \alpha$.

4.2 Key Generation

AA picks $t \xleftarrow{R} \mathbb{Z}_N$ and $\kappa, \gamma, \delta_i \xleftarrow{R} \mathbb{G}_{p_2}, \forall i \in \mathcal{I}_S$.

KeyGen$(PK, MSK, id, \mathcal{S})$: It returns the private key $sk_{id,\mathcal{S}} = (\mathcal{S}, T, T', T'', \{T_i\}_{i\in\mathcal{I}_S})$ with PK, MSK, user identity id and the attribute set $\mathcal{S}$ as inputs, where $T = g^t\kappa, T' = \mathrm{id}, T'' = g^\alpha g^{at}\gamma$, and $T_i = (g^{s_i})^t\delta_i, i \in \mathcal{I}_S$.

AttrGroupKeyGen$(x) \rightarrow (KEK_{TREE_x}, AGK)$: This algorithm takes as input an attribute x. At first, the key encryption key tree is based on users, it can provide the key update information for the unrevoked user, and the user is not revoked to use the key update information to update its private key to realize decryption [34]. In the KEK tree, each attribute $u_i \in \mathcal{U}$ are assigned to the leaf nodes, and each node v_j holds a random key KEK_j. The path key is the node passed from each leaf node to the root node. The key set of the path nodes is the unique path key of each member, which is called $\mathrm{PK_t}$. For any U_j, it has a minimum cover set in the KEK tree that can cover all of the leaf nodes. For example, the path key of user u_1 is $PATH_1 = \{KEK_8, KEK_4, KEK_2, KEK_1\}$.

4.3 Data Encryption

Data owner sets a specified access policy, then uses algorithm **Encrypt** and **ReEncrypt** to encrypt the message.

Encrypt$(PK, M, \mathbb{A})$: Given as inputs a message M, PK, a mapping ρ from $\{1, 2, ..., \ell\}$ to the attribute name universe, an access policy $\mathbb{A}$ corresponding to the LSSS, which has a ℓ by n matrix, and vector $\mathcal{T} = \left(t_{\rho(1)}, t_{\rho(2)}, \ldots, t_{\rho(\ell)}\right)$ which represents the an attribute value, then it picks two random vectors $v = (s, v_2, \ldots, v_n)$ and $v' = (s', v_2', \ldots, v_n')$ over attribute name space and $2\ell + 2$ random subgroup elements $d_1, d_2 \xleftarrow{R} \mathbb{G}_{p_4}$ and $d_{1,x}, d_{2,x} \xleftarrow{R} \mathbb{G}_{p_4}$ for $x \in \{1, 2, ..., \ell\}$. Finally, it selects a random message $\tilde{M} \in \mathbb{G}_T$ and calculates:

$$\mathrm{CT} = \left((A,\rho), \hat{C}, C_1, \hat{C}_1, C_2, \hat{C}_2, \{C_{1,x}, C_{2,x}\}_{x\in[\ell]}\right) \tag{1}$$

where we have $\hat{C} = u^{H(M)}v^{H(\tilde{M})}('H' stands for hash function), C_1 = M \cdot \hat{e}(g,g)^{\alpha\cdot s}, \hat{C}_1 = g^s d_1, C_{1,x} = g^{aA_x\cdot v}(g^{t_{\rho(x)}} \cdot d)^{-s} d_{1,x}, C_2 = \tilde{M} \cdot \hat{e}(g,g)^{\alpha\cdot s'}, \hat{C}_2 = g^{s'}d_2, C_{2,x} = g^{aA_x\cdot v'}(g^{t_{\rho(x)}} \cdot d)^{-s'} d_{2,x}$

ReEncrypt$(CT_{\mathbb{A}}, \{AGK\}) \rightarrow CT'_{\mathbb{A}}$: For access policy $\mathbb{A}$, attribute $\rho(i)$ corresponds to a group key $AGK_{\rho(i)}$, and the re-encryption process is to re-encrypt the CT generated by **Encrypt** using $AGK_{\rho(i)}$ as follows.

$$\mathrm{CT}' = \left((A,\rho), \hat{C}, C_1, \hat{C}_1, C_2, \hat{C}_2, \left\{C'_{1,x}, C'_{2,x}\right\}_{x\in[\ell]}\right) \tag{2}$$

where $C'_{1,x} = (C_{1,x})^{AGK_{\rho(x)}}, C'_{2,x} = (C_{2,x})^{AGK_{\rho(x)}}$

4.4 Data Decryption

Decrypt $(CT', \mathcal{S}, .PK, \{AGK\}, sk_{id,\mathcal{S}}\}) \rightarrow (m/\ \perp)$: It takes as input $\mathrm{PK} = (N, \mathbb{G}, \mathbb{G}_T, \hat{e}, g, g^a, \hat{e}(g,g)^\alpha, u, v)$, the ciphertext $\mathrm{CT}' = \Big((A,\rho), \tilde{C}_1, \hat{C}_1, \left\{C'_{1,x}\right\}_{x\in[\ell]}\Big)$, and a private key $\mathrm{sk}_{id,\mathcal{S}} = (\mathcal{S}, T, T', T'', \{T_i\}_{i\in\mathcal{I}_S})$ with $\mathcal{S} = (\mathcal{I}_S, S)$. For each attribute $\rho(x) \in S$, the user uses specific path keys to recover $AGK_{\rho(x)}$, and then calculates $T^* = (T)^{1/AGK_{\rho(x)}}$. Let $\mathrm{sk}'_{id,\mathcal{S}} = (\mathcal{S}, T^*, T', T'', \{T_i\}_{i\in\mathcal{I}_S})$. The decryption algorithm does the following calculations:

$$\begin{aligned}
&C_2 \cdot \frac{\prod_{x\in\mathcal{X}}(\hat{e}(C'_{2,x}, T^*)\cdot \hat{e}(\hat{C}_2, T_{\rho(x)}))^{w_x}}{\hat{e}(\hat{C}_2, T'')}\\
=&C_2 \cdot \frac{\prod_{x\in\mathcal{X}}(\hat{e}(C_{2,x}, T)\cdot \hat{e}(\hat{C}_2, T_{\rho(x)}))^{w_x}}{\hat{e}(\hat{C}_2, T'')}\\
=&\tilde{M}\cdot \hat{e}(g,g)^{\alpha\cdot s'} \cdot \frac{\prod_{x\in\mathcal{X}}(\hat{e}(g,g)^{aA_x v' t})^{w_x}}{\hat{e}(g^{s'}, T'')}\\
=&\tilde{M}\cdot \hat{e}(g,g)^{\alpha\cdot s'} \cdot \frac{\hat{e}(g,g)^{\sum_{x\in\mathcal{X}}(\omega_x A_x)atv'}}{\hat{e}(g^{s'}, g^\alpha\cdot g^{at})}\\
=&\tilde{M}
\end{aligned} \tag{3}$$

$$\begin{aligned}
&C_1 \cdot \frac{\prod_{x\in\mathcal{X}}(\hat{e}(C'_{1,x}, T^*)\cdot \hat{e}(\hat{C}_1, T_{\rho(x)}))^{w_x}}{\hat{e}(\hat{C}_1, T'')}\\
=&C_1 \cdot \frac{\prod_{x\in\mathcal{X}}(\hat{e}(C_{1,x}, T)\cdot \hat{e}(\hat{C}_1, T_{\rho(x)}))^{w_x}}{\hat{e}(\hat{C}_1, T'')}\\
=&M\cdot \hat{e}(g,g)^{\alpha\cdot s} \cdot \frac{\prod_{x\in\mathcal{X}}(\hat{e}(g,g)^{aA_x vt})^{w_x}}{\hat{e}(g^{s}, T'')}\\
=&M\cdot \hat{e}(g,g)^{\alpha\cdot s} \cdot \frac{\hat{e}(g,g)^{\sum_{x\in\mathcal{X}}(\omega_x A_x)atv}}{\hat{e}(g^{s}, g^\alpha\cdot g^{at})}\\
=&M
\end{aligned} \tag{4}$$

Finally, if $\hat{C} = u^{H(M)}v^{H(\tilde{M})}$, it returns M, which represents DU is allowed to use the $sk_{id,\mathcal{S}}$ to do the decryption operation.

4.5 Traitor Tracing

KeySanityCheck$(par, skid, \mathcal{S})$: Given as inputs PK $= (N, \mathbb{G}, \mathbb{G}_T,\ \hat{e}, g, g^a, \hat{e}(g,g)^{\alpha}, u, v, d)$ and $\text{sk}_{id,\mathcal{S}} = \left(\mathcal{S}, T, T', T'', \{T_i\}_{i\in\mathcal{I}_S}\right)$, then it checks whether $sk_{id,\mathcal{S}}$ is well structured, where $\mathcal{I}_S \subseteq \mathbb{Z}_N$, $T, T'' \in \mathbb{G}$, and $s \in \mathbb{Z}_N$ for any $s \in S, T_i \in \mathbb{G}$ for any $i \in \mathcal{I}_S$. Finally, the correctness of $\hat{e}(g, T'') = \hat{e}(g,g)^{\alpha} \cdot \hat{e}(g^a, T)$ is tested. If $sk_{id,\mathcal{S}}$ satisfies the above conditions, it continues; Otherwise, it is terminated.

Trace$(PK, sk_{id,\mathcal{S}})$: It returns the identity $T' = id$ contained in the key $sk_{id,\mathcal{S}}$ with PK and $sk_{id,\mathcal{S}}$ as inputs.

4.6 Attribute Revocation

For any attribute group $\mathrm{U_j}$, it owns a smallest covering set which covers all leaf nodes. For instance, if attribute u_7, u_8 are revoked and $\mathrm{U_j} = \{u_1, u_2, u_3, u_4, u_5, u_6\}$, then $\mathrm{KEK}(\mathrm{U_j}) = \{\mathrm{KEK}_2, \mathrm{KEK}_6\}$. Attribute authority encrypts AGK'_u by $\{KEK_v\}$ for each $v \in G_u$. AA then sends the encrypted $\{AGK'_u\}_{KEK_{G_u}}$ to the unrevoked users. Finally, we give the definitions of two algorithms **KeyUpdate** and **CTUpdate**, which is used to implement attribute-level revocation.

1) **KeyUpdate** $(\mathcal{S}, sk_{id,\mathcal{S}}, u, AGK'_u) \to sk'_{id,\mathcal{S}}$: Let u be the revoked attribute, $\rho(x') = u$. Unrevoked users recover AGK'_u from $\{AGK'_u\}_{KEK_{G_u}}$ by using a KEK, where $KEK \in (KEK_{G_u} \cap\ PATH_{gid})$. It updates as follows.

$$\begin{aligned} sk'_{id,\mathcal{S}} &= \Big(\mathcal{S}, T^*, T', T'', \{T_i\}_{i\in\mathcal{I}_S}\Big), \\ \forall x \in [l] \backslash \{x'\} &: T^* = (g^t R')^{\frac{1}{AGK_{\rho(x)}}}, \\ x = x' &: T^* = (g^t R')^{\frac{1}{AGK'_u}}\Big). \end{aligned} \tag{5}$$

2) **CTUpdate** $(CT', u, AGK'_u) \to CT^*$: It generates two random vectors $v'' = (s'', v''_2, \ldots, v''_n)^T$, $\hat{v} = (\hat{s}, \hat{v_2}, \ldots, \hat{v_n})^T$. Finally, it outputs the updated CT^*.

$$\mathrm{CT} = \Big((A, \rho), \hat{C}, C''_1, \hat{C}''_1, C''_2, \hat{C}''_2, \{C''_{1,x}, C''_{2,x}\}_{x\in[\ell]}\Big) \tag{6}$$

where $C''_1 = M \cdot \hat{e}(g,g)^{\alpha\cdot s''}, \hat{C}''_1 = g^{s''} d_1, C''_{1,x} = (g^{aA_x\cdot v''}(g^{t_{\rho(x)}} \cdot d)^{-s''} d_{1,x})^{AGK_{\rho(x)}}$, $C''_2 = \tilde{M} \cdot \hat{e}(g,g)^{\alpha\cdot\hat{s}}$, $\hat{C}''_2 = g^{\hat{s}} d_2, C''_{2,x} = (g^{aA_x\cdot\hat{v}}(g^{t_{\rho(x)}} \cdot d)^{-\hat{s}} d_{2,x})^{AGK_{\rho(x)}}$.

5 Security Analysis

Theorem 1: Assume that Zeng's construction [36] is fully secure, then it can be concluded that the scheme constructed in this paper is also fully secure.

The detail of the proof will be given in the full version of this manuscript.

6 Performance Analysis

In Table 2, all schemes support policy hiding. Except for the access structure of AND-gate in scheme [21], the access structure of all other schemes is LSSS; scheme [21] and scheme [23] do not support large attribute domains; scheme [21], scheme [23] and scheme [35] do not support user identity tracing; for attribute level of revocation, none of the above compared schemes support it. Comparing with the above schemes, our scheme is the only one that can support partial policy hiding, large attribute fields, revocability, and traceability under the ensemble order.

Table 2. Comparison of CP-ABE schemes (PH: Policy Hiding; LU: Large Universe)

Schemes	PH	LU	Traceability	Attribute revocation	Expressiveness	Group order
[21]	✓	×	×	×	AND	composite
[23]	✓	×	×	×	LSSS	composite
[35]	✓	✓	×	×	LSSS	composite
[36]	✓	✓	✓	×	LSSS	composite
Ours	✓	✓	✓	✓	LSSS	composite

Table 3. Comparison of storage cost

Scheme	PK		$sk_{id,\mathcal{S}}$	CT	
	$\mathbb{G}_{p_i}$	$\mathbb{G}_T$	$\mathbb{G}_{p_ip_j}$	$\mathbb{G}_{p_ip_j}$	$\mathbb{G}_T$
[21]	$cN+3$	1	0	$cN+1$	1
[23]	$N+5$	1	m+2	4ℓ	2
[35]	4	1	m+2	3ℓ+2	2
[36]	4	1	m+2	2ℓ+2	2
Ours	4	1	m+2	2ℓ+2	2

Next, in Table 4, we give the comparison storage cost, where PK represents the public parameters, $sk_{id,\mathcal{S}}$ represents the private key, and CT represents the encrypted ciphertext. In scheme [21] the public parameter size varies linearly with N(attribute categories' amount) and c(possible values' amount); scheme [23] the public parameter size varies linearly with N; this scheme, scheme [35] and scheme [36] have fixed constant terms for the public parameter size. The scheme [21] does not involve subgroup $\mathbb{G}_{p_ip_j}$, and the number of subgroups $\mathbb{G}_{p_ip_j}$ of other schemes is consistent, all being m+2 (m: amount of user attributes); as for ciphertext size, scheme [35] reduces the amount of subgroup elements to $3\ell+2$, and this scheme and scheme [36] reduce ℓ on top of that to only $2\ell+2$, where ℓ is defined as the matrix A's row size.

Table 4. Comparison of computation overhead

Scheme	Enc		Dec		
	Exp	Exp_T	*Pair*	*Exp*	Exp_T
[21]	$cN+2$	1	$N+1$	0	0
[23]	$7\ell+2$	2	$\|I\|+2$	$\|I\|$	$\|I\|$
[35]	$6\ell+2$	2	$\|I\|+2$	$\|I\|$	$\|I\|$
[36]	$5\ell+2$	2	2	$2\|I\|+1$	0
Ours	$5\ell+4$	2	2	$2\|I\|+1$	0

In Table 4, the computational overhead of scheme [21] is related to the size of c in addition to the number of system attributes; comparing to the scheme [23,35], the computational overhead of our scheme surpasses scheme [23] and is approximately the same as that of scheme [35]; however, its efficiency is lower compared to scheme [36]. Both this scheme and scheme [36] reduce the redundant terms in the ciphertext based on scheme [35] to reduce the exponential operations on $\mathbb{G}$ during encryption; however, because this scheme additionally implements the attribute revocation function, re-encryption with the group key will increase part of the exponential operations on $\mathbb{G}$, and from the viewpoint of computational overhead, sacrificing a certain amount of In terms of computational overhead, it is acceptable to sacrifice some time and space resources to complete the attribute revocation.

The content of Table 4 shows the consumption cost for encryption and decryption based on the JPBC library, and computer configuration used for the above experiments was an Intel i7-11700 CPU @ 2.50GHz CPU with 32GB RAM. It can be noted in Fig. 3 that when the amount of attributes in the attribute domain is used as the independent variable, scheme [21] has the highest encryption efficiency, and the encryption time of this scheme and scheme [36] is approximately the same, second only to scheme [21] scheme [23] has the lowest efficiency, and scheme [35] also has low efficiency. Then, Fig. 4 shows the decryption time consumption. The consumption time of the scheme is strongly related to the amount of pairing operations, and the pairing operations of this scheme and scheme [36] are constant terms, and the decryption time is the least; the amount of pairing operations of both scheme [35] and scheme [36] is $|I|+2$, which grows in a linear fashion with the amount of attributes, so the decryption time is longer; the pairing operations of scheme [21] are determined by the number of total properties of the system, N decryption time is the longest.

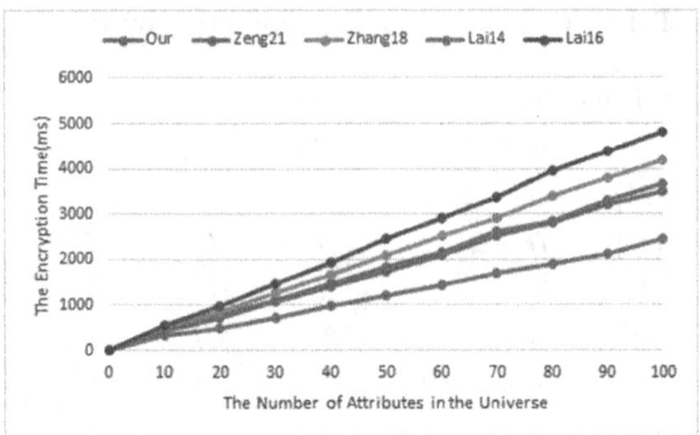

Fig. 3. Encryption cost

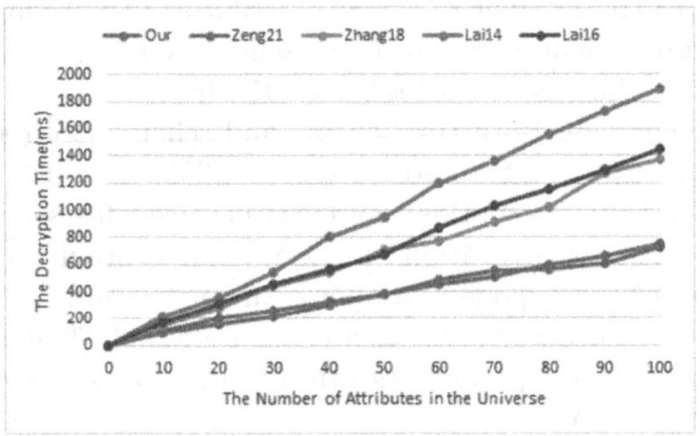

Fig. 4. Decryption cost

7 Conclusion

In this paper, we propose a CP-ABE scheme with partial policy-hiding applied to smart medical systems, which is used to protect patients' privacy information in cloud platforms. Partial policy hiding is used in the encryption phase to ensure that the user's private content cannot be inferred from the access policy; large attribute domains are supported, and new attributes can be added even after the system initializes public parameter generation; for each attribute of each user, the authority generates a corresponding group key and saves it in a binary tree to achieve attribute level revocation; after the user privacy is leaked, the specific user who leaked the information is found according to the user private key. It should be noted that the above functions included in our scheme are all done based on the merge order. This scheme achieves partial policy hiding, and it is challenging to construct a full policy hiding scheme, which can be carried out as a subsequent work.

Acknowledgment. This work was supported in part by the Open Fund of Advanced Cryptography and System Security Key Laboratory of Sichuan Province under Grant

SKLACSS–202102, in part by the Intelligent Terminal Key Laboratory of Sichuan Province under Grant SCITLAB–1019, in part by the Sichuan Science and Technology under Grant 2021JDRC0072 and 2021YFG0164.

References

1. Yuehong, Y., Zeng, Y., Chen, X., Fan, Y.: The internet of things in healthcare: an overview. J. Ind. Inf. Integr. **1**, 3–13 (2016)
2. Xiong, H., Yang, M., Yao, T., Chen, J., Kumari, S.: Efficient unbounded fully attribute hiding inner product encryption in cloud-aided WBANs. IEEE Syst. J. **PP**(99), 1–9 (2021). https://doi.org/10.1109/JSYST.2021.3125455
3. Xiong, H., Hou, Y., Huang, X., Zhao, Y., Chen, C.-M.: Heterogeneous signcryption scheme from IBC to PKI with equality test for WBANs. IEEE Syst. J. **16**(2), 2391–2400 (2022)
4. Wu, T.-Y., et al.: Improved authenticated key agreement scheme for fog-driven IoT healthcare system, Security and Communication Networks (2021)
5. Xiong, H., et al.: An anonymous authentication protocol with delegation and revocation for content delivery networks. IEEE Syst. J. **16**(3), 1–12 (2021)
6. Chen, C.-M., Tie, Z., Wang, E.K., Khan, M.K., Kumar, S., Kumari, S.: Verifiable dynamic ranked search with forward privacy over encrypted cloud data. Peer-to-Peer Netw. Appl. **14**(5), 2977–2991 (2021). https://doi.org/10.1007/s12083-021-01132-3
7. Xiong, H., Chen, J., Mei, Q., Zhao, Y.: Conditional privacy-preserving authentication protocol with dynamic membership updating for VANETs. IEEE Trans. Dependable Secure Comput. **19**(3), 2089–2104 (2022)
8. Xiong, X., Qiao, S., Li, Y., Xiong, F., He, L., Han, N.: Affective impression: sentiment-awareness poi suggestion via embedding in heterogeneous LBSNs. IEEE Trans. Affect. Comput. **13**, 272–284 (2022)
9. Sahai, A., Waters, B.: Fuzzy identity-based encryption. In: Cramer, R. (ed.) EUROCRYPT 2005. LNCS, vol. 3494, pp. 457–473. Springer, Heidelberg (2005). https://doi.org/10.1007/11426639_27
10. Goyal, V., Pandey, O., Sahai, A., Waters, B.: Attribute-based encryption for fine-grained access control of encrypted data. In: Proceedings of the 13th ACM Conference on Computer and Communications Security, pp. 89–98 (2006)
11. Ostrovsky, R., Sahai, A., Waters, B.: Attribute-based encryption with non-monotonic access structures. In: Proceedings of the 14th ACM conference on Computer and communications security, pp. 195–203 (2007)
12. Lewko, A., Okamoto, T., Sahai, A., Takashima, K., Waters, B.: Fully secure functional encryption: attribute-based encryption and (hierarchical) inner product encryption. In: Gilbert, H. (ed.) EUROCRYPT 2010. LNCS, vol. 6110, pp. 62–91. Springer, Heidelberg (2010). https://doi.org/10.1007/978-3-642-13190-5_4
13. Cheung, L., Newport, C.: Provably secure ciphertext policy ABE. In: Proceedings of the 14th ACM conference on Computer and communications security, pp. 456–465 (2007)
14. Wan, Z., Deng, R.H., et al.: HASBE: a hierarchical attribute-based solution for flexible and scalable access control in cloud computing. IEEE Trans. Inf. Forensics Secur. **7**(2), 743–754 (2011)
15. Bethencourt, J., Sahai, A., Waters, B.: Ciphertext-policy attribute-based encryption. In: 2007 IEEE Symposium on Security and Privacy (SP2007), pp. 321–334 (2007)

16. Wang, G., Liu, Q., Wu, J.: Hierarchical attribute-based encryption for fine-grained access control in cloud storage services. In: Proceedings of the 17th ACM Conference on Computer and Communications Security, pp. 735–737 (2010)
17. Nishide, T., Yoneyama, K., Ohta, K.: Attribute-based encryption with partially hidden encryptor-specified access structures. In: Bellovin, S.M., Gennaro, R., Keromytis, A., Yung, M. (eds.) ACNS 2008. LNCS, vol. 5037, pp. 111–129. Springer, Heidelberg (2008). https://doi.org/10.1007/978-3-540-68914-0_7
18. Waters, B.: Ciphertext-policy attribute-based encryption: An expressive, efficient, and provably secure realization. In: International Workshop on Public Key Cryptography, pp. 53–70 (2011)
19. Dong, C., Chen, L., Wen, Z.: When private set intersection meets big data: an efficient and scalable protocol. In: Proceedings of the 2013 ACM SIGSAC conference on Computer & communications security, pp. 789–800 (2013)
20. Yang, K., et al.: An efficient and fine-grained big data access control scheme with privacy-preserving policy. IEEE Internet Things J. **4**(2), 563–571 (2016)
21. Lai, J., Deng, R.H., Li, Y.: Fully secure Cipertext-policy hiding CP-ABE. In: Bao, F., Weng, J. (eds.) ISPEC 2011. LNCS, vol. 6672, pp. 24–39. Springer, Heidelberg (2011). https://doi.org/10.1007/978-3-642-21031-0_3
22. Zhang, Y., Chen, X., Li, J., Wong, D.S., Li, H.: Anonymous attribute-based encryption supporting efficient decryption test. In: Proceedings of the 8th ACM SIGSAC Symposium on Information, Computer and Communications Security, pp. 511–516 (2013)
23. Lai, J., Deng, R.H., Li, Y.: Expressive CP-ABE with partially hidden access structures. In: Proceedings of the 7th ACM symposium on information, computer and communications security, pp. 18–19 (2012)
24. Han, Q., Zhang, Y., Li, H.: Efficient and robust attribute-based encryption supporting access policy hiding in internet of things. Futur. Gener. Comput. Syst. **83**, 269–277 (2018)
25. Katz, J., Schröder, D.: Tracing insider attacks in the context of predicate encryption schemes. ACITA (2011)
26. Liu, Z., Cao, Z., Wong, D.S.: Blackbox traceable CP-ABE: how to catch people leaking their keys by selling decryption devices on eBay. In: Proceedings of the 2013 ACM SIGSAC Conference on Computer & Communications Security, pp. 475–486 (2013)
27. Liu, Z., Cao, Z., Wong, D.S.: White-box traceable ciphertext-policy attribute-based encryption supporting any monotone access structures. IEEE Trans. Inf. Forensics Secur. **8**(1), 76–88 (2012)
28. Wu, A., et al.: Efficient and privacy-preserving traceable attribute-based encryption in blockchain. Annals Telecommun. **74**(7), 401–411 (2019)
29. Han, D., Pan, N., Li, K.-C.: A traceable and revocable ciphertext-policy attribute-based encryption scheme based on privacy protection. IEEE Trans. Dependable Secure Comput. **19**(1), 316–327 (2020)
30. Mei, Q., Xiong, H., Chen, Y.-C., Chen, C.-M.: Blockchain-enabled privacy-preserving authentication mechanism for transportation cps with cloud-edge computing. In: IEEE Transactions on Engineering Management, pp. 1–12 (2022)
31. Xiong, H., et al.: On the design of blockchain-Based ECDSA with fault-tolerant batch verification protocol for blockchain-enabled IoMT. IEEE J. Biomed. Health Inform. **26**(5), 1977–1986 (2021)
32. Pirretti, M., Traynor, P., McDaniel, P., Waters, B.: Secure attribute-based systems. J. Comput. Secur. **18**(5), 799–837 (2010)

33. Wang, W., Zhang, G., Shen, Y.: A CP-ABE scheme supporting attribute revocation and policy hiding in outsourced environment. In: 2018 IEEE 9th International Conference on Software Engineering and Service Science (ICSESS), pp. 96–99 (2018)
34. Liu, Z., Jiang, Z.L., Wang, X., Yiu, S.-M.: Practical attribute-based encryption: outsourcing decryption, attribute revocation and policy updating. J. Netw. Comput. Appl. **108**, 112–123 (2018)
35. Zhang, Y., Zheng, D., Deng, R.H.: Security and privacy in smart health: efficient policy-hiding attribute-based access control. IEEE Internet Things J. **5**(3), 2130–2145 (2018)
36. Zeng, P., Zhang, Z., Lu, R., Choo, K.-K.R.: Efficient policy-hiding and large universe attribute-based encryption with public traceability for internet of medical things. IEEE Internet Things J. **8**(13), 10963–10972 (2021)
37. Huang, X., Xiong, H., Chen, J., Yang, M.: Efficient revocable storage attribute-based encryption with arithmetic span programs in cloud-assisted internet of things. In: IEEE Transactions on Cloud Computing. https://doi.org/10.1109/TCC.2021.3131686
38. Boneh, D., Goh, E.-J., Nissim, K.: Evaluating 2-DNF formulas on ciphertexts. Theor. Crypt. Conf. **3378**, 325–341 (2005)
39. Beimel, A., et al.: Secure schemes for secret sharing and key distribution (1996)
40. Goyal, V.: Reducing trust in the PKG in identity based cryptosystems. In: Menezes, A. (ed.) CRYPTO 2007. LNCS, vol. 4622, pp. 430–447. Springer, Heidelberg (2007). https://doi.org/10.1007/978-3-540-74143-5_24
41. Goyal, V., Lu, S., Sahai, A., Waters, B.: Black-box accountable authority identity-based encryption. In: Proceedings of the 15th ACM Conference on Computer and Communications Security, pp. 427–436 (2008)

Author Index

Printed in the United States
by Baker & Taylor Publisher Services